(한영, 영한)

지식재산 법률용어 사전

Korean-English / English-Korean
Intellectual Property Law Dictionary

특허법원
국제 지식재산권법 연구센터

진 원 사

발간사

오늘날 지식재산 분쟁의 국제적 성격으로 말미암아 동일한 특허 분쟁이 여러 국가에서 동시 다발적으로 제기되거나 동일 · 유사한 쟁점을 가진 지식재산권 분쟁이 여러 국가 법원에서 다루어지는 경우가 흔히 벌어지고 있습니다. 그로 인해 지식재산권에 관한 한 나라의 법제나 판결은 다른 나라의 법원과 지식재산 전문가들에게 중요한 참고 자료로 활용되고 있습니다. 다만 그 과정에서 언어의 차이와 잘못된 번역으로 인해 타국의 법제나 판결을 이해하는 데 어려움이 있고 잘못 이해하는 경우도 종종 발생하고 있습니다. 이러한 용어의 혼동이 활발한 국제 교류의 장애물로 작용하고 있습니다.

이 책은 그와 같은 문제점을 개선하고자, 지식재산 관련 소송에서 사용되고 있는 법률 용어를 검토하여 국어 용어에 대한 적절한 영어 번역례와 영어 용어에 대한 적절한 국어 번역례를 제시하고, 용어에 대한 해설과 사용례를 국어와 영어로 부가함으로써 쉽고 정확하게 국내외 판결이나 자료를 번역하고 이해할 수 있도록 하였습니다. 이를 통해 우리나라의 발전된 지식재산권 법제와 판결을 외국에 널리 소개하는 한편 외국의 판결과 자료들을 정확하게 이해할 수 있을 것으로 기대합니다.

이 책은 올해 개원한 특허법원 『국제 지식재산권법 연구센터(International IP Law Research Center)』 첫 연구 성과물입니다. 지식재산 소송을 전담하는 전문법원인 특허법원은 국제 지식재산소송 및 제도에 대한 심층적인 연구와 외국 전문법원 또는 연구기관과의 국제적 교류를 강화하여 세계 지식재산 허브 법원으로 도약하는 토대를 마련하기 위해 올해 국제 지식재산권법 연구센터를 개원하였습니다. 앞으로도 국제 지식재산권법 연구센터는 지식재산 전문법원이 추구해야 할 바람직한 모습을 설계하고 이론적으로 뒷받침하는 미래지향적 연구를 수행하여 지식재산권법 분야의 발전에 밑거름이 되도록 각고의 노력을 다하고자 합니다.

이 책자의 발간을 위해 오랜 기간 동안 노고를 아끼지 않은 국제 지식재산권법 연구센터 연구위원, 연구원들의 노고에 감사드리고, 이 책자가 지식재산권에 관심이 있는 많은 분들에게 실질적인 도움이 되기를 기대합니다.

2017. 8.

특허법원
국제 지식재산권법 연구센터장 **이 대 경**

일러두기

Korean-English Intellectual Property Law Dictionary

01 이 책은 지식재산권소송에서 자주 접하게 되는 법률용어에 대한 국어 · 영어 번역과 그에 대한 해설 및 사용례를 소개하고 있습니다.

02 구체적으로 이 책은 다음과 같이 구성되어 있습니다.

[1] 제1부 찾아보기

가격침식	price erosion	102
가변요소	phantom elements	102
가압류	provisional seizure	102
가족상표	family of marks	102
가중적 손해배상	enhanced damages	103
가집행	provisional execution	103
가처분	preliminary injunction	103
가출원	provisional application	103

제2부 및 제3부에서 소개된 용어들을 찾아보기 쉽게 일목요연하게 정리하였습니다.

2 제2부 한영사전

보통명칭 그 지정상품을 취급하는 거래계에서 동종업자 및 일반 수요자 사이에 그 상품을 지칭하는 것으로 실제로 사용되고 인식되어 있는 일반적인 명칭, 약칭, 속칭 등으로서 특정인의 업무에 관련된 상품이라고 인식되지 아니하는 명칭.	**generic name, common name** (법제처) Ordinary title, abbreviation or nickname that is actually used and perceived as referring to the good among the ordinary consumers and traders in the relevant marketplace and not perceived as associated with the business of any particular person.
미 **동일인출원** 같은 출원인에 의한 출원. 동시계류출원.	**companion applications** Pending applications filed by the same applicant. Co-pending applications.

국어 용어와 이에 대한 영어 번역 용어를 기재하였고, 법제처 영문 법령이 용어가 별도로 있는 경우 이를 "(법제처)"로 표기하여 추가하였습니다. 미국 지식재산권소송에서 사용되는 용어에 대해서는 용어 앞에 "미"로 표시하였습니다. 용어에 대한 이해를 돕기 위해 해설과 사용례를 국어 및 영어로 소개하였습니다.

일러두기

Korean-English Intellectual Property Law Dictionary

3 제3부 영한사전

aesthetic impression → See. aesthetic sense	**심미감**
aesthetic sense The aesthetic impression a design creates in the observer's mind. A design is sufficiently aesthetic if it creates a sense of pleasure, trendiness, safety or convenience, and is not required to be aesthetically sophisticated or advanced.	**심미감** 디자인이 관찰자에게 불러일으키는 미적 인상. 물품을 보는 자로 하여금 지금까지 볼 수 없었던 특수한 취미감, 유행감, 안전감 혹은 편리감 등을 줄 수 있으면 족하며, 반드시 미학적으로 높은 수준의 우아하고 고상한 것을 요구하는 것은 아님.

한영사전에서 제시된 용어와 해설을 영문 순서로 정리하였습니다. 1개의 국어 용어에 대해 2개의 영어 번역 용어가 있는 경우에는 바람직한 영문 번역 용어에 해설 및 사용례를 기재하고, 나머지 용어는 위 용어를 참조하도록 하였습니다.

03 이 책에서 예문으로 사용한 국어 및 영어 법령과 판결문의 내용은 우리나라 및 미국의 실제 법령 및 판결문의 일부입니다. 우리나라 법령 및 이에 대한 영어 번역은 법제처 웹사이트를, 우리나라 판결문 및 이에 대한 영어 번역은 법원도서관 웹사이트 및 특허법원 발간 영문판례집을, 미국 법령 및 판결문은 미국 법률정보

DB인 Westlaw에서 발췌한 것을 기본으로 하되, 일부 영어 번역은 필요에 따라 적절한 용어로 고쳐서 사용하였으므로 실제와 다를 수 있습니다.

이 책에서 사용된 약어는 다음과 같습니다.

KIPO: Korea Intellectual Property Office (특허청)
IPTAB: Intellectual Property Trial and Appeal Board (특허심판원)
USPTO: United States Patent and Trademark Office (미 특허상표청)
U.S.C.: United States Code (미국 법전)
C.F.R.: Code of Federal Regulations (미국 연방규정집)
F.R.C.P.: Federal Rules of Civil Procedure (미국 연방민사소송규칙)
AIA: Leahy-Smith America Invents Act (미 개정 특허법)
MPEP: Manual of Patent Examining Procedure (미 특허심사지침)
TMEP: Trademark Manual of Examining Procedure (미 상표심사지침)

국제 지식재산권법 연구센터는 특허법원의 세계 IP 허브법원으로의 도약을 뒷받침하기 위해 2017. 3. 특허법원 산하 연구기관으로 설립되어 지식재산권 소송 및 제도에 대한 연구와 국내외 학술교류 업무를 담당하고 있습니다.
이 용어사전은 2017년 연구계획에 따른 연구과제 중 하나인 '지식재산권소송 외국어 법률용어 사전'의 결과물입니다.
위 연구를 수행한 책임자 및 연구자는 아래와 같습니다.

연구책임자: 김환수 국제지식재산권법연구센터 수석연구위원
장현진 국제지식재산권법연구센터 연구위원
연구참여자: 박운정 국제지식재산권법연구센터 연구원
공윤옥 국제지식재산권법연구센터 연구원

Korean-English
Intellectual Property
Law Dictionary

CONTENTS

발간사

일러두기

제1부 찾아보기 11

1. 국어로 찾기 12
2. 영어로 찾기 54

제2부 한영사전 101

– ㄱ～ㅎ 102

제3부 영한사전 299

– A～Z 300

부 록 507

1. 특허법원 침해소송 항소심 심리 매뉴얼(국어) 510
2. 특허법원 침해소송 항소심 심리 매뉴얼(영어) 540
3. 특허법원 심결취소소송 심리 매뉴얼(국어) 580
4. 특허법원 심결취소소송 심리 매뉴얼(영어) 618

2017

지식재산 법률용어사전

Korean-English Intellectual Property Law Dictionary

Korean-English
Intellectual Property
Law Dictionary

제1부
찾아보기

2017

지식재산 법률용어사전

국어로 찾기

가격침식	price erosion	102
가변요소	phantom elements	102
가압류	provisional seizure	102
가족상표	family of marks	102
가중적 손해배상	enhanced damages	103
가집행	provisional execution	103
가처분	preliminary injunction	103
가출원	provisional application	103
각하	dismissal	103
간단하고 흔히 있는 표장	simple and common mark	104
간접침해	indirect infringement	104
간행물	publication	105
감정	appraisal	105
감정인	appraiser	105
감정증인	expert witness	105
갑호증	plaintiff's exhibit	105
강제실시권	compulsory license	105
개량발명	improvement invention	106
개별대리의 원칙	principle of individual representation	106
개시	disclose	106
개시의무	duty of disclosure	106
객관적 관찰	objective observation	106
객관적 창작성	objective creativity	107
거래사회	marketplace	107

(상표의) 거래상의 사용	use in commerce	107
거래상의 인상	commercial impression	108
거래상품	goods in trade	108
거래실정	course of trade	108
거래통념	trade norms	108
거래확장의 원칙	expansion-of-trade doctrine	109
거절	reject	109
거절결정	rejection	109
거절결정 불복소송	trial against rejection	110
거절결정 불복심판	administrative trial against rejection	110
거절이유통지	notice of grounds for rejection/refusal	110
(최초)거절이유통지	Office action	110
거짓표시	false display	111
거짓행위의 죄	crime of fraud	111
검증	inspection	111
(간행물에) 게재된 디자인	design described (in a publication)	111
견본	specimen	111
결정	decision	112
결정계 심사	ex parte reexamination	112
결정계 절차	ex parte prosecution	112
결정계 심판청구	ex parte appeals	112
결정의 취소	revocation of decision	112
결정형(結晶形) 발명	crystal form invention	112

국어로 찾기

결합발명	combination patent	113
결합상표	composite trademark	113
경과규정	transitional provision	114
경과조치	transitional measure	114
경상실시료	running royalty	114
경제적 견련관계	economically relevant relationship	114
경합출원	competing application	114
경험법칙	rule of thumb	115
계류출원	pending application	115
계속사용진술서	affidavit of continued use	115
계속심사청구	request for continued examination	116
계속적 실시료	ongoing royalty	116
계속출원(광의)	continued/continuing application	116
고객흡인력	attractiveness to customers	116
고도(高度)의	highly advanced	117
고소	criminal complaint	117
고안	utility model	117
고안자	deviser	117
고유번호	identification number	117
고유의 식별력	inherent distinctiveness	118
고유필수적 공동소송	inherently compulsory joint litigation	118
고의	willful	118
고의침해	willful infringement	118
공공의 질서	public order	119

공공의 질서 또는 선량한 풍속에 어긋난	against public order or good morals	119
공동발명자	joint inventor	119
공동심판청구	joinder of petition for trial	119
공동연구협약	joint research agreement	119
공동출원인	joint applicants	119
공무원 의제	deemed public officials	120
공서양속에 반하는 상표	immoral or scandalous matter	120
공시송달	public notice in lieu of service	120
공업상 이용가능성	industrial usability	120
공연히 실시된 디자인	publicly practiced design	121
공연히 실시된 발명	publicly practiced invention	121
공용	publicly practiced	121
공유	joint ownership	121
공존사용등록	concurrent use registration	122
공지	public knowledge	122
공지기술	(publicly) known art	122
공지기술 배제의 원칙	principle to exclude publicly known art	122
공지된 디자인	publicly known design	122
공지된 발명	publicly known invention	122
공지 부분을 포함하는 디자인	design containing publicly known parts	123
공지의 예외	prior art exceptions	123
과도한 실험	undue experimentation	123
과실의 추정	presumption of negligence	124

국어로 찾기

과제해결원리	means to solve the problem	124
과태료	surcharge fine for negligence	124
관계의 허위적 암시	false suggestion of connection	124
관계회사	related companies	125
관념	concept	125
관념의 유사	similarity in concept	125
관련디자인	related design	125
관리인	domestic representative	126
관용기술	commonly used art	126
관용표장	commonly used mark	126
관할	Jurisdiction	126
교부	deliver	127
구별성	distinctness	127
구성대비표	feature comparison chart	127
(발명의) 구성요소	component	127
구성요소 일체의 원칙	all elements rule	127
구속력 있는 선례	binding precedent	128
구술심리	oral hearing	128
구제책	remedies	128
(발명의) 구체화	reduction to practice	128
구호	slogan	128
국내단계출원	national stage application	129
국방상 필요한 발명	inventions necessary for national defence	129
국제등록	international registration	129

국제등록기초상표권	basic trademark rights of international registration	129
국제등록명의인	holder of an international registration	130
국제등록부	International Register	130
국제등록의 소멸	extinguishment of international registration	130
국제등록일	date of international registration	130
국제등록 지정국	designated country	130
국제디자인분류	International Classification for Industrial Designs	130
국제사무국	International Bureau	130
국제지식재산연수원	International Intellectual Property Training Institute	131
국제출원인	international applicant	131
권리구제	relief	131
권리남용	abuse of right	131
권리능력	legal capacity	131
권리범위확인소송	action on confirm of the scope of rights	131
권리범위확인심판	(administrative) trial to confirm scope of rights	131
권리불요구	disclaimer	132
권리소진의 원칙	exhaustion doctrine	132
(포기된 출원의) 권리회복청구	petition to revive an application	132
권원의 연속	chain of title	133
균등론	doctrine of equivalents	133

국어로 찾기

국어	영어	쪽
균등침해	infringement by equivalents	133
균일성	uniformity	133
글자체	font	133
금지명령	injunction	134
(영구)금지명령	permanent injunction	134
기각	dismissal	134
기능성	functionality	134
기능식청구항	functional claim	134
기능(수행)실패	failure to function	135
기능적이고 상업적인 변형	functional and commercial modification	135
기만적 표장	deceptive mark	135
기만적 허위표시 표장	deceptively misdescriptive mark	136
기본디자인	principal design	136
기속력	legally binding force	136
기술상식	technological common sense	137
기술설명회	technical explanatory session	137
기술 수준	state of the art	138
기술심리관	(judicial) technical examiners	138
기술적 과제	technical problem	138
기술적 표장	descriptive mark	138
기여도 (특허발명의)	contribution ratio (of a patented invention)	138
기여분	apportionment	138
기여침해	contributory infringement	139

기재불비	lack of sufficient description	139
기재사항	description	139
기초상표권	basic trademark right	139
기판력	res judicata	139
기피	challenge (of a judge)	139
(특허권의) 남용	abuse (of patent right)	140
내재성	inherency	140
내적 증거	intrinsic evidence	140
냄새상표	scent mark	140
니스협정	Nice Agreement	140
다류(多類)출원(제도)	multiple-class application	141
다중종속항	multiple dependent claim	141
단류(單類)출원	single/single-class application	141
단면도	sectional view	141
단순기술표장	merely descriptive mark	141
단체표장	collective mark	141
답변서	written defense	142
당사자계 심판	inter partes review	142
당사자계 재심사	inter partes reexamination	142
대리권	agency authority	142
대리인	agent	142
대비적 관찰	comparative observation	143
대응구성	corresponding elements	143
대체출원	substitute application	143

국어로 찾기

도면	drawing	143
도시(圖示)되고 기재된 바와 같은	as shown and described	143
도시된 바와 같은	as shown	143
도용	misappropriation	143
도형상표	figurative mark	144
독립항	independent claim	144
독점적 실시권, 배타적 실시권	exclusive license	145
독특한 특징	characteristic features	145
동시계류출원	co-pending applications	145
동음이의어 지리적 표시	homonymous geographical indication	145
동일간주원칙	doctrine of legal equivalents	146
동일상표	identical trademark	146
동일상품	identical good	146
동일인출원	companion applications	147
동일한 발명	identical invention	147
동작상표	motion marks	147
드노보 심리(審理)	de novo review	148
등급표시	grade designations	148
등록가능통지	notice of allowability	148
등록결정	decision to register	148
등록결정통지	notice of allowance	148
등록료	registration fee	148
등록료의 보전	payment of remainder	149
등록무효	invalidation	149

등록무효사유	grounds for invalidation	149
등록상표	registered trademark	149
등록실용신안	registered utility model	150
등록유지료	maintenance fees	150
등록일	registration date	150
등록주의	principle of registration	150
등록증	certificate of registration	150
등록취소	cancellation (of registration)	150
등록후재심사	post grant review	150
디자인	design	150
디자인공보	Design Gazette	151
디자인권 존속기간 만료 후의 통상실시권	non-exclusive licenses after expiration of design rights	151
디자인등록원부	Design Register	151
디자인등록출원	application for design registration	151
디자인등록표시	indication of design registration	151
디자인(형태)의 동일 · 유사성	identity or similarity of designs (shapes)	151
디자인창작자	creator of design	152
디자인특허출원	design patent application	152
로카르노협정	Locarno Agreement	152
마드리드 의정서	Madrid Protocol	152
마쿠쉬 청구항	Markush type claim	153
마크맨 심리	Markman hearing	153
명목상의 사용	token use	153

국어로 찾기

명백하고 확실한 증거	clear and convincing evidence	153
명백한 오류 기준	clearly erroneous standard	154
명세서	specification	154
명칭	title	154
명확성	definiteness	154
모델 표시	model designations	154
모방	simulation	154
모방상표	counterfeit mark	155
모양	pattern	155
모인출원	application by unentitled persons	155
모조	imitate	155
모출원(母出願)	parent application	156
몰수	confiscation	156
무권리자	unentitled person	156
무역관련 지적재산권에 관한 협정	TRIPs (Trade-Related Intellectual Property portions of General Agreement on Tariffs and Trade)	156
무임승차	free riding	156
무효심판	trial on invalidation	157
무효처분	invalidation	157
무효처분의 취소	revocation of invalidation	157
(청구항) 무효화	(claim) vitiation	157
문언적 의미	plain meaning	157
문언침해	literal infringement	158
문언해석	literal interpretation	158

문자상표	word mark	158
문장	coat of arms	158
물건을 생산하는 방법의 발명	invention of a process of manufactoring a thing	158
물건의 발명	invention of a thing	159
물상대위	subrogation	159
물품	article of manufacture	159
물품류	classification of goods	159
물품의 기능에 관련된 형태	a form related to a function of the article	160
물품의 기능을 확보하는 데 불가결한 형상	a shape essential for a function of the relevant article	160
물품의 기능적 형태	functional form of a product	160
물품의 기본적 형태	fundamental form of a product	160
미각상표	flavor mark	160
미국 개정 특허법	AIA (Leahy–Smith America Invents Act)	161
미국연방순회항소법원	CAFC (Court of Appeals for the Federal Circuit)	161
미국 특허심판원	PTAB (Patent Trial and Appeal Board)	161
미 상표법	Lanham Act	161
미생물의 기탁	deposit of micro–organisms	161
미완성 발명	incomplete invention	161
바람직한 구현례	preferred embodiment	162
반대신문	cross examination	162
반려	return	162

ㄱㄴ 국어로 찾기

반박	traverse	162
반박증거	rebuttal evidence	162
반복패턴표장	repeating pattern marks	162
반소	counterclaim	163
(간행물의) 반포	distribution (of a publication)	163
반포된 간행물에 게재	description on a publication distributed	163
반포일	date of release	163
발명	invention	163
발명대상	subject matter	163
발명을 특정하여 지칭함	particularly point out the invention	163
발명의 기재 요건	written description requirement	164
발명의 단일성	unity of invention	164
발명의 명칭	title of invention	164
발명의 설명	description (of an invention)	164
발명의 요지	summary of invention	164
발명의 착상	concept	165
발명자	inventor	165
발명주체	inventorship	165
발행일	issue date	165
방법발명	process invention	165
방법청구항	process claim	165
방식흠결출원	informal applications	165
배경기술 기재의무	duty to state technology used for the invention	166

용어	English	쪽
배심재판	jury trial	166
배임행위	malpractice	166
법적판결신청	motion for judgment as a matter of law (JMOL)	166
법정기간	statutory period	166
법정손해배상	statutory damages	166
법정 의견서	amicus curie briefs	167
법정제한요건	statutory bar	167
법정 포기	statutory disclaimer	167
변경출원	conversion of applications	167
변론	pleading	167
변론기일	trial date	168
변론조서	trial record	168
변론준비기일	pretrial hearing	168
변론준비명령	preparatory order for hearing	168
(변론의) 병합	combination	168
병행수입	parallel import	168
(절차)보완명령	order to supplement an application	168
보정	amendment	169
보정각하(결정)	(decision to) dismiss amendment	169
보정명령	order to make an amendment	169
보조등록부	Supplemental Register	170
보조참가인	supplementary intervenor	170
보충심사	supplemental examination	170

국어로 찾기

보통명칭	generic name	170
보통으로 사용하다	use in a common manner	170
보호품종	protected plant variety	171
보호품종의 표시	marking of protected plant variety	171
복수디자인등록출원	multiple-design application	171
복제약	generic drugs	171
본국	country of origin	171
본인출원	pro-se application	172
부가기간	additional period	172
부기적 부분	supplemental portion	172
부당이득	unjust enrichment	172
(특허권의) 부당행사	abuse (of patent right)	172
부등록대상	nonstatutory subject matter	172
부분디자인	partial design	173
부분품	components	173
부수적 금반언	collateral estoppel	173
부정경쟁	unfair competition	173
부정경쟁방지 및 영업비밀보호에 관한 법률	Unfair Competition Prevention and Trade Secret Protection Act	174
부정사용	trademark abuse	174
부품	parts	174
(변론의) 분리	separation	174
분리관찰	compare by element	174
분할	division	175

분할출원	divisional application	175
불가쟁력	incontestability	175
불가항력	force majeure	175
불공정행위	inequitable conduct	176
불리한 추정	adverse inference	176
불변기간	fixed period	176
불사용취소	non-use cancellation	176
불수리처분	disposition refusing to accept application	176
(특허상표청 통지에 대한) 불완전한 반박	incomplete response (to Office action)	177
비교대상고안	cited invention	177
비교대상발명	cited invention	177
비밀누설죄	offense of divulging secrets or confidential information	177
비밀디자인	secret design	178
비밀유지권 포기	waiver of confidentiality	178
비밀유지명령	order to maintain confidentiality	178
비밀유지명령위반죄	breaches of order to maintain confidentiality	178
비밀유지의무	duty of confidentiality	179
비방	disparagement	179
비시각적 상표	non-visual marks	179
비엔나협정	Vienna Agreement	179
비자명성	non-obviousness	179
비전형상표	non-traditional mark	179

국어로 찾기

비특허문헌	non-patent literature	179
사건관리 화상회의	video conference for case management	180
사물관할	subject matter jurisdiction	180
사시도	perspective view	180
사용간주	constructive use	180
사용기반출원	use-based application	180
사용에 의한 식별력	acquired distinctiveness (based on use)	181
사용의사	intent to use (ITU)	181
사용의사 출원	intent-to-use applications	181
(거래상) 사용주장	allegations of use (in commerce)	182
사용진술서	statement of use	182
사전상 부재 증거	negative dictionary evidence	182
사표(社標)	house mark	182
사해심결	administrative trial decision obtained by fraud	182
사후적 고찰	hindsight reconstruction	183
사후지정	subsequent designation	183
산업디자인의 국제등록에 관한 헤이그협정	Hague Agreement Concerning the International Registration of Industrial Designs (the Hague Agreement)	183
산업상 이용가능성	industrial applicability	183
산업재산권의 보호를 위한 파리 협약	the Paris Convention for the Protection of Industrial Property (the Paris Convention)	184

산지(産地)	place of production	184
상거래 관행	generally accepted business practices	184
상고/항소 이유	grounds for appeal	184
상고인/항소인	appellant	184
상당한 주의	due care	184
상대방 당사자	adverse party	185
상식적 선택	common sense selection	185
상업적 성공	commercial success	185
상업적(기능적)인 변형	commercial(functional) modification	185
상위개념	generic concept	185
상표	trademark	186
상표공보	Trademark Official Gazette (TMOG)	186
상표권자	trademark owner	186
상표등록원부	Trademark Register	186
상표등록의 만료	expiration of trademark registration	187
상표등록조약	Trademark Registration Treaty (TRT)	187
상표등록증	certificate of trademark registration	187
상표등록취소사유	grounds to cancel trademark registration	187
상표등록취소심판	(administrative) trial to cancel trademark registration	187
상표를 거래상 사용하고자 하는 진실한 의사	bona fide intention (to use mark in commerce)	188

국어로 찾기

상표법	Trademark Act	188
상표법 시행규칙	Enforcement Rule of the Trademark Act	188
상표법 시행령	Enforcement Decree of the Trademark Act	188
상표심사기준	Trademark Manual of Examining Procedure (TMEP)	188
상표심판항소위원회	Trademark Trial and Appeal Board (TTAB)	188
상표의 국제등록에 관한 마드리드협정	Madrid Agreement Concerning the International Registration of Marks	188
상표의 사용	use of a trademark	189
상표적 사용	use as a trademark	189
상표전문기관	specialized trademark institution	189
상품	good	189
상품류 구분	category of goods	190
상품 및 서비스의 분류	classification of goods/services	190
상품의 허위 또는 기만표시 억제를 위한 마드리드협정	Madrid Agreement for the Repression of False or Deceptive Indications of Source on Goods	190
상품-장소간 연관성(연계성)	goods-place association	190
상호	trade name	191
상호로서의 사용	use of mark as a trade name	191
상호저촉특허	blocking patent	191
색채상표	color mark	191
색채위치의 진술	color location statement	191
생산방법의 추정	presumption of manufacturing process	192

서면심리	written hearing	192
서비스표	service mark	192
서증	documentary evidence	192
석명	clarification	192
선등록상표	prior-registered mark	193
선량한 풍속	good moral	193
선례 구속의 원칙	stare decisis	193
선사용에 의한 통상실시권	non-exclusive licenses based on prior use	193
선서	oath	193
선서를 갈음하는 선언서	declaration in lieu of oath	194
선순위권리자	senior party	194
선의	good faith	194
선출원주의	first-to-file rule	194
선택발명	selection invention	194
선행고안	preceding invention	195
선행근거	antecedent basis	195
선행기술	prior invention	195
선행디자인	prior design	195
선행발명	prior art	195
선행발명의 결합	combination of references/prior arts	195
선행조치	priority action	196
설정등록	registration for establishment of rights	196
소각하 신청	motion to dismiss	196

국어로 찾기

소극적 권리범위확인심판	(administrative) defensive confirmation trial for the scope of rights	196
소급	retroactive	197
소리상표	sound mark	197
소멸	extinguishment	197
소송비용청구	fee shifting	197
소장	complaint	197
소진	exhaustion	197
속지주의	territorial principle	198
(절차의) 속행	continuation (of procedure)	198
손상	tarnishment	198
손실보상청구	claim for compensation for loss	198
손해배상 청구권	claim for damages	199
손해액 추정	presumption of (the amount of) damages	199
송달	service	199
수계	takeover	199
수명법관	commissioned judge	200
수수료	fee	200
수요자 기만	consumer deception	200
수용	expropriation	200
수치한정발명	numerical limitation invention	200
수탁판사	judge sitting by designation	201
승계	succession	201
시각적 유사성	visual similarity	202

시도의 자명성	obvious to try	202
식물 신품종 보호에 관한 국제조약	International Convention for the Protection of New Varieties of Plants	202
식물특허	plant patents	202
식물품종보호법	Plant Varieties Protection Act	202
식별력	distinctiveness	203
식별력이 없는 표장	non-distinctive mark	203
식품의약품안전처	Ministry of Food and Drug Safety	203
신규사항	new matter	203
신규성	novelty	203
신뢰보호의 원칙	principle of trust protection	204
신용회복청구	claim for reinstatement of reputation	204
실사용상표	actually used trademark	204
실시	exploitation	204
실시가능성	enablement	205
실시권	license	205
실시료 과적	royalty stacking	205
실시료 기초	royalty base	205
실시례	embodiment	205
실시의사가 있는 자	willing licensee	205
실용성	utility	206
실용신안공보	Utility Model Gazette	206
실용신안권의 존속기간	term of utility model right	206

국어로 찾기

(청구범위의) 실질적 변경	substantial amendment (to the claims)	206
실체	substance	206
실체적 거절	substantive refusal	206
실체적인 분쟁	actual controversy	207
실효	annulment	207
심결	administrative trial decision	207
심결의 위법사유	erroneous grounds of administrative decision	207
심결취소소송	revocation action of administrative decision	207
심리	hearing	207
심미감	aesthetic sense	207
심미적 기능성	aesthetic functionality	208
심사	examination	208
심사관	examiner	208
심사관 보정	examiner's amendment	208
심사의 보류	suspension of action by office	209
심사청구	requests for examinations	209
심판(특허심판원)	administrative trial	209
심판관	administrative judge	209
심판관합의체	panel of administrative judges	209
심판장	chief administrative judge	209
심판청구	petition for (administrative) trial	209
CA출원(협의의 계속출원)	continuation application	209
아호	pseudonym	210

안정성	stability	210
암시적 표장	suggestive mark	210
약식 신약 허가 신청	abbreviated new drug application (ANDA)	211
약식판결	summary judgment	211
약화(弱化)	blurring	211
양도	assignment	211
양벌규정	joint penal provision	211
양식화	stylized	212
업무상의 신용	business reputation	212
업무표장	business emblem	212
업으로 하다	(to do something) commercially	212
역혼동	reverse confusion	212
연결부	transition	213
연결청구항	linking claim	213
(물품과 서비스의)연관성	relatedness (of the goods or services)	213
연구 또는 시험을 하기 위한 특허발명의 실시	execution of a patented invention for the purpose of research or testing	213
영업방법 발명	business method patent	214
영업비밀	trade secret	214
영업소	place of business	214
예견하다	anticipate	215
예비보정	preliminary amendment	215

국어로 찾기

예측가능성	predictability	215
오감상표	sensory mark	215
오기정정	rectification of clerical errors	215
(발명의) 완성	reduction to practice	216
외관	appearance	216
외관유사	similarity in appearance	216
외국어 등가의 원칙	doctrine of foreign equivalents	216
외적 증거	extrinsic evidence	217
요부	essential part/portion	217
요부관찰	comparison of/by essential parts/portions	217
요약서	abstract	217
요지	substance	218
요지의 변경	material alteration	218
용도발명	use invention	218
용이하게 창작할 수 있는 디자인	easy-to-create design	219
우선권 주장[1]	claim of priority	219
우선권 주장[2]	benefit claim	219
우선심사	accelerated examination	220
우선심사신청 출원	special applications	220
원산지	place of origin	220
원산지 명칭	appellations of origin	220
원특허권자	original patent owner	220
위조	counterfeit	221
위조상표	counterfeit trademark	221

위치상표	positional mark	221
유도 침해	infringement by inducement	221
유럽특허협약 (EPC)	European Patent Convention	221
유사상표	similar mark	222
유사상품	similar goods	222
유사의 폭	range of similarity	222
유사표장	pseudo mark	223
유사필수적 공동소송	quasi-compulsory joint litigation	223
유사한 (기술)분야	analogous art	223
유예기간	grace period	223
유효출원일	effective filing date	224
육성자	breeder	224
… 으로 구성되는 것을 특징으로 하는	consisting of	224
… 을 포함하는 것을 특징으로 하는	comprising	224
음역	transliteration	224
의견서	written argument	225
의견제출기회의 부여	opportunity to submit arguments	225
의료행위	medical practice	225
의사에 반한 공지	publication contrary to the will of the person entitled to a patent	225
의식적 제외	deliberately excluded	225
의약용도	medical usage	225
의약의 조제	dispensing of drugs	226
이격적 관찰	comparison by recollection	226

국어로 찾기

이 사건 발명	subject invention	226
이송명령	writ of certiorari	226
이송신청	motion for transfer	226
이용관계	improvement relationship	226
이용발명	improvement invention	227
(판결) 이유	reason	227
이유 없다	without merit	227
이의신청	opposition	227
이의신청의 경합	competition in opposition	227
이의신청의 병합	consolidation of oppositions	227
이전(移轉)	transfer	228
2차 심사	second examination	228
2차적 고려요소	secondary considerations	228
2차적 의미	secondary meaning	228
2차적 인용문헌	secondary references	229
이해관계인	interested parties	229
인격의 동일성	identity of character	229
인도(引渡)	deliver	229
인용디자인	cited design	230
인용문헌	(cited) references	230
인용상표	cited trademark	230
인적관할	personal jurisdiction	230
일군의 발명	group of inventions	230
1디자인 1디자인등록 출원	one design for one application	231

(출원의) 일련번호	serial number (of application)	231
일반 수요자	ordinary consumers	231
일반승계	general succession	231
일부계속출원	continuation-in-part (CIP) application	231
일부심사등록	partial examination	232
(출원의) 일부포기	partial abandonment (of application)	232
일사부재리	non bis in idem	232
일실이익	lost profit	232
일응의 유리한 사건	prima facie case	232
일응의 자명성	prima facie obviousness	233
임계일	critical date	233
임계적 의의	critical significance	233
임의적 표장	arbitrary mark	233
입증취지	purport of evidence	234
입체상표	three-dimensional trademark	234
입체적 형상	three-dimensional shape	234
자기공지	inventor-initiated disclosure	234
자료제출명령	order to produce documents	235
자명식 중복특허	obviousness-type double patenting (ODP)	235
자문변호사	opinion counsel	235
자백	confession	235
자백간주	regarding as confession/admission	235
자연법칙	law of nature	235

국어로 찾기

자유실시기술	freely exploited/practiced invention	236
자유실시디자인	freely exploited/practiced design	236
잠수함 특허	submarine patent	236
장기간의 필요성	long-felt need	236
장식	ornamentation	236
장식성	ornamentality	237
장치-변환 테스트	machine-or-transformation test	237
장치 청구항	apparatus claims	237
재발행출원	reissue application	237
재심	retrial	238
재심리	de novo review	238
재심사	reexamination	238
재심에 의하여 회복한 특허권에 대한 선사용권자의 통상실시권	non-exclusive license for prior users of patent reinstated through retrial	238
재외자	non-resident	238
재정	adjudication	239
재판적	venue	239
쟁점	issue	239
저명상표	famous trademark	239
저명성	famousness	240
저속한 사항	scandalous matter	240
저장상표	reserved trademark	240
저촉발명	infringing invention	241

저촉심사 (상표)	interference proceeding (trademark)	241
저촉절차 (특허)	interference proceeding (patent)	241
저촉표장	conflicting mark	242
적극적 권리범위확인심판	(administrative) affirmative confirmation trial for the scope of rights	242
전문가 증인	expert witness	242
전문가 진술서	expert witness statement	242
전문심리위원	technical advisors	242
전시	display	243
전용(轉用)	appropriation	243
전용(轉用)사용권	exclusive license	243
전용실시권	exclusive license	244
전자문서	electronic documents	244
전자서명	electronic signature	244
전제부	preamble	244
전체관찰	compare as a whole	245
전체시장가치의 법칙	entire market value rule	245
(심사) 절차	prosecution	245
절차의 보정	amendment of procedure	245
절차 중지 신청	motion to stay	245
점진적 침해의 원칙	doctrine of progressive encroachment	245
정규출원	non-provisional application	246
정당한 불사용의 진술서(선서서)	affidavit/declaration of excusable non-use	246
정당한 이유	good cause	246

국어로 찾기

정보공개진술서	information disclosure statement (IDS)	246
정보통신망	information and communication networks	246
정부에 의한 특허발명의 실시	execution of patented inventions by government	247
정정심판	trial for corrections	247
정정증명서	certificate of correction	247
정정청구	petition for correction	247
정직과 신의성실 의무	duty of candor and good faith	247
제법(製法) 한정 물건발명	product by process claim	247
제조물	manufacture	248
제척	exclusion (of a judge)	248
제척기간	statute of repose	248
제품디자인	product design	248
제품포장	product packaging	248
제호	title (of a book, etc.)	248
젭슨 타입 청구항	jepson type claim	249
조사관	judicial research officer	249
조성물	composition	249
조어상표	coined mark	249
조정	mediation	250
조정전담판사	mediation judge	250
존속기간	term	250
존속기간 갱신	renewal of duration	250
존속기간 만료	expiration of duration	250

존속기간의 연장	extension of duration	250
종국판결	final decision	251
종속항	dependent claim	251
종자	seed	251
종자산업법	Seed Industry Act	251
종합준비서면	comprehensive brief	251
주등록부	Principal Register	251
주로 단지 성(姓)만으로 구성된 표장	(A mark that is) primarily merely a surname	251
(판결)주문	judgment	252
주문자상표 부착방식 (OEM)	OEM (original equipment manufacturing)	252
주변한정주의	peripheral claiming	252
주신문	direct examination	252
주인용문헌	primary references	252
주지관용기술	well-known and commonly used art	253
주지기술	well-known art	253
주지디자인	well-known design	253
주지모양	well-known pattern	253
주지상표	well-known trademark	254
주지저명상표	well-known and famous trademark	254
준비명령	preparatory order	254
준비서면	brief	255
준용	application mutatis mutandis	255
중단	interruption	255

국어로 찾기

중복등록	duplicate registrations	255
중복특허	double patenting	255
중심적 식별력	central distinctiveness	255
중심한정주의	central claiming	256
중용권	intervening rights	256
중의적 표현	double entendre	256
중지	suspension	256
중지명령	cease and desist order	256
증거개시절차	discovery	257
증거보전	preservation of evidence	257
증거설명서	explanatory documents for evidence	257
증거의 우위성	preponderance of evidence	257
증거조사	examination of evidence	257
증명책임	burden of proof	257
증명표장	certification mark	257
증분이익	incremental profit	258
증언녹취	deposition	258
증인소환장	subpoenas to witnesses	258
증인신문사항	a questionnaire for the examination	258
지리적으로 기만적인 허위표시 표장	geographically deceptively misdescriptive marks	258
지리적인 기만적 표장	deceptive geographical marks	259
지리적인 기술적 표장	geographically descriptive marks	259
지리적 표시	geographical indication	259

지리적 표시 단체표장	collective mark with geographical indication	260
지리적 표시 증명표장	certification mark with geographical indication	260
지배적 특징	dominant features	260
지속적 노력	due diligence	260
지정국	designated country	260
지정된 사무소	elected office	261
지정상품	designated good	261
지정상품추가등록	registration of additional designated goods	261
직권(에 의한)	ex officio	261
직권보정	ex officio amendment	261
직권심리	ex officio hearing	261
직권심사	ex officio examination	261
직권조정결정	ex officio decisions of mediation	262
직무발명	employee invention	262
직무발명에 대한 보상	compensation for employee invention	262
직접침해	direct infringement	262
진보성	inventive step	262
(통상적인 상거래에서) 진실한 사용	bona fide use (in the ordinary course of trade)	262
진정상품	genuine goods	263
진정성립	establishment of authenticity	263
질권	pledge	263

국어로 찾기

징벌적 손해배상	punitive damages	264
참가	intervention	264
참고도면	swatch-type drawing	264
참조 조문	reference provisions	264
창작상표	fanciful mark	264
(증거의) 채부	admissibility (of evidence)	265
처분통지서	notice of action	265
청각상표	aural marks	265
청구	claim	265
청구범위 제출유예제도	provisional application	265
청구범위	claims	265
청구원인	cause of action	265
청구의 취지	plaintiff's demand	265
청구인	petitioner	265
청구항	claims	265
청구항 구성요소	claim element	266
청구항 발명	claimed invention	266
청구항 한정	claim limitation	266
청구항 해석	claim construction (interpretation)	266
청산	liquidation	266
최적 실시례	best mode	266
최초 거래상 사용일	date of first use in commerce	267
최초거절이유통지	non-final office action	267
최초사용일	date of first use anywhere	267

최초심사	initial examination	267
최초 청구항	original claim	268
최초 출원	original application	268
최후거절이유통지	final (Office) action	268
추상적 관념	abstract idea	268
추인	confirm	268
추후보완	subsequent completion	268
출원	application	269
출원경과	file history	269
출원경과 금반언의 원칙	file wrapper estoppel	269
출원공개	publication of patent applications	270
출원공고	publication of the application	270
출원데이터시트	application data sheet (ADS)	270
출원변경	modification of the application	270
출원심사청구	request for examinations of applications	270
출원의 기초	filing basis	271
출원의 보정	amendment of application	271
출원의 포기	abandonment of application	271
출원의 회복	recover	271
출원의 회복요청	request to reinstate an application	271
출원일	application filing date	271
출원일자의 회복	request to restore filing date	271
출원포대	file wrapper	272
출처	source	272

국어로 찾기

출처의 오인(혼동)	mistake and confusion as to the source	272
출처표시기능	source indication	272
취소	cancellation	273
(심판청구의) 취하	withdrawal (of request for administrative trial)	273
치환	replacement	273
치환가능성	interchangeability	273
치환자명성	level of obviousness of replacement	274
침해	infringement	274
침해금지청구권	petition (request) for an injunction against infringement	274
침해로 인한 손해	damages for infringement	275
칭송형(稱頌型) 용어(표장)	laudatory terms (mark)	275
크로스 라이센싱	cross licensing	275
타인의 업무와 관련된 물품과 혼동을 가져올 염려가 있는 디자인	design likely to cause confusion with articles associated with others' business	275
통상사용권	non-exclusive license	276
통상실시권	non-exclusive license	276
통상실시권 설정의 재정	adjudication on grant of non-exclusive licenses	276
통상실시권 허락의 심판	trial for grant of non-execlusive licenses	276
통상의 거래	ordinary course of business	276
통상의 관찰자	ordinary observer	277

통상의 기술자	person having ordinary skills in the art	277
투여용법 및 투여용량	administration and dosage (of a medicine)	277
트레이드 드레스	trade dress	277
특허결정	decision to grant patent	278
특허공보	patent gazette	278
특허관리인	patent administrator	278
특허관리전문사업자 (NPE)	non-practicing entity (NPE)	278
특허권	patent right	278
특허권의 존속기간	term of patent	279
특허권의 효력범위	scope of protection of patent	279
특허권자	patentee	279
특허대리인	patent agent	279
특허 대상	patentable subject matter	279
특허등록원부	(patent) register	279
특허료	patent fee	279
특허발명	patented invention	280
특허법원 심결취소소송 심리 매뉴얼	Guideline of Practice and Procedure of Revocation Action in the Patent Court of Korea	280
특허법원 침해소송 항소심 심리 매뉴얼	Guideline of Civil Appellate Practice and Procedure of the Patent Court of Korea	280
특허변호사	patent attorney	280
특허성에 대한 실질적인 새로운 문제 (SNQP)	substantial new question of patentability (SNQP)	280

국어로 찾기

특허심사관	patent examiner	280
특허심사지침	Manual of Patent Examining Procedure (MPEP)	280
특허심판관	administrative patent judge	280
특허심판원	Intellectual Property Trial and Appeal Board (IPTAB)	280
특허억류	patent holdup	280
특허요건	requirements for patent registration	281
특허원부	patent register	281
특허증	patent registration certificate	281
특허청	Korean Intellectual Property Office (KIPO)	281
특허출원에 대한 정보제공	provision of information about patent applications	281
특허취소신청	petition for patent cancellation	281
특허침해	patent infringement	281
특허표시	patent marking	281
특허풀	patent pool	282
특허협력조약 (PCT)	Patent Cooperation Treaty (PCT)	282
TSM기준 (교시, 암시, 동기)	teaching, suggestion and motivation (TSM)	282
(판결의) 파기	reverse (judgment)	282
파라미터 발명	parameter invention	283
파생	derivation	283
파생절차	derivation proceeding	283
판결	decision	283

판사에 의한 재판	bench trial	283
포기[1]	abandonment	283
포기[2]	surrender	283
(지정상품의) 포기[3]	relinquishment	284
표면 장식	surface ornamentation	284
표면 처리	surface treatment	284
표시	indication	284
표어	motto	284
표장	mark	285
표장의 표시	representation of mark	285
표장의 훼손	mutilation of mark	285
표준도면	standard character drawings	286
표준필수특허 (SEP)	standard essential patents (SEP)	286
표준화기구	standard setting organization (SSO)	286
품종	plant variety	286
품종보호공보	Official Reports on Plant Variety Protection	287
품종보호권	plant variety right	287
품종보호권자	holder of plant variety right	287
품종보호심판위원회	plant variety protection tribunal	287
품질보증기능	quality assurance	287
품질오인	mistake as to the quality of goods	287
FRAND	FRAND	288
피상고인 (피항소인)	appellee	288

국어로 찾기

피청구인	defendant	288
하위개념	species	288
한 벌의 물품	a set of articles	288
한정	restriction	289
합리적인 노력	reasonable diligence	289
합리적인 실시료	reasonable royalty	289
합성어 표장	compound word mark	289
항고심판소	Board of Patent Appeals and Interferences	289
항소 (불복심판)	appeal	290
항소이유	grounds of appeal	290
항소장	petition of appeal	290
해결하려는 과제	problem to be solved	290
해쉬태그 표장	hashtag marks	290
해태(懈怠)	doctrine of laches	290
행위능력	legal capacity	290
허가-특허 연계제도	patent linkage system	290
허위표시죄	offense of false marking	291
헤이그협정	Hague Agreement	291
현저한 지리적 명칭	well-known geographical terms	291
현저한 효과	significant effect	291
형상	shape	292
형태	form	292
호칭유사	phonetic similarity	292
호환가능성	substitutability	292

혼동가능성	likelihood of confusion	293
혼동 방지 표시 청구권	right to request an indication to avoid confusion	293
홀로그램 상표	hologram mark	294
화체[1]	be embodied in	294
화체[2]	be associated with	294
화해	settlement	295
확대된 선출원	extended first-to-file rule	295
확인대상 (발명/포장/디자인)	challenging/challenged (invention/mark/design)	295
확인진술서	verified statement	295
확인판결	declaratory judgment	296
환송	remand	296
회복할 수 없는 손해	irreparable harm	296
회피	recusal	296
회피설계	design around	296
효력	effect	296
후각상표	olfactory marks	297
후견감독인	legal guardian	297
후순위권리자	junior party	297
흔히 있는 성 또는 명칭	common surname or name	297
희석	dilution	297

영어로 찾기

abandonment	포기	300
abandonment (of designated goods)	(지정상품의) 포기	300
abandonment of application	출원의 포기	300
abbreviated new drug application (ANDA)	약식 신약 허가 신청	300
abstract	요약서	300
abstract idea	추상적 관념	300
abstraction	추상적 관념	300
abuse (of patent right)	(특허권의) 남용, (특허권의) 부당행사	301
abuse of right	권리남용	301
accelerated examination	우선심사	301
acquired distinctiveness (based on use)	사용에 의한 식별력	301
action to confirmation of the scope of rights	권리범위확인소송	302
actual controversy	실체적인 분쟁	302
actually used trademark	실사용상표	302
additional period	부가기간	302
adjudication	재정	302
adjudication on grant of non-exclusive licenses	통상실시권 설정의 재정	303
administration and dosage (of a medicine)	투여용법 및 투여용량	303
administrative judge	심판관	303
administrative patent judge	특허심판관	304
administrative trial	심판(특허심판원)	304

administrative trial against rejection	거절결정 불복심판	304
administrative trial decision	심결	304
administrative trial decision obtained by fraud	사해심결	304
admissibility (of evidence)	(증거의) 채부	305
admission	자백	305
adverse inference	불리한 추정	305
adverse party	상대방 당사자	305
aesthetic functionality	심미적 기능성	305
aesthetic impression	심미감	305
aesthetic sense	심미감	305
affidavit of continued use	계속사용진술서	306
affidavit/declaration of excusable non-use	정당한 불사용의 진술서(선서서)	306
(administrative) affirmative confirmation trial for the scope of rights	적극적 권리범위확인심판	306
(administrative) affirmative scope of rights trial	적극적 권리범위확인심판	306
against public order or good morals	공공의 질서 또는 선량한 풍속에 어긋난	306
agency authority	대리권	307
agent	대리인	307
AIA (Leahy-Smith America Invents Act)	미국 개정 특허법	307
allegations of use (in commerce)	(거래상) 사용주장	307

영어로 찾기

all elements rule, all-limitation rule	구성요소 일체의 원칙	307
amendment	보정	308
amendment of application	출원의 보정	308
amendment of procedure	절차의 보정	308
amicus curie briefs	법정 의견서	308
analogous art	유사한 (기술)분야	309
annulment	실효	309
antecedent basis	선행근거	309
anticipate	예견하다	309
apparatus claims	장치 청구항	309
appeal	항소(불복심판)	309
appearance	외관	310
appellant	상고인/항소인	310
appellations of origin	원산지 명칭	310
appellee	피상고인(피항소인)	310
application	출원	310
application by unentitled persons	모인출원	310
application data sheet (ADS)	출원데이터시트	310
application filing date	출원일	311
application for design registration	디자인등록출원	311
application mutatis mutandis	준용	311
apportionment	기여분	311
appraisal	감정	311
appropriation	전용(轉用)	312

arbitrary mark	임의적 표장	312
arbitration trademark	임의적 상표	312
article of manufacture	물품	312
as business	업으로 하다	313
as shown	도시된 바와 같은	313
as shown and described	도시(圖示)되고 기재된 바와 같은	313
assignment	양도	313
attractiveness to customers	고객흡인력	313
aural marks	청각상표	313
basic trademark right	기초상표권	314
basic trademark rights of international registration	국제등록기초상표권	314
be associated with	화체	314
be embodied in	화체	314
bench trial	판사에 의한 재판	315
benefit claim	우선권 주장	315
best mode	최적 실시례	315
binding precedent	구속력 있는 선례	315
blocking patent	상호저촉특허	316
blurring	약화(弱化)	316
Board of Patent Appeals and Interferences	항고심판소	316
bona fide intention (to use mark in commerce)	상표를 거래상 사용하고자 하는 진실한 의사	316
bona fide use (in the ordinary course of trade)	(통상적인 상거래에서) 진실한 사용	317

영어로 찾기

breaches of order to maintain confidentiality	비밀유지명령위반죄	317
breeder	육성자	317
brief	준비서면	317
burden of proof	증명책임	317
business emblem	업무표장	317
business method patent	영업방법 발명	317
business reputation	업무상의 신용	318
CAFC (Court of Appeals for the Federal Circuit)	미국연방순회항소법원	318
cancellation	취소	318
cancellation (of registration)	등록취소	318
category of goods	상품류 구분	318
cause of action	청구원인	319
cease and desist order	중지명령	319
central claiming	중심한정주의	319
central distinctiveness	중심적 식별력	319
certificate of correction	정정증명서	319
certificate of registration	등록증	319
certificate of trademark registration	상표등록증	319
certification mark	증명표장	319
certification mark with geographical indication	지리적 표시 증명표장	320
chain of title	권원의 연속	320
challenge (of a judge)	기피	320

challenged/challenging(invention/mark/design)	확인대상(발명/표장/디자인)	320
characteristic features	독특한 특징	321
chief administrative judge	심판장	321
cited design	인용디자인	322
cited invention	비교대상발명, 비교대상고안	322
cited trademark	인용상표	322
claim	청구	322
claim construction (interpretation)	청구항 해석	322
claimed invention	청구항 발명	322
claim element	청구항 구성요소	322
claim for compensation for loss	손실보상청구	323
claim for damages	손해배상 청구권	323
claim for reinstatement of reputation	신용회복청구	323
claim limitation	청구항 한정	324
claim of priority	우선권 주장	324
claims	청구범위, 청구항	324
clarification	석명	324
classification of goods	물품류	325
classification of goods/services	상품 및 서비스의 분류	325
clear and convincing evidence	명백하고 확실한 증거	325
clearly erroneous standard	명백한 오류 기준	325
coat of arms	문장	325

영어로 찾기

coined mark	조어상표	325
co-inventor	공동발명자	326
collateral estoppel	부수적 금반언	326
collective mark	단체표장	326
collective mark with geographical indication	지리적 표시 단체표장	326
color location statement	색채위치의 진술	326
color mark	색채상표	327
combination	(변론의) 병합	327
combination of references/prior arts	선행발명의 결합	327
combination patent	결합발명	327
combined application	다류출원(제도)	328
commercial impression	거래상의 인상	328
(to do something) commercially	업으로 하다	328
commercial name	상호	328
commercial success	상업적 성공	328
commissioned judge	수명법관	329
commonly used art	관용기술	329
commonly used mark	관용표장	329
common sense selection	상식적 선택	330
common surname or name	흔히 있는 성 또는 명칭	330
companion applications	동일인출원	330
comparative observation	대비적 관찰	330
compare as a whole	전체관찰	331

compare by element	분리관찰	331
comparison of/by essential parts/portions	요부관찰	331
comparison by recollection	이격적 관찰	332
compensation for employee invention	직무발명에 대한 보상	332
competing application	경합출원	332
competition in opposition	이의신청의 경합	333
complaint	소장	333
component	(발명의) 구성요소	333
components	부분품	333
composite trademark	결합상표	333
composition	조성물	333
compound	조성물	334
compound word mark	합성어 표장	334
comprehensive brief	종합준비서면	334
comprising	… 을 포함하는 것을 특징으로 하는	334
compulsory license	강제실시권	334
concept	관념, (발명의)착상	334
conception	발명의 착상	335
concurrent use registration	공존사용등록, 공존동의제도	335
confession	자백	335
confidential design	비밀디자인	335
confirm	추인	335
confiscation	몰수	335

영어로 찾기

conflicting mark	저촉표장	336
consisting of	… 으로 구성되는 것을 특징으로 하는	336
consolidation of oppositions	이의신청의 병합	336
constructive use	사용간주	336
consumer deception	수요자 기만	337
continuation (of procedure)	(절차의) 속행	337
continuation application	CA출원(협의의 계속출원)	337
continuation-in-part (CIP) application	일부계속출원	338
continued/continuing application	계속출원(광의)	338
contribution ratio (of a patented invention)	기여도 (특허발명의)	338
contributory infringement	기여침해	338
conversion of applications	변경출원	339
co-pending applications	동시계류출원	339
corresponding elements	대응구성	339
corresponding feature	대응구성	339
counterclaim	반소	339
counterfeit	위조	339
counterfeit mark	모방상표, 위조상표	340
country of origin	본국	340
course of trade	거래실정	340
creator of design	디자인창작자	340
crime of fraud	거짓행위의 죄	340
criminal complaint	고소	340

critical date	임계일	340
critical significance	임계적 의의	341
cross examination	반대신문	341
cross licensing	크로스 라이센싱	341
crystal form invention	결정형(結晶形) 발명	341
damages for infringement	침해로 인한 손해	342
date of first use anywhere	최초사용일	342
date of first use in commerce	최초 거래상 사용일	342
date of international registration	국제등록일	342
date of release	반포일	342
de novo review	드노보 심리(審理), 재심리	342
deceptive geographical marks	지리적인 기만적 표장	343
deceptive intent	기만의 의도	343
deceptively misdescriptive geographic marks	지리적인 기만적 허위표시표장	343
deceptively misdescriptive mark	기만적 허위표시 표장	343
deceptive mark	기만적 표장	343
decision	판결, 결정	344
decision to grant patent	특허결정	344
decision to register	등록결정	344
decision to reject(refuse) an application	거절결정	344
declaration in lieu of oath	선서를 갈음하는 선언서	344
declaration of continued use	계속사용진술서	345
declaratory judgment	확인판결	345

영어로 찾기

deemed public officials	공무원 의제	345
defendant	피청구인	345
(administrative) defensive confirmation trial for the scope of rights	소극적 권리범위확인심판	345
deficiency of description	기재불비	345
definiteness	명확성	346
deliberate infringement	고의침해	346
deliberately excluded	의식적 제외	346
deliver	인도(引渡), 교부	346
dependent claim	종속항	347
deposition	증언녹취	347
deposit of micro-organisms	미생물의 기탁	347
derivation	파생	347
derivation proceeding	파생절차	347
description (of an invention)	(발명의) 설명, 기재사항	347
description on a publication distributed	반포된 간행물에 게재	348
descriptive mark	기술적 표장	348
design	디자인	348
design around	회피설계	348
designated country	(국제등록) 지정국	348
designated good	지정상품	348
design containing publicly known parts	공지 부분을 포함하는 디자인	349
design described (in a publication)	(간행물에) 게재된 의장	349

Design Gazette	디자인공보	349
design likely to cause confusion with articles associated with others' business	타인의 업무와 관련된 물품과 혼동을 가져올 염려가 있는 디자인	349
design patent application	디자인특허출원	350
Design Register	디자인등록원부	350
a design that may be easily created	용이하게 창작할 수 있는 디자인	350
deviser	고안자	350
digital signature	전자서명	350
dilution	희석	350
direct examination	주신문	351
direct infringement	직접침해	351
disclaimer	권리불요구	351
disclose	개시	351
disclosure by applicant	자기공지	351
discovery	증거개시절차	351
dismissal	각하, 기각	352
dismissal of amendment	보정각하(결정)	352
(decision to) dismiss amendment	보정각하(결정)	352
disparagement	비방	352
dispensing of drugs	의약의 조제	352
display	전시	353
disposition refusing to accept application	불수리처분	353
distinctiveness	식별력	353

영어로 찾기

distinctness	구별성	353
distribution (of a publication)	(간행물의) 반포	354
division	분할	354
divisional application	분할출원	354
doctrine of equivalents	균등론	354
doctrine of foreign equivalents	외국어 등가의 원칙	354
doctrine of laches	해태(懈怠)	355
doctrine of legal equivalents	동일 간주 원칙	355
doctrine of progressive encroachment	점진적 침해의 원칙	355
documentary evidence	서증	356
domestic representative	관리인	356
dominant features	지배적 특징	356
double entendre	중의적 표현	356
double patenting	중복특허	357
drawing	도면	357
due diligence	지속적 노력	357
duplicate registrations	중복등록	357
duration	존속기간	357
duty of candor and good faith	정직과 신의성실 의무	357
duty of confidentiality	비밀유지의무	357
duty of disclosure	개시의무	357
duty to state technology used for the invention	배경기술 기재의무	358
easy-to-create design	용이하게 창작할 수 있는 디자인	358

economically relevant relationship	경제적 견련관계	358
effect	효력	359
effective filing date	유효출원일	359
elected office	지정된 사무소	359
electronic documents	전자문서	359
electronic signature	전자서명	359
element	(발명의)구성요소	359
embodiment	실시례	359
employee invention	직무발명	360
enablement	실시가능성	360
Enforcement Decree of the Trademark Act	상표법 시행령	360
Enforcement Rule of the Trademark Act	상표법 시행규칙	360
enhanced damages	가중적 손해배상	360
entire market value rule	전체시장가치의 법칙	360
entrusted judge	수탁판사	360
erroneous grounds of administrative decision	심결의 위법사유	361
essential part/portion	요부	361
establishment of authenticity	진정성립	361
European Patent Convention	유럽특허협약(EPC)	361
examination	심사	361
examination of evidence	증거조사	361
examiner	심사관	362
examiner's amendment	심사관 보정	362

영어로 찾기

exclusion (of a judge)	제척	362
exclusionary implementation righ	독점적 실시권, 배타적 실시권	362
exclusive license	전용실시권, 전용(專用) 사용권, 독점적 실시권, 배타적 실시권	362
executing	실시	363
execution of a patented invention for the purpose of research or testing	연구 또는 시험을 하기 위한 특허발명의 실시	363
execution of patented inventions by government	정부에 의한 특허발명의 실시	363
exercises due care	상당한 주의	363
exhaustion	소진	364
exhaustion doctrine	권리소진의 원칙	364
exhibit	전시	365
ex officio	직권(에 의한)	365
ex officio amendment	직권보정	365
ex officio decisions of mediation	직권조정결정	365
ex officio examination	직권심사	365
ex officio hearing	직권심리	365
expansion-of-trade doctrine	거래확장의 원칙	366
ex parte appeals	결정계 항소	366
ex parte prosecution	결정계 절차	366
ex parte reexamination	결정계 심사	367
expedited examination	우선심사	367
expert witness	전문가 증인, 감정증인	367
expert witness statement	전문가 진술서	367

expiration of duration	존속기간 만료	367
expiration of trademark registration	상표등록의 만료	367
expire	소멸	368
explanatory documents for evidence	증거설명서	368
exploitation	실시	368
expropriation	수용	368
extended first-to-file rule	확대된 선출원	368
extension of duration	존속기간의 연장	368
extinguishment	소멸	368
extinguishment of international registration	국제등록의 소멸	369
extrinsic evidence	외적 증거	369
failure to function	기능(수행)실패	369
false display	거짓표시	369
false indication	거짓표시	370
false suggestion of connection	관계의 허위적 암시	370
fame	저명성	370
family of marks	가족상표	370
famousness	저명성	371
famous trademark	저명상표	371
fanciful mark	창작상표	372
feature comparison chart	구성대비표	372
fee	수수료	372
fee shifting	소송비용청구	372

영어로 찾기

figurative mark	도형상표	372
file history	출원경과	373
file wrapper	출원포대	373
file wrapper estoppel	출원경과 금반언의 원칙	373
filing basis	출원의 기초	374
final (office) action	최후거절이유통지	374
final decision	종국판결	374
final judgment	종국판결	374
first sale doctrine	권리소진의 원칙	374
first-to-file rule	선출원주의	374
fixed period	불변기간	374
flavor mark	미각상표	374
font	글자체	375
force majeure	불가항력	375
forfeiture	몰수	375
form	형태, 모양	375
a form related to a function of the article	물품의 기능에 관련된 형태	375
FRAND	FRAND	376
fraud	거짓행위의 죄	376
freely exploited/practiced design	자유실시디자인	376
freely exploited/practiced invention	자유실시기술	376
free riding	무임승차	376

functional and commercial modification	기능적이고 상업적인 변형	377
functional claim	기능식청구항	377
functional form of a product	물품의 기능적 형태	377
functionality	기능성	377
fundamental form of a product	물품의 기본적 형태	378
general consuming public	일반 수요자	378
generally accepted business practices	상거래 관행	378
general succession	일반승계	378
generic concepts	상위개념	379
generic drugs	복제약	379
generic name	보통명칭	380
genuine goods	진정상품	380
geographical indication	지리적 표시	380
geographically deceptively misdescriptive marks	지리적으로 기만적인 허위표시 표장	380
geographically deceptive marks	지리적인 기만적 표장	381
geographically descriptive marks	지리적인 기술적 표장	381
good	상품	381
good cause	정당한 이유	382
good faith	선의	382
good moral	선량한 풍속	382
goods in trade	거래상품	382
goods-place association	상품-장소간 연관성(연계성)	383
grace period	유예기간	383

영어로 찾기

grade designations	등급표시	383
ground	(판결) 이유	383
grounds for appeal	상고/항소 이유	383
grounds for invalidation	등록무효사유	383
grounds of appeal	항소이유	384
grounds to cancel trademark registration	상표등록취소사유	384
group of inventions	일군의 발명	384
Guideline of Civil Appellate Practice and Procedure of the Patent Court of Korea	특허법원 침해소송 항소심 심리 매뉴얼	384
Guideline of Practice and Procedure of Revocation Action in the Patent Court of Korea	특허법원 심결취소소송 심리 매뉴얼	385
hashtag marks	해쉬태그 표장	385
Hague Agreement	헤이그협정	385
~ have economic ties	경제적 견련관계	385
hearing	심리	385
highly advanced	고도(高度)의	385
hindsight reconstruction	사후적 고찰	385
holder of an international registration	국제등록명의인	386
holder of plant variety right	품종보호권자	386
hologram mark	홀로그램 상표	386
homonymous geographical indication	동음이의어 지리적 표시	386
house mark	사표(社標)	386

identical good	동일상품	387
identical invention	동일한 발명	387
identical trademark	동일상표	387
identification number	고유번호	388
identity of character	인격의 동일성	388
identity or similarity of designs (shapes)	디자인(형태)의 동일 · 유사성	388
imitate	모조	389
immoral or scandalous matter	공서양속에 반하는 상표	389
implementation	실시례	389
improvement invention	이용발명, 개량발명	389
improvement relationship	이용관계	390
including	… 을 포함하는 것을 특징으로 하는	390
in common use	보통으로 사용하다	390
incomplete invention	미완성 발명	390
incomplete response (to Office action)	(특허상표청 통지에 대한) 불완전한 반박	391
incontestability	불가쟁력	391
incremental profit	증분이익	391
independent claim	독립항	391
indication	표시	392
indication of design registration	디자인등록표시	392
indirect infringement	간접침해	392
industrial applicability	산업상 이용가능성	393
industrial usability	공업상 이용가능성	393

영어로 찾기

inequitable conduct	불공정행위	393
informal applications	방식흠결출원	393
information and communication networks	정보통신망	394
information disclosure statement (IDS)	정보공개진술서	394
infringement	침해	394
infringement by equivalents	균등침해	394
infringement by inducement	유도 침해	394
infringing invention	저촉발명	394
inherency	내재성	394
inherent distinctiveness	고유의 식별력	395
inherently compulsory joint litigation	고유필수적 공동소송	395
initial examination	최초심사	395
injunction	금지명령	396
inspection	검증	396
Intellectual Property Trial and Appeal Board (IPTAB)	특허심판원	396
intentionally excluded	의식적 제외	396
intent to use (ITU)	사용의사	396
intent-to-use applications	사용의사 출원	396
interchangeability	치환가능성	397
interested parties	이해관계인	397
interference proceeding (trademark)	저촉심사 (상표)	397

interference proceeding (patent)	저촉절차 (특허)	397
international applicant	국제출원인	397
International Bureau	국제사무국	398
International Classification for Industrial Designs	국제디자인분류	398
International Convention for the Protection of New Varieties of Plants	식물 신품종 보호에 관한 국제조약	398
International Intellectual Property Training Institute	국제지식재산연수원	398
International Register	국제등록부	398
international registration	국제등록	398
inter partes reexamination	당사자계 재심사	398
inter partes review	당사자계 심판	399
interruption	중단	399
intervening rights	중용권	399
intervention	참가	399
intrinsic evidence	내적 증거	399
invalidation	등록무효, 무효처분	399
invention	발명	400
invention at issue	이 사건 발명	400
invention of a process of manufactoring a thing	물건을 생산하는 방법의 발명	400
invention of a thing	물건의 발명	400
inventions necessary for national defence	국방상 필요한 발명	400
inventive step	진보성	400

영어로 찾기

inventor	발명자	401
inventor-initiated disclosure	자기공지	401
inventorship	발명주체	401
investigation officer	조사관	401
IPTAB trial	심판	401
irreparable harm	회복할 수 없는 손해	401
issue	쟁점	401
issue date	발행일	401
Jepson type claim	젭슨 타입 청구항	402
joinder of petition for trial	공동심판청구	402
joint applicants	공동출원인	402
joint inventor	공동발명자	402
joint ownership	공유	402
joint penal provision	양벌규정	403
joint research agreement	공동연구협약	403
judge sitting by designation	수탁판사	403
judge to be in charge	수명법관	403
judgment	(판결)주문	403
judicial research officer	조사관	403
junior party	후순위권리자	403
Jurisdiction	관할	403
jury trial	배심재판	404
Justifiable reason	정당한 이유	404
(publicly) known art	공지기술	404

Korean Intellectual Property Office (KIPO)	특허청	404
lack of sufficient description	기재불비	404
lack of written description	기재불비	404
Lanham Act	미 상표법	404
laudatory terms (mark)	칭송형(稱頌型) 용어(표장)	404
law of nature	자연법칙	405
legal capacity	권리능력, 행위능력	405
legal fiction as public officials	공무원 의제	405
legal guardian	후견감독인	406
legally binding force	기속력	406
letter trademark	문자상표	406
level of obviousness of replacement	치환자명성	406
license	실시권	407
likelihood of confusion	혼동가능성	407
linking claim	연결청구항	408
liquidation	청산	408
literal infringement	문언침해	408
literal interpretation	문언해석	408
Locarno Agreement	로카르노협정	408
long-felt need	장기간의 필요성	408
lost profit	일실이익	409
machine-or-transformation test	장치-변환 테스트	409
Madrid Agreement Concerning the International Registration of Marks	상표의 국제등록에 관한 마드리드협정	409

영어로 찾기

Madrid Agreement for the Repression of False or Deceptive Indications of Source on Goods	상품의 허위 또는 기만표시 억제를 위한 마드리드협정	409
Madrid Protocol	마드리드 의정서	409
maintenance fees	등록유지료	410
malpractice	배임행위	410
Manual of Patent Examining Procedure (MPEP)	특허심사지침	410
manufacture	제조물	410
mark	표장	410
marketplace	거래사회	410
marking of protected plant variety	보호품종의 표시	411
Markman hearing	마크맨 심리	411
Markush type claim	마쿠쉬 청구항	411
material alteration	요지의 변경	411
means plus function claim	기능식청구항	412
means to solve the problem	과제해결원리	412
mediation	조정	412
mediation judge	조정전담판사	412
medical practice	의료행위	412
medical usage	의약용도	412
merely descriptive mark	단순 기술표장	412
method claim	방법청구항	412
Ministry of Food and Drug Safety	식품의약품안전처	413
misappropriation	도용	413

mistake and confusion as to the source	출처의 오인(혼동)	413
mistake as to the quality of goods	품질오인	413
model designations	모델 표시	414
modification of the application	출원변경	414
motion for judgment as a matter of law (JMOL)	법적판결신청	414
motion for transfer	이송신청	414
motion marks	동작상표	414
motion to dismiss	소각하 신청	415
motion to stay	절차 중지 신청	415
motto	표어	415
multiple-class application	다류(多類)출원(제도)	415
multiple dependent claim	다중종속항	415
multiple-design application	복수디자인등록출원	415
mutilation of mark	표장의 훼손	416
national stage application	국내단계출원	416
negative dictionary evidence	사전상 부재 증거	416
new matter	신규사항	417
Nice Agreement	니스협정	417
non bis in idem	일사부재리	417
non-distinctive mark	식별력이 없는 표장	417
non-exclusive license	통상실시권, 통상사용권	418
non-exclusive licenses after expiration of design rights	디자인권 존속기간 만료 후의 통상실시권	418

영어로 찾기

non-exclusive licenses based on prior use	선사용에 의한 통상실시권	418
non-exclusive license for prior users of patent reinstated through retrial	재심에 의하여 회복한 특허권에 대한 선사용권자의 통상실시권	418
non-final office action	최초거절이유통지	419
non-obviousness	비자명성	419
non-patent literature	비특허문헌	419
non-practicing entity (NPE)	특허관리전문사업자 (NPE)	419
non-provisional application	정규출원	419
non-resident	재외자	419
nonstatutory subject matter	부등록대상	420
non-traditional mark	비전형상표	420
non-use cancellation	불사용취소	420
non-visual marks	비시각적 상표	420
notice of action	처분통지서	420
notice of allowability	등록가능통지	421
notice of allowance	등록결정통지	421
notice of grounds for rejection/refusal	거절이유통지	421
novelty	신규성	421
numerical limitation invention	수치한정발명	422
oath	선서	422
objective creativity	객관적 창작성	422
objective observation	객관적 관찰	423

obviousness-type double patenting (ODP)	자명식 중복특허	423
obvious to try	시도의 자명성	423
OEM (original equipment manufacturing)	주문자상표 부착방식 (OEM)	423
offense of divulging secrets or confidential information	비밀누설죄	423
offense of false marking	허위표시죄	424
Office action	(최초)거절이유통지	424
Official Reports on Plant Variety Protection	품종보호공보	424
olfactory marks	후각상표, 냄새상표	424
one design for one application	1디자인 1디자인등록 출원	424
ongoing royalty	계속적 실시료	425
opinion counsel	자문변호사	425
opportunity to submit arguments	의견제출기회의 부여	425
opposition	이의신청	425
oral argument	변론	425
oral hearing	구술심리	425
order	(판결)주문	425
order to make an amendment	보정명령	425
order to maintain confidentiality	비밀유지명령	426
order to produce documents	자료제출명령	426
order to supplement an application	(절차)보완명령	426
ordinary consumers	일반 수요자	427

영어로 찾기

ordinary course of business	통상의 거래	427
ordinary observer	통상의 관찰자	427
original application	최초 출원	427
original claim	최초 청구항	427
original patent owner (right holder)	원특허권자	428
original patent right holder	원특허권자	428
ornamentality	장식성	428
ornamental matter	장식	428
ornamentation	장식	429
overrule	각하, 기각	429
panel of administrative judges	심판관합의체	429
parallel import	병행수입	429
parameter invention	파라미터 발명	429
parent application	모출원(母出願)	429
the Paris Convention for the Protection of Industrial Property (the Paris Convention)	산업재산권의 보호를 위한 파리 협약	430
partial abandonment (of application)	(출원의) 일부포기	430
partial design	부분디자인	430
partial examination	일부심사등록	430
particularly point out the invention	발명을 특정하여 지칭함	430
parts	부품	431
patentability	특허요건	431
patentable subject matter	특허 대상	431

patent administrator	특허관리인	431
patent agent	특허대리인	431
patent attorney	특허변호사	431
Patent Cooperation Treaty (PCT)	특허협력조약 (PCT)	432
patent-drug approval linkage	허가-특허 연계제도	432
patented invention	특허발명	432
patentee	특허권자	432
patent examiner	특허심사관	432
patent fee	특허료	432
patent gazette	특허공보	432
patent holder	특허권자	432
patent holdup	특허억류	432
patent infringement	특허침해	433
patent linkage system	허가-특허 연계제도	433
patent marking	특허표시	433
patent pool	특허풀	433
patent register	특허원부	433
patent registration certificate	특허증	434
patent right	특허권	434
Patent Trial and Appeal Board	미국 특허심판원	434
pattern	모양	434
payment of remainder	등록료의 보전	434
pending application	계류출원	434
peripheral claiming	주변한정주의	434

영어로 찾기

permanent injunction	(영구)금지명령	435
personal jurisdiction	인적관할	435
person having ordinary skills in the art	통상의 기술자	435
perspective view	사시도	435
petition	소장, 청구	435
petitionee	피청구인	435
petitioner	청구인	435
petition (request) for an injunction against infringement	침해금지청구권	435
petition for correction	정정청구	436
petition for patent cancellation	특허취소신청	436
petition for (administrative) trial	심판청구	436
petition of appeal	항소장	436
petition to revive an application	(포기된 출원의) 권리회복청구	436
phantom elements	가변요소	436
phonetic similarity	호칭유사	437
place of business	영업소	437
place of origin	원산지	437
place of production	산지(産地)	437
plain meaning	문언적 의미	438
plaintiff's demand	청구의 취지	438
plaintiff's exhibit	갑호증	438
plant patents	식물특허	438

Plant Varieties Protection Act	식물품종보호법	438
plant variety	품종	438
plant variety protection tribunal	품종보호심판위원회	439
plant variety right	품종보호권	439
pleading	변론	439
pledge	질권	439
positional mark	위치상표	439
post grant review	등록후재심사	440
preamble	전제부	440
preceding invention	선행고안	440
predictability	예측가능성	440
preferred embodiment	바람직한 구현례	440
preliminary amendment	예비보정	440
preliminary injunction	가처분	441
preparatory order	준비명령	441
preparatory order for hearing	변론준비명령	441
preponderance of evidence	증거의 우위성	441
preservation of evidence	증거보전	441
presumption of (the amount of) damages	손해액 추정	441
presumption of manufacturing process	생산방법의 추정	442
presumption of negligence	과실의 추정	442
pretrial hearing	변론준비기일	442

영어로 찾기

previously registered mark	선등록상표	442
price erosion	가격침식	442
prima facie case	일응의 유리한 사건	442
prima facie obviousness	일응의 자명성	443
(A mark that is) Primarily merely a surname	주로 단지 성(姓)만으로 구성된 표장	443
primary references	주인용문헌	443
principal design	기본디자인	443
Principal Register	주등록부	444
principle of general reliance	신뢰보호의 원칙	444
principle of individual representation	개별대리의 원칙	444
principle of registration	등록주의	444
principle of trust protection	신뢰보호의 원칙	444
principle to exclude publicly known art	공지기술 배제의 원칙	444
prior art	선행발명	445
prior art exceptions	공지의 예외	445
prior design	선행디자인	445
prior invention	선행기술	445
priority action	선행조치	445
priority claim	우선권 주장	445
prior-registered mark	선등록상표	445
problem to be solved	기술적 과제	446

process claim	방법청구항	446
process invention	방법발명	446
product by process claim	제법(製法) 한정 물건발명	446
product design	제품디자인	446
product packaging	제품포장	446
pro-se application	본인출원	447
prosecution	(심사) 절차	447
prosecution history	출원경과	447
prosecution history estoppel	출원경과 금반언의 원칙	447
protected plant variety	보호품종	447
protective order	비밀유지명령	447
provisional application[1]	가출원	447
provisional application[2]	청구범위 제출유예제도	447
provisional execution	가집행	448
provisional seizure	가압류	448
provision of information about patent applications	특허출원에 대한 정보제공	448
pseudo mark	유사표장	448
pseudonym	아호	448
publication	간행물	449
publication contrary to the will of the person entitled to a patent	의사에 반한 공지	449
publication of patent applications	출원공개	449
publication of the application	출원공고	449

영어로 찾기

public known	공지	450
publicly known design	공지된 디자인	450
publicly known invention	공지된 발명	450
publicly practiced design	공연히 실시된 디자인	450
publicly practiced invention	공연히 실시된 발명	450
public notice in lieu of service	공시송달	451
public order	공공의 질서	451
public practiced	공용	451
punitive damages	징벌적 손해배상	451
purport of claim	청구의 취지	452
purport of evidence	입증취지	452
quality assurance	품질보증기능	452
quasi-compulsory joint litigation	유사필수적 공동소송	452
questionnaire for examination	증인신문사항	452
range of similarity	유사의 폭	453
ratify	추인	453
reason	(판결) 이유	453
reasonable diligence	합리적인 노력	453
reasonable royalty	합리적인 실시료	454
rebuttal evidence	반박증거	454
recover (an application)	출원의 회복	454
rectification of clerical errors	오기정정	454
recusal	회피	455
reduction to practice	(발명의)완성, (발명의)구체화	455

reexamination	재심사	455
reference provisions	참조 조문	455
(cited) references	인용문헌	455
refusal	거절결정	456
regarding as confession/admission	자백간주	456
(patent) register	특허등록원부	456
registered trademark	등록상표	456
registered utility model	등록실용신안	456
registration date	등록일	456
registration fee	등록료	457
registration for establishment of rights	설정등록	457
registration of additional designated goods	지정상품추가등록	457
reinstate (an application)	출원의 회복	457
reissue application	재발행출원	457
reject	거절결정	458
rejection	거절결정	458
related companies	관계회사	459
related design	관련디자인	459
relatedness (of the goods or services)	(물품과 서비스의)연관성	459
relevant art	유사한 (기술)분야	459
relief	권리구제	459
relief demanded	청구의 취지	459

영어로 찾기

relinquishment	(지정상품의) 포기	459
remand	환송	460
remedies	구제책	460
renewal of duration	존속기간 갱신	460
repeating pattern marks	반복패턴표장	460
replacement	치환	461
reply brief	답변서	461
representation of mark	표장의 표시	461
representative	대리인	462
request for continued examination	계속심사청구	462
request for examinations of applications	출원심사청구	462
request to reinstate an application	출원의 회복요청	462
request to restore filing date	출원일자의 회복	462
requests for examinations (of Patent Applications)	심사청구	462
requirements for patent registration	특허요건	462
reserved trademark	저장상표	462
res judicata	기판력	463
respondent	피청구인	463
response brief	답변서	463
restriction	한정	463
retrial	재심	463
retroactive	소급	463
return	반려	463

reverse (judgment)	(판결의) 파기	464
reverse confusion	역혼동	464
revocation	각하, 기각	464
revocation action of administrative decision	심결취소소송	464
revocation of decision	결정의 취소	464
revocation of invalidation	무효처분의 취소	464
right to request an indication to avoid confusion	혼동 방지 표시 청구권	465
royalty base	실시료 기초	465
royalty stacking	실시료 과적	465
rule of thumb	경험법칙	465
running royalty	경상실시료	465
scandalous matter	저속한 사항	466
scent mark	냄새상표	466
scope of protection of patent	특허권의 효력범위	466
secondary considerations	2차적 고려요소	466
secondary meaning	2차적 의미	466
secondary references	2차적 인용문헌	467
second examination	2차 심사	467
secret design	비밀디자인	467
sectional view	단면도	467
seed	종자	468
Seed Industry Act	종자산업법	468
selection invention	선택발명	468

영어로 찾기

senior party	선순위권리자	469
sensory mark	오감상표	469
separation	(변론의) 분리	469
serial number (of application)	(출원의) 일련번호	469
service	송달	469
service mark	서비스표	469
a set of articles	한 벌의 물품	469
settlement	화해	470
shape	형상	470
a shape essential for a function of the relevant article	물품의 기능을 확보하는 데 불가결한 형상	470
significant effect	현저한 효과	470
similar goods	유사상품	470
similarity in appearance	외관유사	471
similarity in concept	관념의 유사	471
similar mark	유사상표	471
simple and common mark	간단하고 흔히 있는 표장	472
simulation	모방	472
single/single-class application	단류(單類)출원	472
slogan	구호	472
solution principles	과제해결원리	473
sound mark	소리상표	473
source	출처	473
source indicator (indication)	출처표시기능	474
special applications	우선심사신청 출원	474

specialized trademark institution	상표전문기관	474
species	하위개념	474
specification	명세서	474
specimen	견본	475
stability	안정성	475
standard character drawings	표준도면	475
standard essential patents (SEP)	표준필수특허 (SEP)	476
standard setting organization (SSO)	표준화기구	476
stare decisis	선례 구속의 원칙	476
statement	기재사항	476
statement of use	사용진술서	476
state of the art	기술 수준	476
statute of repose	제척기간	477
statutory bar	법정제한요건	477
statutory damages	법정손해배상	477
statutory disclaimer	법정 포기	477
statutory period	법정기간	478
stylized	양식화	478
subject invention	이 사건 발명	478
subject matter	발명대상	478
subject matter jurisdiction	사물관할	478
submarine patent	잠수함 특허	478
subordinate concept	하위개념	478
subpoenas to witnesses	증인소환장	479

영어로 찾기

subrogation	물상대위	479
subsequent completion	추후보완	479
subsequent designation	사후지정	479
substance[1]	요지	480
substance[2]	실체	480
substantial amendment to (the claims)	(청구범위의) 실질적 변경	480
substantial new question of patentability (SNQP)	특허성에 대한 실질적인 새로운 문제 (SNQP)	481
substantive refusal	실체적 거절	481
substitutability	호환가능성	481
substitute application	대체출원	481
substitution	치환	481
succession	승계	481
suggestive mark	암시적 표장	482
summary judgment	약식판결	482
summary of invention	발명의 요지	482
supplementation	추후보완	482
supplemental examination	보충심사	483
supplemental portion	부기적 부분	483
Supplemental register	보조등록부	483
supplementary participant	보조참가인	483
Supplementary Intervention	보조참가	483
superordinate concept	상위개념	483
surcharge	과태료	484

surface ornamentation	표면 장식	484
surface treatment	표면 처리	484
surrender	포기	484
suspension	중지	484
suspension of action by office	심사의 보류	485
swatch–type drawing	참고도면	485
takeover	수계	485
tarnishment	손상	485
teaching, suggestion and motivation (TSM)	TSM기준 (교시, 암시, 동기)	486
technical advisors	전문심리위원	486
(judicial) technical examiners	기술심리관	486
technical explanatory session	기술설명회	486
technological common sense	기술상식	487
term	존속기간	487
term of patent	특허권의 존속기간	487
term of utility model right	실용신안권의 존속기간	487
territorial principle	속지주의	488
three–dimensional shape	입체적 형상	488
three–dimensional trademark	입체상표	488
title	명칭	488
title (of a book, etc.)	제호	489
title of invention	발명의 명칭	489
token use	명목상의 사용	489

영어로 찾기

trade dress	트레이드 드레스	489
trademark	상표	489
trademark abuse	부정사용	490
Trademark Act	상표법	490
Trademark Manual of Examining Procedure (TMEP)	상표심사기준	490
Trademark Official Gazette (TMOG)	상표공보	490
Trademark Owner	상표권자	490
Trademark Register	상표등록원부	491
Trademark Registration Treaty (TRT)	상표등록조약	491
Trademark Trial and Appeal Board (TTAB)	상표심판항소위원회	491
trade name	상호	491
trade norms	거래통념	491
trade secret	영업비밀	491
transfer	이전(移轉)	492
transition	연결부	492
transitional measure	경과조치	492
transitional provision	경과규정	492
transliteration	음역	492
traverse	반박	493
trial against rejection	거절결정 불복소송	493
trial date	변론기일	493
trial for corrections	정정심판	493

trial for grant of non-execlusive licenses	통상실시권 허락의 심판	493
trial minutes	변론조서	494
trial on invalidation	무효심판	494
trial on invalidity (of patents)	무효심판	494
trial record	변론조서	494
trial to cancel trademark registration	상표등록취소심판	494
(administrative) trial to confirm scope of rights	권리범위확인심판	495
TRIPs (Trade-Related Intellectual Property portions of General Agreement on Tariffs and Trade)	무역관련 지적재산권에 관한 협정	495
undue experimentation	과도한 실험	495
unentitled person	무권리자	496
unfair competition	부정경쟁	496
Unfair Competition Prevention and Trade Secret Protection Act	부정경쟁방지 및 영업비밀보호에 관한 법률	496
uniformity	균일성	496
unity of invention	발명의 단일성	497
unjust enrichment	부당이득	497
use as a trademark	상표적 사용	497
use-based application	사용기반출원	497
use in a common manner	보통으로 사용하다	497
use in commerce	(상표의) 거래상의 사용	498
use invention	용도발명	498

영어로 찾기

use of a trademark	상표의 사용	498
use of mark as a trade name	상호로서의 사용	499
use of the mark in commerce	(상표의) 거래상의 사용	499
utility	실용성	499
utility model	고안	499
Utility Model Gazette	실용신안공보	500
venue	재판적	500
verification	검증	500
verified statement	확인진술서	500
video conference for case management	사건관리 화상회의	500
Vienna Agreement	비엔나협정	500
visual similarity	시각적 유사성	500
(claim) vitiation	(청구항) 무효화	501
waiver of confidentiality	비밀유지권 포기	501
well-known and commonly used art	주지관용기술	501
well-known and famous trademark	주지저명상표	502
well-known art	주지기술	502
well-known design	주지디자인	502
well-known geographical terms	현저한 지리적 명칭	503
well-known pattern	주지모양	503
well-known trademark	주지상표	503
willful	고의	504

willful infringement	고의침해	504
willing licensee	실시의사가 있는 자	504
windup	청산	504
withdrawal (of request for administrative trial)	(심판청구의) 취하	504
without merit	이유 없다	504
word mark	문자상표	504
writ of certiorari	이송명령	505
written argument	의견서	505
written defense	답변서	505
written description requirement	발명의 기재 요건	505
written hearing	서면심리	505

2017

지식재산 법률용어사전

Korean-English Intellectual Property Law Dictionary

Korean-English
Intellectual Property
Law Dictionary

제2부
한영사전

2017

지식재산 법률용어사전

ㄱ

가격침식

침해행위로 인하여 그 행위가 없었을 경우 특허권자가 제품을 판매하였을 가격보다 더 낮은 가격에 제품을 판매하게 되어 손해를 입는 경우.

price erosion

A harm caused by acts of infringement when the patent owner is forced to sell its product at a lower price than it could have sold in the absence of the infringing acts.

미 가변요소

출원인이 상표의 일부로 등록하고자 하는 추후 변경 가능한 단어나 영숫자, 기타 구성 부분. 가령 연도 등 날짜를 포함한 표장, 변경될 수 있는 지리적 위치나 모델 번호를 포함한 표장 등에 나타남. (미) TMEP § 1214

phantom elements

A word, alpha-numeric designation, or other component that is subject to change an applicant seeks to register as part of the mark. Examples include marks incorporating a date (usually a year), a geographic location, or a model number that is subject to change. TMEP § 1214.

사용례 반대로 출원인이 표장의 성격에 대한 실질적이고 적절한 공지를 제시하지 않으면서 저촉표장에 대한 포괄적이고 효과적인 검색을 방해하는 **가변요소**의 등록을 하고자 함이 명백할 경우(예: 출원에 '빈칸은 앞으로 변경될 수 있는 부분이다'라고 기재된 경우) 심사관은 하나 이상의 표장에 대한 등록을 하고자 함을 들어 등록거절결정을 하여야 한다. (미) TMEP § 1214.03.

… Otherwise, if it is clear that the applicant is seeking registration of a "**phantom mark**" (e.g., if the application includes a statement that "the blank line represents matter that is subject to change") that would not provide adequate constructive notice of the nature of the mark and that precludes a thorough and effective search for conflicting marks, the examining attorney should issue a refusal of registration … on the ground that the application seeks registration of more than one mark. TMEP § 1214.03.

가압류

가압류란 금전 또는 금전으로 환산할 수 있는 채권에 대한 강제집행을 보전하기 위한 조치로서, 본안판결 선고 시까지 미리 일반 담보가 되는 채무자의 재산을 압류하여 현상을 보전하고, 그 변경을 금지하는 절차를 말함(민사집행법 276조).

provisional seizure

Provisional seizure refers to the attachment to deprive the right to dispose of properties of the debtor to preserve any future execution based on monetary claims until the court renders a judgment on the merit (Civil Execution Act Article 276).

미 가족상표

두드러진 공통의 성질을 공유하여, 그 구성되고 사용되는 방식으로 인해 대중이 개별 상표 뿐 아니라 그 가족상표 내의 공통의 성질까지 상표권자와 관련지어 생각하도록 된 다수의 표장. (미) TMEP § 1207.01(d)(xi).

family of marks

A group of marks having a recognizable common characteristic, wherein the marks are composed and used in such a way that the public associates not only the individual marks, but the common characteristic of the family, with the trademark owner. TMEP § 1207.01(d)(xi).

사용례 2(d)조 하에서 구체적으로 금지

In view of the specific prohibition of Section 2(d) …, the

하는 사항을 고려하면 출원인이 'ALD'라는 낱말로 나타나는 **가족표장**을 지닐 수 있다는 사실은 출원인이 현재 등록하고자 하는 표장이 선등록상표와 혼동을 일으킬 경우에는 아무런 의미가 없다고 보아야 하고, … (미) TMEP § 1207.01(d)(xi); In re Ald, Inc., 148 USPQ 520, 521 (TTAB 1965).

fact that applicant may possess a **family of marks** characterized by the term 'ALD' is of no particular significance herein if the mark for which applicant now seeks registration … is confusingly similar to the previously registered mark … TMEP § 1207.01(d)(xi); In re Ald, Inc., 148 USPQ 520, 521 (TTAB 1965).

가중적 손해배상

enhanced damages

가집행

가집행이란 가집행선고가 있는 미확정의 종국판결 또는 가집행선고가 있는 재판에 의하여 행해지는 강제집행을 말함(민사집행법 제24조, 제56조 제2호).

provisional execution

Provisional execution refers to a compulsory execution on a judgment that is not final or not complete. Provisional execution is commenced when there is an approval thereof by the court accompanied with the subject judgment (Civil Execution Act Article 24, 56(2)).

가처분

재판 전 혹은 도중에 법원이 사건을 판단하기 전에 회복할 수 없는 피해가 발생하는 것을 막기 위한 일시적인 금지명령.

preliminary injunction, provisional disposition (법제처)

A preliminary injunction issued before or during trial to prevent an irreparable harm from occurring before the court has a chance to decide the case.

미 가출원

미 특허법 제 111(b)조에 따라 정규특허출원에 유효한 조기 출원일자를 부여하기 위한 출원. 공식적인 청구항이나 선서나 선언, 선행기술 등의 정보 공개 없이 신청할 수 있다. 가출원은 1년 경과 시 자동으로 포기처리됨. (미) USPTO.

provisional application

A patent application under 35 U.S.C. § 111(b) that provides the means to establish an early effective filing date in a nonprovisional patent application. It allows filing without a formal patent claim, oath or declaration, or any information disclosure (prior art) statement. A provisional application automatically becomes abandoned after one year. USPTO.

각하

각하는 행정기관이 신청서, 심판청구서 등의 수리를 거절하는 행정처분 또는 법원이 당사자의 소송(절차)의 신청에 대하여 관할위반, 당사자적격 흠결 등 부적법을 이유로 배척하는 재판을 말함.

dismissal, rejection

Rejection (or dismissal), in administrative procedures, refers to actions of government agencies or officers rejecting to process applications or complaints. It also means, in litigations, means court decisions rejecting a party's requests, petitions or complaints for the reason that it does not meet the requirements to be heard in court. E.g., lack of jurisdiction or legal standing.

사용례 특허법 제51조(보정**각하**), 제132

Patent Act Article 51 (**Rejection** of Amendments), 132-5

조의5(특허취소신청서 등의 보정**각하**), 제132조의6(보정할 수 없는 특허취소신청의 각하 결정), 제141조(심판청구서 등의 **각하**), 제142조(보정할 수 없는 심판청구의 심결 **각하**)

(Dismissal of Request for Patent Cancellation), 132-6 (Decision Rejecting Incurable Request for Patent Cancellation), 141 (**Dismissal** of Petitions for Trial), 142 (Trial Rulings **Rejecting** Petitions for Trial with Incurable Defects).

간단하고 흔히 있는 표장

상표 부등록 사유임. 여기에 해당되는지 여부는 자타상품에 대한 식별력, 거래의 실정, 그 표장에 대한 독점적 사용이 허용되어도 좋은가 등의 사정을 참작하여 판단함.

simple and common mark, simple and readily available mark (법제처)

A ground for non-registration. A mark may be found simple and common based on its distinctiveness, course of trade and whether exclusive use of the mark may be granted.

사용례 … 이로써 수요자가 누구의 업무에 관련된 상품을 표시하는 것인가를 식별하기에 충분하므로, 이 사건 출원상표는 전체로서 관찰할 때 **간단하고 흔히 있는 표장**만으로 된 상표라고 보기 어렵다(대법원 2004. 11. 26. 선고 2003후2942 판결 참조).

As it is sufficient for consumers to distinguish the goods as to their relevant businesses, the mark at issue, when looked at its entirety, is not considered to be **simple and common** (Supreme Court Decision, 2003Hu2942, decided November 26, 2004).

간접침해

발명의 모든 구성요소를 가진 물건을 실시한 것이 아니고 그 전 단계에 있는 행위를 하였더라도 발명의 모든 구성요소를 가진 물건을 실시하게 될 개연성이 큰 경우에는 장래의 특허권 침해에 대한 권리 구제의 실효성을 높이기 위하여 일정한 요건 아래 이를 특허권의 침해로 간주하는 것(대법원 2009. 9. 10. 선고 2007후3356 판결 참조).

indirect infringement

In order to enhance effectiveness of relief in case of future infringement on the patent right, an act may be considered as infringement of a patent right under certain circumstances even where an article having all components of invention is not implemented and only the act prior to that stage is performed, in case the article having all components of invention is highly likely to be implemented (Supreme Court Decision, 2007Hu3356, decided September 10, 2009).

사용례 다음 각 호의 구분에 따른 행위를 업으로서 하는 경우에는 특허권 또는 전용실시권을 **침해한 것으로 본다**.

1. 특허가 물건의 발명인 경우: 그 물건의 생산에만 사용하는 물건을 생산·양도·대여 또는 수입하거나 그 물건의 양도 또는 대여의 청약을 하는 행위
2. 특허가 방법의 발명인 경우: 그 방법의 실시에만 사용하는 물건을 생산·양도·대여의 청약을 하는 행위(특허법 제127조).

Conducting either of the following activities commercially or industrially shall be **deemed infringement** of a patent or an exclusive license:

1. If the patent is for the invention of a thing: Producing, selling, leasing, or importing a thing used exclusively for producing such thing or offering to sell or lease such thing;
2. If the patent is for the invention of a process: Producing, selling, leasing, or importing a thing used exclusively for executing the process or offering to sell or lease such thing (Patent Act Article 127).

ㄱ

간행물

공개를 목적으로 인쇄 기타의 기계적, 화학적 또는 전자기적 방법으로 복제된 문서, 도화, 사진 등(대법원 1992. 10. 27. 선고 92후377 판결 참조). 특허공보가 가장 대표적인 간행물이고 그 밖에 서적, 논문, 제품의 카탈로그 등을 포함하며 마이크로필름, 컴퓨터 디스크, CD-ROM, 자기필름 등 현재 개발되어 있거나 향후 개발될 매체들 모두 포함.

publication

Documents, drawings or photographs printed or copied either mechanically, chemically or electromagnetically (Supreme Court Decision, 92Hu377, decided October 27, 1992). The most representative type of 'publication' would be official gazettes of patents. Books, journals, catalogs, micro films, computer disk, CD-ROMs, electric films and any kind of media also fall under 'publication.'

감정

특별한 학식 · 경험이 있는 제3자의 판단을 요구하는 증거조사(민사소송법 제334조).

appraisal, expert testimony (법제처)

Examination of evidence in litigation procedure that requires experts' opinion based on special knowledge or experience (Civil Procedure Act Article 334).

사용례 특허권 또는 전용실시권 침해소송에서 법원이 침해로 인한 손해액의 산정을 위하여 **감정**을 명한 때에는 당사자는 감정인에게 **감정**에 필요한 사항을 설명하여야 한다(특허법 제128조의2).

When the court orders **appraisal** in order to calculate the amount of damages in patent infringement cases or exclusive license infringement cases, the parties shall explain to the appraiser matters necessary for the **appraisal** of the damage amount (Patent Act Article 128-2).

감정인

전문적 학식경험에 속하는 법칙, 또는 이를 구체적 사실에 적용하여 얻은 판단을 법원에 보고하는 자(민사소송법 제334조).

appraiser, expert witness (법제처)

A person who reports to the court his/her opinion about a fact pertaining to litigation, based on his/her expertise, special education or experience (Civil Procedure Act Article 334).

감정증인

→ 전문가 증인 참조

expert witness

갑호증

원고가 법원에 제출하는 증거. 피고가 제출하는 증거는 을호증 이라고 함.

plaintiff's exhibit

Evidence submitted to the court by the plaintiff. Cf. Evidence submitted by the defendant is called defendant's exhibit.

강제실시권

공익을 위하여 필요한 경우 특허권자의 의사에 관계없이 행정명령이나 심판을 통하여 국가 또는 제3자에게 특허실시를 허락하도록 강제하는 제도(특허법 제106조, 106조의2, 107조).

compulsory license

Compulsory license is a system where the license of a patent is given to the government or third parties through administrative order or trial with or without consent of the patent holder when there is a public need to execute the patent (Patent Act Articles 106, 106-2, 107).

개량발명

→ 이용발명 참조

improvement invention, use invention

개별대리의 원칙

같은 당사자에 대하여 여러 사람의 소송대리인이 있을 때에는 대리인 각자가 당사자를 대리하는 것.

principle of individual representation

Where there are more than one legal representative for the same party in a lawsuit, each shall be the representative of the party.

개시

정보 등을 드러내 알 수 있게 하는 것.

disclose

To reveal or uncover to make known the information, etc.

사용례 "… 이 사건 제1항 발명의 구성1은 선행발명 1에, 구성2는 선행발명 2에 **개시**되어 있다(특허법원 2016. 9. 29. 선고 2016허2737 판결 참조)."

Element1 of the invention in Claim 1 in this case is disclosed in Prior Art 1, and Element 2 thereof is disclosed in Prior Art 2 (Patent Court Decision, 2016Heo2737, decided September 29, 2016).

미 개시의무

특허출원 및 심사와 관계된 각 개인이 지는, 특허성에 중대한 모든 정보를 특허상표청에 공개하여야 한다는 의무. (미) 37 C.F.R. § 1.56(a).

duty of disclosure

A duty to disclose to USPTO all information known to that individual to be material to patentability, owed by each individual associated with the filing and prosecution of a patent application. 37 C.F.R. § 1.56(a).

객관적 관찰

상표의 유사 여부를 판단할 때 그 상품에 직접 접촉하는 일반인들, 즉 당해 상품의 일반적인 거래자가 그런 종류의 물품을 구입하거나 거래할 경우에 기울이는 통상의 주의력을 기준으로 삼아 관찰 시 출처의 오인, 혼동의 우려가 있는지 판단하는 것.

objective observation

In determining similarity of trademarks, observing whether an ordinary person encountering the good, i.e. an ordinary person in the marketplace who purchases or trades the good, would be misled or confused as to the source of the good when exercising ordinary care.

사용례 상표의 유사 여부는 외관, 호칭 및 관념을 **객관적**, 전체적, 이격적으로 **관찰**하여 지정상품의 거래에서 일반 수요자들이 상표에 대하여 느끼는 직관적 인식을 기준으로 상품의 출처에 관하여 오인·혼동을 일으키게 할 우려가 있는지에 따라 판단하여야 한다(대법원 2014. 3. 20. 선고 2011후3698 전원합의체 판결 참조).

Determination on similarity between trademarks is to be based on whether there are concerns for ordinary consumers to misperceive or confuse the origin of the designated goods in transactions from the perspective of their intuitive perception of the trademark, grounded in an **objective**, overall **observation** of the appearance, name, and conception of the trademark by recollection (Supreme Court Decision, 2011 Hu3698, decided March 20, 2014).

객관적 창작성

objective creativity

사용례 디자인등록을 받기 위해서는 객관적 창작성이 요구됨. **객관적 창작성**은 과거 또는 현존의 모든 것과 유사하지 아니한 독특함만을 말하는 것이 아니고, 과거 및 현존의 것을 기초로 하여 거기에 새로운 미감을 주는 미적 창작이 결합되어 그 전체에서 종전의 디자인과는 다른 미감적 가치가 인정되는 정도면 족하다(대법원 2006. 7. 28. 선고 2005후2922 판결 등 참조).

The **objective creativity** is required for design registration. It does not mean that a design should be unique without any similarity to all past or present designs but is present if aesthetic creation is based on the past or the existing design, combined with artistic creation providing a new aesthetic sense, such that as a whole there can be recognizable aesthetic value that is different from the prior design (Supreme Court Decision, 2005Hu2922, decided July 28, 2006).

거래사회

marketplace, trading society (법제처)

상품, 서비스 등의 거래가 발생하는 시장을 의미함.

A marketplace in which goods or services are traded.

사용례 이 사건 출원상표 · 서비스표가 전체로서 **거래사회**에서 흔히 구호나 광고 문안으로 사용되는 점에 대한 증거가 없고, 일반 수요자가 그와 같이 인식하리라고 볼 만한 자료도 없다(특허법원 2016.2.3 선고 2015허3993판결 참조).

There is no evidence that the mark at issue as a whole is commonly used in slogans or advertising phrases in the **marketplace**, nor is there any data that ordinary consumers would perceive as such (Patent Court Decision, 2015 Heo 3993, decided February 3, 2016).

미 (상표의) 거래상의 사용

use in commerce, use of the mark in commerce

통상의 거래에서의 진실한 상표의 사용.

Bona fide use of a mark in the ordinary course of trade.

사용례 (1) 상표나 서비스표에 있어 출원인, 상표권자 또는 등록권자, 국제등록의 명의인이 미국내 출원, 사용사실주장의 보정, 사용사실진술, 계속사용 또는 정당한 이유에 의한 불사용에 대한 선언서나 선서서에서 특정한 상품 또는 서비스에 또는 그와 관련하여 **거래상 상표를 사용**하는 것, (2) 단체상표나 단체서비스표에 있어, 그 단체의 구성원이 미국내 출원, 사용사실주장의 보정, 사용사실진술, 계속사용 또는 정당한 이유에 의한 불사용에 대한 선언서나 선서서에서 특정한 상품 또는 서비스에 또는 그와 관련하여 **거래상 상표를 사용**하는 것, … (미) 37 C.F.R. §2.2(k).

(1) For a trademark or service mark, **use of the mark in commerce** by an applicant, owner, or holder on or in connection with the goods or services specified in a U.S. application, amendment to allege use, statement of use, or affidavit or declaration of use or excusable nonuse; (2) For a collective trademark or collective service mark, **use of the mark in commerce** by members on or in connection with the goods or services specified in a U.S. application, amendment to allege use, statement of use, or affidavit or declaration of use or excusable nonuse; … 37 C.F.R. §2.2(k).

거래상의 인상

commercial impression

상표 또는 표장이 소비자에게 전달하는 의미나 생각 등을 의미함.

The meaning or idea that a trademark or mark conveys to consumers.

사용례 …, 색채의 **거래상의 인상**은 그 색채가 적용된 물체에 따라 달라질 수 있다. 따라서 색채의 2차적 식별력을 나타내기 위해 제출한 증거에 소비자 인식이 일부 물체에 대해서는 존재하나 다른 물체에 대해서는 그렇지 아니한 것으로 나타날 수 있다. (미) TMEP § 1202.05(a).

… , the **commercial impression** of a color may change depending on the object to which it is applied. Therefore, evidence submitted to demonstrate acquired distinctiveness of a color may show consumer recognition with respect to certain objects, but not for other objects. TMEP § 1202.05(a).

거래상품

goods in trade

상표가 거래상 사용되었다고 하기 위해서는 반드시 거래상품, 즉 타인의 사용을 위해 상업적으로 판매 또는 운송되는 물품에 표시되어야만 함.

A trademark is used in commerce only when it is applied to goods in trade, i.e. goods commercially sold or transported for use by others.

사용례 출원인이 보고서의 판매가 아닌 가입자를 위한 금융보고 서비스를 업으로 하면 보고서는 그 서비스의 최종적 결과를 위한 수단으로 서비스 제공과정에서 사용되는 것에 지나지 않는다. 이로 미루어 볼 때 출원인의 보고서는 **거래상품**이 아니라고 본 심사관의 결정은 정당하였다고 볼 수 밖에 없다. (미) Application of Shareholders Data Corp., 495 F.2d 1360, 1361 (C.C.P.A. 1974).

Applicant is engaged not in the sale of reports but solely in the furnishing of financial reporting services to its subscribers, as it likewise is that the reports submitted to its subscribers are merely incidental to and the ultimate result of its services. Such being the case, we are in full agreement with the Examiner that applicant's reports do not constitute **goods in trade**. Application of Shareholders Data Corp., 495 F.2d 1360, 1361 (C.C.P.A. 1974).

거래실정

course of trade

관련 시장의 성질, 고객층의 재력이나 지식 정도, 전문가인지 여부, 연령, 성별, 당해 상품의 속성과 거래방법, 거래장소, 고장수리 등 사후관리 여부, 현존 및 사용상황, 주지 정도 및 당해 상품과의 관계, 수요자의 일상 언어생활 등을 의미함(대법원 1996. 7. 30. 선고 95후1821 판결 참조). (유사) 거래사정

Course of trade may refer to the characteristics of the relevant market, the financial status or level of knowledge of consumers, their level of expertise, age, sex, the nature and trading methods of the good, the presence and use, as well as how well-known the art is, how it is related to the product and the language used by the consumers on a daily basis (Supreme Court Decision, 95Hu1821, decided July 30, 1996).

거래통념

trade norms

일반적으로 거래시장에서 널리 통하는 개념.

Common ideas socially accepted in the marketplace.

사용례 그렇다면 실사용상표의 사용은 **거래통념**상 이 사건 등록상표와 동일하게 볼 수 있는 형태의 상표 사용에 해당한다고 봄이 타당하다(대법원 2013. 9. 26. 선고 2012후2463 전원합의체 판결 참조).

Therefore, the use of the actually used mark shall constitute a use of a mark deemed identical to the registered mark under the **trade norms** (Supreme Court Decision, 2012 Hu2463, decided September 26, 2013).

미 거래확장의 원칙

expansion-of-trade doctrine

주로 당사자계 절차에서 적용되는 원칙으로, 출원인의 상품 또는 서비스가 이의신청인의 상품 또는 서비스의 자연적인 확장영역에 속하므로 이의신청인의 그 상품 또는 서비스에 관하여 상표사용에 대한 우선권이 출원인의 상품 또는 서비스에까지 확장된다고 주장하는 것. (미) TMEP § 1207.01 (a)(v).

Typically applied in inter partes proceedings where an opposer claims that its priority of use of a mark with respect to its goods/services should be extended to include applicant's goods/services because they are in the natural scope of expansion of opposer's goods/services. TMEP § 1207.01 (a)(v).

사용례 동일상표가 서로 다른 상품류에 사용되고 선사용자의 상품류가 **일반적 혹은 합리적으로 상대방의 상품류에까지 확장될 것인지**가 쟁점인 사안에서, 그 답은 '수요자가 일반적으로 양 상품이 동일한 출처를 가지는 것으로 생각하는지'에 달려있다. J. C. Hall Co. v. Hallmark Cards, Inc., 340 F.2d 960, 963, 52 C.C.P.A. 981, 985 (1965). 일반적 **거래확장**의 문제가 다른 상품류에 적용된 다른 표장 간에 존재할 경우 양 표장 간의 차이점도 고려되어야 한다. J. Wiss & Sons Co. v. W. E. Bassett Co., 462 F.2d 567, 569 (C.C.P.A. 1972).

When the identical marks are being used on different lines of goods, and the issue is whether the prior user's line of goods would **normally or reasonably expand to include the other line of goods**, the answer depends on whether the goods "were of such a nature that purchasers would generally expect them to emanate from the same source." J. C. Hall Co. v. Hallmark Cards, Inc., 340 F.2d 960, 963, 52 C.C.P.A. 981, 985 (1965). We think that where the question of normal **expansion of trade** arises between different marks applied to different lines of goods, the differences between the marks must also be considered. J. Wiss & Sons Co. v. W. E. Bassett Co., 462 F.2d 567, 569 (C.C.P.A. 1972)

거절

reject

→ 거절결정 참조

거절결정

rejection, refusal, decision to reject/refuse an application (법제처)

출원된 산업재산권이 등록요건에 맞지 아니하는 경우 심사관이 등록거절결정을 내리는 것을 말함.

An examiner's decision to refuse to register intellectual property rights when the application therefor fails to meet the requirements for registration.

사용례 심사관은 특허출원이 다음 각 호의 어느 하나의 거절이유(이하 "거절이유"라 한다)에 해당하는 경우에는 **특허거절결**

An examiner shall **determine to reject** a patent application if the patent application falls under any of the following grounds for rejection (hereinafter referred to as "grounds

정을 하여야 한다. 1. 제25조 · 제29조 · 제32조 · 제36조 제1항부터 제3항까지 또는 제44조에 따라 특허를 받을 수 없는 경우 … (특허법 제62조 제1호).

for rejection"). 1. If an invention is unpatentable under any provision of Articles 25, 29, 32, 36 (1) through (3), and 44; … (Patent Act Article 62.1).

거절결정 불복소송

심결취소소송의 하나로, 거절결정 불복심판의 당사자가 해당 심판결정(거절결정)에 불복하여 특허법원에 제기하는 소송.

trial against rejection

A type of revocation action filed with the Patent Court by a patent applicant requesting revocation of a rejection decision of IPTAB.

거절결정 불복심판

특허출원인 등이 자기가 출원한 특허 등에 대하여 특허청이 내린 거절결정에 불복하여 특허심판원에 청구하는 심판. 특허거절결정에 대한 불복심판청구를 기각한 심결의 취소소송에서 법원은 특허거절결정을 유지한 심결의 위법성 여부를 판단하는 것일 뿐 특허출원에 대하여 직접 특허결정 또는 특허거절결정을 하는 것은 아니다(대법원 2014. 7. 10. 선고 2012후3121 판결).

administrative trial against rejection, trial against decision to reject (법제처)

An administrative trial proceeding requested by a party who appeals an examiner's decision to refuse to register a Patent or other rights etc. In an action to revoke administrative decision to dismiss an appeal against rejection of a patent application, the court simply reviews the lawfulness of the administrative decision to uphold the rejection and does not directly decide on the issue of whether to allow or refuse to register the application (Supreme Court Decision, 2012 Hu3121, decided July 10, 2014).

거절이유통지

특허등의 출원인이 특허출원을 한 발명이 특허요건을 갖추지 못하는 등 거절사유에 해당하는 경우 특허심사관은 특허등록을 거절해야 하는데, 이 때 심사관은 출원인에게 거절이유를 통지하고 일정기간 내에 의견제출을 할 기회를 부여하여야 함(특허법 제63조).

notice of grounds for rejection/refusal

When an applicant of patent or other IP rights fails to meet the requirements for patent registration or there are other grounds to reject the application, the patent examiner should reject the application (Patent Act Article 63).

미 (최초)거절이유통지

심사관이 거절이유통지를 하는 것은 출원인에게 출원의 문제점에 대해 고지하기 위함이다. 여기에는 등록거절이유 또는 필요요건 등이 기재된다. 거절이유통지에는 크게 심사관보정, 우선조치, 최초거절이유통지, 최후거절이유통지, 외국등록중상태여부를 묻는 통지 등이 있음. (미) USPTO.

Office action

An examining attorney sends an Office action to notify an applicant about issues with his or her application. This type of action will include the reason why registration is being refused or what requirements must be satisfied. There are several types of Office actions: examiner's amendments, priority actions, non-final Office actions, final Office actions, and suspension inquiry letters. USPTO.

사용례 심사관의 **최초거절이유통지**는 출원인에게 모든 보정요구사항 및 거절이유를

The examining attorney's **first Office action** must be complete, so the applicant will be advised of all requirements

고지할 수 있도록 완전성을 갖추어야 한다. 단 사용주장보정, 또는 사용의사 기반 출원에서 사용사실의 진술에 대한 심사에서 최초로 고려하는 사용 관련 쟁점은 예외로 한다. (미) TMEP § 704.01.

for amendment and all grounds for refusal, with the exception of use-related issues that are considered for the first time in the examination of an amendment to allege use under 15 U.S.C. §1051(c) or a statement of use under 15 U.S.C. §1051(d) in an intent-to-use application. TMEP § 704.01.

거짓표시

false display, false indication

가령 등록을 하지 아니한 상표 또는 상표등록출원을 하지 아니한 상표를 등록상표 또는 등록출원상표인 것같이 상품에 표시하는 행위 등(상표법 제233조).

For example, displaying on goods an unregistered mark or a mark for which no application has been filed as if a valid application or registration of the mark exists (Trademark Act Article 233).

거짓행위의 죄

crime of fraud, fraud

거짓 또는 그 밖의 부정행위로 등록, 존속기간 연장등록, 취소신청에 대한 결정 또는 심결을 받는 경우 거짓행위의 죄가 성립함(특허법 제229조).

Any person who obtains a patent or other rights, registration of an extension, or a trial ruling by fraud or other improper means shall be punished for fraud (Patent Act Article 229).

검증

inspection, verification

법관이 직접 자기의 감각에 의하여 대상의 성질 · 상태를 실험하여 하는 증거조사. 재판부는 필요하다고 인정되는 경우 당사자의 신청에 따라 또는 직권으로 검증절차를 진행할 수 있다(특허법원 심결취소소송 심리매뉴얼 VI.2.가).

Examination of evidence in litigation procedure in which the judge examines the nature and condition of the subject using his or her own sense. If deemed necessary, the Court may conduct verification procedures either upon a party's request or on an ex officio basis (Guideline of Practice and Procedure of Revocation Action in the Patent Court of Korea, VI.2.A).

(간행물에) 게재된 디자인

design described (in a publication)

사용례 "**간행물에 게재된 디자인**"에서 그 게재의 정도는 그 디자인이 속한 분야에서 통상의 지식을 가진 자가 그것을 보고 용이하게 디자인을 창작할 수 있을 정도로 표현되어 있으면 충분하고 … (대법원 2006. 7. 28. 선고 2003후1956판결 참조).

As for "**a design described in a publication**," a design is sufficiently published if it is described to a degree that a person with ordinary knowledge in the industry would be able to easily create the design (Supreme Court Decision, 2003Hu1956, decided July 28, 2006).

견본

specimen

제품, 디자인 등의 전체를 대표하여 본보기가 되는 것.

A sample taken as an example of the whole material or design, etc.

사용례 등록디자인의 보호범위는 디자

The scope of protection of a registered design shall be defined

인등록출원서의 기재사항 및 그 출원서에 첨부된 도면 · 사진 또는 **견본**과 도면에 적힌 디자인의 설명에 따라 표현된 디자인에 의하여 정하여진다(디자인보호법 제93조).

by the design represented in the content of the written application as well as the drawing, picture, **specimen** and description of the design in the drawing, attached to the application (Design Protection Act Article 93).

결정

decision, judgment

미 결정계 심사

ex parte reexamination

특허권자 및 제3자가 등록특허의 재심사를 받기 위한 절차.

A procedure whereby patentees and third parties can seek reexamination of issued patents.

미 결정계 절차

ex parte prosecution

사용례 출원관련 **결정계 절차** 중 발생한 사항에 대한 결정은 그 사안의 성질이나 사건의 상황에 따라 상표심판위원회에 심판청구를 제기함으로써만 검토 가능한 사안, 특허상표청장에게 청구함으로써만 검토할 수 있는 사안, 혹은 둘 다를 통해 검토할 수 있는 사안으로 나뉜다. (미) TMEP § 1201.05.

An action taken on a matter arising during the **ex parte prosecution** of an application for registration may, depending on the nature of the matter and the posture of the case, be reviewable only by appeal to the Board, or only by petition to the Director or by either appeal or petition. The following discussion contains general guidelines for determining whether a matter is appealable or petitionable. TMEP § 1201.05.

미 결정계 심판청구

ex parte appeals

심사관의 최종거절결정에 대한 심판청구. 심판청구를 함에 있어 출원인은 동일한 근거에 의한 2차 거절을 최종거절결정으로 간주할 수 있음.

An appeal from an examiner's final refusal against the application. An applicant may consider a second refusal on the same ground as final for the purpose of appeal.

결정의 취소

revocation of decision

법원은 소가 제기된 경우에 그 청구가 이유 있다고 인정할 경우에는 판결로써 해당 심결 또는 결정을 취소함.

Where the court deems a pleading in a lawsuit is well-grounded, it shall revoke the relevant decision of the examiner or administrative judge by judgment.

결정형(結晶形) 발명

crystal form invention

파라미터 값의 분석치에 의하여 특정되는 화합물의 결정형을 청구범위로 하는 발명.

Crystal form invention refers to an invention that has claims comprised of crystal form of a chemical compound, which is decided by analytic data of parameters.

사용례 **결정형 발명**은 특별한 사정이 없는 한 선행발명에 공지된 화합물이 갖는 효과와 질적으로 다른 효과를 가지고 있거

Unless in exceptional situation, inventive step of a **crystal form invention** can be acknowledged only when it possess effects different in quality from the effects the preceding

나 질적인 차이가 없더라도 양적으로 현저한 차이가 있는 경우에 한하여 그 진보성이 부정되지 않고, 이 때 결정형 발명의 상세한 설명에는 선행발명과의 비교실험자료까지는 아니라고 하더라도 위와 같은 효과가 있음이 명확히 기재되어 있어야만 진보성 판단에 고려될 수 있으며, 만일 그 효과가 의심스러울 때에는 출원일 이후에 출원인 또는 특허권자가 신뢰할 수 있는 비교실험자료를 제출하는 등의 방법에 의하여 그 효과를 구체적으로 주장 · 입증하여야 한다 (대법원 2011. 7. 14. 선고 2010후2865 판결 참조).

invention possess, or if not, at least, there should exist conspicuous differences in effect as measured quantitatively between them. At this time, although the detailed description of the crystal form invention may not state the experimental data, it must explicitly state the above mentioned effects compared to the preceding invention. If the effect of the invention is doubted, the applicant or patent holder shall argue and demonstrate the effect after the application file date (Supreme Court Decision, 2010Hu2865, decided July 14, 2011).

결합발명

이미 존재하는 구성요소를 새로운 방법으로 결합한 발명.

combination patent

A patent granted for an invention that unites existing components in a novel way.

사용례 이 사건 심사의 거절이유는 통상의 기술자가 선행발명1에 선행발명2를 결합하여 이 사건 제1항 발명을 쉽게 발명할 수 있다고 보았으나, 이러한 결합은 선행발명1의 과제해결원리에 반하여 어렵고, 달리 그러한 결합을 할 이유나 동기도 없다 (특허법원2016. 9. 29. 선고2016허2737 판결 참조).

In the rejecting the application, it is alleged that Claim 1 invention of this case can be easily conceived by PHOSITA by combining Prior Art 2 and Prior Art 1. However, such combination is against the solution principle of Prior Art 1, and there is no reason or motivation to combine the two inventions (Patent Court Decision, 2016Heo2737, decided September 29, 2016).

결합상표

두 가지 이상의 구성요소가 결합된 상표. 가령 입체적 형상과 기호·문자·도형 등이 결합한 상표의 경우 입체적 형상 자체에는 식별력이 없더라도 식별력 있는 기호·문자·도형 등과 결합하여 전체적으로 식별력이 인정되면 상표등록을 받을 수 있음.

composite trademark

A trademark that is composed of more than one element. A trademark that is composed of three-dimensional shape and a symbol, letter or figure may still be registered even if the dimensional shape lacks distinctiveness when overall distinctiveness is present in combination with distinctive symbol, letter or figure.

사용례 두 개 이상의 구성 부분이 결합하여 이루어진 이른바 **결합상표**는 상표를 구성하는 전체에 의하여 식별력이 있는지를 판단하여야 한다(특허법원 2016.02.03 선고 2015허3993 판결 참조).

The distinctiveness of a **composite trademark** consisting of two or more element combined should be determined by the entirety of the trademark (Patent Court Decision, 2015 Heo3993, decided February 3, 2016).

경과규정

transitional provision

→ 경과조치 참조

경과조치

transitional measure

법령의 제정 · 개폐가 있는 경우 구법에서 신법으로 이행하는 데 따르는 여러 가지 조치 또는 이에 대한 규정.

The measures and provisions prescribing the measures that are applicable in transition period from an old act to a new one in case of enactment, abolishment or amendment.

사용례 상표등록요건에 관한 상표법의 규정이 개정되면서 그 부칙에서 개정 규정과 관련하여 별도의 **경과규정**을 두지 아니하는 경우에는 특별한 사정이 없는 한 그 개정 전에 출원하여 등록된 상표에 대한 심판 및 소송에 대하여는 종전의 규정에 의하여 형성된 상표법 질서의 안정을 손상시키지 않도록 하기 위하여 원칙적으로 종전의 규정이 적용되어야 하고… (특허법원 2016. 02.03 선고 2010후456판결 참조).

… where the provision of the Trademark Act concerning trademark registration requirements is amended, with no separate **transitional provision** in its addendum, the former provision should apply to adjudication and litigation concerning a trademark registered prior to the amendment, in order to maintain the stability/order of the Trademark Act established under the former provision (Supreme Court Decision, 2010Hu456, decided July 22, 2010).

경상실시료

running royalty

일시불이 아닌 제조 또는 판매 단위당 발생하는 실시료.

The royalty incurred based on the number of units manufactured or sold, as opposed to lump sum.

경제적 견련관계

economically relevant relationship, ~ have economic ties

경제적으로 서로 연결되어 있는 관계.

The relationship of the ones that are tied to each other economically.

사용례 이 사건 등록상표와 선사용상표들은 공통적으로 '나비'의 뜻을 가진 영어단어 'Butterfly'를 그 요부로 하고 있으므로 서로 유사하고, 이 사건 지정상품들은 선사용상표들의 사용상품들과 같이 운동용으로 사용될 수 있는 것들이거나 신발류 또는 의류의 일종으로서 서로 **경제적 견련관계**도 있다고 할 것이다(대법원 2010. 7. 15. 선고 2010후807 판결 참조).

Furthermore, the defendant's registered trademark and the prior used trademarks are similar as they share the English word "Butterfly" as a essential part, and they share an **economically relevant relationship** as the classes of goods for this case and for the prior use trademarks are both used as exercise equipment or as shoes or clothing (Supreme Court Decision, 2010Hu807, decided July 15, 2010).

경합출원

competing application

동일한 발명에 대하여 2인 이상이 출원한

Competing application means applications of 2 or more

경우 이를 경합출원이라 한다. 특허법은 중복특허를 금지하면서 선출원주의를 택하고 있음(특허법 제36조).

applicants that filed patent applications for identical inventions. Patent Law prohibits double patent and provides first-to-file rule (Patent Act Article 36).

사용례 구 특허법(2001. 2. 3. 법률 제6411호로 개정되기 전의 것) 제36조 제3항 등의 적용에 있어 특허권이나 실용신안권의 포기에 의하여 **경합출원**의 하자가 치유되어 제3자에 대한 관계에서 특허권의 효력을 주장할 수 있다고 보는 것은 명문의 근거가 없을 뿐만 아니라 권리자가 포기의 대상과 시기를 임의로 선택할 수 있어 권리관계가 불확정한 상태에 놓이게 되는 등 법적 안정성을 해칠 우려가 있는 점 … (대법원 2007. 1. 12. 선고 2005후3017 판결 참조).

In applying Article 36 (3), etc. of the former Patent Act (amended by Act No. 6411 of February 3, 2001), where there are **competing applications**, even when the owner renounces either the registered patent right or the utility model right, it cannot be deemed that the defect arising from the competing applications is resolved. This is so in light of the following facts: there exists no explicit provision that renunciation of a patent or utility model right resolves a conflict in competing applications or that the right has effect as a patent right to a third party (Supreme Court Decision, 2005Hu3017, decided January 12, 2007).

경험법칙

사회생활에 있어서의 경험법칙 또는 거래상의 관념.

rule of thumb

A principle based on experience in society or concept used as a trade norm.

미 계류출원

출원은 등록되거나 포기되기까지는 계류 중인 것으로 본다. 공고 승인된 출원이나 보조등록부 등록이 승인된 출원, 사용의사에 기한 출원, 복권 또는 회복된 출원의 경우가 모두 계류 중 출원에 해당함. (미) TMEP § 702.03(a).

pending application

An application is pending until it registers or abandons. Pending applications include applications that have been approved for publication or for registration on the Supplemental Register, applications in the Intent-to-Use ("ITU")/Divisional Unit, and revived or reinstated applications. TMEP § 702.03(a).

사용례 항의서 절차는 **계류중인 출원**에 대해서만 밟을 수 있으며 불필요한 지연을 야기하거나 결정계 심사절차의 위상과 객관성을 해하지 아니하고 심사를 지원하는 데에 그 의의가 있다. (미) TMEP § 1715.

The letter of protest procedure applies only to **pending applications** and is intended to aid in examination without causing undue delay and without compromising the integrity and objectivity of the ex parte examination process. TMEP § 1715.

미 계속사용진술서

계속적 사용의 선언. 그 상표가 거래상 사용되고 있다는 등록권자의 확인진술서.

affidavit of continued use, declaration of continued use

Declaration of continued use. a sworn statement, filed by the owner of a registration that the mark is in use in commerce. USPTO.

사용례 법정기간(유예기간 포함)의 잔존기간이 있을 때 상표권자가 사용에 대한 주장, 견본, 수수료와 더불어 새로이 진술서나 선언서를 제출함으로써 거절결정통지에 대응할 경우 특허상표청은 이 새로운 사용진술서 또는 선언서를 심사한다. (미) TMEP § 1604.11.

If there is time remaining in the statutory filing period (including the grace period) and the owner responds to the Office action by submitting a new affidavit or declaration with a claim of use, specimen, and filing fee, the USPTO will examine the new affidavit or declaration of use. TMEP § 1604.11.

미 계속심사청구

request for continued examination

최종 거절결정 되었거나 허여통지를 받은 경우 등 심사절차가 종결된 출원에 대해 청구된 심사절차를 재개하고 심사를 계속할 것을 요청하는 것.

A request filed in an application in which prosecution is closed (e.g., the application is under final rejection or a notice of allowance) that is filed to reopen prosecution and continue examination of the application.

계속적 실시료

ongoing royalty

협상을 통해 또는 법원 명령으로 침해자의 특허의 향후 사용에 대하여 특허권자에게 지급하는 실시료. 과거 침해에 대해 지급하는 실시료와 구분됨.

Royalty paid to the patent owner for the infringer's future use of the patent, either via negotiation or by court order, as opposed to royalties awarded for the past infringement.

미 계속출원(광의)

continued/continuing application

최소 한 명의 발명자를 공동으로 하고 개시사항의 적어도 일부가 공통된 출원이 계류 중일 때 신청한 출원. Transco Products Inc. v. Performance Contracting, Inc., 38 F.3d 551 (Fed. Cir. 1994). 원출원의 출원일을 인정받으면서 출원을 계속적으로 진행시키는 절차. 세 가지 유형, 즉 (협의의)계속출원, 일부계속출원 및 분할출원으로 나뉨. (미) 37 C.F.R. § 1.53(b).

An application filed during the pendency of another application which contains at least part of the disclosure of the other application and names at least one inventor in common with that application. Transco Products Inc. v. Performance Contracting, Inc., 38 F.3d 551 (Fed. Cir. 1994). A continuing application may claim the benefit of the filing date of a prior application. A continuing application may be either a continuation application, continuation-in-part application or divisional application. 37 C.F.R. § 1.53(b).

고객흡인력

attractiveness to customers, customer drawing power (법제처)

상품을 구매하거나 서비스를 이용하도록 고객을 끌어당기는 힘.

The power of trademark to draw or attract customers to buy goods or use services.

사용례 선사용선등록상표에 체화된 영업상의 신용 또는 **고객흡인력** 등의 무형의 가치에 손상을 입히기 위한 것이라고 보기 어렵다(특허법원 2016.02.16 선고 2015허

In view of the following circumstances, it is difficult to see that the initial applicant of the Subject Service Mark or the Plaintiff, as successor in interest to the applicant, damaged intangible value such as business reputation **or**

ㄱ

6558판결 참조).

customer drawing power embodied in the pre-used and pre-registered trademark (Patent Court Decision, 2015Heo 6558, decided February 16, 2016).

고도(高度)의

고도한 것의 의미는 일반적으로 실용신안법상의 고안과 특허법상의 발명을 구분하기 위한 상대적인 개념임.

사용례 "발명"이란 자연법칙을 이용한 기술적 사상의 창작으로서 **고도(高度)한** 것을 말한다(특허법 제2조).

highly advanced

The term "highly advanced" has been introduced to differentiate "device" under the Utility Model Act from "invention" under the Patent Act.

The term "invention" means **highly advanced** creation of a technical idea utilizing the laws of nature (Patent Act Article 2).

고소

범죄의 피해자, 기타 고소권자가 수사기관에 대하여 일정한 범죄사실을 신고하여 그 소추를 구하는 의사표시. 특허권 또는 전용실시권을 침해한 죄는 고소가 없으면 공소(公訴)를 제기할 수 없다(특허법 제225조).

criminal complaint

Criminal complaint refers to a complaint filed by a victim of a crime or a person who holds right to report a crime and requesting investigation to an investigation agency. (2) No person shall be prosecuted for committing a crime of infringement of a patent or an exclusive license without a criminal complaint filed by the injured party (Patent Act Article 225).

고안

실용신안법상 실용신안 등록의 대상. 자연법칙을 이용한 기술적 사상의 창작. 그 중 고도한 것은 특허법상 등록의 대상인 발명에 해당하게 됨(실용신안법 제2조).

utility model, device (법제처)

Subject of registration under the Utility Model Act. Creation of technical ideas applying the law of nature. Such creations that are highly advanced are inventions that may be patented under the Patent Act (Utility Model Act Article 2).

고안자

고안을 한 자.

deviser

A person who devised a utility model.

고유번호

사용례 특허에 관한 절차를 밟는 자 중 산업통상자원부령으로 정하는 자는 특허청장 또는 특허심판원장에게 자신의 **고유번호**의 부여를 신청하여야 한다(특허법 제28조의2 제1항).

identification number

A person specified by Ordinance of the Ministry of Trade, Industry and Energy, who initiate a patent-related procedure, shall apply for issuance of his/her **identification number** to the Commissioner of the Korean Intellectual Property Office or the Director General of the Korean Intellectual Property Trial and Appeal Board (Patent Act Article 28-2(1)).

고유의 식별력

inherent distinctiveness

암시적, 임의적 또는 조어인 표장은 고유의 식별력을 가지고 상품의 출처로서 인식될 수 있다.

A suggestive, arbitrary or fanciful mark is inherently distinctive and identifies the source of the product.

사용례 출원된 포장 상표가 **고유의 식별력**이 없다면 사용에 의한 식별력 또는 2차적 의미의 입증으로 2(f)조 하에 주등록부에 등록하거나 혹은 보조등록부에 등록될 수 있다. (미) TMEP § 1202.02(b)(ii).

If a proposed product packaging mark is not **inherently distinctive**, the mark may be registered on either the Principal Register under §2(f), upon proof that the mark has acquired distinctiveness or secondary meaning, or on the Supplemental Register. TMEP § 1202.02(b)(ii).

고유필수적 공동소송

inherently compulsory joint litigation, indispensable co-litigation (법제처)

공유자 전원이 반드시 공동으로 제기하여야만 하는 소송.

A lawsuit that must be jointly filed by all of the co-owners of rights.

사용례 이른바 **고유필수적 공동소송**이 아닌 사건에서 소송 도중에 당사자를 추가하는 것은 허용될 수 없고, 동일한 특허권에 관하여 2인 이상의 자가 공동으로 특허의 무효심판을 청구하여 승소한 경우에 그 특허권자가 제기할 심결취소소송은 심판청구인 전원을 상대로 제기하여야만 하는 고유필수적 공동소송이라고 할 수 없으므로, 위 소송에서 당사자의 변경을 가져오는 당사자추가신청은 명목이 어떻든 간에 부적법하여 허용될 수 없다(대법원 2009. 5. 28. 선고 2007후1510 판결 참조).

A litigant may not be added in the middle of a case which is not so-called "**inherently indispensable co-litigation.**" In addition, where more than two claimants jointly seek an adjudication on the invalidation of a patent as to the same patent right and thereafter win the adjudication, the litigation for revocation of such adjudication that a patentee will raise cannot be deemed to be an inherently indispensable co-litigation which shall be raised against all claimants. Thus, in this case, the application for adding a litigant which would cause a change of litigant is unlawful and impermissible (Supreme Court Decision, 2007Hu1510, decided May 28, 2009).

고의

willful

→ 고의침해 참조

고의침해

willful infringement, deliberate infringement

사용례 상표권자 또는 전용사용권자는 자기의 상표권 또는 전용사용권을 **고의** 또는 과실로 침해한 자에 대하여 그 침해에 의하여 자기가 받은 손해의 배상을 청구할 수 있다(상표법 제109조).

A trademark right holder or an exclusive licensee may claim damages he/she has incurred against a person who has **willfully** or negligently **infringed** his/her trademark rights or exclusive license (Trademark Act Article 109).

ㄱ

공공의 질서

public order

공공의 질서 또는 선량한 풍속에 어긋난

사용례 상표법 제7조 제1항 제4호에서 '**공공의 질서 또는 선량한 풍속을 문란하게 할 염려가 있는 상표**'라 함은 상표의 구성 자체 또는 그 상표가 그 지정상품에 사용하는 경우에 일반 수요자에게 주는 의미나 내용이 사회공공의 질서에 위반하거나, 사회 일반인의 통상적인 도덕관념인 선량한 풍속에 반하는 경우를 말한다(대법원 2002. 7. 9. 선고 99후451 판결 참조).

against public order or good morals

A trademark that is **against public order or good morals** as defined in Article 7 Paragraph (1) Item 4 of the Trademark Act refers to one that, by its composition or use on the designated goods, conveys a meaning or content that is contrary to public order, or the good morals and customs of ordinary citizen (Supreme Court Decision, 99Hu451, decided July 9, 2002).

공동발명자

공동발명자란 공동 발명의 대상을 발명한 자들 중 어느 1인을 의미함. 2명 이상이 공동으로 발명한 경우에는 특허를 받을 수 있는 권리를 공유한다(특허법 제33조 제2항).

joint inventor, co-inventor

The terms 'joint inventor' and 'co-inventor' mean any one of the individuals who invented the subject matter of a joint invention. If at least two persons jointly make an invention, they are jointly entitled to a patent thereon (Patent Act Article 33(2)).

공동심판청구

동일한 권리에 대하여 2인 이상이 무효심판청구 또는 권리범위확인심판청구를 같이 하는 경우 적용될 수 있는 심판청구 형태. 동일한 특허권에 관하여 무효심판이나 권리범위 확인심판을 청구하는 자가 2인 이상이면 모두가 공동으로 심판을 청구할 수 있다(특허법 제139조 제1항).

joinder of petition for trial, joint filing (법제처)

A type of procedure that applies when two or more persons file petition for invalidation or confirmation of scope of rights for identical patent or other rights. If at least two persons intend to file a petition for trial to invalidate an identical patent or to confirm the scope of rights in a patent, all such petitioners may jointly file a petition for trial (Patent Act Article 139(1)).

공동연구협약

출원발명 분야에서의 실험, 개발, 연구 수행을 위하여 2인 이상 혹은 2개 이상의 단체가 맺는 서면 계약, 지원금, 협력계약. (미) 특허법 100(h)조.

joint research agreement

A written contract, grant, or cooperative agreement entered into by two or more persons or entities for the performance of experimental, developmental, or research work in the field of the claimed invention. Patent Act, 35 U.S.C. § 100 (h).

공동출원인

사용례 **공동출원인**은 하나의 단체가 아

joint applicants

An application by **joint applicants** must be verified by all

닌 개별당사자이므로 공동출원인에 의한 출원은 모든 출원인에 의해 확인되어야 한다. (미) TMEP § 803.03(d).

the applicants, since they are individual parties and not a single entity. TMEP § 803.03(d).

공무원 의제

전문기관 또는 특허문서 전자화기관의 임직원이거나 임직원이었던 사람은 비밀누설죄를 적용하는 경우에는 특허청 소속 직원 또는 직원이었던 사람으로 본다(특허법 제226조의2).

deemed public officials, legal fiction as public officials

Any current or former executive or employee of a specialized agency designated under Article 58 (1), or an agency for digitization of patent documents shall be deemed a current or former employee of the Korean Intellectual Property Office or the Korean Intellectual Property Trial and Appeal Board for the purposes of adjudicating the offence of divulging secrets or confidential information. (Patent Act Article 226-2).

미 공서양속에 반하는 상표

사용례 최소 하나의 표준사전을 포함한 여러 사전이 모두 어느 단어를 비속어로 표시하고 있고 출원인의 그 단어의 사용이 그 저속한 의미로 한정되어 있다면, 사전적 정의만으로 어떤 제시된 표장이 **공서양속에 반하는 내용**으로 이루어져 있음을 충분히 입증할 수 있다. (미) TMEP § 1203.01.

immoral or scandalous matter

Dictionary definitions alone may be sufficient to establish that a proposed mark comprises **scandalous matter**, where multiple dictionaries, including at least one standard dictionary, all indicate that a word is vulgar, and the applicant's use of the word is limited to the vulgar meaning of the word. TMEP § 1203.01.

공시송달

당사자의 송달장소가 불명하여 통상의 송달방법에 의해서는 송달을 실시할 수 없게 되었을 때, 법원에서 송달한 서류를 보관해 두고 송달을 받을 자가 나타나면 언제든지 그것을 그 자에게 교부한다는 것을 법원게시장에 게시함으로써 행하는 송달방법.

public notice in lieu of service, service by publication (법제처)

Where it is impossible to serve a party because the address or the place of business of the party cannot be identified, service may be done by publication on the court bulletin board of the fact that the party may retrieve the document from the court at any time.

공업상 이용가능성

디자인의 공업상 이용가능성이란 공업적 방법에 의하여 양산될 수 있는 것을 의미하고, 공업적 방법이란 원자재에 물리적, 화학적 변화를 가하여 유용한 물품을 제조하는 것을 말하며, 양산이라 함은 동일한 형태의 물품을 반복적으로 계속해서 생산함을 뜻한다(대법원 1994. 9. 9. 선고 93후1247 판결).

industrial usability

Industrial usability of a design means that it can be mass-produced by industrial methods; industrial methods refer to manufacturing a useful product by physically or chemically changing the raw material. Mass-production means repeatedly producing a product in the identical form (Supreme Court Decision, 93Hu1247, decided September 9, 1994).

ㄱ

공연히 실시된 디자인

publicly practiced design

디자인의 내용이 공연히 알려진 또는 불특정 다수인이 알 수 있는 상태에서 실시된 디자인.

A design publicly known or practiced in a state that unspecified number of people may know about the design.

사용례 … '**공연히 실시된 의장(디자인)**'이라 함은 의장의 내용이 공연히 알려진 또는 불특정 다수인이 알 수 있는 상태에서 실시된 의장을 말하는 것이며, 당해 의장과 동일한 형상 모양의 물품을 그 출원일 이전에 동종업자에게 납품한 사실이 있다면 그 의장은 일반사람의 눈에 띔으로써 바로 알려져 모방할 수 있는 것이므로 그의 신규성 내지 비밀성을 잃어 공지로 된다고 할 것이다(대법원 2000. 12. 22. 선고 2000후3012 판결 참조).

"**A publicly practiced design**" refers to a design of which content is publicly known or which has been practiced in a state where unspecified number of people may know about the design. If a good in identical shape of the design was supplied to a merchant in the industry prior to the application date, the design is revealed to the general public and may be simulated. Thus the design lost its novelty or secrecy and is publicly known (Supreme Court Decision, 2000Hu 3012, decided December 22, 2000).

공연히 실시된 발명

publicly practiced invention, publicly executed (법제처)

공연히 실시된 발명은 국내나 국외에서 그 발명이 공연히 알려진 상태 또는 공연히 알려질 수 있는 상태에서 실시되고 있는 것을 의미함(특허법원 1999.1.14. 선고 98허4449 판결 참조). 특허출원 전에 국내 또는 국외에서 공지(公知)되었거나 공연(公然)히 실시된 발명은 특허를 받을 수 없다.

"A publicly practiced invention" means an invention which has been practiced under the conditions where the contents of the invention are to be publicly known or can potentially be publicly known in the Republic of Korea or a foreign country (Patent Court Decision, 98Heo4449, decided January 14, 1999). An invention having industrial applicability, other than the following, is patentable: 1. An invention publicly known or executed in the Republic of Korea or in a foreign country prior to the filing of a patent application is not patentable (Patent Act Article 29(1)).

공용

publicly practiced

→ 공연히 실시된 발명 참조.

공유

joint ownership

하나의 산업재산권등에 관한 권리를 2인 이상이 소유하는 형태를 말하며, 권리 전체에 대하여 각각의 지분별로 소유함.

IP rights is jointly owned when it is owned by two or more persons. Each owner has the ownership in its entirety.

사용례 (특허권의 이전 및 **공유** 등) ③ 특허권이 공유인 경우에는 각 공유자는 계약으로 특별히 약정한 경우를 제외하고는

(Transfer and **Joint Ownership** of Patents) (3) Except as otherwise agreed in writing, no joint owner of a patent may independently execute the patented invention without the

다른 공유자의 동의를 받지 아니하고 그 특허발명을 자신이 실시할 수 있다. ④ 특허권이 공유인 경우에는 각 공유자는 다른 공유자 모두의 동의를 받아야만 그 특허권에 대하여 전용실시권을 설정하거나 통상실시권을 허락할 수 있다(특허법 제99조).

consent of all other joint owners. (4) If a patent is jointly owned, no joint owner of the patent may grant an exclusive or non-exclusive license of the patent, without the consent of all other joint owners (Patent Act Article 99).

미 공존사용등록

공존사용등록, 즉 동일 또는 유사한 표장을 사용할 권리를 지니는 것으로 법원 또는 TTAB의 최종 판결 또는 심판을 얻은 1인 이상이 거래에서 그 표장을 사용하도록 등록하는 것. (미) TMEP § 1207.04(a).

concurrent use registration

Registration of concurrent use, i.e. use of the same or similar marks in commerce by more than one person, all entitled to such use by the final determination of a court of competent jurisdiction or a determination by the Trademark Trial and Appeal Board. TMEP § 1207.04(a).

공지

→ 공지기술 참조

public knowledge

공지기술

해당 기술분야에서 통상의 기술자에게 이미 알려져 있는 기술.

(publicly) known art

An art or technology already publicly known to a person having ordinary skills in the art.

공지기술 배제의 원칙

특허 균등침해의 소극적 성립요건 중 하나. 특허발명과 구분되는 확인대상발명이 공지의 기술에 해당하거나 공지의 기술로부터 진보성이 없는 경우에는 특허침해에 해당하지 아니한다는 원칙(대법원 2001. 8. 21. 선고 98후522 판결 참조).

principle to exclude publicly known art

One of the negative requirements of the doctrine of equivalents. According to this principle, an invention does not constitute patent infringement if the technology has been already publicly known or could have easily been invented by those skilled in the technology from the known prior technology (Supreme Court Decision, 98Hu522, decided August 21, 2001).

공지된 디자인

반드시 불특정 다수인에게 인식되었을 필요는 없더라도 적어도 불특정 다수인이 인식할 수 있는 상태에 놓여 있는 디자인.

publicly known design

A design is publicly known if it is in a state that may be known to unspecified number of people, which does not require actual recognition by such.

공지된 발명

'공지된 발명' 이라 함은 아무런 비밀유지 의무의 부과 없이 공사 실무자들에게 발명의 도면과 샘플을 제공하는 경우와 같이 발명의 내용이 불특정 다수인이 인식할 수 있는 상태에 놓인 것을 말함(대법원 1992. 10.

publicly known invention

Publicly known invention refers to an invention when the content of the invention is left in a situation that many non-specified people can perceive (e.g. when someone distributes drawings and samples of an invention to construction practitioners without imposing any confidential

27. 선고 92후377 판결, 대법원 1996. 6. 14. 선고 95후19 판결 등 참조).

duty) (Supreme Court Decision, 92Hu377, decided December 27, 1992, 95Hu19, decided June 14, 1996).

ㄱ

공지 부분을 포함하는 디자인

디자인의 일부에 공지 부분이 포함되어 있는 경우. 이 경우 그 공지 부분은 창조적 가치가 인정되지 않으나 디자인은 공지 부분도 포함한 통일적 전체로서 판단함.

design containing publicly known parts

A design that includes a publicly known part, which is deemed to have no value as creation. However, the design shall be assessed as a whole, in its entirety including the publicly known part.

사용례 디자인권은 물품의 신규성이 있는 형상, 모양, 색채의 결합에 부여되는 것으로서 **공지의 형상과 모양을 포함한** 출원에 의하여 디자인등록이 되었다 하더라도 공지부분에까지 독점적이고 배타적인 권리를 인정할 수는 없으므로 디자인권의 권리범위를 정함에 있어 공지 부분의 중요도를 낮게 평가하여야 하고, … (대법원 2012. 4. 13. 선고 2011후3469 판결 참조).

The design rights are attached to the novel combination of shapes, patterns and colors of an article. If a design is registered based an application **containing publicly known shape and pattern**, the publicly known parts shall not be the subject of sole and exclusive rights of the design's owner. Therefore the importance of the publicly known parts should be assessed in limited degree (Supreme Court Decision, 2011Hu3469, decided April 13, 2012).

공지의 예외

특허를 받을 수 있는 권리를 가진 자의 발명이 그에 의하여 또는 그 의사에 반하여 공지 또는 공연 실시된 경우 그로부터 12개월 이내에 특허출원을 하면 공지 등이 되지 아니한 발명으로 본다(특허법 제 30조 제1항 참조).

prior art exceptions

If an invention has been laid open by a person entitled to a patent or contrary to the will of the person entitled to a patent, a patent application filed within 12 months from the relevant date shall not be deemed to be publicly known or practiced (Patent Act Article 30(1)).

미 과도한 실험

발명이 실시가능하려면 명세서에 교시된 내용에 따라 통상의 기술자가 과도한 실험 없이 그 발명을 생산하고 사용할 수 있어야 한다. 개시된 내용이 과도한 실험을 요하는지를 결정하기 위해서는 (1) 필요한 실험의 양, (2) 제시된 지침이나 지시의 양, (3) 유효사례의 존부, (4) 발명의 속성, (5) 선행기술수준, (6) 통상의 기술자의 기술수준, (7) 해당 기술분야의 예측가능성 정도, (8) 청구항의 범위가 얼마나 넓은지 등을 고려하여야 한다. (미) In re Wands, 858 F.2d 731, 737 (Fed. Cir. 1988)

undue experimentation

Enablement requires that the specification teach those in the art to make and use the invention without undue experimentation. Factors to determine whether a disclosure would require undue experiment include (1) the quantity of experimentation necessary, (2) the amount of direction or guidance presented, (3) the presence or absence of working examples, (4) the nature of the invention, (5) the state of the prior art, (6) the relative skill of those in the art, (7) the predictability or unpredictability of the art, and (8) the breadth of the claims.

In re Wands, 858 F.2d 731, 737 (Fed. Cir. 1988)

과실의 추정

타인의 특허권 또는 전용실시권을 침해한 자는 그 침해행위에 대하여 과실이 있는 것으로 추정한다(특허법 제130조).

presumption of negligence

A person who infringes a patent or exclusive license of any third person shall be presumed negligent regarding such infringement (Patent Act Article 130).

과제해결원리

과제해결원리의 동일성은 특허 균등침해의 적극적 성립요건 중 하나. 균등침해가 성립하기 위하여는 양 발명의 기술적 사상 내지 과제의 해결원리가 동일하여야 함. → 균등론 참조

means to solve the problem, solution principles

Identity of the principle underlying the solutions of the problems is one of the requirements for infringement by equivalents. Infringement by equivalents is established when two inventions have the same technical idea or principle.

사용례 특허발명과 확인대상발명의 양 발명에서 **과제의 해결원리**가 동일하다는 것은 확인대상발명에서 치환된 구성이 특허발명의 비본질적인 부분이어서 확인대상발명이 특허발명의 특징적 구성을 가지는 것을 의미하는바, 특허발명의 특징적 구성을 파악하기 위하여는 명세서 중 발명의 상세한 설명의 기재와 출원 당시의 공지기술 등을 참작하여 선행기술과 대비하여 볼 때 특허발명에 특유한 해결수단이 기초하고 있는 과제의 해결원리가 무엇인가를 실질적으로 탐구하여야 한다(대법원 2010. 5. 27. 선고 2010후296 판결 참조).

If a patented invention and invention in question share the identical **solution principles**, this means that the element replaced within the invention in question is an inessential part of the patented invention and that the invention in question assumes the characteristic elements of the patented invention. Therefore, in order to grasp the characteristic elements of the patented invention, the detailed descriptions within the specifications and prior art existing at the time of application must be taken into consideration to investigate the solution principle upon which the patented invention establishes a unique solution that is unique to the problem when compared to prior art (Supreme Court Decision, 2010Hu296, decided May 27, 2010).

과태료

금전의 징수를 내용으로 하는 행정벌.

surcharge fine for negligence (법제처)

An administrative punishment that involves forfeiture of money.

미 관계의 허위적 암시

어느 표장이 (1) 타인이나 타 기관이 이전에 사용한 이름 또는 명칭과 동일하거나 이와 유사하고, (2) 독특하고 명백하게 그러한 사람 또는 기관을 나타내는 이름으로 인지되며, (3) 그 표장이 나타내는 사람 또는 기관은 출원인이 그 표장을 사용하여 수행하는 활동과 연관성이 없고, (4) 그 사람 또는 기관이 출원인이 자신의 상품이나 서비스와 관련하여 그 표장을 사용하였을 때 그 사람이나 기관과의 연관성이 추정될 정도

false suggestion of connection

A mark falsely suggests a connection with a person or an institution if: (1) the mark is the same as, or a close approximation of, the name or identity previously used by another person or institution; (2) the mark would be recognized as such, in that it points uniquely and unmistakably to that person or institution; (3) the person or institution named by the mark is not connected with the activities performed by the applicant under the mark; and (4) the fame or reputation of the person or institution is such that, when the mark is used with the applicant's

의 명성을 지닌 경우, 그 표장은 타인이나 타 기관과의 관계를 허위로 암시하는 것으로 간주됨. (미) Univ. of Notre Dame du Lac v. J.C. Gourmet Food Imps. Co., 703 F.2d 1372, 1375-77, 217 USPQ 505,508-10 (Fed. Cir. 1983); TMEP § 1203.03(c)(i).

goods or services, a connection with the person or institution would be presumed. Univ. of Notre Dame du Lac v. J.C. Gourmet Food Imps. Co., 703 F.2d 1372, 1375-77, 217 USPQ 505,508-10 (Fed. Cir. 1983); TMEP § 1203.03(c)(i).

미 관계회사

관계회사가 표장을 사용할 경우 그 사용효과는 그 상품이나 서비스의 성질 또는 품질을 통제하는 당사자에게 귀속된다. (미) TMEP § 1201.03.

related companies

When a mark is used by a related company, use of the mark inures to the benefit of the party who controls the nature and quality of the goods or services. TMEP § 1201.03.

관념

표장이 가지는 의미, 개념.

concept

The meaning or idea of a mark.

사용례 호칭 및 **관념**을 보면, 원고의 등록상표와 피고 제품의 형상은 모두 강아지를 형상화한 도형으로서 '강아지'로 관념되고 '강아지 표'로 호칭될 수 있다(대법원 2013. 1. 24. 선고 2011다18802 판결 참조).

Judging from the sound and **concept**, the plaintiff's registered trademark and the shape of the defendant's product are both figures that embody the shape of a puppy; both can generate the concept of "puppies" and be called as the "puppy marks." (Supreme Court Decision, 2011Da18802, decided January 24, 2013).

관념의 유사

2개의 상표가 가진 의미가 같거나 혼동되기 쉽기 때문에 이들 상표를 붙인 상품이 동일한 제조업자, 판매업자에 의하여 제조 판매하는 상품으로 직감하게 될 염려가 있는 경우.

similarity in concept

Similarity of two trademarks in concept exists when the meanings of the two marks are so identical or confusing that consumers are likely to instinctively believe that the goods with the marks are from the same manufacturer or seller.

사용례 양 상표는 외관 및 호칭에 차이가 있기는 하지만 **관념의 유사를** 압도할 정도에까지 이르렀다고 할 수 없으므로, 관념이 유사한 양 상표를 동일·유사한 지정상품에 함께 사용할 경우 일반 수요자나 거래자로 하여금 상품의 출처에 관하여 오인·혼동을 일으키게 할 염려가 있고, … (대법원 2013. 1. 16. 선고 2011후3322 판결 참조).

While the two trademarks are different in appearance and sound, such difference does not overcome the **similarity in concept**. Therefore, if the conceptually similar marks are both used on identical or similar designated goods, it may cause misconception or confusion to ordinary consumers or traders as to the source of the good, … (Supreme Court Decision, 2011Hu3322, decided January 16, 2013).

관련디자인

기본디자인과만 유사한 디자인으로 그 출

related design

A related design is a design that is only similar to the principal

원일보다 선행하는 타인의 디자인(출원디자인, 등록디자인, 공지디자인)과 유사하지 않은 것.

design and not to others' designs applied, registered or publicly known prior to the application date of the related design.

사용례 디자인등록을 받을 수 있는 권리는 이전할 수 있다. 다만, 기본디자인등록을 받을 수 있는 권리와 **관련디자인**등록을 받을 수 있는 권리는 함께 이전하여야 한다(디자인보호법 제54조 제1항).

A right to have a design registered is transferable: Provided that a right to have a principal design registered and a right to have **related designs** registered shall be transferred together (Design Protection Act Article 54(1)).

관리인

domestic representative, manager (법제처)

재외자의 산업재산권에 관한 대리인으로서, 국내에 주소나 영업소가 있는 자로 재외자를 대리하여 특허권등에 관한 절차를 밟거나 행정청이 한 처분에 대하여 소를 제기할 수 있는 자.

A person who is domiciled or has his/her place of business in the Republic of Korea, acting as an agent who may take actions relating to IP rights or appeal an administrative decision on behalf of a non-resident.

관용기술

commonly used art

「관용기술(慣用技術)」은 주지기술 중 자주 사용되고 있는 기술을 말함. → 주지기술 참조

"Commonly used art" means well-known art which is used widely. → See. Well-known art

관용표장

commonly used mark, customarily used mark (법제처)

특정 종류의 상품을 취급하는 거래계에서 동종업자들 사이에 그 상품을 가리키는 것으로 자유롭고 관용적으로 사용하게 된 표장을 가리킴(대법원 2003. 12. 26. 선고 2003후243 판결).

A mark that is freely and customarily used to refer to a good by those who are in the industry that transacts the good (Supreme Court Decision, 2003Hu243, decided December 26, 2003).

사용례 확인대상표장('매직블럭 매직폼') 중 '매직블럭'은 이 사건 등록상표의 지정상품인 기름 때를 제거하는 연마스펀지 등과 유사한 상품인 세척용 스펀지에 대하여 상표법 제51조 제1항 제3호의 **관용하는 표장**에 해당한다 할 것이다(특허법원 2013. 9. 5. 선고 2012허11375 판결 참조).

'Magic Block' in the challenged mark 'Magicblock Magicform' as at the IPTAB decision of this case, fell into a **customarily used mark** concerning 'cleaning sponge,' for which it was used, under Article 51(1)3 of the Trademark Act, … (Patent Court Decision, 2012Heo11375, decided September 5, 2013).

관할

Jurisdiction

→ 인적 관할권 및 사물 관할권 (물적 관할권) 참조

ㄱ

교부
물건의 인도

deliver
To deliver a product to a person or a place.

사용례 타인의 등록상표와 동일 · 유사한 상표를 그 지정상품과 동일 · 유사한 상품에 사용하거나 사용하게 할 목적으로 **교부** · 판매 · 위조 · 모조 또는 소지하는 행위는 상표권 또는 전용사용권을 침해한 것으로 본다(상표법 제108조 제1항 제2호).

Delivering, selling, forging, imitating, or possessing a trademark identical or similar to a registered trademark of another person for the purpose of using or causing a third party to use such trademark on goods identical or similar to the designated goods (Trademark Act Article 108(1)2).

구별성
식물신품종보호법상 품종보호를 받기 위한 요건 중 하나. 품종보호 출원일 이전까지 일반인에게 알려져 있는 품종과 명확하게 구별되는 품종은 구별성을 갖춘 것으로 본다(식물신품종보호법 제18조 제1항).

distinctness
One of the requirements to be protected under Act on Protection of New Varieties of Plants. The requirements for distinctiveness is provided in Article 18 of the Act. A plant variety shall be deemed distinct if it is clearly distinguishable from any other plant variety, the existence of which is publicly known on the date of filing of the application for protection of the plant variety (Act on Protection of New Varieties of Plants Article 18(1)).

구성대비표
특허발명과 각 선행발명의 대응되는 구성요소를 대비한 표.

feature comparison chart
A chart comparing patented invention and corresponding prior art by elements.

(발명의) 구성요소
발명을 이루는 요소, 부분.

component, element
Elements or parts that constitute an invention.

사용례 의약이라는 물건의 발명에서 대상 질병 또는 약효와 함께 투여용법과 투여용량을 부가하는 경우, 투여용법과 투여용량이 발명의 **구성요소**인지 여부(적극) (대법원 2015. 5. 21. 선고 2014후768 전원합의체판결).

In a case where the administration and dosage of a medicine are added on top of the target disease or efficacy of a pharmaceutical medicine as an invention of a product, whether the administration and dosage constitute an **element** of invention (affirmative) (Supreme Court Decision, 2014Hu 768, decided May 21, 2015).

구성요소 일체의 원칙
청구항의 모든 구성요소는 필수적이고 중요하므로 특허 침해는 침해자가 청구범위의 모든 구성요소를 사용하는 경우에만 성립하고, 그 중 일부만을 실시하는 행위는 원칙적으로 침해를 구성하지 아니함.

all elements rule, all-limitation rule
According to this principle, all elements of a claim is essential and material, therefore each element of a claim must be present in an allegedly infringing device in order to establish infringement.

사용례 … 특허발명의 청구범위가 복수의 구성요소로 되어 있는 경우에는 각 구성요소가 유기적으로 결합된 전체가 특허발명의 요지를 이루는 것이고, 이러한 경우 청구범위를 해석함에 있어서 그 구성요소의 일부를 배제하는 것은 허용될 수 없으며 (대법원 2001. 12. 24. 선고 99후2181 판결 등 참조), 특허발명과 대비되는 확인대상발명이 특허발명의 청구항에 기재된 필수적 구성요소들 중의 일부만을 갖추고 있고 나머지 구성요소가 결여된 경우에는, 소위 **구성요소 완비의 원칙**에 의해, 원칙적으로 그 확인대상발명은 특허발명의 권리범위에 속하지 아니한다(대법원 2000. 11. 14. 선고 98후2351 판결 등 참조).

When a claim of a patented invention is comprised of more than one elements and the elements are organically combined, the whole claim becomes the substance of the patented invention, and therefore, excluding part of the elements while interpreting the patent claims is not allowed. In case the challenged invention consists of only part of the elements of the patented invention and does not include other parts of the patented invention, the challenged invention, in principle, does not fall under the scope of the patented invention according to the **all elements rule** (Supreme Court Decision, 98Hu2351, decided November 14, 2000).

미 구속력 있는 선례

binding precedent

선행 사건에서 있었던 선례는 유사한 쟁점 또는 사실관계을 가진 후행 사건을 판단함에 있어 법원을 구속하거나 설득함.

A prior decision or authority established in a previous legal case that is either binding on or persuasive for a court when deciding subsequent cases with similar issues or facts.

사용례 이러한 지침은 특허상표청이 법에 대해 현재 이해하는 바에 기초한 것으로 미 대법원, 연방순회항소법원 및 그 전신 법원들의 **구속력 있는 선례**와 일관성이 있는 것으로 판단하고 있다. (미) MPEP § 2163 (발명의 상세한 기재 요건에 대한 지침 안내 중)

These Guidelines are based on the Office's current understanding of the law and are believed to be fully consistent with **binding precedent** of the U.S. Supreme Court, as well as the U.S. Court of Appeals for the Federal Circuit and its predecessor courts. MPEP § 2163 (providing guidelines for the written description requirement).

구술심리

oral hearing

구제책

remedies

권리가 침해되었을 때 그로 인한 피해를 보전하여 주기 위한 방법. 금전적 손해배상이나 금지명령 등이 있다.

Measures to make a harmed party whole again when his or her rights are infringed. E.g. Monetary damages or injunction.

(발명의) 구체화

reduction to practice

→ (발명의) 완성 참조

구호

slogan

사용례 또한 이 사건 출원상표 · 서비스

There is also no evidence that the mark at issue as a whole

표가 전체로서 거래사회에서 흔히 **구호**나 광고 문안으로 사용되는 점에 대한 증거가 없고, 일반 수요자가 그와 같이 인식하리라고 볼만한 자료도 없다(특허법원 2016.2.3 선고 2015허3993판결 참조).

is commonly used in **slogans** or advertising phrases in the marketplace, nor is there any data that ordinary consumers would perceive as such (Patent Court Decision, 2015Heo 3993, decided February 3, 2016).

국내단계출원

national stage application

국내 특허관청의 요건을 충족시킴으로써 특허협력조약의 국내단계에 이른 출원.

An application that has entered the national phase of the Patent Cooperation Treaty by the fulfillment of certain requirements in a national patent office.

사용례 미 특허법 371조 하의 **국내단계출원**의 우선권 주장은 특허협력조약에 명시된 기한 및 규정에 따라 하여야 한다. (미) MPEP § 214.3.

For **national stage applications** under Patent Act, 35 U.S.C. § 371, the claim for priority must be made within the time limit set forth in the PCT and the Regulations under the PCT. MPEP § 214.3.

국방상 필요한 발명

inventions necessary for national defence

정부는 국방상 필요한 경우 외국에 특허출원하는 것을 금지하거나 발명자 등에게 특허출원의 발명을 비밀취급하도록 명할 수 있으며(특허법 제41조 제1항), 특허출원된 발명에 대하여 특허를 허여 하지 않거나 특허를 받을 수 있는 권리를 수용할 수 있음(특허법 제41조 제2항).

If necessary for national defence, the government may prohibit filing a patent application with a foreign patent office or order the inventer etc. to keep the invention confidential. Patent Act Article 41(1). When the invention is necessary for national defence, the government may also refuse to grant patent or expropriate the entitlement to patent (Patent Act Article 41(2)).

국제등록

international registration

국내의 산업재산권 등을 여러 체약당사자 영역에서 보호받기 위해 등록하는 것을 의미함. 상표법의 경우 마드리드 의정서, 디자인보호법의 경우 헤이그협정 등.

to protect domestically registered patent or other IP rights in the territories of other parties to the treaties. Registration of trademark under the Madrid Protocol or registration of design under the Hague agreement, etc.

국제등록기초상표권

basic trademark rights of international registration, internationally registered basic trademark rights (법제처)

국제상표등록의 기초가 되는 상표등록. 우리나라를 지정하여 통지된 국제상표등록출원이 등록결정되어 국내 상표등록원부에 등록되어 있는 상표권을 말함.

The basis of an international trademark registration. A registration at the domestic Patent Office which is registered on the International Trademark Register.

국제등록명의인

국제등록명의인은 국제등록의 존속기간을 10년씩 갱신할 수 있다(상표법 제173조 제1항).

holder of an international registration

The holder of an international registration may renew the duration of an international registration every ten years (Trademark Act Article 173(1)).

국제등록부

디자인의 경우 헤이그협정에 의한 국제등록 디자인출원의 등록사항이, 상표의 경우 마드리드의정서에 의한 국제등록상표출원의 등록사항이 각각 기록되는 등록부.

International Register

The Register which records international registration of designs under the Hague Agreement or trademarks under the Madrid Protocol.

국제등록의 소멸

사용례 제1항 및 제2항에 따른 취하 또는 소멸의 효과는 국제상표등록부상 해당 **국제등록이 소멸**된 날부터 발생한다(상표법 제202조 제3항).

extinguishment of international registration

The effect of withdrawal or extinguishment under paragraphs (1) and (2) shall occur from the date the relevant **international registration is extinguished** (Trademark Act Article 202(3)).

국제등록일

국제등록기초상표권의 존속기간은 상표권의 설정등록이 있은 날부터 국제등록일 후 10년이 되는 날까지로 한다(상표법 제198조 제1항).

date of international registration

The duration of internationally registered basic trademark rights shall remain in force until the date ten years elapse after the date of international registration from the date trademark rights are registered and established (Trademark Act Article 198(1)).

국제등록 지정국

산업재산권을 보호받고자 국제출원인이 지정한 국가. 이는 본국에서의 상표등록 또는 상표등록출원을 기초로 함.

designated country

A country designated by the international applicant to protect his or her IP rights. Such designation is based on a IP rights registration or application in the home country.

국제디자인분류

산업디자인의 국제분류 제정을 위한 로카르노협정에 따른 물품 분류.

International Classification for Industrial Designs

Classification of goods pursuant to the Locarno Agreement Establishing an International Classification for Industrial Designs.

국제사무국

특허, 상표, 디자인 등의 국제출원과 등록에 관한 행정적 업무를 담당하는 WIPO 국제사무국.

International Bureau, International Secretariat (법제처)

WIPO International Bureau, in charge of administrative matters relating to international application and registration of patents, trademarks and designs.

국제지식재산연수원

International Intellectual Property Training Institute

국제출원인

지재권의 국제등록을 받으려는 출원인. 대한민국 국민이거나 대한민국에 주소(법인인 경우 영업소의 소재지)를 가진 자여야 함.

international applicant

A person seeking international registration of intellectual property rights; citizenship of the Republic of Korea, or domicile or place of business in the Republic of Korea is required.

권리구제

relief

권리남용

권리자가 상대방에게 고통을 주려는 목적에서 신의성실의 원칙에 반하여 권리를 행사하는 것.

abuse of right

When a person exercises his or her legal right in a manner that is contrary to the duty of good faith with the intent of harming others.

사용례 특허침해소송에서 설령 피고의 기술실시가 원고 특허의 형식적 권리범위에 속한다고 하더라도 원고의 특허가 무효로서 등록이 말소되어야 하기 때문에 원고의 침해청구는 **권리남용**에 해당하여 허용될 수 없다(대법원 2012. 1. 19. 선고 2010다95390 전원합의체 판결 참조).

In patent litigations, even when the defendant's execution of technology falls under the scope of the plaintiff's patented invention, if the plaintiff's patent is manifestly likely to be invalidated, the plaintiff's infringement prohibition claim or damage claim based on that patent right is not allowed as **abuse of rights** (Supreme Court Decision, 2010Da95390, decided January 19, 2012).

권리능력

법적 권리의무의 주체가 될 수 있는 능력

legal capacity

Capacity to have legal rights or legal obligations.

권리범위확인소송

심결취소소송의 하나로, 권리범위확인심판 결정에 불복하여 특허법원에 제기하는 소송.

action on confirm of the scope of rights

An action filed with the Patent Court to revoke IPTAB decisions on the scope of rights.

권리범위확인심판

특허심판원 심판으로서 특허권자가 청구인이 되어 어떤 기술실시가 특허등록된 발명의 청구범위에 포함됨을 확인하여 달라는 내용의 적극적 권리확인심판과 이해관계인이 자신의 기술실시가 특허등록된 발명의 청구범위에 포함되지 않음을 확인하여 달라는 소극적 권리확인심판이 있음(특허법

(administrative) trial to confirm scope of rights

An administrative proceeding filed with IPTAB by a patent holder requesting IPTAB to confirm that the opponent's execution of certain technique falls within the scope of patent holder's registered patent (affirmative scope of rights trial), or by a person executing certain technology seeking to confirm that his or her execution does not fall within the scope of the other party's registered patent rights (defensive

제135조, 상표법 제121조, 디자인보호법 제122조). scope of rights trial).

미 권리불요구

특허권 등의 출원인 또는 등록권자가 그 출원 또는 등록대상의 특정 구성요소 중 한 가지 또는 그 이상에 대하여 배타적 사용권을 주장하지 않는다는 진술. (미) USPTO.

disclaimer

A statement that the applicant or registrant does not claim the exclusive right to use a specified element or elements of the claimed or registered subject matter. USPTO.

권리소진의 원칙

특허품이 적법하게 생산, 판매된 경우에 그 양수인 등이 그 특허제품을 사용하거나 재판매하는 것은 특허침해를 구성하지 아니한다는 원칙으로서, 특허권자가 특허제품을 타인에게 양도함으로써 그 특허권은 정당하게 사용되어 소진되었다는 원칙.

exhaustion doctrine, first sale doctrine

Once a patented product is lawfully manufactured and sold, the use or resale by the assignee does not constitute infringement. By the patentee's assignment of the patented product, the patent rights thereto are duly used and exhausted.

사용례 물건의 발명 또는 물건을 생산하는 방법의 발명에 대한 특허권자 또는 그 특허권자로부터 허락을 받은 실시권자가 우리나라에서 특허물건 또는 특허방법에 의해 생산한 물건을 양도한 경우에는 당해 물건에 관해서는 특허권이 이미 그 목적을 달성하였으므로 소진된다. 그리고 방법의 발명에 대한 특허권자가 우리나라에서 그 방법의 실시에만 사용하는 물건을 양도한 경우에도 양수인 또는 전득자가 그 물건을 이용하여 해당 방법발명을 실시하는 것과 관련하여서는 특허권이 소진되며, 위에서 본 **특허권 소진**의 근거에 비추어 볼 때 물건의 양도가 계약에 의한 경우뿐만 아니라 경매절차에 의한 경우에도 특별한 사정이 없는 한 특허권 소진의 법리는 적용된다(특허법원 2009. 12. 18. 선고 2008허13299 판결 참조).

When a patentee or licencee of a patented invention of a product or patented invention of method to manufacture a product sells the patented product or product made with the patented manufacturing method, the patent right on that product has achieved its purpose and is exhausted. Also, when a patentee of a patented invention of a method sells a product that is only used to execute that method in the territory of Korea, the patent is exhausted with regard to the execution by the buyer or third party that assigned the product from the buyer who use that product to execute the patented method. In light of the **patent exhaustion** theory above, unless any special circumstances exist, legal theory of patent exhaustion applies not only to transfer based on contract but also to transfer in auction procedure (Patent Court Decision, 2008Heo13299, decided December 18, 2009).

(포기된 출원의) 권리회복청구

출원인이 거절이유통지에 기한 내에 답변을 제출하지 않아 출원이 포기되었으나 그 지연이 의도치 않은 것이었을 경우 포기된 출원에 대한 권리를 회복하기 위한 청구를 할 수 있음.

petition to revive an application

When an applicant failed to respond to Office action within the given period and the application was abandoned as a result, the applicant may file a petition to revive the application if the delay was unintentional.

권원의 연속

특정된 토지 등에 대하여, 정부나 권원의 원 출처에서부터 현재의 권리자에게까지 연속적으로 이어져 내려온 그 권리이전의 연속성.

chain of title

A term applied metaphorically to the series of conveyances, or other forms of alienation, affecting e.g., a particular parcel of land, arranged consecutively, from the government or original source of title down to the present holder.

사용례 새로운 상표권자의 이름으로 상표등록을 발행할 것을 요하는 내용의 청구는 양도등록부(Assignment Recordation Branch, ARB)에 등재된 서류에 원 출원인에서 새로운 상표권자까지의 **권원의 연속**이 명백히 나타나지 아니하면 받아들일 수 없다. (미) TMEP § 502.02(a).

A request that a registration issue in the name of a new owner will not be granted unless documents recorded in the Assignment Recordation Branch show clear **chain of title** from the original applicant to the new owner. TMEP § 502.02(a).

균등론

침해대상물의 구성요소의 일부가 특허발명의 대응되는 구성요소와 문언상으로는 동일하지 않더라도('구성요소 완비의 원칙' 참조) 서로 등가관계에 있다면 특허발명의 침해에 해당한다고 보는 이론. 균등침해의 성립요건은 적극적 성립요건으로 ① 과제해결원리 동일성, ② 치환가능성, ③ 치환자명성, 소극적 성립요건으로 ① 공지기술 배제의 원칙, ② 출원경과금반언의 원칙이 있음.

doctrine of equivalents

Even though some elements of the patented invention are not literally identical to the corresponding elements of the infringing subject (see. all-elements rule), infringement may be found if they are equivalent. The requirements for equivalent infringement are: identical principle underlying the solutions, possibility of substitution and obviousness of substitution. Negative requirements relate to principle of excluding publicly known art and file-wrapper estoppel.

균등침해

infringement by equivalents

균일성

식물신품종보호법상 품종보호를 받기 위한 요건 중 하나. 품종의 본질적 특성이 그 품종의 번식방법상 예상되는 변이를 고려한 상태에서 충분히 균일한 경우에는 그 품종은 균일성을 갖춘 것으로 본다(식물신품종보호법 제19조).

uniformity

One of the requirements to be protected under the Act on Protection of New Varieties of Plants. A plant variety shall be deemed uniform if, subject to the variation that may be expected from the particular features of its propagation, it is sufficiently uniform in its relevant characteristics (Act on Protection of New Varieties of Plants Article 19).

글자체

기록이나 표시 또는 인쇄 등에 사용하기 위하여 공통적인 특징을 가진 형태로 만들어진 한 벌의 글자꼴(숫자, 문장부호 및 기호

font

A set of characters (including those in the form of numerals, punctuation marks, and symbols) made in a style with common characteristics for recording, marking, or printing

등의 형태를 포함한다)을 의미(디자인보호법 제2조 제2호).

(Design Protection Act Article 2(2)).

금지명령

특허권자 또는 전용실시권자는 자기의 권리를 침해한 자 또는 침해할 우려가 있는 자에 대하여 그 침해의 금지 또는 예방을 청구할 수 있고, 침해행위를 조성한 물건(물건을 생산하는 방법의 발명인 경우에는 침해행위로 생긴 물건을 포함한다)의 폐기, 침해행위에 제공된 설비의 제거, 그 밖에 침해의 예방에 필요한 행위를 청구할 수 있음(특허법 제126조).

injunction

A patentee or an exclusive licensee may file a complaint to seek injunction against, or prevention of, infringement against a person who infringes, or is likely to infringe, his/her rights. A patentee or an exclusive licensee may also demand the destruction of the means by which the infringement has been committed (including the products obtained by infringement if the relevant invention is a process for manufacturing the products), the removal of the facilities used for infringement, and other measures necessary to prevent infringement (Patent Act Article 126).

미 (영구)금지명령

본안에 대한 최종공판 이후에 내려진 금지명령.

permanent injunction

An injunction granted after a final hearing on the merits.

기각

소송에 있어서 원고의 소에 의한 청구나 상소인의 상소에 의한 불복신청을 이유가 없다고 하여 배척하는 판결 또는 결정.

dismissal

A judgment dismissing the plaintiff's or appellant's request or complaint or appeal as lacking any merits.

기능성

물품의 용도나 목적에 필수적이거나 그 비용 또는 품질에 영향을 미치는 특징.

functionality

A feature is functional if it is essential to the use or purpose of the article or if it affects the cost or quality of the article.

사용례 양 디자인의 공통되는 부분이 그 물품으로서 당연히 있어야할 부분 내지 디자인의 기본적 또는 기능적인 형태인 경우에는 그 중요도를 낮게 평가하여야 하므로 이러한 부분들이 유사하다는 사정만으로는 곧바로 양 디자인이 서로 유사하다고 할 수는 없다(대법원2013. 4. 11. 선고2012후3794 판결참조).

It is incorrect to immediately label the designs similar merely based on the ground of similarities in the dominant features, because the significance of such similarities may be undermined if they constitute parts that the product must contain or relate to the fundamental or **functional** forms of the design (Supreme Court Decision 2012Hu3794 decided April 11, 2013).

기능식청구항

기능식 청구항 중 일부 요소를 구체적 구성으로 기재하지 않고 기능이나 성질, 작용,

functional claim, means plus function claim

A claim in which an element is described in abstract terms such as its function, nature, effect or characteristics rather

특성 등으로 추상화하여 표현한 청구항.

than in specific terms.

미 기능(수행)실패

상표로서의 기능, 즉 자타상품 또는 서비스를 식별하는 출처표시기능 수행에 실패하는 것. (미) TMEP § 1202.17(c).

failure to function

failure to function as a mark, i.e.. as an indicator of the source of the goods or services, identifying and distinguishing them from those of others. TMEP § 1202.17(c).

사용례 표장이 그 상품이나 서비스에 대해 직접적으로 정보를 나타내지 않더라도 타인에게 정보를 전달한다면 **상표로서의 기능 수행에는 실패**할 수 있다. 가령 여러 사람들에 의해 다양한 상품에 빈번하게 표시되는 관용어구나 구호는 장식적으로 사용하지 않더라도 출처표시용도로 인식되지 않을 확률이 높다. (미) TMEP § 1202.17 (c)(i)(A).

Even if a mark does not directly impart information about goods or services, it may nonetheless **fail to function** if it conveys an informational message to others. For example, common phrases and slogans that are frequently displayed by many different parties on various goods are not likely to be viewed as source indicators, even if the matter is being used in a non-ornamental manner. TMEP § 1202.17(c)(i)(A).

기능적이고 상업적인 변형

업계에서 통상의 지식을 가진 자라면 누구나 해당 디자인이 그 물품 또는 기능에 맞도록 하기 위하여 가할 수 있을 것이라고 생각되는 정도의 변화를 말함. (유사)용이하게 창작할 수 있는 정도(디자인보호법 제33조 제2항 참조).

functional and commercial modification

Modifications that any person with ordinary knowledge in the industry would be able to make to render the design suitable for the good or the function. Designs that could have been easily created by a person who has ordinary skill in the art (Design Protection Act Article 33(2)).

사용례 스탠드의 몸체 하단에 받침대를 추가하는 정도의 변형은 같은 업계에 종사하는 사람들이 흔히 취할 수 있는 **기능적이고 상업적인 변형**에 불과한 것이므로, … (특허법원 1999.03.11 선고 98허9604판결 참조).

… [T]he addition of a support stand on the bottom of the body of the lamp is merely a **functional and commercial modification** that can be made by any skilled persons in the art. … (Patent Court Decision, 98Heo9604, decided March 11, 1999).

미 기만적 표장

(1) 상품의 성격, 품질, 기능, 구성, 사용에 대해 허위적인 용어로 되어 있고 (2) 잠재적 수요자가 그 허위표시가 실제로 상품을 나타낸다고 신뢰할 만 하며, (3) 그 허위표시가 당해 상품의 소비자 상당수의 구매결정에 영향을 미칠 만한 기만적 사항으로 구성된 상표.

deceptive mark

A mark that consists of or comprises deceptive matter, as (1) the term is misdescriptive of the character, quality, function, composition or use of the goods; (2) the prospective purchasers are likely to believe that the misdescription actually describes the goods; and (3) the misdescription is likely to affect a significant portion of the relevant consumers' decision to purchase.

사용례 상표법 2(a)하의 **기만적 표장**은 주등록부에 등록될 수 없으며 2(f)에 따라 보조등록부에 등록할 수도 없다. 그러나 출원인은 2(a) 상의 판단기준의 일부 또는 전부를 만족하기 위하여, 표장에 대한 소비자 인식을 나타내는 선언서 등 2차적 식별력 입증을 위한 증거 등을 일응의 유리한 사건에 대한 반박증거로 제시할 수 있다. (미) TMEP § 1203.02(f).

…, [M]ark that are **deceptive** under §2(a) are never registrable on either the Principal Register, even under §2(f) or the Supplemental Register. However, applicants may present evidence of a similar nature to what is often submitted for acquired distinctiveness, such as declarations regarding how the mark is perceived by consumers, as rebuttal evidence to the prima facie case, in an effort to overcome one or all of the prongs of the §2(a) test. TMEP § 1203.02(f).

미 기만적 허위표시 표장

(1) 상품의 성격, 품질, 기능, 구성, 사용에 대해 허위적인 용어로 되어 있으며, (2) 잠재적 수요자가 그 허위표시가 실제로 상품을 나타낸다고 신뢰할 만 하나, (3) 그 허위표시가 당해 상품의 소비자의 구매결정에 중대한 요소까지는 달하지 않는 기만적인 내용으로 구성된 상표.

deceptively misdescriptive mark

A mark that consists of or comprises deceptive matter, as (1) the term is misdescriptive of the character, quality, function, composition or use of the goods and (2) the prospective purchasers are likely to believe that the misdescription actually describes the goods; but the misdescription is not a material factor in the relevant consumers' decision to purchase.

사용례 **기만적 허위표시**에 대한 판단기준은 두 단계로 구성된다. 첫째, 등록을 구하는 내용이 상품을 허위적으로 표시하는지 결정하여야 한다. 만일 그렇다면 그 표장이 또한 기만적인지, 즉 사람들이 그 허위표시를 믿을 만한지 따져보아야 한다. (미) TMEP § 1209.04.

The test for **deceptive misdescriptiveness** has two parts. First we must determine if the matter sought to be registered misdescribes the goods. If so, then we must ask if it is also deceptive, that is, if anyone is likely to believe the misrepresentation. TMEP § 1209.04.

기본디자인

자기의 등록디자인 또는 디자인등록출원한 디자인으로서, 관련디자인과 대비하여 유사의 판단기준이 되는 이미 등록되었거나 등록출원한 디자인(디자인보호법 제35조 참조).

principal design

The principle design in a pending application or registration that is compared with related design to determine similarity (Design Protection Act Article 35).

기속력

법원이나 행정기관이 재판이나 처분에 구속되어 이를 취소하거나 변경할 수 없는 효력.

legally binding force

A court or administrative agency is bound by a prior decision or action and may not revoke or remand the decision or action.

사용례 한편 특허권의 권리범위확인심판은 확인대상발명이 특허권의 효력이 미

Meanwhile, the adjudication on the scope of patent right is a procedure with the limited purpose of confirming whether

치는 객관적인 범위에 속하는지 여부를 확인하는 제한적 목적을 가진 절차일 뿐 침해금지청구권이나 손해배상청구권의 존부와 같은 권리관계까지 확인하거나 확정하는 절차가 아니고, 권리범위확인심판에서의 판단이 특허권침해소송이나 특허무효심판에 **기속력**을 미치는 것도 아니다(대법원 2002. 1. 11. 선고 99다59320 판결).

the cited invention is within the objective scope of the patent right's effectiveness. It is by no means a procedure for confirming or deciding the rights relationship, such as the existence of the right to claim for injunction on infringement or the right to claim damages; nor does its determination carry any **legally binding force** over patent infringement lawsuits or patent invalidation adjudications (Supreme Court Decision 99Da59320, decided January 11, 2002).

기술상식

해당 기술분야에서 널리 알려진 일반적인 지식.

technological common sense

A well-known general knowledge in the technical field.

사용례 따라서 구 특허법 제157조의20에서 정하는 국제특허출원의 특허에 대한 무효사유는 '출원번역문에 기재된 사항이 국제출원명세서 등에 기재된 사항의 범위 내에 없는 경우'를 의미한다. 또한 여기서 국제출원명세서 등에 기재된 사항이란, 국제출원명세서 등에 명시적으로 기재되어 있는 사항이거나 또는 명시적인 기재가 없더라도 발명이 속하는 기술분야에서 통상의 지식을 가진 자라면 출원 시의 **기술상식**에 비추어 보아 출원번역문에 기재되어 있는 사항이 국제출원명세서 등에 기재되어 있는 것과 마찬가지라고 이해할 수 있는 사항이어야 한다(대법원 2014. 4. 30. 선고 2011후767 판결).

Thus, it is reasonable to interpret a patent nullity ground under Article 157-20 of the former Patent Act as "where items stated in the patent application translation were absent in the items stated in the international patent application specification, etc." Further, items stated in the international patent application specification, etc., refer to those explicitly stated in the international patent application specification, etc., or otherwise, items which a person having ordinary knowledge in the art to which the invention pertains would understand the items in the patent application translation to be the same as those in the international patent application specification, etc., in light of **technological common sense** at the time of patent application (Supreme Court Decision, 2011Hu767, decided April 30, 2014).

기술설명회

법원은 기술적 쟁점을 심리하기 위해 변론기일에 앞서 당사자에 의한 기술설명회를 개최할 수 있다.

technical explanatory session

The court may hold a technical explanatory session by the parties before the oral hearing to examine the technical issues.

사용례 사건관리 화상회의에서는 아래 사항을 협의할 수 있고, 협의된 내용에 대하여는 [첨부 7]의 준비명령을 할 수 있다. … ⑤ 당사자에 의한 **기술설명회**의 실시 여부(특허법원 심결취소소송 심리매뉴얼 III.3.다).

In a video conference for case management, the following matters may be discussed and a preparatory order (scheduling order) may be issued based on the results of the discussion. [See. Attachment 7] ⑤ Whether to hold a **technical explanatory session** by the parties (Guideline of Practice and Procedure of Revocation Action in the Patent Court of Korea, III.3.C).

기술 수준

사용례 심사관은 최초거절결정 이전에 인터뷰를 신청하는 출원인에 대하여 발명 당시의 **기술수준**에 대한 일반적 진술과 가장 밀접한 것으로 생각되는 최소 3개의 인용문헌, 그리고 청구항을 가장 폭넓게 해석하였을 때 이 인용문헌과 발명이 어떻게 구별되는지를 설명한 문서를 제출하도록 요구할 수 있다. (미) MPEP § 713.02.

state of the art

Thus, the examiner may require that an applicant requesting an interview before the first Office action provide a paper that includes a general statement of the **state of the art** at the time of the invention, and an identification of no more than three (3) references believed to be the "closest" prior art and an explanation as to how the broadest claim distinguishes over such references. MPEP § 713.02.

기술심리관

(judicial) technical examiners

기술적 과제

사용례 이 사건 제1항 발명은 비교대상발명과는 구체적인 **기술적 과제**가 상이하고, 이를 해결하고자 착안한 원리 내지 방법이 비교대상발명에 내재되어 있거나 비교대상발명으로부터(비교대상발명 이외의 종래기술을 포함하더라도) 용이하게 도출되지도 아니하므로, 목적의 특이성이 인정된다(특허법원2007. 4. 6. 선고2006허6099 판결).

technical problem

The invention in Claim 1 is different from the Prior Art in that specific **technical problems** of these two inventions are different, and the principle or the method made for solving the problems is not inherent in the Prior Art nor easily conceived from the Prior Art (or related arts other than the Prior Art), and as a result, the objective of the invention in Claim 1 is distinct (Patent Court Decision, 2006Heo6009, decided April 6, 2007).

기술적 표장

→ 단순기술표장 참조

descriptive mark

기여도 (특허발명의)

사용례 1심에서 손해액을 산정하기 위해 감정이 실시되지 아니한 경우, 통상의 실시료나 특허발명의 **기여도** 등을 정하기 위해 감정이 필요한 경우, 기타 필요하다고 인정되는 경우, 이에 대한 감정을 실시할 수 있다(특허법원 침해소송 항소심 심리매뉴얼 V.4.가). → 기여분 참조

contribution ratio (of a patented invention)

The Court may conduct an appraisal if an appraisal for calculating the amount of damages was not conducted in the lower court, the appraisal is necessary to determine a reasonable royalty or a **contribution ratio** of a patented invention, or the appraisal is otherwise acknowledged to be necessary (Guideline of Civil Appellate Practice and Procedure of the Patent Court of Korea, V.4.A). → See. apportionment.

기여분

침해된 특허가 전체 제품의 일부에만 적용되었을 때 전체제품의 가치에 침해부분의 가치가 기여하는 기여분을 정하여 배분함.

apportionment

Determining the contribution and allocating value of the infringed part relative to the entire product, when the infringed patent is only applied to the part of the product.

미 기여침해

발명의 중요한 부분을 차지하는 특허등록된 기계장치, 제조물, 조성물 또는 결합물의 구성요소, 방법특허의 실시에 사용할 재료나 장치를 그 특허의 침해를 위하여 제작되었거나 침해를 목적으로 사용되도록 적용되었으며 주로 비침해적 용도의 상업적으로 중요한 물품 또는 재화가 아님을 알면서 미국 내에서 판매 또는 판매의 청약을 하거나 미국으로 수입한 자는 기여침해의 책임이 있다. (미) 특허법 제 271(c)조.

contributory infringement

A party who offers to sell or sell within the United States or imports into the United States a component of a patented machine, manufacture, combination or composition, or a material or apparatus for use in practicing a patented process, constituting a material part of the invention, knowing the same to be especially made or especially adapted for use in an infringement of such patent, and not a staple article or commodity of commerce suitable for substantial noninfringing use, shall be liable as a contributory infringer. Patent Act, 35 U.S.C. § 271(c).

기재불비

특허를 받을 수 없는 불완전한 발명과는 달리, 발명이 완성되었으나 출원시에 기재요건을 만족하지 못한 것. 특허청구항은 1. 발명의 설명에 의하여 뒷받침될 것, 2. 발명이 명확하고 간결하게 적혀 있을 것 등의 기재요건을 갖추어야 한다(특허법 제42조 제4항).

lack of sufficient description, lack of written description, deficiency of description

Distinguished from an incomplete invention, in the case of deficiency of description requirement, an invention is complete at the filing but fails to make a description regularly. Claims shall satisfy the requirements:
1. The invention shall be supported by the description;
2. The invention shall be clearly and concisely described (Patent Act Article 42(4)).

기재사항

사용례 등록상표의 보호범위는 상표등록출원서에 적은 상표 및 **기재사항**에 따라 정해진다(상표법 제91조 제1항).

description, statement (법제처)

The scope of protection of registered trademarks shall be determined by a trademark and **statement** in an application for trademark registration (Trademark Act Article 91(1)).

기초상표권

→ 국제등록기초상표권 참조

basic trademark right

기판력

청구배제효. 이미 그 이유에 대해 판단한 사항을 다시 소송할 수 없다는 원칙.

res judicata

Claim preclusion. The principle that a matter may not, generally, be relitigated once it has been judged on the merits.

기피

법률상 정해진 제척사유 이외에 법관에게 재판의 공정을 기대하기 어려운 사정이 있을 때에 당사자 또는 참가인의 신청에 의하여 당해 법관을 배제시키는 것.

challenge (of a judge)

Excluding a judge from the case by request of the party or the intervenor in case of a situation where the judge cannot be expected to conduct a fair proceeding for reasons other than prescribed by law.

(특허권의) 남용

특허권 등에 기한 합법적인 배타적 권리를 넘어서 이를 부당하게 사용하여 거래를 제한하는 행위를 말하며, 공정거래법 위반행위에 해당할 수 있음.

abuse (of patent right)

Improper use of a patent or other rights by its owner to restrain trade beyond enforcing the exclusive rights lawfully granted under the patent or other rights that may violate antitrust laws.

내재성

하나의 인용선행기술이 출원발명의 특징을 개시하지 않았다 하더라도 그 개시하지 않은 특징이 그 선행기술에 필수적으로 존재한다면 출원발명은 내재적으로 예견되어 그 신규성이 부정된다. (미) Schering Corp. v. Geneva Pharms., Inc., 339 F.3d 1373 (Fed. Cir. 2003).

inherency

An invention is anticipated by inherency and thus lacks novelty when a prior art reference anticipated the invention without disclosing a feature of the claimed invention, if the missing characteristic is necessarily present in the single anticipating reference. Schering Corp. v. Geneva Pharms., Inc., 339 F.3d 1373 (Fed. Cir. 2003).

내적 증거

청구범위 해석을 위해 사용되는 그 출원의 명세서, 도면, 출원경과서류.

intrinsic evidence

Specification, drawings and documents relating to the procedural history of the application, as used for claim construction.

냄새상표

상품의 출처를 표시하기 위해 사용하는 냄새로 된 상표.

scent mark, olfactory mark

A mark that consists of scent used to identify the source of the good.

니스협정

2002년 1월 1일 발효된 표장의 등록을 위한 상품 및 서비스의 국제분류에 관한 니스 협정. 상표 및 서비스표 등록을 위한 상품 및 서비스의 분류체계인 니스국제상품분류표를 정립함. 회원국의 상표청은 각 상표등록에 관련된 공문서 및 공지에 니스분류표 하에서 그 상품 또는 서비스가 속하는 상품류 또는 서비스류의 번호를 표시하여야 함.

Nice Agreement

The Nice Agreement Concerning the International Classification of Goods and Services for the Purposes of the Registration of Marks, effective January 1, 2002. The aim of the Trademark Law Treaty (TLT) is to standardize and streamline national and regional trademark registration procedures. The great majority of the provisions of the TLT concern the procedure before a trademark office which can be divided into three main phases: application for registration; changes after registration; and renewal.

다류(多類)출원(제도)

동일한 표장을 하나의 출원을 통해 여러 분류 하의 상품, 서비스, 단체 또는 그 모두에 대해 등록하고자 하는 출원.

multiple-class application, combined application

An application to register the same mark for goods, services, and/or a collective membership organization in multiple classes in a single application.

다중종속항

앞에 기재된 하나 이상의 독립항 또는 종속항을 선택적으로 인용하고 이를 한정하는 종속항.

multiple dependent claim

A dependent claim that further limits and refers back in the alternative to more than one preceding independent or dependent claim.

단류(單類)출원

분류표에서 하나의 분류에 속하는 상품이나 서비스에 대해서만 등록하고자 하는 출원.

single/single-class application

An application in which the designated goods or services all fall into a single category in the classification schedule.

단면도

사용례 청구된 디자인의 바깥 표면의 정확한 윤곽이나 구성이 도면의 도로부터 명백하지 않고, 내부 구조의 특징을 표현하려는 시도가 아닌 경우에는, 그 디자인의 형상을 명확하게 하기 위하여 **단면도**가 포함될 수 있다. (미) MPEP 1503.02.

sectional view

Where the exact contour or configuration of the exterior surface of a claimed design is not apparent from the views of the drawing, and no attempt is made to illustrate features of internal construction, a **sectional view** may be included to clarify the shape of said design. MPEP 1503.02.

미 단순기술표장

특정 상품이나 서비스의 성분이나 품질, 성격, 기능, 특성, 목적이나 용도를 설명하는 표장.

merely descriptive mark

A mark is considered merely descriptive if it describes an ingredient, quality, characteristic, function, feature, purpose or use of the specified goods or services.

사용례 단순히 기술적인 보편적 기호와 다른 기술적이거나 보통명칭, 기타 출처표시기능이 없는 사항으로 구성된 표장은 전체적으로 **단순기술표장**에 해당하고 심사관은 이에 대해 상표법 2(e)(1)에 따라 거절결정을 하여야 한다. (미) TMEP § 1202.17(d)(i).

If a mark consists of a merely descriptive universal symbol and other descriptive, generic, or otherwise non-source-indicating matter, then the mark is **merely descriptive** in its entirety and the examining attorney must issue a refusal under §2(e)(1). TMEP § 1202.17(d)(i).

단체표장

상품을 생산 · 제조 · 가공 · 판매하거나 서

collective mark

A mark intended to be used directly by a corporation jointly

비스를 제공하는 자가 공동으로 설립한 법인이 직접 사용하거나 그 소속 단체원에게 사용하게 하기 위한 표장(상표법 제2조 제1항 제3호).

incorporated by persons who produce, manufacture, process or sell goods, or who provide services, or intended to be used by its members (Trademark Act Article 2(1)3).

답변서

피고가 원고의 청구를 다투는 경우에는 소장의 부본을 송달받은 날부터 30일 이내에 답변서를 제출하여야 한다(민사소송법 제256조 제1항).

written defense, reply brief, response brief

Where a defendant contests the claim of a plaintiff, he/she shall submit a written defence within 30 days from the date of receiving a service of a duplicate of the written complaint (Civil Procedure Act Article 256(1)).

미 당사자계 심판

제3자가 특허 등의 무효를 청구할 수 있는 심판절차.

inter partes review

A procedure for third parties to seek invalidation of patents.

사용례 **당사자계 심판** 청구일 이전에 청구인 또는 실제 이해관계를 가진 당사자가 특허의 무효를 주장하는 민사소송을 제기하였다면 당사자계 심판을 개시하여서는 아니 된다. (미) 특허법 제315(a)(1)조.

An **inter partes review** may not be instituted if, before the date on which the petition for such a review is filed, the petitioner or real party in interest filed a civil action challenging the validity of a claim of the patent. Patent Act, 35 U.S.C. § 315(a)(1).

미 당사자계 재심사

2012년 9월 16일 이후로는 당사자계 재심사를 신청할 수 없음. 미 개정특허법으로 당사자계 재심사는 신설된 당사자계심판절차로 대체됨. (미) MPEP § 2601.

inter partes reexamination

No requests for inter partes reexamination may be filed on or after September 16, 2012. Under the Leahy-Smith America Invents Act (the AIA), the inter partes reexamination is replaced by the new inter partes review process. MPEP § 2601.

대리권

→ 대리인 참조

agency authority

대리인

소송절차 또는 행정절차를 대신하여 수행할 권한을 위임받은 자. '**대리인**이나 대표자'라 함은 일반적으로 국외에 있는 상표에 관한 권리를 가진 자의 그 상품을 수입하여 판매 · 광고하는 대리점, 특약점, 위탁판매업자, 총대리점 등을 가리키는 것인바, … (특허법원 2014. 6. 19. 선고 2013허10027 판결 참조).

agent, representative

A person authorized to carry out the litigation or administrative procedure as a representative. The term "**agent or representative**" generally means an agency, distributor, consigned seller, or general agency importing product from a person that has right to an overseas trademark and selling and advertising the product … (Patent Court Decision, 2013Heo10027, decided June 19, 2014).

대비적 관찰

양 상표를 나란히 놓고 외관, 호칭, 관념을 비교 관찰하는 방법.

사용례 … 다만 예외적으로 고가의 정밀제품과 같이 꼼꼼히 따져서 구매하는 것이 통례인 경우에는 이격적 관찰이 아닌 **대비적 관찰**을 할 수도 있을 것이다(특허법원 1999.09.09 선고 99허6008 판결 참조).

comparative observation

Comparing trademarks side by side, in appearance, sound and concept.

However, a **comparative observation** may be exceptionally more desirable than comparison by recollection as the good is a high-priced and elaborated one that requires careful consideration before purchase (Patent Court Decision, 99Heo6008, decided September 9, 1999).

대응구성

사용례 선행발명 1, 2는 기술분야가 동일하고, 선행발명 1, 2의 **대응구성**들의 결합에 기술적 어려움이 없으며, … (특허법원 2016. 9. 29. 선고 2016허2737 판결 참조).

corresponding elements, corresponding feature

Prior Arts 1 and 2 are within the same technical field, and there is no technical difficulty in combining **corresponding features** of Prior Arts 1 and 2 (Patent Court Decision, 2016Heo2737, decided September 29, 2016).

미 대체출원

출원인이 현 출원을 신청하기 전에 포기한 이전 출원과 사실상 동일한 출원. 대체출원으로는 이전 출원의 출원일을 인정받을 수 없음.

substitute application

An application that is, in essence, a duplicate of a prior application by the same applicant abandoned before the filing of the substitute application. A substitute application does not obtain the benefit of the filing date of the prior application.

도면

특허출원서에는 발명의 설명 · 청구범위를 적은 명세서와 필요한 도면 및 요약서를 첨부하여야 한다(특허법 제42조 제2항).

drawing

A patent application filed under paragraph (1) shall be accompanied by a specification containing the description of the invention and the claims, necessary drawings, and an abstract (Patent Act Article 42(2)).

도시(圖示)되고 기재된 바와 같은

→ '도시된 바와 같은' 참조

as shown and described

도시된 바와 같은

출원에서 도면은 "도시된 바와 같은" 의 청구범위 용어를 사용함으로써 청구범위에 포함됨. (미) MPEP 1504.04.

as shown

The drawing in an application is incorporated into the claim by use of the claim language "as shown." MPEP 1504.04.

도용

타인의 산업재산권등을 무단으로 사용하는 행위.

misappropriation

The act of using registered IP rights without lawful authority to do so.

사용례 특허청 또는 특허심판원 직원이나 그 직원으로 재직하였던 사람이 디자인등록출원 중인 디자인(헤이그협정 제11조에 따라 연기 신청된 국제디자인등록출원 중인 디자인을 포함한다)에 관하여 직무상 알게 된 비밀을 누설하거나 **도용**한 경우에는 5년 이하의 징역 또는 5천만원 이하의 벌금에 처한다(디자인보호법 제225조 제1항).

Any employee of the Korean Intellectual Property Office or the Intellectual Property Trial and Appeal Board that divulges or misappropriates confidential information which becomes known to him/her about a design claimed in a pending application for design registration (including designs claimed in a pending application for international design registration, for which a request for deferment has been filed under Article 11 of the Hague Agreement) in the course of performing his/her duties shall be punished by imprisonment with labor for not more than five years or by a fine not exceeding 50 million won (Design Protection Act Article 225(1)).

도형상표

figurative mark

상품의 출처를 표시하기 위해 사용하는 도형으로 된 상표.

A mark that consists of figures used to identify the source of the good.

사용례 특히 **도형상표**들에 있어서는 그 외관이 주는 지배적 인상이 동일·유사하여 두 상표를 동일·유사한 상품에 다 같이 사용하는 경우 일반 수요자에게 상품의 출처에 관하여 오인·혼동을 일으킬 염려가 있다면 두 상표는 유사하다고 보아야 한다(대법원 2016. 7. 14. 선고 2015후1348 판결 참조).

Two **figurative marks** shall be deemed similar when the dominant images created by the appearances of the marks are identical or similar and there is likelihood of confusion and misconception as to the source of the goods among ordinary consumers when the marks are both used on identical or similar goods (Supreme Court Decision, 2015Hu1348, decided July 14, 2016).

독립항

independent claim

특허 청구항 중 다른 청구항을 인용하지 않는 청구항.

A claim that does not refer back to or depend on another claim.

사용례 법 제42조 제8항에 따른 청구범위의 청구항(이하 "청구항"이라 한다)을 기재할 때에는 독립청구항(이하 "**독립항**"이라 한다)을 기재하여야 하며, 그 독립항을 한정하거나 부가하여 구체화하는 종속청구항(이하 "종속항"이라 한다)을 기재할 수 있다. 이 경우 필요한 때에는 그 종속항을 한정하거나 부가하여 구체화하는 다른 종속항을 기재할 수 있다(특허법시행령 제5조 제1항).

When claims within the scope of claims under Article 42 (8) of the Act (hereinafter referred to as "claims") are stated, such claims shall be stated in the form of independent claims (hereinafter referred to as "**independent claims**"), but dependent claims may be added to limit or additionally specify such independent claims (hereinafter referred to as "dependent claims"). If it is necessary in such cases, other dependent claims may be added to limit or additionally specify such dependent claims (Enforcement Decree of Patent Act Article 5(1)).

독점적 실시권, 배타적 실시권

exclusive license, exclusionary implementation right

권리자가 그 권리에 대해 독점적으로 허락한 실시권.

The license granted by a right holder for exclusive practice of the right.

사용례 다만 대법원은 특허의 일부 또는 전부가 출원 당시 공지공용의 것인 경우까지 청구범위에 기재되어 있다는 이유만으로 권리범위를 인정하여 독점적 · **배타적인 실시권**을 부여할 수는 없으므로 권리범위확인심판에서도 특허무효의 심결 유무에 관계없이 그 권리범위를 부정할 수 있다고 보고 있으나(대법원 2014. 3. 20. 선고 2012후4162 전원합의체 판결 참조).

It is true that the Supreme Court's view is that, when the patent application pertains in whole or in part to public knowledge or public use at the time of its filing, a monopolistic, **exclusive implementation right** may not be granted by acknowledging its scope of rights for the mere reason that they are indicated in the claims (Supreme Court Decision, 2012Hu4162, decided March 20, 2014).

ㄷ

미 독특한 특징

characteristic features

공지디자인에 대하여 신규성 또는 비자명성을 가지는 특징이라고 출원인이 생각하는 디자인의 특정한 특징. (미) 37 C.F.R. § 1.71(c).

A particular feature of the design that is considered by applicant to be a feature of novelty or nonobviousness over the prior art. 37 C.F.R. § 1.71(c).

사용례 명세서에는 등록하고자 하는 디자인의 신규성 또는 진보성을 지니는 특정한 특징을 묘사하는 '**독특한 특징**'에 대한 진술이 허용될 수 있는데, 이러한 진술은 '해당 디자인의 독특한 특징은 [1]에 존재한다'거나 그림을 통한 묘사와 결합하여 사용될 경우에는 '그 독특한 특징은 [2]에 존재한다'와 같은 문구를 사용하여야 한다. (미) MPEP § 1503.01.

A "**characteristic features**" statement describing a particular feature of novelty or nonobviousness in the claimed design may be permissible in the specification. Such a statement should be in terms such as "The characteristic feature of the design resides in [1]," or if combined with one of the Figure descriptions, in terms such as "the characteristic feature of which resides in [2]." MPEP § 1503.01.

미 동시계류출원

co-pending applications

→ 동일인출원 참조

동음이의어 지리적 표시

homonymous geographical indication

같은 상품에 대한 지리적 표시가 타인의 지리적 표시와 발음은 같지만 해당 지역이 다른 지리적 표시를 말함(상표법 제2조 제1항 제5호).

A geographical indication that has the same pronunciation with but refers to a different location from another geographical indication used by another person for the same good (Trademark Act Article 2(1)5).

미 **동일간주원칙** 상표법에서, 사진상의 묘사와 등가의 단어가 수요자들에게 동일한 심상을 불러일으켜 혼동을 일으킬 가능성이 있다는 인식에 기반한 원칙.	**doctrine of legal equivalents** A doctrine under trademark law based on a recognition that a pictorial depiction and equivalent wording are likely to impress the same mental image on purchasers and thus may cause likelihood of confusion.
사용례 수요자들에게 어느 표장과 다른 표장의 일부를 동일한 것으로 간주할 만큼 지속적으로 동일한 상업적 인상을 불러일으킨다면 그 표장은 다른 표장의 일부와 **동일하게 간주된다**. (미) TMEP § 1212.02(f)(ii)(B).	A mark is the **legal equivalent** of a portion of another mark if it creates the same, continuing commercial impression such that the consumer would consider the mark to be the same as the portion of the other mark. TMEP § 1212.02(f)(ii)(B).
동일상표 동일한 상표. 등록된 상표와 물리적으로 동일한 경우뿐 아니라 상표의 동일성을 해치지 않을 정도로 변형하여 사용하는 경우, 즉 거래통념상 동일성이 인정되는 형태의 상표까지 포함됨.	**identical trademark** An identical trademark includes not only physically identical one to a registered mark but also those that have modified the registered mark within a degree that does not interfere with the identity and are deemed identical under the trade norms.
사용례 … 위와 같은 불사용으로 인한 상표등록취소 제도의 취지에 비추어 볼 때, 여기서 '등록상표를 사용'한다고 함은 등록상표와 동일한 상표를 사용한 경우를 말하고 유사상표를 사용한 경우는 포함되지 아니하나, '**동일한 상표**'에는 등록상표 그 자체뿐만 아니라 거래통념상 등록상표와 동일하게 볼 수 있는 형태의 상표도 포함된다고 할 것이다(대법원 2013. 9. 26. 선고 2012후2463 전원합의체 판결 참조).	In light of the purpose of the aforementioned trademark cancellation system by reason of non-use, using a "registered trademark" means using a trademark which is identical to the registered trademark, and does not include similar trademarks; however, "**identical trademark**" may include not just the registered trademark itself, but also trademarks that can be perceived as identical to a registered trademark in terms of trade norms (Supreme Court Decision, 2012Hu2463, decided September 26, 2013).
동일상품 지정상품 그 자체 또는 거래사회의 통념상 이와 동일하게 볼 수 있는 상품. 양 상품의 품질·용도·형상·사용방법·유통경로 및 공급자와 수요자 등 상품의 속성과 거래의 실정을 종합적으로 고려하여 객관적으로 판단함.	**identical good** Goods identical or deemed identical to the designated good under the norms of the marketplace. The determination is made in an objective manner based on thorough consideration of the characteristics of the goods and course of trade such as the quality, use, form, and usage of the goods, distribution channels, suppliers and consumers.
사용례 보석 장신구인 '진주 반지, 산호 반지'에 이 사건 등록상표를 사용한 것은	… The use of the registered trademark at issue on "pearl rings, coral rings," types of jewelery ornaments, is not use

거래사회의 통념상 이 사건 등록상표의 지정상품인 '진주, 산호'와 **동일성 있는 물품**에 대하여 등록상표를 사용한 것이라고 할 수 없다(대법원 2008. 5. 29. 선고 2006후2967 판결 참조).

the mark on **goods identical** to the designated goods, "pearls and corals." (Supreme Court Decision, 2006Hu2967, decided May 29, 2008).

미 동일인출원

같은 출원인에 의한 출원. 동시계류출원.

companion applications

Pending applications filed by the same applicant. Co-pending applications.

사용례 **동일인출원**이 이의신청을 위해 공지되었거나 등록되었을 경우 심사관은 그 **동일인출원** 또는 등록 상의 상품이나 서비스의 분류 또는 명칭이 인용가능한 것이라 가정할 수 있다. 단 그 분류 또는 명칭이 명백히 오류가 있을 때에는 그러하지 아니하다. (미) TMEP § 702.03(a)(iv).

If a **companion application** has been published for opposition or has registered, the examining attorney may presume that the classification and identification of goods or services in the companion application or registration are acceptable, unless the identification or classification is clearly wrong. TMEP § 702.03(a)(iv).

동일한 발명

두 발명이 서로 동일한 발명인지 여부는 대비되는 두 발명의 실체를 파악하여 따져보아야 할 것이지 표현양식에 따른 차이에 따라 판단할 것은 아니므로, 대비되는 두 발명이 각각 물건의 발명과 방법의 발명으로 서로 발명의 범주가 다르다고 하여 곧바로 동일한 발명이 아니라고 단정할 수 없다(대법원 2007. 1. 12. 선고 2005후3017 판결 참조).

identical invention

In judging if two inventions are identical, the actual substance of the two inventions compared shall be examined, rather than the differences as to how they are described, such that even when the two inventions compared fall under the different categories of "invention of a product" and "invention of a process," it shall not be automatically determined that they do not constitute identical inventions (Supreme Court Decision, 2005Hu3017, January 12, 2007).

동작상표

짧은 시간 사이에 반복되는 동작을 그 표장의 특성으로 포함하고 있는 상표.

motion marks

Marks that include a repetitive motion of short duration, i.e. motion, as a feature. TMEP § 807.11.

사용례 **동작상표**가 실제로 상품을 특정, 식별하며 출처를 표시함을 입증하기 위해 출원인은 그 표장이 상품 또는 서비스에 혹은 그와 관련하여 어떻게 사용되는지를 나타내기에 충분하게 그 동작을 묘사하고 표장에 필요한 설명에 일치하는 견본을 제출하여야 한다. (미) TMEP § 904.03(l).

To show that a **motion mark** actually identifies and distinguishes the goods/services and indicates their source, an applicant must submit a specimen that depicts the motion sufficiently to show how the mark is used on or in connection with the goods/services, and that matches the required description of the mark. TMEP § 904.03(l).

미 드노보 심리(審理) — de novo review

하급심의 사실 판단에 구속되지 않고 사건을 새롭게 검토하는 기준.

Anew. A standard of review that no deference is given to the lower court's factual findings.

등급표시 — grade designations

등급 지정은 어느 상품이 그 정해진 범위 내에서 특정 수준의 품질을 보유함을 나타내기 위해 사용됨.

Grade designations are used to indicate that a particular product has a certain level of quality within a set range.

미 등록가능통지 — notice of allowability

사용례 최종거절결정 전후로 출원이 등록허여를 위한 요건을 만족하는 모든 경우, 출원인에게 **등록가능통지** 양식 PTOL-37로 이를 신속히 통지하여야 한다. (미) MPEP § 1302.03.

In all instances, both before and after final rejection, in which an application is placed in condition for allowance, applicant should be notified promptly of allowability of the claims by a **Notice of Allowability** PTOL-37. MPEP §1302.03.

등록결정 — decision to register

사용례 특허청장은 제212조에 따라 준용되는 제68조에 따른 상표**등록결정**이 있는 경우에는 지정상품의 분류를 전환하여 등록하여야 한다(상표법 제211조).

Where a **decision to register** a trademark under Article 68 applied mutatis mutandis pursuant to Article 212 is made, the Commissioner of the Korean Intellectual Property Office shall register the conversion of the classification of designated goods (Trademark Act Article 211).

미 등록결정통지 — notice of allowance

출원인에게 법에 따른 특허권등을 소유할 자격이 있음을 알리는 내용의 통지. 미 상표법 상 등록결정통지는 사용의사에 기한 출원에 대해서만 발행되며, 아직 상표가 등록되었다는 의미는 아님. (미) USPTO.

A notification to the applicant that he or she is entitled to a patent or other rights under the law. In trademark law, Notices of allowance are only issued for applications that have been filed based on “intent to use” and does not mean that the mark has registered yet. USPTO.

사용례 심사결과 출원인이 법에 따라 특허권을 허여받을 자격이 있는 것으로 나타날 경우 1.33에 따른 주소로 **등록결정통지**를 발송하게 된다. (미) 37 C.F.R. § 1.311.

If, on examination, it appears that the applicant is entitled to a patent under the law, a **notice of allowance** will be sent to the applicant at the correspondence address indicated in § 1.33. 37 C.F.R. § 1.311.

등록료 — registration fee

특허권등의 설정등록, 존속기간갱신등록, 지정상품추가등록 등을 받기 위해 납부하는 금액.

Fee to establish patent or other IP rights, to renew their terms or add designated goods.

사용례 제90조 제1항에 따른 디자인권의 설정등록을 받으려는 자는 설정등록을 받으려는 날부터 3년분의 디자인등록료(이하 "**등록료**"라 한다)를 내야 하며, 디자인권자는 그 다음 해부터의 등록료를 그 권리의 설정등록일에 해당하는 날을 기준으로 매년 1년분씩 내야 한다(디자인보호법 제79조 제1항).

A person granted a design right registered under Article 90 (1) shall pay a design registration fee (hereinafter referred to as "**registration fee**") for three years from the date the grant of the right is registered, and the owner of a design right shall pay a registration fee for one year thereafter on or before each anniversary of the registration date of the grant of the relevant right (Design Protection Act Article 79(1)).

등록료의 보전

등록료의 일부를 납부하지 아니하여 부족한 부분을 보태어 채우는 것.

payment of remainder

To pay off any unpaid balance of registration fee.

등록무효

일단 유효하게 성립된 산업재산권등을 일정한 법정사유로 인하여 심판절차에 의해 등록일로 소급하여 그 효력을 상실시키는 것.

invalidation

To retroactively void any effect of validly established IP registration due to statutory grounds through trial proceedings.

등록무효사유

산업재산권의 등록이 무효로 되어야 하는 사유. 무효심판 청구에 대한 심결로 결정하며, 확정 시 그 산업재산권은 처음부터 없었던 것으로 간주.

grounds for invalidation

Grounds to invalidate a registered intellectual property rights. Where an administrative trial decision to invalidate a registration becomes final and conclusive, such intellectual property rights shall be deemed never to have existed.

사용례 …그 심결취소소송인 원심절차에서 원고는 이 사건 심결의 위법사유로서 이 사건 등록디자인이 비교대상디자인 등으로부터 용이하게 창작할 수 있는 디자인에 해당하지 않으므로 같은 법 제5조 제2항 소정의 **등록무효사유**가 존재하지 않는다는 주장만을 하였을 뿐이고, … (대법원 2011. 3. 24. 선고 2010후3509 판결 참조).

Following the Tribunal's decision, the plaintiff filed an appeal in the court below seeking reversal of the decision where the plaintiff alleged Article 5 (2) of the Act is not a valid **ground to invalidate** the registered design at issue because the design was not easily creatable from other comparable designs (Supreme Court Decision, 2010Hu3509, decided March 24, 2011).

등록상표

상표권자 또는 출원인은 등록상표 또는 상표등록출원의 지정상품을 추가하여 상표등록을 받을 수 있다. 이 경우 추가등록된 지정상품에 대한 상표권의 존속기간 만료일은 그 **등록상표**권의 존속기간 만료일로 한다(상표법 제86조 제1항).

registered trademark

A trademark owner or applicant may add designated goods in the registration or application. In such cases, the expiration date of the trademark on the subsequently added designated goods shall be the expiration date of the **registered trademark** (Trademark Act Article 86(1)).

ㄷ

등록실용신안
실용신안등록을 받은 고안.

registered utility model
A device for which a utility model has been granted.

등록유지료

maintenance fees

등록일

registration date

등록주의
사용 여부와 관계없이 등록에 의하여 권리를 인정하는 주의.

principle of registration
The principle that one shall be entitled to IP rights, whether or not the IP rights is actually used, by registration.

등록증

certificate of registration

등록취소
일단 유효하게 등록된 산업재산권 등이 사후의 일정한 사유에 의하여 그 등록의 효력을 장래에 대하여 상실시키는 것을 말함.

cancellation (of registration)
To prospectively remove any effect of IP rights due to a certain cause arising after a valid registration.

미 등록후재심사
개정 특허법에 신설된 절차로, 이에 따라 제3자가 특허의 발행 또는 재발행일로부터 9개월 내에 하나 또는 복수의 특허를 취소할 것을 청구할 수 있음.

post grant review
Under this new procedure added by the AIA, third parties may file a petition seeking to cancel one or more patent claims within nine months of a patent's issue or reissue date.

사용례 복수의 **등록후재심사**를 이 장하에 동일한 특허에 대하여 청구하였고 그 중 복수의 청구가 324조 하에 등록후재심사의 대상이 될 자격이 있다고 판단할 경우 특허상표청장은 각 청구를 단일한 등록후재심사 사건으로 병합할 수 있다. (미) 특허법 제325(c)조.

If more than one petition for a **post-grant review** under this chapter is properly filed against the same patent and the Director determines that more than one of these petitions warrants the institution of a post-grant review under section 324, the Director may consolidate such reviews into a single post-grant review. Patent Act, 35 U.S.C. § 325(c).

디자인
물품(물품의 부분 및 글자체를 포함한다)의 형상·모양·색채 또는 이들을 결합한 것으로서 시각을 통하여 미감을 일으키게 하는 것 (디자인보호법 제2조 제1호).

design
The term "design" means a shape, pattern, or color of an article (including parts of an article (excluding those defined under Article 42) and fonts; the same shall apply hereinafter), which invokes a sense of beauty through visual perception; … (Design Protection Act Article 2.1).

디자인공보

디자인공보는 디자인의 설명, 도면 또는 사진 등 등록디자인에 관한 사항을 게재하며, 디자인보호법 제212조 제1항에 따라 등록디자인공보와 공개디자인공보로 나뉨(디자인보호법 시행령 제10조).

Design Gazette

The Design Gazette published under Article 212 (1) of the Act shall be classified into the Design Gazette for Registration and the Design Gazette for Publication (Enforcement Decree of the Design Protection Act Article 10).

디자인권 존속기간 만료 후의 통상실시권

특허출원일 전 또는 특허출원일과 같은 날에 출원되어 등록된 디자인권이 그 특허권과 저촉되는 경우 그 디자인권의 존속기간이 만료될 때에는 그 디자인권자는 그 디자인권의 범위에서 그 특허권에 대하여 통상실시권을 가지거나 그 디자인권의 존속기간 만료 당시 존재하는 그 특허권의 전용실시권에 대하여 통상실시권을 가짐(특허법 제105조 제1항).

non-exclusive licenses after expiration of design rights

If a design right claimed in an application filed on or before the filing date of a patent application and registered accordingly conflicts with the patent, the holder of the design right at the expiration of the term of the design right shall have a non-exclusive license of the patent within the scope of the design right or a non-exclusive license of the exclusive license that exists on the patent at the expiration of the term of the design right, within the scope of the design right (Patent Act Article 105(1)).

디자인등록원부

디자인권과 전용실시권 또는 통상실시권의 설정, 이전, 소멸, 회복 등의 사항을 등록함(디자인보호법 제88조 제1항).

Design Register

The following matters shall be recorded in the Design Register: the grant, transfer, extinguishment, or reinstatement of design rights, exclusive or non-exclusive licenses (Design Protection Act Article 88(1)).

디자인등록출원

디자인등록출원은 1디자인마다 1디자인등록출원으로 한다(디자인보호법 제 40조 제1항).

application for design registration

Each design shall be applied for registration under a separate application (Design Protection Act Article 40(1)).

디자인등록표시

물품, 물품의 용기나 포장 등에 그 디자인이 디자인등록을 받은 사실을 표시하는 것. 디자인권자 · 전용실시권자 또는 통상실시권자는 등록디자인에 관한 물품 또는 그 물품의 용기나 포장 등에 디자인등록의 표시를 할 수 있다(디자인보호법 제214조).

indication of design registration

Indication of the fact that the design embodied in a product, its container or package is registered. A design right-holder or an exclusive or non-exclusive licensee may place a mark indicating design registration on products to which the registered design is applied or containers or packaging materials of such products (Design Protection Act Article 214).

디자인(형태)의 동일 · 유사성

2개의 디자인을 비교할 때, 그 디자인을 구

identity or similarity of designs (shapes)

Identity or similarity of designs is what creates identical

ㄷ

성하는 형상 · 모양 · 색채 또는 이들을 결합한 것, 즉 형태가 외관상 서로 동일·유사한 미감을 일으키게 하는 것.

or similar aesthetic sense between the shapes (i.e. the configurations, forms, colors or their combination) that constitute the two designs when compared in their appearance.

사용례 동일하거나 유사한 디자인에 대하여 다른 날에 2 이상의 디자인등록출원이 있는 경우에는 먼저 디자인등록출원한 자만이 그 디자인에 관하여 디자인등록을 받을 수 있다(디자인보호법 제46조 제1항).

If at least two applications are filed on different dates for registration of an **identical or similar design**, only the first applicant to file an application may have his/her design registered (Design Protection Act Article 46(1)).

디자인창작자

디자인 등록을 받을 수 있는 주체로서, 사실행위로서의 창작자를 의미.

creator of design

One who is entitled to register a design and who actually created the design.

미 디자인특허출원

신규성, 독창성, 장식성을 갖춘 디자인이 물품에 허가 없이 사용되는 것을 막기 위한 특허출원.

design patent application

An application for a patent to protect against the unauthorized use of new, original, and ornamental designs for articles of manufacture.

ㄹ

로카르노협정

디자인의 국제분류에 관한 로카르노협정. 산업디자인 분류법인 로카르노 분류체계를 정립함. 회원국의 산업디자인 담당기관은 각 디자인의 기탁 또는 등록에 관련된 공문서에 로카르노분류 하에서 그 상품이 속하는 분류 및 세분류의 번호를 표시하여야 함. WIPO.

Locarno Agreement

Locarno Agreement Establishing an International Classification for Industrial Designs. The Locarno Agreement establishes a classification for industrial designs (the Locarno Classification). The competent offices of the Contracting States must indicate in official documents reflecting the deposit or registration of industrial designs the numbers of the classes and subclasses of the Classification to which the goods incorporating the designs belong WIPO.

ㅁ

마드리드 의정서

표장의 국제등록에 관한 마드리드협정에 대한 의정서. 상표권자로 하여금 '국제출원'이라 불리는 단일출원을 함으로써 마드리드 의정서에 가입한 체약국 어디에서나 그

Madrid Protocol

The "Protocol Relating to the Madrid Agreement Concerning the International Registration of Marks" (Madrid Protocol). An international treaty that allows a trademark owner to seek registration in any of the countries that have joined

상표를 등록할 수 있도록 하는 조약.

the Madrid Protocol by filing a single application, called an "international application."

마쿠쉬 청구항

마쿠쉬 청구항이란 대안적인 형태로서 "A, B, C로 구성된 그룹에서 선택된"과 같은 형태를 의미함. (미) Ex parte Markush, 1925 C.D. 126 (Comm'r Pat. 1925).

Markush type claim

A Markush-type claim recites alternatives in a format such as "selected from the group consisting of A, B and C." Ex parte Markush, 1925 C.D. 126 (Comm'r Pat. 1925).

사용례 마쿠쉬 그룹(위 예의 A, B, C)는 일반적으로 알려진 물리적 또는 화학적 집단 또는 기술집단에 속해야 한다. 그러나 마쿠쉬 그룹이 방법항이나 조성물 발명 청구항에 사용되는 경우에는(즉, 단일한 화합물로 구성되지 않은 경우에는), 그 그룹의 구성원들이 청구된 관계에서의 기능을 하기 위한 적어도 하나의 기능을 보유하는 것으로 명세서에 개시되어 있고, 그것들의 성질 또는 선행기술에 비추어 구성원 모두가 그 성질을 갖고 있음이 명백하면 충분하다. (미) MPEP 2173.05(h).

The members of the Markush group (A, B, and C in the example above) ordinarily must belong to a recognized physical or chemical class or to an art-recognized class. However, when the Markush group occurs in a claim reciting a process or a combination (not a single compound), it is sufficient if the members of the group are disclosed in the specification to possess at least one property in common which is mainly responsible for their function in the claimed relationship, and it is clear from their very nature or from the prior art that all of them possess this property. MPEP § 2173.05(h).

미 마크맨 심리

1심 단계에서 내적 증거 및 외부증거를 고려하여 청구항을 해석하기 위한 변론전 심리. 청구항 해석 심리라고도 함.

Markman hearing

A district-court level pretrial hearing held for the purpose of claim construction based on intrinsic and extrinsic evidence. Also known as a claim construction hearing.

명목상의 사용

상표에 대한 권리를 확보해 두기 위한 목적으로만 상표를 사용하는 것.

token use

Use of a mark solely for the purpose of reserving rights in the mark.

사용례 따라서, 다른 종류의 거래에서 판촉목적으로 상품에 상표를 사용한 것이나 단순한 **명목상의 사용**은 랜햄법 상 '사용'에 해당하지 아니한다. (미) Emergency One, Inc. v. Am. FireEagle, Ltd., 228 F.3d 531, 536 (4th Cir. 2000).

Thus, neither promotional use of the mark on goods in a different course of trade nor mere **token use** constitute "use" under the Lanham Act. Emergency One, Inc. v. Am. Fire Eagle, Ltd., 228 F.3d 531, 536 (4th Cir. 2000)

미 명백하고 확실한 증거

'증거의 우월성'보다는 높으나 '합리적 의심의 여지가 없는' 증명보다는 낮은 입증책

clear and convincing evidence

A higher standard than "preponderance of evidence" but lower than "beyond a reasonable doubt" standard regarding

ㅁ

임 충족 여부 판단의 기준.

burden of proof.

미 명백한 오류 기준

하급심의 사실관계 판단에 대한 검토 기준. 이 기준 하에서 항소법원은 하급심이 오류를 범하였다는 확신이 있지 않는 한 하급심의 판결을 유지하게 됨.

clearly erroneous standard

A standard of review in reviewing a lower court's treatment of factual issues. The lower court's judgment will be upheld unless the appellate court is firmly convinced that an error has been committed.

명세서

특허발명의 발명의 설명, 청구범위 등이 상세하게 기재된 서면. 특허출원시 출원서에 첨부하여 제출하여야 하며 특허법상 요건에 따라 구체적으로 명확하게 적어야 함.

specification

A document that includes detailed explanation of the invention, patent claims, etc. When filing patent application, specification shall be attached to the written application. Specification shall meet the specificity required by the relevant provisions of the Patent Act.

명칭

상표권은 자기의 성명 · 명칭 또는 상호 · 초상 · 성명 · 인장 또는 저명한 아호 · 예명 · 필명과 이들의 저명한 약칭을 상거래 관행에 따라 사용하는 상표에는 그 효력이 미치지 않는다(상표법 제90조 제1항 제1호).

title

A trademark shall not be effective when it uses his or her own name, title, or trade name, portrait, signature, seal, or well-known pseudonym, stage name, pen name, and the well-known abbreviated title thereof, in accordance with generally accepted business practices (Trademark Act Article 90(1)1).

명확성

특허 청구항에서 출원인이 본인의 발명이라 믿는 대상을 특정하여 밝히고 이에 대해 명확하게 청구하여야 한다는 요건.

definiteness

The requirement that patent claims must particularly point out and distinctly claim the subject matter that the applicant regards as his or her invention.

미 모델 표시

모델 표시는 다양한 상품에 대해 특정한 스타일이나 타입, 특정 제품라인 내의 상품의 디자인을 특정하기 위해서나 동일한 생산라인의 다른 자동차 부품 타입을 구별하기 위해 사용됨. (미) TMEP § 1202.16.

model designations

Model designations appear in connection with a wide variety of products to identify a specific style, type, or design of a product within a particular line of goods, or to distinguish between different types of automobile parts within a single product line. TMEP § 1202.16.

모방

물품을 대상으로 한 디자인에 관한 청구범위가 잘 알려지거나 자연적으로 발생되는 물건이나 사람을 모방한 경우, 이는 청구된 디자인이 독창성이 부족하여 등록을 받을 수 없다.

simulation

claim directed to a design for an article which simulates a well known or naturally occurring object or person should be rejected as nonstatutory subject matter in that the claimed design lacks originality.

모방상표

정당한 권원이 없이 원상표와 유사하게 모방하여 부착된 상표.

counterfeit mark

A mark that imitates the original trademark without legitimate authority to do so.

사용례 위 규정의 취지는 특정인의 주지상표가 국내에서 등록되어 있지 않음을 기화로 제3자가 이를 모방한 상표를 등록하여 사용함으로써 … 주지상표권자에게 손해를 가하거나 이러한 **모방상표**를 이용하여 부당한 이익을 얻을 목적으로 사용하는 상표는 그 등록을 허용하지 않는다는 데에 있다(대법원 2014. 2. 27. 선고 2013후2484 판결 참조).

The purpose of the above regulation is to prohibit registration of a trademark by a third party who imitates a well-known mark not registered in the territory of Korea … to cause harm to the owner of the well-known mark or gain undue profit from the use of the **counterfeit mark** (Supreme Court Decision, 2013Hu2484, decided February 27, 2014).

모양

사용례 디자인이란 형상 · **모양** · 색채 또는 이들을 결합한 것으로서 시각을 통하여 미감을 일으키게 하는 것을 말한다(디자인보호법 제2조 제1호).

pattern, form

The term "design" means a shape, **pattern**, or color of an article [including parts of an article (excluding those defined under Article 42) and fonts; the same shall apply hereinafter], which invokes a sense of beauty through visual perception (Design Protection Act Article 2.1).

모인출원

어떤 발명에 대하여 특허를 받을 권리가 없는 자가 한 특허출원.

application by unentitled persons

A patent application filed by a person who does not have the right to hold a patent of such invention.

사용례 발명자가 아닌 자로서 특허를 받을 수 있는 권리의 승계인이 아닌 자(이하 "무권리자"라 한다)가 한 특허출원이 제33조 제1항 본문에 따른 특허를 받을 수 있는 권리를 가지지 아니한 사유로 제62조 제2호에 해당하여 특허를 받지 못하게 된 경우에는 그 **무권리자의 특허출원** 후에 한 정당한 권리자의 특허출원은 무권리자가 특허출원한 때에 특허출원한 것으로 본다(특허법 제34조).

If a patent application filed by a person who is not an inventor nor a successor to an entitlement to a patent (hereinafter referred to as "unentitled person") falls under subparagraph 2 of Article 62 on the ground that the person has no entitlement to a patent under the main body of Article 33 (1) and no patent is granted to such person, the patent application filed by a legitimate right-holder subsequent to **the patent application filed by the unentitled person** shall be deemed filed on the date of filing of the patent application by the unentitled person (Patent Act Article 34).

모조

타인의 등록상표와 동일 · 유사한 상표를 그 지정상품과 동일 · 유사한 상품에 사용하거나 사용하게 할 목적으로 교부 · 판매 · 위조 · 모조 또는 소지하는 행위는 상표

imitate

The following Delivering, selling, forging, imitating, or possessing a trademark identical or similar to a registered trademark of another person for the purpose of using or causing a third party to use such trademark on goods identical

ㅁ

권 침해에 해당한다(상표법 제108조 제1항 제2호).

or similar to the designated goods shall be deemed an infringement of trademark rights. (Trademark Act Article 108(1)2).

모출원(母出願)

parent application

몰수

confiscation, forfeiture

형법상 형의 일종으로 범죄행위와 관련된 재산의 박탈을 내용으로 하는 재산형. 지식재산권 또는 전용실시권을 침해한 행위를 조성한 물건 또는 그 침해행위로부터 생긴 물건은 이를 몰수함. 범죄와 관련한 재산을 박탈하는 국가의 행위.

Pecuniary punishment under criminal law to take away property relevant to the crime. Goods that are the subject of infringement of intellectual property rights or exclusive licenses thereof, or goods obtained from such acts of infringement, shall be confiscated. Government action forfeiting the assets related to a crime.

무권리자

unentitled person, person without rights (법제처)

특허권등의 권리자가 아닌 자로서, 창작자나 발명가 또는 권리의 승계인이 아닌 자.

A person who is neither the creator/inventor of IP rights nor a legitimate successor to such right.

무역관련 지적재산권에 관한 협정

TRIPs (Trade-Related Intellectual Property portions of General Agreement on Tariffs and Trade)

보호대상 지식재산권은 저작권 및 저작인접권, 서비스표를 포함한 상표, 원산지명칭을 포함한 지리적 표시, 산업디자인, 식물품종보호를 포함한 특허, 집적회로 배치설계, 영업비밀과 테스트 데이터 등의 비공개정보 등이 있다. 회원국은 조약에 따른 지식재산권 보호에 있어 자국민과 타 회원국의 국민을 동등하게 대우하여야 함. WTO.

The areas of intellectual property that it covers are: copyright and related rights; trademarks including service marks; geographical indications including appellations of origin; industrial designs; patents including the protection of new varieties of plants; the layout-designs of integrated circuits; and undisclosed information including trade secrets and test data. The basic obligation on each Member country is to accord the treatment in regard to the protection of intellectual property provided for under the Agreement to the persons of other Members. WTO.

무임승차

free riding

사용례 나아가 이미 국내 또는 해외의 거래자 또는 수요자간에 특정인의 상표라고 현저하게 인식될 수 있을 정도로 알려져 있고 또 상표권자의 선전, 광고 및 다년간의 지속적인 사용을 통하여 영업상 신용이나 고객흡인력 등의 무형의 재산적 가치(GOODWILL)가 축적된 상표를 모방하여

Furthermore, if the trademark is already conspicuously known as belonging to a particular source among traders or consumers in Korea and overseas and has accumulated business reputation and customer appeal through years' of continued use, **free riding** on the intangible financial value of the trademark by filing application for a mark that imitates lacks justification under the legal reasoning relating to the

출원함으로써 위 무형의 재산적 가치에 **무임승차**(FREE RIDE)하려는 것도 구 상표법 제9조 제1항 제4호에 관한 법리상 그 사회적 타당성을 결여한 것이고 … (특허법원 1999.04.15 선고 99허31 판결 참조).

previous Trademark Act, Article 9(1)4, … (Patent Court Decision 99Heo31, decided April 15, 1999).

무효심판

trial on invalidation, trial on invalidity (of patents)

이해관계자들이 권리자를 상대로 등록된 권리의 무효를 구하기 위하여 특허심판원에 제기하는 심판.

An action filed with the IPTAB by interested persons in order to invalidate the IP rights registration.

사용례 이해관계인(제2호 본문의 경우에는 특허를 받을 수 있는 권리를 가진 자만 해당한다) 또는 심사관은 특허가 다음 각 호의 어느 하나에 해당하는 경우에는 무효심판을 청구할 수 있다. 이 경우 청구범위의 청구항이 둘 이상인 경우에는 청구항마다 청구할 수 있다(특허법 제133조 제1항).

(1) In any of the following cases, an interested party or examiner may file a petition for trial to seek invalidation of a patent. In such cases, when the claim contains at least two claims, a petition for trial for invalidation may be filed for each claim: Provided, That any person may file a petition for trial for invalidation on any of the following grounds (excluding the ground specified in subparagraph 2), if three months have not passed since the date when the registration of the patent is published after the grant of the patent is registered (Patent Act Article 133(1)).

무효처분

invalidation

무효처분의 취소

revocation of invalidation

사용례 특허청장 또는 특허심판원장은 제1항에 따른 무효처분 또는 제2항 본문에 따른 **무효처분의 취소**처분을 할 때에는 그 보정명령을 받은 자에게 처분통지서를 송달하여야 한다(디자인보호법 제18조 제3항).

When the Commissioner of the Korean Intellectual Property Office or the Director General of the Intellectual Property Trial and Appeal Board invalidates a procedure under paragraph (1) or **revokes the invalidation** of the proceeding under the body of paragraph (2), he/she shall give notice of the disposition to the person ordered to amend the procedure (Design Protection Act Article 18(3)).

미 (청구항) 무효화

(claim) vitiation

침해가 의심되는 고안이 청구항의 한정사항을 무효화 또는 제거한다면 침해물이라 할 수 없음. 구성요소 완비의 법칙에 의한 필연적 결과.

An accused device cannot be infringing if it would effectively vitiate (or eliminate) any claim limitation. A natural conclusion from all-elements rule.

문언적 의미

plain meaning

발명 당시 그 발명이 속하는 기술 분야의

The ordinary and customary meaning given to a term by

ㅁ

통상의 기술자가 그 용어에 부여한 일반적이고 관용적인 의미. (미) MPEP § 2111.01.

those of ordinary skill in the art at the time of the invention. MPEP § 2111.01.

문언침해

청구범위의 문언해석에 의하여 당해 특허의 구성요소를 모두 사용하는 경우에 성립하는 침해로서, 가장 기본적인 침해유형.

literal infringement

The most basic type of infringement, which is established when, literally interpreted, the accused device uses all elements of the patented invention.

문언해석

청구범위를 해석함에 있어서 청구범위에 표현된 문언이 일반적, 객관적으로 어떠한 의미를 나타내는지 해당 기술분야의 통상의 기술자를 기준으로 해석해야 한다. 특허발명은 청구범위에 '기재된' 사항에 의하여 보호범위가 결정되므로 발명의 설명이나 도면에 나타난 것이라도 청구범위에 기재되지 않은 사항은 원칙적으로 보호범위에서 제외됨.

literal interpretation

A patent claim shall be interpreted based on the general, objective meaning of the expression of the word in the claim, and how persons skilled in the art would interpret the word. The protection scope of a patented invention is decided by what is written in the claim, therefore a matter included in detailed description or drawing is excluded from protection if it is not disclosed in the claim.

문자상표

한글·한자·로마자·외국어·숫자 등의 문자로 구성된 상표

word mark, letter trademark

A mark that comprises of letters, such as Korean, Chinese, Roman characters, other foreign languages or numbers.

사용례 이 사건 출원상표 'APP STORE'는 "적용, 응용, 응용 프로그램" 등의 의미가 있는 'Application'의 약어인 'APP'과 "백화점, 가게, 저장(소)" 등의 의미가 있는 'STORE'가 결합하여 구성된 **문자상표**로서, … (특허법원 2014. 5. 8. 선고 2013허9126 판결 참조).

"APP STORE," the trademark of this case, is a **letter trademark** combining "APP," abbreviation of "Application" which means "application, application program, etc.," and "STORE," meaning "department store, store, storage, etc.," … (Patent Court Decision, 2013Heo9126, decided May 8, 2014).

문장

국가나 단체 또는 집안 따위를 나타내기 위하여 사용하는 상징적인 표지.

coat of arms

The distinctive heraldic design, emblem or shield of family, corporation, or country.

물건을 생산하는 방법의 발명

물건의 발명, 방법의 발명과 함께 특허법상 인정되는 발명의 유형 중 하나.

invention of a process of manufactoring a thing

A type of invention recognized by the Patent Act together with 'invention of a thing' and 'invention of a process.'

사용례 **물건을 생산하는 방법**의 발명인

An **invention of a process of manufacturing a thing**: Using,

경우: 나목의 행위 외에 그 방법에 의하여 생산한 물건을 사용 · 양도 · 대여 또는 수입하거나 그 물건의 양도 또는 대여의 청약을 하는 행위(특허법 제2조).

selling, leasing, or importing a thing manufactured by the process or offering to sell or lease such thing, other than the activities specified in item (b) (Patent Act Article 2).

물건의 발명

invention of a thing

방법의 발명, 물건을 생산하는 방법의 발명과 함께 특허법상 인정되는 발명의 유형 중 하나.

A type of invention recognized by the Patent Act together with 'invention of a process' and 'invention of a process of manufacturing a thing.'

사용례 **물건의 발명**인 경우: 그 물건을 생산 · 사용 · 양도 · 대여 또는 수입하거나 그 물건의 양도 또는 대여의 청약(양도 또는 대여를 위한 전시를 포함한다. 이하 같다)을 하는 행위(특허법 제2조).

An **invention of a thing**: Manufacturing, using, selling, leasing, importing the thing or offering to sell or lease the thing (including displaying a thing for the purpose of sale or lease; hereinafter the same shall apply) (Patent Act Article 2).

물상대위

subrogation

담보권자가 담보목적물의 멸실, 훼손, 공용징수 등으로 인하여 담보설정자가 받을 금전 기타 물건에 대하여 담보권을 행사하는 것(민법 제342조).

A pledge may also be exercised against money or other things which the pledger is entitled to receive by reason of the loss, damage or expropriation of the pledged article. In such case, an attachment must be levied thereon prior to their payment or delivery (Civil Act Article 342).

물품

article of manufacture

발명, 상표 또는 디자인 등이 화체 또는 적용된 대상.

The subject an invention, trademark or design is embodied in or applied to.

사용례 물품에 적용된 여하한 표시, 대조적인 색채나 재질, 그래픽 표현물, 또는 다른 장식. 표면 처리는 **물품**에 적용되거나 화체된 것이어야 한다. 표면 처리는, 그 자체로는 (즉, 특정한 물품에 적용되거나 화체되지 않은 상태로는) 미 특허법 제171조에 따른 디자인특허의 올바른 대상이라 할 수 없다. (미) MPEP 1503.02.IV.

Any indicia, contrasting color or materials, graphic representations, or other ornamentation applied to the article. Surface treatment must be applied to or embodied in an **article of manufacture**. Surface treatment, per se (i.e., not applied to or embodied in a specific article of manufacture), is not proper subject matter for a design patent under 35 U.S.C. 171. MPEP 1503.02.IV.

물품류

classification of goods, category of products (법제처)

로카르노협정에 따른 물품의 구분.

Classification of goods under the Locarno Agreement.

ㅁ

물품의 기능에 관련된 형태

물품의 기능에 관련된 형태라도 그것이 수요자에게 심미감을 줄 수 있는 부분이라면 디자인의 지배적인 특징으로 판단할 수 있는 것이지만, 그러한 기능적인 요소가 디자인의 지배적인 특징이 되기 위해서는 표현된 물품에서 보는 사람의 주의를 끌 수 있거나 형태적인 특징을 가장 잘 나타낼 수 있어야 한다(특허법원 2015. 9. 10. 선고 2015허3801 판결 참조).

a form related to a function of the article

Even if a form is related to a function of the article, it may be a dominant feature of the design if it appeals to the aesthetic sense of purchasers. However, for such a functional element to be a dominant feature of the design, it must attract the attention of the observer or represent the characteristics of the shape in the applied article (Patent Court Decision, 2015Heo3801, decided September 10, 2015).

물품의 기능을 확보하는 데 불가결한 형상

물품의 기능을 확보하기 위해 필연적으로 결정되어 버린 형상으로서 대체가능성이 없는 것뿐만 아니라 물리적으로 대체가능성이 있다고 하더라도 그 분야에서 그러한 형상의 변화를 추구하는 것이 예외적인 경우. 물품의 기능을 확보하는 데에 불가결한 형상만으로 된 디자인은 디자인등록을 받을 수 없다(디자인보호법 제34조).

a shape essential for a function of the relevant article

A shape necessitated by the article's function. It is unsubstitutable or, even if physically substitutable, such substitution would be exceptional in the field. A design that solely consists of a shape essential to a function of the article (Design Protection Act Article 34).

물품의 기능적 형태

양 디자인의 공통되는 부분이 그 물품으로서 당연히 있어야 할 부분 내지 디자인의 기본적 또는 기능적인 형태인 경우에는 그 중요도를 낮게 평가하여야 하므로 이러한 부분들이 유사하다는 사정만으로는 곧바로 양 디자인이 서로 유사하다고 할 수는 없다(특허법원 2015. 4. 23. 선고 2014허6858판결 참조).

functional form of a product

It is incorrect to immediately label the designs as similar merely based on the ground of similarities in the dominant features, because the significance of such similarities may be undermined if they constitute parts that the product must contain or relate to the fundamental or functional forms of the design (Patent Court Decision, 2014Heo6858, decided April 23, 2015).

물품의 기본적 형태

디자인의 골격이 되는 기본형태로서 그 형태를 갖춤으로써 그 물품이라고 인식되고 명명될 수 있는 것.

fundamental form of a product

The shape of an article that is the basis of the design, and is required to perceive and identify the article as such.

미각상표

미각적인 수단에 의하여 자타상품을 식별하는 표장.

flavor mark

A mark that provides distinctiveness by taste.

미 미국 개정 특허법 — AIA (Leahy-Smith America Invents Act)

미 미국연방순회항소법원 — CAFC (Court of Appeals for the Federal Circuit)

미 미국 특허심판원 — PTAB (Patent Trial and Appeal Board)

미 미 상표법 — Lanham Act

미생물의 기탁

미생물에 관계되는 발명에 대하여 특허출원을 하려는 자는 특허출원 전에 해당 기관에 특허청장이 정하여 고시하는 방법에 따라 해당 미생물을 기탁하여야 함.

deposit of micro-organisms

A person who wishes to file a patent application for an invention related to a micro-organism shall deposit the micro-organism with authorities, prior to filing the patent application, in the manner prescribed and publicly notified by the Commissioner of the Korean Intellectual Property Office.

미완성 발명

미완성 발명은 특허보호의 대상이 될 만한 발명에 이르지 못하였다고 평가되는 경우를 말한다.

incomplete invention

Incomplete invention refers to an invention that is not complete enough to be subject to protection of patent.

사용례 **미완성 발명**은 특허보호의 대상이 될 만한 발명에 이르지 못하였다고 평가되는 경우로서, 단순한 과제 또는 착상의 제기에 그치고 그 실현방법을 모르는 것, 발명의 목적을 달성하기 위한 수단의 일부 또는 그 전부가 결여되어 발명의 목적달성이 실제로 불가능한 것, 과제의 해결수단이 막연하여 구체화할 수 없는 것 또는 그 수단만 가지고는 목적을 달성할 수 없는 것, 발명의 반복재현이 불가능한 것 등을 말한다(특허법원 2002. 10. 10. 선고 2001허4722 판결 참조).

Incomplete invention refers to an invention that is not complete enough to be subject to protection of patent, which includes mere proposal of a problem or idea and not knowing method for materialization, cases in which the purpose of the invention is impossible to achieve because lack of all or part of the means necessary to achieve the purpose, cases in which means to solve technical problems is too remote and cannot be concrete, cases in which the purpose cannot be achieved with only that method, and inventions that cannot be repeated (Patent Court Decision, 2001Heo4722, decided December, 2002).

바람직한 구현례

발명자가 제시하는 출원의 출원발명을 수행하는 최적의 실시례.

preferred embodiment

How the inventor sets forth the best mode for carrying out the claimed invention in the application.

반대신문

소송에서 상대방 측 증인에 대해 행하는, 그 증언 또는 성품에 대한 신뢰성을 떨어뜨리기 위한 신문.

cross examination

Examination of a witness in litigation when the testimony supports the other party, to discredit the testimony or the witness's character.

반려

상표등록출원에 대한 보완명령을 받은 자가 지정기간 내에 보완하지 아니한 경우 출원서류를 반려한다(상표법 시행규칙 제25조 제6항).

return

In case the recipient of the order to supplement the application fails to comply within the designated period, the application documents shall be returned(Enforcement Rule of the Trademark Act, Article. 25(6)).

반박

사용례 출원의 청구항이나 재심사대상 특허가 거절 또는 이의신청의 대상이 되었을 때에는 그 거절 또는 이의신청을 **반박**하기 위해 제출하는 증거는 그 근거가 별도로 명시되지 아니하였을 경우 이 조항에 따라 선서 또는 선언서와 함께 제출되어야 한다. (미) MPEP § 1.132.

traverse

When any claim of an application or a patent under reexamination is rejected or objected to, any evidence submitted to **traverse** the rejection or objection on a basis not otherwise provided for must be by way of an oath or declaration under this section. MPEP § 1.132.

반박증거

출원인이 거절결정을 막기 위해 특허상표청의 통지에 대해 제출함. 가령 특허출원에 대한 반박증거에는 상업적 성공, 오래 되었으나 해결되지 않은 필요, 타인의 실패 등 2차적 고려사항(Graham v. John Deere Co. 판례 참조)과 예상치 못한 결과에 대한 증거가 포함될 수 있음. (미) MPEP § 2141.01.

rebuttal evidence

Submitted by the applicant in response to an Office action to avoid rejection. Rebuttal evidence regarding a patent application, for example, may include evidence of secondary considerations, such as commercial success long felt but unsolved needs, [and] failure of others (Graham v. John Deere Co.), and may also include evidence of unexpected results. MPEP § 2141.01.

반복패턴표장

디자인, 숫자, 글자, 기타 다른 문자의 반복되는 단일한 구성요소 또는 반복적 조합으로, 제품 포장이나 상품의 표면, 서비스의 광고나 제공과 관련된 물건에 패턴으로 나타나는 표장. (미) TMEP § 1202.19.

repeating pattern marks

A mark composed of a single repeated element or a repeated combination of designs, numbers, letters, or other characters, forming a pattern that is displayed on the surface of goods, on product packaging, or on materials associated with the advertising or provision of services. TMEP § 1202.19.

사용례 **반복패턴**으로 형성된 인상은 가령 그 패턴이나 패턴이 사용되는 물품의 성질, 그 물품에서 패턴이 사용된 위치, 사용 시 패턴의 구성요소의 크기나 범위 등 여러 요소에 의해 변할 수 있다. 따라서 대부분의 경우 표장을 정확히 묘사하기 위해서는 **반복패턴**의 특정한 표시방법이나 위치가 도면에 반드시 나타나야 할 것이다. (미) TMEP § 1202.19(a).

The impression created by a **repeating pattern** may change depending on a number of factors, including the nature of the pattern and the item it appears on, the particular placement of the pattern on the item, and the size and scale of the elements in the pattern as applied. Thus, in most cases, to accurately depict the mark, a drawing showing the particular manner of display and placement of the **repeating pattern** is necessary. TMEP § 1202.19(a).

반소

소송에서 피고가 원고의 소에 반박하기 위하여 제기하는 소

counterclaim

A claim by a defendant in a litigation made to rebut the plaintiff's claim.

(간행물의) 반포

간행물을 불특정다수인이 볼 수 있는 상태에 두는 것.

distribution (of a publication)

Putting a publication in a state where it can be viewed by unspecified number of people.

반포된 간행물에 게재

불특정 다수의 일반 공중이 인식할 수 있는 상태에 놓인 공개를 목적으로 인쇄 기타 방법으로 복제된 문서, 도화, 사진 등에 기재된 것.

description on a publication distributed

A description disclosed on documents, drawings or pictures, etc., printed or copied, in order to be publicized and is in a condition that unspecified general public can recognize.

반포일

date of release

발명

자연법칙을 이용한 기술적 사상의 창작으로서 고도한 것.

invention

Highly advanced creation of a technical idea utilizing the laws of nature.

미 발명대상

사용례 명세서는 그 발명자 또는 공동발명자가 발명으로 간주하는 **발명대상**을 특정하게 지칭하고 구별되도록 청구하는 하나 이상의 청구항으로 끝을 맺어야 한다. (미) 특허법 제112(b)조.

subject matter

The specification shall conclude with one or more claims particularly pointing out and distinctly claiming the **subject matter** which the inventor or a joint inventor regards as the invention. 35 U.S.C. § 112(b).

발명을 특정하여 지칭함

발명의 범위가 구별되도록 청구범위에 이

particularly point out the invention

A requirement to grant patent that claims must specify and

를 특정하여 지칭하고 정의하여야 한다는 특허 허여의 요건. 청구범위의 명확성 판단을 위한 기준으로 사용됨.

identify the distinct scope of the invention, used as a standard to determine whether the claims are sufficiently clear.

발명의 기재 요건

written description requirement

특허는 그 특허를 받고자 하는 기술을 설명하여야 한다는 원칙을 반영. → 기재불비 참조.

The written description requirement implements the principle that a patent must describe the technology that is sought to be patented. → See. lack of sufficient description

사용례 **발명의 기재요건** 충족을 위해 특허명세서에는 발명자가 그 출원발명을 소유하고 있는 것으로 통상의 기술자가 합리적으로 결론지을 수 있을 만큼 충분히 상세하게 기재되어야 한다. (미) MPEP § 2163.

To satisfy the **written description requirement**, a patent specification must describe the claimed invention in sufficient detail that one skilled in the art can reasonably conclude that the inventor had possession of the claimed invention. MPEP § 2163.

발명의 단일성

unity of invention

국제출원이 하나의 발명 또는 단일한 일반적 발명의 관념을 이룬다고 할 만큼 연결된 다수의 발명만을 대상으로 하여야 한다는 요건. PCT Rule 13.1.

The requirement that an international application shall relate to one invention only or to a group of inventions so linked as to form a single general inventive concept. PCT Rule 13.1.

발명의 명칭

title of invention

사용례 **발명의 명칭**은 500자를 넘지 않아야 하며 최대한 짧고 구체적이어야 한다. (미) 37 C.F.R. § 1.72(a).

The **title of the invention** may not exceed 500 characters in length and must be as short and specific as possible. 37 C.F.R. § 1.72(a).

발명의 설명

description (of an invention)

특허 명세서에 청구항과 함께 포함되는 부분으로서 그 발명이 속하는 통상의 지식을 가진 사람이 그 발명을 쉽게 실시할 수 있도록 명확하고 상세하게 기재될 것을 요함 (특허법 제42조 제3항).

A description included in the patent specification with the patent claims, which is required to be clearly detailed in such manner that person skilled in the art can easily execute the invention(Patent Act Article 42(3)).

발명의 요지

summary of invention

특허성 판단을 위하여 파악하여야 할 발명의 핵심적 내용. 미국출원의 경우 명세서의 별도의 항목.

The essence of a claimed invention that must be identified to determine patentability. A separate section in the specification as for U.S. applications.

사용례 발명의 상세한 설명에 앞서 발

A brief **summary of the invention** indicating its nature and

명의 목적 등을 포함한 발명의 속성과 내용을 표시한 간략한 **발명의 요지**를 기재하여야 한다. 발명의 요지를 기재할 때는 출원 발명에 부합하도록 하여야 하며 요지에 설명한 목적은 청구된 발명의 목적이어야 한다. (미) 37 C.F.R. § 1.73.

substance, which may include a statement of the object of the invention, should precede the detailed description. Such summary should, when set forth, be commensurate with the invention as claimed and any object recited should be that of the invention as claimed. 37 C.F.R. § § 1.73.

발명의 착상

concept, conception

이후에 구현될 완성된 발명에 대한 명확하고 영구적인 아이디어가 발명자의 마음속에 형성되는 것을 가리킴.

The formation in the mind of the inventor of the definite and permanent idea of the complete invention that is thereafter reduced to practice.

사용례 구 특허법 102(e)조 하의 거절결정은 인용발명에서 개시된 사항이 출원인의 연구에서 기인하였고 인용발명의 출원일 이전에 출원인이 발명을 **착상**하였음을 증명함으로써 극복할 수 있다. (미) MPEP § 2136.05.

A showing that the reference disclosure arose from applicant's work coupled with a showing of **conception** by the applicant before the filing date of the reference will overcome the pre-AIA Patent Act, 35 U.S.C. § 102(e) rejection. MPEP §2136.05.

발명자

inventor

발명주체

inventorship

미 발행일

issue date

특허출원이 특허가 되는 날. 발행일은 곧 특허권 행사를 시작할 수 있는 날임.

The date that a patent application becomes a patent. The issue date is the date from which patent rights can be exercised.

방법발명

process invention

물건의 발명, 물건을 생산하는 방법의 발명과 함께 특허법상 인정되는 발명의 유형 중 하나.

A type of invention recognized by the Patent Act together with 'invention of a thing' and 'invention of a process of manufacturing a thing'.

방법청구항

process claim, method claim

무언가를 실행하는 방법에 대한 청구로, 주로 일련의 단계로 설명된다.

A claim covering a way of doing something, typically conveyed as a series of steps.

미 방식흠결출원

informal applications

불완전 출원. 즉 출원일자를 받기에 필요한 최소한의 요건을 만족시키지 못한 출원을

Incomplete applications. Applications that do not meet the minimum requirements for receipt of a filing date. TMEP

ㅂ

가리킴. (미) TMEP § 202. (미)

§ 202.

사용례 출원일자를 받기 위한 37 C.F.R. 2.21조의 최소요건을 충족시키지 못하는 1조나 44조 하의 상표출원이 심사를 위해 심사관에게 배정될 때가 있다. 이 경우 해당 사건에 대한 통지를 발행하기 전에 오류를 발견한 심사관은 그 출원을 **방식상 흠결**이 있는 것으로 분류하여야 한다. (미) TMEP § 204.03.

Sometimes an application under §1 or §44 that does not meet the minimum requirements of 37 C.F.R. §2.21 for receipt of a filing date is erroneously referred to an examining attorney for examination. In this situation, if the examining attorney discovers the error before issuing an action in the case, then the examining attorney should have the **application declared informal**. TMEP § 204.03.

배경기술 기재의무

duty to state technology used for the invention

특허출원서에 첨부되는 명세서의 발명의 설명에는 배경기술을 기재하여야 함(특허법 제42조 제3항 제2호).

In the description of invention in the specification attached to the application, the technology used for the invention shall be stated(Patent Act Article 42(3)2).

배심재판

jury trial

배임행위

malpractice

미 법적판결신청

motion for judgment as a matter of law (JMOL)

배심원의 숙고 이전 혹은 신청인이 패소하여야 한다고 본 배심원 평결 이후 상대방에게 승소평결을 내릴 만큼 법적으로 충분한 증거가 없었음을 근거로 재판부가 승소판결을 내려줄 것을 요청하는 당사자 신청.

A party's request that the court enter a judgment in its favor before the case is submitted to the jury or after a contrary jury verdict on the ground that there is no legally sufficient evidence on which a jury could find for the other party.

미 법정기간

statutory period

미 특허법 133조 하의 법정기간은 37 C.F.R. § 1.136조에 따라 연장될 수 있는데, 단 거절이유통지일로부터 6개월의 법정기간을 초과할 수 없다. (미) MPEP § 710.02(d).

Extensions of the statutory period under Patent Act, 35 U.S.C. § 133 may be obtained under 37 C.F.R. § § 1.136, provided the extension does not go beyond the 6-month statutory period from the date of the Office action (Patent Act, 35 U.S.C. § 133). MPEP § 710.02(d).

법정손해배상

statutory damages, legal damages (법제처)

산업재산권을 침해 당한경우 원고가 입증하지 않더라도 법률에 근거하여 받을 수 있는 손해의 배상액.

Damages a plaintiff in an infringement suit may recover without meeting any burden of proof pursuant to applicable statutory law prescribing the amount of damages.

사용례 상표권자가 이 규정에 의한 손

For a trademark owner to seek damages hereunder, the owner

해배상을 청구하려면, 상표권 침해 당시 해당 등록상표를 상표권자가 실제 사용하고 있었어야 하고, 침해자가 사용한 상표가 상표권자의 등록상표와 같거나 동일성이 있어야 하며, 동일성 요건을 갖추지 못한 경우에는 통상의 방법으로 손해를 증명하여 배상을 청구하여야지 위 규정에서 정한 **법정손해배상**을 청구할 수는 없고, … (대법원 2016. 9. 30. 선고 2014다59712판결 참조)

must have used the registered mark at issue at the time of the infringement, the mark used by the infringer must be identical or deemed to have identicality with the owner's mark. In the absence of identicality, the owner must prove the damages as in other cases and shall not be entitled to seek **statutory damages** as prescribed in the foregoing(Supreme Court Decision, 2014Da59712, decided September 30, 2016).

미 법정 의견서

소의 결과에 이해관계를 지닌 이가 청원 또는 법원의 요청에 의하여 법원에 제출하는 의견서.

amicus curie briefs

A brief submitted to the court, by petition or upon request of the court, by someone who has interest in the outcome of the lawsuit.

미 법정제한요건

사용례 인용문헌의 공개일이 출원인 또는 특허권자의 유효출원일보다 1년 이상 앞서는 경우. 이러한 인용문헌은 37 C.F.R. § 1.131(a)(2)에 인용된 구 특허법 102(b)조 하의 **법정제한요건**에 해당한다. (미) MPEP § 715.

statutory bar

Where the reference publication date is more than 1 year prior to applicant's or patent owner's effective filing date. Such a reference is a "**statutory bar**" under pre-AIA Patent Act, 35 U.S.C. § 102(b) as referenced in 37 C.F.R. § § 1.131(a)(2). MPEP § 715.

미 법정 포기

미 특허법 253조 하의 포기는 법정 포기와 존속기간 포기의 두 종류로 나뉨. 특허권자는 어떠한 청구항에 대하여도 그 특허에 대한 본인의 이해관계의 범위를 진술한 법정 포기를 할 수 있음. 또한 존속기간 포기를 통해 그 특허의 잔존특허기간을 포기하거나 공중에 이를 개방할 수 있도록 함.

statutory disclaimer

There are two types of disclaimers under § 253: statutory disclaimers and terminal disclaimers. A patentee may make a statutory disclaimer of any complete claim, stating therein the extent of his or her interest in such patent. A patentee may make a terminal disclaimer to disclaim or dedicate to the public the remaining time of the term of the patent granted.

변경출원

실용신안출원 등은 그 출원서에 최초로 첨부된 명세서 또는 도면에 기재된 사항의 범위에서 그 출원을 (특허출원으로) 변경할 수 있음.

conversion of applications

An applicant for registration of a utility model may convert the application into a patent application within the scope of the features described in the specification or drawings accompanying the initial application for registration of the utility model.

변론

당사자가 직접 또는 소송대리인을 통해 법

pleading, oral argument

Actions of parties of a litigation arguing, demonstrating,

ㅂ

정에서 재판장의 지휘 하에 주장과 입증, 공격과 방어를 하는 행위.

offending and defending at the court under the instruction of the presiding judge by oneself or through its legal counsel.

변론기일

법정에서 변론이 열리는 기일.

trial date

The date the trial is held at court.

변론조서

변론기일의 재판 진행사항과 내용이 기록된 공식문서.

trial record, trial minutes, protocol of pleadings (법제처)

Official transcript in which the process and content of the court proceeding on the trial date is recorded.

변론준비기일

변론기일 전에 주장과 증거의 정리를 위해 필요한 경우 재판장에 의해 열리는 기일.

pretrial hearing, preperatory hearing (법제처)

A date set up by the presiding judge when it is necessary to organize the arguments and evidence.

변론준비명령

재판장이 당사자에게 변론준비를 하도록 하는 명령.

preparatory order for hearing

An order issued by the presiding judge to the parties to prepare for the pleading.

(변론의) 병합

법원의 소송진행방식 중 하나로서, 법원이 별개의 사건으로 접수된 소송사건들을 병합하여 그 변론을 함께 진행하는 것.

combination

One of court practices to combine cases that were separately filed, to process the hearings together.

병행수입

산업재산권자의 허락 없이 모조품이 아닌 제품을 다른 나라로부터 수입하는 것.

parallel import

A non-counterfeit product imported from another country without permission of the intellectual property owner.

사용례 **병행 수입** 그 자체는 위법성이 없는 정당한 행위로서 상표권 침해 등을 구성하지 아니함은 원심의 판단과 같으므로 병행수입업자가 상표권자의 상표가 부착된 상태에서 상품을 판매하는 행위는 당연히 허용될 것인바, … (대법원 2002. 9. 24. 선고 99다42322 판결 참조).

By itself, **parallel import** is neither illegal nor unlawful and does not constitute infringement of trademark rights, as held by the lower court. Therefore, there is no doubt that sale of goods by parallel importers with the trademark owner's mark affixed to the good is permissible(Supreme Court Decision, 99Da42322, decided September 24, 2002).

(절차)보완명령

등록을 받으려는 취지가 명확하게 표시되지 아니하는 등의 경우에 특허청장이 등록

order to supplement an application

Where the purpose for which an applicant intends to obtain IP rights registration is not clearly indicated, the

을 받으려는 자에게 적절한 기간을 정하여 보완할 것을 명하는 것.

Commissioner of the Korean Intellectual Property Office shall order the person to supplement the application in due time.

사용례 제2항에 따른 **보완명령**을 받은 자가 상표등록출원을 보완하는 경우에는 절차보완에 관한 서면(이하 이 조에서 "절차보완서"라 한다)을 제출하여야 한다(상표법 제37조 제3항).

Where a person **ordered to supplement an application** under paragraph (2) supplements this application for trademark registration, he/she shall submit a document concerning the complement of procedures (hereafter in this Article, referred to as "document concerning the complement of procedures") (Trademark Act Article 37(3).

보정

신청 또는 청구 등에 부적법 또는 불명확 등의 사유가 있는 경우 이를 보완하거나 출원 이후 수정을 가하는 것. 출원의 요지를 변경하지 아니하는 범위 이내에서만 허용됨.

amendment

Amending unlawfulness or ambiguousness of a petition or application. Modification made after the application is filed. Amendment is permissible only if it would keep the substance of the application unchanged.

사용례 심사관은 제57조에 따른 출원공고결정을 할 때에 상표등록출원서에 적힌 사항이 명백히 잘못된 경우에는 직권으로 **보정**(이하 이 조에서 "직권보정"이라 한다)을 할 수 있다(상표법 제59조 제1항).

Where any matter mentioned in a written application for trademark registration is clearly incorrect when an examiner decides to publish an application under Article 57, he/she may make any **amendments** ex officio (hereinafter referred to as "ex officio amendment") (Trademark Act Article 59(1)).

보정각하(결정)

출원인이 제출한 보정서가 부적법한 경우 이를 결정으로 거부하는 것.

(decision to) dismiss amendment, dismissal of amendment

Administrative decision to refuse to accept an improper request for amendment.

보정명령

보정을 명하는 명령.

order to make an amendment

Order to amend an application.

사용례 특허청장 또는 특허심판원장은 제46조에 따른 **보정명령**을 받은 자가 지정된 기간에 그 보정을 하지 아니하면 특허에 관한 절차를 무효로 할 수 있다(특허법 제16조 제1항).

When a person **ordered to make an amendment** under Article 46 fails to do so within a specified period, the Commissioner of the Korean Intellectual Property Office or the Director General of the Korean Intellectual Property Trial and Appeal Board may invalidate the patent-related procedure(Patent Act Article 16(1)).

ㅂ

미 보조등록부

특허상표청의 부차적 상표등록부. 주등록부에는 등록될 수 없으나 출원인의 상품이나 서비스를 식별할 수는 있는 상표를 등록한다. 보조등록부에 등록된 상표는 저촉표장으로부터 보호되는 등 다양한 보호를 받으나 상표법의 일부 혜택으로부터 제외됨. (미) USPTO.

Supplemental Register

Secondary trademark register for the USPTO. It allows for registration of certain marks that are not eligible for registration on the Principal Register, but are capable of distinguishing an applicant's goods or services. Marks registered on the Supplemental Register receive protection from conflicting marks and other protections, but are excluded from receiving the advantages of certain sections of the Trademark Act of 1946. USPTO.

보조참가인

소송결과에 이해관계가 있는 제3자는 한 쪽 당사자를 돕기 위하여 법원에 계속중인 소송에 참가할 수 있다. 다만, 소송절차를 현저하게 지연시키는 경우에는 그러하지 아니하다(민사소송법 제71조).

supplementary intervenor

Any third party interested in the result of a lawsuit may intervene in the lawsuit pending before the court in order to assist either party: Provided, That the same shall not apply where it may retard the litigation procedures significantly(Civil Procedure Act Article 71).

미 보충심사

특허등록 이후에도 특허권자가 특허상표청에 특허와 관련 있는 정보를 고려 또는 정정하도록 요청할 수 있도록 하는 개정 특허법으로 신설된 제도. (미) 특허법 제257(a)조.

supplemental examination

A new proceeding introduced by AIA that allows patentees to request the USPTO to consider or correct information believed to be relevant to the patent. Patent Act, 35 U.S.C. § 257(a).

보통명칭

그 지정상품을 취급하는 거래계에서 동종업자 및 일반 수요자 사이에 그 상품을 지칭하는 것으로 실제로 사용되고 인식되어 있는 일반적인 명칭, 약칭, 속칭 등으로서 특정인의 업무에 관련된 상품이라고 인식되지 아니하는 명칭.

generic name, common name (법제처)

Ordinary title, abbreviation or nickname that is actually used and perceived as referring to the good among the ordinary consumers and traders in the relevant marketplace and not perceived as associated with the business of any particular person.

보통으로 사용하다

사용례 다음 각 호의 어느 하나에 해당하는 상표를 제외하고는 상표등록을 받을 수 있다.

1. 그 상품의 보통명칭을 **보통으로 사용하는** 방법으로 표시한 표장만으로 된 상표

5. 흔히 있는 성(姓) 또는 명칭을 **보통으로 사용하는** 방법으로 표시한 표장만으로 된 상표(상표법 제33조 제1항).

use in a common manner, in common use

Trademark registration may be obtained, excluding the following trademarks:

1. A trademark consisting solely of a mark indicating, **in a common manner**, the common name of the goods;

5. A trademark consisting solely of a mark indicating a common surname or name according to the method **in common use**(Trademark Act Article 33(1)).

보호품종

식물신품종보호법상 품종보호 요건을 갖추어 품종보호권이 주어진 품종.

protected plant variety

A plant variety for which a plant variety right is granted as it meets requirements for plant variety protection under the Act on Protection of New Varieties of Plants.

보호품종의 표시

품종보호권자, 전용실시권자 또는 통상실시권자는 해당 품종이 보호품종임을 표시할 수 있다(식물신품종보호법 제88조).

marking of protected plant variety

The holder of a plant variety right, exclusive license holder or non-exclusive license holder may label the relevant plant variety as a protected plant variety(Act on Protection of New Varieties of Plants Article 88).

복수디자인등록출원

물품류 구분에서 같은 물품류에 속하는 물품에 대해 100 이내의 디자인을 1디자인등록출원으로 출원하는 것. 1 디자인마다 분리하여 표현하여야함(디자인보호법 제41조).

multiple-design application

Applying for multiple designs of the same classification, not exceeding one hundred, in a single application. Each design must be separately described(Design Protection Act Article 41).

사용례 디자인등록출원인은 디자인권의 설정등록일부터 3년 이내의 기간을 정하여 그 디자인을 비밀로 할 것을 청구할 수 있다. 이 경우 **복수디자인등록출원**된 디자인에 대하여는 출원된 디자인의 전부 또는 일부에 대하여 청구할 수 있다(디자인보호법 제43조 제1항).

An applicant for design registration may request that the design be kept secret for a prescribed period of up to three years from the date of registration for establishment of the design right. It may be also requested to keep confidential all or some of designs claimed in an **application for multiple designs registration**(Design Protection Act Article 43(1)).

복제약

처음 개발된 신물질로 만든 의약품을 오리지널 의약품이라고 하며, 오리지널 의약품의 화학성분 분석을 통해 오리지널 의약품과 동일한 유효성분, 제형, 용량, 효과, 용법 등을 동일하게 복제하여 만든 약을 복제약이라 함.

generic drugs

A drug made of a newly developed substance is called an original drug. A drug that is made to imitate the original drug and have the same effective substance, formulation, volume, effect and administration method via chemical analysis of the original drug is called a generic drug.

본국

country of origin

사용례 상표법 44조에 의한 출원의 도면은 출원인의 **본국**에 정히 등록된 표장의 등록증 상의 도면에 나타난 표장을 실질적

In an application under section 44 of the Act, the drawing of the mark must be a substantially exact representation of the mark as it appears in the drawing in the registration

ㅂ

으로 동일하게 표현하여야 한다. (미) 37 C.F.R. § 2.51(c).

certificate of a mark duly registered in the applicant's **country of origin**. 37 C.F.R. § 2.51(c).

본인출원

대리인 자격을 보유한 대리인의 도움을 받지 아니하고 직접 출원을 제출하기로 한 독립된 발명자의 출원.

pro-se application

Applications filed by an independent inventor who has elected to file the application on his or her own without the services of a licensed representative.

부가기간

심판장은 도서·벽지 등 교통이 불편한 지역에 있는 자를 위하여 산업통상자원부령으로 정하는 바에 따라 직권으로 불변기간에 대하여 부가기간을 정할 수 있다(상표법 제162조 제4항).

additional period

The period under paragraph (3) shall be fixed: Provided, That the presiding judge may determine an additional period to the fixed period for those in the area with poor transportation, such as islands and remote rural areas, on his/her own authority, as prescribed by Ordinance of the Ministry of Trade, Industry and Energy(Trademark Act Article 162(4)).

부기적 부분

부수적 부분. 상표 유사 판단에 영향을 미치지 않음.

supplemental portion

Ancillary part. A part that does not affect the similarity or dissimilarity of a mark.

사용례 상표의 **부기적인 부분**의 삭제는 상표등록출원의 요지를 변경하지 아니하는 것으로 본다(상표법 제40조 제2항 제4호).

Where an amendment made under paragraph (1) falls under any of the following, the substance of the relevant application for trademark registration shall be deemed unchanged: … 4. Omission of **supplemental portion** of the trademark (Trademark Act Article 40(2)4).

부당이득

타인이 법률상 원인 없이 자기의 재산 또는 노무로 인하여 이익을 얻은 경우에 그로 인하여 손해를 입은 자가 그 타인을 상대로 위 이익의 반환을 청구할 수 있음.

unjust enrichment

An injured party may seek to recover benefits from a person who is enriched with the benefit from the injured party's property or labor without legal ground.

(특허권의) 부당행사

→ (특허권의) 남용 참조

abuse (of patent right)

미 부등록대상

사용례 디자인이 물품에 화체되거나 적

nonstatutory subject matter

The claim is rejected under 35 U.S.C. 171 as directed to

용된 것이 아니므로, 청구범위는 35 U.S.C. 171에 따라 **부등록대상**인 것으로 되어 거절된다. (미) MPEP § 1504.01.

nonstatutory subject matter because the design is not shown embodied in or applied to an article. MPEP § 1504.01.

부분디자인

물품의 부분에 대한 디자인.

partial design

A design applied to a part of an article.

사용례 휴대폰 케이스를 대상물품으로 하여 우측 [그림 1]과 같은 사시도에서 회색으로 표현된 케이스 본체 부분을 제외한 나머지 부분, 즉 대상물품 상부의 [그림 2] 부분과 하단 뒷면에 돌출된 [그림 3] 부분만을 보호받고자 **부분디자인**으로 출원된 이 사건 출원디자인은 … (대법원 2013. 2. 15. 선고 2012후3343 판결 참조).

The proposed design at issue, applied as a **partial design** on the subject article of a cellular phone cover, to be granted protection limited to Drawing 2 part in the upper side of the article and Drawing 3 projected at the back bottom, exclusive of the main body of the cover, described in gray color in the perspective view in [Drawing 1], … (Supreme Court Decision, 2012Hu3343, decided February 15, 2013).

부분품

→ 부품 참조

components

미 부수적 금반언

판결에 의하여 이미 결정된 쟁점을 동일한 당사자가 동일한 방식으로 다른 법원에서 다툴 수 없다는 금반언의 원칙.

collateral estoppel

The principle of estoppel that an issue that has been decided by judgment cannot be taken to another court by the same litigants in the same manner.

사용례 기판력, **부수적 금반언**, 선례구속의 원칙에 따라 출원인이 패한 기존의 결정은 동일한 사실관계와 쟁점에 기초하여 동일한 표장을 등록하고자 하는 이후의 출원에 대해서도 구속력을 지닐 수 있다. (미) TMEP § 1217.

A prior adjudication against an applicant may be dispositive of a later application for registration of the same mark on the basis of the same facts and issues, under the doctrine of res judicata, **collateral estoppel**, or stare decisions. TMEP § 1217.

부정경쟁

국내에 널리 인식된 타인의 성명, 상호, 상표, 상품의 용기 · 포장, 그 밖에 타인의 상품임을 표시한 표지와 동일하거나 유사한 것을 사용하거나 이러한 것을 사용한 상품을 판매 · 반포 또는 수입 · 수출하여 타인의 상품과 혼동하게 하는 행위 등(부정경쟁방지법 제2조 제1호).

unfair competition

An act of causing confusion with another person's goods by using marks identical or similar to, another person's name, trade name, trademark, or container or package of goods, or any other mark indicating another person's goods, which is widely known in the Republic of Korea; or by selling, distributing, importing, or exporting goods bearing such marks(Unfair Competition Prevention Act, Art.2.1).

부정경쟁방지 및 영업비밀보호에 관한 법률	**Unfair Competition Prevention and Trade Secret Protection Act**
국내에 널리 알려진 타인의 상표 · 상호(商號) 등을 부정하게 사용하는 등의 부정경쟁행위와 타인의 영업비밀을 침해하는 행위를 방지하여 건전한 거래질서를 유지함을 목적으로 하는 법률.	The purpose of this Act is to maintain orderly trade by preventing acts of unfair competition such as improper use of domestically well-known trademarks and trade names, and by preventing infringement of trade secrets.
부정사용	**trademark abuse**
지정상품 또는 이와 유사한 상품에 등록상표 또는 이와 유사한 상표를 사용함으로써 수요자에게 상품의 품질을 오인하게 하거나 타인의 업무와 관련된 상품과의 혼동을 불러일으키게 한 경우. 상표등록취소심판 청구의 근거가 됨(상표법 제119조 제1항 제5호.).	When use of a registered or similar mark on a designated or similar good, creating misconception of quality of the good or confusion with a good associated with other person's business. Grounds for cancellation of a trademark(Trademark Act Article 119(1)5).
사용례 … 따라서 같은 취지의 원심판단은 정당하고, 거기에 상고이유의 주장과 같은 상표 **부정사용**의 고의에 관한 법리오해 등의 위법이 없다(대법원 2012. 10. 11. 선고 2012후2227 판결).	Therefore, the judgment below was correct; and contrary to the arguments in the grounds of appeal, there was no error of law on the intent element for **trademark abuse** (Supreme Court Decision, 2012Hu2227, decided October 11, 2012).
부품	**parts**
물품 전체의 일부. 그 부분만을 따로 분리하여 교체할 수 있고(호환가능성), 또 분리된 부분만으로 독립된 거래의 대상(독립거래가능성)이 된다면 디자인 보호의 대상이 되는 물품으로 봄.	A part of an article. A part is also an article, eligible for design protection if the part may be separated for replacement and can be an independent subject of transaction.
(변론의) 분리	**separation**
사용례 법원은 변론의 제한 · **분리** 또는 병합을 명하거나, 그 명령을 취소할 수 있다(민사소송법 제141조).	A court may order a limitation, **separation** or combination of pleadings, or may cancel such order(Civil Procedure Act Article 141).
분리관찰	**compare by element, separately viewed** (법제처)
복수의 구성부분으로 되어 있어 식별력을 발휘하는 부분의 요부가 2 이상일 경우, 각각의 요부를 대비하여 비교함으로써 유사 여부를 판단하는 방법.	Determining similarity of that consists of multiple elements and with more than one essential part that makes the trademark distinctive, by comparing each essential part of a good with a corresponding part of another.

사용례 위 인정사실에 의하면, 이 사건 출원상표 는 숫자 '360'에 영어 소문자 'do'를 붙여 쓴 '360do'와 '솔, 솔질하다, 칫솔질하다'라는 뜻의 영어 대문자 'BRUSH'가 결합된 것으로서 '360do'와 'BRUSH'로 **분리관찰**이 가능하고, (특허법원 2016.05.04 선고 2015허5043판결 참조).

The subject mark '360do BRUSH' is a combination of number '360,' English lower-case letters 'do' and English capital letters 'BRUSH' meaning 'a brush, to brush and to brush teeth' and can be **separately viewed** as '360do' and 'BRUSH', … (Patent Court Decision, 2015Heo5043, decided May 4, 2016).

분할

지정상품이 둘 이상인 경우에 그 권리를 지정상품별로 나누는 것.

division

Where there are at least two designated goods the relevant trademark rights may be divided for each of the designated goods.

분할출원

특허출원인은 둘 이상의 발명을 하나의 특허출원으로 한 경우에는 그 특허출원의 출원서에 최초로 첨부된 명세서 또는 도면에 기재된 사항의 범위에서 법정 기간에 그 일부를 하나 이상의 특허출원으로 분할할 수 있음(특허법 제 52조 제1항).

divisional application

An applicant who has filed a single patent application for two or more inventions may divide the application into two or more applications within the scope of the features described in the specification or drawings accompanying the initial patent application, within the statutory period(Patent Act Article 52(1)).

미 불가쟁력

등록일로부터 계속 5년간 거래상 사용되어 왔고 아직도 거래상 사용되고 있는 상품 또는 서비스의 등록표장의 효력을 다툴 수 없음, 즉 불가쟁력을 가지게 됨. (미) 상표법 제 15조.

incontestability

A trademark registration is incontestable if the mark has been in continuous use in commerce for a period of five years after the date of registration. 15 U.S.C. § 1065.

사용례 **불가쟁력**을 지닌 상표의 등록소유권이 있다 하여 출원인이 다른 상품이나 서비스에 대해 동일한 상표를 등록할 수는 없으며 이는 그 상품 또는 서비스가 다툴 수 없는 등록상표와 긴밀한 연관성이 있다 하더라도 마찬가지이다. (미) TMEP § 1216.02.

Ownership of an **incontestable** registration does not give the applicant a right to register the same mark for different goods or services, even if they are closely related to the goods or services in the incontestable registration. TMEP § 1216.02.

불가항력

사용례 '정당한 이유'라 함은 질병 기타 천재 등의 **불가항력**에 의하여 영업을 할 수 없는 경우뿐만 아니라 … 상표권자의 귀책사유로 인하지 아니한 상표 불사용의 경

force majeure

A "justifiable cause" refers not only to the circumstances where a party is prevented from engaging in his or her business due to illness or **force majeure** events such as act of God, … but also to non-use the party shall not be held

우도 포함된다고 할 것이다(대법원 2000. 4. 25. 선고 97후3920 판결 참조).

responsible(Supreme Court Decision, 97Hu3920, decided April 25, 2000).

불공정행위

특허의 출원인이 정직과 신의성실의 의무를 위반하는 것

inequitable conduct

A patent applicant engages in inequitable conduct when he or she breaches the duty to proceed with the patent application in good faith and candor.

불리한 추정

진술하지 않거나 요청한 증거를 제출하지 않는 경우 관련 당사자에 불리하게 적용되는 추정.

adverse inference

A legal inference, adverse to the concerned party, drawn from silence or absence of requested evidence.

불변기간

심판장은 도서 · 벽지 등 교통이 불편한 지역에 있는 자를 위하여 산업통상자원부령으로 정하는 바에 따라 직권으로 불변기간에 대하여 부가기간을 정할 수 있다(상표법 제162조 제4항).

fixed period

The period under paragraph (3) shall be fixed: Provided, That the presiding judge may determine an additional period to the fixed period for those in the area with poor transportation, such as islands and remote rural areas, on his/her own authority, as prescribed by Ordinance of the Ministry of Trade, Industry and Energy(Trademark Act Article 162(4)).

불사용취소

등록상표를 그 지정상품에 대하여 3년 이상 국내에서 사용하고 있지 아니한 경우. 상표등록취소의 사유가 됨(상표법 119조 1항 제3호).

non-use cancellation

When a registered trademark was not used on the designated goods in the Republic of Korea for at least three consecutive years. Grounds for trademark cancellation(Trademark Act Article 119(1)3).

사용례 위 전단지가 일시적으로 사용되었다고 해서 이를 **불사용 취소**를 면탈하기 위한 형식적인 사용에 불과하다고 단정할 수는 없으며, … (특허법원 2016.12.29 선고 2016허2904판결 참조).

The temporariness of the use of the above leaflet does not necessarily mean that such use was only for the purpose of avoiding a **non-use cancellation**(Patent Court Decision, 2016Heo2904, decided December 29, 2016).

불수리처분

특허출원서가 법령이 정한 방식에 위반되고 보정조차도 불가능할 정도로 그 위반의 정도가 중대한 경우에는 특허청에 의하여 불수리처분을 받게 되는데 이때는 출원 자체를 없었던 것으로 함(특허법 시행규칙 제

disposition refusing to accept application

In case a patent application does not meet the statutory requirements, and the defect is too significant that it cannot be cured, the KIPO refuses to accept the application and it is deemed that there was no application in the first place(Enforcement Regulation of the Patent Act Article

11조 제1항).

11(1)).

미 (특허상표청 통지에 대한) 불완전한 반박

(1) 특허상표청 통지 중 하나 이상의 거절사항이나 한정요구에 반박하지 않았거나 (2) 서명 누락 (3) 권한 없는 자의 서명 (4) 반박기간이 종료되었을 때 최후 통지에 대한 반박이 모든 거절이유를 해결하지 못하거나 모든 요구사항을 충족하지 못하였고 출원인이 적시에 항소를 신청하지 못하였을 경우 출원인의 특허상표청 통지에 대한 반박은 불완전한 것으로 본다. 일반적으로 출원을 포기하지 않기 위해서는 통지가 발행된 일로부터 6개월 내에 완전한 반박서를 제출하여야 한다. 37 C.F.R. § 2.65(a); TMEP § 718.03. (미)

incomplete response (to Office action)

An applicant's response to an Office action that (1) does not address one or more of the requirements or refusals made in the Office action; (2) is unsigned; (3) is signed by an unauthorized person; or (4) is a response to a final action that does not overcome all refusals or satisfy all requirements, when the response period has expired, and the applicant has not timely filed a notice of appeal. Generally, a complete response must be filed within six months from the date of issuance of the Office action to avoid abandonment. 37 C.F.R. § 2.65(a); TMEP § 718.03.

비교대상고안

→ 비교대상발명 참조

cited invention

비교대상발명

특허의 신규성 또는 진보성 판단 기준이 되는 기술. → 선행발명 참조

cited invention

An art or technology which is used as a basis to determine novelty or inventive step of an invention. Prior art, prior invention. → See. prior invention

사용례 원심은, 아래와 같은 이유를 들어, 확인대상발명은 그 발명이 속하는 기술분야에서 통상의 지식을 가진 사람(이하 '통상의 기술자'라 한다)이 그 판시 **비교대상발명**들과 주지관용기술로부터 용이하게 실시할 수 있는 자유실시기술에 해당하므로, 명칭을 '저용량의 엔테카비르 제제 및 그의 용도'로 하는 이 사건 특허발명의 청구범위 제1항(이하 '이 사건 제1항 발명'이라 한다)과 대비할 필요 없이 그 권리범위에 속하지 아니한다고 판단하였다(대법원 2015. 5. 21. 선고 2015후768 판결 참조).

On the grounds as laid out below, the lower court determined that the challenged invention is not subsumed in the scope of the right of the instant Patented Invention (patent registration number omitted) Claim 1 (hereinafter "Invention Claim 1"), titled, "low dosage entecavir tablet and its uses," without even having to contrast the two, since it constitutes the state-of-the-art technology that a person of ordinary skill in the art (hereinafter "a person with ordinary skill") can easily implement based on the **cited inventions** and generally known art in practice(Supreme Court Decision, 2015Hu768, decided May 21, 2015).

비밀누설죄

특허청 또는 특허심판원 직원이나 그 직원

offense of divulging secrets or confidential information

Any employee of the Korean Intellectual Property Office

으로 재직하였던 사람이 디자인등록출원 중인 디자인(헤이그협정 제11조에 따라 연기 신청된 국제디자인등록출원 중인 디자인을 포함한다)에 관하여 직무상 알게 된 비밀을 누설하거나 도용한 경우에는 5년 이하의 징역 또는 5천만원 이하의 벌금에 처한다(디자인보호법 제225조 제1항, 특허법 제226조 등).

or the Intellectual Property Trial and Appeal Board that divulges or misappropriates confidential information which becomes known to him/her about a design claimed in a pending application for design registration (including designs claimed in a pending application for international design registration, for which a request for deferment has been filed under Article 11 of the Hague Agreement) in the course of performing his/her duties shall be punished by imprisonment with labor for not more than five years or by a fine not exceeding 50 million won (Design Protection Act Article 225, Patent Act Article 226, etc.).

비밀디자인

디자인등록출원인의 청구에 의하여 설정등록일로부터 3년 이내의 지정기간 동안 공개되지 않는 디자인(디자인보호법 제43조 제1항).

secret design, confidential design

An applicant for design registration may request that the design be kept secret for a prescribed period of up to three years from the date of registration for establishment of the design right (Design Protection Act Article 43(1)).

미 비밀유지권 포기

계속심사출원은 다음의 범위 내에서 특허법 제122조 하의 출원인의 비밀을 유지 받을 권리에 대한 포기가 포함된 것으로 본다. (미) 37 C.F.R. § § 1.53(d)(6)

waiver of confidentiality

A CPA (Continued Prosecution Applications) is construed to include a waiver of confidentiality by the applicant under Patent Act, 35 U.S.C. § 122 to the extent that … 37 C.F.R. § § 1.53(d)(6).

비밀유지명령

법원은 특허권 또는 전용실시권의 침해에 관한 소송에서 그 당사자가 보유한 영업비밀에 대하여 다음 각 호의 사유를 모두 소명한 경우에는 그 당사자의 신청에 따라 결정으로 다른 당사자(법인인 경우에는 그 대표자), 당사자를 위하여 소송을 대리하는 자, 그 밖에 그 소송으로 인하여 영업비밀을 알게 된 자에게 그 영업비밀을 그 소송의 계속적인 수행 외의 목적으로 사용하거나 그 영업비밀에 관계된 이 항에 따른 명령을 받은 자 외의 자에게 공개하지 아니할 것을 명할 수 있음.

order to maintain confidentiality, protective order

If a party establishes a prima facie case of the party's trade secret on any of the following grounds in legal proceedings on infringement of a patent or exclusive license, the court may, upon the party's request, order the other party (if the party is a corporation, its representative), the person who represents the other party in the legal proceedings, or any other person who becomes aware of the trade secret in the course of the legal proceedings not to use the trade secret for any purpose other than to proceed in the legal proceedings, and not to disclose the trade secret to any person other than the persons in receipt of the order under this paragraph in connection with the trade secret.

비밀유지명령위반죄

breaches of order to maintain confidentiality

비밀유지의무

변호사와 의뢰인 간에 있었던 비밀사항의 소통에 대해 공개를 거부할 변호사의 의무. (미) 비밀유지특권.

duty of confidentiality

An attorney's duty to keep the content of communication with his or her client confidential. Cf. Attorney-client privilege. (US)

미 비방

사용례 출원인의 상품을 타인의 상품과 식별할 수 있도록 하는 어떠한 상표도 다음 각 항의 어느 하나에 해당하는 경우를 제외하고는 그 본질적 특성을 이유로 주등록부에 등록이 거절되지 아니한다.
(a)공서양속에 반하는 사항, 기만적이거나 중상적인 사항 또는 다른 자(생사를 묻지 아니한다), 기관, 종교 또는 국가의 상징을 **비방**하거나 그 관계를 허위로 암시 또는 모욕하거나 악평을 가할 수 있는 사항으로 구성되는 것, … (미) 상표법 제2(a)조.

disparagement

No trademark by which the goods of the applicant may be distinguished from the goods of others shall be refused registration on the principal register on account of its nature unless it—
(a) Consists of or comprises immoral, deceptive, or scandalous matter; or matter which may **disparage** or falsely suggest a connection with persons, living or dead, institutions, beliefs, or national symbols, or bring them into contempt, or disrepute; … 15 U.S.C. § 1052(a).

비시각적 상표

소리(음악, 또는 단어와 음악), 냄새, 기타 완전히 비시각적인 사항으로만 된 상표.

non-visual marks

A trademark consists solely of a sound (e.g., music or words and music), a scent, or other completely non-visual matter.

비엔나협정

도형상표의 국제분류설정에 관한 비엔나 협정

Vienna Agreement

The Vienna Agreement Establishing an International Classification of the Figurative Elements of Marks

미 비자명성

미국 특허요건의 하나. → 진보성 참조

non-obviousness

one of the requirements for patent registration under US patent act. → See. inventive step

비전형상표

상표는 전형상표와 비전형상표로 구분되고, 비전형상표는 그 자체가 식별력을 갖추거나 사용에 의하여 식별력을 취득하여야만 식별력이 인정된다.

non-traditional mark

Trademarks can be classified into traditional and non-traditional marks. The latter may be distinctive only if it is distinctive by itself or has acquired distinctiveness by use.

비특허문헌

특허 또는 공개된 특허출원은 아니나 특허 심사절차에서 관련성이 있는 인용문헌으로 인용된 문서 또는 간행물.

non-patent literature

Documents and publications that are not patents or published patent applications but are cited as references for being relevant in a patent prosecution.

사용례 검색분야 결정시에는 국내특허(출원공개를 포함한다), 해외특허문헌, **<u>비특허문헌</u>**의 3가지 인용출처를 검토하여야 한다. (미) MPEP § 904.02.

When determining the field of search, three reference sources must be considered: domestic patents (including patent application publications), foreign patent documents, and **<u>non-patent literature</u>** (NPL). MPEP § 904.02.

ㅅ

사건관리 화상회의

video conference for case management

재판장은 당사자의 의견을 들어 양쪽 당사자와 영상·음성의 송수신에 의하여 동시에 통화를 할 수 있는 방법으로 절차 진행에 관한 사항을 협의할 수 있다.

After hearing opinions of the parties, the presiding judge may discuss procedural matters of the case with the parties simultaneously through video and audio communication means.

미 사물관할

subject matter jurisdiction

특정 대상에 관한 결정을 내릴 그 법원의 권한.

A court's authority to make decisions over a particular subject matter.

사시도

perspective view

사시도는 3차원 디자인의 외관을 명확하게 도시하기 위하여 추천되는 것이고 제출될 수 있다. 사시도가 제출되는 경우에는, 표면이 사시도에서 명확하게 이해되고 완전히 도시된 경우 일반적으로 이들 표면은 다른 도면에서는 도시될 필요가 없다. (미) MPEP § 1503.02.

Perspective views are suggested and may be submitted to clearly show the appearance of three dimensional designs. If a perspective view is submitted, the surfaces shown would normally not be required to be illustrated in other views if these surfaces are clearly understood and fully disclosed in the perspective. MPEP § 1503.02.

사용간주

constructive use

실제로 그렇지 아니하더라도 법적으로 사용한 것으로 간주함.

Deemed as use even in the absence of actual use.

사용례 상표법 7(c), 60f(b)항 하에서, 사용의사에 근거한 출원을 포함하여 주등록부에 등록하기 위한 출원신청은 표장의 **<u>추정적 사용</u>**으로 본다. 단 이는 그 출원이 등록으로 이어질 때에만 그러하다. (미) TMEP § 201.02.

Under 15 U.S.C. §§1057(c) and 1141f(b), filing any application for registration on the Principal Register, including an intent-to-use application, constitutes **<u>constructive use</u>** of the mark, provided the application matures into a registration. TMEP § 201.02.

미 사용기반출원

use-based application

거래상 상표의 사용에 기반한 상표등록출

An application for trademark registration based on use of

원. (미) USPTO.

the mark in commerce. USPTO.

사용례 CSI는 표장 'COACH'를 학생용 표준능력시험 대비 교재에 대하여 등록하고자 하는 Triumph의 **사용기반출원**에 대한 이의신청을 기각하기로 하는 상표심판항소위원회의 최종결정에 대한 항소를 제기하였다. Coach Servs., Inc. v. Triumph Learning LLC, 668 F.3d 1356, 1360 (Fed. Cir. 2012).

Coach Services, Inc("CSI"). appeals from the final decision of the Trademark Trial and Appeal Board("the Board") dismissing its opposition to Triumph Learning, LLC's ("Triumph") **use-based applications** to register the mark COACH for educational materials used to prepare students for standardized tests. Coach Servs., Inc. v. Triumph Learning LLC, 668 F.3d 1356, 1360 (Fed. Cir. 2012).

사용에 의한 식별력

acquired distinctiveness (based on use)

식별력이 없거나 미약한 상표였더라도 특정인이 상당한 기간에 걸쳐 독점적, 계속적으로 그 상표를 사용한 결과 일반 수요자나 거래자에게 그 상표가 누구의 업무에 관련된 상품을 표시하는가가 현저하게 인식되어 식별력을 취득하는 것.

Distinctiveness of a mark, originally with little or no distinctiveness, acquired from use by a particular person in a continuous and exclusive manner for a significant period time, creating conspicuous perception among ordinary consumers or traders as to whose good the mark identifies.

사용례 상표의 사용기간, 사용횟수 및 사용의 계속성, 그 상표가 부착된 상품의 생산·판매량 및 시장점유율, 광고·선전의 방법, 횟수, 내용, 기간 및 그 액수, 상품품질의 우수성, 상표사용자의 명성과 신용, 상표의 경합적 사용의 정도 및 태양 등을 종합적으로 고려할 때 당해 상표가 사용된 상품에 관한 거래자 및 수요자의 대다수에게 특정인의 상품을 표시하는 것으로 인식되기에 이르렀다면 **사용에 의한 식별력**의 취득을 인정할 수 있다(대법원 2008. 9. 25. 선고 2006후2288 판결 참조).

A mark can be said as having **acquired distinctiveness** by use if the majority of traders and consumers of the good would perceive the mark as identifying a particular source, judging in entirety from the length, frequency and continuity of use of the mark, the quantity of production and sales and market share of the good to which the mark is affixed, the method, frequency, content, period of and amount spent for its advertisement and promotion, the quality of the good, the reputation and credit of the users of the mark, the degree and modality of any competition in using the mark(Supreme Court Decision, 2006Hu2288, decided September 25, 2008).

미 사용의사

intent to use (ITU)

사용의사에 기반한 출원을 출원인의 영업의 승계인이 아닌 자에게 사용사실주장을 제출하기 전에 양도할 경우 그 출원은 무효로 되고, 그 출원으로 인한 등록은 취소되어야 한다. (미) TMEP § 501.01(a).

The assignment of an intent-to-use application to someone who is not the successor to the applicant's business before filing an allegation of use renders the application void, and any resulting registration must be cancelled. TMEP § 501.01(a).

미 사용의사 출원

intent-to-use applications

사용의사에 기한 출원.

Applications filed based on intent to use.

미 (거래상) 사용주장

미 상표법 1(b) 하의 사용의사에 기한 출원 계류 중 그 상표를 거래상 사용하였다는 1(c)에 따른 사용사실에 기한 권리 주장. (미) 상표법 제1조.

allegations of use (in commerce)

Allegation under 1(c) of the Trademark Act that the applicant has made use of the mark in commerce while the application under 1(b) (intent to use) is pending, to claim benefits of such use. 15 U.S.C. § 1051.

미 사용진술서

상표의 거래상 사용에 대해 증언하는 출원인 또는 출원인을 대신하여 서명할 권한이 있는 자가 서명하고 선서한 문서. (미) USPTO.

statement of use

A sworn statement signed by the applicant or a person authorized to sign on behalf of the applicant attesting to use of the mark in commerce. USPTO.

미 사전상 부재 증거

어느 단어가 사전이나 지도에 없다는 증거.

negative dictionary evidence

Evidence that a term is absent from dictionaries or atlases.

사용례 **사전상 부재 증거**는 그 단어에 성(姓)이 아닌 다른 의미가 없음을 입증할 수 있다. (미) TMEP § 1211.02(b)(vi).

Negative dictionary evidence may demonstrate the lack of non-surname significance of a term. TMEP § 1211.02(b)(vi).

사표(社標)

제품이 '제품표장'에 의해 식별된다면 이와 대비하여 그러한 다양한 제품의 제조업자 또는 판매업자를 식별하는 표장. 주로 화학, 약품, 출판, 식품업계에서 사용됨. 한 제품에 제품상표와 사표 모두를 표시할 수도 있음. (미) TMEP § 1402.03(b).

house mark

Marks that identify the manufacturer or seller over a wide variety of goods rather than the goods, which are often themselves identified by a "product mark." House marks are often used in the chemical, pharmaceutical, publishing, and food industries. A product may bear both a productmark and a house mark. TMEP § 1402.03(b).

사용례 Bose는 또한 WAVE, WAVE 상표와 빈번히 함께 표시되는 BOSE **사표(社標)**의 상표권자이기도 하다. 본 소송의 목적상 QSC와 상표심리위원회 모두 BOSE **사표**는 공중의 인지도가 매우 높으며 상표법상 '저명상표'에 해당함을 인정한다. (미) Bose Corp. v. QSC Audio Prod., Inc., 293 F.3d 1367, 1369 (Fed. Cir. 2002)

Bose also owns its **house mark** BOSE that frequently accompanies the ACOUSTIC WAVE and WAVE marks. For purposes of this litigation, QSC and the Board accept that the BOSE **house mark** enjoys extensive public recognition and renown and in trademark parlance is therefore "famous." Bose Corp. v. QSC Audio Prod., Inc., 293 F.3d 1367, 1369 (Fed. Cir. 2002)

사해심결

타인을 사해할 목적으로 얻은 심결. 심판의 당사자가 공모하여 제3자의 권리 또는 이익을 사해할 목적으로 심결을 하게 한 경우

administrative trial decision obtained by fraud

An administrative decision obtained by an action filed for the purpose of harming others. If the parties to an administrative patent trial conspire to obtain a trial decision

에는 제3자는 그 확정된 심결에 대하여 재심을 청구할 수 있다(디자인보호법 제159조).

by fraud with intent to infringe a third party's right or interest, the third party may file a petition for a retrial on the judgment that has become final and conclusive (Design Protection Act Article 159(1)).

사후적 고찰

어떤 발명의 진보성을 판단함에 있어 그 판단대상이 된 발명의 명세서에 개시되어 있는 기술을 알고 있음을 전제로 하여 사후적으로 통상의 기술자가 그 발명을 용이하게 발명할 수 있는지 판단하는 오류(대법원 2007. 8. 24. 선고 2006후138 판결 참조).

hindsight reconstruction

Hindsight reconstruction is an error of determining inventiveness based on whether or not a person skilled in the art can easily create the invention at issue in hindsight assuming that the person already knows the technology disclosed in the specification of the invention (Supreme Court Decision, 2006Hu138, decided August 24, 2007).

사후지정

국제출원할 당시에는 마드리드 의정서 체약국이 아니었던 국가, 보호가 불필요하여 지정하지 않았던 국가, 거절 · 무효 · 포기 등으로 보호되지 않았으나 현재는 해당 사유가 해소된 국가에 대해서 국제등록 후 신청하여 상표에 대한 보호를 받는 것.

subsequent designation

Designating a country for trademark protection subsequent to the international registration when the protection was unavailable at the time the international application was filed because the country was not a party to the Madrid Protocol or protection in the territory of the country was unnecessary at the time of filing, or protection was denied by refusal, invalidation or abandonment but such circumstances have changed.

산업디자인의 국제등록에 관한 헤이그협정

세계지식재산기구(WIPO) 국제사무국에 하나의 국제출원서를 제출하여 여러 체약당사자 영역에서 디자인을 보호받을 수 있도록 한 협정.

Hague Agreement Concerning the International Registration of Industrial Designs (the Hague Agreement)

The Hague Agreement allows a design to receive extended protection in the territory of the parties to the Agreement by filing a single application at the WIPO International Bureau.

산업상 이용가능성

발명이 특허등록이 되기 위한 요건의 하나(특허법 제29조 제1항 본문). 특허법의 궁극적 목적은 기술발전 촉진을 통한 산업발전이바지이므로(특허법 제1조), 발명이 특허를 받기 위하여는 산업상 이용가능성이 있어야 함.

industrial applicability

One of the requirements for patent registration (Patent Act Article 29(1)). Since the ultimate purpose of patent law is to promote industrial development by facilitating technological development (Patent Act Article 1), an invention must have industrial applicability in order to be patented.

산업재산권의 보호를 위한 파리 협약

the Paris Convention for the Protection of Industrial Property (the Paris Convention)

파리협약. 특허, 실용신안, 디자인, 상표, 서비스표, 상호, 원산지표시 또는 원산지명칭의 보호 및 부당경쟁의 방지를 목적으로 함.

The Paris Convention. It is intended to protect patents, utility models, industrial designs, trademarks, service marks, trade names, indications of source or appellations of origin, and to repress unfair competition.

산지(産地)

place of production

지정상품이 생산되는 지역의 지리적 명칭

The geographical name of the region that produces the designated good.

상거래 관행

generally accepted business practices

사용례 상표권(지리적 표시 단체표장권은 제외한다)은 다음 각 호의 어느 하나에 해당하는 경우에는 그 효력이 미치지 아니한다. 1. 자기의 성명 · 명칭 또는 상호 · 초상 · 서명 · 인장 또는 저명한 아호 · 예명 · 필명과 이들의 저명한 약칭을 **상거래 관행**에 따라 사용하는 상표 … (상표법 제90조 제1항 제1호).

Where trademark rights (excluding the right to a collective mark with geographical indication) fall under any of the following, trademark rights shall not effect the same: Any trademark using his/her own name, title, or trade name, portrait, signature, seal, or well-known pseudonym, stage name, pen name, and the well-known abbreviated title thereof, in accordance with **generally accepted business practices** (Trademark Act Article 90(1)1)

상고/항소 이유

grounds for appeal

사용례 (**상고이유**) 상고는 판결에 영향을 미친 헌법 · 법률 · 명령 또는 규칙의 위반이 있다는 것을 이유로 드는 때에만 할 수 있다(민사소송법 제423조).

(**Grounds for Appeal** to Supreme Court) An appeal to the Supreme Court may be filed only when stating as the grounds therefore that there has been a violation of the Constitution, Acts, administrative decrees, or regulations, which has affected the judgment (Civil Procedure Act Article 423).

상고인/항소인

appellant

상당한 주의

due care, considerable attention (법제처)

보통의 신중하고 합리적인 당사자가 그 상황 하에서 타인에게 피해를 입히지 않기 위해 기울이는 노력. 특정한 상황 하에서 합리적으로 취할 것으로 기대되는 판단의 정도, 주의, 신중함, 결단, 행동 등을 가리킴.

The care exercised by an ordinary prudent and reasonable party to avoid inflicting harm to another under the circumstance. The level of judgment, care, prudence, determination, and action that a person would be reasonably expected to exercise under the given circumstances.

사용례 전용사용권자 또는 통상사용권자가 지정상품 또는 이와 유사한 상품에 등록상표 또는 이와 유사한 상표를 사용함으

Where an exclusive licensee or a non-exclusive licensee causes the misunderstanding of the quality of goods or confusion with goods related to another person's business

로써 수요자에게 상품의 품질을 오인하게 하거나 타인의 업무와 관련된 상품과의 혼동을 불러일으키게 한 경우. 다만, 상표권자가 **상당한 주의**를 한 경우는 제외한다 (상표법 제119조 제1항 제2호).

by using a registered trademark or a trademark similar to the registered trademark on the designated goods, or goods similar to the designated goods: Provided, That the foregoing shall not apply where the trademark right holder **pays considerable attention** … (Trademark Act Article 119(1)2).

상대방 당사자

adverse party

미 상식적 선택

common sense selection

KSR 판례(550 U.S. 398 (2007))에서 제시된 비자명성 판단 기준. → 교시, 암시, 동기 참조.

A standard to determine non-obviousness as provided in the KSR case, 550 U.S. 398 (2007). → See. teaching, suggestion, motivation; see also common sense selection.

상업적 성공

commercial success

진보성 판단에 있어서의 2차적 고려사항. 진보성에 관한 일응의 증명이 성립되면 이에 대한 객관적 증거로써 이를 반박할 증명책임이 출원인에게로 전환되는데, 2차적 고려사항에 대한 예로는 상업적 성공, 전문가 증언 및 타인에 의한 디자인의 복제 등이 있음.

One of the secondary factors in determining non-obviousness. Once a prima facie case of obviousness has been established, the burden shifts to the applicant to rebut it, if possible, with objective evidence of nonobviousness. Examples of secondary considerations are commercial success, expert testimony and copying of the design by others.

사용례 피고가 내세우는 **상업적 성공**은 단지 특허발명의 진보성 여부를 판단하는 데 있어 하나의 참고자료에 불과할 뿐이고, 이 사건 특허발명에 진보성을 인정할 수 있는지 여부는 결국 발명의 목적, 구성 및 효과를 토대로 통상의 기술자가 선행기술에 의하여 이를 쉽게 발명할 수 있는지에 따라 판단되어야 하는데, 앞서 살핀 바와 같이 이 사건 특허발명의 정정청구항 1이 선행발명 3, 9로부터 쉽게 발명할 수 있을 것으로 보이는 이상, 피고의 위 주장도 받아들이지 않는다(특허법원 2017. 1. 13.선고 2016허3174 판결 참조).

The **commercial success** argued by the Defendant is no more than one of the references to look at in determining inventiveness of the patented invention. Inventiveness is determined by whether or not a person with ordinary skills in the art can easily invent it based on prior arts judging from the objective, composition and effect of the invention. However, as seen from above, it appears that such a person can easily invent the corrected Claim 1 from Prior Arts 3 and 9. Defendant's argument is thus rejected (Patent Court Decision 2016Heo3174, decided January 13, 2017).

상업적(기능적)인 변형

commercial(functional) modification

→ 기능적이고 상업적인 변형 참조.

상위개념

generic concept, superordinate concept

출원발명이 상위개념으로 표현되어 있고

If a claimed invention is expressed in a generic concept

ㅅ

인용발명은 하위개념으로 표현되어 있다면, 청구항에 나타난 발명은 신규성이 부정됨. '상위개념'은 동일한 과 또는 속에 속하는 사항을 포괄하는 개념 또는 공통된 성질을 가지는 복수의 사항을 포괄하는 개념으로 정의됨.

and a cited invention is expressed in a specific concept, the invention in the claims is not novel. "Generic concepts" is defined as concepts integrating matters in the same family or the same genus, or those integrating a plurality of matters with the common characteristic.

사용례 선행 또는 공지의 발명에 구성요건이 상위개념으로 기재되어 있고 위 **상위개념**에 포함되는 하위개념만을 구성요건 중의 전부 또는 일부로 하는 이른바 선택발명의 신규성을 부정하기 위해서는 선행발명이 선택발명을 구성하는 하위개념을 구체적으로 개시하고 있어야 하고, 이에는 선행발명을 기재한 선행문헌에 선택발명에 대한 문언적인 기재가 존재하는 경우 외에도 그 발명이 속하는 기술분야에서 통상의 지식을 가진 자가 선행문헌의 기재 내용과 출원시의 기술 상식에 기초하여 선행문헌으로부터 직접적으로 선택발명의 존재를 인식할 수 있는 경우도 포함된다(대법원 2009. 10. 15. 선고 2008후736판결 참조).

In order to deny the novelty of the so-called selection invention, which means an invention whose elements are stated in the preceding or already publicized invention as a **generic concept** and entirely or partly consist of a subordinate concept derived from the above generic concept, a preceding invention has disclosed subordinate concepts comprising the selection invention in a concrete manner. The novelty of selective invention is also denied when a person with ordinary knowledge in the technology to which the invention pertains can recognize the existence of selective invention directly from the preceding literature, based on the contents stated in the preceding literature and his common sense in the technology at the time of application, as well as when wordings concerning the selection invention exist in the preceding literature stating the preceding invention (Supreme Court Decision, 2008Hu736, decided October 15, 2009).

상표

'상품을 생산, 가공, 증명, 판매하는 것을 업으로 영위하는 자'가 사용하는 표장(상표법 제2조 제1항 제1호).

trademark

A mark used to distinguish goods (including services or goods related to the provision of services except goods on which a geographical indication is used; hereinafter the same shall apply) of one business from those of others (Trademark Act Article 2(1)1).

상표공보

Trademark Official Gazette (TMOG)

상표권자

등록상표에 대한 상표권을 가진 자. 등록상표를 그 지정상품에 사용할 권리를 독점함.

trademark owner, trademark right holder (법제처)

A person who has the ownership of the registered trademark. The owner of a trademark has exclusive rights to use the mark on the designated goods.

상표등록원부

등록상표에 대한 상표권, 전용사용권, 통상

Trademark Register

The register is managed by the KIPO and keeps record

사용권의 설정, 이전, 변경, 소멸 등의 사항을 기록하는 장부로서 특허청에서 관리함(상표법 제80조).

of the establishment, transfer, amendment, extinguishment of trademark rights, exclusive or non-exclusive licenses among others (Trademark Act Article 80).

상표등록의 만료

expiration of trademark registration

등록권자가 존속기간의 종료시까지 상표등록을 갱신하지 못하였을 때 상표등록이 그 효력을 잃는 것.

Trademark registration becomes no longer active when the registrant failed to renew the trademark registration by the end of the term.

상표등록조약

Trademark Registration Treaty (TRT)

본 조약에 따라 상표의 소유자는 제네바의 국제사무국에 국제등록을 함으로써 본 조약의 동맹국에 각각 자기의 상표를 등록시킨 것과 동일한 권리를 향유할 수 있음.

Under TRT, a trademark owner may enjoy the same rights as trademark owners in each of the member states to the Treaty by registering the mark with the International Bureau in Geneva.

상표등록증

certificate of trademark registration

상표등록취소사유

grounds to cancel trademark registration, grounds to revoke trademark registration (법제처)

상표의 부정사용, 불사용, 상표권자의 오인 또는 혼동행위 등 상표법 119조 1항에 규정된 상표 등록의 취소사유.

Grounds to cancel trademark registration as prescribed under Trademark Act Art.119(1), such as abuse or nonuse of trademark or acts causing misconception or confusion by trademark owner.

상표등록취소심판

(administrative) trial to cancel trademark registration, trial to revoke trademark registration (법제처)

상표등록취소의 청구에 따른 심판. 상표법 제119조 제1항 제4호 및 제6호에 해당하는 사유에 근거한 취소심판은 이해관계인이, 그 외의 제119조 제1항의 사유에 근거한 취소심판은 누구든지 청구할 수 있음(상표법 제119조 제5항).

Administrative trial proceeding held pursuant to the petition to cancel a trademark registration. A proceeding held based on the Trademark Act Art.119(1)4 and (1)6 shall be filed by interested parties. Proceedings based on all the other grounds under Art.119(1) may be requested by anyone (Trademark Act Article 119(5)).

사용례 등록상표가 다음 각 호의 어느 하나에 해당하는 경우에는 그 **상표등록의 취소심판**을 청구할 수 있다. 1. 상표권자가 고의로 지정상품에 등록상표와 유사한 상표를 사용하거나 지정상품과 유사한 상품

Where a registered trademark falls under any of the followings, a **trial to revoke the trademark registration** may be requested: Where a trademark right holder causes the misunderstanding of the quality of goods or confusion with goods related to another person's business among consumers

에 등록상표 또는 이와 유사한 상표를 사용함으로써 수요자에게 상품의 품질을 오인하게 하거나 타인의 업무와 관련된 상품과 혼동을 불러일으키게 한 경우 … (상표법 제119조 제1항 제1호).

by wilfully using a trademark similar to the registered trademark on the designated goods, or using the registered trademark or a similar trademark on goods similar to the designated goods; … (Trademark Act Article 119(1)1).

미 **상표를 거래상 사용하고자 하는 진실한 의사**

거래상 상표를 사용하고자 하는 진실한 의사. 상표를 거래상 사용하고자 하는 진실한 의사를 가진 자는 … 정해진 수수료를 지불하고 특허상표청장이 정한 양식에 따라 확인진술서와 출원서를 제출함으로써 주등록부에 상표를 등록할 것을 요청할 수 있다. (미) 상표법 제1(b)(1)조.

bona fide intention (to use mark in commerce)

Intention to use a trademark in commerce in good faith. A person who has a bona fide intention, …, to use a trademark in commerce may request registration of its trademark on the principal register hereby established by paying the prescribed fee and filing in the Patent and Trademark Office an application and a verified statement, in such form as may be prescribed by the Director. 15 U.S.C. § 1051(b)(1)).

상표법

Trademark Act

상표법 시행규칙

Enforcement Rule of the Trademark Act

상표법 시행령

Enforcement Decree of the Trademark Act

미 **상표심사기준**

미 특허상표청의 상표등록출원의 처리실무 및 절차에 대한 참고자료. 특허상표청 심사관, 상표출원인, 상표권자, 출원인 및 상표권자의 변호사와 대리인을 위한 지침을 제시함. (미) USPTO.

Trademark Manual of Examining Procedure (TMEP)

A reference work on the practices and procedures relative to prosecution of applications to register marks in the USPTO. It contains guidelines for USPTO examining attorneys, trademark applicants and owners, and attorneys and representatives for trademark applicants and owners. USPTO.

미 **상표심판항소위원회**

Trademark Trial and Appeal Board (TTAB)

상표의 국제등록에 관한 마드리드 협정

마드리드협정은 마드리드의정서와 함께 마드리드시스템을 주관함. 마드리드시스템 하에서 상표권자는 자국의 상표청을 통해

Madrid Agreement Concerning the International Registration of Marks

The Madrid Agreement governs the Madrid System along with the Madrid Protocol. The Madrid System allows trademark owners to file a single application with the

국제사무국에 일괄적으로 수수료를 지불하고 하나의 언어(영어 또는 프랑스어, 스페인어)로 된 단일한 출원을 신청함으로써 국제등록을 통해 지정한 회원국 각각에서 그 상표를 보호받을 수 있음. WIPO.

International Bureau (through the office of the home country), in one language (English, French or Spanish) and paying one set of fees for international registration and enjoy protection of their rights in each of the designated contracting parties. WIPO.

상표의 사용

상품 또는 상품의 포장에 상표를 표시하는 행위, 상품 또는 상품의 포장에 상표를 표시한 것을 양도 또는 인도하거나 양도 또는 인도할 목적으로 전시 · 수출 또는 수입하는 행위, 상품에 관한 광고 · 정가표(定價票) · 거래서류, 그 밖의 수단에 상표를 표시하고 전시하거나 널리 알리는 행위(상표법 제2조 제1항 제11호).

use of a trademark

Displaying a trademark on goods or packages of goods; transferring or delivering goods or packages of goods on which a trademark is displayed, or exhibiting, exporting, or importing such goods for the purpose of transfer or delivery; displaying a trademark on advertisements for goods, price tags, transaction documents, or other means, and exhibiting or giving wide publicity to the trademark (Trademark Act Article 2(1)11).

사용례 … 위와 같은 불사용으로 인한 상표등록취소 제도의 취지에 비추어 볼 때, 여기서 '**등록상표를 사용**'한다고 함은 등록상표와 동일한 상표를 사용한 경우를 말하고 유사상표를 사용한 경우는 포함되지 아니하나, '동일한 상표'에는 등록상표 그 자체뿐만 아니라 거래통념상 등록상표와 동일하게 볼 수 있는 형태의 상표도 포함된다고 할 것이다(대법원 2013. 9. 26. 선고 2012후2463 전원합의체 판결 참조).

In light of the purpose of the aforementioned trademark cancellation system by reason of non-use, **using a "registered trademark"** means using a trademark which is identical to the registered trademark, and does not include similar trademarks; however, "identical trademark" may include not just the registered trademark itself, but also trademarks that can be perceived as identical to a registered trademark in terms of trade norms (Supreme Court Decision, 2012Hu2463, decided September 26, 2013).

상표적 사용

상표의 사용에 해당하기 위해서는 그 사용이 반드시 '상표적 사용'이어야 함. 디자인적 사용, 순수한 상호로서만의 사용 등과 대비되는 개념.

use as a trademark

To state a mark is used, the use must be a "use as a mark," in contrast to use as a design or use merely as a trade name.

상표전문기관

특허청장의 지정에 따라 상표검색, 상품분류 등을 수행하는 전문기관(상표법 제51조 참조).

specialized trademark institution

A specialized institution that performs trademark search and/or classification of goods upon designation by the Commissioner of the Korean Intellectual Property Office (Trademark Act Article 51).

상품

'반복하여 거래대상이 되는 유체물', '교환

good

A tangible and transportable object that repeatedly functions

가치를 가지고 독립된 상거래의 목적물이 되는 물품' 등. 상표법은 상품의 개념에 대하여 규정하고 있지 아니하므로, 이에 해당하는지 여부는 상표법의 목적과 거래사회의 통념을 고려하여 결정하여야 함.

as a subject of transactions; an article that has value for exchange and is the subject of independent commercial transaction. The Trademark Act does not define what a "good" is; it shall be determined based on the objective of the Act and trade norms.

상품류 구분

상표등의 출원을 하고자 하는 자는 상품류 구분상 1류 구분 이상의 상품을 지정하여 상표마다 출원하여야 한다.

category of goods

Any person who intends to file an application for trademark or other rights shall file an application for each right and designate at least one category of goods in accordance with the classification of goods.

사용례 심사관은 상품분류전환등록신청이 다음 각 호의 어느 하나에 해당하는 경우에는 그 신청에 대하여 상품분류전환등록거절결정을 하여야 한다. … 2. 상품분류전환등록신청의 지정상품이 **상품류 구분**과 일치하지 아니하는 경우(상표법 제210조 제1항 제2호).

Where an application for registration of the conversion of the classification of goods falls under any of the following, an examiner shall decide to reject registration of the conversion of the classification of goods against such application: … 2. Where goods in the application for registration of the conversion of the classification of goods are inconsistent with the classification of the **category of goods**; … (Trademark Act Article 210(1)2).

상품 및 서비스의 분류

상품 및 서비스는 국제조약에 따른 국제시스템 하에 분류되며 특허청은 상표출원에 포함된 모든 상품과 서비스를 이에 따라 분류함. 니스 협정 참조.

classification of goods/services

Goods and services are classified by an international system, according to international treaties to which the Republic of Korea is a signatory. All goods and services included in trademark applications are classified by the KIPO according to this system. → See. Nice Agreement.

상품의 허위 또는 기만표시 억제를 위한 마드리드협정

허위로 혹은 기만적으로 회원국이나 그 회원국 내의 장소를 원산국이나 원산지로 출처를 표시하는 상품은 수입시 압류하거나 수입을 금지하거나 기타 수입과 관련한 조치 및 제재를 받도록 하는 협정. WIPO.

Madrid Agreement for the Repression of False or Deceptive Indications of Source on Goods

According to this Agreement, all goods bearing a false or deceptive indication of source, by which one of the Contracting States, or a place situated therein, is directly or indirectly indicated as being the country or place of origin, must be seized on importation, or such importation must be prohibited, or other actions and sanctions must be applied in connection with such importation. WIPO.

상품-장소간 연관성(연계성)

소비자가 어느 상품의 잘 알려진 출처로 어

goods-place association

An association between goods and a place is present when

느 장소를 연상할 때 상품-장소간 연계성이 존재함.

consumers identify as a known source of the product.

사용례 표장이 희미하거나 불분명한 경우 공중은 **상품과 장소 또는 서비스와 장소를 연결**지어 생각하지 않을 것이다. (미) TMEP § 1210.01(b).

If the mark is remote or obscure, the public is unlikely to make a **goods/place or services/place association**. TMEP § 1210.01(b).

상호

본인의 사업이나 직업 등을 나타내기 위해 사용하는 명칭.

trade name

Any name used by a person to identify his or her business or occupation.

미 상호로서의 사용

사용례 심사관은 상표로 등록하고자 하는 사항이 **상호로서의 사용에 그친다**고 판단할 경우 주등록부와 보조등록부 등록을 모두 거절하여야 한다. (미) TMEP § 1202.01.

use of mark as a trade name

If the examining attorney determines that matter for which registration is requested **is merely a trade name**, registration must be refused both on the Principal Register and on the Supplemental Register. TMEP § 1202.01.

상호저촉특허

서로 상대방 특허발명을 침해하지 않고는 실시할 수 없는 저촉 관계에 있는 2개 이상의 특허. 문제 해결을 위해 당사자들은 보통 크로스 라이선스 계약을 체결함.

blocking patent

Two or more patented inventions block each other when one cannot be practiced without infringing the other, and vice versa. The parties commonly agree to a cross-license to resolve the issue.

색채상표

특정 대상에 사용된 하나 또는 그 이상의 색채로만 된 상표.

color mark

Marks that consist solely of one or more colors used on particular objects.

사용례 상품에 대해 사용된 표장에 있어 색채는 그 상품 표면의 전체나 일부, 또는 그 상품의 포장의 전체나 일부에 대해 사용될 수 있다. 가령 **색채상표**는 샐러드 그릇에 사용된 보라색, 삽의 손잡이에 사용된 분홍색, 상품포장의 전체 또는 일부에 사용된 파란색 바탕의 분홍색 원 등으로 구성될 수 있다. (미) TMEP § 1202.05.

For marks used in connection with goods, color may be used on the entire surface of the goods, on a portion of the goods, or on all or part of the packaging for the goods. For example, a **color trademark** might consist of purple used on a salad bowl, pink used on the handle of a shovel, or a blue background and a pink circle used on all or part of a product package. TMEP § 1202.05.

미 색채위치의 진술

그 표장에서 색채가 구현되는 위치를 특정

color location statement

A statement submitted by an applicant that submits a color

하기 위하여 채색한 도면이 출원인에 의하여 제출되는 것. (미) 37 C.F.R. § 2.52(b)(1).

drawing to specify where the color appears on the mark. 37 C.F.R. § 2.52(b)(1).

사용례 **색채위치의 진술**이 부정확, 불완전하거나 도면에 나타난 색채와 불일치할 경우 색채위치설명은 도면에 묘사된 색채와 일치하도록 정정되어야 한다. (미) TMEP § 807.07(a)(ii).

If the **color location statement** is incorrect, incomplete, or inconsistent with the color(s) shown on the drawing, the color location statement must be corrected to conform to the color(s) depicted on the drawing. TMEP § 807.07(a)(ii).

생산방법의 추정

presumption of manufacturing process

물건을 생산하는 방법의 발명에 관하여 특허가 된 경우에 그 물건과 동일한 물건은 그 특허된 방법에 의하여 생산된 것으로 추정한다(특허법 제129조).

Where a patent has been granted for inventing a manufacturing process of a thing, any product identical to the thing shall be deemed manufactured by the patented process (Patent Act Article 129).

서면심리

written hearing, paper hearing (법제처)

서면만으로 신청/청구의 당부를 심리하는 것.

To hear and determine the merits of a petition/trial solely based on written documents.

사용례 심판은 구술심리 또는 **서면심리**로 한다. 다만, 당사자가 구술심리를 신청한 경우에는 서면심리만으로 결정할 수 있다고 인정되는 경우 외에는 구술심리를 하여야 한다(상표법 제141조 제1항).

A **hearing** in a trial shall be either oral or **on paper**: Provided, That where a party applies for an oral hearing, the oral hearing shall be held except where it is deemed that a decision may be made only by a paper hearing (Trademark Act Article 141(1)).

서비스표

service mark

서비스의 출처를 표시하고 자타서비스를 식별하기 위한 단어, 명칭, 기호, 고안. 서비스표는 상품이 아닌 서비스를 특정하고 출처를 식별한다는 점 외에는 상표와 동일함. '상표'나 '표장'이 상표와 서비스표를 모두 가리키기도 함.

A word, name, symbol or device that is to indicate the source of the services and to distinguish them from the services of others. A service mark is the same as a trademark except that it identifies and distinguishes the source of a service rather than a product. The terms "trademark" and "mark" are often used to refer to both trademarks and service marks.

서증

documentary evidence

석명

clarification

사실을 설명하여 내용을 밝힘.

To explain and clarify facts.

사용례 … 다음 각 호의 어느 하나에

The substance of the relevant application for trademark

해당하는 경우에는 상표등록출원의 요지를 변경하지 아니하는 것으로 본다. … 3. 불명료한 기재의 **석명**(상표법 제40조 제2항).

registration shall be deemed unchanged in any of the following: … 3. **Clarification** of ambiguous statements (Trademark Act Article 40(2)).

선등록상표

prior-registered mark, previously registered mark

사용례 지정상품에 관하여 그 수요자들이 이 사건 등록상표와 **선등록상표**를 오인·혼동한 사례는 보이지 않는다(특허법원 2015. 12. 18. 선고 2015허5432 판결 참조).

It does not appear that consumers of the designated goods were mistaken or confused between the mark at issue and the **prior-registered** trade mark (Patent Court Decision, 2015Heo5432, decided December 18, 2015).

선량한 풍속

good moral

사용례 따라서 이 사건 출원발명은 공공의 질서 또는 **선량한 풍속**을 문란하게 하거나 공중의 위생을 해할 염려가 있는 발명에 해당하므로, … (특허법원 2016. 7. 8. 선고 2016허229 판결 참조).

The Subject Invention is deemed as an invention in breach of the public order and **good moral**s or an invention likely to damage the public hygiene, … (Patent Court Decision, 2016Heo229, decided July 8, 2016).

미 선례 구속의 원칙

stare decisis

이미 결정된 판례를 따름. 선례를 지킴. 기존 판결을 유지함.

To stand by decided cases; to uphold precedents; to maintain former adjudications.

사용례 기판력, 부수적 금반언, **선례구속의 원칙**에 따라 출원인이 패한 기존의 결정은 동일한 사실관계와 쟁점에 기초하여 동일한 표장을 등록하고자 하는 이후의 출원에 대해서도 구속력을 지닐 수 있다. (미) TMEP § 1217.

A prior adjudication against an applicant may be dispositive of a later application for registration of the same mark on the basis of the same facts and issues, under the doctrine of res judicata, collateral estoppel, or **stare decisis**. TMEP § 1217.

선사용에 의한 통상실시권

non-exclusive licenses based on prior use

특허출원 시에 그 특허출원된 발명의 내용을 알지 못하고 그 발명을 하거나 그 발명을 한 사람으로부터 알게 되어 국내에서 그 발명의 실시사업을 하거나 이를 준비하고 있는 자는 그 실시하거나 준비하고 있는 발명 및 사업목적의 범위에서 그 특허출원된 발명의 특허권에 대하여 통상실시권을 가짐.

A person may obtain nonexclusive license to practice a patented invention if he or she was commercially practicing or preparing to commercially practice the invention at the time of the filing of the application, provided that he or she created the invention or learned of the invention from the inventor, without knowledge of the patent application, and that the nonexclusive license is limited to the commercial scope the person is practicing or preparing to practice the invention.

선서

oath

ㅅ

미 선서를 갈음하는 선언서

법에 규정된 선서는 서면으로 된 선언서로 대체할 수 있음. 가령 특허출원의 경우 출원인이 (1) 그 출원을 작성하거나 허가하였고 (2) 본인이 출원에 청구한 발명의 최초 발명자 또는 최초 공동발명자라 믿으며 (3) 선언서에 고의적인 허위진술이 있을 경우 18 U.S.C. § 1001에 따라 벌금이나 5년 이하의 금고형에 처해질 수 있음을 인지함을 선언한 선언서로 선서를 대신할 수 있음.

declaration in lieu of oath

A written declaration may be submitted in lieu of oath required by law. E.g. a patent application may be accompanied by a declaration in lieu of oath if the applicant declares that he or she (1) made or authorized the application, (2) believes that he or she is the original inventor or an original joint inventor of a claimed invention in the application; and (3) acknowledges that any willful false statement made in the declaration is punishable under 18 U.S.C. § 1001 by fine or imprisonment of not more than five (5) years, or both.

선순위권리자

저촉심사에서 선출원의 출원인 혹은 발명자를 가리킴. → 저촉심사 참조

senior party

The applicant or inventor of an earlier-filed patent application in an interference proceeding. → See. interference proceeding.

선의

good faith

선출원주의

1. 동일한 발명에 대하여 다른 날에 둘 이상의 특허출원이 있는 경우에는 먼저 특허출원한 자만이 그 발명에 대하여 특허를 받을 수 있다는 원칙(특허법 제36조 제1항) 2. 먼저 출원한 발명자의 특허권을 인정하는 제도. 한국과 마찬가지로 미국도 AIA 이후로는 선출원주의를 따름.

first-to-file rule

1. According to this rule, where at least two patent applications for an identical invention are filed on different dates, only the applicant of the application having the earlier filing date is entitled to a patent on the invention (Patent Act Article 36(1)). 2. The patent regime that grants patent rights to the inventor of the claimed invention with earlier filing date than others.

선택발명

선택발명은 인용발명에는 상위개념으로 표현되어 있으나 청구항에 기재된 발명은 하위개념으로 표현된 발명으로, 인용발명에는 직접적으로 개시되어 있지 아니한 사항을 발명의 필수 구성요소의 일부로 하여 선택한 발명을 의미함.

selection invention

"A selection invention" is an invention which comprises indispensible elements with a more specific concept selected from a generic concept disclosed in a cited invention, wherein the specific concept is not directly disclosed in the cited invention.

사용례 선행 또는 공지의 발명에 구성요건이 상위개념으로 기재되어 있고 위 상위개념에 포함되는 하위개념만을 구성요건 중의 전부 또는 일부로 하는 이른바 **선택발명**의 신규성을 부정하기 위해서는 선행발

In order to deny the novelty of the so-called **selection invention**, which means an invention whose elements are stated in the preceding or already publicized invention as a generic concept and entirely or partly consist of a subordinate concept derived from the above generic concept,

명이 선택발명을 구성하는 하위개념을 구체적으로 개시하고 있어야 하고, 이에는 선행발명을 기재한 선행문헌에 선택발명에 대한 문언적인 기재가 존재하는 경우 외에도 그 발명이 속하는 기술분야에서 통상의 지식을 가진 자가 선행문헌의 기재 내용과 출원시의 기술 상식에 기초하여 선행문헌으로부터 직접적으로 선택발명의 존재를 인식할 수 있는 경우도 포함된다(대법원 2009. 10. 15. 선고 2008후736 판결 참조).

a preceding invention has disclosed subordinate concepts comprising the selection invention in a concrete manner. The novelty of selective invention is also denied when a person with ordinary knowledge in the technology to which the invention pertains can recognize the existence of selective invention directly from the preceding literature, based on the contents stated in the preceding literature and his common sense in the technology at the time of application, as well as when wordings concerning the selection invention exist in the preceding literature stating the preceding invention (Supreme Court Decision, 2008Hu736, decided October 15, 2009).

선행고안

→ 선행발명 참조

preceding invention

선행근거

사용례 신규사항이란 최초의 명세서, 도면 또는 청구범위에 대한 **선행 근거**가 없는 대상을 말한다. (미) MPEP 1504.04.I.B.

antecedent basis

New matter is subject matter which has no **antecedent basis** in the original specification, drawings or claim. MPEP 1504.04.I.B.

선행기술

→ 선행발명 참조

prior invention

선행디자인

→ 선행발명 참조

prior design

선행발명

특허출원 당시 공지되었거나 공연히 실시된 기술 또는 발명. 특허의 신규성 또는 진보성 판단 기준이 됨.

prior art

Technology or invention that are published or publicly known at the time of the patent application. It is used as a basis to determine novelty or inventive step of an invention. Prior art is referred to as "prior art" in litigation but as "cited invention" in KIPO's examination process.

선행발명의 결합

사용례 선행발명을 결합할 동기는 선행발명에서 전체적으로 암시될 경우뿐 아니라 그 개량이 기술독립적이며 **선행발명의 결합**이 더 바람직한, 즉 가령 견고성, 가격, 위생, 속도, 무게, 크기, 내구성, 효율 측면

combination of references/prior arts

An implicit motivation to combine exists not only when a suggestion may be gleaned from the prior art as a whole, but when the 'improvement' is technology-independent and the **combination of references** results in a product or process that is more desirable, for example because it is stronger,

ㅅ

에서 더 나은 제품이나 방법으로 이어질 경우에도 내포되어 있다. (미) DyStar Textilfarben GmbH & Co. Deutschland KG v. C.H. Patrick Co., 464 F.3d 1356, 1360 (Fed. Cir. 2006).

cheaper, cleaner, faster, lighter, smaller, more durable, or more efficient. DyStar Textilfarben GmbH & Co. Deutschland KG v. C.H. Patrick Co., 464 F.3d 1356, 1360 (Fed. Cir. 2006).

미 선행조치

심사관은 출원인과 출원의 문제점을 의논한 뒤 그 의견교환과정을 서면으로 확인하는 목적으로 선행조치를 발송함. 여기에는 거절이유나 특정 출원요건의 충족 방법 등이 포함된다.

priority action

An examining attorney sends a priority action after having consulted with the applicant regarding problems with the application, to confirm in writing what was discussed. This type of action will include reasons why registration is being refused and/or how to satisfy certain application requirements.

설정등록

등록주의를 채택하고 있는 한국 등의 나라에서 산업재산권은 등록에 의해 권리가 발생하며, 권리를 발생시키기 위한 등록을 설정등록이라 함.

registration for establishment of rights

In countries that adopt the principle of registration such as the Republic of Korea, intellectual property rights arise from registration. Registration to give rise to such rights is referred to as registration for establishment of rights.

사용례 상표권은 **설정등록**에 의하여 발생한다(상표법 제82조 제1항).

Trademark rights shall come into existence by obtaining trademark registration and **establishing** trademark rights (Trademark Act Article 82(1)).

소각하 신청

당사자 합의나 재판관할 부재 등 여러 가지 이유로 법원에 정식으로 소를 각하할 것을 요청하는 것.

motion to dismiss

Formal request for the court to dismiss a case for various reasons, such as lack of jurisdiction or settlement between the parties.

소극적 권리범위확인심판

→ 권리범위확인심판 참조.

(administrative) defensive confirmation trial for the scope of rights, defensive scope of rights trial

사용례 … 원고가 2007. 3. 21. 피고를 상대로 특허심판원에 이 사건 **소극적 권리범위확인심판**을 제기하였으나 특허심판원이 2008. 4. 28. 확인대상표장이 이 사건 등록상표의 권리범위에 속한다는 이유로 청구를 기각하는 심결을 한 점, … (대법원 2011. 2. 24. 선고 2008후4486 판결 참조).

The plaintiff filed a lawsuit seeking **defensive confirmation trial for the scope of rights** on March 21, 2007 against the defendant in the Korean Intellectual Property Tribunal. The Tribunal rendered a decision on April 28, 2008 dismissing the plaintiff's claim … on the ground that the trademark at issue belonged to the scope of the already registered trademark (Supreme Court Decision, 2008Hu4486, decided February 24, 2011).

소급

사용례 행위능력 또는 법정대리권이 없거나 상표에 관한 절차를 밟는 데 필요한 권한의 위임에 흠이 있는 자가 밟은 절차는 보정(補正)된 당사자나 법정대리인이 추인(追認)하면 행위를 한 때로 **소급**하여 그 효력이 발생한다(상표법 제9조).

retroactive

Procedures followed by a person who has no legal capacity or authority of legal representation, or who has any defect in the delegation of authority necessary to follow trademark-related procedures shall take effect **retroactive** to the time he/she performed an act if the party whose defect has been rectified or his/her legal representative confirms such procedures (Trademark Act Article 9).

소리상표

소리만으로 된 상표.

sound mark

A mark that solely consists of sound.

사용례 **소리상표**는 듣는 이에게 '특정한 형태나 상태를 떠올리게 하고' 그 '상품이나 서비스와 소리 사이에 연관성을 형성'할 경우 출처표시기능을 한다. (미) In re Gen. Electric Broad. Co.,199 USPQ 560, 563 (TTAB 1978).

Sound marks function as source indicators when they "assume a definitive shape or arrangement" and "create in the hearer's mind an association of the sound" with a good or service. In re Gen. Electric Broad. Co.,199 USPQ 560, 563 (TTAB 1978).

소멸

사용례 상표권자가 사망한 날부터 3년 이내에 상속인이 그 상표권의 이전등록을 하지 아니한 경우에는 상표권자가 사망한 날부터 3년이 되는 날의 다음 날에 상표권이 **소멸**된다(상표법 제106조 제1항).

extinguishment

Where a successor of a deceased trademark owner fails to register transfer of the trademark rights within three years after the death of the owner, the trademark rights shall be **extinguished** on the day following the date on which three years have passed since the owner's death (Trademark Act Article 106(1)).

소송비용청구

법원이 승소자에게 합리적인 변호사비용을 청구할 수 있도록 하는 예외적인 경우. (미) 특허법 제285조.

fee shifting

The court in exceptional cases may award reasonable attorney fees to the prevailing party. 35 U.S.C. § 285.

소장

complaint

소진

사용례 특별한 사정이 없는 한 상표권자 등이 국내에서 등록상표가 표시된 상품을 양도한 경우에는 당해 상품에 대한 상표권은 그 목적을 달성한 것으로서 **소진**되고, 그로써 상표권의 효력은 당해 상품을 사용,

exhaustion

In case where a trademark owner has assigned goods on which a registered trademark is displayed in Korea, the trademark right is **exhausted** as for the good, and the effect of the trademark right shall not extend to the acts of using, transferring or leasing the good (Supreme Court Decision,

양도 또는 대여한 행위 등에는 미치지 않는다(대법원 2003. 4. 11. 선고 2002도3445 판결 참조).

2002Do3445, decided April 11, 2003).

속지주의

국가의 영토를 기준으로 하여 그 영토 내에서 법을 적용하는 원칙. 산업재산권법에는 속지주의 원칙이 적용되며, 따라서 어느 한 국가의 산업재산제도에 따라 인정되는 특정 산업재산권의 효력은 그 나라 영토 내에만 미치고 영토 밖에서는 미치지 않음.

territorial principle

The principle that application of a country's laws is limited to the territory of the country. Industrial property laws are subject to the territorial principle. Therefore, an industrial property right acknowledged in a certain country under its system is effective only in the territory of that country and does not have effect outside the territory.

(절차의) 속행

특허청장 또는 심판장은 특허에 관한 절차가 특허청 또는 특허심판원에 계속(係屬) 중일 때 특허권 또는 특허에 관한 권리가 이전되면 그 특허권 또는 특허에 관한 권리의 승계인에 대하여 그 절차를 속행(續行)하게 할 수 있다(특허법 제19조).

continuation (of procedure)

Where a patent or any other right in a patent is transferred while a patent-related procedure is pending in the Korean Intellectual Property Office or the Korean Intellectual Property Trial and Appeal Board, the Commissioner of the Korean Intellectual Property Office or the presiding judge may permit the successor to the patent or the right in the patent to continue the patent-related procedure (Patent Act Article 19).

미 손상

사용례 Victoria's Secret 측의 상표가 저명성을 갖추었다는 주장에 대해서는 청구인들도 다투지 아니하므로, 원심에서 남은 쟁점은 청구인의 상표의 사용이 피청구인의 상표의 품질을 희석시켰는가 하는 것이다. 원심은 상표희석은 '제품 특정기능의 약화 또는 상표와 제품간의 긍정적 연관성을 손상시킴으로써' 상표를 '침식'시킨다는 전제에서 출발하여, 우선 양 상표는 희석을 야기할 만큼 충분히 유사하다고 판단하고, '피고의 상표가 Victoria's Secret 상표에 미치는 **손상**의 효과를 고려할 때 원고의 상표를 희석시킨다고 보아야 한다'고 판시하였다. (미) Moseley v. V Secret Catalogue, Inc., 537 U.S. 418, 425 (2003).

tarnishment

Noting that petitioners did not challenge Victoria's Secret's claim that its mark is "famous," the only question it had to decide was whether petitioners' use of their mark diluted the quality of respondents' mark. Reasoning from the premise that dilution "corrodes" a trademark either by " 'blurring its product identification or by damaging positive associations that have attached to it,' " the court first found the two marks to be sufficiently similar to cause dilution, and then found "that Defendants' mark dilutes Plaintiffs' mark because of its **tarnishing** effect upon the Victoria's Secret mark." Moseley v. V Secret Catalogue, Inc., 537 U.S. 418, 425 (2003).

손실보상청구

타인의 적법한 행위(국가의 수용 등)로 인

claim for compensation for loss

Claim for remedy for economic damage caused by legitimate

하여 경제적 피해를 입은 경우 그 보전을 해줄 것을 청구하는 것.

action of other person (e.g. expropriation by government).

손해배상 청구권

타인의 위법한 행위(특허침해, 민법상 불법행위 등)로 인하여 경제적 피해를 입은 경우 그 보전을 해줄 것을 청구하는 것.

claim for damages

Claim for remedy for economic damage caused by illegal action of other person (e.g. patent infringement, illegal acts under the Civil Act).

사용례 따라서 상표권자가 이 규정에 의한 **손해배상을 청구**하려면, 상표권 침해 당시 해당 등록상표를 상표권자가 실제 사용하고 있었어야 하고, 침해자가 사용한 상표가 상표권자의 등록상표와 같거나 동일성이 있어야 하며, 동일성 요건을 갖추지 못한 경우에는 통상의 방법으로 손해를 증명하여 배상을 청구하여야지 위 규정에서 정한 법정손해배상을 청구할 수는 없고, 이러한 법리는 서비스표의 경우에도 동일하게 적용된다(대법원 2016. 9. 30. 선고 2014다59712판결 참조).

Thus, for a trademark owner to **claim for damages** under the said provision: (a) the trademark holder should have been actually using the registered trademark at the time of infringement; (b) the trademark used by the infringer shall be the same as, or has identical elements to, the trademark holder's registered trademark; and (c) when such identity requirement is not met, the victim may not claim for the legally stipulated damages under the above provision, but instead shall claim for damages by proving injury using ordinary methods. Such a legal doctrine applies likewise to service marks (Supreme Court Decision, 2014Da59712, decided September 30, 2016).

손해액 추정

손해배상을 청구하는 경우 그 권리를 침해한 자가 그 침해행위를 하게 한 물건을 양도하였을 때에는 그 물건의 양도수량에 특허권자 또는 전용실시권자가 그 침해행위가 없었다면 판매할 수 있었던 물건의 단위수량당 이익액을 곱한 금액을 특허권자 또는 전용실시권자가 입은 손해액으로 할 수 있다(특허법 제128조).

presumption of (the amount of) damages

If the infringer has sold the infringing products to third parties, the amount of loss may be calculated by multiplying the quantity of the sold products by the profit per unit of the product that the patentee or the exclusive licensee could have sold but for the infringement (Patent Act Article 128).

송달

사용례 준비서면은 그것에 적힌 사항에 대하여 상대방이 준비하는 데 필요한 기간을 두고 제출하여야 하며, 법원은 상대방에게 그 부본을 **송달**하여야 한다(민사소송법 제273조).

service

Briefs shall be submitted in such a way that the other party may have sufficient period to prepare for the matters as stated therein, and the court shall **serve** a duplicate thereof on the other party (Civil Procedure Act Article 273).

수계

takeover, resumption (법제처)

ㅅ

수명법관

법원합의부의 재판장으로부터 법률에 정해진 일정한 사항의 처리를 위임받은 그 합의부원인 법관을 말함.

commissioned judge

A judge who is entrusted with the handling of certain matters prescribed by law from the presiding judge of the judicial panel.

사용례 법원은 소송의 정도와 관계없이 화해를 권고하거나, **수명법관** 또는 수탁판사로 하여금 권고하게 할 수 있다(민사소송법 제145조 제1항).

A court may, irrespective of the progress of litigation, recommend a compromise, or have a **commissioned judge** or an entrusted judge recommend it (Civil Procedure Act Article 145(1)).

수수료

사용례 상표에 관한 절차를 밟는 자는 **수수료**를 내야 한다. 다만, 제117조 제1항 및 제118조 제1항에 따라 심사관이 무효심판을 청구하는 경우에는 수수료를 면제한다(상표법 제78조 제1항).

fee

Any person who follows trademark-related procedures shall pay **fees**: Provided, That where an examiner requests a trial to invalidate a trademark pursuant to Articles 117 (1) and 118 (1), he/she shall be exempted from the fees (Trademark Act Article 78(1)).

수요자 기만

타인의 상표를 모방하여 자기상표로 등록출원하는 등 수요자를 속이는 것.

consumer deception

Deceiving consumers by filing an application of a mark imitating a trademark of another person.

사용례 그렇다면 이 사건 등록상표가 상표법 제7조 제1항 제11호의 '**수요자를 기만**할 염려가 있는 상표'에 해당하는지 여부를 판단함에 있어서는 선사용서비스표들의 구성 중 이 사건 등록상표의 등록결정시에 식별력을 취득한 'coffee bean' 부분을 그 사용서비스업인 '커피전문점경영업, 커피전문점체인업'에 관하여 요부로 보아 상표의 유사 여부를 살피고 등록상표가 수요자를 기만할 염려가 있는 상표에 해당하는지 여부를 판단할 수 있다 할 것이다(대법원 2013. 3. 28. 선고 2011후835 판결 참조).

Therefore, in order to determine whether the trademark of this case constitutes "trademark that may mislead or **deceive consumers**" in accordance with Article 7(1) subparag. 11 of the Trademark Act, the decision shall be made based on the similarity of the marks with the "coffeebean" portion as the essential part concerning 'coffee shop business, coffee franchise business' as the service of use, since the portion of the previously used service marks had acquired distinctiveness by the time of the decision to register the registered mark (Supreme Court Decision, 2011Hu835, decided March 28, 2013).

수용

특정한 공익사업을 위하여 개인의 재산권을 법률에 의하여 강제적으로 취득하는 것을 말함.

expropriation

An action based on law acquiring private properties by force for a specific project in public interest.

수치한정발명

발명의 구성요건 중 예컨대 온도나 배합비

numerical limitation invention

Inventions that use numerical values to express the scope

율과 같이 일정한 범위를 가지는 구성요소에 관하여 수치를 한정한 발명을 수치한정발명이라 함. 이때 수치한정발명에 신규성 또는 진보성이 인정되기 위하여는 한정된 수치범위 내외에서 현저한 작용효과가 있어야 하는데, 이러한 현저한 작용효과를 임계적 의의라 지칭함.

of its elements (e.g., temperature, mix ratio) is called numerical limitation invention. In order for a numerical limitation invention to have novelty or an inventive step, the numerical limit must yield significant effect. The significance of this effect is called critical significance.

사용례 특허등록된 발명이 그 출원 전에 공지된 발명이 가지는 구성요소의 범위를 수치로써 한정하여 표현한 경우에 있어, 그 특허발명의 과제 및 효과가 공지된 발명의 연장선상에 있고 **수치한정**의 유무에서만 차이가 있는 경우에는 그 한정된 수치범위 내외에서 현저한 효과의 차이가 생기지 않는다면 그 특허발명은 그 기술분야에서 통상의 기술자가 통상적이고 반복적인 실험을 통하여 적절히 선택할 수 있는 정도의 단순한 수치한정에 불과하여 진보성이 부정된다(대법원 2010. 8. 19. 선고 2008후4998 판결 참조).

In the case of a patented invention which uses specific numerical values to express the scope of elements for an invention already publicly known at the time of application, if there is a difference only in the **numerical limitation** while the object and functional effects of the patented invention are in line with those of publicly known inventions, and if no substantial difference in functional effect occurs within the limited numerical range, the patented invention lacks the requisite “inventive step” since it is no more than a simple numerical limitation that a person having ordinary skill in the art can properly derive through ordinary and repetitive experiments (Supreme Court Decision, 2008Hu4998, decided August 19, 2010).

수탁판사

judge sitting by designation, entrusted judge (법제처)

법원으로부터 특정한 소송행위에 대하여 촉탁을 받은 판사. 다른 관할구역에서의 증거조사도 가능.

Judge who has accepted the entrustment from the court for the subject matter. An entrusted judge can investigate evidence in other jurisdiction.

사용례 법원은 제297조의 규정에 따라 수명법관 또는 **수탁판사**에게 문서에 대한 증거조사를 하게 하는 경우에 그 조서에 적을 사항을 정할 수 있다(민사소송법 제354조 제1항).

Where a court requires, pursuant to the provisions of Article 297, a commissioned judge or an **entrusted judge** to conduct an examination of evidence as to a document, it may determine the matters to be entered in the relevant protocol (Civil Procedure Act Article 354(1)).

승계

succession

사용례 특허권 또는 특허에 관한 권리에 관하여 밟은 절차의 효력은 그 특허권 또는 특허에 관한 권리의 **승계**인에게 미친다(특허법 제18조).

The effects of a procedure taken with respect to a patent or any other right in a patent shall extend to the **successor** to the patent or the right in the patent (Patent Act Article 18).

시각적 유사성

사용례 쟁점의 대상이 둘 다 디자인표장이라면 표장의 유사성은 주로 **시각적 유사성**을 바탕으로 결정되어야 한다. 이 경우 표장이 대부분의 경우 거래사회에서 그 구체적인 성질보다는 일반적인 성질에 대해 이격적으로 관찰하는 경우가 대비관찰보다 흔하다는 사실을 염두에 두어야 한다. 따라서 양 표장 간의 차이에도 불구하고 혼동을 일으킬 만한 유사성이 존재할 수 있다. (미) TMEP § 1207.01(c).

visual similarity

When the marks at issue are both design marks, the similarity of the marks must be decided primarily on the basis of **visual similarity**. In this situation, consideration must be given to the fact that the marks usually will not be viewed side-by-side in the marketplace and a purchaser's recollection of design marks is often of a general, rather than specific, nature; thus the marks may be confusingly similar despite differences between them. TMEP § 1207.01(c).

시도의 자명성

KSR 판례에서 제시된 비자명성 판단 기준. → TSM기준 (교시, 암시, 동기) 및 상식적 선택 참조.

obvious to try

A standard to determine non-obviousness as provided in the KSR case, 550 U.S. 398 (2007) → See. TSM; common sense selection.

식물 신품종 보호에 관한 국제조약

1961년 12월 2일 파리에서 채택, 1968년 8월 10일 발효됨. 이 조약에 기초하여 형성된 동맹(International Union for the Protection of New Varieties of Plants, UPOV)의 약칭으로 일반적으로 'UPOV 조약'이라고도 함.

International Convention for the Protection of New Varieties of Plants

This convention was adopted in Paris on December 2, 1961 and came into force on August 10, 1968. It is also called 'UPOV Convention' since the International Union for the Protection of New Varieties of Plants (UPOV) was established by this convention.

식물특허

덩기줄기식물(tuber propagated plant)나 야생식물을 제외한 배양된 변종, 돌연변이, 교잡종, 새로 발견된 묘목, 무성생식이 가능한 식물의 독특하고 새로운 품종을 발명 또는 발견한 자는 그에 대한 특허를 받을 수 있다. (미) 특허법 제161조.

plant patents

Whoever invents or discovers and asexually reproduces any distinct and new variety of plant, including cultivated sports, mutants, hybrids, and newly found seedlings, other than a tuber propagated plant or a plant found in an uncultivated state, may obtain a patent therefor … Patent Act, 35 U.S.C. § 161.

미 식물품종보호법

식물품종의 보호에 대한 미국 법령. 본 법은 육성자에게 최장 25년 간 새로운 식물종에 대한 독점적 통제권을 줌. 특허권과 유사한 권리가 주어지는 것이지만 식물특허는 무성생식 식물에만 적용된다는 점에서 차이가 있음.

Plant Varieties Protection Act

A U.S. statute on plant varieties protection. The Act gives breeders up to 25 years of exclusive control over new plant varieties. The rights granted under the Act should not be confused with plant patents, which are limited to asexually reproduced plants.

식별력

자타의 상품을 일반수요자나 소비자로 하여금 식별하게 할 수 있는 상표로서의 기능.

distinctiveness

A function of a trademark that allows ordinary purchasers or consumers to distinguish the trademark owner's goods from others'.

사용례 수요자들에게 현저하게 인식되어 있는 타인의 상품이나 영업과 혼동을 일으키게 하거나 그 **식별력** 또는 명성을 손상시킬 염려가 있는 상표는 상표등록을 받을 수 없다(상표법 제34조 제1항 제11호).

None of the following trademarks shall be registered: … Any trademark likely to cause confusion with goods or business of another person remarkably recognized by consumers or to dilute their **distinctiveness** or reputation (Trademark Act Article 34(1)11).

식별력이 없는 표장

전체적으로 보아서 자타상품의 식별력이 없거나 공익상 특정인에게 독점시키는 것이 적당하지 아니한 표장.

non-distinctive mark

A mark that does not overall, unsuitable for trademark registration because it lacks distinctiveness or it is improper to grant exclusive right to a particular person for the sake of public interest.

사용례 … 이 사건 출원상표는 거래계에서 흔히 쓰일 수 있는 구호나 광고문안 정도로 인식되는 표장이 아니고, 공익상 특정인에게 독점시키는 것이 적합하지 않은 경우에도 해당하지 않으며 … '기타 **식별력이 없는 표장**'의 구체적인 인정 사유들 중 어디에도 해당하지 않는다(특허법원 2017. 04. 14 선고 2016허8322 판결 참조).

The proposed mark at issue is not perceived as a slogan or advertising phrase that may be commonly used in the marketplace, and it cannot be stated that a grant of exclusive rights of the mark to a particular person is inappropriate for the sake of public interest; … and thus does not have any grounds to conclude that the mark falls under the category of other **non-distinctive marks** (Patent Court Decision, 2016Heo8322, decided April 14, 2017).

식품의약품안전처

Ministry of Food and Drug Safety

신규사항

최초의 명세서, 도면 또는 청구범위에서 선행 근거가 없는 대상. 신규사항을 도입하는 청구범위에 대한 보정은 거절되어야 함.

new matter

Subject matter which has no antecedent basis in the original specification, drawings or claim. An amendment to the claim which introduces new matter shall be rejected.

신규성

특허요건의 하나. 특허를 받을 수 있는 발명이기 위해서는 특허 출원 전에 국내 또는 국외에서 공지되었거나 공연히 실시된 발명 등에 해당하지 아니하여야 함.

novelty

One of the requirements for patent registration. In order to be patentable, an invention shall not be publicly known or executed in the Republic of Korea or in a foreign country prior to the filing of a patent application.

신뢰보호의 원칙

신뢰보호원칙이란 행정청의 공적견해표명에 대한 보호가치 있는 신뢰를 가진 국민이 그 신뢰에 기초하여 어떠한 행위를 하였을 때, 위 신뢰는 보호되어야 한다는 원칙.

principle of trust protection, principle of general reliance

The principle that a citizen's trust on a government agency's public expression of its opinion should be protected, when the citizen acted in reliance of the trust and such trust deserves protection.

사용례 그러나 다음과 같은 이유로 이 사건 출원발명에 대한 거절결정이 **신뢰보호원칙**에 위배되어 위법하다고 할 수는 없다(특허법원 2016. 7. 8. 선고 2016허229 판결 참조).

However, it cannot be said that the final rejection on the Subject Invention is illegal due to violation of the **principle of trust protection** on the following grounds (Patent Court Decision, 2016Heo229, decided July 8, 2016).

신용회복청구

법원은 고의나 과실로 특허권 또는 전용실시권을 침해함으로써 특허권자 또는 전용실시권자의 업무상 신용을 떨어뜨린 자에 대해서는 특허권자 또는 전용실시권자의 청구에 의하여 손해배상을 갈음하여 또는 손해배상과 함께 특허권자 또는 전용실시권자의 업무상 신용회복을 위하여 필요한 조치를 명할 수 있음(특허법 제131조).

claim for reinstatement of reputation

Upon request of a patentee or exclusive licensee, the court may order the person who has degraded the business reputation of the patentee or exclusive licensee by intentionally or negligently infringing the patent or exclusive license to take necessary measures to reinstate the business reputation of the said patentee or exclusive licensee, in lieu of or in addition to damages therefor (Patent Act Article 131).

실사용상표

사용례 … 또 영문자 부분 'CONTINENTAL'은 그 한글 음역 부분 '콘티넨탈'의 병기 없이도 '콘티넨탈'로 동일하게 호칭될 것으로 보이므로, 이 사건 등록상표 중 상단의 영문자 부분만으로 된 **실사용상표**는 일반 수요자나 거래자에게 이 사건 등록상표 그 자체와 동일한 호칭과 관념을 일으킨다고 할 것이다(특허법원 2016. 7. 8. 선고 2016허229 판결 참조).

actually used trademark

Additionally, it appears that the "CONTINENTAL" portion will be also called "continental" without the Korean transliteration "콘티넨탈" -the **actually used trademark**- which was composed of the upper line's English letters, will cause consumers or traders to conceive a name and concept which is identical to the registered trademark at issue (Patent Court Decision, 2016Heo229, decided July 8, 2016).

실시

물건발명의 경우 물품을 생산 · 사용 · 양도 · 대여 · 수출 또는 수입하거나 그 물품을 양도 또는 대여하기 위한 청약행위, 방법발명의 경우 그 방법에 의하여 생산한 물건을 사용 · 양도 · 대여 또는 수입하거나 그 물건의 양도 또는 대여의 청약을 하는 행위(특허법 제2조).

exploitation, executing (법제처)

As for a product invention, acts of producing, using, assigning, leasing, exporting or importing an article, acts of offer to assign or acts to assign or lease the article; for a process invention, acts to use, assign, lease or import articles manufactured with the process, or to offer to assign or lease the article (Patent Act Article 2).

실시가능성
명세서가 통상의 기술자가 과도한 실험 없이 발명을 생산하고 실시할 수 있도록 전체적으로 명확하고 간결하며 정확하게 기재되어야 한다는 요건.

enablement
The requirement that a specification must describe in "full, clear, concise, and exact terms" how to make and use the invention such that any person skilled in the art can do so without undue experimentation.

사용례 디자인특허출원의 특허 허여 필수요건은 장식성, 신규성, 비자명성, **실시가능성**, 명확성이다. (미) MPEP § 1504.

In design patent applications, ornamentality, novelty, nonobviousness, **enablement** and definiteness are necessary prerequisites to the grant of a patent. MPEP § 1504.

실시권
산업재산권을 실시할 수 있는 권리. 전용실시권과 통상실시권으로 구분됨.

license
Right to execute an industrial property right. A license may either be exclusive or non-exclusive.

사용례 특허권자는 그 특허권에 대하여 타인에게 **통상실시권**을 허락할 수 있다(특허법 제102조 제1항).

A patentee may grant a **non-exclusive license** of the patent to others (Patent Act Article 102(1)).

실시료 과적
단일제품이 복수의 특허를 침해할 경우 발생하는, 복수의 실시료 책정으로 과도한 부담이 주어지는 경우.

royalty stacking
A problem that occurs in case of a single product infringing multiple patents as the multiple royalty burdens are likely to be excessive.

실시료 기초
합리적 실시료 또는 FRAND 실시료 산정 시의 기준이 되는 제품이나 서비스. 주로 하위시장 제품의 소매가를 활용함.

royalty base
Product or service used to determine reasonable royalty. Downstream retail price is often used.

실시례
발명이 제작, 사용, 실행되고 표현되는 방식

embodiment, implementation
A manner in which an invention is made, used, practiced, or expressed.

실시의사가 있는 자
특허의 실시자로서 협상의 용의가 있는 특허권자와 구속력 있는 실시권계약을 협상할 용의가 있는 자. 합리적 실시료 또는 FRAND 실시료 결정 시 사용되는, 침해행위 시작 직전 시점에 가상의 협상을 하고자 하는 당사자의 개념.

willing licensee
An implementer of a patent who is willing to negotiate a binding license agreement with a willing licensor. A concept used to determine reasonably royalty or FRAND royalty as a party to a hypothetical negotiation to ascertain the royalty just before the infringing acts began.

실용성

어떤 발명이 특허성을 갖추기 위해서는 구체적이고 실질적이며 믿을만한 실용성이 있어야 한다.

utility

To be patentable, an invention must have specific, substantial, and credible utility.

실용신안공보

Utility Model Gazette

실용신안권의 존속기간

실용신안권의 존속기간은 제21조 제1항에 따라 실용신안권을 설정등록한 날부터 실용신안등록출원일 후 10년이 되는 날까지로 한다(실용신안법 제22조 제1항).

term of utility model right

The term of a utility model right shall commence on the registration date of the establishment of the utility model right under Article 21 (1), and shall expire on the tenth anniversary of the filing date of the application for the utility model registration (Utility Model Act Article 22(1)).

(청구범위의) 실질적 변경

사용례 구 특허법 제133조의2, 제136조 제3항의 규정 취지는 무효심판의 피청구인이 된 특허권자에게 별도의 정정심판을 청구하지 않더라도 무효심판절차 내에서 정정청구를 할 수 있게 해주되, **청구범위를 실질적으로 확장하거나 변경**하는 것은 허용하지 아니하고, 제3자의 권리를 침해할 우려가 없는 범위 내에서의 청구범위의 감축이나 오기를 정정하고 기재상의 불비를 해소하여 바르게 하는 오류의 정정은 허용하는 데 있다(대법원 2016. 11. 25. 선고 2014후2184 판결 참조).

substantial amendment (to the claims)

The purport of Articles 133-2 and 136(3) of the former Patent Act (amended by Act No. 9381, Jan. 30, 2009) is to: (a) enable the patent-holder as the respondent in a patent invalidation trial to petition for correction in the invalidation trial procedure without having to file for a separate trial for correction; (b) prohibit any **substantial extension of, or amendment to, the claims**; but (c) allow for a reduction in the number of claims, rectification of clerical errors, and clarification of ambiguous indications, to the extent they are not likely to infringe on third party rights (Supreme Court Decision, 2014Hu2184, decided November 25, 2016).

실체

사용례 두 발명이 서로 동일한 발명인지 여부는 대비되는 두 발명의 **실체**를 파악하여 따져보아야 할 것이지 표현양식에 따른 차이에 따라 판단할 것은 아니므로, 대비되는 두 발명이 각각 물건의 발명과 방법의 발명으로 서로 발명의 범주가 다르다고 하여 곧바로 동일한 발명이 아니라고 단정할 수 없다(대법원 2007. 1. 12. 선고 2005후3017 판결 참조).

substance

The actual **substance** of the two inventions compared shall be examined, rather than the differences as to how they are described, such that even when the two inventions compared fall under the different categories of "invention of a product" and "invention of a process," it shall not be automatically determined that they do not constitute identical inventions (Supreme Court Decision, 2005Hu3017, decided January 12, 2007).

실체적 거절

식별력의 부재 또는 혼동가능성 등 실체적

substantive refusal

A refusal based on substantive reasons such as likelihood

사유에 근거한 거절결정.

of confusion or lack of distinctiveness.

실체적인 분쟁

소송에는 법원의 판결을 구하기 위해서는 가상의 사건이 아닌 법원이 해결할 수 있는 두 당사자 간의 실체적인 분쟁이 있어야 함.

actual controversy

A real dispute must be present between two parties, capable of being resolved by the court, as opposed to a hypothetical case brought in an attempt to get the court to issue an advisory opinion.

실효

사용례 (재정의 **실효**) 재정을 받은 자가 제110조 제2항 제2호에 따른 지급시기까지 대가(대가를 정기 또는 분할하여 지급할 경우에는 최초의 지급분)를 지급하지 아니하거나 공탁을 하지 아니한 경우에는 그 재정은 효력을 잃는다(특허법 제113조).

annulment

(**Annulment** of Adjudication) If a person for whom adjudication has been made fails to pay the consideration (the initial installment, if the consideration is to be paid periodically or in installments) or fails to pay it into the competent court, the adjudication shall become null and void (Patent Act Article 113).

심결

심판사건에 대하여 심판관합의체가 내리는 종국적인 판단.

administrative trial decision, trial ruling (법제처)

A final disposition by the panel of administrative judges to rule on an administrative trial.

심결의 위법사유

erroneous grounds of administrative decision

심결취소소송

특허권, 실용신안권, 디자인권, 상표권에 관한 거절결정, 무효심판, 권리범위확인심판에 대한 심결 등에 대하여 그 취소를 구하는 소송. 심결취소소송은 2심제 구조를 취하며 1심은 특허법원이 전속 관할함.

revocation action of administrative decision

Actions filed to seek revocation of the administrative decisions of KIPO (IPTAB) regarding KIPO examiner's rejection on the application, decisions from invalidation trials, or confirmation of the scope of rights and etc. Revocation of administrative action involves a two-tiered trial system, with the Patent Court being the sole court of first instance.

심리

hearing

심미감

디자인이 관찰자에게 불러일으키는 미적 인상. 물품을 보는 자로 하여금 지금까지 볼 수 없었던 특수한 취미감, 유행감, 안전감 혹은 편리감 등을 줄 수 있으면 족하며, 반드시 미학적으로 높은 수준의 우아하고 고상한 것을 요구하는 것은 아님.

aesthetic sense, aesthetic impression

The aesthetic impression a design creates in the observer's mind. A design is sufficiently aesthetic if it creates a sense of pleasure, trendiness, safety or convenience, and is not required to be aesthetically sophisticated or advanced.

사용례 … 양 디자인 사이에 위와 같은 차이점이 존재하기는 하나, 그 차이의 정도가 양 디자인의 지배적인 특징을 나타내는 위 유사점 ④, ⑤로 말미암은 유사성을 상쇄하여 양 디자인이 전체적으로 다른 **심미감**을 나타낼 정도로는 보기 어렵고, … (특허법원 2015. 4. 23. 선고 2014허6858 판결 참조).

Despite the aforementioned differences, the dissimilarity does not rise to the degree that offsets the similarity brought by the points ④ and ⑤ above, which represent the dominant features of the designs, so as to display distinct **aesthetic senses** as a whole (Patent Court Decision, 2014Heo6858, decided April 23, 2015).

미 심미적 기능성

aesthetic functionality

기능적인데 불과한 제품 또는 제품포장이 심미적이고 눈에 띄는 특징을 지니고 이 특징이 그 제품의 상업적 성공에 중요한 영향을 미치는 경우 트레이드 드레스나 상표로 보호받을 수 없다고 보는 것.

The doctrine that merely functional product or packaging that are aesthetically pleasing and appealing to the eyes, which play an important role in the commercial success of the product, are not eligible for trade dress or trademark protection.

사용례 출원상표가 장식적 성격을 띄는지 여부가 쟁점일 때 '**심미적 기능성**'은 적용되지 않으므로 이를 논하는 것은 부적합하다. (미) TMEP § 1202.02(a)(vi).

Where the issue presented is whether the proposed mark is ornamental in nature, it is improper to refer to "**aesthetic functionality**," because the doctrine of "functionality" is inapplicable to such cases. TMEP § 1202.02(a)(vi).

심사

examination

심사관

examiner

미 심사관 보정

examiner's amendment

출원에 대한 보정사항의 서면확인. 그 출원의 담당심사관은 출원인 또는 그 대리인과 협의 후에 그 출원을 보정함. (미) USPTO.

A written confirmation of an amendment made to an application. The examiner assigned to the application will make the amendment after consultation with an applicant or the applicant's attorney. USPTO.

사용례 심사관은 필요한 보정이 출원인의 확인을 거칠 필요가 없을 때는 언제든지 **심사관 보정**으로 그 출원을 보정할 수 있다. 필요한 경우 심사관 보정을 통해 상품 또는 서비스의 명칭을 보정하거나 권리불요구사항의 등록, 법인설립현황의 추가, 주등록부에서 보조등록부로의 이전 등을 할 수 있다. (미) TMEP § 707.

The examining attorney may issue an **examiner's amendment** whenever the required amendment does not have to be verified by the applicant. For example, in appropriate circumstances, an examiner's amendment may be used to amend the identification of goods/services, enter a disclaimer, add the state of incorporation, or amend from the Principal to the Supplemental Register. TMEP § 707.

미 **심사의 보류**

특허상표청의 절차를 정당하고 충분한 사유에 따라 합리적인 기간 동안 중지함. '절차의 중지'란 심사관이 이를 중지함을 가리키며, 출원인이 답변할 시간을 중지시키거나 연장함을 뜻하지 아니함. (미) 37 C.F.R. §2.67; TMEP § 716.

suspension of action by office

Suspending action by the Patent and Trademark Office for a reasonable time for good and sufficient cause. The term "suspension of action" means suspending action by the examining attorney. It does not mean suspending or extending an applicant's time to respond. 37 C.F.R. §2.67; TMEP § 716.

심사청구

특허출원에 대하여 심사청구가 있을 때에만 이를 심사한다. 누구든지 특허출원에 대하여 특허출원일부터 5년 이내에 특허청장에게 출원심사의 청구를 할 수 있다(특허법 제59조).

requests for examinations

A patent application shall be examined only upon receipt of a request for examination. Any person may file a request for examination of a patent application with the Commissioner of the Korean Intellectual Property Office within five years from the filing date of the patent application.

심판(특허심판원)

산업재산권의 무효나 등록거절결정 등에 대하여 위법 · 부당성을 심사하는 행정적 절차.

administrative trial, IPTAB trial

An administrative trial proceeding to determine lawfulness or legality of administrative decisions such as to invalidate or refuse to register industrial property rights.

심판관

특허심판원에 제기된 심판에 대해 직무상 독립하여 심판하는 역할을 함.

administrative judge

Administrative judges of the Intellectual Property Trial and Appeal Board who will make independent rulings in administrative trials.

심판관합의체

심판은 3인 또는 5인의 심판관의 합의체가 행하며 합의는 심판관 중 과반수에 의하여 결정함. 심판의 합의는 공개하지 아니함.

panel of administrative judges, panel for trial (법제처)

An administrative trial shall be conducted by a panel consisting of three or five administrative judges. A consensus shall be reached by a majority decision and shall not be disclosed.

심판장

chief administrative judge, presiding judge (법제처)

심판청구

petition for (administrative) trial

미 **CA출원(협의의 계속출원)**

선출원된 동시계류 정규출원, 미국을 지정

continuation application

An application for the invention(s) disclosed in a prior-

국으로 하는 국제출원 또는 국제디자인출원에 개시된 발명을 대상으로 하는 출원. (미) MPEP § 201.07.

filed copending nonprovisional application, international application designating the United States, or international design application designating the United States. MPEP § 201.07.

ㅇ

아호

작가 등이 본래의 이름 외에 사용하는 이름.

pseudonym

A name that a person (such as a writer) uses instead of his or her real name.

사용례 상표권(지리적 표시 단체표장권은 제외한다)은 다음 각 호의 어느 하나에 해당하는 경우에는 그 효력이 미치지 아니한다. 1. 자기의 성명 · 명칭 또는 상호 · 초상 · 서명 · 인장 또는 저명한 **아호** · 예명 · 필명과 이들의 저명한 약칭을 상거래 관행에 따라 사용하는 상표 … (상표법 제90조 제1항 제1호).

Where trademark rights (excluding the right to a collective mark with geographical indication) fall under any of the following, trademark rights shall not effect the same: 1. Any trademark using his/her own name, title, or trade name, portrait, signature, seal, or well-known **pseudonym**, stage name, pen name, and the well-known abbreviated title thereof, in accordance with generally accepted business practices; … (Trademark Act Article 90(1)1).

안정성

식물신품종보호법상 품종보호를 받기 위한 요건의 하나. 품종의 본질적 특성이 반복적으로 증식된 후(1대 잡종 등과 같이 특정한 증식주기를 가지고 있는 경우에는 매 증식주기 종료 후를 말한다)에도 그 품종의 본질적 특성이 변하지 아니하는 경우에는 그 품종은 안정성을 갖춘 것으로 본다(식물신품종 보호법 제20조).

stability

One of the requirements for protection of plant varieties under the Act on the Protection of New Varieties. A plant variety shall be deemed stable as if its relevant characteristics remain unchanged after repeated propagation (at the end of each cycle of propagation in the case of a particular cycle of propagation, such as a first filial generation hybrid) (Act on the Protection of New Varieties Article 20).

암시적 표장

해당 상품이나 서비스에 사용되었을 때 그 성질을 추측하기 위해서 상상력, 사고력, 지각력을 요하는 표장.

suggestive mark

A mark that, when applied to the goods or services at issue, requires imagination, thought or perception to reach a conclusion as to the nature of those goods or services.

사용례 … 일반적으로 조어상표의 식별력은 **암시적 상표**, 기술적 상표, 보통명칭 상표 등에 비해 높게 평가된다(특허법원 2013. 11. 22. 선고 2013허5445 판결 참조).

Generally, coined marks are considered more distinctive than **suggestive**, descriptive or generic marks (Patent Court Decision, 2013Heo5445, decided November 22, 2013).

미 약식 신약 허가 신청

미국 Hatch-Waxman법(21 U.S.C. §355(b)(2))에 따른 제네릭 의약품에 대한 허가 신청.

abbreviated new drug application (ANDA)

Application for a generic drug for an approved drug under Hatch-Waxman Act (21 U.S.C. §355(b)(2)).

미 약식판결

사실심리 없는 판결은 중대한 사실에 대한 진정한 쟁점이 부재하며 신청인이 법에 따라 승소할 권리가 있음을 신청(motion)을 통해 보임으로써 얻어내는 판결. (미) F.R.C.P. § 56(a).

summary judgment

A judgment granted upon a motion that shows there is no genuine dispute as to any material fact and the movant is entitled to a favorable judgment as a matter of law. F.R.C.P. § 56(a).

약화(弱化)

어느 상표를 타인이 유사하지 아니한 상품에 정당한 권한 없이 사용함으로써 그 상표가 지니는 기존의 판매력을 감소시키는 것. (미) Mead Data Central, Inc. v. Toyota Motor Sales, U.S.A., Inc., 875 F.2d 1026, 1031 (2d Cir.1989).

blurring

The whittling away of an established trademark's selling power through its unauthorized use by others upon dissimilar products. Mead Data Central, Inc. v. Toyota Motor Sales, U.S.A., Inc., 875 F.2d 1026, 1031 (2d Cir.1989).

사용례 나아가 두 명칭이 구별은 가능하다 하더라도, “R” Us 접미사 부분의 동일성과 매장에서 판매되는 해당 아동용품의 유사성을 고려하면 “Kids ‘r’ Us” 표장은 “Toys “R” Us” 상표의 제품식별력을 **약화**시킨다고밖에 볼 수 없다. 원고 상표의 식별력은 Kids ‘r’ Us를 포함하여 “R” Us를 사용한 명칭이 늘어날수록 감소할 것이 명백하고 이로 인해 상표가 가지는 판매력도 희석된다. (미) Toys R Us, Inc. v. Canarsie Kiddie Shop, Inc., 559 F. Supp. 1189, 1208 (E.D.N.Y. 1983).

Furthermore, although the two names are distinguishable, the identity of the “R” Us suffixes and the similarity of the children's products sold by the stores compels me to conclude that the name Kids ‘r’ Us is likely to **blur** Toys “R” Us' product identification. Clearly, the distinctiveness of plaintiff's mark is being “whittled away” by a proliferation of “R” Us names, including Kids ‘r’ Us, and the mark's accompanying selling power is being diluted. Toys R Us, Inc. v. Canarsie Kiddie Shop, Inc., 559 F. Supp. 1189, 1208 (E.D.N.Y. 1983).

양도

‘양도’란 권리를 이전하는 행위로서 유 · 무상 여부에 관계없음.

assignment

assignment refer to transfer of ownership, regardless of whether it is paid for or not.

양벌규정

법인의 대표자나 법인 또는 개인의 대리인 · 사용인 기타 종업원이, 업무에 관하여 일정한 위법행위를 하였을 경우에, 현실의 행위자를 처벌하는 이외에도 그 사업주체인

joint penal provision

Provisions that attach liability to the principal or the corporation for certain unlawful acts of its agent, representative or employee in relation to the business of the principal or the corporation, along with the wrongdoer

ㅇ

법인 또는 개인도 처벌하는 규정.

themselves.

미 양식화

사용례 보통명칭에 본질적인 식별력은 없으나 상표로서 기능할 수 있는 표현 또는 디자인을 형성하도록 **양식화** 되었을 경우 그 표장은 보통명칭에 대한 권리불요구를 포함하여 보조등록부에 등록될 수 있다. (미) TMEP § 1209.03(w).

stylized

If generic wording is **stylized** to create a display or design that is not inherently distinctive, but is nonetheless capable of functioning as a mark, the mark may be registered on the Supplemental Register with a disclaimer of the generic wording. TMEP § 1209.03(w).

업무상의 신용

사용례 상표권자 또는 전용사용권자의 **업무상 신용**을 떨어뜨린 자에 대해서는 상표권자 또는 전용사용권자의 청구에 의하여 손해배상을 갈음하거나 손해배상과 함께 상표권자 또는 전용사용권자의 업무상 신용회복을 위하여 필요한 조치를 명할 수 있다(상표법 제113조).

business reputation

The court may order a person who has damaged **business reputation** of a trademark right holder or an exclusive licensee by wilfully or negligently infringing the trademark rights or the exclusive license to pay damages at the request of the trademark right holder or the exclusive licensee, or order the person to take measures necessary to reinstate the business reputation of the trademark right holder or the exclusive licensee along with compensation for damages (Trademark Act Article 113).

업무표장

영리를 목적으로 하지 아니하는 업무를 하는 자가 그 업무를 나타내기 위하여 사용하는 표장을 말함. 적십자 등(상표법 제2조 제1항 제9호.)

business emblem

A mark used by a person who engages in not-for-profit business to identify his/her business. E.g. "Red Cross" (Trademark Act Article 2(1)9).

업으로 하다

상품을 생산, 가공, 증명, 판매하는 사업을 계속적 반복적으로 행하는 것.

사용례 "지리적 표시 증명표장"이란 지리적 표시를 증명하는 것을 **업으로 하는** 자가 타인의 상품에 대하여 그 상품이 정해진 지리적 특성을 충족한다는 것을 증명하는 데 사용하는 표장을 말한다(상표법 제2조 제1항 제8호).

(to do something) commercially, as business

Conducting business of producing, processing, certifying or selling goods in a continuous and repetitive manner.

The term "certification mark with geographical indication" means a mark used by a person who **commercially** certifies a geographical indication to certify that goods of others meet specified geographical characteristics (Trademark Act Article 2(1)8).

역혼동

선발사용자의 상표는 무명의 존재인데, 후

reverse confusion

Reverse confusion is created where a mark put to use in

발사용자의 상표가 주지 또는 저명해져서 선발사용자의 상표가 오히려 후발사용자의 그것이 아닌가 하는 혼동을 초래하는 경우.

commerce earlier has not gained fame while another mark that entered the market later became well known or famous, causing confusion that the former may belong to the source of the latter.

사용례 설령 피고 표장이 뒤늦게 주지성을 획득하였다고 하더라도, 피고의 행위는 이른바 **역혼동**에 해당하여 위법하다(서울고등법원 2013.08.29 선고 2013나6058 참조).

Even if the defendant's mark became well-known later, the act created **reverse confusion** and was illegal (Seoul High Court Decision, 2013Na6058, decided August 29, 2013).

연결부

transition

특허청구항 중 '…로 구성되는 것을 특징으로 하는', '본질적으로 …로 이루어지는', '…로 포함되는 것을 특징으로 하는'과 같은 용어를 이름.

The transitional phrases such as "comprising", "consisting essentially of" and "consisting of" used in patent claims.

미 연결청구항

linking claim

연결청구항과 그 청구항이 연결하는 발명들은 대개 제품만에 대한 것이거나 방법만에 대한 것(즉 분할 가능한 제품발명을 연결한 제품 청구항 또는 분할가능한 방법발명을 연결한 방법 청구항)이다. (미) MPEP § 809.

Linking claims and the inventions they link together are usually either all directed to products or all directed to processes (i.e., a product claim linking properly divisible product inventions, or a process claim linking properly divisible process inventions). MPEP § 809.

(물품과 서비스의)연관성

relatedness (of the goods or services)

혼동가능성의 결정 요소 중 하나. 물품/서비스가 혼동될 수 있는지가 아닌, 공중이 그 출처를 혼동할 것인지가 기준임.

A factor in finding likelihood of confusion. The test is not whether the goods or services are related; it must be determined whether the public would confuse the source of the goods or services.

사용례 서비스가 명칭에 나타난 상품을 명백히 포함한다면 일반적으로 **연관성**이 있다 할 것이다. 가령 '맥주 제조 및 판매' 서비스와 '맥주'라는 상품 등이 이에 해당한다. TMEP § 1207.01(a)(ii).

Relatedness would generally be recognized when the services clearly include or encompass the goods in the identification, such as when the services are "brew pubs" and the goods are "beer" … TMEP § 1207.01(a)(ii).

연구 또는 시험을 하기 위한 특허발명의 실시

execution of a patented invention for the purpose of research or testing

연구 또는 시험을 하기 위한 특허발명의 실

The effects of a patent shall not extent to the execution

ㅇ

시에 대해서는 특허권의 효력이 미치지 않음(특허법 제96조 제1항).

of a patented invention for the purpose of research or testing (Patent Act Article 96(1)).

영업방법 발명

정보기술을 이용하여 영업방법을 구현하는 발명으로서, 컴퓨터상에서 소프트웨어에 의한 정보처리가 하드웨어를 이용하여 구체적으로 실현되고 있어야 하며, 명세서의 기재만으로는 통상의 기술자가 컴퓨터상에서 소프트웨어에 의한 정보처리가 하드웨어를 이용하여 구체적으로 어떻게 실현되는지 알 수 없다면, 그 발명은 산업상 이용할 수 있는 발명이 아님(대법원 2008. 12. 24. 선고 2007후265 판결 참조).

business method patent

An invention that uses information technology to materialize a business method. The information processing of the software on the computer shall be realized by using the hardware. A person skilled in the art must be able to learn specifically by the description of the specification how the information process of the software on the computer gets realized by using the hardwarc (Suprcmc Court Dccision, 2007Hu265, decided December 24, 2008).

영업비밀

'영업비밀'이란 공공연히 알려져 있지 아니하고 독립된 경제적 가치를 가지는 것으로서, 합리적인 노력에 의하여 비밀로 유지된 생산방법, 판매방법, 그 밖에 영업활동에 유용한 기술상 또는 경영상의 정보를 말한다(부정경쟁방지 및 영업비밀보호에 관한 법률 제2조 제2호).

trade secret

The term "trade secret" means information, including a production method, sale method, useful technical or business information for business activities, that is not known publicly, is the subject of reasonable efforts to maintain its secrecy, and has independent economic value (Unfair Competition Prevention and Trade Secret Protection Act 2(2)).

사용례 정보제출시 경우에 따라 관련 정보의 중요하지 않은 부분을 적절히 삭제하는 등의 방법을 통해 정당한 **영업비밀**이 공개되지 않도록 할 수 있다. (미) MPEP § 724.

In some circumstances, it may be possible to submit the information in such a manner that legitimate **trade secrets**, etc., will not be disclosed, e.g., by appropriate deletions of nonmaterial portions of the information. MPEP § 724.

영업소

사용례 국내에 주소 또는 **영업소**가 없는 자(이하 "재외자"라 한다)는 재외자(법인의 경우에는 그 대표자)가 국내에 체류하는 경우를 제외하고는 그 재외자의 특허에 관한 대리인으로서 국내에 주소 또는 영업소가 있는 자(이하 "특허관리인"이라 한다)에 의해서만 특허에 관한 절차를 밟거나 이 법 또는 이 법에 따른 명령에 따라 행정청이 한 처분에 대하여 소(訴)를 제기할 수 있다(특허법 제5조 제1항).

place of business

No person with no domicile or **place of business** in the Republic of Korea (hereinafter referred to as "overseas resident") shall initiate any patent-related procedure or file legal proceedings against a disposition made by an administrative authority under this Act or an order issued under this Act, unless he/she is represented by an agent with respect to his/her patent, who has a domicile or place of business in the Republic of Korea (hereinafter referred to as "patent administrator"), except where the overseas resident (or the representative if the overseas resident is a corporation) sojourns in the Republic of Korea (Patent Act Article 5(1)).

예견하다

하나의 선행문헌이 청구항의 모든 구성요소를 포함하고 있는 경우 선행문헌으로부터 청구항 발명이 예측되며, 이러한 청구항 발명은 신규성 결여로 거절됨.

anticipate

A single prior art reference anticipates a claim when it contains all the elements of the claim. Such a claim is rejected for lack of novelty.

미 예비보정

최초거절사유통지의 발송일 혹은 그 이전에 특허상표청에 도달한 보정. (미) 37 C.F.R. § 1.115(a).

preliminary amendment

an amendment that is received in the Office on or before the mail date of the first Office action under § 1.104. 37 C.F.R. § 1.115(a).

예측가능성

통상의 기술자가 출원발명의 공개 또는 공지된 결과를 추정할 가능성. 통상의 기술자가 선행기술로부터 출원발명의 대상의 변화로 인한 효과를 쉽게 예견할 수 있다면 예측가능성이 있다고 본다.

predictability

The ability of one skilled in the art to extrapolate the disclosed or known results to the claimed invention. If one skilled in the art can readily anticipate the effect of a change within the subject matter to which the claimed invention pertains, then there is predictability in the art.

오감상표

오감에 호소하는 색채나, 입체적인 형상, 냄새, 동작, 소리, 트레이드드레스 등으로 구성된 상표.

sensory mark

A mark that appeals to one or more of the five senses of human, consisting of color, three-dimensional shape, smell, sound, motion or trade dress.

오기정정

출원발명 또는 특허발명의 명세서, 도면의 오류나 불분명한 기재를 정정하는 것.

rectification of clerical errors

To correct ambiguity or errors in the specification and drawings of a patent or an application.

사용례 구 특허법 제133조의2, 제136조 제3항의 규정 취지는 무효심판의 피청구인이 된 특허권자에게 별도의 정정심판을 청구하지 않더라도 무효심판절차 내에서 정정청구를 할 수 있게 해주되, 청구범위를 실질적으로 확장하거나 변경하는 것은 허용하지 아니하고, 제3자의 권리를 침해할 우려가 없는 범위 내에서의 청구범위의 감축이나 **오기를 정정**하고 기재상의 불비를 해소하여 바르게 하는 오류의 정정은 허용하는 데 있다(대법원 2016. 11. 25. 선고 2014후2184 판결 참조).

The purport of Articles 133-2 and 136(3) of the former Patent Act (amended by Act No. 9381, Jan. 30, 2009) is to: enable the patent-holder as the respondent in a patent invalidation trial to petition for correction in the invalidation trial procedure without having to file for a separate trial for correction; prohibit any substantial extension of, or amendment to, the claims; but allow for a reduction in the number of claims, **rectification of clerical errors**, and clarification of ambiguous indications, to the extent they are not likely to infringe on third party rights (Supreme Court Decision, decided November 25, 2016).

(발명의) 완성

발명은 착상으로 시작되어 구현으로 완성된다. 발명의 구현은 발명의 물리적 형상을 만들어 내는 것과 같이 실제적일 수도 있으며, 개시요건을 만족시키는 특허출원을 제기함으로써 의제적으로 할 수도 있음.

reduction to practice

Starting with conception, an invention is complete when it is reduced to practice. Reduction to practice may be actual such as constructing a physical embodiment of the invention, or constructive by filing a patent application that satisfies the disclosure requirements.

외관

물품이나 표장의 외부적 형태로서, 시각을 통해 감지되는 외부적 형상 등을 의미.

appearance

Visibly recognizable outer configuration of a product or a mark.

외관유사

대비되는 두 개의 상표에 표시된 문자 · 도형 · 기호 · 입체적 형상 · 색채 등 상표의 외관상의 형상을 시각에 호소하여 관찰하였을 경우 그들이 상품의 식별표지로서 서로 혼동되기 쉬운 것을 말함.

similarity in appearance

Two marks are similar in appearance when visible comparison of their appearance, such as the word, figure, symbol, dimensional shape and color, indicate that they are likely to create confusion when used as identifiers of goods.

사용례 이 사건 등록상표는 닻줄을 휘감은 검은색의 닻 모양의 도형만으로 구성되어 있는 반면 이 사건 견장은 오각형 도형의 중앙 바로 윗 부분에 닻줄이 없는 닻 모양의 도형과 오각형 도형의 아랫 부분에 학년을 표시하는 띠 형상의 선 등을 포함하고 있는 차이가 있어서, 전체적으로 관찰하여 볼 때 이 사건 등록상표와 이 사건 견장은 그 **외관이 유사**하지 아니하다(대법원 2010. 7. 29. 선고 2008후4721 판결).

The registered trademark here consists only of a diagram in the shape of a black anchor and cable twined around it, while the shoulder emblem incorporates an anchor-shaped diagram positioned directly above the center of a pentagon, with lines on the bottom representing the grade of a cadet. On the whole, the registered trademark and the shoulder emblem are not **similar in appearance** (Supreme Court Decision, 2008Hu4721, decided July 29, 2010).

미 외국어 등가의 원칙

외국어(미국 소비자의 상당수에게 익숙한 언어) 단어와 등가의 영단어는 서로 혼동을 야기할 만큼 유사하다 할 수 있다고 보는 원칙. (미) TMEP § 1207.01(b)(vi).

doctrine of foreign equivalents

A doctrine that a foreign word (from a language familiar to an appreciable segment of American consumers) and the English equivalent may be held to be confusingly similar. TMEP § 1207.01(b)(vi).

사용례 심사관이 **외국어 등가의 원칙**을 적용해야 하는지는 그 외국어 표장이 관련 수요자에 갖는 의의에 따라, 가령 사전, 인터넷, LexisNexis® 증거 등을 포함한 기록상 증거를 분석하여 결정한다. 만일 증거에 관련 영문번역이 문자 그대로의 직역으로

Whether an examining attorney should apply the **doctrine of foreign equivalents** turns upon the significance of the foreign mark to the relevant purchasers, which is based on an analysis of the evidence of record, including, for example, dictionary, Internet, and LexisNexis® evidence. If the evidence shows that the relevant English translation

나타나며 다른 반대되는 의미나 관련된 의미가 존재한다는 증거가 없다면 일반적으로 외국어 등가의 원칙을 적용해야 한다고 할 수 있다. (미) TMEP § 1207.01(b)(vi) (A).

is literal and direct, and no contradictory evidence of shades of meaning or other relevant meanings exists, the doctrine generally should be applied by the examining attorney. TMEP § 1207.01(b)(vi)(A).

미 외적 증거

마크맨 심리에 사용되는 내적 증거가 아닌 전문가 증언, 학술논문, 특허권자의 증언, 출원에 인용되지 않은 선행기술 등의 증거.

extrinsic evidence

Evidence used in a Markman hearing, other than intrinsic evidence, such as expert witness testimony, scholarly articles, testimony of the patentee, prior arts not referenced in the application.

요부

산업재산권 등에서 수요자의 주의를 끌어 자타권리를 구별하는 부분.

essential part/portion

The part of an industrial property that particularly attracts consumer attention. The portion that distinguishes one's rights from others'.

사용례 이 경우 디자인을 보는 사람의 주의를 가장 끌기 쉬운 부분을 **요부**로서 파악하고 이것을 관찰하여 심미감에 차이가 생기게 하는지 여부의 관점에서 그 유사 여부를 결정하여야 하며 … (특허법원 2015. 4. 23. 선고 2014허6858 판결 참조).

The most discernible features of the designs that attract the ordinary observer's attention is to be perceived as the **essential parts**, and the question of similarity depends on whether the comparison of those features provide any aesthetic differences (Patent Court Decision, 2014Heo6858, decided April 23, 2015).

요부관찰

산업재산권 등의 동일유사 여부를 판단 시 일반 수요자의 관점에서 차이가 생기게 하는지 여부의 관점에서 그 유사 여부를 결정하는 방법. 전체관찰에 대한 보완적 방법.

comparison of/by essential parts/portions

It is a method of determining the similarity of Patent or other IP rights by whether they create different sense to ordinary consumers. Used as a supplement to the method of observation in entirety.

사용례 양 디자인에 있어서 가장 주의를 끌기 쉬운 **요부**는 신발 앞부분의 토끼의 특징적인 얼굴 모습인 눈, 코, 입 및 긴 수염과 길다란 귀의 모습에 있다 할 것인바 양 디자인의 지배적인 특징이 서로 유사하여 일반수요자가 느끼는 심미감에 차이가 없다 할 것이고, … (대법원 1996. 1. 26. 선고 95후1135 판결 참조).

The **essential part** that drags most attention in both designs is the eyes, nose, mouth, long beard and long ears on the front of the shoes, which are characteristics of a rabbit. Therefore, the dominant features of both designs are similar and create little difference in aesthetic sense in ordinary purchasers' mind (Supreme Court Decision, 95Hu1135, decided January 26, 1996).

요약서

특허 등의 명세서에서 공개된 기술 등에 대

abstract

A concise statement of the technical disclosure in the

한 요약 기재. 특허출원서에는 요약서를 첨부하여야 한다(특허법 제 42조 제2항).

specification. A patent application filed shall be accompanied by an abstract (Patent Act Article 42(2))

사용례 **요약서**는 기술정보로서의 용도로 사용하여야 하며, 특허발명의 보호범위를 정하는 데에는 사용할 수 없다(특허법 제43조).

An **abstract** shall be used only for technical information, and shall not define the scope of the invention for which protection is sought (Patent Act Article 43).

요지

substance, gist (법제처)

최초 출원서에 기재되어 있는 실질적 내용

The substantive content made in the initial application.

사용례 디자인등록출원인은 최초의 디자인등록출원의 **요지**를 변경하지 아니하는 범위에서 디자인등록출원서의 기재사항, 디자인등록출원서에 첨부한 도면, 도면의 기재사항이나 사진 또는 견본을 보정할 수 있다(디자인보호법 제48조 제1항).

An applicant for design registration may amend any statement made in the application, drawing attached to the application, statement in the drawing, picture or specimen, to the extent that the **gist** of the initial application remains unchanged (Design Protection Act Article 48(1)).

요지의 변경

material alteration

사용례 일반적으로 추가 검색이 필요한 구성요소의 부가는 **요지의 변경**에 해당한다. 그러나 새로운 검색이 필요한지가 중대한 변경의 존부 결정에 고려해야 할 요소이기는 하나 반드시 결정적 요소인 것은 아니다. (미) TMEP § 807.14.

As a general rule, the addition of any element that would require a further search will constitute a **material alteration**. However, while the question of whether a new search would be required is a factor to be considered in deciding whether an amendment would materially alter a mark, it is not necessarily the determining factor. TMEP § 807.14.

용도발명

use invention

미지의 속성의 발견에 기초하여 어떠한 효능을 발휘하는 새로운 용도를 제공하는 발명을 의미함.

An invention offering invention offering a new use based on the discovery of an unknown feature of a specific effect.

사용례 의약용도발명이란 의약물질이 가지는 특정의 약리효과라는 미지의 속성의 발견에 기초하여 의약으로서의 효능을 발휘하는 새로운 용도를 제공하는 발명을 의미한다. 그런데 의약물질은 다양한 속성을 가지고 있으므로, 의약물질 자체가 알려져 있더라도 그 구체적인 약리효과는 다각도의 시험을 거쳐야 비로소 밝혀지는 경우가 많고, 약리효과에 기초한 새로운 용도를 개발하기 위하여는 오랜 기간의 임상시험

Invention of pharmaceutical use means an invention offering a new use in which the pharmaceutical substance demonstrates efficacy as a medicine based on the discovery of an unknown feature of a specific pharmacological effect. Meanwhile, as a pharmaceutical substance has diverse features, even when the pharmaceutical substance itself is known, in many instances its concrete pharmacological effect is only revealed by undergoing a multi-faceted experiment. Also, developing a new use based on pharmacological effect demands cost and effort over a prolonged period of clinical

에 따른 비용과 노력이 소요되는 점에서, 이와 같은 용도의 개발을 특허로써 보호하여 장려할 필요가 있다(대법원 2015. 5. 21. 선고 2014후768 전원합의체판결 참조).

trials. In this regard, it is necessary to protect and encourage such development of use by means of patent (Supreme Court Decision, 2014Hu768, decided May 21, 2015).

용이하게 창작할 수 있는 디자인

easy-to-create design, design that may be easily created

그 디자인이 속하는 분야에서 통상의 지식을 가진 자가 용이하게 창작할 수 있는 디자인.

A design that may be easily created by a person who has ordinary skills in the art to which the design pertains.

사용례 전체적으로 볼 때 다른 미감적 가치가 인정되지 않는 상업적 · 기능적 변형에 불과하거나, 또는 그 디자인 분야에서 흔한 창작수법이나 표현방법에 의해 이를 변경 · 조합하거나 전용하였음에 불과한 디자인 등과 같이 창작수준이 낮은 디자인은 그 디자인이 속하는 분야에서 통상의 지식을 가진 자가 **용이하게 창작할 수 있는** 것이어서 디자인등록을 받을 수 없다(대법원 2010. 5. 13. 선고 2008후2800 판결 참조).

If they are mere commercial and functional modifications without any other aesthetic value seen as a whole, … , or designs of a low creative level like designs, etc. which are modified, combined or used pursuant to creative or expressive methods frequently used in such design area, design registration will not be granted since a person with ordinary skill in the art to which the design pertains could **easily create** them (Supreme Court Decision, 2008Hu2800, decided May 13, 2010).

우선권 주장[1]

claim of priority, priority claim

조약에 따라 국제출원의 출원일을 그 우선권 주장이 인정되는 최초 제1국에서의 출원시로 보도록 하는 것.

To make the filing date of application of international registration as the filing date in the first country that a valid priority claim is recognized.

사용례 조약에 따라 대한민국 국민에게 상표등록출원에 대한 우선권을 인정하는 당사국의 국민이 그 당사국 또는 다른 당사국에 상표등록출원을 한 후 같은 상표를 대한민국에 상표등록출원 하여 **우선권을 주장**하는 경우에는 제35조를 적용할 때 그 당사국에 출원한 날을 대한민국에 상표등록 출원한 날로 본다(상표법 제46조 제1항).

Where a citizen of a State party which recognizes the priority of an application for trademark registration filed by a citizen of the Republic of Korea in accordance with the treaty **claims priority** by filing an application for registration of the same trademark with the Republic of Korea after he/she has filed an application for trademark registration with the State party or other State parties, the date the application for trademark registration is filed with the State party shall be deemed the date the application for trademark registration is filed with the Republic of Korea when Article 35 is applied (Trademark Act Article 46(1)).

미 우선권 주장[2]

benefit claim

미 특허법 119(e), 120, 365(c)조에 따라 미국 내 가출원 등 선출원에 기한 출원인의

The claiming by an applicant of benefit from an earlier filed application under 35 U.S.C. §§ 119(e), 120 and 365(c)

ㅇ

우선권 주장.

such as a U.S. provisional application.

사용례 개정특허법 102(d)조는 **우선권 주장**이 근거한 선출원에 등록거절결정에서 근거로 삼은 미국 특허문헌 상의 대상이 묘사되었을 것을 요한다. (미) MPEP § 2154.01(b).

AIA Patent Act, 35 U.S.C. § 102(d) requires that a prior-filed application to which a priority or **benefit claim** is made must describe the subject matter from the U.S. patent document relied upon in a rejection. MPEP § 2154.01(b).

우선심사

accelerated examination, preferential examination

사용례 특허청장은 특정한 경우 등록출원에 대하여는 심사관에게 다른 등록출원에 **우선하여 심사**하게 할 수 있다.

The Commissioner of the Korean Intellectual Property Office may order an examiner to **preferentially examine** an application first among other applications

미 우선심사신청 출원

special applications

특정 요건을 만족하여 우선심사의 대상이 된 출원. 에너지원 개발에 중대한 기여를 할 발명이거나 잘못 취소되거나 만료된 상표등록의 대상인 경우 등이 있음.

Applications that receive expedited examination when certain requirements are met, e.g. the invention will materially contribute to the development of energy resources; or the trademark registration was inadvertently cancelled or expired.

원산지

place of origin

사용례 "증명표장"이란 상품의 품질, **원산지**, 생산방법 또는 그 밖의 특성을 증명하고 관리하는 것을 업(業)으로 하는 자가 타인의 상품에 대하여 그 상품이 품질, **원산지**, 생산방법 또는 그 밖의 특성을 충족한다는 것을 증명하는 데 사용하는 표장을 말한다(상표법 제2조 제1항 제7호).

The term "certification mark" means a mark used by a person who commercially certifies and manages the quality, **place of origin**, methods of production, or other characteristics of goods to certify that goods of others meet quality criteria, the **place of origin**, methods of production, or other characteristics; … (Trademark Act Article 2(1)7).

원산지 명칭

appellations of origin

원특허권자

original patent owner, original right holder

사용례 상표등록출원일 전 또는 상표등록출원일과 동일한 날에 출원되어 등록된 특허권이 그 상표권과 저촉되는 경우 그 특허권의 존속기간이 만료되는 때에는 그 **원특허권자**는 원특허권의 범위에서 그 등록상표의 지정상품과 동일 · 유사한 상품에 대하여 그 등록상표와 동일 · 유사한 상표

Where patent rights registered after filing an application for the patent before the filing date of a trademark application or on the same date as the filing of a trademark application is in conflict with such trademark right, and the duration of the patent rights expires, the **original patent right holder** shall have the right to use a trademark identical or similar to such registered trademark on goods identical or similar

를 사용할 권리를 가진다(상표법 제98조 제1항).

to designated goods of the registered trademark to the extent of the original patent rights (Trademark Act Article 98).

위조

사용례 타인의 등록상표와 동일 · 유사한 상표를 그 지정상품과 동일 · 유사한 상품에 사용하거나 사용하게 할 목적으로 교부 · 판매 · **위조** · 모조 또는 소지하는 행위는 상표권(지리적 표시 단체표장권은 제외한다) 또는 전용사용권을 침해한 것으로 본다(상표법 제108조 제1항 제2호).

counterfeit, forgery (법제처)

Delivering, selling, **forging**, imitating, or possessing a trademark identical or similar to a registered trademark of another person for the purpose of using or causing a third party to use such trademark on goods identical or similar to the designated goods; ··· (Trademark Act Article 108(1)2).

위조상표

counterfeit trademark

위치상표

기호 · 문자 · 도형 각각 또는 그 결합이 일정한 형상이나 모양을 이루고, 이러한 일정한 형상이나 모양이 지정상품의 특정 위치에 부착되는 것에 의하여 자타상품을 식별하게 되는 표장.

positional mark

A mark which is a consistent image or shape formed by an individual sign, letter, figure, or the combination thereof and distinguishes the designated good from other products by being attached to a certain location of the product, location of the product.

사용례 **위치상표**에서는 지정상품에 일정한 형상이나 모양 등이 부착되는 특정 위치를 설명하기 위하여 지정상품의 형상을 표시하는 부분을 필요로 하게 된다(대법원 2012. 12. 20. 선고 2010후2339 전원합의체 판결 참조).

A **position mark** requires space for labeling in order to explain where an image or shape is specifically located on the designated product (Supreme Court Decision, 2010Hu2339, decided December 20, 2012).

미 유도 침해

특허의 직접침해를 적극적으로 유도하는 행위. 특허권의 직접침해를 유도하려는 고의와 제3자에 의한 특허권의 직접침해를 요함.

infringement by inducement

Active inducement of direct infringement. Infringement by inducement requires an intent to induce direct infringement of a patent a third party's direct infringement of the patent.

유럽특허협약 (EPC)

유럽특허협약이란, 유럽특허청을 설립하여 유럽에서 특허를 심사하기 위한 시스템과 기본법을 만들기 위한 국제 협약을 말함.

European Patent Convention

The European Patent Convention is the international agreement establishing the European Patent Organisation, whose main branch is the European Patent Office, as well as the system and underlying law for granting and examination of European Patents.

ㅇ

유사상표

등록상표와 동일한 것은 아니나 외관, 호칭, 관념의 면에서 유사하여 이를 동일, 유사 상품에 사용할 경우 거래통념상 상품 출처의 혼동을 일으킬 염려가 있는 상표.

similar mark

A mark that is not identical with but similar to the registered trademark in appearance, sound and concept, and therefore likely to cause confusion of source of goods under trade norms.

사용례 또한, 저명상표의 경우 상표 자체로서는 **유사상표**라고 할 수 없는 상표라도 양 상표의 구성이나 관념 등을 비교하여 그 상표에서 타인의 저명상표 또는 상품 등이 용이하게 연상되거나 타인의 상표 또는 상품 등과 밀접한 관련성이 있는 것으로 인정되어 상품의 출처에 오인·혼동을 일으키는 경우에는 등록될 수 없다(특허법원 2009. 12. 11. 선고 2009허6311 판결 참조).

If a trademark, when compared in composition and conception, is easily associated with others' well-known trademark or goods, or recognized as having close relation with others' trademark or goods, which can cause misconception and confusion about the origin of goods, the registration cannot be granted, even though those trademarks are not similar (Patent Court Decision, 2009Heo6311, decided December 11, 2009).

유사상품

용도, 수요자, 거래형태 등이 중첩되는 상품.

similar goods

Goods with overlapping usage, consumers and course of dealing.

사용례 양 상품의 품질, 형상, 용도가 전혀 다르고, 그 생산 부문, 판매 부문, 수요자의 범위 역시 중첩된다고 보기 어려우므로, **양 상품은 거래통념상 유사하지 않다**고 할 것이다(특허법원 2009. 12. 11. 선고 2009허6311 판결 참조).

Since the two goods have significantly different quality, shape and use and their range of production, sales or consumer pool seldom overlap, **the two goods are not similar** under trade norms (Patent Court Decision, 2009Heo6311, decided December 11, 2009).

유사의 폭

상표 또는 디자인의 유사성 판단에 있어 적용되는 상표 또는 디자인의 유사 범위. 구체적인 거래실정에 따라 좁아질 수도, 넓어질 수도 있음.

range of similarity

The scope of similarity applied in determining the similarity of trademarks or designs. It may be broad or narrow depending on the particular course of trade.

사용례 등록디자인에 의하여 비로소 창작되거나 채택된 모티브인 경우 모티브의 동일성만으로도 동일한 심미감을 형성할 것이므로 양 디자인의 **유사의 폭**은 넓게 보아야 할 것인바, … (특허법원 2008. 9. 11. 선고 2007허8559 판결 참조).

In case of a motif created or adopted for the first time by the registered design, use of the same motive would create the identical aesthetic feel. Therefore, the **range of similarity** of both designs should be viewed as broad (Patent Court Decision, 2007Heo8559, decided September 11, 2008).

미 **유사표장**

대안적 또는 의도적으로 바꾼 스펠링으로 된 문자표장을 검색하기 위해 사용. 유사표장검색으로 해당 문자표장과 매우 유사하거나 발음상 동등한 스펠링을 찾을 수 있음. (미) USPTO.

pseudo mark

A way of locating a word mark that is comprised of an alternative or intentionally corrupted spelling of an English word. The pseudo mark search locates spellings that are very similar or phonetically equivalent to the word mark. USPTO.

유사필수적 공동소송

특정 당사자들이 반드시 공동으로 소송을 수행할 필요는 없으나 합일확정이 요청되어 승패를 일률적으로 하여야 할 공동소송 형태.

quasi-compulsory joint litigation

A form of joint litigation by certain parties who are not necessarily required to jointly pursue the litigation in the first place but requested joinder and who shall now be subject to a uniform disposition.

사용례 원고의 이 사건 당사자참가신청을 통한 등록무효 심판청구가 새로운 심판청구로서의 실질을 갖고 있고 그에 따라 ooo의 이 사건 심판청구와 유사필수적 공동심판관계에 놓이게 된다 하더라도, 그 신청서를 각하한 이 사건 결정이 이미 확정되어 그 위법성을 더 이상 다툴 수 없는 이상, 이 사건 심결취소소송에서도 이를 다툴 수 없는 것은 마찬가지이다(특허법원 2016. 06. 10. 선고 2015허8424판결 참조).

Even if the plaintiff's claim to invalidate the registration through intervention has substantive merits as a claim for a new trial and therefore is a **quasi-compulsory joint litigation** to that of ooo's petition, the decision to dismiss the petition is already confirmed and its lawfulness can no longer be disputed. As such, it may not be an issue in the present proceeding to revoke the administrative decision (Patent Court Decision, 2015Heo8424, decided June 10, 2016).

유사한 (기술)분야

진보성 판단에서 통상의 기술자가 발명의 기술적 과제를 해결하기 위해 참고할 수 있는 기술. 유사 기술은 발명과 동일한 기술분야에 속하거나 다른 기술분야이더라도 해당 과제에 합리적으로 관련이 있어야 함.

analogous art, relevant art

In a non-obviousness analysis, an analogous art refers to the art that a person having ordinary skill in the art would have referred to in attempting to solve the problem addressed by the innovation. It must be either within the same field of endeavor as the invention, or from a different filed but reasonably pertinent to the same problem.

사용례 1차적인 인용문헌에 대한 변형으로 인하여 형태상의 변화가 초래된다면, 1차적 및 이차적 인용문헌 모두 **유사한 분야**에 관한 것이어야 한다. (미) MPEP § 1504.03.

When a modification to a primary reference involves a change in configuration, both the primary and secondary references must be from **analogous arts**. MPEP § 1504.03.

미 **유예기간**

구 특허법 하에서는 1년의 신규성 의제기간이 허락되어 출원 전 1년의 기간 동안 발

grace period

Before the AIA, a one-year grace period before filing is allowed to an inventor during which the inventor can disclose

ㅇ

명을 공지하거나 이용하여도 신규성을 상실하지 아니하였음. 개정 특허법 하에서는 이러한 기간은 진정한 발명자의 공개에만 적용되며 타인의 공개가 있었을 시 신규성이 상실됨. 단 타인의 공개 이전에 진정한 발명자의 공개가 선행되었을 때는 예외로 함.

or use the invention without losing its novelty. Under the revised statute, the period is only given to disclosures by the actual inventor but not others, unless disclosure by others is subsequent to disclosure of the actual inventor.

유효출원일

경우에 따라, 특허 또는 특허출원의 실제 출원일 또는 우선권을 주장할 수 있는 최초 출원일.

effective filing date

The actual filing date of the patent or the application for the patent, or the filing date of the earliest application for which the patent or application is entitled to a right of priority, as applicable.

육성자

"육성자"란 품종을 육성한 자나 이를 발견하여 개발한 자를 말한다(식물신품종보호법 제2조 제3호).

breeder

The term "breeder" means a person who either breeds, or discovers and develops a plant variety (Act on Protection of New Varieties of Plants Article 2.3).

… 으로 구성되는 것을 특징으로 하는

특허청구항의 연결부 중 하나. 폐쇄형, 청구항에 기재된 구성요소로만 이루어진 발명을 보호범위로 함.

consisting of

A transitional phrase in patent claims. It provides a closed-ended claim that only includes the components described in the claims.

… 을 포함하는 것을 특징으로 하는

특허청구항의 연결부 중 하나. 개방형, 해당 청구항의 구성요소 이외에 다른 구성요소도 포함될 수 있는 것으로 해석.

comprising, including

A transitional phrase in patent claims. The open-ended language leaves room to include elements not described in the claims.

음역

외국어의 음을 대응되는 알파벳 또는 언어로 변경하여 표시하는 것.

transliteration

To change foreign letters into corresponding characters of another language based on pronunciation.

사용례 마찬가지로, 비라틴문자를 포함하는 상표의 출원은 반드시 그 문자의 **음역**과 함께 영어 번역문이나 상표의 해당 부분은 영어로 아무 의미를 갖지 않음을 진술하는 내용을 포함하여야 한다. (미) 37 C.F.R. §2.32(a)(10).

Similarly, an application for a mark that comprises non-Latin characters must include a **transliteration** of those characters, and either an English translation or a statement that this portion of the mark has no meaning in English. 37 C.F.R. §2.32(a)(10).

의견서

written argument

의견제출기회의 부여

사용례 심사관은 특허거절결정을 하려는 경우 특허출원인에게 거절이유를 통지하고, 기간을 정하여 **의견서를 제출할 수 있는 기회**를 주어야 한다(특허법 제63조 제1항).

opportunity to submit arguments

When an examiner intends to determine to reject a patent application. he/she shall notify the applicant of the grounds for rejection and provide the applicant with an **opportunity to submit written arguments** within a specified period(Patent Act Article 63(1)).

의료행위

사용례 한편, 사람의 질병을 진단 · 경감 · 치료 · 처치하고 예방하거나 건강을 증진하는 등의 **의료행위**에 관한 발명은 특허의 대상에서 제외되므로 … (대법원 1991. 3. 12. 선고 90후250 판결 참조).

medical practice

Meanwhile, inventions concerning **medical practices**, such as diagnosis, alleviation, therapy, and treatment of human disease, are excluded from patentability … (Supreme Court Decision, 90Hu250, decided March 12, 1991).

의사에 반한 공지

특허출원 전에 발명이 공개된 경우 원칙적으로 신규성 요건이 부정되어 특허를 받을 수 없으나, 특허법은 출원전 공개가 의사에 반한 공지인 경우 일정한 요건 하에 신규성이 부정되지 않도록 예외를 두고 있음.

publication contrary to the will of the person entitled to a patent

In order to be patentable, an invention shall not be publicly known prior to the filing of a patent application. However, when the invention became publicly known against the will of the person entitled to the patent, the inventions may not be deemed as publicly known under certain circumstances.

의식적 제외

특허발명의 청구범위에서 의식적으로 제외된 부분은 이후 균등론을 바탕으로 특허의 권리범위에 속함을 주장할 수 없음. 대상제품이 특허발명의 출원, 등록과정 등에서 특허발명의 청구범위로부터 의식적으로 제외된 것에 해당하는지 여부는 명세서뿐만 아니라 출원에서부터 특허될 때까지 특허청 심사관이 제시한 견해 및 특허출원인이 제출한 보정서와 의견서 등에 나타난 특허출원인의 의도 등을 참작하여 판단하여야 함(대법원 2006. 6. 30. 선고 2004다51771 판결 참조).

deliberately excluded, intentionally excluded

A patentee is barred from arguing the portion intentionally excluded from the claims as falling within the scope of the patent rights based on the doctrine of equivalents. When determining whether or not the subject product was deliberately excluded from the patented invention's claim during the patented invention's application process, not only the specification of the invention but also the opinions of the examiners and the intent of the applicant reflected in his/her amendment and opinion documents shall be considered (Supreme Court Decision, 2004Da51771, June 30, 2006).

의약용도

medical usage

의약의 조제

"조제"란 일정한 처방에 따라서 두 가지 이상의 의약품을 배합하거나 한 가지 의약품을 그대로 일정한 분량으로 나누어서 특정한 용법에 따라 특정인의 특정된 질병을 치료하거나 예방하는 등의 목적으로 사용하도록 약제를 만드는 것을 말한다 (약사법 제2조 제11호).

dispensing of drugs

The term "dispensing of drug" means dispensing drugs for the purposes of treatment, prevention, etc. of a certain disease for a specific individual in accordance with the specific directions by mixing at least two drugs or by dividing one kind of drug into certain dosages according to a specific prescription (Pharmaceutical Affairs Act Article 2.11).

이격적 관찰

2개의 상표들을 각각 때와 장소를 달리하여 접하는 경우 상표를 접하는 자가 상표를 착각하는지의 여부를 관찰하여 그 유사여부를 판단하는 방법.

comparison by recollection, arm's length observation (법제처)

A method of determining similarity of marks by looking at whether an observer who sees the two marks in different time and place would confuse one mark with another.

사용례 두 개의 상표를 놓고 그 외관, 호칭, 관념 등을 객관적, 전체적, **이격적으로 관찰**하여 거래상 일반 수요자나 거래자가 상표에 대하여 느끼는 직관적 인식을 기준으로 하여 … (특허법원 2009. 6. 4. 선고 2009허450 판결 참조).

On the basis of what general consumers or traders in the course of trade intuitively recognize with respect to the trademark, after an objective, comprehensive and **arm's length observation** of the two trademarks' appearances, sounds and meanings, etc. (Patent Court Decision, 2009Heo450, decided June 4, 2009).

이 사건 발명

subject invention, invention at issue

미 이송명령

writ of certiorari

이송신청

사건을 다른 재판지로 이송하기 위한 신청.

motion for transfer

A motion to transfer the case to another district.

이용관계

이용관계는 후 발명이 선 특허발명의 기술적 구성에 새로운 기술적 요소를 부가하는 것으로서 후 발명이 선 특허발명의 요지를 전부 포함하고 이를 그대로 이용하되, 후 발명 내에 선 특허발명이 발명으로서의 일체성을 유지하는 경우에 성립하는 것이며, 이는 선 특허발명과 동일한 발명뿐만 아니라 균등한 발명을 이용하는 경우도 마찬가지이다(대법원 2001. 8. 21. 선고 98후522 판결). 이용관계에 있는 경우에는 후 발명

improvement relationship, use relationship (법제처)

The subsequent invention in the improvement relationship adds a new technological element to the technical composition of the previous invention, contains all the main substance of the previous invention and applies them as they are. The patented invention as incorporated in the subsequent invention must maintain its consistency as an invention. The relationship is formed not only when the subsequent invention uses an invention identical to the patented invention but also an equivalent one (Supreme Court Decision, 98Hu522,

은 선 특허발명의 권리범위에 속하게 된다.

decided August. 21, 2001). The subsequent invention falls within the scope of the previous patented invention.

이용발명

이용 대상이 되는 특허발명의 구성요소를 모두 그대로 가지고 있으면서 여기에 새로운 구성요소를 부가하여 특허성을 취득한 경우를 말한다. 특허법 제98조는 특허권자가 선출원 특허발명을 이용하여 특허받은 경우에는 선출원 특허권자의 동의를 얻지 아니하고는 자기의 특허발명을 업으로서 실시할 수 없다고 규정함으로써 이용발명에 대하여 규정하고 있으므로, 이용발명의 실시는 이용대상이 되는 특허발명의 침해가 됨.

improvement invention, use invention

An invention that includes all the components of the patented invention that is being used but adds new components to obtain patentabiltiy. Since Patent Act Article 98 provides that a patent holder who earned his/her patent right by using an earlier-applied patent invention may not execute his/her patent without the permission of the owner of the earlier-applied patent, executing use invention may constitute infringement of the patent used by the use invention.

(판결) 이유

reason, ground

이유 없다

without merit

사용례 원고의 청구는 이유 있으므로 이를 인용한다.

원고의 청구는 **이유 없으므로** 이를 기각한다.

The Plaintiff's petition is well grounded and therefore shall be granted.

The Plaintiff's petition is **without merit** and therefore dismissed.

이의신청

opposition, formal objection (법제처)

등록거절이유 등이 있는 경우 누구든지 출원공고일부터 2개월 내에 특허청장에게 이의신청을 할 수 있다.

Any person can file for opposition to the Commissioner of KIPO within two months of the publication of an application if there is a reason to believe that registration should be denied.

이의신청의 경합

competition in opposition, competition in formal objections (법제처)

이의신청의 병합

consolidation of oppositions, consolidation of formal objections (법제처)

동일한 건에 대한 이의신청사건을 일괄처리하기 위하여 하나로 하여 합치는 것.

Consolidation of different oppositions regarding the same application to process them together.

ㅇ

사용례 심사관합의체는 둘 이상의 이의신청을 **병합**하거나 분리하여 심사 · 결정할 수 있다(상표법 제64조).

A panel of examiners may examine or decide on at least two formal objections by consolidating or dividing them (Trademark Act Article 64).

이전(移轉)

transfer

특허권은 이전할 수 있다(특허법 제99조 제1항).

A patent is transferable (Patent Act Article 99(1)).

미 2차 심사

second examination

사용진술서의 심사. 재심사와 구부하여야 함. (미) TMEP § 1109.07.

Examination of the statement of use. To be distinguished with reconsideration. TMEP § 1109.07.

사용례 최초심사 이후 상당한 시간이 지났을 경우 그 표장은 지정상품 또는 서비스와 관련하여 기술적 표장 또는 보통명칭이 되었을 수도 있다. 이 경우 최초심사에서는 기술적 표장 또는 보통명칭으로서의 사용에 대한 증거를 제출할 수 없었으므로 **2차 심사**에서 요청을 하거나 또는 거절결정을 하여야 한다. (미) TMEP § 1102.01.

Where a significant length of time has elapsed since the initial examination, a mark may have become descriptive or even generic with respect to the goods/services. In such a case, since the evidence of the descriptive or generic use would not have been available during initial examination, the requirement or refusal must be issued during **second examination**. TMEP § 1102.01.

2차적 고려요소

secondary considerations

비자명성에 대한 객관적인 증거. 2차적 고려에 대한 예로는, 상업적 성공, 전문가 증언, 및 타인에 의한 디자인의 복제가 있음.

Objective evidence regarding inventive step, such as commercial success, expert testimony, copying of the design by others, etc.

사용례 상업적 성공 및 타인에 의한 디자인의 복제와 같은 **2차적 고려요소**도 디자인 청구범위의 자명성의 평가에 관련될 수 있다. 비자명성의 증거는 자명성에 관한 일응의 증명이 평가될 때에 제출될 수 있으며, 이전의 자명성 거절에 대한 반박에서 제출될 수 있다. (미) MPEP § 1504.03.I.D.

Secondary considerations, such as commercial success and copying of the design by others, are relevant to the evaluation of obviousness of a design claim. Evidence of nonobviousness may be present at the time a prima facie case of obviousness is evaluated or it may be presented in rebuttal of a prior obviousness rejection. MPEP § 1504.03.I.D.

2차적 의미

secondary meaning

상표로 선택된 단어가 특정 상품에 장기간 사용됨으로써 특정 상품의 출처를 나타내는 것으로 일반인에게 알려지게 되는 것.

Secondary meaning is created when the word used as a trademark are used on a particular good for a long period of time so as to the public would associate the word as indicating the source of the good.

사용례 어디에서도 상표가 모든 분류에 2차적 의미 없이 '출원인의 지정상품이 타인의 상품과 식별되는' 상표를 반드시 포함하여야 한다, 즉 모든 분류에 본질적인 식별력을 지닌 상표를 포함하여야 한다고 요하고 있지 아니하다. … Qualitex 판례에서 … 본 법원은 색채를 상표로 보호가능하다고 판시하였으나, 단 **2차적 의미**를 입증하였을 때에만 그러하다고 하였다. (미) Wal-Mart Stores, Inc. v. Samara Bros., 529 U.S. 205, 21112 (2000).

Nothing , …, demands the conclusion that every category of mark necessarily includes some marks "by which the goods of the applicant may be distinguished from the goods of others" without secondary meaning that in every category some marks are inherently distinctive. … In Qualitex, … [w]e held that a color could be protected as a trademark, but only upon a showing of **secondary meaning**. Wal-Mart Stores, Inc. v. Samara Bros., 529 U.S. 205, 21112 (2000).

2차적 인용문헌

사용례 통상의 지식을 가진 디자이너의 관점에서 그 특징을 삭제하거나, 관련된 이차적 인용문헌에서의 특징으로 치환하거나 이를 추가함으로써 1차적 인용문헌을 변형하는 것에 대한 동기가 있었을 것이라면, 35 U.S.C. §103(a)에 따른 거절은 적절한 것이다. **2차적 인용문헌**이 고려되기 위하여는, **2차적 인용문헌**에서의 특징을 사용하여 기본적인 디자인을 변형하는 것에 대한 암시가 공지디자인에 존재하여야 한다. (미) MPEP § 1504.03.II.A.

secondary references

A rejection under 35 U.S.C. §103 would be appropriate if a designer of ordinary skill would have been motivated to modify a primary reference by deleting features thereof or by interchanging with or adding features from pertinent secondary references. In order for **secondary references** to be considered, there must be some suggestion in the prior art to modify the basic design with features from the **secondary references**. MPEP § 1504.03.II.A.

이해관계인

이해관계인은 특허료를 내야 할 자의 의사와 관계없이 특허료를 낼 수 있다(특허법 제80조 제1항).

interested parties

Any interested party may pay patent fees, regardless of the wishes of a person liable to pay the patent fees (Patent Act Article 80(1)).

인격의 동일성

사용례 자기의 성명 · 상호 등 **인격의 동일성**을 표시하는 수단을 상거래 관행에 따라 상표로 사용하는 자로서 제1항 제1호의 요건을 갖춘 자는 해당 상표를 그 사용하는 상품에 대하여 계속 사용할 권리를 가진다(상표법 제99조 제2항).

identity of character

Any person who uses a means indicating the **identity of his/her character**, such as his/her name and trade name, as his/her trademark in accordance with generally accepted business practices, and meets requirements under paragraph (1) 1 shall have the right to continuously use the trademark on goods on which he/she uses the relevant trademark (Trademark Act Article 99(2)).

인도(引渡)

물건에 대한 현실적인 지배권을 이전하는 것.

deliver

Transferring the actual possession of an object.

ㅇ

사용례 타인의 등록상표 또는 이와 유사한 상표가 표시된 지정상품과 동일·유사한 상품을 양도 또는 **인도**하기 위하여 소지하는 행위는 상표권(지리적 표시 단체표장권은 제외한다) 또는 전용사용권을 침해한 것으로 본다(상표법 제108조 제1항 제4호).

The following shall be deemed infringement of trademark rights (excluding the right to collective mark with geographical indication) or an exclusive license: … Possessing goods identical or similar to the designated goods bearing a registered trademark of another person or any other similar trademark for the purpose of transferring or **delivering** such goods (Trademark Act Article 108(1)4).

인용디자인

cited design

인용문헌

(cited) references

특허심사절차에서 관련성이 있는 것으로 인용된 문헌. 크게 국내특허, 특허출원공고, 해외특허, 비특허문헌으로 나눌 수 있음.

Documents cited as relevant in a patent prosecution. References may be categorized into: domestic patents and patent application publications; foreign patents; and non-patent literature.

사용례 디자인 사례에서의 쟁점은 결합하고자 하는 **인용문헌**이 기계적으로 유사한 기술분야에 속하는지가 아닌 한 디자인의 특정한 장식적 특징이 그 외관상 다른 디자인에 적용된 것으로 암시할 만큼 서로 연관되어 있는가이다. (미) In re Glavas, 230 F.2d 447, 450, 109 USPQ 50, 52 (CCPA 1956).

The question in design cases is not whether the **references** sought to be combined are in analogous arts in the mechanical sense, but whether they are so related that the appearance of certain ornamental features in one would suggest the application of those features to the other. In re Glavas, 230 F.2d 447, 450, 109 USPQ 50, 52 (CCPA 1956).

인용상표

cited trademark

인적관할

personal jurisdiction

법원이 소송 당사자에 대해 판결을 내릴 권한.

A court's power to make decisions over parties.

일군의 발명

group of inventions

일군의 발명에 대하여 1특허출원을 하기 위하여는 다음 각호의 요건을 갖추어야 한다. 1. 청구된 발명간에 기술적 상호관련성이 있을 것 2. 청구된 발명들이 동일하거나 상응하는 기술적 특징을 가지고 있을 것. 이 경우 기술적 특징은 발명 전체로 보아 선행기술에 비하여 개선된 것이어야 한다(특허법시행령 제6조).

A single patent application for a group of inventions shall meet the following requirements: 1. The inventions described in the application shall be technologically correlated; 2. The inventions described in the application shall have the same or corresponding technological features. In such case, the technological features shall be those improved than the prior technology in light of the invention at large (Enforcement Decree of Patent Act Article 6).

1디자인 1디자인등록 출원

one design for one application, doctrine of one-design for one-registration application (법제처)

하나의 출원에는 하나의 디자인만을 표시하여야 하는 원칙.

The principle that one application is allowed to display one design embodied in one article.

(출원의) 일련번호

serial number (of application)

일반 수요자

ordinary consumers, general consuming public

사용례 상표권자 또는 사용권자가 위 등록상표에서 영문자나 그 한글 음역 중 어느 한 부분이 생략된 형태의 상표를 사용하더라도, **일반 수요자**나 거래자에게는 위 등록상표와 동일하게 호칭·관념되는 같은 상표가 사용된다고 인식되어 그에 대한 신뢰가 형성될 것이므로, 그 상표들 사이의 동일성을 부정한다면 일반 수요자나 거래자의 신뢰를 깨뜨리는 결과가 초래된다(대법원 2013. 9. 26. 선고 2012후2463 전원합의체 판결 참조).

Even if the trademark owner or licensee uses a trademark which omits either the English letters or their transliteration in Korean, denying the identicalness of the trademarks will result in destroying the trust of **ordinary consumers** or traders, since general consumers or traders will recognize that the trademark shares the same name and concept as the above trademark, and their trust will be based on such understanding (Supreme Court Decision, 2012Hu2463, decided September 26, 2013).

일반승계

general succession

→ 양도 참조

사용례 상표등록출원의 승계는 상속이나 그 밖의 **일반승계**의 경우를 제외하고는 출원인 변경신고를 하지 아니하면 그 효력이 발생하지 아니한다(상표법 제48조 제1항).

No succession to an application for trademark registration shall take effect unless a report on the change of the applicant is filed, except in cases of inheritance and other **general succession** (Trademark Act Article 48(1)).

미 일부계속출원

continuation-in-part (CIP) application

선행하는 정규출원의 전부 또는 상당한 일부를 반복하고 이에 개시되지 아니한 사항을 부가하여 선행 정규출원이 유효한 동안 제출한 출원. (미) MPEP § 1504.20.

An application filed during the lifetime of an earlier nonprovisional application, repeating some substantial portion or all of the earlier nonprovisional application and adding matter not disclosed in the earlier nonprovisional application. MPEP § 1504.20.

사용례 '**일부계속출원**'으로 제출된 디자인특허출원은 선출원에서 개시된 디자인의 형상이나 구성을 변경할 경우 그 선출원

design application filed as a "**continuation-in-part**" that changes the shape or configuration of a design disclosed in an earlier application is not entitled to the benefit of

일의 이익을 주장할 수 없다. (미) MPEP § 1504.20.

the filing date of the earlier application. MPEP§ 1504.20.

일부심사등록

디자인등록출원이 디자인등록요건 중 일부만을 갖추고 있는지를 심사하여 등록하는 것(디자인보호법 제2조 제6호). 디자인 일부심사등록에 대한 이의신청을 취하하면 그 이의신청은 처음부터 없었던 것으로 본다(디자인보호법 제75조 제2항).

partial examination

a design is registered if an application successfully passes an examination as to whether it meets only some of the requirements for design registration (Design Protection Act Article 2.6). If a written opposition to registration of a partially-examined design is withdrawn, the written opposition shall be deemed to have never existed (Design Protection Act Article 75(2)).

(출원의) 일부포기

거절결정 대상이 되는 특정 상품 또는 서비스에 대해서만 출원을 포기하는 것.

사용례 **출원의 일부포기**는 특허상표청의 통지에 거절결정이나 한정요구가 특정 상품 또는 서비스, 분류에만 제한되어 있음이 명시되어 있을 때에만 가능하다. (미) TMEP § 718.02(a).

partial abandonment (of application)

Abandonment of application only as to particular goods or services that are subject to a refusal or other decisions.

Partial abandonment applies only if the Office action expressly states that a refusal or requirement is limited to only certain goods/services/class(es). TMEP § 718.02(a).

일사부재리

사용례 (**일사부재리**) 이 법에 따른 심판의 심결이 확정되었을 때에는 그 사건에 대해서는 누구든지 동일 사실 및 동일 증거에 의하여 다시 심판을 청구할 수 없다. 다만, 확정된 심결이 각하심결인 경우에는 그러하지 아니하다(특허법 제163조).

non bis in idem

(Non Bis In Idem) If a trial ruling rendered under this Act becomes final and conclusive, no person may demand re-trial, based on the same facts and evidence: Provided, That the foregoing shall not apply where the final and conclusive trial ruling is a rejection (Patent Act Article 163).

일실이익

침해가 없었더라면 그로 인한 피해를 입은 당사자가 얻을 수 있었을 이익.

lost profit

The profit that an infringed party would have made had it not been for the infringement.

미 일응의 유리한 사건

심사관이 일응의 유리한 사건을 제시하지 못하면 출원인은 비자명성 입증을 위해 2차적 증거를 제출할 어떠한 의무도 없다. 반면 심사관이 일응의 유리한 사건을 제시하였다면 증거 또는 주장을 제시할 책임은

prima facie case

If the examiner does not produce a prima facie case, the applicant is under no obligation to submit secondary evidence to show nonobviousness. If, however, the examiner does produce a prima facie case, the burden of coming forward with evidence or arguments shifts to the applicant who may

출원인에게로 전환되는데, 출원인은 출원 발명이 선행기술에서 예측할 수 없는 개선된 특성을 지니고 있음을 나타내는 비교실험데이터 등 비자명성에 대한 추가적인 증거를 제시할 수 있다. (미) MPEP § 2142.

submit additional evidence of nonobviousness, such as comparative test data showing that the claimed invention possesses improved properties not expected by the prior art. MPEP § 2142.

미 일응의 자명성

사용례 Graham v. John Deere Co., 383 U.S. 1, 148 USPQ 459 (1966) 판례에 따른 사실조사가 수행된 후에는, 심사관은 이들이 **일응의 자명성**이라는 결론을 뒷받침하는지 판단하여야 한다. **일응의 자명성**이 성립하기 위하여는, 모든 청구범위 한정이 공지디자인에서 교시되거나 암시되어야 한다. (미) MPEP § 1504.03.II.

prima facie obviousness

Once the factual inquiries mandated under Graham v. John DeereCo., 383 U. S. 1, 148 USPQ 459 (1966), have been made, the examiner must determine whether they support a conclusion of **prima facie obviousness**. To establish **prima facie obviousness**, all the claim limitations must be taught or suggested by the prior art. MPEP § 1504.03.II.

미 임계일

특허출원일로부터 1년 이전이 되는 날. 구 특허법 제102(b)조 하에서 발명이 임계일 이전에 미국 내 공용되거나 세계 어디에서든 특허를 받았거나 묘사되었을 경우 그 발명에 대한 특허는 신규성 결여로 무효가 된다.

critical date

The date one year prior to the date a patent application is filed. Under pre-AIA Patent Act, 35 U.S.C. § 102(b), the patent will be invalid for lack of novelty if the invention was in public use in the United States, or patented or described anywhere in the world, prior to the critical date.

임계적 의의

수치한정의 임계적 의의가 인정되기 위해서는 수치한정 사항을 경계로 특성 즉, 발명의 작용 · 효과에 현저한 변화가 있어야 하는 것으로, ①수치한정의 기술적 의미가 발명의 설명에 기재되어 있어야 하고, ②상한치 및 하한치가 임계치라는 것이 발명의 설명 중의 실시례 또는 보조 자료 등으로부터 입증되어야 한다(특허법원 1998. 11. 6. 선고 98허2481 판결 참조).

critical significance

For the critical significance of the numerical limitation to be acknowledged, a remarkable change in the effect of the invention is required across the boundary of the numerical limitation and the following conditions should be satisfied: 1) The technical meaning of the numerical limitation should be described in the description, 2) the embodiments in the detailed description or supplemental materials should prove that the upper and lower limits of the numerical limitation is critical (Patent Court Decision, 98Heo2481, November 11, 1998).

임의적 표장

이미 존재하는 용어 중에서 임의로 선택하여 이루어진 표장으로 특정상품 또는 서비스와 관련되어 사용되었을 때, 그 상품 또는 서비스의 품질, 특성을 암시하거나 묘사

arbitrary mark

The marks that consist of arbitrarily chosen existing words that do not imply or depict the quality or characteristics of particular goods or services when used in connection with the goods or services. E.g. “Apple” Computers.

ㅇ

하지 않는 단어나 도형을 의미함. 예. "애플"컴퓨터.

사용례 이 건 출원상표는 일견 식별력이 없는 흔한 단어가 의외의 상품을 지정상품으로 하여 사용됨으로써 독특한 식별력을 가지게 되는 상표인 **임의적 상표**(arbitrary mark)에 해당한다(특허법원 1999. 4. 8. 선고 99허819 판결 참조).

The mark at issue is an **arbitrary mark** that has gained unique distinctiveness by using a common and non-distinctive word on the designated good, one that is not expected to be associated with the word (Patent Court Decision, 99Heo819, decided April 8, 1999).

입증취지

purport of evidence

입체상표

3차원의 입체적 형상으로 구성된 상표.

three-dimensional trademark

A mark that consists of a three-dimensional shape.

사용례 **입체상표**는 입체적 형상만으로 된 상표여야 하는 것은 아니다. 입체적 형상과 문자가 결합된 상표도 그 자체로서 상표등록 받을 수 있어야 한다(특허법원 2014. 9. 19. 선고 2014허2344 판결 참조).

A 3D mark does not necessarily have to be a **trademark** consisting of a **dimensional** shape alone. A mark combining a dimensional shape with a word should also surely be granted trademark registration (Patent Court Decision, 2014Heo 2344, decided September 19, 2014).

입체적 형상

입체적 형상과 기호 · 문자 등이 결합된 상표에서 입체적 형상에는 식별력이 없고 문자 등에 식별력 있는 경우, 식별력이 없는 입체적 형상은 출처표시기능을 할 수 없으므로, 그와 유사한 입체적 형상의 상품간의 관계에서 출처의 혼동 우려가 없다(특허법원 2014. 9. 19. 선고 2014허2344 판결 참조).

three-dimensional shape, dimensional shape (법제처)

In the case of a mark combining a dimensional shape with a device or word, if the dimensional shape lacks distinctiveness but the word is distinctive, the non-distinctive dimensional shape cannot function as a source identifier, and thus, there is no likelihood of confusion arising with respect to the goods having a similar dimensional shape (Patent Court Decision, 2014Heo2344, decided September 19, 2014).

ㅈ

자기공지

특허출원 전에 발명이 공개된 경우 원칙적으로 신규성 요건이 부정되어 특허를 받을 수 없으나(특허법 제29조 제1항) 자기공지의 예외에 해당하거나(특허법 제30조 제1항

inventor-initiated disclosure, disclosure by applicant

An invention publicly known prior to the filing of a patent application shall not be patented in principle (Patent Act

제1호) 의사에 반한 공지(제30조 제1항 제2호) 등의 경우에는 일정한 요건 하에 신규성이 부정되지 아니함.

Article 29(1)). However, novelty is not denied if certain requirements are met, such as an exceptional case when the inventor initiated the disclosure (Patent Act Article 30(1)1), or the disclosure was against the inventor's will (Patent Act Article 30(1)2).

자료제출명령

order to produce documents, order to submit documents (법제처)

소송에서 법원이 당사자의 신청에 의하여 상대방 당사자에게 해당 침해의 증명 또는 침해로 인한 손해액의 산정에 필요한 자료를 제출하도록 하는 명령. 법원은 특허권 또는 전용실시권 침해소송에서 당사자의 신청에 의하여 상대방 당사자에게 해당 침해의 증명 또는 침해로 인한 손해액의 산정에 필요한 자료의 제출을 명할 수 있다. 다만, 그 자료의 소지자가 그 자료의 제출을 거절할 정당한 이유가 있으면 그러하지 아니하다(특허법 제132조 제1항).

Upon receipt of a request from either party to legal proceedings on infringement of a patent or exclusive license, the court may order the other party to submit documents necessary to assess losses caused by the relevant infringement. Upon receipt of a request from either party to legal proceedings on infringement of a patent or exclusive license, the court may order the other party to submit documents necessary for assessing losses caused by the relevant infringement: Provided, That the foregoing shall not apply where the person possessing the documents has a reasonable ground to refuse to submit them (Patent Act Article 132(1)).

미 자명식 중복특허

obviousness-type double patenting (ODP)

→ 중복특허 참조

자문변호사

opinion counsel

자백

confession, admission

자백간주

regarding as confession/admission

당사자가 변론에서 상대방이 주장하는 사실을 명백히 다투지 아니한 때에는 그 사실을 자백한 것으로 본다. 다만, 변론 전체의 취지로 보아 그 사실에 대하여 다툰 것으로 인정되는 경우에는 그러하지 아니하다(민사소송법 제150조 제1항).

When a party has failed to evidently contest at his/her pleading the facts alleged by the other party, he/she shall be deemed to have confessed such facts: Provided, That the same shall not apply where it is deemed that a contest has been made against such facts, in view of the purports of entire pleadings (Civil Procedure Act Article 150(1)).

자연법칙

law of nature

특허의 대상이 되는 '발명'에 해당하기 위한 요건. 특허를 받을 수 있는 '발명'에 해당하기 위하여는 자연법칙을 이용한 기술적 사상의 창작으로서 고도한 것이어야 함(특허법 제2조 제1호).

A requirement for patentable 'invention.' In order to be patentable, an 'invention' shall be highly advanced creation of a technical idea utilizing the laws of nature (Patent Act Article 2.1).

자유실시기술

어떤 기술의 실시형태가 외형상 특허발명의 구성과 동일하거나 그 균등의 범주에 속한다 하더라도 그것이 당해 특허발명 이외에 이미 존재하는 공지의 자유기술을 실시하는 것인 때에는 특허발명에 대한 침해를 구성하지 않는다는 항변.

freely exploited/practiced invention

A defense that even when an execution of a technology apparently has the same composition with a patented invention or is equivalent with the patented invention, the execution does not constitute infringement of the patent if it is an act merely executing a pre-existing publicly known state-of-the-art technology.

자유실시디자인

사용례 확인대상디자인은 그 디자인이 속하는 분야에서 통상의 지식을 가진 사람이 선행디자인 2~9로부터 쉽게 창작할 수 있는 **자유실시디자인**에 불과하므로, 이 사건 등록디자인과 대비할 필요도 없이 이 사건 등록디자인의 보호범위에 속하지 않는다(특허법원 2017. 3. 24. 선고 2013허7526 판결 참조).

freely exploited/practiced design

The challenged design is merely a **freely exploited design** that can be easily created by a person with ordinary knowledge in the field from prior designs No.2-9, and comparison with the registered design at issue is unnecessary to conclude that it does not fall within the scope of protection of the registered design (Patent Court Decision, 2013Heo7526, decided March 24, 2017).

미 잠수함 특허

출원인이 계속출원제도를 악용하여 특허심사를 지연시킴으로써 타인이 자신의 특허의 존재를 모르고 사용할 때 등록하여 권리를 행사하는 경우. '특허심사절차에서의 태만'을 들어 항변할 수 있음.

submarine patent

Submarine patents are those used by an applicant who waits to enforce patent rights until a third party uses the invention not knowing the existence of the pending application, abusing the continuation application process. In response, an affected party can argue procedural laches.

장기간의 필요성

그 발명이 속하는 기술 분야에서 오랫동안 그 과제의 존재를 인지하고 있었으나 해결하지 못한 경우 장기간의 필요성이 인정됨.

long-felt need

Long-felt need is established when an art recognized problem existed in the art for a long period of time without solution.

장식

장식적 특성만을 지닌 대상. 장식은 자타상품 식별력이 없어 상표로서 기능하지 아니함.

ornamentation, ornamental matter

Subject matter that is merely a decorative feature. A mere ornamentation does not distinguish the applicant's goods and thus does not function as a trademark.

사용례 본질적인 식별력도 2차적 출처 표시기능도 없는 **장식**도 출원인이 그 대상이 지정상품에 관련하여 식별력을 취득하였음을 입증할 경우 미 상표법 2(f)조에 따라 주등록부에 등록될 수 있다. (미) TMEP § 1202.03(2).

Ornamental matter that is neither inherently distinctive nor a secondary source indicator may be registered on the Principal Register under §2(f), if the applicant establishes that the subject matter has acquired distinctiveness as a mark in relation to the goods. TMEP § 1202.03(2).

장식성

물품은 기능성과 장식성을 모두 갖출 수 있는데, 디자인권은 그 디자인의 장식적 측면에만 연관되어 있다.

ornamentality

Articles of manufacture may possess both functional and ornamental characteristics. A design right only concerns the ornamental aspects of the design.

사용례 디자인특허는 그 디자인의 **장식적 측면**만을 보호하는 것이다. OddzOn의 특허 구현 제품과 같은 공기역학적 안정성을 갖기 위해서는 프로펠러축과 지느러미 부분이 필수적임이 입증되었으므로 이러한 일반적 특성은 기능적이며 따라서 디자인으로서 보호될 수 없다. (미) OddzOn Prod., Inc. v. Just Toys, Inc., 122 F.3d 1396, 1404 (Fed. Cir. 1997).

A design patent only protects the **ornamental aspects** of the design. Because the presence of a tailshaft and fins has been shown to be necessary to have a ball with similar aerodynamic stability to OddzOn's commercial embodiment, such general features are functional and thus not protectable as such. OddzOn Prod., Inc. v. Just Toys, Inc., 122 F.3d 1396, 1404 (Fed. Cir. 1997).

미 장치-변환 테스트

방법발명에 대한 청구항의 내용이 특정한 기계에 전형적이거나 사소하지 않은 방식으로 구현되었거나 물품의 상태를 변형시키는 것일 때 특허적격성을 지닌다고 보는 판단기준.

machine-or-transformation test

A test on patent eligibility that requires a claim to a process invention to be implemented by a particular machine in a non-conventional and non-trivial manner or transforms an article from one state to another.

미 장치 청구항

기계 혹은 구조물 발명에 대한 청구항.

apparatus claims

Claims of an invention of a machine or structure.

미 재발행출원

특허의 결함 있는 명세서나 도면, 혹은 청구가능한 범위보다 넓거나 좁게 청구하였을 경우와 같은 오류로 인하여 특허가 그 전체 또는 부분이 작용이 불가능하거나 무효로 간주되었을 때 특허권자가 그 특허를 포기(surrender)하고 법에 정한 수수료를 납부하면 특허상표청장은 원출원에 개시된 발명에 대하여 그 특허를 재발행하여야 하며 이는 신규 또는 보정된 출원과 일관되고 원 특허의 잔존기간 동안 유효하다. 재발행출원에는 신규사항이 포함되어서는 아니된다. 단 실무적으로는 특허의 재발행으로 자동적으로 원 특허는 포기된 것으로 보며 물리적으로 문서를 제출할 필요는 없다. (미) MPEP § 1416.

reissue application

Whenever any patent is, through error, deemed wholly or partly inoperative or invalid, by reason of a defective specification or drawing, or by reason of the patentee claiming more or less than he had a right to claim in the patent, the Director shall, on the surrender of such patent and the payment of the fee required by law, reissue the patent for the invention disclosed in the original patent, and in accordance with a new and amended application, for the unexpired part of the term of the original patent. No new matter shall be introduced into the application for reissue. In practice, surrender is automatic upon the grant of the reissue patent and no physical surrender is required. MPEP § 1416.

재심

당사자는 확정된 특허취소결정 또는 확정된 심결에 대하여 재심을 청구할 수 있다(특허법 제178조 제1항).

retrial

Any party may file a petition for retrial against the final and conclusive trial ruling (Patent Act Article 178(1)).

재심리

→ 드노보 심리 참조

de novo review

재심사

특허출원인은 그 특허출원에 관하여 특허거절결정등본을 송달받은 날부터 30일 기간이 연장된 경우 그 연장된 기간을 말한다) 이내에 그 특허출원의 명세서 또는 도면을 보정하여 해당 특허출원에 관한 재심사(이하 "재심사"라 한다)를 청구할 수 있다(특허법 제67조의2 제1항).

reexamination

A patent applicant may file a request to re-examine his/her patent application (hereinafter referred to as "re-examination") after amending the specification or drawings of the patent application within 30 days (referring to an extension, if the period is extended) after receipt of a certified copy of the decision to reject the patent application (Patent Act Article 67-2(1)).

재심에 의하여 회복한 특허권에 대한 선사용권자의 통상실시권

특허취소결정 또는 심결이 확정된 후 재심청구 등록 전에 국내에서 선의로 그 발명의 실시사업을 하고 있는 자 또는 그 사업을 준비하고 있는 자는 실시하고 있거나 준비하고 있는 발명 및 사업목적의 범위에서 그 특허권에 관하여 통상실시권을 가진다(특허법 제182조).

non-exclusive license for prior users of patent reinstated through retrial

A person who executes, or prepares to execute, the relevant patent commercially or industrially, in good faith, in the Republic of Korea after the relevant trial ruling becomes final and conclusive, but before the petition filed for retrial is registered shall be granted a non-exclusive license of the patent within the scope of subject matter of the patented invention that the person executes or prepares to execute, or the objectives of the business (Patent Act Article 182).

재외자

국내에 주소나 영업소가 없는 자.

non-resident

A person who is not domiciled or does not have his/her place of business in the Republic of Korea.

사용례 **재외자**인 외국인은 다음 각 호의 어느 하나에 해당하는 경우를 제외하고는 상표권 또는 상표에 관한 권리를 누릴 수 없다. 1. 그 외국인이 속하는 국가에서 대한민국 국민에 대하여 그 국민과 같은 조건으로 상표권 또는 상표에 관한 권리를 인정하는 경우 … (상표법 제27조 제1호)

No **non-resident** foreigner shall be entitled to enjoy trademark rights or the rights relating to the trademark, except in any of the following cases: 1. Where a state to which such foreigner is a citizen recognizes trademark rights or the rights relating to the trademark owned by a citizen of the Republic of Korea on the same conditions as those of its citizen; … (Trademark Act Article 27.1).

재정

사용례 특허발명을 실시하려는 자는 특허발명이 다음 각 호의 어느 하나에 해당하고, 그 특허발명의 특허권자 또는 전용실시권자와 합리적인 조건으로 통상실시권 허락에 관한 협의를 하였으나 합의가 이루어지지 아니하는 경우 또는 협의를 할 수 없는 경우에는 특허청장에게 통상실시권 설정에 관한 **재정**을 청구할 수 있다(특허법 제107조 제1항).

adjudication

If a patented invention falls under any of the following, and a person who intends to execute the patented invention fails, or is unable, to reach agreement with the patentee or exclusive licensee of the patented invention on the grant of a non-exclusive license under reasonable terms and conditions, although the person has negotiated the agreement, the person may file a petition for **adjudication** on the grant of the non-exclusive license with the Commissioner of the Korean Intellectual Property Office (Patent Act Article 107(1)).

재판적

사건의 재판에 적절하거나 재판이 가능한 장소.

venue

The proper or possible place for the trial of a case.

쟁점

당사자에게 다툼이 있는 사항 즉, 사실상 또는 법률상 쟁점.

issue

The subject matter in dispute between parties, factual or legal.

저명상표

그 상표가 수요자에게 널리 알려져 있을 뿐 아니라 그 상품이 갖는 품질의 우수성 때문에 상표의 수요자뿐만 아니라 일반대중에게까지 양질감을 획득하고 있어 상품의 출처뿐만 아니라 그 영업주체를 표시하는 힘까지 갖게 된 상표. 따라서 단순한 주지상표와는 구별됨. 저명상표에 해당하는지 여부는, 그 상표의 사용, 공급, 영업활동의 기간, 방법, 태양 및 거래범위 등과 그 거래실정 또는 사회통념상 객관적으로 널리 알려졌느냐의 여부 등이 기준이 됨.

famous trademark

A famous mark is a mark not only widely known to the consumers of the designated good but also has gained an impression of high quality among the general public due to its superior quality and thus serves as a source indicator for the business. It is therefore distinguished from well-known marks. Whether a trademark is famous is determined by the usage and supply of the mark, the method and period the good is marketed, the broadness of customer basis and course of trade, as well as how widely known it is when objectively viewed under social norms.

사용례 선사용상표들의 국내외에서의 영업기간, 방법 및 형태, 연간 매출액, 국내외에서 공적인 기관 및 언론 등을 통하여 알려진 정도 등 제반 사정을 종합하면, 선사용상표들은 이 사건 등록상표의 출원일인 2006. 2. 28. 무렵에 거래자나 일반 소비자들 사이에서 현저하게 알려진 **저명상표**였다고 봄이 상당하다(특허법원 2009. 12.

In view of pre-use trademarks' foreign and domestic business operation periods, methods and forms, annual sales volumes, popularity through foreign and domestic public authorities and media, etc. revealed by the above facts, pre-use trademarks were **famous trademarks** conspicuously known among traders or general consumers around Feb. 28, 2006 when the registered trademark of this case was applied for (Patent Court Decision, 2009Heo6311, decided December

ㅈ

11. 선고 2009허6311 판결 참조).

11, 2009).

저명성

저명한 아호, 예명, 필명과 이들의 서명한 약칭을 상거래 관행에 따라 사용하는 상표에는 타 상표권의 효력이 미치지 아니함(상표법 제90조 제1항 제1호). 이때 타인의 명칭 등이 저명한지는 그 사용기간, 방법, 태양, 사용량 및 거래의 범위와 상품거래의 실정 등을 고려하여 사회통념상 또는 지정상품과 관련한 거래사회에서 타인의 명칭 등이 널리 인식될 수 있는 정도에 이르렀는지 여부에 따라 판단하여야 함(특허법원 2016. 5. 19. 선고 2015허7292 판결 참조).

famousness, fame

Any trademark using his/her own name, title, or trade name, portrait, signature, seal, or well-known pseudonym, stage name, pen name, and the well-known abbreviated title thereof, in accordance with generally accepted business practices. (Trademark Act Article 90(1)). Famousness of a name is determined based on whether the name is widely recognized in the relevant marketplace, judging from the period, manner, type and frequency of use, the scope and practice of trading of goods using the name, among others (Patent Court Decision, 2015Heo7292, decided May 19, 2016).

사용례 이 사건 그룹가수의 명칭과 같은 구성의 선사용상표 1 및 선사용서비스표는 피고의 '음반, 음원' 등의 사용상품 및 '가수공연업, 음악공연업, 방송출연업, 광고모델업' 등의 사용서비스업에 대하여 관계 거래자 이외에 일반공중의 대부분에까지 널리 알려지게 됨으로써 **저명성**을 획득하였다고 보아야 하고 … (대법원 2015. 10. 15. 선고 2013후1207 판결 참조).

The Trademark in Prior Use 1 and the Service Mark in Prior Use, of the same composition as the name of the group, shall be deemed to have acquired **famousness** by being widely known not only to traders in the industry but also to most of the general public, in connection with the Defendant's goods of "phonorecord albums and music source files" and such services as "singer and musical performances, broadcast appearances, and advertisement endorsements" (Supreme Court Decision, 2013Hu1207, decided October 15, 2015).

미 저속한 사항

→ 공서양속에 반하는 상표 참조.

scandalous matter

저장상표

경쟁사에 대하여 선점을 위해 불확정한 미래에 사용할 목적으로 등록을 받은 상표.

reserved trademark

A trademark registered for the purpose of preserving it earlier than the applicant's competitor and using it in the unforeseeable future.

사용례 상표법 제73조 제1항 제3호는 상표권자·전용사용권자 또는 통상사용권자중 어느 누구도 정당한 이유 없이 등록상표를 그 지정상품에 대하여 취소심판청구일전 계속하여 3년 이상 국내에서 사용하고 있지 아니한 경우를 상표등록의 취소사유로 규정하고 있는바, 이는 사용되지 아니

Under the Trademark Act, Article 73(1)3, a registered trademark may be cancelled if on the ground that none of the trademark owner, exclusive or non-exclusive licensee used the trademark, without just cause, for three consecutive years or more prior to the date the cancellation action was filed. This is to cancel registration of a **reserved trademark** with no intent to use by extinguishing registration of such

하는 상표의 등록을 말소시킴으로써 사용 의사가 없는 **저장상표**를 등록취소 시키고, … (특허법원 2011. 10. 26. 선고 2011허5946 참조).

an unused mark (Patent Court Decision, 2011 Heo5946, decided October 26, 2011).

저촉발명

특허권자 · 전용실시권자 또는 통상실시권자는 특허발명이 그 특허발명의 특허출원일 전에 출원된 타인의 특허발명등록실용신안 또는 등록디자인이나 그 디자인과 유사한 디자인을 이용하거나 특허권이 그 특허발명의 특허출원일 전에 출원된 타인의 디자인권 또는 상표권과 저촉되는 경우에는 그 특허권자 · 실용신안권자 · 디자인권자 또는 상표권자의 허락을 받지 아니하고는 자기의 특허발명을 업으로서 실시할 수 없다(특허법 제98조).

infringing invention

No patentee, exclusive licensee, nor non-exclusive licensee shall commercially or industrially execute any patented invention on which he/she has the right to execute, without permission from the patent holder, the holder of a registered utility model, design, or trademark, if the patented invention uses another person's patented invention or registered utility model or design claimed in an application filed prior to the filing date of the patent application or any similar design or infringes another person's registered design or trademark claimed in an application filed prior to the filing date of the patent application (Patent Act Article 98).

미 저촉심사 (상표)

다른 출원 또는 등록과 저촉관계에 놓인 출원인이나 다른 출원과 저촉관계에 놓인 등록권자가 등록을 받을 수 있는지 결정하는 TTAB의 절차. 이는 특허상표청장을 상대로 특수한 상황이 존재함, 즉 저촉심사를 하지 아니하면 청구인이 부당한 피해를 입을 것임을 청구를 통해 입증하여야만 가능함. (미) TMBP § 102.02.

interference proceeding (trademark)

A proceeding in which the TTAB determines which, if any, of the owners of conflicting applications (or of one or more applications and one or more registrations which are in conflict), is entitled to registration. The proceeding is declared by the Office only upon petition to the Director showing extraordinary circumstances therefor, that is, that the party who filed the petition would be unduly prejudiced without an interference. TMBP § 102.02.

사용례 **저촉심사**관계는 출원인의 상품 또는 서비스와 관련하여 사용될 때에는 혼동, 오인 또는 기만행위가 될 염려가 있을 정도로 타인에 의하여 전에 등록되었거나 타인이 전에 등록출원을 한 표장과 거의 유사한 표장의 등록출원을 한 경우에 존재한다. (미) 상표법 제16조.

Interference exists when an application is made for the registration of a mark which so resembles a mark previously registered by another, or for the registration of which another has previously made application, as to be likely when used on or in connection with the goods or services of the applicant to cause confusion or mistake or to deceive. 15 U.S.C. § 1066.

미 저촉절차 (특허)

개정특허법에 의하여 파생절차로 대체됨. → 파생절차 참조

interference proceeding (patent)

Replaced by derivation proceeding under the AIA. → See. derivation proceeding.

ㅈ

저촉표장

타인의 권리 또는 법률에 저촉되는 표장. 상표권자 · 전용사용권자 또는 통상사용권자는 그 등록상표를 사용할 경우에 그 사용 상태에 따라 그 상표등록출원일 전에 출원된 타인의 특허권 · 실용신안권 · 디자인권 또는 그 상표등록출원일 전에 발생한 타인의 저작권과 저촉되는 경우에는 지정상품 중 저촉되는 지정상품에 대한 상표의 사용은 특허권자 · 실용신안권자 · 디자인권자 또는 저작권자의 동의를 받지 아니하고는 그 등록상표를 사용할 수 없다(상표법 제92조 제1항).

conflicting mark

A mark that conflicts with laws or others' rights. Where a trademark right holder, an exclusive licensee or a non-exclusive licensee uses his/her registered trademark, in which case his/her use of the registered trademark is in conflict with another person's patent right, utility model right or design right for which the application was filed prior to the filing date of an application for such trademark registration or another person's copyright created prior to the filing date of an application for such trademark registration depending on how the trademark is used, he/she shall not use the registered trademark on designated goods in conflict with the relevant rights of others without the consent of the patentee, the holer of the utility model right, the holder of design right, or the holder of the copyright, respectively (Trademark Act Article 92(1)).

적극적 권리범위확인심판

→ 권리범위확인심판 참조

(administrative) affirmative confirmation trial for the scope of rights, affirmative scope of rights trial

전문가 증인

사용례 **전문가 증인**을 신청할 때에는 증인의 전문성과 객관성을 확인할 수 있는 전문가 증인 기본 사항 확인서를 첨부하여야 하고, 전문가 증인이 채택되면 전문가 증인의 증언이 담긴 증인 진술서와 증인신문사항을 제출하여야 한다(특허법원 심결취소소송 심리매뉴얼 V.3.).

expert witness

If a party files a request for an expert witness, the party shall attach a basic declaration of the **expert witness** that can confirm the expertise and objectivity of the witness. If the request is accepted, the party shall submit a witness statement containing the testimony of the expert witness and a questionnaire for witness examination (Patent Court Guideline of Practice and Procedure of Revocation Action V.3.A).

전문가 진술서

expert witness statement

전문심리위원

전문적인 지식을 필요로 하는 소송절차에서 설명 또는 의견을 기재한 서면을 제출하거나 기일에 출석하여 설명이나 의견을 진술할 수 있는 전문성을 갖춘 자(민사소송법 제164조의2 제2항).

technical advisors, professional examiners (법제처)

Professional examiners are those who have the expertise to submit a report stating explanation or opinion, or provide explanation or opinion in court in litigations that require specialized knowledge on the matter (Civil Procedure Act Article 164-2(2)).

사용례 법원은 소송관계를 분명하게 하거나 소송절차를 원활하게 진행하기 위하여 직권 또는 당사자의 신청에 따른 결정으로 **전문심리위원**을 지정하여 소송절차에 참여하게 할 수 있다(민사소송법 제164조의2 제1항).

In order to clarify litigation relations or to smoothly proceed with litigation procedures, the court may designate **professional examiners** ex officio or upon application of parties and have them participate in the litigation procedures (Civil Procedure Act Article 164-2(1)).

전시

‘전시’란 다중이 열람할 수 있는 상태에 놓이는 것을 말한다. 상품 또는 상품의 포장에 상표를 표시한 상품을 양도 또는 인도할 목적이 있어야 하고, 이러한 주관적인 의사 없는 전시 · 수출 · 수입행위는 이에 해당하지 아니함.

display, exhibit

A good is displayed if it is in a state that can be seen by the general public, for the purpose of transferring or delivering the good bearing the mark on it or its package. Exhibition, import or export without such purpose shall not qualify as display under the Trademark Act.

전용(轉用)

사용례 … 국내에서 널리 알려진 형상 · 모양 · 색채 또는 이들의 결합(이하 ‘주지형태’라고 한다)을 거의 그대로 모방 또는 **전용**하였거나, 이를 부분적으로 변형하였다고 하더라도 전체적으로 볼 때 다른 미감적 가치가 인정되지 않는 상업적 · 기능적 변형에 불과하거나, … (대법원 2016. 6. 9. 선고 2014후614 판결 참조).

appropriation

… (a) a design imitating or **appropriating** a shape, pattern, or color, or a combination thereof, that is widely known in the Republic of Korea almost as it is; (b) notwithstanding the partial transformation, in its totality a design that is merely a commercial and functional transformation without any other recognized aesthetic value; or … (Supreme Court Decision, 2014Hu614, decided June 9, 2016).

전용(轉用)사용권

상표권자 등의 동의에 따라 지정상품에 관하여 등록상표를 독점적으로 사용할 권리.

exclusive license

A right to exclusively use the registered rights in relation to the designated good as granted by trademark or other rights owner.

사용례 **전용사용권**은 그 설정계약이 해지되면 등록 여부에 관계없이 그 효력을 상실하며, 종전과 동일한 내용으로 전용사용권설정계약을 부활하는 묵시적 합의가 있었다고 하더라도 새로이 설정등록을 하지 않고서는 상표법상의 전용사용권을 취득할 수 없는 것이어서, 2000. 4. 28. 이후에는 피고를 인용상표들에 대한 전용사용권자라고 할 수 없다(대법원 2004. 9. 13. 선고 2002후703 판결 참조).

Exclusive licenses lose validity regardless of whether they are registered or not once the contract establishing such rights is terminated, and further, even if a tacit agreement for restoring the contract with the same terms and conditions existed, one cannot acquire an exclusive right for the use of the Trademark under the Trademark Act unless its establishment is newly registered. Thus, the defendant cannot be viewed as an exclusive license holder as to Trademark 1 and 2 from April 28, 2000 (Supreme Court Decision, 2002Hu703, decided September 13, 2004).

전용실시권

가령 특허의 경우, 특허권자로부터 허여받아 특허발명의 실시를 독점할 수 있는 권리. 특허권의 전용실시권의 설정은 등록하여야 한다. 특허권자는 그 특허권에 대하여 타인에게 전용실시권을 설정할 수 있다. 전용실시권을 설정받은 전용실시권자는 그 설정행위로 정한 범위에서 그 특허발명을 업으로서 실시할 권리를 독점한다(특허법 제100조).

exclusive license

In case of patents, for example, a right to exclusively exploit the patented invention as granted by the patent owner. Establishment of exclusive license of patent rights requires registration. A patentee may grant an exclusive license of the patent to other persons. An exclusive licensee with the exclusive license shall have the sole right to commercially or industrially execute the patented invention to the extent prescribed at the grant of the license (Patent Act Article 100).

전자문서

특허에 관한 절차를 밟는 자는 이 법에 따라 특허청장 또는 특허심판원장에게 제출하는 특허출원서, 그 밖의 서류를 산업통상자원부령으로 정하는 방식에 따라 전자문서화하고, 이를 정보통신망을 이용하여 제출하거나 이동식 저장장치 등 전자적 기록매체에 수록하여 제출할 수 있다(특허법 제28조의3 제1항).

electronic documents

A person who initiates a patent-related procedure may convert a patent application and other documents to be filed with the Commissioner of the Korean Intellectual Property Office or the Director General of the Korean Intellectual Property Trial and Appeal Board under this Act, into electronic documents by the method prescribed by Ordinance of the Ministry of Trade, Industry and Energy, and submit them via an information and communications network or by means of any electronic recording medium, such as a portable storage device (Patent Act Article 28-3(1)).

전자서명

사용례 전자문서로 특허에 관한 절차를 밟으려는 자는 미리 특허청장 또는 특허심판원장에게 전자문서 이용신고를 하여야 하며, 특허청장 또는 특허심판원장에게 제출하는 전자문서에 제출인을 알아볼 수 있도록 **전자서명**을 하여야 한다(특허법 제28조의4 제1항).

electronic signature, digital signature

A person who intends to take a patent-related procedure using electronic documents shall report such use of electronic documents to the Commissioner of the Korean Intellectual Property Office or the Director General of the Korean Intellectual Property Trial and Appeal Board, and shall affix his/her **digital signature** on electronic documents submitted to the Commissioner of the Korean Intellectual Property Office or the Director General of the Korean Intellectual Property Trial and Appeal Board to identify the person who submits the documents (Patent Act Article 28-4(1)).

전제부

청구항의 서두.

사용례 젭슨 형식 청구항 작성은 **전제부**의 대상이 타인의 선행기술임을 암묵적으로 인정하는 것으로 간주된다. (미) MPEP § 2129.

preamble

The introductory statement of the claim.

Drafting a claim in Jepson format … is taken as an implied admission that the subject matter of the **preamble** is the prior art work of another. MPEP § 2129.

전체관찰	**compare as a whole**
사용례 … 이들이 이 사건 출원상표를 각각 식별력이 약한 "Ace"와 "Link"의 두 부분으로 분리하여 "Ace" 또는 "Link"만으로 호칭하고 관념할 것으로 보기는 어려우므로, 이 사건 출원상표와 인용상표들을 비교함에 있어서 원칙으로 돌아가 **전체로서 관찰**하여 그 외관, 호칭 및 관념을 비교, 검토하여 판단하여야 한다고 본 다음, … (대법원 2001. 4. 27. 선고 2000후2453 판결 참조).	It is unlikely that they would separate the proposed mark into "Ace" and "Link," both parts with little distinctiveness, and call or think of the mark as either "Ace" or "Link." Therefore, in comparing the proposed mark at issue and cited marks, we shall refer to the basic principle. Our determination shall be based on **comparison as a whole**, comparing and examining their appearance, name and concept (Supreme Court Decision, 2000Hu2453, decided April 27, 2001).
미 **전체시장가치의 법칙**	**entire market value rule**
침해의 손해배상액을 산정할 때 특허가 적용된 부품만이 아닌 전체제품의 가격으로 산정하는 방법.	The method that awards damages for infringement based on the amount of the price of the entire product, rather than the parts to which the patent is applied.
(심사) 절차	**prosecution**
출원에 대한 특허청의 일련의 심사절차.	The entire process for the application in the KIPO.
절차의 보정	**amendment of procedure**
사용례 특허청장 또는 특허심판원장은 상표에 관한 절차가 다음 각 호의 어느 하나에 해당하는 경우에는 **보정**을 명하여야 한다(상표법 제39조).	The Commissioner of the Korean intellectual Property Office or the Director General of the Intellectual Property Trial and Appeal Board shall order a relevant person to **amend procedures** within a fixed period, if any of the following applies: … (Trademark Act Article 39).
절차 중지 신청	**motion to stay**
일시적으로 절차를 중지하는 법원의 명령을 구하는 신청.	A motion for the court order to temporarily stop the proceeding.
미 **점진적 침해의 원칙**	**doctrine of progressive encroachment**
소 제기의 태만을 근거로 한 적극적 항변에 대한 공격적 대응수단. 점진적 침해를 주장하는 원고는 일반적으로 (1) 지연기간 동안 당해 사건에서 주장하는 침해행위에 대해 소를 제기하지 않은 것이 합리적 결론이었으며 (2) 피고가 그 침해행위의 내용에 중대한 변경을 가하였고 (3) 침해행위에 중대	Progressive encroachment is an offensive countermeasure to the affirmative defense of laches. As a general rule, a plaintiff invoking the doctrine should establish that: (1) during the period of the delay the plaintiff could reasonably conclude that it should not bring suit to challenge the allegedly infringing activity; (2) the defendant materially altered its infringing activities; and (3) suit was not unreasonably

ㅈ

한 변경이 일어난 이후로는 소 제기를 비합리적으로 지연시키지 아니하였음을 입증하여야 함. (미) Oriental Fin. Grp., Inc. v. Coope- rativa de Ahorro y Credito Oriental, 698 F.3d 9, 21 (1st Cir. 2012).

delayed after the alteration in infringing activity. Oriental Fin. Grp., Inc. v. Cooperativa de Ahorro y Credito Oriental, 698 F.3d 9, 21 (1st Cir. 2012).

미 정규출원

가출원과 구분되는, '일반적' 의미의 특허출원.

non-provisional application

The "regular" type of patent applications, as distinguished from provisional applications.

미 정당한 불사용의 진술서(선서서)

표장이 거래상 사용되고 있지 않으나 그 불사용이 특별한 사정으로 인한 정당한 불사용에 의한 것이며, 상표를 포기하고자 하는 의사에 의한 것이 아님에 대하여 등록권자가 제출한 확인진술서. (미) USPTO.

affidavit/declaration of excusable non-use

A sworn statement, filed by the owner of a registration, that the mark is not in use in commerce due to special circumstances that excuse such nonuse and is not due to any intention to abandon the mark. USPTO.

정당한 이유

불사용으로 인한 상표등록취소 등에 대한 항변의 근거.

good cause, justifiable reason

A defense to cancellation of trademark based on nonuse.

사용례 '**정당한 이유**'라 함은 질병 기타 천재 등의 불가항력에 의하여 영업을 할 수 없는 경우뿐만 아니라 상표권자의 귀책사유로 인하지 아니한 상표 불사용의 경우도 포함된다고 할 것이다(대법원 2000. 4. 25. 선고 97후3920 판결 참조).

An "**good cause**" includes not only the circumstances where a party is prevented from engaging in his or her business due to illness or reasons of force majure such as acts of God, ··· but also to non-use the party shall not be held responsible (Supreme Court Decision, 97Hu3920, decided April 25, 2000).

미 정보공개진술서

출원발명의 특허성 판단에 중요한 정보를 제출할 출원인의 의무를 수행하기 위하여 미 특허법 111(a)조 하에 출원된 정규특허출원에 대한 특허상표청의 검토를 위하여 제출된 특허, 간행물, 미국내 출원 및 기타 정보를 포함하는 문서.

information disclosure statement (IDS)

An IDS shall include patents, publications, U.S. applications, or other information submitted for consideration by the USPTO in a nonprovisional patent application filed under § 111(a) to comply with applicant's duty to submit information which is material to patentability of the claimed invention.

정보통신망

information and communication networks

정부에 의한 특허발명의 실시

정부는 특허발명이 국가 비상사태, 극도의 긴급상황 또는 공공의 이익을 위하여 비상업적(非商業的)으로 실시할 필요가 있다고 인정하는 경우에는 그 특허발명을 실시하거나 정부 외의 자에게 실시하게 할 수 있다(특허법 제106조의2 제1항).

execution of patented inventions by government

If the Government deems it necessary to non-commercially execute a patented invention due to a national or dire emergency, or for the public interests, it may directly execute the patented invention or authorize any person other than the Government to execute it on its behalf (Patent Act Article 106-2(1)).

정정심판

특허권자는 다음 각 호의 어느 하나에 해당하는 경우에는 특허발명의 명세서 또는 도면에 대하여 정정심판을 청구할 수 있다.
1. 청구범위를 감축하는 경우,
2. 잘못 기재된 사항을 정정하는 경우,
3. 분명하지 아니하게 기재된 사항을 명확하게 하는 경우(특허법 제136조 제1항).

trial for corrections

In any of the following cases, a patentee may file a petition for trial to correct the specification or drawings of his/her patented invention: Provided, That the foregoing shall not apply where a trial to invalidate a patent or to invalidate a correction is pending in the Korean Intellectual Property Trial and Appeal Board:
1. Where he/she intends to reduce the number of claims;
2. Where he/she intends to rectify a clerical error;
3. Where he/she intends to clarify an ambiguous description (Patent Act Article 136(1)).

미 정정증명서

특허의 오류를 정정하기 위해 특허상표청이 발행하는 증명서.

certificate of correction

A certificate issued by the USPTO to correct a mistake in a patent.

정정청구

petition for correction

미 정직과 신의성실 의무

특허출원 준비 및 심사과정과 연관된 각 사람, 재심사 절차에서 특허권자와 연관된 개인은 특허상표청과의 절차에서 정직과 신의성실의 의무를 지니며 이는 개인이 알고 있는 특허성 결정에 중대한 모든 정보를 특허상표청에 개시할 의무를 포함한다.

duty of candor and good faith

Each individual associated with the preparation and prosecution of patent applications or Each individual associated with the patent owner in a reexamination proceeding has a duty of candor and good faith in dealing with the Office, which includes a duty to disclose to the Office all information known to that individual to be material to patentability.

ㅈ

제법(製法) 한정 물건발명

물건의 발명임에도 그 청구범위에 그 물건의 제조방법이 기재되는 경우로서, 그 제조방법의 기술적 특징을 고려하여 진보성을

product by process claim

A claim for a product invention that describes its manufacturing process. A product-by-process claim raises the issue of whether the technological characteristics of the

판단할 것인가 아니면 최종산물인 물건만을 기준으로 진보성을 판단할 것인가 문제가 있음.

process should be taken into consideration or only the final product must be assessed in determining non-obviousness.

제조물

manufacture

사용례 새롭고 유용한 방법, 기계장치, **제조물**, 조성물, 또는 이들에 대한 새롭고 유용한 개량을 한 자는 법정 조건 및 요건이 적용되는 경우를 예외로 하고 누구든지 특허를 받을 수 있다. (미) 특허법 101조.

Whoever invents or discovers any new and useful process, machine, **manufacture**, or composition of matter, or any new and useful improvement thereof, may obtain a patent therefor, subject to the conditions and requirements of this title. Patent Act, 35 U.S.C. § 101.

제척

exclusion (of a judge)

법관이 사건과 특수한 관계에 있는 경우 당해 사건에서 법률상 당연히 배제되는 것.

Disqualifying a judge from discharging his or her authority by law as to a certain case to which he or she has a special relation.

제척기간

statute of repose

권리의 법적 안정성 확보나 업무상의 신용보호 등을 위하여 심판을 청구(소송을 제기)할 수 있도록 한정된 기간.

The period within which parties can file actions for (administrative) trial, often limited to promote legal stability of rights and protect business reputation.

제품디자인

product design

사용례 **제품디자인** 트레이드 드레스로 구성된 표장은 결코 본질적인 식별력이 있다 할 수 없으며 출원인이 미 상표법 2(f)조에 따라 그 표장이 식별력을 취득하였음을 입증하지 아니하면 주등록부에 등록될 수 없다. (미) TMEP § 1202.02(b)(i).

A mark that consists of **product design** trade dress is never inherently distinctive and is not registrable on the Principal Register unless the applicant establishes that the mark has acquired distinctiveness under §2(f). TMEP § 1202.02(b)(i).

제품포장

product packaging

사용례 **제품포장**에 대한 출원표장에 본질적인 식별력이 없을 경우 그 표장은 미 상표법 2(f)조에 따라 사용에 의한 식별력 또는 2차적 의미를 입증함으로써 주등록부에 등록되거나 보조등록부에 등록될 수 있다. (미) TMEP § 1202.02(b)(ii).

If a proposed **product packaging** mark is not inherently distinctive, the mark may be registered on either the Principal Register under §2(f), upon proof that the mark has acquired distinctiveness or secondary meaning, or on the Supplemental Register. TMEP § 1202.02(b)(ii).

제호

title (of a book, etc.)

서적의 제호는 그것이 보통 일반적으로 사

As long as a title of a book is not commonly used and

용되는 것이 아니고 그 저작물의 내용을 직접 표시하는 것이 아닌 한은 서적이나 필름 등의 상표로서 사용되는 경우에는 다른 상품과 식별하는 능력이 있고 출처표시로서의 기능도 있다고 할 것이나, … (대법원 1995. 9. 26. 선고 95다3381 판결 참조).

does not directly indicate the content of the work of art, it is distinctive and works as a source identifier when used as a mark for books or films (Supreme Court Decision, 95Da3381, decided September 26, 1995).

젭슨 타입 청구항

jepson type claim

전제부와 특징부로 나뉘어 기재하는 젭슨 타입으로 기재된 청구항. 이 경우 전제부는 발명의 기술분야를 한정하는 경우, 발명의 기술이 적용되는 대상물품을 한정하는 경우, 공지의 기술로 생각하여 권리의 보호범위에서 제외하는 경우 등 여러 가지로 해석이 가능함. 특징부는 전제부와 조합하여 보호하고자 하는 그 발명의 기술적 특징을 가리킴.

A claim written in Jepson format, divided into the preamble and the body. The preamble may be construed as a limitation on the technical field of the invention, limitation on the product to which the technology of the invention is applied, or exclusion from the sought protection as it is deemed publicly known. The body is the technical characteristics of the claimed invention for which protection is sought in combination with the preamble.

조사관

judicial research officer, investigation officer

조성물

composition, compound

사용례 가령, 독립항에서 '적어도 20%의 나트륨'을 포함하는 것을 특징으로 하는 **조성물**에 대해 설명하고 종속항에서 나트륨 이외의 재료의 구체적 양을 기재하여 그 총 합이 명백히 나트륨을 제외하고 100%에 달하였다면 '적어도'라는 한정에 대한 모호성이 발생하였고 … (미) MPEP § 2173.05(c).

For example, when an independent claim recites a **composition** comprising "at least 20% sodium" and a dependent claim sets forth specific amounts of nonsodium ingredients which add up to 100%, apparently to the exclusion of sodium, an ambiguity is created with regard to the "at least" limitation … MPEP § 2173.05(c).

조어상표

coined mark

만들어진 말인 조어로 된 상표. 일반적으로 조어상표의 식별력은 암시적 상표, 기술적 상표, 보통명칭 상표 등에 비해 높게 평가됨(특허법원 2013. 11. 22. 선고 2013허5445 판결 참조).

A mark that consists of coined words. Generally, coined marks are considered to be more distinctive than suggestive mark, descriptive mark or generic mark (Patent Court Decision, 2013Heo5445, decided November 22, 2013).

사용례 이 사건 출원상표는 사전에 등재되지 않은 **조어**이고, 그 구성 문자도 띄어쓰기 없이 연결되어 있으나, 'air'와 'fryer' 모두 비교적 쉬운 영어단어이므로,

Although the mark is a **coined word** which is not registered in the dictionary, and the words constituting the mark are linked without spacing between the words, since both 'air' and 'fryer' are relatively easy English words, general

ㅈ

우리나라의 영어보급수준에 비추어 볼 때, 일반 수요자나 거래자는 이 사건 출원상표를 'air'와 'fryer'가 결합된 것임을 쉽게 인식할 수 있다(특허법원 2015. 4. 10. 선고 2014허4876 판결 참조).

consumers or traders are able to easily recognize that the mark is a combination of 'air' and 'fryer' in light of the knowledge level regarding English in Korea (Patent Court Decision, 2014Heo4876, decided April 10, 2015).

조정

mediation

조정전담판사

조기조정 절차에 회부된 사건은 원칙적으로 조정전담판사가 담당한다. 조정담당판사는 당사자와 협의하여 법원 외의 적당한 장소에서 조정절차를 진행할 수 있다(특허법원 침해소송 심리매뉴얼 VI.1.나).

mediation judge

In principle, the mediation judge shall be in charge of cases referred to an early mediation proceeding. Upon discussions with the parties, the mediation judge may conduct mediation proceedings at suitable locations other than the Court (Patent Court Guideline of Civil Practice and Procedure, VI.1.B).

존속기간

특허권의 존속기간은 제87조 제1항에 따라 특허권을 설정등록한 날부터 특허출원일 후 20년이 되는 날까지로 한다(특허법 제88조 제1항).

term, duration

The term of a patent shall begin on the registration date of the grant of the patent right under Article 87 (1) and last for 20 years from the filing date of the patent application (Patent Act Article 88(1)).

존속기간 갱신

상표권의 존속기간은 존속기간갱신등록신청에 의하여 10년씩 갱신할 수 있다(상표법 제83조 제2항).

renewal of duration

The duration of trademark rights may be renewed for another ten years by filing an application to register the renewal of the duration (Trademark Act Article 83(2)).

존속기간 만료

expiration of duration

존속기간의 연장

특허발명을 실시하기 위하여 다른 법령에 따라 허가를 받거나 등록 등을 하여야 하고, 그 허가 또는 등록 등(이하 "허가등"이라 한다)을 위하여 필요한 유효성 · 안전성 등의 시험으로 인하여 장기간이 소요되는 대통령령으로 정하는 발명인 경우에는 제88조 제1항에도 불구하고 그 실시할 수 없었던 기간에 대하여 5년의 기간까지 그 특허권의 존속기간을 한 차례만 연장할 수 있다(특허법 제89조 제1항).

extension of duration

Notwithstanding Article 88 (1), the term of a patent on an invention may be extended only once by up to five years to compensate for the period during which the invention cannot be executed, if the invention is specified by Presidential Decree and requires permission, registration, etc. under any other statute (hereinafter referred to as "permission, etc.") to execute patented invention but it takes a long time to undergo necessary tests for validity, safety, etc. for such permission, registration, etc. (Patent Act Article 89(1)).

종국판결

final decision, final judgment

종속항

특허청구항 중 독립항이나 다른 종속항을 인용하여 이를 한정하거나 부가하여 구체화하는 청구항.

dependent claim

A claim that refers back to and further limits a preceding dependent or independent claim. A dependent claim includes by reference every limitation of the claim on which it depends.

종자

「종자산업법」 제2조 제1호에 따른 종자 및 「수산종자산업육성법」 제2조 제3호에 따른 수산식물종자를 말함(식물신품종보호법 제2조 제1호).

seed

The seed as defined in subparagraph 1 of Article 2 of the Seed Industry Act as well as the seed of aquatic plants defined in subparagraph 3 of Article 2 of the Fisheries Seed Industry Promotion Act (Act on New Varieties of Plants Article 2.1).

종자산업법

Seed Industry Act

종합준비서면

사용례 **종합준비서면**을 제외한 나머지 준비서면에는 이미 주장한 내용을 반복하여 기재하지 않는다(특허법원 침해소송매뉴얼 VII.1.가.⑤).

comprehensive brief

In briefs other than the **comprehensive briefs**, arguments that have been previously made shall not be repeated (Patent Court Guideline of Civil Practice and Procedure, VII.1.A.5).

미 주등록부

미 특허상표청의 주된 상표등록부. 주등록부에 등록된 상표는 상표법 하의 모든 권리를 가짐. (미) USPTO.

Principal Register

Primary trademark register of the USPTO. When a mark has been registered on the Principal Register, the mark is entitled to all the rights provided by the Trademark Act. USPTO.

미 주로 단지 성(姓)만으로 구성된 표장

일반 수요자가 보기에 전체적으로 그 표장이 주로 성만을 나타내는 경우.

(A mark that is) primarily merely a surname

When the primary significance of the mark as a whole to the purchasing public is merely a surname.

사용례 상표로 등록하고자 하는 단어가 상표법상 **주로 단지 성만으로 구성**되었는지는 각각의 사례에 따라서만 판단할 수 있을 것이다. 영업과 관련이 있는 자의 성을 따라 정한 상표라 하더라도 일반적인 의미도 가지는 단어라면 상표법상 주로 단지 성

The question of whether a word sought to be registered is **primarily merely a surname** within the meaning of the statute can be resolved only on a case by case basis. Even though a mark may have been adopted because it is the surname of one connected with the business, it may not be primarily merely a surname under the statute because

만으로 된 상표에 해당하지 않는 것도 가능하다. 공중에게는 일반적 의미가 주된 의미일 가능성이 높기 때문이다. (미) In re Etablissements Darty Et Fils, 759 F.2d 15, 17 (Fed. Cir. 1985).

it is also a word having ordinary language meaning. The language meaning is likely to be the primary meaning to the public. In re Etablissements Darty Et Fils, 759 F.2d 15, 17 (Fed. Cir. 1985).

(판결)주문

판결은 재판장이 판결원본에 따라 주문을 읽어 선고하며, 필요한 때에는 이유를 간략히 설명할 수 있다(민사소송법 제206조).

judgment, order

The presiding judge shall pronounce a judgment by reading the text thereof pursuant to the original of judgment, and if deemed necessary, he/she may briefly explain the grounds therefor (Civil Procedure Act Article 206).

주문자상표 부착방식 (OEM)

자신의 상표가 아니라 주문자가 요구하는 상표로 상품을 생산하여 주는 주문자상표 부착생산 방식.

OEM (original equipment manufacturing)

Manufacturing products under a trademark requested by the client company instead of the manufacturer's own.

주변한정주의

출원인이 청구항을 직접 정의하는 중심한정주의의 반대개념으로, 배타적 권리를 주장하는 정확한 경계를 표시하게 하는 주의.

peripheral claiming

A regime in which an applicant delineates the precise boundaries of the claimed area of exclusivity, in contrast to central claiming in which the applicant defines the claim directly.

주신문

전문가 증인에 대한 주신문은 전문가증인 진술서의 범위 내에서 하여야 한다. 전문가 증인에게 주신문에서 제시하거나 인용하는 모든 자료는 증인신문기일 전에 증거로 제출되어야 한다(특허법원 침해소송매뉴얼 V.2.다).

direct examination

The direct examination of the expert witness by the party who requests for the witness shall be made within the scope of the statement of the expert witness. All materials presented or cited in the direct examination shall be submitted as evidence before the date designated for examining the witness (Patent Court Guideline of Civil Practice and Procedure, V.2.C).

주인용문헌

사용례 자명성의 판단을 뒷받침하기 위해서는 **주인용문헌**에 디자인 관념 이상의 것이 있어야 하며, 주장하는 디자인과 실질적으로 동일한 외관이 나타나야 한다. (미) MPEP § 1504.03.

primary references

Therefore, in order to support a holding of obviousness, a **primary reference** must be more than a design concept; it must have an appearance substantially the same as the claimed design. MPEP § 1504.03.

주지관용기술

well-known and commonly used art

사용례 원심은, 아래와 같은 이유를 들어, 확인대상발명은 그 발명이 속하는 기술분야에서 통상의 지식을 가진 사람(이하 '통상의 기술자'라 한다)이 그 판시 비교대상발명들과 **주지관용기술**로부터 용이하게 실시할 수 있는 자유실시기술에 해당하므로, 명칭을 '저용량의 엔테카비르 제제 및 그의 용도'로 하는 이 사건 특허발명(특허등록번호 생략)의 청구범위 제1항(이하 '이 사건 제1항 발명'이라 한다)과 대비할 필요 없이 그 권리범위에 속하지 아니한다고 판단하였다(대법원 2015. 5. 21. 선고 2014후768 전원합의체판결 참조).

As to the ground of appeal on whether the challenged invention is the state-of-the-art technologyA. On the grounds as laid out below, the lower court determined that the challenged invention is not subsumed in the scope of the right of the instant Patented Invention (patent registration number omitted) Claim 1 (hereinafter "Invention Claim 1"), titled, "low dosage entecavir tablet and its uses," without even having to contrast the two, since it constitutes the state-of-the-art technology that a person of ordinary skill in the art (hereinafter "a person with ordinary skill") can easily implement based on the cited inventions and **well-known and commonly used art** (Supreme Court Decision, 2014Hu768, decided May 21, 2015).

주지기술

well-known art

그 기술에 관해 상당히 다수의 문헌이 존재하거나, 또는 업계에 알려져 있거나, 혹은 예시할 필요가 없을 정도로 잘 알려진 기술과 같이 그 기술분야에서 일반적으로 알려진 기술.

A "well-known art" means a technology generally known in the relevant technical field, e.g., those appeared in many prior art documents, those widely known throughout the industry, or those well-known to the extent that there is no need to present examples.

주지디자인

well-known design

주지의 형상이나 모양을 거의 그대로 이용하거나 전용하여 물품에 표현하였거나 이들을 물품에 이용 또는 전용함에 있어서 그 디자인이 속하는 분야에서 통상의 지식을 가진 자라면 누구나 그 디자인이 그 물품에 맞도록 하기 위하여 가할 수 있을 정도의 변화에 지나지 아니한 디자인.

A design that adopts or appropriates well-known shape or pattern, or a design with immaterial change from such well-known shape or pattern that a person with ordinary knowledge in the field would be able to make to apply the design to the article.

사용례 … 따라서 이 사건 등록디자인은 통상의 디자이너가 **주지디자인**인 자연물로서의 화강암 무늬 등에 의하여 용이하게 창작할 수 있는 디자인에 해당한다(특허법원 2014. 4. 11. 선고 2014허447 판결 참조).

… Therefore, the registered design at issue may be easily created by an ordinary designer based on granite pattern in nature, a **well-known design** (Patent Court Decision, 2014Heo447, decided April 11, 2014).

주지모양

well-known pattern

한 국가 내에서 널리 알려진 모양. 물방울

A widely known shape in the country that may be identified

ㅈ

모양이나 체크모양 등과 같이 명칭으로써 그 모양을 특정할 수 있는 것.

by name, such as droplet shape or checkered shape.

사용례 이 사건 등록디자인은 국내에서 널리 알려진 **주지**의 형상, **모양**인 기린무늬, 거북등무늬 등을 단순 변형한 것으로서, … (특허법원 2016.03.31 선고 2015허8370 판결 참조).

The Subject Design is just a simple transformation of the pattern on the turtlebacks or giraffes which is a domestically **well-known** figure or **shape**, … (Patent Court Decision, 2015Heo8370, decided March 31, 2016).

주지상표

타인의 상품을 표시하는 것이라고 수요자간에 현저하게 인식되어 있는 상표. 주지상표로서 타인의 상표등록을 배제하려면 그 상표가 특정인의 상품에 사용되는 것임이 수요자 또는 거래자간에 널리 인식되어 있을 것이 필요하고, 구체적으로 그 상표가 주지인가의 여부는 그 사용, 공급, 영업활동의 기간, 방법, 태양, 사용량, 거래범위 등과 거래실정이나 사회통념상 객관적으로 널리 알려졌느냐의 여부가 일응의 기준이 된다고 할 것이다(대법원 1994. 1. 25. 선고 93후268 판결 참조).

well-known trademark

A mark conspicuously perceived among purchasers as indicating goods of another person. To prevent another person's trademark from being registered on the ground that it is well-known, widespread recognition among purchasers or traders that the mark is used by a particular source must be shown. More specifically, a prima facie case may be established based on the usage and supply of the mark, the method and period the good is marketed, the broadness of customer basis and course of trade, as well as how widely known it is when objectively viewed under social norms (Supreme Court Decision, 93Hu268, decided January 25, 1994).

주지저명상표

사용례 상표권자가 오인·혼동을 일으킬 만한 대상상표의 존재를 알면서 그 대상상표와 동일·유사한 실사용상표를 사용하면 상표 부정사용의 고의가 있다 할 것이고, 특히 그 대상상표가 **주지·저명 상표인 경우에는** 그 대상상표나 그 표장상품의 존재를 인식하지 못하였다는 등의 특별한 사정이 없는 한 고의의 존재를 추정할 수 있다(대법원 2012. 10. 11. 선고 2012후2227 판결 참조).

well-known and famous trademark

When a trademark owner uses a prior used trademark that is same or similar to a subject trademark while being fully aware of the latter's existence - which will likely result in misconception or confusion - and thus had the intent of trademark abuse. Additionally, if the subject trademark is **well-known and famous,** it is assumed that the aforementioned intent existed; provided that there were no unique circumstances, such as the trademark owner being unaware of the subject trademark or the products it marks (Supreme Court Decision, 2012Hu2227, decided October 11, 2012).

준비명령

사용례 항소장에 항소이유 기재가 충분하지 아니한 경우 항소사건이 접수된 직후 항소인에게 항소이유가 기재된 준비서면 제출을 명한다(특허법원 침해소송 항소심

preparatory order

An order issued to the appellant to submit a brief stating the ground of appeal immediately upon submission of a notice of appeal with insufficient statement of appeal (Guidelines of Civil Appelate Practice and Procedure of Patent Court

심리메뉴얼 2. 나.).

of Korea 2. B).

준비서면

사실, 주장 등을 기재한 소송절차 상의 서류.

brief

A document containing statement of facts, claim, etc. in litigation.

준용

사용례 실용신안에 관하여는 「특허법」 제3조부터 제7조까지, 제7조의2, 제8조부터 제25조까지, 제28조, 제28조의2부터 제28조의5까지의 규정을 **준용**한다(실용신안법 제3조).

application mutatis mutandis

Articles 3 through 7, 7-2, 8 through 25, 28, and 28-2 through 28-5 of the Patent Act shall **apply mutatis mutandis** to utility models (Utility Model Act Article 3).

중단

사용례 상표에 관한 절차가 **중단**되거나 중지된 경우에는 그 기간의 진행은 정지되고 그 절차의 수계 통지를 하거나 그 절차를 속행한 때부터 전체 기간이 새로 진행된다(상표법 제26조).

interruption

Where trademark-related procedures are **interrupted** or suspended, the running of the relevant period shall be suspended and the entire period shall recommence from the time the resumption of the procedures is notified or such procedures are continued (Trademark Act Article 26).

중복등록

같은 등록부 상의 동일한 등록.

duplicate registrations

Identical registrations on the same register.

중복특허

특허권자가 동일한 발명에 대하여 이중으로 특허를 등록하는 것을 방지하기 위한 원칙.

double patenting

The double patenting doctrine generally prevents a patentee from receiving two patents for the same invention.

중심적 식별력

등록상표의 전부 또는 일부 구성이 등록결정 당시에는 식별력이 없거나 미약하였다고 하더라도 그 등록상표를 전체로서 또는 일부 구성 부분을 분리하여 사용함으로써 권리범위확인심판의 심결 시점에 이르러서는 수요자 사이에 누구의 상품을 표시하는 것인지 현저하게 인식될 정도가 되어 중심적 식별력을 가지게 된 경우에는, 이를 기초로 상표의 유사 여부를 판단하여야 한다(대법원 2014. 3. 20. 선고 2011후3698 전원합의체 판결 참조).

central distinctiveness

Thus, in cases where the composition of a registered trademark, in whole or in part, may have had little or no distinctiveness at the time of registration, but the use of a trademark, in whole or in component part separately, has allowed the trademark to acquire central distinctiveness for consumers to manifestly recognize whose product it is by the time of adjudication decision on the scope of right, the similarity of trademarks should be determined based on that central distinctiveness (Supreme Court Decision, 2011Hu 3698, decided March 20, 2014).

ㅈ

중심한정주의

발명의 바람직한 구현례를 설명하는 청구항에 그와 균등한 범위까지 포함되는 것으로 간주하는 청구항 해석의 방법.

central claiming

A claiming regime in which a claim recites the preferred embodiment of the invention but is deemed to cover a range of equivalents to that preferred embodiment.

미 중용권

재발행 시 청구항이 수정되었을 경우 신뢰에 기초한 중용권이 발생함. 제3자는 기존 특허의 청구항에 의지할 수 있음.

intervening rights

Claims that were modified at reissue, for any reason, are subject to a reliance-type interest (intervening rights). Third parties may rely on the claims of an issued patent.

중의적 표현

한 가지 이상의 해석이 가능한 단어나 표현. 상표법에서는 그 상품 또는 서비스에 적용되었을 때 이중의 의미 또는 의의를 갖는 표현을 가리킴.

double entendre

A word or expression capable of more than one interpretation. For trademark purposes, an expression that has a double connotation or significance as applied to the goods or services.

사용례 마지막으로 특허상표청은 DialAMattress가 MATTRESS.COM이 **중의적 표현**이라는 증거를 제시하지 못하였으며 MATTRESS.COM이 연상기호에 해당하지도 않는다고 주장하였다. 본 법원은 MATTRESS.COM이 보통명칭에 해당한다는 TTAB의 결론이 상당한 증거에 의해 뒷받침되었다는 특허상표청의 주장에 동의한다. (미) In re 1800Mattress.com IP, LLC, 586 F.3d 1359, 1362 (Fed. Cir. 2009).

Finally, the PTO asserts that DialAMattress presented no evidence that MATTRESS.COM is a **double entendre** evoking a quality of comfort, and it is not a mnemonic. We agree with the PTO that substantial evidence supported the Board's conclusion that the mark MATTRESS.COM is generic. In re 1800Mattress.com IP, LLC, 586 F.3d 1359, 1362 (Fed. Cir. 2009).

중지

특허청장 또는 심판관이 천재지변이나 그 밖의 불가피한 사유로 그 직무를 수행할 수 없는 경우에는 특허청 또는 특허심판원에 계속 중인 절차는 그 사유가 없어질 때까지 중지된다(상표법 제25조 제1항).

suspension

Where the Commissioner of the Korean Intellectual Property Office or an examiner is unable to perform any of his/her duties due to a natural disaster or other extenuating circumstances, procedures pending in the Korean Intellectual Property Office or the Intellectual Property Trial and Appeal Board shall be suspended until such circumstance ceases to exist (Trademark Act Article 25(1)).

중지명령

불법행위에 대해 중지를 명하는 법원 또는 행정기관의 명령.

cease and desist order

An order of a court or an administrative agency to an individual or a business to stop a purportedly illegal activity.

미 증거개시절차

discovery

사용례 양 당사자가 37 C.F.R. § 42.51(a)(1) 하의 의무적 **증거개시절차**에 대한 합의에 실패할 경우 일방 당사자의 신청으로 증거개시를 요청할 수 있다. (미) 37 C.F.R. § 42.51(a)(2).

Where the parties fail to agree to the mandatory **discovery** set forth in paragraph (a)(1), a party may seek such discovery by motion. 37 C.F.R. § 42.51(a)(2).

증거보전

preservation of evidence

소송계속 전 또는 소송계속 중에 특정의 증거를 미리 조사해 두었다가 본안소송에서 사실을 인정하는 데 사용하기 위한 증거조사방법(민사소송법 제375조).

Collecting particular evidence prior to or during continuation of a litigation for factfinding in the main proceeding (Civil Procedure Act Article 375).

증거설명서

explanatory documents for evidence

미 증거의 우위성

preponderance of evidence

소송당사자가 그 입증책임을 충족시켰는지를 판단하기 위한 입증기준. 공정하고 중립적인 사람이 소송의 쟁점에 대하여 어느 한 쪽으로 마음을 정할 수 있을 만큼 증거의 비중이 기울어졌다고 보는 것.

A standard of proof applied to determine whether a party has met his or her burden of proof. The greater weight of the evidence that is sufficient to incline a fair and impartial mind to one side on the issue.

증거조사

examination of evidence

증명책임

burden of proof

증거로 주장을 뒷받침할 당사자의 의무.

A party's duty to substantiate his or her argument with evidence.

사용례 출원인이 청구된 기능을 수행하는 선행기술의 구성요소의 비균등성을 입증함에 있어 그 **증명책임**을 만족하였는지 결정하기 위하여는 다음과 같은 요소가 고려되며 … (미) MPEP § 2184.

When deciding whether an applicant has met the **burden of proof** with respect to showing nonequivalence of a prior art element that performs the claimed function, the following factors may be considered. … MPEP § 2184.

증명표장

certification mark

상품의 품질, 원산지, 생산방법 또는 그 밖의 특성을 증명하고 관리하는 것을 업으로 하는 자가 타인의 상품에 대하여 그 상품이 품질, 원산지, 생산방법 또는 그 밖의 특성

A mark used by a person who commercially certifies and manages the quality, place of origin, methods of production, or other characteristics of goods to certify that goods of others meet quality criteria, the place of origin, methods

을 충족한다는 것을 증명하는 데 사용하는 표장(상표법 제2조 제1항 제7호).

of production, or other characteristics (Trademark Act Article 2(1)7).

증분이익

침해제품의 시장 진입 이전 시점을 기준으로 특허권자가 특허제품 1대를 추가로 판매함으로써 얻었을 이익.

incremental profit

The profit a patent owner would have gained by selling additional unit of the patented product prior to the infringing good's entry into the market.

미 증언녹취

사용례 **증언녹취**는 구두 또는 서면질문에 따라 상대방에 최소 10일의 사전 고지에 따라 증언녹취장소에서 선서 또는 서약을 집행할 수 있는 직책에 있는 자 앞에서 할 수 있다. (미) 37 C.F.R. § 11.51(a).

deposition

Depositions may be taken upon oral or written questions, upon not less than ten days' written notice to the other party, before any officer authorized to administer an oath or affirmation in the place where the deposition is to be taken. 37 C.F.R. § 11.51(a).

증인소환장

증인에 대한 재판출석요청.

subpoenas to witnesses

A writ to summon a witness to appear in a court proceeding.

증인신문사항

전문가증인의 신문을 위해 필요한 사항(전문가증인 진술서 및 증인신문사항의 제출기한, 증인신문시간의 제한, 전문가증인의 증언의 신빙성을 탄핵하는 주장 및 증거의 제출기한 등)에 대해서는 준비명령을 할 수 있다(특허법원 침해소송 심리매뉴얼 VI.2. 나).

a questionnaire for the examination

The Court may issue a preparatory order for examination of an expert witness (e.g. deadlines for submission of affidavit and a questionnaire for the direct examination, limitation of the time for examination, and deadlines for submission of arguments and evidence for impeaching the credibility of the expert witness testimony) (Patent Court Guideline of Civil Practice and Procedure, VI.2.B).

미 지리적으로 기만적인 허위표시 표장

표장은 (1) 그 주된 의의가 일반적으로 알려진 지리적 위치에 대한 것이고, (2) 그 상품이나 서비스는 표장에 나타난 장소를 출처로 하지 아니하며, (3) 소비자들은 상품 또는 서비스가 표장에 나타난 장소를 출처로 한다고 믿을 것이라 보여지며, (4) 이러한 허위표시가 해당 분야의 소비자들이 그 상품을 구매하거나 서비스를 사용하기로 결정하는 데에 상당부분 중대한 요소로 작용할 경우 지리적인 기만적 허위표시 표장이라 함. (미) TMEP § 1210.01(b).

geographically deceptively misdescriptive marks

A mark is geographically deceptively misdescriptive if: (1) the primary significance of the mark is a generally known geographic location; (2) the goods or services do not originate in the place identified in the mark; (3) purchasers would be likely to believe that the goods or services originate in the geographic place identified in the mark; and (4) the misrepresentation is a material factor in a significant portion of the relevant consumer's decision to buy the goods or use the services. TMEP § 1210.01(b).

사용례 이 사건 표장[NORMANDIE CAMAMBERT]의 주된 의미는 일반적으로 알려진 지리적 위치, 즉 프랑스 노르망디의 명칭에 있다. 치즈와 노르망디 사이에는 상품-장소간 연관성이 존재한다. 출원인의 상품은 노르망디에서 생산되지 않으며 앞으로도 그러할 것이다. 당해 표장의 상품의 지리적 출처에 대한 허위표시는 상품의 구매결정에 중대한 요소로 작용한다. 따라서 NORMANDIE CAMAMBERT 표장은 지정상품인 치즈에 대하여 주로 **지리적으로 기만적인 허위표시 표장**으로, 출원인의 표장은 상표법 2(e)(3)에 따라 등록불가하다. (미) In re Cheezwhse.com, Inc., 85 U.S.P.Q. 2d 1917 (TTAB 2008).

The primary significance of the mark is the name of a generally-known geographic location, i.e., Normandy, France. A goods/place association exists between cheese and Normandy. Applicant's goods do not or will not originate in or from Normandy. The mark's misrepresentation of the geographic origin of the goods is or would be material to the decision to purchase the goods. Thus, we conclude that NORMANDIE CAMEMBERT is primarily **geographically deceptively misdescriptive** of "cheese," and that applicant's mark accordingly is unregistrable under Trademark Act Section 2(e)(3). In Re Cheezwhse.com, Inc., 85 U.S.P.Q.2d 1917 (TTAB Feb. 1, 2008).

미 지리적인 기만적 표장

deceptive geographical marks, geographically deceptive marks

→ 지리적인 기술적 표장 참조.

미 지리적인 기술적 표장

geographically descriptive marks

표장은 (1) 그 주된 의의가 일반적으로 알려진 지리적 위치에 대한 것이고, (2) 그 상품이나 서비스는 표장에 나타난 장소를 출처로 하며, (3) 소비자들은 상품 또는 서비스가 표장에 나타난 장소를 출처로 한다고 믿을 것이라 보여질 때 주로 지리적인 기술적 표장이라 함. (미) TMEP § 1210.01(a).

A mark is primarily geographically descriptive if (1) the primary significance of the mark is a generally known geographic location; (2) the goods or services originate in the place identified in the mark; and (3) purchasers would be likely to believe that the goods or services originate in the geographic place identified in mark. TMEP § 1210.01(a).

지리적 표시

geographical indication

상품의 특정 품질 · 명성 또는 그 밖의 특성이 본질적으로 특정지역에서 비롯된 경우에 그 지역에서 생산 · 제조 또는 가공된 상품임을 나타내는 표시(상표법 제2조 제1항 제4호).

An indication used to identify goods produced, manufactured, or processed in a specific area in cases where a certain quality, reputation or other characteristic of goods has essentially originated from such specific area (Trademark Act Article 2(1)4).

사용례 타인의 상품을 표시하는 것이라고 수요자들에게 널리 인식되어 있는 상표(**지리적 표시**는 제외한다)와 동일 · 유사한 상표로서 그 타인의 상품과 동일 · 유사한 상품에 사용하는 상표는 상표등록을 받을 수 없다(상표법 제34조 제1항 9).

None of the following trademarks shall be registered: … 9. Any trademark identical or similar to a trademark (excluding a **geographical indication**) widely recognized by consumers as indicating the goods of another person, which is used on goods identical or similar to the goods of another person; … (Trademark Act Article 34(1)9).

지리적 표시 단체표장

지리적 표시를 사용할 수 있는 상품을 생산·제조 또는 가공하는 자가 공동으로 설립한 법인이 직접 사용하거나 그 소속 단체원에게 사용하게 하기 위한 표장(상표법 제2조 제1항 제6호).

collective mark with geographical indication

A mark intended to be used directly by a corporation incorporated by persons who produce, manufacture, or process goods on which a geographical indication may be used, or is intended to be used by its members (Trademark Act Article 2(1)6).

지리적 표시 증명표장

지리적 표시를 증명하는 것을 업으로 하는 자가 타인의 상품에 대하여 그 상품이 정해진 지리적 특성을 충족한다는 것을 증명하는 데 사용하는 표장(상표법 제2조 제1항 제8호).

certification mark with geographical indication

A mark used by a person who commercially certifies a geographical indication to certify that goods of others meet specified geographical characteristics (Trademark Act Article 2(1)8).

지배적 특징

사용례 … 양 디자인 사이에 위와 같은 차이점이 존재하기는 하나, 그 차이의 정도가 양 디자인의 **지배적인 특징**을 나타내는 위 유사점 ④, ⑤로 말미암은 유사성을 상쇄하여 양 디자인이 전체적으로 다른 심미감을 나타낼 정도로는 보기 어렵다(특허법원 2015. 4. 23. 선고 2014허6858 판결 참조).

dominant features

Despite the aforementioned dissimilarity, it is difficult to say that the extent of dissimilarity is significant enough to extinguish the similarity of the **dominant features** stated above in points ④ and ⑤ (Patent Court Decision, 2014Heo6858, decided April 23, 2015).

미 지속적 노력

발명의 착상일을 곧 발명일로 하기 위하여는 발명자는 착상으로부터 발명의 구현에 이르기까지 지속적인 노력을 기울였어야 함.

due diligence

To establish a conception date as the date of invention, the inventor must have worked diligently following conception to reduce the invention to practice.

지정국

국제출원을 하려는 자가 그 지식재산권을 보호받으려는 국가. 국제등록의 명의인(이하 "국제등록명의인"이라 한다)은 국제등록된 지정국을 추가로 지정(이하 "사후지정"이라 한다)하려는 경우에는 산업통상자원부령으로 정하는 바에 따라 특허청장에게 사후지정을 신청할 수 있다(상표법 제172조 제1항).

designated country

The country the person who intends to file an international application seeks protection of his or her intellectual property. Where a holder of an international registration (hereinafter referred to as "holder of an international registration")intends to additionally designate a designated country internationally registered (hereinafter referred to as "subsequent designation"), he/she may file an application for subsequent designation with the Commissioner of the Korean Intellectual Property Office, as prescribed by Ordinance of the Ministry of Trade, Industry and Energy (Trademark Act Article 172(1)).

지정된 사무소 — **elected office**

지정상품 — **designated good**

상표등록을 받고자 하는 경우 상품 분류에 따라 지정상품을 하나 이상 정하여 신청을 하여야 한다(상표법 제38조).

Any person who intends to file an application for trademark registration shall file an application for each trademark by designating at least one category of goods in accordance with the classification of goods (Trademark Act Article 38).

사용례 선등록상표보다 먼저 출원되어 등록된, **지정상품**을 '전기매트리스, 전열식 카펫' 등으로 하고 '명품한솔'로 구성된 상표에 관한 상표권을 취득하였다고 하더라도… (특허법원 2015. 4. 23. 선고 2014허6858 판결 참조).

Even if the Plaintiff had obtained rights to the trademark "명품한솔" used on the **designated goods** ("electric mattress, electric carpet") for which application for registration was filed earlier than the previously registered trademark … (Patent Court Decision, 2014Heo6858, decided April 23, 2015).

지정상품추가등록 — **registration of additional designated goods**

상표권자 또는 출원인은 등록상표 또는 상표등록출원의 지정상품을 추가하여 상표등록을 받을 수 있다(상표법 제86조 제1항).

A trademark right holder or an applicant may obtain trademark registration by adding designated goods to the registered trademark or to the application for trademark registration (Trademark Act Article 86(1)).

직권(에 의한) — **ex officio**

당사자의 신청이 아닌 법원 또는 심판기관의 권한에 의함.

By the authority of court or administrative trial board, rather than by request of parties.

직권보정 — **ex officio amendment**

심사관이 출원서 또는 도면에 적힌 사항이 명백히 잘못된 경우 출원자의 신청에 의하지 아니하고도 그러한 사항을 보정하는 것.

Amendment of clear error in an application or drawing by the examiner, without request of the applicant.

직권심리 — **ex officio hearing**

심판관이 당사자 또는 참가인이 신청하지 아니한 이유에 대해 심리하는 것. 이 경우 심판관은 당사자 또는 참가인에게 그 이유에 대해 진술할 기회를 주어야 함.

An administrative judge may hold hearings about grounds a party or an intervenor did not mention in his or her application. In such cases, the administrative judge shall give them an opportunity to state their opinions on such grounds.

직권심사 — **ex officio examination**

직권조정결정

사용례 종자위원회는 당사자 간에 합의가 이루어지지 아니한 경우 또는 신청인의 주장이 이유 있다고 판단되는 경우에는 당사자들의 이익과 그 밖의 모든 사정을 고려하여 신청 취지에 반하지 아니하는 한도에서 직권으로 조정을 갈음하는 결정(이하 "**직권조정결정**"이라 한다)을 할 수 있다 (식물신품종보호법 제123조 제1항).

ex officio decisions of mediation

Where parties fail to reach an agreement or a requester's claim is deemed reasonable, the Seed Commission may make an ex officio decision in lieu of mediation (hereinafter referred to as "**ex officio decision of mediation**") and insofar as it does not go against the intent of the request, taking into consideration the interests of the parties and all other circumstances (Act on Protection of New Varieties of Plants Article 123(1)).

직무발명

종업원, 법인의 임원 또는 공무원이 그 직무에 관하여 발명한 것이 성질상 사용자·법인 또는 국가나 지방자치단체의 업무 범위에 속하고 그 발명을 하게 된 행위가 종업원 등의 현재 또는 과거의 직무에 속하는 발명을 말함(발명진흥법 제2조 제2호).

employee invention

An invention that an employee, executive officer of a corporation, or public official makes in connection with his/her duties, where it falls within the scope of business of the employer, the corporation, the State, or the competent local government and the activities that have led to the invention fall within the present or past duties of the employee, etc. (Invention Promotion Act Article 2.2).

직무발명에 대한 보상

종업원 등은 직무발명에 대하여 특허 등을 받을 수 있는 권리나 특허권 등을 계약이나 근무규정에 따라 사용자등에게 승계하게 하거나 전용실시권을 설정한 경우에는 정당한 보상을 받을 권리를 가진다(발명진흥법 제15조 제1항).

compensation for employee invention

An employee, etc. shall be entitled to fair compensation where the employer, etc. succeeds, under a contract or employment regulations, to the right to acquire patent, etc., or a patent, right, etc., for an employee's invention, or are to be granted an exclusive license in the patent right, etc. (Invention Promotion Act Article 15(1)).

직접침해

권한 없이 특허발명에 대하여 생산, 사용, 판매의 청약, 판매 또는 수입을 한 자는 직접침해에 대한 책임이 있음.

direct infringement

A person is liable for direct infringement if he or she makes, uses, offers to sell, sells or imports any patented invention without authority.

진보성

특허요건의 하나(특허법 제29조 제2항). 특허출원 전에 통상의 기술자가 선행발명에 의하여 쉽게 발명할 수 있는 발명에 해당하는 경우 특허를 받을 수 없음.

inventive step, inventiveness, non-obviousness

One of the requirements for patent registration (Patent Act Article 29(2)). An invention is not patentable if a person skilled in the art would have come up with the invention at issue based on prior arts before the filing of the application.

(통상적인 상거래에서) 진실한 사용

사용정도, 거래의 성질이나 수준, 해당 업

bona fide use (in the ordinary course of trade)

Bona fide use is found based on the amount of use, the

계의 일반적 사용방법 등을 바탕으로 판단함.

nature or quality of the transaction and what is typical use in the particular industry.

진정상품

genuine goods

진정한 상표권자에 의해 적법하게 제조되어 유통된 상품.

A product lawfully manufactured and distributed by the true owner of registered trademark.

사용례 …사실관계가 이러하다면 국외에서 제조·판매되는 상품과 국내 전용사용권자가 제조·판매하는 상품 사이에 품질상 아무런 차이가 없다거나 그 제조·판매의 출처가 동일한 것이라고 할 수 없고, … 이러한 경우에는 이른바 **진정상품**의 병행수입이라고 하더라도 국내 전용사용권을 침해하는 것으로서 허용되지 않는다고 보아야 할 것이다(대법원 1997. 10. 10. 선고 96도2191 판결 참조).

Based on the foregoing facts, we shall not conclude that there is no difference in quality between the goods manufactured and sold abroad and the goods manufactured and sold by the exclusive licensee in Korea, or that both goods are manufactured and sold by the same source. … In such cases, parallel import of the so-called **genuine goods** infringes the exclusive license in Korea and therefore is not allowed (Supreme Court Decision, 96Do2191, decided October 10, 1997).

진정성립

establishment of authenticity

제출된 서증에 대하여, 문서가 작성명의인의 의사에 의하여 작성되었음을 말함.

Establishment of the fact that a submitted documentary evidence was created at the will of the person identified as the author of the document.

사용례 문서에 대한 **진정성립**의 인정여부는 법원이 모든 증거자료와 변론 전체의 취지에 터 잡아 자유심증에 따라 판단하는 것이고, 사문서의 진정성립에 관한 증명방법에 관하여는 특별한 제한이 없으나 그 증명 방법은 신빙성이 있어야 하고, … (대법원 2010. 6. 24. 선고 2009다10980 판결 참조).

Whether or not the **authenticity** of a document is **established** is determined at the discretion of the court based on the overall evidence and arguments submitted. While there is no particular limitation, the method of authentication of private document must be credible (Supreme Court Decision, 2009Da10980, decided June 24, 2010).

질권

pledge

사용례 전용사용권 또는 통상사용권을 목적으로 하는 **질권**의 설정·이전(상속이나 그 밖의 일반승계에 의한 경우는 제외한다)·변경·포기에 의한 소멸 또는 처분의 제한은 등록하지 아니하면 제3자에 대항할 수 없다(상표법 제100조 제2항, 특허법 제121조).

Establishment, transfer (excluding transfer by inheritance or other general succession), amendment, extinguishment by abandonment or restrictions on disposition of a **pledge**, the object of which is to acquire the exclusive license or the non-exclusive license (Trademark Act Article 100(1)2, Patent Act Article 121).

미 징벌적 손해배상

고의침해 시 침해자에게 인정된 손해의 최대 3배까지 증액하여 배상하도록 함. Halo 미 대법원 판결 이후 침해의 고의는 더 이상 객관적인 무모함(recklessness)이 아닌 침해자의 주관적 인지에 따라 결정되며, 그 입증책임 기준도 '명백하고 확실한 증거(clear and convincing evidence)'에서 '증거의 우월성(preponderance of evidence)'으로 완화되었다. (미) Halo Elecs., Inc. v. Pulse Elecs., Inc., 136 S. Ct. 1923, 1927, 195 L. Ed. 2d 278 (2016).

punitive damages

An infringer may be liable for punitive damages up to three times of the amount found in case of willful infringement. Willfulness is now determined by subjective knowledge of the infringer instead of objective recklessness. In addition, the burden of proof is now easier to satisfy, as the applicable standard has changed to preponderance of evidence from clear and convincing evidence. Halo Elecs., Inc. v. Pulse Elecs., Inc., 136 S. Ct. 1923, 1927, 195 L. Ed. 2d 278 (2016).

ㅊ

참가

이해관계가 있는 제3자 또는 행정청이 당해 사건에 참가하는 것.

intervention

A third party or administrative agency that has an interest in matters at issue joining the lawsuit.

참고도면

사용례 패턴의 특성이나 패턴이 표시되는 물품의 종류, 물품에서 패턴이 차지하는 특정한 위치, 적용 시 패턴에서 그 구성요소가 갖는 크기나 범위에 따라 반복패턴이 주는 인상이 달라질 수 있으므로, **참고도면**은 보통 등록하고자 하는 표장의 성질을 적절히 묘사하지 못할 것이다. (미) TMEP § 1202.19(a)(iii).

swatch-type drawing

These **swatch-type drawings** usually will not adequately depict the nature of the mark for which registration is sought, because the impression created by a repeating pattern may change depending on the nature of the pattern, the type of item on which the pattern appears, the particular placement of the pattern on that item, and the size and scale of the elements in the pattern as applied. TMEP § 1202.19(a)(iii).

참조 조문

reference provisions

창작상표

상표 또는 서비스표로의 기능만을 위해 만들어진 단어로 된 상표. 그 언어에 없는 말(예: PEPSI, KODAK, EXXON)이거나 보통의 용례를 완전히 벗어난 경우(예: FLIVVER. FLIVVER는 실패, 실수 등의 뜻을 가지며 저가의 승용차를 지정상품으로 하여 사용됨).

fanciful mark

Fanciful marks comprise terms that have been invented for the sole purpose of functioning as a trademark or service mark. Such marks comprise words that are either unknown in the language (e.g., PEPSI, KODAK, EXXON) or are completely out of common usage (e.g., FLIVVER for low-priced vehicle).

(증거의) 채부 — admissibility (of evidence)

처분통지서 — notice of action

특허청장 또는 특허심판원장은 무효처분 또는 무효처분의 취소처분을 할 경우에는 그 보정명령을 받은 자에게 처분통지서를 송달하여야 한다(상표법 제18조, 디자인보호법 제18조).

Where the Commissioner of the Korean Intellectual Property Office or the Director General of the Intellectual Property Trial and Appeal Board invalidates procedures or revokes the invalidation, he/she shall serve a notice of his/her action on a person ordered to make an amendment (Trademark Act Article 18; Design Protection Act Article 18).

청각상표 — aural marks

→ 소리상표 참조

→ See. sound marks.

청구 — claim, complaint, petition

청구범위 제출유예제도 — provisional application

출원일 확보 등을 위하여 특허출원서에 청구범위를 생략한 채 발명의 설명만을 기재하여 임시로 제출한 출원.

A temporary application mainly submitted to secure a filing date, containing explanation as to the invention but without claims.

청구범위 — claims

발명을 정의하여 특허권자에게 부여되는 배타적 권리의 범위. 특허발명의 보호범위는 청구범위에 적혀 있는 사항에 의하여 정하여진다(특허법 제97조).

Claims define the invention and are the scope of exclusive rights granted to the patent owner. The scope of protection of a patented invention shall be determined by the descriptions of the claims (Patent Act Article 97).

청구원인 — cause of action

청구의 취지 — plaintiff's demand, relief demanded, purport of claim

소로써 달성하려는 사회경제적 목적, 소의 결론. 심판을 청구하려는 자는 심판청구서에 반드시 청구의 취지 및 그 이유를 기재하여야 함.

The conclusion of the plaintiff's action, i.e. the social and economic objective the plaintiff seeks to achieve by filing the action. Any person who intends to request a trial shall state a relief demanded in the suit and any grounds therefor.

청구인 — petitioner

청구항 — claims

→ 청구범위 참조

청구항 구성요소

→ 구성요소 참조

claim element

사용례 정보가 충분히 제공되지 않아 하나 이상의 필수적인 **청구항의 구성요소**나 구성요소 간 관계가 통상의 기술자가 과도한 실험 없이는 개발할 수 없을 정도이어서 실시가능성에 의문이 제기되는 경우는 흔히 발생한다. 이 경우 심사관은 구체적으로 어떤 정보가 필요하며 발명이 실시가능하기 위하여 그 정보가 왜 필요한지도 설명하여야 한다. (미) MPEP § 2164.06(a).

It is common that doubt arises about enablement because information is missing about one or more essential **claim elements** or relationships between elements which one skilled in the art could not develop without undue experimentation. In such a case, the examiner should specifically identify what information is missing and why the missing information is needed to provide enablement. MPEP § 2164.06(a).

청구항 발명

특허 또는 특허출원의 청구항에서 정의된 발명의 대상.

claimed invention

The subject matter defined by a claim in a patent or an application for a patent.

청구항 한정

사용례 항고심판소에서는 '모발 성장을 회복시킨다'는 **청구항의 한정**을 모발이 원상태로 회복되어야 하는 것으로 해석하였는데 법원은 이를 청구항 한정의 부정확한 해석인 것으로 판시하였다. (미) MPEP § 2111 (In re Cortright, 165 F.3d 1353, 1359 (Fed. Cir. 1999) 인용).

claim limitation

The Board's construction of the **claim limitation** "restore hair growth" as requiring the hair to be returned to its original state was held to be an incorrect interpretation of the limitation. MPEP § 2111 (citing In re Cortright, 165 F.3d 1353, 1359 (Fed. Cir. 1999)).

청구항 해석

사용례 청구항의 특징부에서 출원발명의 모든 한정사항을 완전하고 있는 그대로 설명하고 전제부는 출원발명의 한정사항에 대해 뚜렷한 정의를 제시하지 아니하며 발명의 목적이나 의도된 용도 등만을 진술할 경우, 전제부는 한정사항을 포함하는 것으로 간주되지 아니하고 **청구항 해석**에 있어 아무 비중을 갖지 아니한다. (미) MPEP § 2111.02.

claim construction (interpretation)

If the body of a claim fully and intrinsically sets forth all of the limitations of the claimed invention, and the preamble merely states, for example, the purpose or intended use of the invention, rather than any distinct definition of any of the claimed invention's limitations, then the preamble is not considered a limitation and is of no significance to **claim construction**. MPEP § 2111.02.

청산

liquidation, windup

미 최적 실시례

명세서에는 최적의 실시례 또는 바람직한

best mode

The specification must set forth the best mode, or preferred

구현례를 기재하여야 함. 개정 특허법에는 최적 실시례를 기재하지 않는 것을 무효 사유의 기초로 보는 규정을 삭제함.

embodiment. The America Invents Act eliminated failure to set forth best mode as a basis for patent invalidity.

사용례 명세서에는 발명의 상세한 기재와 그 발명과 관련되거나 가장 근접한 분야에서 통상의 기술자라면 누구든지 똑같이 이를 생산하고 사용할 수 있을 만큼 전체적이고 명확, 간결, 정확한 용어로 된 그 발명을 생산하고 사용하는 방법과 과정, 그리고 그 발명을 실시하는 발명자나 공동발명자가 고려하기에 **최적의 실시례**를 제시하여야 한다. (미) 특허법 112(a)조.

The specification shall contain a written description of the invention, and of the manner and process of making and using it, in such full, clear, concise, and exact terms as to enable any person skilled in the art to which it pertains, or with which it is most nearly connected, to make and use the same, and shall set forth the **best mode** contemplated by the inventor or joint inventor of carrying out the invention. 35 U.S.C. § 112(a).

미 최초 거래상 사용일

date of first use in commerce

상표가 표시된 상품을 최초로 판매하거나 운송한 일자, 서비스를 최초로 개시한 일자. 단 그러한 사용이 통상의 거래에서의 진실한 사용이며 미국 의회가 합법적으로 규제할 수 있는 상거래 상의 사용에 해당하여야 함.

The date when the goods were first sold or transported, or the services were first rendered, under the mark in a type of commerce that may be lawfully regulated by the U.S. Congress, if such use is bona fide and in the ordinary course of trade.

최초거절이유통지

non-final office action

새로운 흠결사항에 대한 특허청의 통지로 주로 심사 초기단계에 해당함. 출원인은 출원이 포기되는 것을 막기 위해 그 통지에 대해 정해진 기간 이내에 반박하여야 함.

An Office action letter that raises new issues in the initial phase of the examination process. Applicants must respond to non-final Office action letters within a given time to avoid abandonment of the application.

미 최초사용일

date of first use anywhere

상표가 표시된 상품을 최초로 판매하거나 운송한 일자, 서비스를 최초로 개시한 일자. 단 그러한 사용이 통상의 거래에서의 진실한 사용에 해당하여야 함. (미) TMEP § 903.01.

The date when the goods were first sold or transported, or the services were first rendered, under the mark, if such use is bona fide and in the ordinary course of trade. TMEP § 903.01.

미 최초심사

initial examination

사용례 **최초 심사**에서 심사관이 주등록부에 등록하기 위한 출원의 표장이 이의신청을 위해 공지될 조건을 갖추었다고 판단하면 그 출원을 공지하도록 허가한다. (미) TMEP § 704.01.

If, on **initial examination**, the examining attorney finds the mark in an application for registration on the Principal Register to be in condition for publication for opposition, the examining attorney will approve the application for publication. TMEP § 704.01.

ㅊ

최초 청구항

original claim

미 최초 출원

original application

사용례 **최초출원**신청으로 이론적으로는 그 시점에 발명이 구현된 것으로 간주하여야 하나, 해당 출원을 이후 포기함으로써 그 효과 또한 포기한 것이다. 그러나 최초출원신청은 발명의 착상에 대한 증거가 된다. (미) In re Costello, 717 F.2d 1346, 1350 (Fed. Cir. 1983).

While the filing of the **original application** theoretically constituted a constructive reduction to practice at the time, the subsequent abandonment of that application also resulted in an abandonment of the benefit of that filing as a constructive reduction to practice. The filing of the original application is, however, evidence of conception of the invention. In re Costello, 717 F.2d 1346 (Fed. Cir. 1983).

최후거절이유통지

final (Office) action

이전의 최초 통지부터 계속되는 출원의 거절이유를 다시 나열하고 종국적으로 미해결되었음을 알리는 통지.

An Office action that restates all outstanding issues from previous non-final office action(s) and holds these issues final.

추상적 관념

abstract idea, abstraction

추상적 관념, 자연법칙, 자연현상은 특허적격성이 결여됨.

Abstract ideas, as well as the laws of nature and natural phenomena are not patentable subject matter.

사용례 방법청구항이 **추상적 관념**을 설명하는 것인지 결정하려면 그 청구항을 전체적으로 판단하여야 하고 단지 자연법칙이나 수학적 알고리즘에 기반한다는 이유만으로 특허적격성이 없는 것은 아님을 상기하여야 한다. (미) Digitech Image Techs., LLC v. Elecs. for Imaging, Inc., 758 F.3d 1344, 1350 (Fed. Cir. 2014).

In determining whether a process claim recites an **abstract idea**, we must examine the claim as a whole, keeping in mind that an invention is not ineligible just because it relies upon a law of nature or mathematical algorithm. Digitech Image Techs., LLC v. Elecs. for Imaging, Inc., 758 F.3d 1344, 1350 (Fed. Cir. 2014).

추인

confirm, ratify

행위능력 또는 법정대리권이 없거나 필요한 권한의 위임에 흠이 있는 자가 밟은 절차는 보정(보정)된 당사자나 법정대리인이 추인하면 행위를 한 때로 소급하여 그 효력이 발생한다.

Procedures followed by a person who has no legal capacity or authority of legal representation, or who has any defect in the delegation of authority shall take effect retroactive to the time he/she performed an act if the party whose defect has been rectified or his/her legal representative confirms such procedures.

추후보완

subsequent completion, supplementation

특허에 관한 절차를 밟은 자가 책임질 수 없는 사유로 다음 각 호의 어느 하나에 해

If a person who has initiated a patent-related procedure fails to complete the procedure within either of the following

당하는 기간을 지키지 못한 경우에는 그 사유가 소멸한 날부터 2개월 이내에 지키지 못한 절차를 추후 보완할 수 있다. 다만, 그 기간의 만료일부터 1년이 지났을 때에는 그러하지 아니하다(특허법 제17조).

periods due to a cause not attributable to him/her, he/she may subsequently complete the procedure within 2 months after the cause ceases to exist: Provided, That the foregoing shall not apply where one year has passed since the expiration of the specified period (Patent Act Article 17).

출원

특허나 상표 등의 등록요청서류. 각 법에 정해진 요건을 만족시켜야만 출원일자를 받을 수 있음.

application

A document by which a person requests registration of a patent, trademark, etc. An application must satisfy the requirements prescribed in the relevant laws to receive a filing date.

출원경과

file history, prosecution history

출원경과 금반언의 원칙

공지기술에 의한 등록거절을 피하기 위한 목적 등으로 청구범위를 감축하거나 또는 좁게 해석하여야 한다고 주장함으로써 특허를 받은 경우, 나중에 출원 중에 포기한 보호범위를 균등론에 의하여 회복하는 것은 허용되지 않는다는 원칙.

file wrapper estoppel, prosecution history estoppel

A patent owner whose application was granted based on the argument that the claims must be reduced or narrowly interpreted, in order to avoid refusal on the ground of publicly known art, shall not be allowed to reclaim his or her rights by the doctrine of equivalents if the rights were so waived in the application.

사용례 확인대상별명이 특허발명의 권리범위에 속한다고 할 수 있기 위하여는 특허발명의 각 구성요소와 구성요소 간의 유기적 결합관계가 확인대상별명에 그대로 포함되어 있어야 할 것이고, 다만 확인대상별명에 구성요소의 치환 내지 변경이 있더라도 양 발명에서 과제의 해결원리가 동일하며, 그러한 치환에 의하더라도 특허발명에서와 같은 목적을 달성할 수 있고 실질적으로 동일한 작용효과를 나타내며, 그와 같이 치환하는 것을 그 발명이 속하는 기술분야에서 통상의 지식을 가진 자가 용이하게 생각해 낼 수 있을 정도로 자명하다면, 확인대상별명이 특허발명의 출원시에 이미 공지된 기술 내지 공지기술로부터 당업자가 용이하게 발명할 수 있었던 기술에 해당하거나 특허발명의 **출원절차를 통하여 확인대상별명의 치환된 구성요소가 청구범위로부터 의식적으로 제외된 것에 해당**하는

In order for the invention in quetion to be within the scope of patented invention, the organic composite relationship between each element of the patented invention shall be included in the invention in quetion. However, even if there is a substitution or modification of the element of the invention in quetion, where the substituted element of the invention in quetion is considered equivalent to the corresponding element of the patented invention, then the invention in quetion is still within the scope of the patented invention if the principles of establishing both inventions are the same, the invention in quetion could achieve the same objective and essentially obtain the same effect even though it is due to the substitution and it is self-evident that such substitution is that a person having ordinary skill in the technology (skilled in the technology) could easily have made, unless there are special circumstances such that the technology has been already publicly known or could have easily been invented by those skilled in the technology

ㅊ

등의 특별한 사정이 없는 한, 확인대상별명의 치환된 구성요소는 특허발명의 대응되는 구성요소와 균등관계에 있는 것으로 보아 확인대상별명은 여전히 특허발명의 권리범위에 속한다고 보아야 한다(대법원 2001. 8.21, 선고, 98후522, 판결 참조).

from the known prior technology or that the substituted element of the invention in quetion and therefore, this substituted element was **purposefully excluded from the scope of the request for a patent during the application procedure** (Supreme Court Decision, 98Hu522, decided August 21, 2001).

출원공개

publication of patent applications, laying-open of applications (법제처)

특허청장은 특허출원일로부터 1년 6개월이 지난 후 또는 그 전이라도 특허출원인이 신청한 경우에는 그 특허출원에 관하여 특허공보에 게재하여 출원공개를 하여야 한다(특허법 제64조 제1항).

The Commissioner of the Korean Intellectual Property Office shall publish a patent application in the Patent Gazette to lay it open, filing date of the patent application (Patent Act Article 64(1)).

출원공고

publication of the application

사용례 심사관은 상표등록출원에 대하여 거절이유를 발견할 수 없는 경우에는 **출원공고**결정을 하여야 한다 … (상표법 제57조 제1항).

Where an examiner fails to discover any grounds for rejection of an application for trademark registration, he/she shall decide to **publish such application**: … (Trademark Act Article 57(1)).

미 출원데이터시트

application data sheet (ADS)

가출원의 경우 미 특허법 111(b)조, 정규출원은 111(a)조, 정규 국제디자인출원이나 국내단계출원의 경우 371조에 따라 제출할 수 있으며, 119, 120, 121, 365, 386조 하에서 선출원에 기한 우선권을 주장할 경우 37 C.F.R. § 1.55조나 1.78조에 따라 반드시 제출하여야 함. 출원의 일부를 구성. (미) 37 C.F.R. § 1.76(a).

A sheet or sheets that may be submitted in a provisional application under Patent Act, 35 U.S.C. § 111(b), a nonprovisional application under Patent Act, 35 U.S.C. § 111(a), a nonprovisional international design application, or a national stage application under Patent Act, 35 U.S.C. § 371 and must be submitted when required by § 1.55 or 1.78 to claim priority to or the benefit of a prior-filed application under Patent Act, 35 U.S.C. § 119, 120, 121, 365, or 386. The application data sheet is part of the application for which it has been submitted. 37 C.F.R. § 1.76(a).

출원변경

modification of the application

출원의 주체나 내용의 동일성을 유지하면서 출원의 형식만을 변경하는 것. 예를 들어 특허출원을 실용신안등록출원으로 변경하는 것.

Making procedural modification to an application while maintaining the identity of the applicant or the substance. E.g. modifying a patent application into a utility model application.

출원심사청구

request for examinations of applications

미 출원의 기초

미국 내 상표등록출원의 법정 기초. 출원인은 상표 또는 서비스표의 출원을 함에 있어서 최소 1개의 출원의 기초를 명시하고 그에 필요한 요건을 만족하여야 함. (미) 37 C.F.R. §2.32(a)(5).

filing basis

The statutory basis for filing an application for registration of a mark in the United States. An applicant must specify and meet the requirements of one or more bases in a trademark or service mark application. 37 C.F.R. §2.32(a)(5).

출원의 보정

amendment of application

출원의 포기

명시적 출원포기 또는 정해진 기한 내에 필요한 조치를 취하지 못함으로 인하여 계류 출원목록에서 출원이 삭제되는 것.

abandonment of application

Removal of an application from the docket of pending applications, either by express abandonment or failure to take proper action within the specified period.

출원의 회복

등록료의 보전 등으로 출원의 효력을 회복하는 것.

recover, reinstate

Reinstating the effectiveness of application, for example by paying outstanding balance of registration fee.

사용례 제2항에 따라 상표등록출원, 지정상품추가등록출원 또는 상표권(…)이 회복된 경우에는 그 상표등록출원등의 효력은 제72조 제3항 또는 제74조에 따른 납부기간이 지난 후 상표등록출원등이 **회복**되기 전에 그 상표와 동일 · 유사한 상표를 그 지정상품과 동일 · 유사한 상품에 사용한 행위에는 미치지 아니한다(상표법 제77조 제3항).

Where an application for trademark registration, an application for registration of additional designated goods or a bundle of trademark rights (…) has been recovered pursuant to paragraph (2), such application for trademark registration, etc. shall not effect an act of using a trademark identical or similar to such trademark on goods identical or similar to such designated goods before the application for trademark registration, etc. is **recovered** after the period for payment under Article 72 (3) or 74 expires (Trademark Act Article 77(3)).

출원의 회복요청

request to reinstate an application

출원일

법에 규정된 대로 출원에 필요한 모든 요소가 특허청에 제출된 일자.

application filing date

The date on which all the elements for an application as set forth in the law are received by the KIPO.

출원일자의 회복

사용례 출원일자 발급 거부가 특허상표청의 실수로 인한 것이라 보는 출원인은 그

request to restore filing date

If an applicant believes that the USPTO committed an error in denying the application a filing date, the applicant may

ㅊ

출원일자의 회복요청을 할 수 있다. (미) TMEP § 204.02.

submit a request to restore the filing date. TMEP § 204.02.

출원포대

file wrapper

출처

source

사용례 둘 이상의 지리적 표시 등록단체표장이 서로 동음이의어 지리적 표시에 해당하는 경우 각 단체표장권자와 그 소속 단체원은 지리적 **출처**에 대하여 수요자가 혼동하지 아니하도록 하는 표시를 등록단체표장과 함께 사용하여야 한다(상표법 제223조).

Where at least two registered collective marks with geographical indication correspond to a mutually homonymous geographical indication, each collective mark right holder and its members shall use a mark that prevents consumers from being confused about the geographical **source** along with its registered collective mark (Trademark Act Article 223).

출처의 오인(혼동)

mistake and confusion as to the source

사용권자가 등록상표 구성의 일부를 변경, 가감, 축소, 확대하여 변형 사용함으로써 타인이 사용하는 상표와 오인 또는 혼동을 일으키는 경우를 의미함.

When a trademark owner or licensee changes, modifies, limits or expands a part or parts of the registered trademark and thereby causing misconception or confusion with other person's trademark.

사용례 상표권자가 **오인 · 혼동**을 일으킬 만한 대상상표의 존재를 알면서 그 대상상표와 동일 · 유사한 실사용상표를 사용하면 상표 부정사용의 고의가 있다 할 것이고, 특히 그 대상상표가 주지 · 저명 상표인 경우에는 그 대상상표나 그 표장상품의 존재를 인식하지 못하였다는 등의 특별한 사정이 없는 한 고의의 존재를 추정할 수 있다(대법원 2012. 10. 11. 선고 2012후2227판결 참조).

When a trademark owner uses a prior used trademark that is same or similar to a subject trademark while being fully aware of the latter's existence - which will likely result in **mistake or confusion** - and thus had the intent of trademark abuse. Additionally, if the subject trademark is widely recognized and well-known, it is assumed that the aforementioned intent existed; provided that there were no unique circumstances, such as the trademark owner being unaware of the subject trademark or the products it marks (Supreme Court Decision, 2012Hu2227, decided October 11, 2012).

출처표시기능

source indication

동일한 상표가 사용된 상품은 동일한 출처(source)에서 생산되어 동일한 판로(channel)를 거쳐 판매된다는 것을 수요자에게 나타내는 상표의 기능.

A function of trademark; indicating to consumers that goods that use the same trademark are produced by the same source and sold through the same channel.

사용례 상표는 기본적으로 당해 상표가 부착된 상품의 출처가 특정한 영업주체임을 나타내는 상품**출처표시기능**과 이에 수

Given that a trademark's main functions boil down to **source indication** that the goods to which the mark is affixed come from a particular business, along with quality assurance…

반되는 품질보증기능이 주된 기능이라는 점 등에 비추어 볼 때, … (대법원 2002. 9. 24. 선고 99다42322 판결 참조).

(Supreme Court Decision, 99Da42322, decided September 24, 2002).

취소

cancellation

(심판청구의) 취하

withdrawal (of request for administrative trial)

심사청구인이 해당 심사청구를 철회하는 등의 의사표시로서 이를 취하하면 처음부터 심판청구가 없었던 것으로 됨. 심판청구는 심결이 확정될 때까지 취하할 수 있다. 다만, 답변서가 제출된 후에는 상대방의 동의를 받아야 한다(특허법 제161조 제1항).

A petitioner's act of withdrawing an already filed request. Withdrawal renders the petition as if it was never filed in the first place. A petition for trial may be voluntarily withdrawn before a trial ruling becomes final and conclusive: Provided, That once the defendant has submitted a response, his/her consent shall be obtained to withdraw such petition (Patent Act Article 161(1)).

치환

replacement, substitution

사용례 확인대상발명이 특허발명의 권리범위에 속한다고 할 수 있기 위해서는 특허발명의 청구범위에 기재된 각 구성요소와 그 구성요소 간의 유기적 결합관계가 확인대상발명에 그대로 포함되어 있어야 한다. 한편, 확인대상발명에서 특허발명의 청구범위에 기재된 구성 중 **치환** 내지 변경된 부분이 있는 경우에도, 양 발명에서 과제의 해결원리가 동일하고, 그러한 **치환**에 의하더라도 특허발명에서와 같은 목적을 달성할 수 있고 실질적으로 동일한 작용효과를 나타내며, 그와 같이 **치환**하는 것이 그 발명이 속하는 기술분야에서 통상의 지식을 가진 사람이라면 누구나 용이하게 생각해 낼 수 있는 정도로 자명하다면 확인대상발명은 전체적으로 특허발명의 청구범위에 기재된 구성과 균등한 것으로서 여전히 특허발명의 권리범위에 속한다고 보아야 한다(대법원 2010.5.27, 선고, 2010후296, 판결 참조).

An invention in question falls under the scope of the patent right of a patented invention only when each element and the whole combination of its components as specified within the scope of the patent claim for the patented invention are intact within the invention in question. Even in cases where an invention in question contains portions which **replace or substitute** elements included in the scope of a patent claim for a patented invention, if both inventions share the same solution principle, if such a replacement still makes it possible to achieve the goal of the patented invention and enables an identical effect on an actual level, and if this **replacement** is self-evident to the extent that any person of ordinary skill in the pertinent field of technology could have easily conceived it, then the invention in question must be seen as equivalent in whole to the elements specified in the scope of the patent claim for a patented invention (Supreme Court Decision, 2010Hu296, decided May 27, 2010).

치환가능성

interchangeability

특허 균등침해의 요건의 하나. 균등침해가 성립하기 위해서는 치환에 의하더라도 특허발명에서와 같은 목적을 달성할 수 있고

One of requirements of infringement by equivalents. The requirement is met when the invention in question, even if by replacement, achieves the same objective and enables

실질적으로 동일한 작용효과를 나타내야 함.

a practically identical effect as the patented invention.

치환자명성

특허 균등침해의 요건의 하나. 균등침해가 성립하기 위하여는 그와 같이 치환하는 것을 그 발명이 속하는 분야에서 통상의 지식을 가진 자가 용이하게 생각해 낼 수 있을 정도로 자명해야 한다는 것.

level of obviousness of replacement

One of the requirements of infringement by equivalents. The requirement is met if the replacement is self-evident to the extent that any person of ordinary skill in the pertinent field of technology could have easily conceived it.

사용례 확인대상발명이 특허발명의 권리범위에 속한다고 할 수 있기 위해서는 특허발명의 청구범위에 기재된 각 구성요소와 그 구성요소 간의 유기적 결합관계가 확인대상발명에 그대로 포함되어 있어야 한다. 한편, 확인대상발명에서 특허발명의 청구범위에 기재된 구성 중 치환 내지 변경된 부분이 있는 경우에도, 양 발명에서 과제의 해결원리가 동일하고, 그러한 치환에 의하더라도 특허발명에서와 같은 목적을 달성할 수 있고 실질적으로 동일한 작용효과를 나타내며, **그와 같이 치환하는 것이 그 발명이 속하는 기술분야에서 통상의 지식을 가진 사람이라면 누구나 용이하게 생각해 낼 수 있는 정도로 자명하다면** 확인대상발명은 전체적으로 특허발명의 청구범위에 기재된 구성과 **균등**한 것으로서 여전히 특허발명의 권리범위에 속한다고 보아야 한다(대법원 2010. 5. 27. 선고 2010후296 판결 참조).

An invention in question falls under the scope of the patent right of a patented invention only when each element and the whole combination of its components as specified within the scope of the patent claim for the patented invention are intact within the invention in question. Even in cases where an invention in question contains portions which replace or substitute elements included in the scope of a patent claim for a patented invention, if both inventions share the same solution principle, if such a replacement still makes it possible to achieve the goal of the patented invention and enables an identical effect on an actual level, and **if this replacement is self-evident to the extent that any person of ordinary skill in the pertinent field of technology could have easily conceived it**, then the invention in question must be seen as **equivalent** in whole to the elements specified in the scope of the patent claim for a patented invention (Supreme Court Decision, 2010Hu296, decided May 27, 2010).

침해

특허나 저작권, 상표권자의 배타적 권리를 침범하는 행위.

infringement

An act that interferes with the exclusive rights of a patent, copyright, or trademark owner.

침해금지청구권

특허권 등의 소유권자 또는 전용실시권자는 자기의 권리를 침해한 자 또는 침해할 우려가 있는 자에 대하여 그 침해의 금지 또는 예방을 청구할 수 있음.

petition (request) for an injunction against infringement

An owner of patent or other rights, or an exclusive licensee thereof, may seek an injunction for prohibition or prevention of infringement against a person who infringes or is likely to infringe on his/her rights.

ㅋ

침해로 인한 손해

침해행위로 발생한 손실에 대한 금전적 배상.

damages for infringement

Monetary award to compensate for the loss incurred by the act of infringement.

미 칭송형(稱頌型) 용어(표장)

상품 또는 서비스의 품질이나 우수성을 나타내는 단어. 칭송형 용어는 미 상표법 2(e)(1)조의 단순기술표장으로 분류됨. (미) TMEP § 1209.03(k).

laudatory terms (mark)

Terms that attribute quality or excellence to goods or services. Laudatory terms are merely descriptive under§2(e)(1). TMEP § 1209.03(k).

사용례 상품이 가지고 있는 것으로 주장하는 이점을 묘사하는 **칭송형 표장**은 단순히 압축적으로 그 상품의 성질이나 품질을 묘사하는 것이므로 기술적 표장이다. … 따라서, 소비자들이 즉각적으로 THE ULTIMATE BIKE RACK을 Nett Designs의 자전거 거치대의 우수성을 드러내는 찬사적 및 기술적인 문구로 간주할 것이라는 TTAB의 결정을 뒷받침하는 상당한 증거가 존재한다. (미) In re Nett Designs, Inc., 236 F.3d 1339, 1342 (Fed. Cir. 2001).

Laudatory marks that describe the alleged merit of the goods are descriptive because they simply describe the characteristics or quality of the goods in a condensed form. … Accordingly, substantial evidence supports the Board's finding that consumers will immediately regard THE ULTIMATE BIKE RACK as a laudatory descriptive phrase that touts the superiority of Nett Designs' bike racks. In re Nett Designs, Inc., 236 F.3d 1339, 1342 (Fed. Cir. 2001).

ㅋ

크로스 라이센싱

상호간에 서로가 가진 특허권의 실시를 양해하는 것.

cross licensing

Where parties grant licenses to each other in exchange for license of the other's patent.

ㅌ

타인의 업무와 관련된 물품과 혼동을 가져올 염려가 있는 디자인

사용례 원고는, 이 사건 등록디자인이 그 출원 전에 이미 공지된 디자인들과 유사하거나 그 디자인들로부터 용이하게 창작할 수 있는 디자인에 해당함은 물론 **타인의 업무에 관계되는 물품과 혼동을 가져올 염**

design likely to cause confusion with articles associated with others' business

The plaintiff filed an action to invalidate design registration, claiming that the registered design at issue is similar to designs that were publicly known prior to its application or **is likely to create confusion with articles associated with others' business** … and therefore the registration shall be

려가 있는 디자인에 해당하므로 … 그 등록이 무효로 되어야 한다고 주장하면서 등록무효심판을 청구하였는데, … (특허법원 2010. 2. 11. 선고 2009허7765 판결).

invalidated. … (Patent Court Decision, 2009Heo7765, decided February 11, 2010).

통상사용권

→ 통상실시권 참조

non-exclusive license

통상실시권

등록권리에 대한 자신의 사용권을 유지하면서 다른 사람에게도 사용하도록 허락하는 것.

non-exclusive license

By granting a non-exclusive license, a right holder keeps his or her right to use the registered right along with the licensee.

사용례 특허권자는 그 특허권에 대하여 타인에게 **통상실시권**을 허락할 수 있다(특허법 제102조 제1항).

A patentee may grant a **non-exclusive license** of the patent to others (Patent Act Article 102).

통상실시권 설정의 재정

제3자가 특허법 제107조 각호 중 어느 하나에 해당하는 사유로 인하여 특허발명을 실시할 필요가 있고, 그와 같은 실시를 위하여 특허권자 또는 전용실시권자와 합리적인 조건 하에 협의를 시도하였음에도 통상실시권 설정계약이 이루어지지 않은 경우, 또는 그와 같은 협의를 할 수 없는 경우 그 제3자는 특허청장에게 통상실시권 설정에 관한 재정을 청구할 수 있음(특허법 제107조 제1항).

adjudication on grant of non-exclusive licenses

If a patented invention falls under any grounds elaborated in Article 107(1), and a person who intends to execute the patented invention fails, or is unable, to reach agreement with the patentee or exclusive licensee of the patented invention on the grant of a non-exclusive license under reasonable terms and conditions, although the person has negotiated the agreement, the person may file a petition for adjudication on the grant of the non-exclusive license with the Commissioner of the Korean Intellectual Property Office (Patent Act Article 107(1)).

통상실시권 허락의 심판

특허출원을 한 자가 선출원 특허발명 등을 이용하는 관계에 있거나 저촉 관계에 있는 경우, 후출원 특허권자가 선출원자의 허락 없이 후출원 특허발명을 실시하면 선출원자의 권리를 침해하게 되지만, 특허법은 선출원자가 정당한 이유 없이 실시허락을 하지 않는 경우 후출원자가 필요한 범위 내에서 심판을 통해 실시권 허락을 받도록 함.

trial for grant of non-execlusive licenses

In case a patented invention uses or interferes with an earlier-filed patented invention, the patent owner of the later-filed invention infringes the rights of the earlier-filed patent if he or she exploits the invention without permission of the earlier-filed patent's owner. However, the permission may be granted via administrative trial if necessary if the owner of earlier-filed patent refuses to grant license without just cause.

통상의 거래

ordinary course of business

통상의 관찰자

ordinary observer

사용례 디자인의 유사 여부는 이를 구성하는 각 요소를 분리하여 개별적으로 대비할 것이 아니라 그 외관을 전체적으로 대비 관찰하여, **보는 사람(통상의 관찰자)**으로 하여금 상이한 심미감을 느끼게 하는지의 여부에 따라 판단하여야 하고, … (특허법원 2015. 4. 23. 선고 2014허6858 판결 참조).

In determining the question of similarity of the designs in contention, a judge or an examiner is not to compare individual features that comprise the designs separately, but rather must consider whether an **ordinary observer** is able to identify differing aesthetic features by comparing and contrasting each designs' over all appearance (Patent Court Decision, 2014Heo6858, decided April 23, 2015).

통상의 기술자

person having ordinary skills in the art

출원시에 당해 기술분야의 기술상식을 보유하고 있고, 연구개발을 위하여 통상의 수단 및 능력을 자유롭게 구사할 수 있으며, 출원시의 기술수준에 있는 모든 것을 입수하여 자신의 지식으로 할 수 있고, 발명의 과제와 관련되는 기술분야의 지식을 자신의 지식으로 할 수 있는 가상의 인물.

A hypothetical person that possesses the technological common sense at the time of the patent application, who can utilize ordinary means and ability for research and development with ease, collect all the information in the state of the art at the time of the application and make it his/her own, and process the knowledge in the technological field relevant to the technical problem of the invention.

투여용법 및 투여용량

administration and dosage (of a medicine)

사용례 의약이라는 물건의 발명에서 대상 질병 또는 약효와 함께 **투여용법과 투여용량**을 부가하는 경우, 투여용법과 투여용량이 발명의 구성요소인지 여부(적극) 및 투여용법과 투여용량이라는 새로운 의약용도가 부가되어 신규성과 진보성 등의 특허요건을 갖춘 의약에 대해서 새롭게 특허권이 부여될 수 있는지 여부(적극) 이 법리가 권리범위확인심판에서 심판청구인이 심판의 대상으로 삼은 확인대상발명이 공지기술로부터 용이하게 실시할 수 있는지를 판단할 때에도 마찬가지로 적용되는지 여부(적극) (대법원 2015. 5. 21. 선고 2014후768 전원합의체판결 참조).

In a case where the **administration and dosage** of a medicine are added on top of the target disease or efficacy of a pharmaceutical medicine as an invention of a product, whether the administration and dosage constitute an element of invention (affirmative), and whether a patent may be newly granted to a pharmaceutical medicine meeting the patentability requirements including novelty and non-obviousness by adding a new pharmaceutical use, namely, administration and dosage (affirmative) / Whether this legal principle likewise applies when determining whether the challenged invention brought by the petitioner as the subject matter of a trial to confirm the scope of a patent right could be easily implemented from the publicly known art (affirmative) (Supreme Court Decision, 2014Hu768, decided May 21, 2015).

트레이드 드레스

trade dress

제품디자인이나 제품포장, 색채, 외관상의 식별력 있는 비기능적 구성요소.

A product's design, product packaging, color, or other distinguishing nonfunctional element of appearance.

사용례 일반적으로 **트레이드 드레스**는 그 특성이 물건의 용도나 목적에 필수적이거나 그 비용 또는 품질에 영향을 미칠 경우 기능적이며 상표로 사용할 수 없다. (미) QualitexCo. v. Jacobson Prods. Co., 514 U.S. 159, 165, 34 USPQ2d 1161, 1163-64 (1995) ; TMEP § 1202.02(a).

In general terms, **trade dress** is functional, and cannot serve as a trademark, if a feature of that trade dress is "essential to the use or purpose of the article or if it affects the cost or quality of the article." QualitexCo. v. Jacobson Prods. Co., 514 U.S. 159, 165 (1995); TMEP § 1202.02(a).

특허결정

심사관은 특허출원에 대하여 거절이유를 발견할 수 없으면 특허결정을 하여야 한다(특허법 제66조).

decision to grant patent; determination to grant patent (법제처)

If an examiner finds no ground to reject a patent application, he/she shall determine to grant a patent (Patent Act Article 66).

특허공보

patent gazette

특허관리인

국내에 주소 또는 영업소가 없는 자(이하 "재외자"라 한다)는 재외자(법인의 경우에는 그 대표자)가 국내에 체류하는 경우를 제외하고는 그 재외자의 특허에 관한 대리인으로서 국내에 주소 또는 영업소가 있는 자(이하 "특허관리인"이라 한다)에 의해서만 특허에 관한 절차를 밟거나 이 법 또는 이 법에 따른 명령에 따라 행정청이 한 처분에 대하여 소를 제기할 수 있다(특허법 제5조 제1항).

patent administrator

No person with no domicile or place of business in the Republic of Korea (hereinafter referred to as "overseas resident") shall initiate any patent-related procedure or file legal proceedings against a disposition made by an administrative authority under this Act or an order issued under this Act, unless he/she is represented by an agent with respect to his/her patent, who has a domicile or place of business in the Republic of Korea (hereinafter referred to as "patent administrator"), except where the overseas resident (or the representative if the overseas resident is a corporation) sojourns in the Republic of Korea (Patent Act Article 5(1)).

특허관리전문사업자 (NPE)

특허기술을 이용한 상품의 제조 또는 판매, 서비스 공급 등은 하지 아니하면서도 특허를 실시하는 자 등에 대한 특허권의 행사를 통하여 수익을 창출하는 것을 사업활동으로 하는 사업자를 말함.

non-practicing entity (NPE)

A business entity engaging in business activities to make profits by exercising a patent over patent licensees, etc., rather than manufacturing or selling products or providing services by applying the patented technology.

특허권

특허권은 설정등록에 의하여 발생한다(특허법 제87조 제1항).

patent right

A patent shall take effect when the grant of the patent is registered (Patent Act Article 87(1)).

E

특허권의 존속기간

특허권의 존속기간은 제87조 제1항에 따라 특허권을 설정등록한 날부터 특허출원일 후 20년이 되는 날까지로 한다(특허법 제88조 제1항).

term of patent

The term of a patent shall begin on the registration date of the grant of the patent right under Article 87 (1) and last for 20 years from the filing date of the patent application (Patent Act Article 88(1)).

특허권의 효력범위

특허발명의 보호범위는 청구범위에 적혀 있는 사항에 의하여 정하여진다(특허법 제97조).

scope of protection of patent

The scope of protection of a patented invention shall be determined by the descriptions of the claims (Patent Act Article 97).

특허권자

특허권의 소유권자. 특허권자는 특허가 발행된 자뿐 아니라 그 권원의 승계자를 포함한다.

patentee, patent holder

A patent owner. Patentees include not only the one to whom the patent was issued but also the successors in title to the patentee.

미 특허대리인

USPTO의 변리사시험(patent bar)을 통과하여 특허의 출원 및 심사과정에서 타인을 대리할 자격을 가진 자.

patent agent

Those who are authorized to represent others in patent application and prosecution by passing USPTO's patent bar.

미 특허 대상

일반적으로 새롭고 유용한 방법, 기계장치, 제조물, 조성물, 또는 이들에 대한 새롭고 유용한 개량은 법에 의한 조건이나 요건이 적용되는 경우를 예외로 하고 무엇이든 특허 대상이 된다. (미) 특허법 101조.

patentable subject matter

In general, any new and useful process, machine, manufacture, or composition of matter, or any new and useful improvement thereof, subject to the conditions and requirements under the law. 35 U.S.C. § 101.

특허등록원부

특허청에 있는, 특허권 등의 설정, 이전, 소멸, 회복, 처분의 제한 또는 존속기간의 연장 등을 등록하는 장부.

(patent) register

A book in the KIPO that is used to enter the grant, expiration, reinstatement of patents or other rights, restrictions on the disposal and the extension of terms, etc.

특허료

특허권의 설정등록을 받으려는 자는 설정등록을 받으려는 날로부터 3년분의 특허료를 내야 한다(특허법 제79조).

patent fee

A person who intends to register the establishment of patent rights shall pay patent fees for three years from the date he or she intends to register the patent rights (Patent Act Article 79).

특허발명
특허를 받은 발명.

patented invention
Invention for which a patent has been granted.

특허법원 심결취소소송 심리 매뉴얼

Guideline of Practice and Procedure of Revocation Action in the Patent Court of Korea

특허법원 침해소송 항소심 심리 매뉴얼

Guideline of Civil Appellate Practice and Procedure of the Patent Court of Korea

미 **특허변호사**
USPTO의 변리사시험(patent bar exam) 및 해당 주의 변호사 시험(bar exam)을 통과하여 특허의 출원 및 심사과정뿐만 아니라 소송에서까지 타인을 대리할 자격을 가진 자.

patent attorney
Those who are authorized to represent others in patent application, prosecution and litigation in court by passing USPTO's patent bar and a state bar exam in the U.S.

미 **특허성에 대한 실질적인 새로운 문제 (SNQP)**
재심사를 청구한 각 청구항에 영향을 미치는 특허성에 관한 실질적인 새로운 문제가 있어야 한다는 재심사 개시를 위한 요건.

substantial new question of patentability (SNQP)
The requirement for reexamination that there must be a substantial new question of patentability that affects all claims raised in the request for reexamination.

특허심사관
특허청에 소속되어 특허 등 산업재산권의 출원을 심사하는 자.

patent examiner
KIPO examiners who review applications for patent and other industrial rights.

미 **특허심사지침**

Manual of Patent Examining Procedure (MPEP)

특허심판관
특허심판원에 소속되어 특허심판을 담당하는 자.

administrative patent judge
Administrative judges who preside over administrative patent trials in the Intellectual Property Trial and Appeal Board.

특허심판원

Intellectual Property Trial and Appeal Board (IPTAB)

특허억류
특허권자의 특허기술이 표준필수특허가 됨

patent holdup
An opportunistic move by a patentee, whose patented

에 따라 기회주의적으로 그 특허의 가치 자체를 상회하는 실시료를 요구하는 것. 이를 방지하기 위해 보통 FRAND 확약을 요구한다.

technology is an SEP, to demand royalties exceeding the value of the patent itself. As a preventive measure, patentees are often required to make FRAND commitment.

E

특허요건

발명이 특허로 등록되기 위한 요건. 신규성, 진보성, 산업상 이용가능성.

requirements for patent registration, patentability

The requirements an invention must to be patented. Novelty, inventiveness and industrial applicability.

특허원부

patent register

특허증

patent registration certificate

특허청

Korean Intellectual Property Office (KIPO)

특허출원에 대한 정보제공

특허출원에 관하여 누구든지 그 특허출원이 거절이유에 해당하여 특허될 수 없다는 취지의 정보를 증거와 함께 특허청장에게 제공할 수 있다. 다만, 제42조 제3항 제2호, 같은 조 제8항 및 제45조에 따른 요건을 갖추지 아니한 경우에는 그러하지 아니하다(특허법 제63조의2).

provision of information about patent applications

Any person may provide the Commissioner of the Korean Intellectual Property Office with information that a patent application is ineligible for a patent as it falls under a ground for rejection, along with evidentiary documents: Provided, That the foregoing shall not apply where the patent application fails to meet any of the requirements prescribed under Articles 42 (3) 2 and (8) and Article 45 (Patent Act Article 63-2).

특허취소신청

누구든지 특허권의 설정등록일부터 등록공고일 후 6개월이 되는 날까지 그 특허가 다음 각 호의 어느 하나에 해당하는 경우에는 특허심판원장에게 특허취소신청을 할 수 있다(특허법 제132조의2 제1항).

petition for patent cancellation

In any of the following cases, Any person may file a petition for the cancellation to the Director General of the Intellectual Property Trial and Appeal Board, if six month have not passed since the date when the registration of the patent is published after the grant of the patent is registered (Patent Act Article 132-2(1)).

특허침해

특허권자 또는 전용실시권자의 허락 없이 권리자의 의사에 반하여 특허를 실시하는 것.

patent infringement

Execution of a patent in the absence of a permission by the patent owner or an exclusive licensee against their will.

특허표시

특허권자, 전용실시권자 또는 통상실시권

patent marking

A patentee or exclusive or non-exclusive licensee may mark

자는 다음 각 호의 구분에 따른 방법으로 특허표시를 할 수 있다. 1. 물건의 특허발명의 경우: 그 물건에 특허표시 2. 물건을 생산하는 방법의 특허발명의 경우: 그 방법에 따라 생산된 물건에 특허표시 3. 물건에 특허표시를 할 수 없는 경우: 그 물건의 용기 또는 포장에 특허표시(특허법 제223조).

his/her products as patented in any of the following relevant manners: 1. If the patent is for the invention of a thing: The patent shall be marked on the thing; 2. If the patent is for the invention of a process for manufacturing a thing: The patent shall be marked on the thing manufactured by the process; 3. If it is impossible to mark the patent on a thing: The patent shall be marked on the containers or packaging of the thing (Patent Act Article 223).

특허풀

특정 제품의 생산 등에 필요한 다수의 특허를 하나의 풀(pool)로 묶어 그 소속 기업들 간 크로스 라이센싱 등을 통해 각 기술마다 개별적으로 실시권을 얻을 때 발생하는 부담을 줄이는 등의 기능을 수행함.

patent pool

A patent pool put together multiple patents that are essential to manufacture a particular product, for example, and allows its member companies to cross-license their patented technologies that belong to the pool, which lowers the burden of individually obtaining licenses for each patent in the pool.

특허협력조약 (PCT)

외국의 여러나라에 동일한 발명에 대한 특허를 받고자 하는 출원인이 소정의 방식에 따라 지정국을 표시하여 하나의 국제출원을 수리관청에 제출하면 각 지정국에 위 국제출원일에 정규의 출원이 있었던 것으로 효력을 인정받는 것을 특징으로 하는 조약.

Patent Cooperation Treaty (PCT)

According to this treaty, a patent applicant who is planning to apply patent registration in several foreign countries may file a single application in a prescribed form designating the countries he/she is willing to have the patent registered, then it is deemed that the applicant filed application in the designated countries on the date he/she filed international application.

TSM기준 (교시, 암시, 동기)

선행기술에 통상의 기술자로 하여금 그 선행기술을 결합하도록 하는 교시, 암시, 동기가 있었을 경우 그 발명은 특허를 받을 수 없다고 하는 자명성에 대한 테스트 KSR 판례의 '상식적 선택' 기준에 의하여 제한됨. → 상식적 선택 및 시도의 자명성 참조.

teaching, suggestion and motivation (TSM)

An obviousness test that provides teaching, suggestion or motivation to combine the prior arts by a person having ordinary skills in the art found in the prior arts renders the invention unpatentable. Limited by "common sense selection" test in KSR v. Teleflex, 550 U.S. 398 (2007). → See. common sense selection; obvious to try.

ㅍ

(판결의) 파기

사용례 원심판결을 **파기**하고, 사건을 특허법원에 환송한다(대법원 2016. 11. 25. 선고 2014후2184 판결 참조).

reverse (judgment)

Judgment of the lower court is **reversed**, and the cases is remanded to the Patent Court of Korea (Supreme Court Decision, 2014Hu2184, decided November 25, 2016).

파라미터 발명

파라미터 발명은 물리, 화학 분야에서 표준적이거나 흔하게 사용되지 않는 특성값을 창출하고 복수의 특성값 간 상관관계를 이용하여 산술적으로 파라미터화하여 이를 발명의 필수적 구성요소의 일부로 하는 발명을 말함.

parameter invention

A parameter invention is an invention in which an applicant creates a certain parameter which is not standard or commonly used in physics or chemistry, parameterizes it arithmetically by using the correlation among plural parameters, and employs it as a part of essential elements of the invention.

미 파생

사용례 **파생**은 타인에 의한 완전한 발명의 착상이 이루어졌다는 것과 그 착상에 대하여 파생행위를 하였다고 주장되는 당사자가 발명에 대한 지식을 가지고 있음이 입증된 날보다 그 이전 날짜에 그 당사자 상호간에 소통이 이루어졌을 것을 요한다. (미) MPEP § 2137.

derivation

Derivation requires complete conception by another and communication of that conception by any means to the party charged with derivation prior to any date on which it can be shown that the one charged with derivation possessed knowledge of the invention. MPEP § 2137.

미 파생절차

미 개정특허법에 따라 신설된 절차로, 발명자가 제3자의 선출원된 출원 또는 등록에 대하여 그 특허대상이 발명자 본인의 작업으로부터 파생되었음을 주장할 수 있도록 하며 저촉심사를 대체함.

derivation proceeding

A new proceeding established under the America Invents Act that allows an inventor to challenge an earlier filed third party application or patent claiming subject matter that was derived from the inventor's own work. This proceeding replaces the interference proceeding.

판결

decision, judgment

판사에 의한 재판

배심원 없이 판사 앞에서 행해지는 재판.

bench trial

A trial before a judge without a jury.

포기[1]

사용례 특허권 · 전용실시권 또는 통상실시권을 **포기**한 때에는 특허권 · 전용실시권 또는 통상실시권은 그때부터 소멸된다(특허법 제120조).

abandonment

A patent or exclusive or non-exclusive license shall be extinguished at the time the patent or the exclusive or non-exclusive license is **abandoned** (Patent Act Article 120).

미 포기[2]

출원의 포기와 다른 미국 특유의 제도. 특허 또는 상표의 재발행 또는 등록취소를 목적으로 함.

surrender

To be distinguished from abandonment of application. A patent or trademark is surrendered for the purpose of reissue or cancellation of registration.

사용례 상표권자의 신청에 따라 특허상표청장은 어느 상표등록이든지 취소를 위하여 **포기**하도록 할 수 있다. 상표등록이 취소되면 그에 따라 필요한 사항이 특허상표청에 기록되어야 한다. (미) 상표법 제7(e)조.

Upon application of the owner the Director may permit any registration to be **surrendered** for cancellation, and upon cancellation appropriate entry shall be made in the records of the United States Patent and Trademark Office. … 15 U.S.C. § 1057(e).

(지정상품의) 포기[3]

relinquishment, abandonment (of designated goods)

해당 지정상품에 대한 상표권의 포기. 상표권, 전용사용권, 통상사용권, 질권 등을 포기하였을 경우 그 해당 권리는 그때부터 소멸된다(상표법 제103조).

Where trademark rights, exclusive license, non-exclusive license, or pledge is relinquished, the trademark rights, exclusive license, non-exclusive license, or pledge shall be extinguished henceforth (Trademark Act Article 103).

표면 장식

surface ornamentation

발명적 신규성 또는 비자명성은 디자인이 화체된 물품 또는 디자인에 적용되거나 화체된 표면 장식의 장식적인 형상이나 구성에 있다. (미) MPEP § 1504.

The inventive novelty or unobviousness resides in the ornamental shape or configuration of the article in which the design is embodied or the surface ornamentation which is applied to or embodied in the design. MPEP § 1504.

미 표면 처리

surface treatment

물품에 적용된 여하한 표시, 대조적인 색채나 재질, 그래픽 표현물, 또는 다른 장식. 표면 처리는 물품에 적용되거나 화체된 것이어야 함. 표면 처리는, 그 자체로는 (즉, 특정한 물품에 적용되거나 화체되지 않은 상태로는) 35 U.S.C. § 171에 따른 디자인특허의 올바른 대상이 아님. (미) MPEP § 1503.02.IV.

Any indicia, contrasting color or materials, graphic representations, or other ornamentation applied to the article. Surface treatment must be applied to or embodied in an article of manufacture. Surface treatment, per se (i.e., not applied to or embodied in a specific article of manufacture), is not proper subject matter for a design patent under 35 U.S.C. 171. MPEP § 1503.02.IV.

표시

indication

상표권자 · 전용사용권자 또는 통상사용권자는 등록상표를 사용할 때에 해당 상표가 등록상표임을 표시할 수 있다(상표법 제222조).

Where a trademark right holder, an exclusive licensee, or a non-exclusive licensee uses a registered trademark, he/she may indicate that the relevant trademark is the registered trademark (Trademark Act Article 222).

표어

motto

사용례 이 사건 출원상표/서비스표는 그 지정상품/서비스업과 관련하여 '차이를 만들기 위하여 디자인(고안, 계획) 된', '차

The trademark/service mark at issue is recognized as having the meaning of "designed to make difference," "distinguished design," "devised (planned) to make difference" when used

별화 된 디자인', '차별화를 시키기 위하여 고안된(계획된)' 등의 의미로 인식되므로, 설령 지정상품/서비스업의 품질, 효능 등을 표시하는 표장에 해당되지 않는다고 하더라도, 일반 수요자로서는 이를 특정인의 상표로 인식한다기보다는 흔히 쓰일 수 있는 구호 또는 **표어**나 광고문안 정도로 인식할 것으로 보여진다(특허법원 2013. 3. 14. 선고 2012허10129 판결 참조).

in relation to the designated good or service. Hence, even if it is not a mark that indicates the quality or benefit of the designated good or service, general consumers would likely recognize the trademark/service mark at issue not as a particular person's trademark but as a slogan, **motto** or advertisement phrase that may be commonly used (Patent Court Decision, 2012Heo10129, decided March 14, 2013).

표장

기호, 문자, 도형, 소리, 냄새, 입체적 형상, 홀로그램 · 동작 또는 색채 등으로서 그 구성이나 표현방식에 상관없이 상품의 출처(출처)를 나타내기 위하여 사용하는 모든 표시(상표법 제2조 제1항 제2호).

mark

All indications used to identify the source of goods, irrespective of the composition or methods of the expression thereof, which include any sign, letter, figure, sound, smell, three-dimensional shape, hologram, movement, color, etc. (Trademark Act Article 2(1)2).

표장의 표시

출원인이 등록하고자 하는 표장의 명확한 묘사. 모든 출원에는 상표가 표현되어야 함.

representation of mark

A clear depiction of the mark an applicant seeks to register. Every application must include a representation of the mark.

사용례 단순히 기술적이거나 주로 지리적으로 기술적인 표장으로 문자를 대체하는 디자인이 보통의 사항이나 단순히 기술적 혹은 지리적으로 기술적인 사항의 정확한 사진적 **표현**에 해당한다면 심사관은 출원인에게 보조등록부 등록 또는 2(f)조 하에 주등록부 등록을 위해 보정하도록 하여야 한다. 또한 출원인은 보통명칭으로의 단어사용이나 보통의 사항에 대한 정확한 사진적 **표현**에 해당하는 모든 부분에 대한 권리를 포기하여야 한다. (미) TMEP § 1213.05 (g)(iii).

If the mark is otherwise merely descriptive or primarily geographically descriptive, and the design replacing a letter is an accurate pictorial **representation** of generic, merely descriptive, or geographically descriptive matter, the examining attorney must require the applicant to amend to the Supplemental Register or seek registration on the Principal Register under Trademark Act §2(f). The applicant must disclaim any generic wording or any accurate pictorial **representation** of generic matter. TMEP § 1213.05(g)(iii).

표장의 훼손

표장의 도면에 나타난 표시가 완전한 표장을 보여준다 할 수 없어 필수적이고 완전한 대상이 도면에서 누락되었다고 하여야 할 경우. (미) TMEP § 807.12(d).

mutilation of mark

When the representation on a drawing of a mark does not constitute a complete mark so as to conclude essential and integral subject matter is missing from the drawing. TMEP § 807.12(d).

사용례 In re Schecter Bros. Modular

In re Schecter Bros. Modular Corp.,182 USPQ 694 (TTAB

Corp.,182 USPQ 694 (TTAB 1974) (표장의 일부가 "RAINAIRE"과 그 그림자 이미지인 것으로 견본에 보여지는 경우, "RAINAIRE"가 그 표장의 필수적인 인상을 만들어내는 것이어서 도면에서 그림자 이미지를 삭제한 것은 **표장의 훼손**이라 볼 수 없다고 본 사례). (미) TMEP § 807.12(d).

1974) (where specimens show mark consisting in part of "RAINAIRE" together with its shadow image, it is not a **mutilation** of mark to delete shadow image from drawing since "RAINAIRE" creates the essential impression); … TMEP § 807.12(d).

미 표준도면

구 typed drawing. 그 제출된 표현방식에 대해 특별한 주장을 하지 아니하는 표장에 사용되는 도면을 가리킨다. 이 경우 도면은 반드시 흰색 바탕에 검은색으로 표장을 나타내야 하며 37 C.F.R. 2.52(a)조의 요건을 만족시켜야 함. (미) TMEP § 807.03; 807.03(a).

standard character drawings

Formerly "typed" drawing. Standard character drawing refers to those that applicants who seek to register a mark without any claim as to the manner of display submit. The drawing must show the mark in black on a white background and comply with the requirements of 37 C.F.R. § 2.52(a). TMEP §§ 807.03; 807.03(a).

사용례 **표준도면**은 디자인 요소, 색채, 문자의 특별한 스타일이나 크기에 대한 주장을 포함하는 특수양식도면으로 보정될 수 없다. 단 심사관이 그 보정이 중대한 변경이 아니라고 결정하는 경우에는 그렇지 아니하다. (미) 37 C.F.R. § 2.72; TMEP § 807.03(d).

A **standard character drawing** cannot be amended to a special form drawing containing a design element, color, or a claim to a distinctive style or size of lettering, unless the examining attorney determines that the amendment is not material. 37 C.F.R. §2.72; TMEP § 807.03(d).

표준필수특허 (SEP)

표준화기구가 지정한 표준을 준수하여 제품을 생산 또는 서비스를 제공하는 데에 필수적인 기술에 대한 특허.

standard essential patents (SEP)

A patent for a technology which is essential to manufacture products or provide services in compliance with a standard set by a Standard Setting Organization.

표준화기구

표준의 설정을 추진하는 등 기타 표준화 활동을 수행하는 단체 및 기구. 일반적으로 소속 회원들이 FRAND 조건에 따라 실시권을 허락할 것을 요구함. → FRAND 참조.

standard setting organization (SSO)

Organizations that promote setting standards and engage in other standardization-related activities. SSOs generally require their members to grant license under FRAND terms.

품종

'품종'이란 식물학에서 통용되는 최저분류 단위의 식물군으로서 제16조에 따른 품종보호 요건을 갖추었는지와 관계없이 유전적으로 나타나는 특성 중 한 가지 이상의 특성이 다른 식물군과 구별되고 변함없이

plant variety

The term "plant variety" means a plant grouping within a single botanical taxon of the lowest known rank, which, irrespective of whether the conditions for the grant of a plant variety right under Article 12 are fully met, can be defined by the expression of the characteristics resulting

증식될 수 있는 것을 말함(식물신품종보호법 제2조 제2호).

from a given genotype or combination of genotypes distinguished from any other plant grouping, by the expression of at least one of the said characteristics, and considered as units with regard to its suitability for being propagated unchanged (Act on Protection of New Varieties of Plants Article 2.2).

품종보호공보

Official Reports on Plant Variety Protection

품종보호권

plant variety right

품종보호권자

holder of plant variety right

품종보호심판위원회

plant variety protection tribunal

품종보호에 관한 심판과 재심을 관장하기 위하여 농림축산식품부에 품종보호심판위원회(이하 "심판위원회"라 한다)를 둔다(식물신품종보호법 제90조 제1항).

A Plant Variety Tribunal (hereinafter referred to as the "Tribunal") shall be established within the Ministry of Agriculture, Food and Rural Affairs to take charge of adjudication and re-adjudication on plant variety protection (Act on Protection of New Varieties of Plants Article 90(1)).

품질보증기능

quality assurance

수요자로 하여금 그 상표가 부착된 상품은 동일한 성능과 품질을 가지고 있다고 기대할 수 있도록 하는 상표의 기능.

A function of trademark, which is to assure consumers to expect that goods with the trademark to all show identical performance and quality.

사용례 상표는 기본적으로 당해 상표가 부착된 상품의 출처가 특정한 영업주체임을 나타내는 상품출처표시기능과 이에 수반되는 **품질보증기능**이 주된 기능이라는 점 등에 비추어 볼 때, … (대법원 2002. 9. 24. 선고 99다42322 판결 참조).

Given that a trademark's main functions boil down to source indication that the goods to which the mark is affixed come from a particular business, along with **quality assurance** … (Supreme Court Decision, 99Da42322, decided September 24, 2002).

품질오인

mistake as to the quality of goods, mislead consumers about the quality of goods (법제처)

사용례 제33조에도 불구하고 다음 각 호의 어느 하나에 해당하는 상표에 대해서는 상표등록을 받을 수 없다. … 12. 상품의 **품질을 오인**하게 하거나 수요자를 기만할 염려가 있는 상표(상표법 제34조 제1항).

Notwithstanding Article 33, none of the following trademarks shall be registered: … 12. Any trademark which is likely to **mislead** consumers about the **quality** of goods or deceive consumers (Trademark Act Article 34(1)).

FRAND

공정하고 합리적이며 비차별적인. 불공정 행위의 방지를 목적으로 대개 표준필수특허의 특허권자에게 공정하고 합리적이며 비차별적인 실시권을 허여하도록 요구하는 조건.

FRAND

Fair, Reasonable and Non-Discriminatory. A term that requires the patentee, often a standard and essential patent holder, to grant fair, reasonable and non-discriminatory licenses for the purpose of preventing unfair practices.

피상고인 (피항소인)

appellee

피청구인

defendant, respondent, petitionee

ㅎ

하위개념

사용례 선행 또는 공지의 발명에 구성요건이 상위개념으로 기재되어 있고 위 상위개념에 포함되는 **하위개념**만을 구성요건 중의 전부 또는 일부로 하는 이른바 선택발명의 신규성을 부정하기 위해서는 선행발명이 선택발명을 구성하는 하위개념을 구체적으로 개시하고 있어야 하고, 이에는 선행발명을 기재한 선행문헌에 선택발명에 대한 문언적인 기재가 존재하는 경우 외에도 그 발명이 속하는 기술분야에서 통상의 지식을 가진 자가 선행문헌의 기재 내용과 출원시의 기술 상식에 기초하여 선행문헌으로부터 직접적으로 선택발명의 존재를 인식할 수 있는 경우도 포함된다(대법원 2009. 10. 15. 선고 2008후736 판결).

species, subordinate concept

In order to deny the novelty of the so-called selection invention, which means an invention whose elements are stated in the preceding or already publicized invention as a generic concept and entirely or partly consist of a **subordinate concept** derived from the above generic concept, a preceding invention has disclosed subordinate concepts comprising the selection invention in a concrete manner. The novelty of selective invention is also denied when a person with ordinary knowledge in the technology to which the invention pertains can recognize the existence of selective invention directly from the preceding literature, based on the contents stated in the preceding literature and his common sense in the technology at the time of application, as well as when wordings concerning the selection invention exist in the preceding literature stating the preceding invention (Supreme Court Decision, 2008Hu736, decided October 15, 2009).

한 벌의 물품

둘 이상의 물품이 짝을 이루는 경우.

a set of articles

Where two or more articles are used as one set.

사용례 **한 벌의 물품**으로 동시에 사용되는 경우 그 **한 벌의 물품**의 디자인이 한 벌 전체로서 통일성이 있을 때에는 1디자인으로 디자인등록을 받을 수 있다(디자인보호법 제42조 제1항).

Where at least two articles are used together as **a set of articles**, a design for the set of products may be registered as one design, if the design for **the set of articles** is unitary (Design Protection Act Article 42(1)).

한정

restriction

미 합리적인 노력

reasonable diligence

→ 지속적 노력 참조

→ 지속적 노력 참조

사용례 **합리적인 노력**을 입증하기 위해 근거로 든 노력은 해당 사건의 발명의 구현과 직접적으로 연관되어야 한다. (미) MPEP § 2138.06.

The work relied upon to show **reasonable diligence** must be directly related to the reduction to practice of the invention in issue. MPEP § 2138.06.

합리적인 실시료

reasonable royalty

특허대상인 물품을 업으로 생산, 사용, 판매하고자 하는 자가 지불할 의향이 있으며 지불하고도 그 물품의 생산, 사용, 판매로 시장에서 합리적인 이익을 얻을 수 있을 정도의 금액. (미) Trans-World Mfg. Corp. v. Al Nyman & Sons, Inc., 750 F.2d 1552, 1568 (Fed. Cir. 1984)

The amount that a person, desiring to manufacture, use, or sell a patented article, as a business proposition, would be willing to pay as a royalty and yet be able to make, use, or sell the patented article, in the market, at a reasonable profit. Trans-World Mfg. Corp. v. Al Nyman & Sons, Inc., 750 F.2d 1552, 1568 (Fed. Cir. 1984).

사용례 제(1)항에 따라 **합리적인 실시료**를 받을 권리는 특허등록 이후 6년 이내에 제기된 소에 따라서만 인정될 수 있다. (미) 특허법 154(d)(3)조.

The right under paragraph (1) to obtain a **reasonable royalty** shall be available only in an action brought not later than 6 years after the patent is issued. 35 U.S.C. § 154(d)(3).

합성어 표장

compound word mark

두 개 이상의 단어 또는 단어와 음절로 구성되었고 하나의 단어로 표현된 표장.

A mark comprised of two or more distinct words, or words and syllables, that are represented as one word.

사용례 표장이 도면에 **합성어 표장**으로 묘사되어 있으나 견본은 두 개의 별도의 단어로 나타내거나 혹은 그 반대의 경우, 심사관은 도면의 표장이 견본 상의 표장을 실질적으로 정확하게 나타내고 있는지, 도면의 보정이 표장의 중대한 변경에 해당할 것인지 혹은 둘 다를 결정하여야 한다. (미) TMEP § 807.12(e).

If the drawing depicts the mark as a **compound word mark**, but the specimen shows the mark as two separate words, or vice versa, the examining attorney must determine whether the mark on the drawing is a substantially exact representation of the mark on the specimen and/or whether an amendment of the drawing would be a material alteration of the mark TMEP § 807.12(e).

미 항고심판소

Board of Patent Appeals and Interferences

특허심판원의 전신.

The predecessor of the Patent Trial and Appeal Board.

항소 (불복심판) — **appeal**

항소이유 — **grounds of appeal**

항소장 — **petition of appeal**

해결하려는 과제 — **problem to be solved**

미 해쉬태그 표장 — **hashtag marks**

해쉬 기호(#)나 '해쉬태그'(HASHTAG)라는 단어로 이루어진 표장. 출원인의 상품 또는 서비스의 출처표시 기능을 수행할 때에 한하여 상표 또는 서비스표로 등록할 수 있음. (미) TMEP § 1202.18.

A mark consisting of or containing the hash symbol (#) or the term HASHTAG. Registrable as a trademark or service mark only if it functions as an identifier of the source of the applicant's goods or services. TMEP § 1202.18.

미 해태(懈怠) — **doctrine of laches**

원고가 침해소송을 제기하기까지 불합리하게 지연하였음을 주장하는 형평법상의 항변. 특허권자가 쟁점이 되는 침해사실을 알았거나 혹은 합리적으로 알았어야 하는 때로부터 6년 이상이 지난 뒤에 소를 제기한다면 해태가 추정되고 특허권자는 지연에 대한 합당한 사유의 존재를 입증하여야 함. 해태로 인해 소 제기 자체가 금지되지는 않으나 소 제기일 이전에 발생한 손해에 대해서는 배상받을 수 없음.

An equitable defense that the plaintiff unreasonably delayed in asserting an infringement claim. If a patentee files suit more than six years after she became (or reasonably should have become) aware of the alleged infringement, a presumption of laches arises and the patentee must present legitimate reasons for the delay. This defense does not bar the plaintiff's action entirely, but prevents the recovery of any damages accrued prior to the filing of the action.

행위능력 — **legal capacity**

자기의 권리 · 의무에 변동이 일어나도록 스스로 행위할 수 있는 능력.

The capacity to act by oneself so as to bring about changes in one's rights or obligations.

사용례 **행위능력** 또는 법정대리권이 없거나 상표에 관한 절차를 밟는 데 필요한 권한의 위임에 흠이 있는 자가 밟은 절차는 보정(補正)된 당사자나 법정대리인이 추인(追認)하면 행위를 한 때로 소급하여 그 효력이 발생한다(상표법 제9조).

Procedures followed by a person who has no **legal capacity** or authority of legal representation, or who has any defect in the delegation of authority necessary to follow trademark-related procedures shall take effect retroactive to the time he/she performed an act if the party whose defect has been rectified or his/her legal representative confirms such procedures (Trademark Act Article 9).

허가-특허 연계제도 — **patent linkage system, patent-drug approval linkage**

복제약 제조사가 식품의약품안전처에서 관

리하는 등재목록에 등재된 특허를 이용하여 복제약을 제조·판매하기 위해 품목허가신청을 하는 경우 45일 내에 해당 특허의 특허권자에게 품목허가신청 사실을 통지하도록 강제하고, 통지를 받은 특허권자는 복제약 제조사를 상대로 침해금지소송을 제기하면서 통지받은 날로부터 9개월 간 판매금지신청을 할 수 있게 하는 제도.

Under the system, a generic drug company that files application with the Korean Ministry of Food and Drug Safety ("MFDS") to sell a certain generic drug, using a pharmaceutical patent listed on the patent list managed by the MFDS must give notice to the patent holder of the above patent within 45 days of the application. After the patent holder receives the notice, it is entitled to request MFDS to prohibit the sale of the generic drug for up to 9 months, after filing suit against the generic drug company for infringement.

허위표시죄

특허된 것이 아닌 물건에 특허표시 또는 이와 혼동하기 쉬운 표시를 하는 경우 허위표시죄로 처벌 된다(특허법 제 228조).

offense of false marking

Any person who commit marking "patented" or any similar misleading word on any unpatented thing shall be punished for offense of false marking (Patent Act Article 228).

헤이그협정

산업디자인의 국제등록에 관한 헤이그협정.

Hague Agreement

The Hague Agreement concerning the International Registration of Industrial Designs.

현저한 지리적 명칭

현저한 지리적 명칭이나 그 약서 또는 지도만으로 된 상표는 상표등록을 받을 수 없다(상표법 제33조 제1항 제4호).

well-known geographical terms, conspicuous goegraphical name (법제처)

A trademark consisting solely of a conspicuous geographical name, the abbreviation thereof, or a map may not be obtained trademark registration (Trademark Act Article 33(1)4).

사용례 구 상표법 하에서의 상표의 유사여부를 판단함에 있어서는 상표의 구성 중 **현저한 지리적 명칭**에 해당하는 부분은 사용의 결과 수요자 간에 특정인의 상표로 현저하게 인식되어 있는지의 여부에 관계없이 자타상품을 식별할 수 있는 요부가 된다고 할 수 없다(대법원 2006. 1. 26. 선고 2004후1175 판결 참조).

In determining similarity of trademarks under the old Trademark Act, the part of a trademark that constitutes **well-known geographical name** cannot be an essential part that distinguishes one's product from another's, regardless of whether the trademark is conspicuously recognized as belonging to a specified person by consumers as a result of usage (Supreme Court Decision, 2004Hu1175, decided January 26, 2006).

현저한 효과

사용례 이상에서 살핀 바를 종합하면, 이 사건 등록고안 중 청구항 1은 그 일부 구성에서 선행고안1과 분명한 차이가 있고, 통상의 기술자가 선행고안 1, 2 또는 주지관용기술에 의하여 그와 같은 차이를 극히

significant effect

To sum the above explanations, Claim 1 of the patented invention has a clear difference from Prior Art 1 in terms of part or the structure, and PHOSITA cannot easily overcome the difference with Prior Arts 1, 2 or common general knowledge, and Claim 1 has a **significant effect**. Thus, it

ㅎ

쉽게 극복할 수 없으며, 그로 인한 **작용효과 역시 현저**하므로, 그 진보성이 부정되지 않는다고 보아야 한다(특허법원 2016.05.27 선고 2015허666판결 참조).

is considered that its inventive step is not rejected (Patent Court Decision, 2015Heo666, decided May 27, 2016).

형상

물품의 윤곽. 모든 디자인은 형상을 수반함.

shape

The contours of an article. All designs have shapes.

사용례 "디자인"이란 물품[물품의 부분(제42조는 제외한다) 및 글자체를 포함한다. 이하 같다]의 **형상** · 모양 · 색채 또는 이들을 결합한 것으로서 시각을 통하여 미감(美感)을 일으키게 하는 것을 말한다(디자인보호법 제2조 제1호).

The term "design" means a **shape**, pattern, or color of an article [including parts of an article (excluding those defined under Article 42) and fonts; the same shall apply hereinafter], which invokes a sense of beauty through visual perception (Design Protection Act Article 2.1).

형태

형상 · 모양 · 색채 또는 이들의 결합.

form

Shape, pattern, color or combination thereof.

사용례 "글자체"란 기록이나 표시 또는 인쇄 등에 사용하기 위하여 공통적인 특징을 가진 **형태**로 만들어진 한 벌의 글자꼴(숫자, 문장부호 및 기호 등의 형태를 포함한다)을 말한다(디자인보호법 제2조 제2호).

The term "font" means a set of characters (including those in the **form** of numerals, punctuation marks, and symbols) made in a style with common characteristics for recording, marking, or printing (Design Protection Act Article 2.2).

호칭유사

일반 거래자들이 대비되는 상표를 부르는 호칭이 서로 동일 · 유사하게 들림으로써 상표를 오인 · 혼동하는 것인데 그로 인하여 당해 상품의 출처에 대하여 혼동을 일으킬 염려가 있는 경우 상표 유사로 판단될 수 있음.

phonetic similarity

Similarity in pronunciation of marks that causes misconception or confusion between the marks among ordinary purchasers. Such marks are similar if there is likelihood of confusion as to the source of the goods.

사용례 인용상표도 그 한글표기는 비록 "한라"라고 표시되어 있으나… "할라"로 **호칭되어 유사**하며 … (대법원 1984. 9. 11. 선고 82후62 판결 참조).

While the cited mark is written as "한라" in Korean, it is called as "HALLA", which is **phonetically similar** … (Supreme Court Decision, 82Hu62, decided September 11, 1984).

호환가능성

어느 물건의 일부인 부품을 그 부분만을 따로 분리하여 교체할 수 있는 가능성.

substitutability

The possibility a part of an article can be separated and replaced.

사용례 이러한 물품이 의장등록의 대상이 되기 위해서는 통상의 상태에서 독립된 거래의 대상이 되어야 하고, 그것이 부품인 경우에는 다시 호환성을 가져야 하나, 이는 반드시 실제 거래사회에서 현실적으로 거래되고 다른 물품과 호환될 것을 요하는 것은 아니고, 그러한 독립된 거래의 대상 및 **호환의 가능성**만 있으면 의장등록의 대상이 된다고 할 것이다(대법원 1998.12.4.선고 98후2900 판결).

For such an article to be registered as a design, it shall be a subject matter of an independent dealing in its ordinary state. In case of a component to another article, it must also be substitutable. However, it is not to say that there must be actual trading of the component in the marketplace and substituted by other articles; merely the possibility of independent trading and **substituabiliy** shall suffice (Supreme Court Decision, 98Hu2900, decided December 4, 1998).

혼동가능성

likelihood of confusion

상표나 서비스표의 등록거절이유. 이미 등록되었거나 출원 중인 상표와 혼동을 일으킬 가능성이 있으므로 거절하는 것.

A basis for refusing registration of a trademark or service mark because it is likely to conflict with a mark or marks already registered or pending.

사용례 **혼동가능성**의 판단은 그 표장이 대비적 관찰을 하였을 때 식별가능한지가 아닌 그 상품 또는 서비스의 출처에 있어 **혼동을 일으킬 수 있을 만큼** 충분히 유사하다 할 것인지를 기준으로 한다. (미) TMEP § 1207.01(b).

The test of **likelihood of confusion** is not whether the marks can be distinguished when subjected to a side-by-side comparison, but whether the marks are sufficiently similar that there is a **likelihood of confusion** as to the source of the goods or services. TMEP § 1207.01(b).

사용례 1. 입체적 형상과 기호·문자 등이 결합된 상표에서 입체적 형상에는 식별력이 없고 문자 등에 식별력이 있는 경우, 식별력이 없는 입체적 형상은 출처표시 기능을 할 수 없으므로, 그와 유사한 입체적 형상의 상품간의 관계에서 출처의 **혼동우려**가 없다. 수요자들은 식별력이 있는 문자 등으로부터 누구의 업무에 관련된 상품을 표시하는 것인가를 어렵지 않게 인식할 수 있을 것으로 보인다(특허법원 2014.9.19. 선고 2014허2344).

1. In the case of a mark combining a dimensional shape with a device or word, if the dimensional shape lacks distinctiveness but the word is distinctive, the non-distinctive dimensional shape cannot function as a source identifier, and thus, there is no **likelihood of confusion** arising with respect to the goods having a similar dimensional shape. It appears that the consumers can easily recognize whose goods the mark identifies by the distinctive word (Patent Court Decision, 2014Heo2344, decided on September 19, 2014).

혼동 방지 표시 청구권

right to request an indication to avoid confusion

선사용자에게 자기의 상품과 선사용자의 상품간의 출처의 오인이나 혼동을 방지할 수 있는 적당한 표시를 할 것을 청구할 수 있는 상표권자나 전용사용권자의 권리.

The right of a trademark owner or exclusive licensee to request a prior user to mark his or her goods to avoid misconception or confusion of source between the goods.

사용례 상표권자나 전용사용권자는 제1

An trademark owner or exclusive licensee of a trademark

항에 따라 상표를 사용할 권리를 가지는 자에게 그 자의 상품과 자기의 상품 간에 출처의 오인이나 **혼동을 방지하는 데 필요한 표시를 할 것을 청구**할 수 있다(상표법 제99조 제3항).

may request a party who has the right to use the mark under paragraph (1) to make an **indication on the good necessary to avoid misconception or confusion** as to the source of the goods of both parties (Trademark Act Article 99(3)).

홀로그램 상표

hologram mark

홀로그램으로 구성된 상표.

A trademark that consists of holograms.

사용례 "표장"이란 기호, 문자, 도형, 소리, 냄새, 입체적 형상, **홀로그램** · 동작 또는 색채 등으로서 그 구성이나 표현방식에 상관없이 상품의 출처(출처)를 나타내기 위하여 사용하는 모든 표시를 말한다(상표법 제2조 제1항 제2호).

The term "mark" means all indications used to identify the source of goods, irrespective of the composition or methods of the expression thereof, which include any sign, letter, figure, sound, smell, three-dimensional shape, **hologram**, movement, color, etc. (Trademark Act Article 2(1)2).

화체[1]

be embodied in

디자인을 물품에 표현함.

A design is embodied in an article.

사용례 명세서는 다음 항목을 순서대로 포함하여야 한다: (1) 출원인의 이름, 디자인의 명칭, 및 디자인이 **화체된** 물품의 속성과 용도에 대한간단한 설명을 언급하는 전제부. (미) 37 C.F.R. § 1.154(b).

The specification should include the following sections in order: (1) Preamble, stating the name of the applicant, title of the design, and a brief description of the nature and intended use of the article in which the design **is embodied**. 37 C.F.R. § 1.154.

화체[2]

be associated with

상표에 그 상표권자의 영업상 신용이 나타남.

A trademark is associated with the good will of the trademark owner.

사용례 구 상표법 제7조 제1항 제12호는 국내 또는 외국의 수요자 간에 특정인의 상표라고 현저하게 인식되어 있는 이른바 주지상표가 국내에서 등록되어 있지 않음을 기화로 제3자가 이를 모방한 상표를 등록하여 사용함으로써 주지상표에 **화체**된 영업상의 신용이나 고객흡인력 등의 무형의 가치에 손상을 입히거나 주지상표권자의 국내에서의 영업을 방해하는 등의 방법으로 주지상표권자에게 손해를 가하거나 이러한 모방상표를 이용하여 부당한 이익을 얻을 목적으로 사용하는 상표는 그 등록을 허용하지 않는다는 취지이다(대법원 2010. 7. 15. 선고 2010후807 판결 참조).

The purpose of Article 7 (1) subparagraph 12 of the former Trademark Act is to disallow the registration of a trademark identical or similar to a trademark which is well recognized as indicating the goods of a particular person by consumers within or outside the Republic of Korea, and which is used for unjust purposes such as obtaining unjust profits or inflicting harm on the prior trademark holder through the loss of intangible value (e.g. good will or customer appeal **associated with** the well-known trademark) or obstructing business within Korea (Supreme Court Decision, 2010Hu 807, decided July 15, 2010).

화해

settlement

확대된 선출원

후출원 발명과 동일한 내용이 선출원 발명의 최초 명세서에 기재되어 있으면, 양발명의 청구범위가 동일하지 않더라도, 심사관은 이를 근거로 후출원 발명을 등록거절할 수 있는 원칙.

extended first-to-file rule

The rule that allows a patent examiner to reject an application when the invention for which the patent application is filed is identical to the invention described in the original specification of an earlier-filed patent application, even if the scope of claims of the inventions are not identical.

확인대상 (발명/포장/디자인)

권리범위확인의 대상이 되는 발명, 표장, 디자인. 해당 발명, 표장, 디자인에 대하여 적극적 권리범위확인심판의 경우 challenged, 소극적 권리범위확인심판의 경우 challenging으로 쓸 수 있음.

challenging/challenged (invention/mark/design), subject to confirmation (법제처)

The invention, mark or design subject to confirmation in a scope of rights confirmation action. *Challenged* in an action for affirmative adjudication on the scope of rights; *challenging* in a defensive scope of rights action.

사용례 따라서 상표권의 권리범위확인 심판 및 그 심결취소청구 사건에서 등록상표와 **확인대상표장**의 유사 여부를 판단하기 위한 요소가 되는 등록상표의 식별력은 상표의 유사 여부를 판단하는 기준시인 심결 시를 기준으로 판단하여야 한다(대법원 2014. 3. 20. 선고 2011후3698 전원합의체 판결).

Therefore, in the context of adjudication on the scope of right and petition for revocation of the adjudicated decision, the distinctiveness of a trademark, which is an element to determine the similarity between a registered trademark and a **challenged mark**, is to be determined at the time of adjudication, which is also the reference point for determining the similarity of trademarks (Supreme Court Decision, 2011Hu3698, decided March 20, 2014).

사용례 원심은, 아래와 같은 이유를 들어, **확인대상발명**은 그 발명이 속하는 기술분야에서 통상의 지식을 가진 사람(이하 '통상의 기술자'라 한다)이 그 판시 비교대상발명들과 주지관용기술로부터 용이하게 실시할 수 있는 자유실시기술에 해당하므로, 명칭을 '저용량의 엔테카비르 제제 및 그의 용도'로 하는 이 사건 특허발명(특허등록번호 생략)의 청구범위 제1항(이하 '이 사건 제1항 발명'이라 한다)과 대비할 필요 없이 그 권리범위에 속하지 아니한다고 판단하였다(대법원 2015. 5. 21. 선고 2014후768 전원합의체판결 참조).

On the grounds as laid out below, the lower court determined that the **challenged invention** is not subsumed in the scope of the right of the instant Patented Invention (patent registration number omitted) Claim 1 (hereinafter "Invention Claim 1"), titled, "low dosage entecavir tablet and its uses," without even having to contrast the two, since it constitutes the state-of-the-art technology that a person of ordinary skill in the art (hereinafter "a person with ordinary skill") can easily implement based on the cited inventions and generally known art in practice (Supreme Court Decision, 2014Hu768, decided May 21, 2015).

미 확인진술서

선서서 또는 선서를 통해 서약하였거나 선

verified statement

a statement that is sworn to, made under oath or in an

언서로 보완하고 서명한 진술서. (미) 37 C.F.R. § 2.2(n).

affidavit, or supported by a declaration and signed. 37 C.F.R. § 2.2(n).

사용례 …에 따른 상표나 서비스표의 출원에서 출원인은 그 상표를 거래상 사용하고자 하는 진실한 의도를 가지고 있음에 대한 **확인진술서**를 제출하여야 한다. **확인진술서**가 최초 출원시 함께 제출되지 않았을 경우에는 여기에 출원인이 출원일자에 상표를 거래상 사용하고자 하는 진실한 의도를 가지고 있었음을 주장하여야 한다. (미) TMEP § 806.01(b).

In a trademark or service mark application based on …, the applicant must submit a **verified statement** that the applicant has a bona fide intention to use the mark in commerce. If the verified statement is not filed with the initial application, the **verified statement** must also allege that the applicant had a bona fide intention to use the mark in commerce as of the application filing date. TMEP § 806.01(b).

확인판결

declaratory judgment

판결의 집행 또는 손해배상액 산정 없이 당사자간 법적 관계와 당사자의 권리만을 결정하는 판결.

A judgment of a court only defining the rights and legal relationship of the parties without enforcement or award of damages.

환송

remand

상급심 법원이 재심리를 위해 사건을 하급심 법원으로 돌려보냄.

Appellate court sending back the case to the inferior court for additional hearings.

사용례 원심판결을 파기하고, 사건을 특허법원에 **환송**한다(대법원 2016.11.25. 선고 2014후2184판결 참조).

Judgment of the lower court is reversed, and the cases is **remanded** to the Patent Court of Korea (Supreme Court Decision, 2014Hu2184, decided November 25, 2016).

회복할 수 없는 손해

irreparable harm

금전적 배상으로 회복할 수 없는 손해. 침해로 인한 잠정적 금지명령 시 판단근거가 되는 요소 중 하나.

A harm that cannot be corrected by monetary compensation. One of the factors in granting preliminary injunctive relief in case of infringement.

회피

recusal, avoidance (법제처)

법관 스스로 제척 또는 기피의 원인이 있다고 인정한 때에 직무의 집행을 피하는 것.

To voluntarily avoid discharging authority on cases when a judge believes there is a reason to be excluded or avoided.

회피설계

design around

특허권자의 권리를 침해하지 않기 위하여 특허발명에 대한 대안을 찾는 것.

To find an alternative to a patented invention so that it would not infringe the patentee's rights.

효력

effect

사용례 다음 각 호의 어느 하나에 해당

In any of the following cases, the **effect** of a design right

하는 경우에 디자인권의 **효력**은 해당 심결이 확정된 후 재심청구 등록 전에 선의로 수입 또는 국내에서 생산하거나 취득한 물품에는 미치지 아니한다. 1. 무효가 된 디자인권(디자인등록취소결정에 대한 심판에 의하여 취소가 확정된 디자인권을 포함한다)이 재심에 의하여 회복된 경우 … (디자인보호법 제161조 제1항).

shall not extend to the goods imported or domestically produced or acquired in good faith after the relevant trial decision became final and conclusive but before a petition filed for an administrative patent retrial is registered: 1. Where an invalidated design right (including a design right that has been finally and conclusively revoked in a trial on a determination to revoke design registration) is restored in the retrial; … (Design Protection Act Article 161(1)).

후각상표

→ 냄새상표 참조.

olfactory marks

후견감독인

legal guardian

미 후순위권리자

저촉심사에서 선순위 권리자가 아닌 자. 후순위권리자는 본인이 최초 발명자임을 입증할 책임을 진다.

junior party

A party other than the senior party in an interference proceeding. A junior party bears the burden of proof to show that he or she is the first inventor.

흔히 있는 성 또는 명칭

흔히 있는 성 또는 명칭을 보통으로 사용하는 방법으로 표시한 표장은 상표등록대상이 되지 아니함(상표법 제33조 제1항 제5호).

common surname or name (법제처)

A trademark consisting solely of a mark indicating a common surname or name according to the method in common use may not be registered(Trademark Act Article 33(1)5).

희석

상표권 침해의 한 유형. 타인이 동일, 유사하지 않은 상품에 상표권자의 허락 없이 당해 상표를 사용함으로써 상표의 식별력을 흐리게 하거나 상표의 이미지를 훼손하는 경우 비록 그 상표사용행위가 소비자에게 오인혼동을 주거나 수요자를 기만할 우려가 없더라도 상표권 침해를 구성한 것으로 본다는 것임.

dilution

A type of trademark infringement. Use of a registered trademark by a third party on goods that are neither identical nor similar to the designated good of the registered mark may still constitute infringement when it blurs the distinctiveness of the mark or tarnish its reputation, even if the use of the mark does not cause misconception, confusion among purchasers or deceive them.

사용례 제43조(c)에 따라 식별력 약화에 의한 **희석** 또는 명성 손상에 의한 **희석**을 야기할 우려가 있는 표장은 제13조에 따라 제기되는 절차를 따르는 경우에 한하여 그 등록을 거절할 수 있다. (미) 상표법 제2(f)조.

A mark which would be likely to cause **dilution** by blurring or **dilution** by tarnishment under section 43(c), may be refused registration only pursuant to a proceeding brought under section 13. 15 U.S.C. § 1052(f).

2017

지식재산 법률용어사전

Korean-English Intellectual Property Law Dictionary

Korean-English
Intellectual Property
Law Dictionary

제3부
영한사전

2017

지식재산 법률용어사전

A

abandonment

포기

Example A patent or exclusive or non-exclusive license shall be extinguished at the time the patent or the exclusive or non-exclusive license is **abandoned** (Patent Act Article 120).

특허권 · 전용실시권 또는 통상실시권을 **포기**한 때에는 특허권 · 전용실시권 또는 통상실시권은 그때부터 소멸된다(특허법 제120조).

abandonment (of designated goods)

(지정상품의) 포기

→ See. relinquishment.

abandonment of application

출원의 포기

abbreviated new drug application (ANDA)

미 약식 신약 허가 신청

Application for a generic drug for an approved drug under Hatch-Waxman Act (21 U.S.C. §355(b)(2)).

미국 Hatch-Waxman법(21 U.S.C. §355(b)(2))에 따른 제네릭 의약품에 대한 허가 신청.

abstract

요약서

A concise statement of the technical disclosure in the specification. A patent application filed shall be accompanied by an abstract (Patent Act Article 42(2)).

특허 등의 명세서에서 공개된 기술에 대한 요약 기재. 특허출원서에는 요약서를 첨부하여야 한다(특허법 제42조 제2항).

Example An abstract shall be used only for technical information, and shall not define the scope of the invention for which protection is sought (Patent Act Article 43).

요약서는 기술정보로서의 용도로 사용하여야 하며, 특허발명의 보호범위를 정하는 데에는 사용할 수 없다(특허법 제43조).

abstract idea

추상적 관념

Abstract ideas, as well as the laws of nature and natural phenomena are not patentable subject matter.

추상적 관념, 자연법칙, 자연현상은 특허적격성이 결여됨.

Example In determining whether a process claim recites an **abstract idea**, we must examine the claim as a whole, keeping in mind that an invention is not ineligible just because it relies upon a law of nature or mathematical algorithm. Digitech Image Techs., LLC v. Elecs. for Imaging, Inc., 758 F.3d 1344, 1350 (Fed. Cir. 2014).

방법청구항이 **추상적 관념**을 설명하는 것인지 결정하려면 그 청구항을 전체적으로 판단하여야 하고 단지 자연법칙이나 수학적 알고리즘에 기반한다는 이유만으로 특허적격성이 없는 것은 아님을 상기하여야 한다. Digitech Image Techs., LLC v. Elecs. for Imaging, Inc., 758 F.3d 1344, 1350 (Fed. Cir. 2014).

abstraction

추상적 관념

→ See. abstract idea.

A

abuse (of patent right)

Improper use of a patent or other rights by its owner to restrain trade beyond enforcing the exclusive rights lawfully granted under the patent or other rights that may violate antitrust laws.

(특허권의) 남용, (특허권의) 부당행사

특허권 등에 기한 합법적인 배타적 권리를 넘어서 이를 부당하게 사용하여 거래를 제한하는 행위를 말하며, 공정거래법 위반행위에 해당할 수 있음.

abuse of right

When a person exercises his or her legal right in a manner that is contrary to the duty of good faith with the intent of harming others.

Example In patetent litigations, even when the defendant's execution of technology falls under the scope of the plaintiff's patented invention, if the plaintiff's patent is manifestly likely to be invalidated, the plaintiff's infringement prohibition claim or damage claim based on that patent right is not allowed as **abuse of rights** (Supreme Court Decision, 2010Da95390, decided January 19, 2012).

권리남용

권리자가 상대방에게 고통을 주려는 목적에서 신의성실의 원칙에 반하여 권리를 행사하는 것.

특허침해소송에서 설령 피고의 기술실시가 원고 특허의 형식적 권리범위에 속한다고 하더라도 원고의 특허가 무효로서 등록이 말소되어야 하기 때문에 원고의 침해청구는 **권리남용**에 해당하여 허용될 수 없음(대법원 2012. 1. 19. 선고 2010다95390 전원합의체 판결 참조).

accelerated examination

The Commissioner of the Korean Intellectual Property Office may order an examiner to preferentially examine an application first among other applications.

우선심사

특허청장은 특정한 경우 등록출원에 대하여는 심사관에게 다른 디자인등록출원에 우선하여 심사하게 할 수 있다.

acquired distinctiveness (based on use)

Distinctiveness of a mark, originally with little or no distinctiveness, acquired from use by a particular person in a continuous and exclusive manner for a significant period time, creating conspicuous perception among ordinary consumers or traders as to whose good the mark identifies.

Example A mark can be said as having **acquired distinctiveness** by use if the majority of traders and consumers of the good would perceive the mark as identifying a particular source, judging in entirety from the length, frequency and continuity of use of the mark, the quantity of production and sales and market share of the good to which the mark is affixed, the method, frequency, content, period of and amount spent for its advertisement and promotion, the quality of the good, the reputation and credit of the users of the mark, the degree

사용에 의한 식별력

식별력이 없거나 미약한 상표였더라도 특정인이 상당한 기간에 걸쳐 독점적, 계속적으로 그 상표를 사용한 결과 일반 수요자나 거래자에게 그 상표가 누구의 업무에 관련된 상품을 표시하는가가 현저하게 인식되어 식별력을 취득하는 것.

상표의 사용기간, 사용횟수 및 사용의 계속성, 그 상표가 부착된 상품의 생산 · 판매량 및 시장점유율, 광고 · 선전의 방법, 횟수, 내용, 기간 및 그 액수, 상품품질의 우수성, 상표사용자의 명성과 신용, 상표의 경합적 사용의 정도 및 태양 등을 종합적으로 고려할 때 당해 상표가 사용된 상품에 관한 거래자 및 수요자의 대다수에게 특정인의 상품을 표시하는 것으로 인식되기에 이르렀다면 사용에 의한 식별력의 취득을 인정할

and modality of any competition in using the mark (Supreme Court Decision, 2006Hu2288, decided September 25, 2008).

수 있다(대법원 2008. 9. 25. 선고 2006후2288 판결 참조).

action to confirmation of the scope of rights

An action filed with the Patent Court to revoke IPTAB decisions on the scope of right.

권리범위확인소송

심결취소소송의 하나로, 권리범위확인심판 결정에 불복하여 특허법원에 제기하는 소송.

actual controversy

A real dispute must be present between two parties, capable of being resolved by the court, as opposed to a hypothetical case brought in an attempt to get the court to issue an advisory opinion.

실체적인 분쟁

소송에는 법원의 판결을 구하기 위해서는 가상의 사건이 아닌 법원이 해결할 수 있는 두 당사자 간의 실체적인 분쟁이 있어야 함.

actually used trademark

Example Additionally, it appears that the "CONTINENTAL" portion will be also called "continental" without the Korean transliteration "콘티넨탈" -the **actually used trademark**- which was composed of the upper line's English letters, will cause consumers or traders to conceive a name and concept which is identical to the registered trademark at issue (Patent Court Decision, 2016Heo229, decided July 8, 2016).

실사용상표

… 또 영문자 부분 'CONTINENTAL'은 그 한글 음역 부분 '콘티넨탈'의 병기 없이도 '콘티넨탈'로 동일하게 호칭될 것으로 보이므로, 이 사건 등록상표 중 상단의 영문자 부분만으로 된 **실사용상표**는 일반 수요자나 거래자에게 이 사건 등록상표 그 자체와 동일한 호칭과 관념을 일으킨다고 할 것이다(특허법원 2016. 7. 8. 선고 2016허229 판결 참조).

additional period

The period under paragraph (3) shall be fixed: Provided, That the presiding judge may determine an additional period to the fixed period for those in the area with poor transportation, such as islands and remote rural areas, on his/her own authority, as prescribed by Ordinance of the Ministry of Trade, Industry and Energy (Trademark Act Article 162(4)).

부가기간

심판장은 도서 · 벽지 등 교통이 불편한 지역에 있는 자를 위하여 산업통상자원부령으로 정하는 바에 따라 직권으로 불변기간에 대하여 부가기간을 정할 수 있다(상표법 제162조 제4항).

adjudication

If a patented invention falls under any of the following, and a person who intends to execute the patented invention fails, or is unable, to reach agreement with the patentee or exclusive licensee of the patented invention on the grant of a non-exclusive license under reasonable terms and

재정

특허발명을 실시하려는 자는 특허발명이 다음 각 호의 어느 하나에 해당하고, 그 특허발명의 특허권자 또는 전용실시권자와 합리적인 조건으로 통상실시권 허락에 관한 협의를 하였으나 합의가 이루어지지 아

conditions, although the person has negotiated the agreement, the person may file a petition for adjudication on the grant of the non-exclusive license the Commissioner of the Korean Intellectual Property Office (Patent Act Article 107(1)).

니하는 경우 또는 협의를 할 수 없는 경우에는 특허청장에게 통상실시권 설정에 관한 재정을 청구할 수 있다(특허법 제107조 제1항).

adjudication on grant of non-exclusive licenses

If a patented invention falls under any grounds elaborated in Article 107(1), and a person who intends to execute the patented invention fails, or is unable, to reach agreement with the patentee or exclusive licensee of the patented invention on the grant of a non-exclusive license under reasonable terms and conditions, although the person has negotiated the agreement, the person may file a petition for adjudication on the grant of the non-exclusive license with the Commissioner of the Korean Intellectual Property Office (Patent Act Article 107(1)).

통상실시권 설정의 재정

제3자가 특허법 제107조 각호 중 어느 하나에 해당하는 사유로 인하여 특허발명을 실시할 필요가 있고, 그와 같은 실시를 위하여 특허권자 또는 전용실시권자와 합리적인 조건 하에 협의를 시도하였음에도 통상실시권 설정계약이 이루어지지 않은 경우, 또는 그와 같은 협의를 할 수 없는 경우 그 제3자는 특허청장에게 통상실시권 설정에 관한 재정을 청구할 수 있음(특허법 제107조 제1항).

administration and dosage (of a medicine)

Example In a case where the **administration and dosage** of a medicine are added on top of the target disease or efficacy of a pharmaceutical medicine as an invention of a product, whether the administration and dosage constitute an element of invention (affirmative), and whether a patent may be newly granted to a pharmaceutical medicine meeting the patentability requirements including novelty and non-obviousness by adding a new pharmaceutical use, namely, administration and dosage (affirmative) / Whether this legal principle likewise applies when determining whether the challenged invention brought by the petitioner as the subject matter of a trial to confirm the scope of a patent right could be easily implemented from the publicly known art (affirmative) (Supreme Court Decision, 2014Hu 768, decided May 21, 2015).

투여용법 및 투여용량

의약이라는 물건의 발명에서 대상 질병 또는 약효와 함께 **투여용법과 투여용량**을 부가하는 경우, 투여용법과 투여용량이 발명의 구성요소인지 여부(적극) 및 투여용법과 투여용량이라는 새로운 의약용도가 부가되어 신규성과 진보성 등의 특허요건을 갖춘 의약에 대해서 새롭게 특허권이 부여될 수 있는지 여부(적극) 이 법리가 권리범위확인심판에서 심판청구인이 심판의 대상으로 삼은 확인대상발명이 공지기술로부터 용이하게 실시할 수 있는지를 판단할 때에도 마찬가지로 적용되는지 여부(적극)(대법원 2015. 5. 21. 선고 2014후768 전원합의체판결 참조).

administrative judge

Administrative judges of the Intellectual Property Trial and Appeal Board who will make independent rulings in administrative trials (Trademark Act Article 129, Design Protection Act Article 130).

심판관

특허심판원에 제기된 심판에 대해 직무상 독립하여 심판하는 역할을 함(상표법 제129조, 디자인보호법 제130조).

administrative patent judge

Administrative judges who preside over administrative patent trials in the Intellectual Property Trial and Appeal Board.

특허심판관

특허심판원에 소속되어 특허심판을 담당하는 자.

administrative trial

An administrative trial proceeding to determine lawfulness or legality of administrative decisions such as to invalidate or refuse to register industrial property rights.

심판(특허심판원)

산업재산권의 무효나 등록거절결정 등에 대하여 위법 · 부당성을 심사하는 행정적 절차.

administrative trial against rejection

An administrative trial proceeding requested by a party who appeals an examiner's decision to refuse to register a Patent or other rights etc. If a person has an objection to a ruling rejecting a patent application or to a ruling rejecting an application to register the extended term of a patent, he/she may file a petition for trial within 30 days from the date when he/she is served with a certified copy of the ruling (Patent Act Article 132-17).

거절결정 불복심판

특허출원인 등이 자기가 출원한 특허 등에 대하여 특허청이 내린 거절결정에 불복하여 특허심판원에 청구하는 심판. 특허거절결정 또는 특허권의 존속기간의 연장등록거절결정을 받은 자가 결정에 불복할 때에는 그 결정등본을 송달받은 날로부터 30일 이내에 심판을 청구할 수 있다(특허법 제132조의17).

• trial against decision to reject (법제처)

Example In an action to revoke **administrative decision to dismiss an appeal against rejection** of a patent application, the court simply reviews the lawfulness of the administrative decision to uphold the rejection and does not directly decide on the issue of whether to allow or refuse to register the application (Supreme Court Decision, 2012Hu3121, decided July 10, 2014).

특허거절결정에 대한 **불복심판청구를 기각한 심결**의 취소소송에서 법원은 특허거절결정을 유지한 심결의 위법성 여부를 판단하는 것일 뿐 특허출원에 대하여 직접 특허결정 또는 특허거절결정을 하는 것은 아니다(대법원 2014. 7. 10. 선고 2012후3121 판결).

administrative trial decision

A final disposition by the panel of administrative judges to rule on an administrative trial.

심결

심판사건에 대하여 심판관합의체가 내리는 종국적인 판단

• trial ruling (법제처)

administrative trial decision obtained by fraud

An administrative decision obtained by an action filed for the purpose of harming others. If the parties to an administrative patent trial conspire to obtain a trial decision by fraud with intent to infringe a third party's right or interest,

사해심결

타인을 사해할 목적으로 얻은 심결. 심판의 당사자가 공모하여 제3자의 권리 또는 이익을 사해할 목적으로 심결을 하게 한 경우에는 제3자는 그 확정된 심결에 대하

the third party may file a petition for a retrial on the judgment that has become final and conclusive (Design Protection Act Article 159).

여 재심을 청구할 수 있다(디자인보호법 제159조).

admissibility (of evidence)

(증거의) 채부

admission

자백

adverse inference

불리한 추정

A legal inference, adverse to the concerned party, drawn from silence or absence of requested evidence.

진술하지 않거나 요청한 증거를 제출하지 않는 경우 관련 당사자에 불리하게 적용되는 추정.

adverse party

상대방 당사자

aesthetic functionality

미 심미적 기능성

The doctrine that merely functional product or packaging that are aesthetically pleasing and appealing to the eyes, which play an important role in the commercial success of the product, are not eligible for trade dress or trademark protection.

기능적인데 불과한 제품 또는 제품포장이 심미적이고 눈에 띄는 특징을 지니고 이 특징이 그 제품의 상업적 성공에 중요한 영향을 미치는 경우 트레이드 드레스나 상표로 보호받을 수 없다고 보는 것.

Example Where the issue presented is whether the proposed mark is ornamental in nature, it is improper to refer to "**aesthetic functionality**," because the doctrine of "functionality" is inapplicable to such cases. TMEP § 1202.02(a)(vi).

출원상표가 장식적 성격을 띄는 지 여부가 쟁점일 때 '**심미적 기능성**'은 적용되지 않으므로 이를 논하는 것은 부적합하다. (미) TMEP § 1202.02(a)(vi).

aesthetic impression

심미감

→ See. aesthetic sense.

aesthetic sense

심미감

The aesthetic impression a design creates in the observer's mind. A design is sufficiently aesthetic if it creates a sense of pleasure, trendiness, safety or convenience, and is not required to be aesthetically sophisticated or advanced.

디자인이 관찰자에게 불러일으키는 미적 인상. 물품을 보는 자로 하여금 지금까지 볼 수 없었던 특수한 취미감, 유행감, 안전감 혹은 편리감 등을 줄 수 있으면 족하며, 반드시 미학적으로 높은 수준의 우아하고 고상한 것을 요구하는 것은 아님.

Example Despite the aforementioned differences, the dissimilarity does not rise to the degree that offsets the similarity brought by the points ④ and ⑤ above, which represent the dominant features of the designs, so as to display distinct **aesthetic senses** as a whole (Patent Court Decision, 2014Heo6858, decided April 23, 2015).

… 양 디자인 사이에 위와 같은 차이점이 존재하기는 하나, 그 차이의 정도가 양 디자인의 지배적인 특징을 나타내는 위 유사점 ④, ⑤로 말미암은 유사성을 상쇄하여 양 디자인이 전체적으로 다른 **심미감**을 나타낼 정도로는 보기 어렵고, … (특허법원 2015. 4. 23. 선고 2014허6858 판결 참조).

affidavit of continued use

Declaration of continued use. a sworn statement, filed by the owner of a registration that the mark is in use in commerce. USPTO.

미 계속사용진술서

계속적 사용의 선언. 그 상표가 거래상 사용되고 있다는 등록권자의 확인진술서.

Example If there is time remaining in the statutory filing period (including the grace period) and the owner responds to the Office action by submitting a new affidavit or declaration with a claim of use, specimen, and filing fee, the USPTO will examine the new affidavit or declaration of use. TMEP § 1604.11.

법정기간(유예기간 포함)의 잔존기간이 있을 때 상표권자가 사용에 대한 주장, 견본, 수수료와 더불어 새로이 진술서나 선언서를 제출함으로써 거절결정통지에 대응할 경우 특허상표청은 이 새로운 사용진술서 또는 선언서를 심사한다. (미) TMEP § 1604.11.

affidavit/declaration of excusable non-use

A sworn statement, filed by the owner of a registration, that the mark is not in use in commerce due to special circumstances that excuse such nonuse and is not due to any intention to abandon the mark. USPTO.

미 정당한 불사용의 진술서(선서서)

표장이 거래상 사용되고 있지 않으나 그 불사용이 특별한 사정으로 인한 정당한 불사용에 의한 것이며, 상표를 포기하고자 하는 의사에 의한 것이 아님에 대하여 등록권자가 제출한 확인진술서. (미) USPTO.

(administrative) affirmative confirmation trial for the scope of rights

→ See. administrative trial on confirmation of the scope of rights.

적극적 권리범위확인심판

(administrative) affirmative scope of rights trial

→ See. administrative trial on confirmation of the scope of rights.

적극적 권리범위확인심판

against public order or good morals

공공의 질서 또는 선량한 풍속에 어긋난

Example A trademark that is **against public order or good morals** as defined in Article 7 Paragraph (1) Item 4 of the TA refers to one that, by its composition or use on the designated goods, conveys a meaning or content that is contrary to public order, or the good morals and customs of ordinary citizens (Supreme Court Decision, 99Hu451, decided July 9, 2002).

상표법 제7조 제1항 제4호에서 '**공공의 질서 또는 선량한 풍속을 문란하게 할 염려가 있는 상표**'라 함은 상표의 구성 자체 또는 그 상표가 그 지정상품에 사용하는 경우에 일반 수요자에게 주는 의미나 내용이 사회 공공의 질서에 위반하거나, 사회일반인의 통상적인 도덕관념인 선량한 풍속에 반하는 경우를 말한다(대법원 2002. 7. 9. 선고 99후451 판결 참조).

agency authority

대리권

→ See. agent.

agent

대리인

A person authorized to carry out the litigation or administrative procedure as a representative.

소송절차 또는 행정절차를 대신하여 수행할 권한을 위임받은 자.

Example The term "**agent** or representative" generally means an agency, distributor, consigned seller, or general agency importing product from a person that has right to an overseas trademark and selling and advertising the product … (Patent Court Decision, 2013Heo10027, decided June 19, 2014).

'**대리인**이나 대표자'라 함은 일반적으로 국외에 있는 상표에 관한 권리를 가진 자의 그 상품을 수입하여 판매 · 광고하는 대리점, 특약점, 위탁판매업자, 총대리점 등을 가리키는 것인바, … (특허법원 2014. 6. 19. 선고 2013허10027 판결 참조).

AIA (Leahy-Smith America Invents Act)

미 미국 개정 특허법

allegations of use (in commerce)

미 (거래상) 사용주장

Allegation under 1(c) of the Trademark Act that the applicant has made use of the mark in commerce while the application under 1(b) (intent to use) is pending, to claim benefits of such use. 15 U.S.C. § 1051.

미 상표법 1(b) 하의 사용의사에 기한 출원 계류 중 그 상표를 거래상 사용하였다는 1(c)에 따른 사용사실에 기한 권리 주장. (미) 상표법 제1조

all elements rule, all-limitation rule

구성요소 일체의 원칙

According to this principle, all elements of a claim is essential and material, therefore each element of a claim must be present in an allegedly infringing device in order to establish infringement.

청구항의 모든 구성요소는 필수적이고 중요하므로 특허 침해는 침해자가 청구범위의 모든 구성요소를 사용하는 경우에만 성립하고, 그 중 일부만을 실시하는 행위는 원칙적으로 침해를 구성하지 아니함.

Example When a claim of a patented invention is comprised of more than one elements and the elements are organically

특허발명의 청구범위가 복수의 구성요소로 되어 있는 경우에는 각 구성요소가 유기적

combined, the whole claim becomes the substance of the patented invention, and therefore, excluding part of the elements while interpreting the patent claims is not allowed. In case the challenged invention consists of only part of the elements of the patented invention and does not include other parts of the patented invention, the challenged invention, in principle, does not fall under the scope of the patented invention according to the **all elements rule** (Supreme Court Decision, 98Hu2351, decided November 14, 2000).

으로 결합된 전체가 특허발명의 요지를 이루는 것이고, 이러한 경우 청구범위를 해석함에 있어서 그 구성요소의 일부를 배제하는 것은 허용될 수 없으며(대법원 2001. 12. 24. 선고 99후2181 판결 등 참조), 특허발명과 대비되는 확인대상발명이 특허발명의 청구항에 기재된 필수적 구성요소들 중의 일부만을 갖추고 있고 나머지 구성요소가 결여된 경우에는, 소위 **구성요소 완비의 원칙**에 의해, 원칙적으로 그 확인대상발명은 특허발명의 권리범위에 속하지 아니한다(대법원 2000. 11. 14. 선고 98후2351 판결 등 참조).

amendment

보정

Amending unlawfulness or ambiguousness of a petition or application. Modification made after the application is filed. Amendment is permissible only if it would keep the substance of the application unchanged.

신청 또는 청구 등에 부적법 또는 불명확 등의 사유가 있는 경우 이를 보완하거나 출원 이후 수정을 가하는 것. 출원의 요지를 변경하지 아니하는 범위 이내에서만 허용됨.

Example Where any matter mentioned in a written application for trademark registration is clearly incorrect when an examiner decides to publish an application under Article 57, he/she may make any amendments ex officio (hereinafter referred to as "ex officio amendment") (Trademark Act Article 59(1)).

심사관은 제57조에 따른 출원공고결정을 할 때에 상표등록출원서에 적힌 사항이 명백히 잘못된 경우에는 직권으로 **보정**(이하 이 조에서 "직권보정"이라 한다)을 할 수 있다(상표법 제59조 제1항).

amendment of application

출원의 보정

amendment of procedure

절차의 보정

Example The Commissioner of the Korean intellectual Property Office or the Director General of the Intellectual Property Trial and Appeal Board shall order a relevant person to **amend procedures** within a fixed period, if any of the following applies: … (Trademark Act Article 39).

특허청장 또는 특허심판원장은 상표에 관한 절차가 다음 각 호의 어느 하나에 해당하는 경우에는 **보정**을 명하여야 한다(상표법 제39조).

amicus curie briefs

미 법정 의견서

A brief submitted to the court, by petition or upon request of the court, by someone who has interest in the outcome

소의 결과에 이해관계를 지닌 이가 청원 또는 법원의 요청에 의하여 법원에 제출하는

of the lawsuit.

의견서.

analogous art

In a non-obviousness analysis, an analogous art refers to the art that a person having ordinary skill in the art would have referred to in attempting to solve the problem addressed by the innovation. It must be either within the same field of endeavor as the invention, or from a different filed but reasonably pertinent to the same problem.

유사한 (기술)분야

진보성 판단에서 통상의 기술자가 발명의 기술적 과제를 해결하기 위해 참고할 수 있는 기술. 유사 기술은 발명과 동일한 기술분야에 속하거나 다른 기술분야이더라도 해당 과제에 합리적으로 관련이 있어야 함.

Example When a modification to a primary reference involves a change in configuration, both the primary and secondary references must be from **analogous arts**. MPEP § 1504.03.

1차적인 인용문헌에 대한 변형으로 인하여 형태상의 변화가 초래된다면, 1차적 및 이차적 인용문헌 모두 **유사한 분야**에 관한 것이어야 한다. (미) MPEP § 1504.03.

annulment

실효

Example (**Annulment** of Adjudication) If a person for whom adjudication has been made fails to pay the consideration (the initial installment, if the consideration is to be paid periodically or in installments) or fails to pay it into the competent court, the adjudication shall become null and void (Patent Act Article 113).

(재정의 **실효**) 재정을 받은 자가 제110조 제2항 제2호에 따른 지급시기까지 대가(대가를 정기 또는 분할하여 지급할 경우에는 최초의 지급분)를 지급하지 아니하거나 공탁을 하지 아니한 경우에는 그 재정은 효력을 잃는다(특허법 제113조).

antecedent basis

선행근거

Example New matter is subject matter which has no **antecedent basis** in the original specification, drawings or claim. MPEP 1504.04.I.B.

신규사항이란 최초의 명세서, 도면 또는 청구범위에 대한 **선행근거**가 없는 대상을 말한다. (미) MPEP 1504.04.I.B.

anticipate

A single prior art reference anticipates a claim when it contains all the elements of the claim. Such a claim is rejected for lack of novelty.

예견하다

하나의 선행문헌이 청구항의 모든 구성요소를 포함하고 있는 경우 선행문헌으로부터 청구항 발명이 예측되며, 이러한 청구항 발명은 신규성 결여로 거절됨.

apparatus claims

Claims of an invention of a machine or structure.

미 장치 청구항

기계 혹은 구조물 발명에 대한 청구항.

appeal

항소(불복심판)

appearance
Visibly recognizable outer configuration of a product or a mark.

외관
물품이나 표장의 외부적 형태로서, 시각을 통해 감지되는 외부적 형상 등을 의미.

appellant

상고인/항소인

appellations of origin

원산지 명칭

appellee

피상고인(피항소인)

application
A document by which a person requests registration of a patent, trademark, etc. An application must satisfy the requirements prescribed in the relevant laws to receive a filing date.

출원
특허나 상표 등의 등록요청서류. 각 법에 정해진 요건을 만족시켜야만 출원일자를 받을 수 있음.

application by unentitled persons
A patent application filed by a person who does not have the right to hold a patent of such invention.

모인출원
어떤 발명에 대하여 특허를 받을 권리가 없는 자가 한 특허출원.

Example If a patent application filed by a person who is not an inventor nor a successor to an entitlement to a patent (hereinafter referred to as "unentitled person") falls under subparagraph 2 of Article 62 on the ground that the person has no entitlement to a patent under the main body of Article 33 (1) and no patent is granted to such person, the patent application filed by a legitimate right-holder subsequent to **the patent application filed by the unentitled person** shall be deemed filed on the date of filing of the patent application by the unentitled person (Patent Act Article 34).

발명자가 아닌 자로서 특허를 받을 수 있는 권리의 승계인이 아닌 자(이하 "무권리자"라 한다)가 한 특허출원이 제33조 제1항 본문에 따른 특허를 받을 수 있는 권리를 가지지 아니한 사유로 제62조 제2호에 해당하여 특허를 받지 못하게 된 경우에는 그 **무권리자의 특허출원** 후에 한 정당한 권리자의 특허출원은 무권리자가 특허출원한 때에 특허출원한 것으로 본다(특허법 제34조).

application data sheet (ADS)
A sheet or sheets that may be submitted in a provisional application under Patent Act, 35 U.S.C. § 111(b), a nonprovisional application under Patent Act, 35 U.S.C. § 111(a), a nonprovisional international design application,or a national stage application under Patent Act, 35 U.S.C. § 371 and must be submitted when required by § 1.55 or

미 출원데이터시트
가출원의 경우 미 특허법 111(b)조, 정규출원은 111(a)조, 정규 국제디자인출원이나 국내단계출원의 경우 371조에 따라 제출할 수 있으며, 119, 120, 121, 365, 386조 하에서 선출원에 기한 우선권을 주장할 경우 37 C.F.R. § 1.55조나 1.78조에 따라 반드시 제

1.78 to claim priority to or the benefit of a prior-filed application under Patent Act, 35 U.S.C. § 119, 120, 121, 365, or 386. The application data sheet is partof the application for which it has been submitted. 37 C.F.R. § 1.76(a).

출하여야 함. 출원의 일부를 구성.

A

application filing date

출원일

The date on which all the elements for an application as set forth in the law are received by the KIPO.

법에 규정된 대로 출원에 필요한 모든 요소가 특허청에 제출된 일자.

application for design registration

디자인등록출원

Each design shall be applied for registration under a separate application (Design Protection Act Article 40(1)).

디자인등록출원은 1디자인마다 1디자인등록출원으로 한다(디자인보호법 제40조 제1항).

application mutatis mutandis

준용

Example Articles 3 through 7, 7-2, 8 through 25, 28, and 28-2 through 28-5 of the Patent Act shall **apply mutatis mutandis** to utility models (Utility Model Act Article 3).

실용신안에 관하여는 「특허법」 제3조부터 제7조까지, 제7조의2, 제8조부터 제25조까지, 제28조, 제28조의2부터 제28조의5까지의 규정을 **준용**한다(실용신안법 제3조).

apportionment

기여분

Determining the contribution and allocating value of the infringed part relative to the entire product, when the infringed patent is only applied to the part of the product.

침해된 특허가 전체 제품의 일부에만 적용되었을 때 전체제품의 가치에 침해부분의 가치가 기여하는 기여분을 정하여 배분함.

appraisal

감정

Examination of evidence in litigation procedure that requires experts' opinion based on special knowledge or experience (Civil Procedure Act Article 334)

특별한 학식 · 경험이 있는 제3자의 판단 요구하는 증거조사(민사소송법 제334조).

- expert testimony (법제처)

Example When the court orders **appraisal** in order to calculate the amount of damages in patent infringement cases or exclusive license infringement cases, the parties shall explain to the appraiser matters necessary for the **appraisal** of the damage amount (Patent Act Article 128-2).

특허권 또는 전용실시권 침해소송에서 법원이 침해로 인한 손해액의 산정을 위하여 **감정**을 명한 때에는 당사자는 감정인에게 **감정**에 필요한 사항을 설명하여야 한다(특허법 제128조의2).

appropriation

전용(轉用)

Example … (a) a design imitating or **appropriating** a shape, pattern, or color, or a combination thereof, that is widely known in the Republic of Korea almost as it is; (b) notwithstanding the partial transformation, in its totality a design that is merely a commercial and functional transformation without any other recognized aesthetic value; or … (Supreme Court Decision, 2014Hu614, decided June 9, 2016).

… 국내에서 널리 알려진 형상 · 모양 · 색채 또는 이들의 결합(이하 '주지형태'라고 한다)을 거의 그대로 모방 또는 **전용**하였거나, 이를 부분적으로 변형하였다고 하더라도 전체적으로 볼 때 다른 미감적 가치가 인정되지 않는 상업적 · 기능적 변형에 불과하거나, … (대법원 2016. 6. 9. 선고 2014후614 판결 참조).

arbitrary mark

임의적 표장

The marks that consist of arbitrarily chosen existing words that do not imply or depict the quality or characteristics of particular goods or services when used in connection with the goods or services. E.g. "Apple" Computers.

이미 존재하는 용어 중에서 임의로 선택하여 이루어진 표장으로 특정상품 또는 서비스와 관련되어 사용되었을 때, 그 상품 또는 서비스의 품질, 특성을 암시하거나 묘사하지 않는 단어나 도형을 의미함. 예. "애플"컴퓨터.

Example The mark at issue is an **arbitrary mark** that has gained unique distinctiveness by using a common and non-distinctive word on the designated good, one that is not expected to be associated with the word (Patent Court Decision, 99Heo819, decided April 8, 1999).

이 건 출원상표는 일견 식별력이 없는 흔한 단어가 의외의 상품을 지정상품으로 하여 사용됨으로써 독특한 식별력을 가지게 되는 상표인 **임의적 상표**(arbitrary mark)에 해당한다(특허법원 1999. 4. 8. 선고 99허819 판결 참조).

arbitration trademark

임의적 상표

→ See. arbitrary marks.

article of manufacture

물품

The subject an invention, trademark or design is embodied in or applied to.

발명, 상표 또는 디자인 등이 화체 또는 적용된 대상.

Example Any indicia, contrasting color or materials, graphic representations, or other ornamentation applied to the article. Surface treatment must be applied to or embodied in an **article of manufacture**. Surface treatment, per se (i.e., not applied to or embodied in a specific **article of manufacture**), is not proper subject matter for a design patent under 35 U.S.C. 171. (미) MPEP 1503.02.IV.

물품에 적용된 여하한 표시, 대조적인 색채나 재질, 그래픽 표현물, 또는 다른 장식. 표면 처리는 **물품**에 적용되거나 화체된 것이어야 한다. 표면 처리는, 그 자체로는 (즉, 특정한 **물품**에 적용되거나 화체되지 않은 상태로는) 미 특허법 제171조에 따른 디자인특허의 올바른 대상이라 할 수 없다. MPEP 1503.02.IV.

A

as business

→ See. (to do something) commercially.

업으로 하다

as shown

The drawing in an application is incorporated into the claim by use of the claim language "as shown." MPEP 1504.04.

도시된 바와 같은

출원에서 도면은 "도시된 바와 같은" 의 청구범위 용어를 사용함으로써 청구범위에 포함됨. (미) MPEP 1504.04.

as shown and described

The description in an application is incorporated into the claim by use of the language "as shown and described." MPEP 1504.04.

도시(圖示)되고 기재된 바와 같은

출원에서 설명은, "도시되고 기재된 바와 같은"의 용어를 사용함으로써 청구범위에 포섭됨. (미) MPEP 1504.04.

assignment

Assignment refer to transfer of ownership, regardless of whether it is paid for or not.

양도

'양도'란 권리를 이전하는 행위로서 유 · 무상 여부에 관계없음.

attractiveness to customers

The power of trademark to draw or attract customers to buy goods or use services.

고객흡인력

상품을 구매하거나 서비스를 이용하도록 고객을 끌어당기는 힘.

Example In view of the following circumstances, it is difficult to see that the initial applicant of the Subject Service Mark or the Plaintiff, as successor in interest to the applicant, damaged intangible value such as business reputation or **customer drawing power** embodied in the pre-used and pre-registered trademark (Patent Court Decision, 2015Heo 6558, decided February 16, 2016).

선사용선등록상표에 체화된 영업상의 신용 또는 **고객흡인력** 등의 무형의 가치에 손상을 입히기 위한 것이라고 보기 어렵다(특허법원 2016.02.16 선고 2015허6558판결 참조).

• customer drawing power (법제처)

aural marks

→ See. sound marks.

청각상표

B

basic trademark right

기초상표권

→ See. basic trademark rights [or application/registration] of international registration.

basic trademark rights of international registration

국제등록기초상표권

The basis of an international trademark registration. A registration at the domestic Patent Office which is registered on the International Trademark Register.

국제상표등록의 기초가 되는 상표등록. 우리나라를 지정하여 통지된 국제상표등록출원이 등록결정되어 국내 상표등록원부에 등록되어 있는 상표권을 말함.

• internationally registered basic trademark rights. (법제처)

be associated with

화체

A trademark is associated with the good will of the trademark owner.

상표에 그 상표권자의 영업상 신용이 나타남.

Example The purpose of Article 7 (1) subparagraph 12 of the former Trademark Act is to disallow the registration of a trademark identical or similar to a trademark which is well recognized as indicating the goods of a particular person by consumers within or outside the Republic of Korea, and which is used for unjust purposes such as obtaining unjust profits or inflicting harm on the prior trademark holder through the loss of intangible value (e.g. good will or customer appeal **associated with** the well-known trademark) or obstructing business within Korea (Supreme Court Decision, 2010Hu807, decided July 15, 2010).

구 상표법 제7조 제1항 제12호는 국내 또는 외국의 수요자 간에 특정인의 상표라고 현저하게 인식되어 있는 이른바 주지상표가 국내에서 등록되어 있지 않음을 기화로 제3자가 이를 모방한 상표를 등록하여 사용함으로써 주지상표에 **화체**된 영업상의 신용이나 고객흡인력 등의 무형의 가치에 손상을 입히거나 주지상표권자의 국내에서의 영업을 방해하는 등의 방법으로 주지상표권자에게 손해를 가하거나 이러한 모방상표를 이용하여 부당한 이익을 얻을 목적으로 사용하는 상표는 그 등록을 허용하지 않는다는 취지이다(대법원 2010. 7. 15. 선고 2010후807 판결 참조).

be embodied in

화체

A design is embodied in an article.

디자인을 물품에 표현하는 경우

Example The specification should include the following sections in order: (1) Preamble, stating the name of the applicant, title of the design, and a brief description of the nature and intended use of the article in which the design **is embodied**. 37 C.F.R. § 1.154.

명세서는 다음 항목을 순서대로 포함하여야 한다: (1) 출원인의 이름, 디자인의 명칭, 및 디자인이 **화체**된 물품의 속성과 용도에 대한간단한 설명을 언급하는 전제부. (미) 37 C.F.R. § 1.154(b).

bench trial

A trial before a judge without a jury.

판사에 의한 재판

배심원 없이 판사 앞에서 행해지는 재판.

benefit claim

The claiming by an applicant of benefit from an earlier filed application under 35 U.S.C. §§ 119(e), 120 and 365(c) such as a U.S. provisional application. → Cf. Claim of priority.

미 우선권 주장

미 특허법 119(e), 120, 365(c)조에 따라 미국 내 가출원 등 선출원에 기한 출원인의 우선권 주장.

Example AIA Patent Act, 35 U.S.C. § 102(d) requires that a prior-filed application to which a priority or **benefit claim** is made must describe the subject matter from the U.S.patent document relied upon in a rejection. MPEP § 2154.01(b).

개정특허법 102(d)조는 **우선권 주장**이 근거한 선출원에 등록거절결정에서 근거로 삼은 미국 특허문헌 상의 대상이 묘사되었을 것을 요한다. (미) MPEP § 2154.01(b).

best mode

The specification must set forth the best mode, or preferred embodiment The America Invents Act eliminated failure to set forth best mode as a basis for patent invalidity.

미 최적 실시례

명세서에는 최적의 실시례 또는 바람직한 구현례를 기재하여야 함(미국 특허법 제112조). 개정 특허법에는 최적 실시례를 기재하지 않는 것을 무효 사유의 기초로 보는 규정을 삭제함.

Example The specification shall contain a written description of the invention, and of the manner and process of making and using it, in such full, clear, concise, and exact terms as to enable any person skilled in the art to which it pertains, or with which it is most nearly connected, to make and use the same, and shall set forth the **best mode** contemplated by the inventor or joint inventor of carrying out the invention. 35 U.S.C. § 112(a).

명세서에는 발명의 상세한 기재와 그 발명과 관련되거나 가장 근접한 분야에서 통상의 기술자라면 누구든지 똑같이 이를 생산하고 사용할 수 있을 만큼 전체적이고 명확, 간결, 정확한 용어로 된 그 발명을 생산하고 사용하는 방법과 과정, 그리고 그 발명을 실시하는 발명자나 공동발명자가 고려하기에 **최적의 실시례**를 제시하여야 한다. (미) 특허법 112(a)조.

binding precedent

A prior decision or authority established in a previous legal case that is either binding on or persuasive for a court when deciding subsequent cases with similar issues or facts.

미 구속력 있는 선례

선행 사건에서 있었던 선례 또는 법원은 유사한 쟁점 또는 사실관계를 가진 후행 사건을 판단함에 있어 법원을 구속하거나 설득함.

Example These Guidelines are based on the Office's current understanding of the law and are believed to be fully consistent with **binding precedent** of the U.S. Supreme Court,

이러한 지침은 특허상표청이 법에 대해 현재 이해하는 바에 기초한 것으로 미 대법원, 연방순회항소법원 및 그 전신 법원들의 **구속력있는 선례**와 일관성이 있는 것으로

as well as the U.S. Court of Appeals for the Federal Circuit and its predecessor courts. MPEP § 2163 (providing guidelines for the written description requirement).

판단하고 있다. (미) MPEP § 2163 (발명의 상세한 기재 요건에 대한 지침 안내 중)

blocking patent

Two or more patented inventions block each other when one cannot be practiced without infringing the other, and vice versa. The parties commonly agree to a cross-license to resolve the issue.

상호저촉특허

서로 상대방 특허발명을 침해하지 않고는 실시할 수 없는 저촉 관계에 있는 2개 이상의 특허. 문제 해결을 위해 당사자들은 보통 크로스 라이선스 계약을 체결함.

blurring

The whittling away of an established trademark's selling power through its unauthorized use by others upon dissimilar products. Mead Data Central, Inc. v. Toyota Motor Sales, U.S.A., Inc., 875 F.2d 1026, 1031 (2d Cir.1989).

약화(弱化)

어느 상표를 타인이 유사하지 아니한 상품에 정당한 권한 없이 사용함으로써 그 상표가 지니는 기존의 판매력을 감소시키는 것. (미) Mead Data Central, Inc. v. Toyota Motor Sales, U.S.A., Inc., 875 F.2d 1026, 1031 (2d Cir.1989).

Example Furthermore, although the two names are distinguishable, the identity of the "R" Us suffixes and the similarity of the children's products sold by the stores compels me to conclude that the name Kids 'r' Us is likely to **blur** Toys "R" Us' product identification. Clearly, the distinctiveness of plaintiff's mark is being "whittled away" by a proliferation of "R" Us names, including Kids 'r' Us, and the mark's accompanying selling power is being diluted. Toys R Us, Inc. v. Canarsie Kiddie Shop, Inc., 559 F. Supp. 1189, 1208 (E.D.N.Y. 1983).

나아가 두 명칭이 구별은 가능하다 하더라도, "R" Us 접미사 부분의 동일성과 매장에서 판매되는 해당 아동용품의 유사성을 고려하면 "Kids 'r' Us" 표장은 "Toys "R" Us" 상표의 제품식별력을 **약화**시킨다고밖에 볼 수 없다. 원고 상표의 식별력은 Kids 'r' Us를 포함하여 "R" Us를 사용한 명칭이 늘어날수록 감소할 것이 명백하고 이로 인해 상표가 가지는 판매력도 희석된다. (미) Toys R Us, Inc. v. Canarsie Kiddie Shop, Inc., 559 F. Supp. 1189, 1208 (E.D.N.Y. 1983).

Board of Patent Appeals and Interferences

The predecessor of the Patent Trial and Appeal Board.

미 항고심판소

특허심판원의 전신.

bona fide intention (to use mark in commerce)

Intention to use a trademark in commerce in good faith. A person who has a bona fide intention, …, to use a trademark in commerce may request registration of its trademark on the principal register hereby established by paying the prescribed fee and filing in the Patent and Trademark Office an application and a verified statement, in such form as

미 상표를 거래상 사용하고자 하는 진실한 의사

거래상 상표를 사용하고자 하는 진실한 의사. 상표를 거래상 사용하고자 하는 진실한 의사를 가진 자는 … 정해진 수수료를 지불하고 특허상표청장이 정한 양식에 따라 확인진술서와 출원서를 제출함으로써 주등록

may be prescribed by the Commissioner. 15 U.S.C. § 1051(b)(1)).

부에 상표를 등록할 것을 요청할 수 있다. (미) 상표법 제1(b)(1)조.

bona fide use (in the ordinary course of trade)

Bona fide use is found based on the amount of use, the nature or quality of the transaction and what is typical use in the particular industry.

(통상적인 상거래에서) 진실한 사용

사용정도, 거래의 성질이나 수준, 해당 업계의 일반적 사용방법 등을 바탕으로 판단함.

B

breaches of order to maintain confidentiality

비밀유지명령위반죄

breeder

The term "breeder" means a person who either breeds, or discovers and develops a plant variety; … (Act on Protection of New Varieties of Plants Article 2.3).

육성자

"육성자"란 품종을 육성한 자나 이를 발견하여 개발한 자를 말한다(식물신품종보호법 제2조 제3호).

brief

A document containing statement of facts, claim, etc. in litigation.

준비서면

사실, 주장 등을 기재한 소송절차 상의 서류.

burden of proof

A party's duty to substantiate his or her argument with evidence.

증명책임

증거로 주장을 뒷받침할 당사자의 의무.

Example When deciding whether an applicant has met the **burden of proof** with respect to showing nonequivalence of a prior art element that performs the claimed function, the following factors may be considered. … MPEP § 2184.`

출원인이 청구된 기능을 수행하는 선행기술의 구성요소의 비균등성을 입증함에 있어 그 **증명책임**을 만족하였는지 결정하기 위하여는 다음과 같은 요소가 고려되며 … (미) MPEP § 2184.

business emblem

A mark used by a person who engages in not-for-profit business to identify his/her business. E.g. "Red Cross" (Trademark Act Article 2(1)9).

업무표장

영리를 목적으로 하지 아니하는 업무를 하는 자가 그 업무를 나타내기 위하여 사용하는 표장을 말함. 적십자 등(상표법 제2조 제1항 제9호).

business method patent

An invention that uses information technology to materialize a business method. The information processing of the software on the computer shall be realized by using the hardware. A person skilled in the art must be able to learn

영업방법 발명

정보기술을 이용하여 영업방법을 구현하는 발명으로서, 컴퓨터상에서 소프트웨어에 의한 정보처리가 하드웨어를 이용하여 구체적으로 실현되고 있어야 하며, 명세서의

specifically by the description of the specification how the information process of the software on the computer gets realized by using the hardware (Supreme Court Decision, 2007Hu265, decided December 24, 2008).

기재만으로는 통상의 기술자가 컴퓨터상에서 소프트웨어에 의한 정보처리가 하드웨어를 이용하여 구체적으로 어떻게 실현되는지 알 수 없다면, 그 발명은 산업상 이용할 수 있는 발명이 아님(대법원 2008. 12. 24 선고 2007후265판결 참조).

business reputation

업무상의 신용

Example The court may order a person who has damaged **business reputation** of a trademark right holder or an exclusive licensee by wilfully or negligently infringing the trademark rights or the exclusive license to pay damages at the request of the trademark right holder or the exclusive licensee, or order the person to take measures necessary to reinstate the business reputation of the trademark right holder or the exclusive licensee along with compensation for damages (Trademark Act Article 113).

… 상표권자 또는 전용사용권자의 **업무상 신용**을 떨어뜨린 자에 대해서는 상표권자 또는 전용사용권자의 청구에 의하여 손해배상을 갈음하거나 손해배상과 함께 상표권자 또는 전용사용권자의 업무상 신용회복을 위하여 필요한 조치를 명할 수 있다(상표법 제113조).

C

CAFC (Court of Appeals for the Federal Circuit)

미 미국연방순회항소법원

cancellation

취소

cancellation (of registration)

To prospectively remove any effect of IP rights due to a certain cause arising after a valid registration.

등록취소

일단 유효하게 등록된 산업재산권 등이 사후의 일정한 사유에 의하여 그 등록의 효력을 장래에 대하여 상실시키는 것을 말함.

category of goods

Any person who intends to file an application for trademark or other rights shall file an application for each right and designate at least one category of goods in accordance with the classification of goods.

상품류 구분

상표 등의 출원을 하고자 하는 자는 상품류 구분상 1류 구분 이상의 상품을 지정하여 상표마다 출원하여야 한다.

Example Where goods in the application for registration of the conversion of the classification of goods are

상품분류전환등록신청의 지정상품이 **상품류 구분**과 일치하지 아니하는 경우 상품분

inconsistent with the classification of the **category of goods** (Trademark Act Article 210(1)2).

류전환등록거절결정을 하여야 한다(상표법 제210조 제1항 제2호).

cause of action

청구원인

cease and desist order

An order of a court or an administrative agency to an individual or a business to stop a purportedly illegal activity.

중지명령

불법행위에 대해 중지를 명하는 법원 또는 행정기관의 명령.

central claiming

A claiming regime in which a claim recites the preferred embodiment of the invention but is deemed to cover a range of equivalents to that preferred embodiment.

중심한정주의

발명의 바람직한 구현례를 설명하는 청구항에 그와 균등한 범위까지 포함되는 것으로 간주하는 청구항 해석의 방법.

central distinctiveness

Thus, in cases where the composition of a registered trademark, in whole or in part, may have had little or no distinctiveness at the time of registration, but the use of a trademark, in whole or in component part separately, has allowed the trademark to acquire central distinctiveness for consumers to manifestly recognize whose product it is by the time of adjudication decision on the scope of right, the similarity of trademarks should be determined based on that central distinctiveness (Supreme Court Decision, 2011Hu 3698, decided March 20, 2014).

중심적 식별력

등록상표의 전부 또는 일부 구성이 등록결정 당시에는 식별력이 없거나 미약하였다고 하더라도 그 등록상표를 전체로서 또는 일부 구성 부분을 분리하여 사용함으로써 권리범위확인심판의 심결 시점에 이르러서는 수요자 사이에 누구의 상품을 표시하는 것인지 현저하게 인식될 정도가 되어 중심적 식별력을 가지게 된 경우에는, 이를 기초로 상표의 유사 여부를 판단하여야 한다(대법원 2014. 3. 20. 선고 2011후3698 전원합의체 판결 참조).

certificate of correction

A certificate issued by the USPTO to correct a mistake in a patent.

미 정정증명서

특허의 오류를 정정하기 위해 특허상표청이 발행하는 증명서.

certificate of registration

등록증

certificate of trademark registration

상표등록증

certification mark

A mark used by a person who commercially certifies and manages the quality, place of origin, methods of production, or other characteristics of goods to certify that goods of

증명표장

상품의 품질, 원산지, 생산방법 또는 그 밖의 특성을 증명하고 관리하는 것을 업으로 하는 자가 타인의 상품에 대하여 그 상품이

C

others meet quality criteria, the place of origin, methods of production, or other characteristics (Trademark Act Article 2(1)7).

품질, 원산지, 생산방법 또는 그 밖의 특성을 충족한다는 것을 증명하는 데 사용하는 표장을 의미함(상표법 제2조 제1항 제7호).

certification mark with geographical indication

지리적 표시 증명표장

A mark used by a person who commercially certifies a geographical indication to certify that goods of others meet specified geographical characteristics (Trademark Act Article 2(1)8).

지리적 표시를 증명하는 것을 업으로 하는 자가 타인의 상품에 대하여 그 상품이 정해진 지리적 특성을 충족한다는 것을 증명하는 데 사용하는 표장(상표법 제2조 제1항 제8호).

chain of title

권원의 연속

A term applied metaphorically to the series of conveyances, or other forms of alienation, affecting e.g., a particular parcel of land, arranged consecutively, from the government or original source of title down to the present holder.

특정된 토지 등에 대하여, 정부나 권원의 원 출처에서부터 현재의 권리자에게까지 연속적으로 이어져 내려온 그 권리이전의 연속성.

Example A request that a registration issue in the name of a new owner will not be granted unless documents recorded in the Assignment recordation Branch show clear **chain of title** from the original applicant to the new owner. TMEP § 502.02(a).

새로운 상표권자의 이름으로 상표등록을 발행할 것을 요하는 내용의 청구는 양도등록부(Assignment Rcordation Branch, ARB)에 등재된 서류에 원 출원인에서 새로운 상표권자까지의 **권원의 연속**이 명백히 나타나지 아니하면 받아들일 수 없다. (미) TMEP § 502.02(a).

challenge (of a judge)

기피

Excluding a judge from the case by request of the party or the intervenor in case of a situation where the judge cannot be expected to conduct a fair proceeding for reasons other than prescribed by law.

법률상 정해진 제척사유 이외에 법관에게 재판의 공정을 기대하기 어려운 사정이 있을 때에 당사자 또는 참가인의 신청에 의하여 당해 법관을 배제시키는 것.

challenged/challenging(invention/mark/design)

확인대상(발명/표장/디자인)

The invention, mark or design subject to confirmation in a scope of rights confirmation action. *Challenged* in an action for affirmative adjudication on the scope of rights; *challenging* in a defensive scope of rights action.

권리범위확인의 대상이 되는 발명, 표장, 디자인. 해당 발명, 표장, 디자인에 대하여 적극적 권리범위확인심판의 경우 challenged, 소극적 권리범위확인심판의 경우 challenging으로 쓸 수 있음.

Example Therefore, in the context of adjudication on the scope of right and petition for revocation of the adjudicated decision, the distinctiveness of a trademark, which is an

따라서 상표권의 권리범위확인심판 및 그 심결취소청구 사건에서 등록상표와 **확인대상표장**의 유사 여부를 판단하기 위한 요소가 되는 등록상표의 식별력은 상표의 유사

element to determine the similarity between a registered trademark and a **challenged mark**, is to be determined at the time of adjudication, which is also the reference point for determining the similarity of trademarks (Supreme Court Decision, 2011Hu3698, decided March 20, 2014).

여부를 판단하는 기준시인 심결 시를 기준으로 판단하여야 한다(대법원 2014. 3. 20. 선고 2011후3698 전원합의체 판결 참조.

• subject to confirmation (법제처)

Example On the grounds as laid out below, the lower court determined that the **challenged invention** is not subsumed in the scope of the right of the instant Patented Invention (patent registration number omitted) Claim 1 (hereinafter "Invention Claim 1"), titled, "low dosage entecavir tablet and its uses," without even having to contrast the two, since it constitutes the state-of-the-art technology that a person of ordinary skill in the art (hereinafter "a person with ordinary skill") can easily implement based on the cited inventions and generally known art in practice (Supreme Court Decision, 2014Hu768, decided May 21, 2015).

원심은, 아래와 같은 이유를 들어, **확인대상발명**은 그 발명이 속하는 기술분야에서 통상의 지식을 가진 사람(이하 '통상의 기술자'라 한다)이 그 판시 비교대상발명들과 주지관용기술로부터 용이하게 실시할 수 있는 자유실시기술에 해당하므로, 명칭을 '저용량의 엔테카비르 제제 및 그의 용도'로 하는 이 사건 특허발명(특허등록번호 생략)의 청구범위 제1항(이하 '이 사건 제1항 발명'이라 한다)과 대비할 필요 없이 그 권리범위에 속하지 아니한다고 판단하였다(대법원 2015. 5. 21. 선고 2014후768 전원합의체판결 참조).

characteristic features

A particular feature of the design that is considered by applicant to be a feature of novelty or nonobviousness over the prior art. 37 C.F.R. § 1.71(c).

미 독특한 특징

공지디자인에 대하여 신규성 또는 비자명성을 가지는 특징이라고 출원인이 생각하는 디자인의 특정한 특징. (미) 37 C.F.R. § 1.71(c).

Example A "**characteristic features**" statement describing a particular feature of novelty or nonobviousness in the claimed design may be permissible in the specification. Such a statement should be in terms such as "The characteristic feature of the design resides in [1]," or if combined with one of the Figure descriptions, in terms such as "the characteristic feature of which resides in [2]." MPEP § 1503.01.

명세서에는 등록하고자 하는 디자인의 신규성 또는 진보성을 지니는 특정한 특징을 묘사하는 '**독특한 특징**'에 대한 진술이 허용될 수 있는데, 이러한 진술은 '해당 디자인의 독특한 특징은 [1]에 존재한다'거나 그림을 통한 묘사와 결합하여 사용될 경우에는 '그 독특한 특징은 [2]에 존재한다'와 같은 문구를 사용하여야 한다. (미) MPEP § 1503.01.

chief administrative judge

심판장

• presiding judge (법제처)

C

cited design

인용디자인

cited invention

비교대상발명, 비교대상고안

An art or technology which is used as a basis to determine novelty or inventive step of an invention. Prior art, prior invention. → See. prior invention

특허의 신규성 또는 진보성 판단 기준이 되는 기술.

Example On the grounds as laid out below, the lower court determined that the challenged invention is not subsumed in the scope of the right of the instant Patented Invention (patent registration number omitted) Claim 1 (hereinafter "Invention Claim 1"), titled, "low dosage entecavir tablet and its uses," without even having to contrast the two, since it constitutes the state-of-the-art technology that a person of ordinary skill in the art (hereinafter "a person with ordinary skill") can easily implement based on the **cited inventions** and generally known art in in practice (Supreme Court Decision, 2015Hu768, decided May 21, 2015).

2014후768 원심은, 아래와 같은 이유를 들어, 확인대상발명은 그 발명이 속하는 기술분야에서 통상의 지식을 가진 사람(이하 '통상의 기술자'라 한다)이 그 판시 **비교대상발명**들과 주지관용기술로부터 용이하게 실시할 수 있는 자유실시기술에 해당하므로, 명칭을 '저용량의 엔테카비르 제제 및 그의 용도'로 하는 이 사건 특허발명의 청구범위 제1항(이하 '이 사건 제1항 발명'이라 한다)과 대비할 필요 없이 그 권리범위에 속하지 아니한다고 판단하였다(대법원 2015. 5. 21. 선고 2015후768 판결 참조).

cited trademark

인용상표

claim

청구

claim construction (interpretation)

청구항 해석

Example If the body of a claim fully and intrinsically sets forth all of the limitations of the claimed invention, and the preamble merely states, for example, the purpose or intended use of the invention, rather than any distinct definition of any of the claimed invention's limitations, then the preamble is not considered a limitation and is of no significance to **claim construction**. MPEP § 2111.02.

청구항의 특징부에서 출원발명의 모든 한정사항을 완전하고 있는 그대로 설명하고 전제부는 출원발명의 한정사항에 대해 뚜렷한 정의를 제시하지 아니하며 발명의 목적이나 의도된 용도 등만을 진술할 경우, 전제부는 한정사항을 포함하는 것으로 간주되지 아니 하고 **청구항 해석**에 있어 아무 비중을 갖지 아니한다. (미) MPEP § 2111.02.

claimed invention

청구항 발명

The subject matter defined by a claim in a patent or an application for a patent.

특허 또는 특허출원의 청구항에서 정의된 발명의 대상.

claim element

청구항 구성요소

→ See. element.

Example It is common that doubt arises about enablement because information is missing about one or more essential **claim elements** or relationships between elements which one skilled in the art could not develop without undue experimentation. In such a case, the examiner should specifically identify what information is missing and why the missing information is needed to provide enablement. MPEP § 2164.06(a).

정보가 충분히 제공되지 않아 하나 이상의 필수적인 **청구항의 구성요소**나 구성요소 간 관계가 통상의 기술자가 과도한 실험 없이는 개발할 수 없을 정도이어서 실시가능성에 의문이 제기되는 경우는 흔히 발생한다. 이 경우 심사관은 구체적으로 어떤 정보가 필요하며 발명이 실시가능하기 위하여 그 정보가 왜 필요한지도 설명하여야 한다. (미) MPEP § 2164.06(a).

C

claim for compensation for loss

손실보상청구

Claim for remedy for economic damage caused by legitimate action of other person (e.g. expropriation by government).

타인의 적법한 행위(국가의 수용 등)로 인하여 경제적 피해를 입은 경우 그 보전을 해줄 것을 청구하는 것.

claim for damages

손해배상 청구권

Claim for remedy of economical damage caused by illegal action of other person. Ie. Patent infringement, illegal action under Civil Act.

타인의 위법한 행위(특허침해, 민법상 불법행위 등)로 인하여 경제적 피해를 입은 경우 그 보전을 해줄 것을 청구하는 것.

Example Thus, for a trademark owner to **claim for damages** under the said provision: (a) the trademark holder should have been actually using the registered trademark at the time of infringement; (b) the trademark used by the infringer shall be the same as, or have identical elements to, the trademark holder's registered trademark; and (c) when such identity requirement is not met, the victim may not claim for the legally stipulated damages under the above provision, but instead shall claim for damages by proving injury using ordinary methods. Such a legal doctrine applies likewise to service marks (Supreme Court Decision, 2014Da59712, decided September 30, 2016).

따라서 상표권자가 이 규정에 의한 **손해배상을 청구**하려면, 상표권 침해 당시 해당 등록상표를 상표권자가 실제 사용하고 있었어야 하고, 침해자가 사용한 상표가 상표권자의 등록상표와 같거나 동일성이 있어야 하며, 동일성 요건을 갖추지 못한 경우에는 통상의 방법으로 손해를 증명하여 배상을 청구하여야지 위 규정에서 정한 법정 손해배상을 청구할 수는 없고, 이러한 법리는 서비스표의 경우에도 동일하게 적용된다(대법원 2016. 9. 30. 선고 2014다59712판결 참조).

claim for reinstatement of reputation

신용회복청구

Example Upon request of a patentee or exclusive licensee, the court may order the person who has degraded the business reputation of the patentee or exclusive licensee by intentionally or negligently infringing the patent or exclusive license to take necessary measures to reinstate the business reputation of the said patentee or exclusive licensee, in lieu

법원은 고의나 과실로 특허권 또는 전용실시권을 침해함으로써 특허권자 또는 전용실시권자의 업무상 신용을 떨어뜨린 자에 대해서는 특허권자 또는 전용실시권자의 청구에 의하여 손해배상을 갈음하여 또는 손해배상과 함께 특허권자 또는 전용실시

of or in addition to damages therefor (Patent Act Article 131).

권자의 업무상 신용회복을 위하여 필요한 조치를 명할 수 있음(특허법 제131조).

claim limitation

청구항 한정

Example The Board's construction of the **claim limitation** "restore hair growth" as requiring the hair to be returned to its original state was held to be an incorrect interpretation of the limitation. MPEP § 2111 (citing In re Cortright, 165 F.3d 1353, 1359 (Fed. Cir. 1999)).

항고심판소에서는 '모발 성장을 회복시킨다'는 **청구항의 한정**을 모발이 원 상태로 회복되어야 한다고 해석하였는데 법원은 이를 청구항 한정의 부정확한 해석인 것으로 판시하였다. (미) MPEP § 2111 (In re Cortright, 165 F.3d 1353, 1359 (Fed. Cir. 1999) 인용).

claim of priority

우선권 주장

To make the filing date of application of international registration as the filing date in the first country that a valid priority claim is recognized.

조약에 따라 국제출원의 출원일을 그 우선권 주장이 인정되는 최초 제1국에서의 출원시로 보도록 하는 것.

Example Where a citizen of a State party which recognizes the priority of an application for trademark registration filed by a citizen of the Republic of Korea in accordance with the treaty **claims priority** by filing an application for registration of the same trademark with the Republic of Korea after he/she has filed an application for trademark registration with the State party or other State parties, the date the application for trademark registration is filed with the State party shall be deemed the date the application for trademark registration is filed with the Republic of Korea when Article 35 is applied (Patent Act Article 46(1)).

조약에 따라 대한민국 국민에게 상표등록출원에 대한 우선권을 인정하는 당사국의 국민이 그 당사국 또는 다른 당사국에 상표등록출원을 한 후 같은 상표를 대한민국에 상표등록출원하여 **우선권을 주장**하는 경우에는 제35조를 적용할 때 그 당사국에 출원한 날을 대한민국에 상표등록출원한 날로 본다(특허법 제46조 제1항).

claims

청구범위, 청구항

Claims define the invention and are the scope of exclusive rights granted to the patent owner. The scope of protection of a patented invention shall be determined by the descriptions of the claims (Patent Act Article 97).

발명을 정의하여 특허권자에게 부여되는 배타적 권리의 범위. 특허발명의 보호범위는 청구범위에 적혀 있는 사항에 의하여 정하여진다(특허법 제97조).

clarification

석명

To explain and clarify facts.

사실을 설명하여 내용을 밝힘.

Example The substance of the relevant application for trademark registration shall be deemed unchanged in any

… 다음 각 호의 어느 하나에 해당하는 경우에는 상표등록출원의 요지를 변경하지

of the following: ··· 3. **Clarification** of ambiguous statements (Trademark Act Article 40(2)).

아니하는 것으로 본다. ···
3. 불명료한 기재의 **석명** (상표법 제40조 제2항).

classification of goods

Classification of goods under the Locarno Agreement.

물품류

로카르노협정에 따른 물품의 구분.

• category of products (법제처)

classification of goods/services

Goods and services are classified by an international system, according to international treaties to which the Republic of Korea is a signatory. All goods and services included in trademark applications are classified by the KIPO according to this system. → See. Nice Agreement.

상품 및 서비스의 분류

상품 및 서비스는 국제조약에 따른 국제시스템 하에 분류되며 특허청은 상표출원에 포함된 모든 상품과 서비스를 이에 따라 분류함. 니스 협정 참조.

clear and convincing evidence

A higher standard than "preponderance of evidence" but lower than "beyond a reasonable doubt" standard regarding burden of proof.

미 명백하고 확실한 증거

'증거의 우월성'보다는 높으나 '합리적 의심의 여지가 없는' 증명보다는 낮은 입증책임 충족 여부 판단의 기준.

clearly erroneous standard

A standard of review in reviewing a lower court's treatment of factual issues. The lower court's judgment will be upheld unless the appellate court is firmly convinced that an error has been committed.

미 명백한 오류 기준

하급심의 사실관계 판단에 대한 검토 기준. 이 기준 하에서 항소법원은 하급심이 오류를 범하였다는 확신이 있지 않는 한 하급심의 판결을 유지하게 됨.

coat of arms

The distinctive heraldic design, emblem or shield of family, corporation, or country.

문장

국가나 단체 또는 집안 따위를 나타내기 위하여 사용하는 상징적인 표지.

coined mark

A mark that consists of coined words. Generally, coined marks are considered to be more distinctive than suggestive mark, descriptive mark or generic mark (Patent Court Decision, 2013Heo5445, decided November 22, 2013).

조어상표

만들어진 말인 조어로 된 상표. 일반적으로 조어상표의 식별력은 암시적 상표, 기술적 상표, 보통명칭 상표 등에 비해 높게 평가됨(특허법원 2013. 11. 22. 선고 2013허5445 판결 참조).

Example Although the mark is a **coined word** which is not registered in the dictionary, and the words constituting the

이 사건 출원상표는 사전에 등재되지 않은 **조어**이고, 그 구성 문자도 띄어쓰기 없이

mark are linked without spacking between the words, since both 'air' and 'fryer' are relatively easy English words, general consumers or traders are able to easily recognize that the mark is a combination of 'air' and 'fryer' in light of the knowledge level regarding English in Korea (Patent Court Decision, 2014Heo4876, decided April 10, 2015).

연결되어 있으나, 'air'와 'fryer' 모두 비교적 쉬운 영어단어이므로, 우리나라의 영어 보급수준에 비추어 볼 때, 일반 수요자나 거래자는 이 사건 출원상표를 'air'와 'fryer'가 결합된 것임을 쉽게 인식할 수 있다(특허법원 2015. 4. 10. 선고 2014허4876 판결 참조).

co-inventor

공동발명자

→ See. joint inventor.

collateral estoppel

미 부수적 금반언

The principle of estoppel that an issue that has been decided by judgment cannot be taken to another court by the same litigants in the same manner.

판결에 의하여 이미 결정된 쟁점을 동일한 당사자가 동일한 방식으로 다른 법원에서 다툴 수 없다는 금반언의 원칙.

Example A prior adjudication against an applicant may be dispositive of a later application for registration of the same mark on the basis of the same facts and issues, under the doctrine of res judicata, **collateral estoppel**, or stare decisions. TMEP § 1217.

기판력, **부수적 금반언**, 선례구속의 원칙에 따라 출원인이 패한 기존의 결정은 동일한 사실관계와 쟁점에 기초하여 동일한 표장을 등록하고자 하는 이후의 출원에 대해서도 구속력을 지닐 수 있다. (미) TMEP § 1217.

collective mark

단체표장

A mark intended to be used directly by a corporation jointly incorporated by persons who produce, manufacture, process or sell goods, or who provide services, or intended to be used by its members (Trademark Act Article 2(1)3).

상품을 생산 · 제조 · 가공 · 판매하거나 서비스를 제공하는 자가 공동으로 설립한 법인이 직접 사용하거나 그 소속 단체원에게 사용하게 하기 위한 표장.

collective mark with geographical indication

지리적 표시 단체표장

A mark intended to be used directly by a corporation incorporated by persons who produce, manufacture, or process goods on which a geographical indication may be used, or is intended to be used by its members (Trademark Act Article 2(1)6).

지리적 표시를 사용할 수 있는 상품을 생산 · 제조 또는 가공하는 자가 공동으로 설립한 법인이 직접 사용하거나 그 소속 단체원에게 사용하게 하기 위한 표장을 말함 (상표법 제2조 제1항 제6호).

color location statement

미 색채위치의 진술

A statement submitted by an applicant that submits a color drawing to specify where the color appears on the mark. 37 C.F.R. § 2.52(b)(1).

그 표장에서 색채가 구현되는 위치를 특정하기 위하여 채색한 도면이 출원인에 의하여 제출되는 것. (미) 37 C.F.R. § 2.52(b)(1).

Example If the **color location statement** is incorrect, incomplete, or inconsistent with the color(s) shown on the drawing, the color location statement must be corrected to conform to the color(s) depicted on the drawing. TMEP § 807.07(a)(ii).

색채위치의 진술이 부정확, 불완전하거나 도면에 나타난 색채와 불일치할 경우 색채위치설명은 도면에 묘사된 색채와 일치하도록 정정되어야 한다. (미) TMEP § 807.07(a)(ii).

color mark

색채상표

Marks that consist solely of one or more colors used on particular objects.

특정 대상에 사용된 하나 또는 그 이상의 색채로만 된 상표.

Example For marks used in connection with goods, color may be used on the entire surface of the goods, on a portion of the goods, or on all or part of the packaging for the goods. For example, a **color trademark** might consist of purple used on a salad bowl, pink used on the handle of a shovel, or a blue background and a pink circle used on all or part of a product package. TMEP § 1202.05.

상품에 대해 사용된 표장에 있어 색채는 그 상품 표면의 전체나 일부, 또는 그 상품의 포장의 전체나 일부에 대해 사용될 수 있다. 가령 **색채상표**는 샐러드 그릇에 사용된 보라색, 삽의 손잡이에 사용된 분홍색, 상품포장의 전체 또는 일부에 사용된 파란색 바탕의 분홍색 원 등으로 구성될 수 있다. (미) TMEP § 1202.05.

combination

(변론의) 병합

One of court practices to combine cases that were separately filed, to process the hearings together.

법원의 소송진행방식 중 하나로서, 법원이 별개의 사건으로 접수된 소송사건들을 병합하여 그 변론을 함께 진행하는 것.

combination of references/prior arts

선행발명의 결합

Example [A]n implicit motivation to combine exists not only when a suggestion may be gleaned from the prior art as a whole, but when the 'improvement' is technology-independent and the **combination of references** results in a product or process that is more desirable, for example because it is stronger, cheaper, cleaner, faster, lighter, smaller, more durable, or more efficient. DyStar Textilfarben GmbH & Co. Deutschland KG v. C.H. Patrick Co., 464 F.3d 1356, 1360 (Fed. Cir. 2006).

선행발명을 결합할 동기는 선행발명에서 전체적으로 암시될 경우뿐 아니라 그 개량이 기술독립적이며 **선행발명의 결합**이 더 바람직한, 즉 가령 견고성, 가격, 위생, 속도, 무게, 크기, 내구성, 효율 측면에서 더 나은 제품이나 방법으로 이어질 경우에도 내포되어 있다. (미) DyStar Textilfarben GmbH & Co. Deutschland KG v. C.H. Patrick Co., 464 F.3d 1356, 1360 (Fed. Cir. 2006).

combination patent

결합발명

A patent granted for an invention that unites existing components in a novel way.

이미 존재하는 구성요소를 새로운 방법으로 결합한 발명.

Example In the rejecting the application, it is alleged that Claim 1 invention of this case can be easily conceived by PHOSITA by combining Prior Art 2 and Prior Art 1. However, such combination is against the solution principle of Prior Art 1, and there is no reason or motivation to combine the two inventions (Patent Court Decision, 2016Heo2737, decided September 29, 2016).

이 사건 심사의 거절이유는 통상의 기술자가 선행발명 1에 선행발명 2를 결합하여 이 사건 제1항 발명을 쉽게 발명할 수 있다고 보았으나, 이러한 결합은 선행발명 1의 과제해결원리에 반하여 어렵고, 달리 그러한 결합을 할 이유나 동기도 없다(특허법원 2016. 9. 29. 선고2016허2737 판결참조).

combined application

다류출원(제도)

→ See. multiple-class application.

commercial impression

거래상의 인상

The meaning or idea that a trademark or mark conveys to consumers.

상표 또는 표장이 소비자에게 전달하는 의미나 생각 등을 의미함.

Example the **commercial impression** of a color may change depending on the object to which it is applied. Therefore, evidence submitted to demonstrate acquired distinctiveness of a color may show consumer recognition with respect to certain objects, but not for other objects. TMEP § 1202.05(a).

색채의 **거래상의 인상**은 그 색채가 적용된 물체에 따라 달라질 수 있다. 따라서 색채의 2차적 식별력을 나타내기 위해 제출한 증거에 소비자 인식이 일부 물체에 대해서는 존재하나 다른 물체에 대해서는 그렇지 아니한 것으로 나타날 수 있다. (미) TMEP § 1202.05(a).

(to do something) commercially

업으로 하다

Conducting business of producing, processing, certifying or selling goods in a continuous and repetitive manner.

상품을 생산, 가공, 증명, 판매하는 사업을 계속적 반복적으로 행하는 것.

Example The term "certification mark with geographical indication" means a mark used by a person who **commercially** certifies a geographical indication to certify that goods of others meet specified geographical characteristics (Trademark Act Article 2(1)8).

"지리적 표시 증명표장"이란 지리적 표시를 증명하는 것을 **업으로 하는** 자가 타인의 상품에 대하여 그 상품이 정해진 지리적 특성을 충족한다는 것을 증명하는 데 사용하는 표장을 말한다(상표법 제2조 제1항 제8호).

commercial name

상호

→ See. trade name.

commercial success

상업적 성공

One of the secondary factors in determining non-obviousness. Once a prima facie case of obviousness has been established, the burden shifts to the applicant to rebut it, if possible,

진보성 판단에 있어서의 2차적 고려사항. 진보성에 관한 일응의 증명이 성립되면 이에 대한 객관적 증거로써 이를 반박할 증명

with objective evidence of nonobviousness. Examples of secondary considerations are commercial success, expert testimony and copying of the design by others.

책임이 출원인에게로 전환되는데, 2차적 고려사항에 대한 예로는 상업적 성공, 전문가 증언 및 타인에 의한 디자인의 복제 등이 있음.

Example The **commercial success** argued by the Defendant is no more than one of the references to look at in determining inventiveness of the patented invention. Inventiveness is determined by whether or not a person with ordinary skills in the art can easily invent it based on prior arts judging from the objective, composition and effect of the invention. However, as seen from above, it appears that such a person can easily invent the corrected Claim 1 from Prior Arts 3 and 9. Defendant's argument is thus rejected (Patent Court Decision 2016Heo3174, decided January 13, 2017).

… 피고가 내세우는 **상업적 성공**은 단지 특허발명의 진보성 여부를 판단하는 데 있어 하나의 참고자료에 불과할 뿐이고, 이 사건 특허발명에 진보성을 인정할 수 있는지 여부는 결국 발명의 목적, 구성 및 효과를 토대로 통상의 기술자가 선행기술에 의하여 이를 쉽게 발명할 수 있는지에 따라 판단되어야 하는데, 앞서 살핀 바와 같이 이 사건 특허발명의 정정청구항 1이 선행발명 3, 9로부터 쉽게 발명할 수 있을 것으로 보이는 이상, 피고의 위 주장도 받아들이지 않는다(특허법원 2017. 1. 13.선고 2016허3174 판결 참조).

commissioned judge

A judge who is entrusted with the handling of certain matters prescribed by law from the presiding judge of the judicial panel.

수명법관

법원합의부의 재판장으로부터 법률에 정해진 일정한 사항의 처리를 위임받은 그 합의부원인 법관을 말함.

Example A court may, irrespective of the progress of litigation, recommend a compromise, or have a **commissioned judge** or an entrusted judge recommend it (Civil Procedure Act Article 145(1)).

법원은 소송의 정도와 관계없이 화해를 권고하거나, **수명법관** 또는 수탁판사로 하여금 권고하게 할 수 있다(민사소송법 제145조 제1항).

commonly used art

"Commonly used art" means well-known art which is used widely. → See. Well-known art.

관용기술

「관용기술(慣用技術)」은 주지기술 중 자주 사용되고 있는 기술을 말함. → 주지기술 참조

commonly used mark

A mark that is freely and customarily used to refer to a good by those who are in the industry that transacts the good (Supreme Court Decision, 2003Hu243, decided December 26, 2003).

관용표장

특정 종류의 상품을 취급하는 거래계에서 동종업자들 사이에 그 상품을 가리키는 것으로 자유롭고 관용적으로 사용하게 된 표장을 가리킴(대법원 2003. 12. 26. 선고 2003후243 판결 참조.

Example 'Magic Block' in the challenged mark 'Magicblock

확인대상표장('매직블럭 매직폼') 중 '매직

Magicform' as at the IPTAB decision of this case, fell into a **customarily used mark** concerning 'cleaning sponge,' for which it was used, under Article 51(1)3 of the Trademark Act, … (Patent Court Decision, 2012Heo11375, decided September 5, 2013).

블럭'은 이 사건 등록상표의 지정상품인 기름 때를 제거하는 연마스펀지 등과 유사한 상품인 세척용 스펀지에 대하여 상표법 제51조 제1항 제3호의 **관용하는 표장**에 해당한다 할 것이다(특허법원 2013. 9. 5. 선고 2012허11375 판결 참조).

• customarily used mark (법제처)

common sense selection

미 상식적 선택

A standard to determine non-obviousness as provided in the KSR case, 550 U.S. 398 (2007). → See. teaching, suggestion, motivation; see also common sense selection.

KSR 판례(550 U.S. 398 (2007))에서 제시된 비자명성 판단 기준. → 교시, 암시, 동기 참조.

common surname or name (법제처)

흔히 있는 성 또는 명칭

A trademark consisting solely of a mark indicating a common surname or name according to the method in common use may not be obtained the trademark registration (Trademark Act Article 33(1)5).

흔히 있는 성 또는 명칭을 보통으로 사용하는 방법으로 표시한 표장만으로 된 상표는 상표등록을 받을 수 없다(상표법 제33조 제1항 제5호).

companion applications

미 동일인출원

Pending applications filed by the same applicant. Co-pending applications.

같은 출원인에 의한 출원. 동시계류출원.

Example If a **companion application** has been published for opposition or has registered, the examining attorney may presume that the classification and identification of goods or services in the companion application or registration are acceptable, unless the identification or classification is clearly wrong. TMEP § 702.03(a)(iv).

동일인출원이 이의신청을 위해 공지되었거나 등록되었을 경우 심사관은 그 동일인출원 또는 등록 상의 상품이나 서비스의 분류 또는 명칭이 인용가능한 것이라 가정할 수 있다. 단 그 분류 또는 명칭이 명백히 오류가 있을 때에는 그러하지 아니하다. (미) TMEP § 702.03(a)(iv).

comparative observation

대비적 관찰

Comparing trademarks side by side, in appearance, sound and concept.

양 상표를 나란히 놓고 외관, 호칭, 관념을 비교 관찰하는 방법.

Example However, a **comparative observation** may be exceptionally more desirable than comparison by recollection as the good is a high-priced and elaborated one that requires careful consideration before purchase (Patent Court Decision, 99Heo6008, decided September 9, 1999).

… 다만 예외적으로 고가의 정밀제품과 같이 꼼꼼히 따져서 구매하는 것이 통례인 경우에는 이격적 관찰이 아닌 **대비적 관찰**을 할 수도 있을 것이다(특허법원 1999.09.09 선고 99허6008 판결 참조).

compare as a whole

전체관찰

Example It is unlikely that they would separate the proposed mark into "Ace" and "Link," both parts with little distinctiveness, and call or think of the mark as either "Ace" or "Link." Therefore, in comparing the proposed mark at issue and cited marks, we shall refer to the basic principle. Our determination shall be based on **comparison as a whole**, comparing and examining their appearance, name and concept (Supreme Court Decision, 2000Hu2453, decided April 27, 2001).

… 이들이 이 사건 출원상표를 각각 식별력이 약한 "Ace"와 "Link"의 두 부분으로 분리하여 "Ace" 또는 "Link"만으로 호칭하고 관념할 것으로 보기는 어려우므로, 이 사건 출원상표와 인용상표들을 비교함에 있어서 원칙으로 돌아가 **전체로서 관찰**하여 그 외관, 호칭 및 관념을 비교, 검토하여 판단하여야 한다고 본 다음, … (대법원 2001. 4. 27. 선고 2000후2453 판결 참조).

compare by element

분리관찰

Determining similarity of that consists of multiple elements and with more than one essential part that makes the trademark distinctive, by comparing each essential part of a good with a corresponding part of another.

복수의 구성부분으로 되어 있어 식별력을 발휘하는 부분의 요부가 2 이상일 경우, 각각의 요부를 대비하여 비교함으로써 유사 여부를 판단하는 방법.

Example The subject mark '360do BRUSH' is a combination of number '360,' English lower-case letters 'do' and English capital letters 'BRUSH' meaning 'a brush, to brush and to brush teeth' and can be **separately viewed** as '360do' and 'BRUSH', … (Patent Court Decision, 2015Heo5043, decided May 4, 2016).

위 인정사실에 의하면, 이 사건 출원상표는 숫자 '360'에 영어 소문자 'do'를 붙여 쓴 '360do'와 '솔, 솔질하다, 칫솔질하다'라는 뜻의 영어 대문자 'BRUSH'가 결합된 것으로서 '360do'와 'BRUSH'로 **분리관찰**이 가능하고, … (특허법원 2016.05.04 선고 2015허5043판결 참조).

• separately viewed (법제처)

comparison of/by essential parts/portions

요부관찰

It is a method of determining the similarity of Patent or other IP rights by whether they create different sense to ordinary consumers. Used as a supplement to the method of observation in entirety.

산업재산권 등의 동일유사 여부를 판단 시 일반 수요자의 관점에서 차이가 생기게 하는지 여부의 관점에서 그 유사 여부를 결정하는 방법. 전체관찰에 대한 보완적 방법.

Example The **essential part** that drags most attention in both designs is the eyes, nose, mouth, long beard and long ears on the front of the shoes, which are characteristics of a rabbit. Therefore, the dominant features of both designs are similar and create little difference in aesthetic sense in ordinary purchasers' mind (Supreme Court Decision, 95Hu1135, decided January 26, 1996).

양 디자인에 있어서 가장 주의를 끌기 쉬운 **요부**는 신발 앞부분의 토끼의 특징적인 얼굴 모습인 눈, 코, 입 및 긴 수염과 길다란 귀의 모습에 있다 할 것인바 양 디자인의 지배적인 특징이 서로 유사하여 일반수요자가 느끼는 심미감에 차이가 없다 할 것이고, … (대법원 1996. 1. 26. 선고 95후1135 판결 참조).

comparison by recollection

A method of determining similarity of marks by looking at whether an observer who sees the two marks in different time and place would confuse one mark with another.

이격적 관찰

2개의 상표들을 각각 때와 장소를 달리하여 접하는 경우 상표를 접하는 자가 상표를 착각하는지의 여부를 관찰하여 그 유사여부를 판단하는 방법.

Example On the basis of what general consumers or traders in the course of trade intuitively recognize with respect to the trademark, after an objective, comprehensive and **arm's length observation** of the two trademarks' appearances, sounds and meanings, etc. (Patent Court Decision, 2009Heo 450, decided June 4, 2009).

두 개의 상표를 놓고 그 외관, 호칭, 관념 등을 객관적, 전체적, **이격적으로 관찰**하여 거래상 일반 수요자나 거래자가 상표에 대하여 느끼는 직관적 인식을 기준으로 하여 … (특허법원 2009. 6. 4. 선고 2009허450 판결 참조).

• arm's length observation (법제처)

compensation for employee invention

An employee, etc. shall be entitled to fair compensation where the employer, etc. succeeds, under a contract or employment regulations, to the right to acquire patent, etc., or a patent, right, etc., for an employee's invention, or are to be granted an exclusive license in the patent right, etc. (Invention Promotion Act Article 15(1)).

직무발명에 대한 보상

종업원등은 직무발명에 대하여 특허 등을 받을 수 있는 권리나 특허권 등을 계약이나 근무규정에 따라 사용자등에게 승계하게 하거나 전용실시권을 설정한 경우에는 정당한 보상을 받을 권리를 가진다(발명진흥법 제15조 제1항).

competing application

Competing application means applications of 2 or more applicants that filed patent applications for identical inventions. Patent Law prohibits double patent and provides first-to-file rule (Patent Act Article 36).

경합출원

동일한 발명에 대하여 2인 이상이 출원한 경우 이를 경합출원이라 한다. 특허법은 중복특허를 금지하면서 선출원주의를 택하고 있음(특허법 제36조).

Example In applying Article 36 (3), etc. of the former Patent Act (amended by Act No. 6411 of February 3, 2001), where there are **competing applications**, even when the owner renounces either the registered patent right or the utility model right, it cannot be deemed that the defect arising from the competing applications is resolved. This is so in light of the following facts: there exists no explicit provision that renunciation of a patent or utility model right resolves a conflict in competing applications or that the right has effect as a patent right to a third party (Supreme Court Decision, 2005Hu3017, decided January 12, 2007).

구 특허법(2001. 2. 3. 법률 제6411호로 개정되기 전의 것) 제36조 제3항 등의 적용에 있어 특허권이나 실용신안권의 포기에 의하여 **경합출원**의 하자가 치유되어 제3자에 대한 관계에서 특허권의 효력을 주장할 수 있다고 보는 것은 명문의 근거가 없을 뿐만 아니라 권리자가 포기의 대상과 시기를 임의로 선택할 수 있어 권리관계가 불확정한 상태에 놓이게 되는 등 법적 안정성을 해칠 우려가 있는 점 … (대법원 2007. 1. 12. 선고 2005후3017 판결 참조).

competition in opposition

이의신청의 경합

- competition in formal objections (법제처)

complaint

소장

component

(발명의) 구성요소

Elements or parts that constitute an invention.

발명을 이루는 요소, 부분.

Example In a case where the administration and dosage of a medicine are added on top of the target disease or efficacy of a pharmaceutical medicine as an invention of a product, whether the administration and dosage constitute an **element** of invention(affirmative) (Supreme Court Decisions, 2014Hu768, decided May 21, 2015).

의약이라는 물건의 발명에서 대상 질병 또는 약효와 함께 투여용법과 투여용량을 부가하는 경우, 투여용법과 투여용량이 발명의 **구성요소**인지 여부(적극)(대법원 2015. 5. 21. 선고 2014후768 전원합의체판결 참조).

components

부분품

→ See. parts.

composite trademark

결합상표

A trademark that is composed of more than one element. A trademark that is composed of three-dimensional shape and a symbol, letter or figure may still be registered even if the dimensional shape lacks distinctiveness when overall distinctiveness is present in combination with distinctive symbol, letter or figure.

두 가지 이상의 구성요소가 결합된 상표. 가령 입체적 형상과 기호·문자·도형 등이 결합한 상표의 경우 입체적 형상 자체에는 식별력이 없더라도 식별력 있는 기호·문자·도형 등과 결합하여 전체적으로 식별력이 인정되면 상표등록을 받을 수 있음.

Example The distinctiveness of a **composite trademark** consisting of two or more element combined should be determined by the entirety of the trademark (Patent Court Decision, 2015Heo3993, decided February 3, 2016).

두 개 이상의 구성부분이 결합하여 이루어진 이른바 **결합상표**는 상표를 구성하는 전체에 의하여 식별력이 있는지를 판단하여야 한다(특허법원 2016.02.03 선고 2015허3993 판결 참조).

composition

조성물

Example For example, when an independent claim recites a **composition** comprising “at least 20% sodium” and a dependent claim sets forth specific amounts of nonsodium ingredients which add up to 100%, apparently to the exclusion

가령, 독립항에서 ‘적어도 20%의 나트륨’을 포함하는 것을 특징으로 하는 **조성물**에 대해 설명하고 종속항에서 나트륨 이외의 재료의 구체적 양을 기재하여 그 총 합이 명

of sodium, an ambiguity is created with regard to the "at least" limitation … MPEP § 2173.05(c).

백히 나트륨을 제외하고 100%에 달하였다면 '적어도'라는 한정에 대한 모호성이 발생하였고 … (미) MPEP § 2173.05(c).

compound

조성물

→ See. composition.

compound word mark

합성어 표장

A mark comprised of two or more distinct words, or words and syllables, that are represented as one word.

두 개 이상의 단어 또는 단어와 음절로 구성되었고 하나의 단어로 표현된 표장.

Example If the drawing depicts the mark as a **compound word mark**, but the specimen shows the mark as two separate words, or vice versa, the examining attorney must determine whether the mark on the drawing is a substantially exact representation of the mark on the specimen and/or whether an amendment of the drawing would be a material alteration of the mark. TMEP § 807.12(e).

표장이 도면에 **합성어 표장**으로 묘사되어 있으나 견본은 두 개의 별도의 단어로 나타내거나 혹은 그 반대의 경우, 심사관은 도면의 표장이 견본 상의 표장을 실질적으로 정확하게 나타내고 있는지, 도면의 보정이 표장의 중대한 변경에 해당할 것인지 혹은 둘 다를 결정하여야 한다(TMEP § 807.12(e)).

comprehensive brief

종합준비서면

Example In briefs other than the **comprehensive briefs**, arguments that have been previously made shall not be repeated (Guideline of Civil Practice and Procedure of the Patent Court of Korea, VII.1.A.5).

종합준비서면을 제외한 나머지 준비서면에는 이미 주장한 내용을 반복하여 기재하지 않는다(특허법원 침해소송 항소심 매뉴얼 VII.1.가.⑤).

comprising

… 을 포함하는 것을 특징으로 하는

A transitional phrase in patent claims. The open-ended language leaves room to include elements not described in the claims.

특허청구항의 연결부 중 하나. 개방형, 해당 청구항의 구성요소 이외에 다른 구성요소도 포함될 수 있는 것으로 해석.

compulsory license

강제실시권

Compulsory license is a system where the license of a patent is given to the government or third parties through administrative order or trial with or without consent of the patent holder when there is a public need to execute the patent (Patent Act Articles 106, 106-2, 107).

공익을 위하여 필요한 경우 특허권자의 의사에 관계없이 행정명령이나 심판을 통하여 국가 또는 제3자에게 특허실시를 허락하도록 강제하는 제도(특허법 제106조, 106조의2, 107조).

concept

관념, (발명의)착상

The meaning or idea of a mark.

표장이 가지는 의미, 개념.

Example Judging from the sound and **concept**, the plaintiff's registered trademark and the shape of the defendant's product are both figures that embody the shape of a puppy; both can generate the concept of "puppies" and be called as the "puppy marks" (Supreme Court Decision, 2011Da18802, decided January 24, 2013).

호칭 및 **관념**을 보면, 원고의 등록상표와 피고 제품의 형상은 모두 강아지를 형상화한 도형으로서 '강아지'로 관념되고 '강아지 표'로 호칭될 수 있다(대법원 2013. 1. 24. 선고 2011다18802 판결 참조).

conception

발명의 착상

The formation in the mind of the inventor of the definite and permanent idea of the complete invention that is thereafter reduced to practice.

이후에 구현될 완성된 발명에 대한 명확하고 영구적인 아이디어가 발명자의 마음속에 형성되는 것을 가리킴.

Example A showing that the reference disclosure arose from applicant's work coupled with a showing of **conception** by the applicant before the filing date of the reference will overcome the pre-AIA Patent Act, 35 U.S.C. § 102(e) rejection. MPEP §2136.05.

구 특허법 102(e)조 하의 거절결정은 인용발명에서 개시된 사항이 출원인의 연구에서 기인하였고 인용발명의 출원일 이전에 출원인이 발명을 **착상**하였음을 증명함으로써 극복할 수 있다. (미) MPEP § 2136.05.

concurrent use registration

미 공존사용등록, 공존동의제도

Registration of concurrent use, i.e. use of the same or similar marks in commerce by more than one person, all entitled to such use by the final determination of a court of competent jurisdiction or a determination by the Trademark Trial and Appeal Board. TMEP § 1207.04(a).

공존사용등록, 즉 동일 또는 유사한 표장을 사용할 권리를 지니는 것으로 법원 또는 TTAB의 최종 판결 또는 심판을 얻은 1인 이상이 거래에서 그 표장을 사용하도록 등록하는 것. (미) TMEP § 1207.04(a).

confession

자백

confidential design

비밀디자인

→ See. secret design.

confirm

추인

→ See. ratify

confiscation

몰수

Pecuniary punishment under criminal law to take away property relevant to the crime. Goods that are the subject of infringement of intellectual property rights or exclusive licenses thereof, or goods obtained from such acts of

형법상 형의 일종으로 범죄행위와 관련된 재산의 박탈을 내용으로 하는 재산형. 지식재산권 또는 전용실시권을 침해한 행위를 조성한 물건 또는 그 침해행위로부터 생긴

infringement, shall be confiscated. Government action forfeiting the assets related to a crime.

물건은 이를 몰수함. 범죄와 관련한 재산을 박탈하는 국가의 행위.

conflicting mark

A mark that conflicts with laws or others' rights. Where a trademark right holder, an exclusive licensee or a non-exclusive licensee uses his/her registered trademark, in which case his/her use of the registered trademark is in conflict with another person's patent right, utility model right or design right for which the application was filed prior to the filing date of an application for such trademark registration or another person's copyright created prior to the filing date of an application for such trademark registration depending on how the trademark is used, he/she shall not use the registered trademark on designated goods in conflict with the relevant rights of others without the consent of the patentee, the holer of the utility model right, the holder of design right, or the holder of the copyright, respectively (Trademark Act Article 92(1)).

저촉표장

타인의 권리 또는 법률에 저촉되는 표장. 상표권자 · 전용사용권자 또는 통상사용권자는 그 등록상표를 사용할 경우에 그 사용 상태에 따라 그 상표등록출원일 전에 출원된 타인의 특허권 · 실용신안권 · 디자인권 또는 그 상표등록출원일 전에 발생한 타인의 저작권과 저촉되는 경우에는 지정상품 중 저촉되는 지정상품에 대한 상표의 사용은 특허권자 · 실용신안권자 · 디자인권자 또는 저작권자의 동의를 받지 아니하고는 그 등록상표를 사용할 수 없다(상표법 제92조 제1항).

consisting of

A transitional phrase in patent claims. It provides a closed-ended claim that only includes the components described in the claims.

… 으로 구성되는 것을 특징으로 하는

특허청구항의 연결부 중 하나. 폐쇄형, 청구항에 기재된 구성요소로만 이루어진 발명을 보호범위로 함.

consolidation of oppositions

Consolidation of different oppositions regarding the same application to process them together.

이의신청의 병합

동일한 건에 대한 이의신청사건을 일괄처리하기 위하여 하나로 하여 합치는 것.

Example A panel of examiners may examine or decide on at least two formal objections by **consolidating** or dividing them (Trademark Act Article 64).

심사관합의체는 둘 이상의 이의신청을 **병합**하거나 분리하여 심사 · 결정할 수 있다(상표법 제64조).

• consolidation of formal objections (법제처)

constructive use

Deemed as use even in the absence of actual use.

사용간주

실제로 그렇지 아니하더라도 법적으로 사용한 것으로 간주함.

Example Under 15 U.S.C. §§1057(c) and 1141f(b), filing

상표법 7(c), 60f(b)항 하에서, 사용의사에

any application for registration on the Principal Register, including an intent-to-use application, constitutes **constructive use** of the mark, provided the application matures into a registration. TMEP § 201.02.

근거한 출원을 포함하여 주등록부에 등록하기 위한 출원신청은 표장의 **추정적 사용**으로 본다. 단 이는 그 출원이 등록으로 이어질 때에만 그러하다. (미) TMEP § 201.02.

consumer deception

수요자 기만

Deceiving consumers by filing an application of a mark imitating a trademark of another person.

타인의 상표를 모방하여 자기상표로 등록출원하는 등 수요자를 속이는 것.

C

Example Therefore, in order to determine whether the trademark of this case constitutes "trademark that may mislead or **deceive consumers**" in accordance with Article 7(1) subparag. 11 of the Trademark Act, the decision shall be made based on the similarity of the marks with the "coffeebean" portion as the essential part concerning 'coffee shop business, coffee franchise business' as the service of use, since the portion of the previously used service marks had acquired distinctiveness by the time of the decision to register the registered mark (Supreme Court Decision, 2011Hu835, decided March 28, 2013).

그렇다면 이 사건 등록상표가 상표법 제7조 제1항 제11호의 '**수요자를 기만**할 염려가 있는 상표'에 해당하는지 여부를 판단함에 있어서는 선사용서비스표들의 구성 중 이 사건 등록상표의 등록결정시에 식별력을 취득한 'coffee bean' 부분을 그 사용서비스업인 '커피전문점경영업, 커피전문점체인업'에 관하여 요부로 보아 상표의 유사 여부를 살피고 등록상표가 수요자를 기만할 염려가 있는 상표에 해당하는지 여부를 판단할 수 있다 할 것이다(대법원 2013. 3. 28. 선고 2011후835 판결 참조).

continuation (of procedure)

(절차의) 속행

Example Where a patent or any other right in a patent is transferred while a patent-related procedure is pending in the Korean Intellectual Property Office or the Korean Intellectual Property Trial and Appeal Board, the Commissioner of the Korean Intellectual Property Office or the presiding judge may permit the successor to the patent or the right in the patent to **continue** the patent-related procedure (Patent Act Article 19).

특허청장 또는 심판장은 특허에 관한 절차가 특허청 또는 특허심판원에 계속(係速) 중일 때 특허권 또는 특허에 관한 권리가 이전되면 그 특허권 또는 특허에 관한 권리의 승계인에 대하여 그 절차를 **속행(續行)**하게 할 수 있다(특허법 제19조).

continuation application

미 CA출원(협의의 계속출원)

An application for the invention(s) disclosed in a prior-filed copending nonprovisional application, international application designating the United States, or international design application designating the United States. MPEP § 201.07.

선출원된 동시계류 정규출원, 미국을 지정국으로 하는 국제출원 또는 국제디자인출원에 개시된 발명을 대상으로 하는 출원. (미) MPEP § 201.07.

continuation-in-part (CIP) application

An application filed during the lifetime of an earlier nonprovisional application, repeating some substantial portion or all of the earlier nonprovisional application and adding matter not disclosed in the earlier nonprovisional application. MPEP § 1504.20.

Example design application filed as a "**continuation-in-part**" that changes the shape or configuration of a design disclosed in an earlier application is not entitled to the benefit of the filing date of the earlier application. MPEP§ 1504.20.

미 일부계속출원

선행하는 정규출원의 전부 또는 상당한 일부를 반복하고 이에 개시되지 아니한 사항을 부가하여 선행 정규출원이 유효한 동안 제출한 출원. (미) MPEP § 1504.20.

'**일부계속출원**'으로 제출된 디자인특허출원은 선출원에서 개시된 디자인의 형상이나 구성을 변경할 경우 그 선출원일의 이익을 주장할 수 없다. (미) MPEP § 1504.20.

continued/continuing application

An application filed during the pendency of another application which contains at least part of the disclosure of the other application and names at least one inventor in common with that application. Transco Products Inc. v. Performance Contracting, Inc., 38 F.3d 551 (Fed. Cir. 1994). A continuing application may claim the benefit of the filing date of a prior application. A continuing application may be either a continuation application, continuation-in-part application or divisional application. 37 C.F.R. § 1.53(b).

미 계속출원(광의)

최소 한 명의 발명자를 공동으로 하고 개시사항의 적어도 일부가 공통된 출원이 계류중일 때 신청한 출원. Transco Products Inc. v. Performance Contracting, Inc., 38 F.3d 551 (Fed. Cir. 1994). 원출원의 출원일을 인정받으면서 출원을 계속적으로 진행시키는 절차. 세 가지 유형, 즉 CA출원, 일부계속출원 및 분할출원으로 나뉨. (미) 37 C.F.R. § 1.53(b).

contribution ratio (of a patented invention)

Example The Court may conduct an appraisal if an appraisal for calculating the amount of damages was not conducted in the lower court, the appraisal is necessary to determine a reasonable royalty or a **contribution ratio** of a patented invention, or the appraisal is otherwise acknowledged to be necessary (Guideline of Civil Practice and Procedure of the Patent Court of Korea, V.4.A). → See. apportionment

기여도 (특허발명의)

1심에서 손해액을 산정하기 위해 감정이 실시되지 아니한 경우, 통상의 실시료나 특허발명의 **기여도** 등을 정하기 위해 감정이 필요한 경우, 기타 필요하다고 인정되는 경우, 이에 대한 감정을 실시할 수 있다(특허법원 침해소송 항소심 심리매뉴얼 V.4.가). → 기여분 참조

contributory infringement

A party who offers to sell or sell within the United States or imports into the United States a component of a patented machine, manufacture, combination or composition, or a material or apparatus for use in practicing a patented process, constituting a material part of the invention, knowing the same to be especially made or especially adapted for use

미 기여침해

발명의 중요한 부분을 차지하는 특허등록된 기계장치, 제조물, 조성물 또는 결합물의 구성요소, 방법특허의 실시에 사용할 재료나 장치를 그 특허의 침해를 위하여 제작되었거나 침해를 목적으로 사용되도록 적용되었으며 주로 비침해적 용도의 상업적

in an infringement of such patent, and not a staple article or commodity of commerce suitable for substantial noninfringing use, shall be liable as a contributory infringer. Patent Act, 35 U.S.C. § 271(c).

으로 중요한 물품 또는 재화가 아님을 알면서 미국 내에서 판매 또는 판매의 청약을 하거나 미국으로 수입한 자는 기여침해의 책임이 있다. (미) 특허법 제 271(c)조.

conversion of applications

변경출원

An applicant for registration of a utility model may convert the application into a patent application within the scope of the features described in the specification or drawings accompanying the initial application for registration of the utility model.

실용신안출원 등은 그 출원서에 최초로 첨부된 명세서 또는 도면에 기재된 사항의 범위에서 그 출원을 (특허출원으로) 변경할 수 있음.

C

co-pending applications

미 동시계류출원

→ See. companion applications.

corresponding elements

대응구성

→ See. corresponding feature.

corresponding feature

대응구성

Example Prior Arts 1 and 2 are within same technical field, and there is no technical difficulty in combining **corresponding features** of Prior Arts 1 and 2." (Patent Court Decision, 2016Heo2737, decided September 29, 2016)

선행발명 1, 2는 기술분야가 동일하고, 선행발명 1, 2의 **대응구성**들의 결합에 기술적 어려움이 없으며, … (특허법원 2016. 9. 29. 선고 2016허2737 판결 참조).

counterclaim

반소

A claim by a defendant in a litigation made to rebut the plaintiff's claim.

소송에서 피고가 원고의 소에 반박하기 위하여 제기하는 소

counterfeit

위조

Example Delivering, selling, **forging**, imitating, or possessing a trademark identical or similar to a registered trademark of another person for the purpose of using or causing a third party to use such trademark on goods identical or similar to the designated goods; … (Trademark Act Article 108(1)2).

타인의 등록상표와 동일·유사한 상표를 그 지정상품과 동일·유사한 상품에 사용하거나 사용하게 할 목적으로 교부·판매·**위조**·모조 또는 소지하는 행위는 상표권(지리적 표시 단체표장권은 제외한다) 또는 전용사용권을 침해한 것으로 본다(상표법 제108조 제1항 제2호).

• forgery (법제처)

counterfeit mark

A mark that imitates the original trademark without legitimate authority to do so.

모방상표, 위조상표

정당한 권원이 없이 원상표와 유사하게 모방하여 부착된 상표.

country of origin

Example In an application under section 44 of the Act, the drawing of the mark must be a substantially exact representation of the mark as it appears in the drawing in the registration certificate of a mark duly registered in the applicant's **country of origin**. 37 C.F.R. § 2.51(c).

본국

상표법 44조에 의한 출원의 도면은 출원인의 **본국**에 정히 등록된 표장의 등록증 상의 도면에 나타난 표장을 실질적으로 동일하게 표현하여야 한다. (미) 37 C.F.R. § 2.51(c).

course of trade

Course of trade may refer to the characteristics of the relevant market, the financial status or level of knowledge of consumers, their level of expertise, age, sex, the nature and trading methods of the good, the presence and use, as well as how well-known the art is, how it is related to the product and the language used by the consumers on a daily basis (Supreme Court Decision, 95Hu1821, decided July 30, 1996).

거래실정

가령 관련 시장의 성질, 고객층의 재력이나 지식 정도, 전문가인지 여부, 연령, 성별, 당해 상품의 속성과 거래방법, 거래장소, 고장수리 등 사후관리 여부, 현존 및 사용상황, 주지 정도 및 당해 상품과의 관계, 수요자의 일상 언어생활 등을 가리킨다(대법원 1996. 7. 30. 선고 95후1821 판결 참조). (유사) 거래사정

creator of design

One who is entitled to register a design and who actually created the design.

디자인창작자

디자인 등록을 받을 수 있는 주체로서, 사실행위로서의 창작자를 의미

crime of fraud

→ See. fraud.

거짓행위의 죄

criminal complaint

Criminal complaint refers to a complaint filed by a victim of a crime or a person who holds right to report a crime and requesting investigation to an investigation agency. No person shall be prosecuted for committing a crime of infringement of a patent or an exclusive license without a criminal complaint filed by the injured party (Patent Act Article 225).

고소

범죄의 피해자, 기타 고소권자가 수사기관에 대하여 일정한 범죄사실을 신고하여 그 소추를 구하는 의사표시. 특허권 또는 전용실시권을 침해한 죄는 고소가 없으면 공소(公訴)를 제기할 수 없다(특허법 제225조).

critical date

The date one year prior to the date a patent application is filed. Under pre-AIA Patent Act, 35 U.S.C. § 102(b),

미 임계일

특허출원일로부터 1년 이전이 되는 날. 구 특허법 제102(b)조 하에서 발명이 임계일

the patent will be invalid for lack of novelty if the invention was in public use in the United States, or patented or described anywhere in the world, prior to the critical date.

이전에 미국 내 공용되거나 세계 어디에서든 특허를 받았거나 묘사되었을 경우 그 발명에 대한 특허는 신규성 결여로 무효가 된다.

critical significance

For the critical significance of the numerical limitation to be acknowledged, a remarkable change in the effect of the invention is required across the boundary of the numerical limitation and the following conditions should be satisfied: 1) The technical meaning of the numerical limitation should be described in the description, 2) the embodiments in the detailed description or supplemental materials should prove that the upper and lower limits of the numerical limitation is critical (Patent Court Decision, 98Heo2481, November 11, 1998).

임계적 의의

수치한정의 임계적 의의가 인정되기 위해서는 수치한정 사항을 경계로 특성 즉, 발명의 작용 · 효과에 현저한 변화가 있어야 하는 것으로, ①수치한정의 기술적 의미가 발명의 설명에 기재되어 있어야 하고, ②상한치 및 하한치가 임계치라는 것이 발명의 설명 중의 실시례 또는 보조 자료 등으로부터 입증되어야 한다(특허법원 1998. 11. 6. 선고 98허2481 판결 참조).

cross examination

Examination of a witness in litigation when the testimony supports the other party, to discredit the testimony or the witness's character.

반대신문

소송에서 상대방 측 증인에 대해 행하는, 그 증언 또는 성품에 대한 신뢰성을 떨어뜨리기 위한 신문.

cross licensing

Where parties grant licenses to each other in exchange for license of the other's patent.

크로스 라이센싱

상호간에 서로가 가진 특허권의 실시를 양해하는 것.

crystal form invention

Crystal form invention refers to an invention that has claims comprised of crystal form of a chemical compound, which is decided by analytic data of parameters.

결정형(結晶形) 발명

파라미터 값의 분석치에 의하여 특정되는 화합물의 결정형을 청구범위로 하는 발명.

Example Unless in exceptional situation, inventive step of a **crystal form invention** can be acknowledged only when it possess effects different in quality from the effects the preceding invention possess, or if not, at least, there should exist conspicuous differences in effect as measured quantitatively between them. At this time, although the detailed description of the crystal form invention may not state the experimental data, it must explicitly state the above mentioned effects compared to the preceding invention. If the effect of the invention is doubted, the applicant or patent

결정형 발명은 특별한 사정이 없는 한 선행발명에 공지된 화합물이 갖는 효과와 질적으로 다른 효과를 가지고 있거나 질적인 차이가 없더라도 양적으로 현저한 차이가 있는 경우에 한하여 그 진보성이 부정되지 않고, 이 때 결정형 발명의 상세한 설명에는 선행발명과의 비교실험자료 까지는 아니라고 하더라도 위와 같은 효과가 있음이 명확히 기재되어 있어야만 진보성 판단에 고려될 수 있으며, 만일 그 효과가 의심스러울 때에는 출원일 이후에 출원인 또는 특허권

holder shall argue and demonstrate the effect after the application file date (Supreme Court Decision, 2010Hu2865, decided July 14, 2011).

자가 신뢰할 수 있는 비교실험자료를 제출하는 등의 방법에 의하여 그 효과를 구체적으로 주장입증하여야 한다(대법원 2011. 7. 14. 선고 2010후2865 판결 참조).

D

damages for infringement

Monetary award to compensate for the loss incurred by the act of infringement.

침해로 인한 손해

침해행위로 발생한 손실에 대한 금전적 배상.

date of first use anywhere

The date when the goods were first sold or transported, or the services were first rendered, under the mark, if such use is bona fide and in the ordinary course of trade. TMEP § 903.01.

미 최초사용일

상표가 표시된 상품을 최초로 판매하거나 운송한 일자, 서비스를 최초로 개시한 일자. 단 그러한 사용이 통상의 거래에서의 진실한 사용에 해당하여야 함. (미) TMEP § 903.01.

date of first use in commerce

The date when the goods were first sold or transported, or the services were first rendered, under the mark in a type of commerce that may be lawfully regulated by the U.S. Congress, if such use is bona fide and in the ordinary course of trade.

미 최초 거래상 사용일

상표가 표시된 상품을 최초로 판매하거나 운송한 일자, 서비스를 최초로 개시한 일자. 단 그러한 사용이 통상의 거래에서의 진실한 사용이며 미국 의회가 합법적으로 규제할 수 있는 상거래 상의 사용에 해당하여야 함.

date of international registration

The duration of internationally registered basic trademark rights shall remain in force until the date ten years elapse after the date of international registration from the date trademark rights are registered and established (Trademark Act Article 198(1)).

국제등록일

국제등록기초상표권의 존속기간은 상표권의 설정등록이 있은 날부터 국제등록일 후 10년이 되는 날까지로 한다(상표법 제198조 제1항).

date of release

반포일

de novo review

Anew. A standard of review that no deference is given to the lower court's factual findings.

미 드노보 심리(審理), 재심리

하급심의 사실 판단에 구속되지 않고 사건을 새롭게 검토하는 기준.

deceptive geographical marks

→ See. geographically descriptive marks.

미 지리적인 기만적 표장

deceptive intent

기만의 의도

Example Whenever any patent is, through error without any **deceptive intent**, deemed wholly or partly inoperative or invalid, by reason of a defective specification or drawing, or by reason of the patentee claiming more or less than he had a right to claim in the patent, the Director shall, on the surrender of such patent and the payment of the fee required by law, reissue the patent for the invention disclosed in the original patent, and … Patent Act, 35 U.S.C. § 251.

명세서나 도면의 흠결을 근거로, 혹은 특허권자가 청구항에서 실제 청구할 수 있는 범위보다 넓거나 혹은 좁게 청구하였음을 근거로 그 특허가 **기만의 의도** 없는 오류로 전체 또는 부분적으로 작용하지 않거나 무효한 것으로 간주되는 경우, 특허상표청장은 그 특허 및 법으로 정한 수수료의 납부로 최초 특허에 개시된 발명에 대한 특허를 재발행할 수 있으며 … (미) 특허법 제 251조

deceptively misdescriptive geographic marks

→ See. geographically deceptively misdescriptive marks.

미 지리적인 기만적 허위표시 표장

deceptively misdescriptive mark

A mark that consists of or comprises deceptive matter, as (1) the term is misdescriptive of the character, quality, function, composition or use of the goods and (2) the prospective purchasers are likely to believe that the misdescription actually describes the goods; but the misdescription is not a material factor in the relevant consumers' decision to purchase.

기만적 허위표시 표장

(1) 상품의 성격, 품질, 기능, 구성, 사용에 대해 허위적인 용어로 되어 있으며, (2) 잠재적 수요자가 그 허위표시가 실제로 상품을 나타낸다고 신뢰할 만 하나, (3) 그 허위표시가 당해 상품의 소비자의 구매결정에 중대한 요소까지는 달하지 않는 기만적인 내용으로 구성된 상표

Example The test for **deceptive misdescriptiveness** has two parts. First we must determine if the matter sought to be registered misdescribes the goods. If so, then we must ask if it is also deceptive, that is, if anyone is likely to believe the misrepresentation. TMEP § 1209.04.

기만적 허위표시에 대한 판단기준은 두 단계로 구성된다. 첫째, 등록을 구하는 내용이 상품을 허위적으로 표시하는지 결정하여야 한다. 만일 그렇다면 그 표장이 또한 기만적인지, 즉 사람들이 그 허위표시를 믿을 만한지 따져보아야 한다. (미) TMEP § 1209.04.

deceptive mark

A mark that consists of or comprises deceptive matter, as (1) the term is misdescriptive of the character, quality, function, composition or use of the goods; (2) the prospective purchasers are likely to believe that the misdescription actually describes the goods; and (3) the misdescription is

미 기만적 표장

(1) 상품의 성격, 품질, 기능, 구성, 사용에 대해 허위적인 용어로 되어 있고 (2) 잠재적 수요자가 그 허위표시가 실제로 상품을 나타낸다고 신뢰할 만 하며, (3) 그 허위표시가 당해 상품의 소비자 상당수의 구매결

D

likely to affect a significant portion of the relevant consumers' decision to purchase.

정에 영향을 미칠 만한 기만적 사항으로 구성된 상표

Example …, [M]arks that are **deceptive** under §2(a) are never registrable on either the Principal Register, even under §2(f) or the Supplemental Register. However, applicants may present evidence of a similar nature to what is often submitted for acquired distinctiveness, such as declarations regarding how the mark is perceived by consumers, as rebuttal evidence to the prima facie case, in an effort to overcome one or all of the prongs of the §2(a) test. TMEP § 1203.02(f).

상표법 2(a)하의 **기만적 표장**은 주등록부에 등록될 수 없으며 2(f)에 따라 보조등록부에 등록할 수도 없다. 그러나 출원인은 2(a)상의 판단기준의 일부 또는 전부를 만족하기 위하여, 표장에 대한 소비자 인식을 나타내는 선언서 등 2차적 식별력 입증을 위한 증거 등을 일응의 유리한 사건에 대한 반박증거로 제시할 수 있다. (미) TMEP § 1203.02(f).

decision

판결, 결정

decision to grant patent

특허결정

If an examiner finds no ground to reject a patent application, he/she shall determine to grant a patent (Patent Act Article 66).

심사관은 특허출원에 대하여 거절이유를 발견할 수 없으면 특허결정을 하여야 한다(특허법 제66조).

- determination to grant patent (법제처)

decision to register

등록결정

Example Where a **decision to register** a trademark under Article 68 applied mutatis mutandis pursuant to Article 212 is made, the Commissioner of the Korean Intellectual Property Office shall register the conversion of the classification of designated goods (Trademark Act Article 211).

특허청장은 제212조에 따라 준용되는 제68조에 따른 상표**등록결정**이 있는 경우에는 지정상품의 분류를 전환하여 등록하여야 한다(상표법 제211조).

decision to reject(refuse) an application

거절결정

→ See. rejection.

declaration in lieu of oath

미 선서를 갈음하는 선언서

A written declaration may be submitted in lieu of oath required by law. E.g. a patent application may be accompanied by a declaration in lieu of oath if the applicant declares that he or she (1) made or authorized the application, (2) believes that he or she is the original inventor or an original joint inventor of a claimed invention in the

법에 규정된 선서는 서면으로 된 선언서로 대체할 수 있음. 가령 특허출원의 경우 출원인이 (1) 그 출원을 작성하거나 허가하였고 (2) 본인이 출원에 청구한 발명의 최초 발명자 또는 최초 공동발명자라 믿으며 (3) 선언서에 고의적인 허위진술이 있을 경우

application; and (3) acknowledges that any willful false statement made in the declaration is punishable under 18 U.S.C. § 1001 by fine or imprisonment of not more than five (5) years, or both.

18 U.S.C. § 1001에 따라 벌금이나 5년 이하의 금고형에 처해질 수 있음을 인지함을 선언한 선언서로 선서를 대신할 수 있음.

declaration of continued use

→ See. affidavit of continued use.

미 계속사용진술서

declaratory judgment

A judgment of a court only defining the rights and legal relationship of the parties without enforcement or award of damages.

확인판결

판결의 집행 또는 손해배상액 산정 없이 당사자간 법적 관계와 당사자의 권리만을 결정하는 판결.

deemed public officials

Any current or former executive or employee of a specialized agency or an agency for digitization of patent documents shall be deemed a current or former employee of the Korean Intellectual Property Office or the Korean Intellectual Property Trial and Appeal Board for the purposes of the offence of divulging secrets or confidential information (Patent Act Article 226-2).

공무원 의제

전문기관 또는 특허문서 전자화기관의 임직원이거나 임직원이었던 사람은 비밀누설죄를 적용하는 경우에는 특허청 소속 직원 또는 직원이었던 사람으로 본다(특허법 제226조의2).

defendant

피청구인

(administrative) defensive confirmation trial for the scope of rights

→ See. trials to confirm scope of right.

소극적 권리범위확인심판

Example The plaintiff filed a lawsuit seeking **defensive confirmation trial for the scope of rights** on March 21, 2007 against the defendant in the Korean Intellectual Property Tribunal. The Tribunal rendered a decision on April 28, 2008 dismissing the plaintiff's claim … on the ground that the trademark at issue belonged to the scope of the already registered trademark (Supreme Court Decision, 2008Hu 4486, decided February 24, 2011).

… 원고가 2007. 3. 21. 피고를 상대로 특허심판원에 이 사건 **소극적 권리범위확인심판**을 제기하였으나 특허심판원이 2008. 4. 28. 확인대상표장이 이 사건 등록상표의 권리범위에 속한다는 이유로 청구를 기각하는 심결을 한 점, … (대법원 2011. 2. 24. 선고 2008후4486 판결 참조).

deficiency of description

→ See. lack of sufficient description.

기재불비

definiteness

The requirement that patent claims must particularly point out and distinctly claim the subject matter that the applicant regards as his or her invention.

명확성

특허 청구항에서 출원인이 본인의 발명이라 믿는 대상을 특정하여 밝히고 이에 대해 명확하게 청구하여야 한다는 요건.

deliberate infringement

고의침해

deliberately excluded

A patentee is barred from arguing the portion intentionally excluded from the claims as falling within the scope of the patent rights based on the doctrine of equivalents. When determining whether or not the subject product was deliberately excluded from the patented invention's claim during the patented invention's application process, not only the specification of the invention but also the opinions of the examiners and the intent of the applicant reflected in his/her amendment and opinion documents shall be considered (Supreme Court Decision, 2004Da51771, June 30, 2006).

의식적 제외

특허발명의 청구범위에서 의식적으로 제외된 부분은 이후 균등론을 비탕으로 특허의 권리범위에 속함을 주장할 수 없음. 대상제품이 특허발명의 출원, 등록과정 등에서 특허발명의 청구범위로부터 의식적으로 제외된 것에 해당하는지 여부는 명세서뿐만 아니라 출원에서부터 특허될 때까지 특허청 심사관이 제시한 견해 및 특허출원인이 제출한 보정서와 의견서 등에 나타난 특허출원인의 의도 등을 참작하여 판단하여야 함 (대법원 2006. 6. 30. 선고 2004다51771 판결 참조).

deliver

Transferring the actual possession of an object.

인도(引渡), 교부

물건에 대한 현실적인 지배권을 이전하는 것.

Example **Delivering**, selling, forging, imitating, or possessing a trademark identical or similar to a registered trademark of another person for the purpose of using or causing a third party to use such trademark on goods identical or similar to the designated goods (Trademark Act Article 108(1)2).

타인의 등록상표와 동일·유사한 상표를 그 지정상품과 동일·유사한 상품에 사용하거나 사용하게 할 목적으로 **교부**·판매·위조·모조 또는 소지하는 행위는 상표권 또는 전용사용권을 침해한 것으로 본다 (상표법 제108조 제1항 제2호) .

Example The following shall be deemed infringement of trademark rights (excluding the right to collective mark with geographical indication) or an exclusive license: … Possessing goods identical or similar to the designated goods bearing a registered trademark of another person or any other similar trademark for the purpose of transferring or **delivering** such goods (Trademark Act Article 108(1)4).

타인의 등록상표 또는 이와 유사한 상표가 표시된 지정상품과 동일·유사한 상품을 양도 또는 **인도**하기 위하여 소지하는 행위는 상표권(지리적 표시 단체표장권은 제외한다) 또는 전용사용권을 침해한 것으로 본다 (상표법 제108조 제1항 제4호).

dependent claim

A claim that refers back to and further limits a preceding dependent or independent claim. A dependent claim includes by reference every limitation of the claim on which it depends.

종속항

특허청구항 중 독립항이나 다른 종속항을 인용하여 이를 한정하거나 부가하여 구체화하는 청구항.

deposition

Example **Depositions** may be taken upon oral or written questions, upon not less than ten days' written notice to the other party, before any officer authorized to administer an oath or affirmation in the place where the deposition is to be taken. 37 C.F.R. § 11.51(a).

미 증언녹취

증언녹취는 구두 또는 서면질문에 따라 상대방에 최소 10일의 사전 고지에 따라 증언녹취장소에서 선서 또는 서약을 집행할 수 있는 직책에 있는 자 앞에서 할 수 있다. (미) 37 C.F.R. § 11.51(a).

deposit of micro-organisms

A person who wishes to file a patent application for an invention related to a micro-organism shall deposit the micro-organism with authorities, prior to filing the patent application, in the manner prescribed and publicly notified by the Commissioner of the Korean Intellectual Property Office.

미생물의 기탁

미생물에 관계되는 발명에 대하여 특허출원을 하려는 자는 특허출원 전에 해당 기관에 특허청장이 정하여 고시하는 방법에 따라 해당 미생물을 기탁하여야 함.

derivation

Example **Derivation** requires complete conception by another and communication of that conception by any means to the party charged with derivation prior to any date on which it can be shown that the one charged with derivation possessed knowledge of the invention. MPEP § 2137.

미 파생

파생은 타인에 의한 완전한 발명의 착상이 이루어졌다는 것과 그 착상에 대하여 파생행위를 하였다고 주장되는 당사자가 발명에 대한 지식을 가지고 있음이 입증된 날보다 그 이전 날짜에 그 당사자 상호간에 소통이 이루어졌을 것을 요한다. (미) MPEP § 2137.

derivation proceeding

A new proceeding established under the America Invents Act that allows an inventor to challenge an earlier filed third party application or patent claiming subject matter that was derived from the inventor's own work. This proceeding replaces the interference proceeding.

미 파생절차

미 개정특허법에 따라 신설된 절차로, 발명자가 제3자의 선출원된 출원 또는 등록에 대하여 그 특허대상이 발명자 본인의 작업으로부터 파생되었음을 주장할 수 있도록 하며 저촉심사를 대체함.

description (of an invention)

A description included in the patent specification with the patent claims, which is required to be clearly detailed in

(발명의) 설명, 기재사항

특허 명세서에 청구항과 함께 포함되는 부분으로서 그 발명이 속하는 통상의 지식을

D

such manner that person skilled in the art can easily execute the invention (Patent Act Article 42(3)).

가진 사람이 그 발명을 쉽게 실시할 수 있도록 명확하고 상세하게 기재될 것을 요함(특허법 제42조 제3항).

description on a publication distributed

A description disclosed on documents, drawings or pictures, etc., printed or copied, in order to be publicized and is in a condition that public can recognize.

반포된 간행물에 게재

불특정 다수의 일반 공중이 인식할 수 있는 상태에 놓인 공개를 목적으로 인쇄 기타 방법으로 복제된 문서, 도화, 사진 등에 기재된 것.

descriptive mark

→ See. merely descriptive mark.

기술적 표장

design

The term "design" means a shape, pattern, or color of an article (including parts of an article (excluding those defined under Article 42) and fonts; the same shall apply hereinafter), which invokes a sense of beauty through visual perception; … (Design Protection Act Article 2.1).

디자인

물품(물품의 부분 및 글자체를 포함한다)의 형상 · 모양 · 색채 또는 이들을 결합한 것으로서 시각을 통하여 미감을 일으키게 하는 것(디자인보호법 제2조 제1호).

design around

To find an alternative to a patented invention so that it would not infringe the patentee's rights.

회피설계

특허권자의 권리를 침해하지 않기 위하여 특허발명에 대한 대안을 찾는 것.

designated country

A country designated by the international applicant to protect his or her IP rights. Such designation is based on a IP rights registration or application in the home country. Where a holder of an international registration (hereinafter referred to as "holder of an international registration") intends to additionally designate a designated country internationally registered (hereinafter referred to as "subsequent designation"), he/she may file an application for subsequent designation with the Commissioner of the Korean Intellectual Property Office, as prescribed by Ordinance of the Ministry of Trade, Industry and Energy (Trademark Act Article 172(1)).

(국제등록) 지정국

산업재산권을 보호받고자 국제출원인이 지정한 국가. 이는 본국에서의 상표등록 또는 상표등록출원을 기초로 함. 국제등록의 명의인(이하 "국제등록명의인"이라 한다)은 국제등록된 지정국을 추가로 지정(이하 "사후지정"이라 한다)하려는 경우에는 산업통상자원부령으로 정하는 바에 따라 특허청장에게 사후지정을 신청할 수 있다(상표법 제172조 제1항).

designated good

Any person who intends to file an application for trademark registration shall file an application for each trademark by designating at least one category of goods in accordance with the classification of goods (Trademark Act Article 38).

지정상품

상표등록을 받고자 하는 경우 상품 분류에 따라 지정상품을 하나 이상 정하여 신청을 하여야 한다(상표법 제38조).

Example [E]ven if the Plaintiff had obtained rights to the trademark "명품한솔" used on the **designated goods** ("electric mattress, electric carpet") for which application for registration was filed earlier than the previously registered trademark ··· (Patent Court Decision, 2014Heo6858, decided April 23, 2015).

선등록상표보다 먼저 출원되어 등록된, **지정상품**을 '전기매트리스, 전열식 카펫' 등으로 하고 '명품한솔'로 구성된 상표에 관한 상표권을 취득하였다고 하더라도 ··· (특허법원 2015. 4. 23. 선고 2014허6858 판결 참조).

design containing publicly known parts

공지 부분을 포함하는 디자인

A design that includes a publicly known part, which is deemed to have no value as creation. However, the design shall be assessed as a whole, in its entirety including the publicly known part.

디자인의 일부에 공지부분이 포함되어 있는 경우. 이 경우 그 공지부분은 창조적 가치가 인정되지 않으나 디자인은 공지부분도 포함한 통일적 전체로서 판단함.

Example The design rights are attached to the novel combination of shapes, patterns and colors of an article. If a design is registered based an application **containing publicly known shape and pattern**, the publicly known parts shall not be the subject of sole and exclusive rights of the design's owner. Therefore the importance of the publicly known parts should be assessed in limited degree (Supreme Court Decision, 2011Hu3469, decided April 13, 2012).

디자인권은 물품의 신규성이 있는 형상, 모양, 색채의 결합에 부여되는 것으로서 **공지의 형상과 모양을 포함한** 출원에 의하여 디자인등록이 되었다 하더라도 공지부분에까지 독점적이고 배타적인 권리를 인정할 수는 없으므로 디자인권의 권리범위를 정함에 있어 공지부분의 중요도를 낮게 평가하여야 하고, ··· (대법원 2012. 4. 13. 선고 2011후3469 판결 참조).

design described (in a publication)

(간행물에) 게재된 의장

Example As for **"a design described in a publication,"** a design is sufficiently published if it is described to a degree that a person with ordinary knowledge in the industry would be able to easily create the design (Supreme Court Decision, 2003Hu1956, decided July 28, 2006).

"간행물에 게재된 의장"에서 그 게재의 정도는 그 의장이 속한 분야에서 통상의 지식을 가진 자가 그것을 보고 용이하게 의장을 창작할 수 있을 정도로 표현되어 있으면 충분하고 ··· (대법원 2006. 7. 28. 선고 2003후1956판결 참조).

Design Gazette

디자인공보

The Design Gazette published under Article 212 (1) of the Act shall be classified into the Design Gazette for Registration and the Design Gazette for Publication (Enforcement Decree of the Design Protection Act Article 10).

디자인공보는 디자인의 설명, 도면 또는 사진 등 등록디자인에 관한 사항을 게재하며, 등록디자인공보와 공개디자인공보로 나뉨 (디자인보호법 시행령 제10조).

design likely to cause confusion with articles associated with others' business

타인의 업무와 관련된 물품과 혼동을 가져올 염려가 있는 디자인

Example The plaintiff filed an action to invalidate design registration, claiming that the registered design at issue is similar to designs that were publicly known prior to its application or **is likely to create confusion with articles associated with others' business** … and therefore the registration shall be invalidated. … (Patent Court Decision, 2009Heo7765, decided February 11, 2010).

원고는, 이 사건 등록디자인이 그 출원 전에 이미 공지된 디자인들과 유사하거나 그 디자인들로부터 용이하게 창작할 수 있는 디자인에 해당함은 물론 **타인의 업무에 관계되는 물품과 혼동을 가져올 염려가 있는 디자인**에 해당하므로 … 그 등록이 무효로 되어야 한다고 주장하면서 등록무효심판을 청구하였는데, … (특허법원 2010. 2. 11. 선고 2009허7765 판결 참조.

design patent application

미 디자인특허출원

An application for a patent to protect against the unauthorized use of new, original, and ornamental designs for articles of manufacture.

신규성, 독창성, 장식성을 갖춘 디자인이 물품에 허가없이 사용되는 것을 막기 위한 특허출원.

Design Register

디자인등록원부

The following matters shall be recorded in the Design Register: the grant, transfer, extinguishment, or reinstatement of design rights, exclusive or non-exclusive licenses (Design Protection Act Article 88(1)).

디자인권과 전용실시권 또는 통상실시권의 설정, 이전, 소멸, 회복 등의 사항을 등록함 (디자인보호법 제88조 제1항).

a design that may be easily created

용이하게 창작할 수 있는 디자인

→ See. easy-to-create design.

deviser

고안자

A person who devised a utility model.

고안을 한 자.

digital signature

전자서명

dilution

희석

A type of trademark infringement. Use of a registered trademark by a third party on goods that are neither identical nor similar to the designated good of the registered mark may still constitute infringement when it blurs the distinctiveness of the mark or tarnish its reputation, even if the use of the mark does not cause misconception, confusion among purchasers or deceive them.

상표권 침해의 한 유형. 타인이 동일, 유사하지 않은 상품에 상표권자의 허락 없이 당해 상표를 사용함으로써 상표의 식별력을 흐리게 하거나 상표의 이미지를 훼손하는 경우 비록 그 상표사용행위가 소비자에게 오인혼동을 주거나 수요자를 기만할 우려가 없더라도 상표권 침해를 구성한 것으로 본다는 것임.

Example A mark which would be likely to cause **dilution**

제43조(c)에 따라 식별력 약화에 의한 **희석**

by blurring or **dilution** by tarnishment under section 43(c), may be refused registration only pursuant to a proceeding brought under section 13. 15 U.S.C. § 1052(f).

또는 명성 손상에 의한 **희석**을 야기할 우려가 있는 표장은 제13조에 따라 제기되는 절차를 따르는 경우에 한하여 그 등록을 거절할 수 있다. (미) 상표법 제 2(f)조.

direct examination

The direct examination of the expert witness by the party who requests for the witness shall be made within the scope of the statement of the expert witness. All materials presented or cited in the direct examination shall be submitted as evidence before the date designated for examining the witness (Guideline of Civil Practice and Procedure, V.2.다).

주신문

전문가 증인에 대한 주신문은 전문가증인 진술서의 범위 내에서 하여야 한다. 전문가 증인에게 주신문에서 제시하거나 인용하는 모든 자료는 증인신문기일 전에 증거로 제출되어야 한다(특허법원 침해소송 항소심 매뉴얼 V.2.다).

direct infringement

A person is liable for direct infringement if he or she makes, uses, offers to sell, sells or imports any patented invention without authority.

직접침해

권한 없이 특허발명에 대하여 생산, 사용, 판매의 청약, 판매 또는 수입을 한 자는 직접침해에 대한 책임이 있음.

disclaimer

A statement that the applicant or registrant does not claim the exclusive right to use a specified element or elements of the claimed or registered subject matter. USPTO.

미 권리불요구

특허권 등의 출원인 또는 등록권자가 그 출원 또는 등록대상의 특정 구성요소 중 한 가지 또는 그 이상에 대하여 배타적 사용권을 주장하지 않는다는 진술. (미) USPTO.

disclose

To reveal or uncover to make known the information, etc.

개시

정보 등을 드러내 알 수 있게 하는 것.

Example Element 1 of the invention in Claim 1 in this case is disclosed in Prior Art 1, and Element 2 thereof is disclosed in Prior Art 2 (Patent Court Decision, 2016Heo2737, decided September 29, 2016).

… 이 사건 제1항 발명의 구성1은 선행발명 1에, 구성2는 선행발명 2에 **개시**되어 있다 (특허법원 2016. 9. 29. 선고 2016허2737 판결 참조).

disclosure by applicant

→ See. inventor-initiated disclosure.

자기공지

discovery

미 증거개시절차

Example Where the parties fail to agree to the mandatory **discovery** set forth in paragraph (a)(1), a party may seek such discovery by motion. 37 C.F.R. § 42.51(a)(2).

양 당사자가 37 C.F.R. § 42.51(a)(1)하의 의무적 **증거개시절차**에 대한 합의에 실패할 경우 일방 당사자의 신청으로 증거개시를 요청할 수 있다. 37 C.F.R. § 42.51(a)(2).

dismissal

각하, 기각

1. Rejection (or dismissal), in administrative procedures, refers to actions of government agencies or officers rejecting to process applications or complaints. It also means, in litigations, it means court decisions rejecting a party's requests, petitions or complaints for the reason that it does not meet the requirements to be heard in court. E.g., lack of jurisdiction or legal standing.
2. A judgment dismissing the plaintiff's or appellant's request or complaint or appeal.

1. 각하는 행정기관이 신청서, 심판청구서 등의 수리를 거절하는 행정처분 또는 법원이 당사자의 소송(절차)상의 신청에 대하여 관할위반, 당사자적격 흠결 등 부적법을 이유로 배척하는 재판을 말함.
2. 소송에 있어서 원고의 소에 의한 청구나 상소인의 상소에 의한 불복신청을 이유가 없다고 하여 배척하는 판결 또는 결정.

Example Patent Act Article 51 (Rejection of Amendments), 132-5 (**Dismissal** of Request for Patent Cancellation), 132-6 (Decision Rejecting Incurable Request for Patent Cancellation), 141 (**Dismissal** of Petitions for Trial), 142 (Trial Rulings Rejecting Petitions for Trial with Incurrable Defects).

특허법 제51조(보정각하), 제132조의5(특허취소신청서 등의 보정**각하**), 제132조의6(보정할 수 없는 특허취소신청의 각하 결정), 제141조(심판청구서 등의 **각하**), 제142조(보정할 수 없는 심판청구의 심결각하),

dismissal of amendment

보정각하(결정)

→ See. (decision to) dismiss amendment.

(decision to) dismiss amendment

보정각하(결정)

Administrative decision to refuse to accept an improper request for amendment.

출원인이 제출한 보정서가 부적법한경우 이를 결정으로 거부하는 것.

disparagement

미 비방

Example No trademark by which the goods of the applicant may be distinguished from the goods of others shall be refused registration on the principal register on account of its nature unless it—
(a) Consists of or comprises immoral, deceptive, or scandalous matter; or matter which may **disparage** or falsely suggest a connection with persons, living or dead, institutions, beliefs, or national symbols, or bring them into contempt, or disrepute; ··· 15 U.S.C. § 1052(a).

출원인의 상품을 타인의 상품과 식별할 수 있도록 하는 어떠한 상표도 다음 각 항의 어느 하나에 해당하는 경우를 제외하고는 그 본질적 특성을 이유로 주등록부에 등록이 거절되지 아니한다.
(a) 공서양속에 반하는 사항, 기만적이거나 중상적인 사항 또는 다른 자(생사를 묻지 아니한다), 기관, 종교 또는 국가의 상징을 **비방**하거나 그 관계를 허위로 암시 또는 모욕하거나 악평을 가할 수 있는 사항으로 구성되는 것, ··· (미) 상표법 제2(a)조.

dispensing of drugs

의약의 조제

The term “dispensing of drug” means dispensing drugs for

“조제”란 일정한 처방에 따라서 두 가지 이

the purposes of treatment, prevention, etc. of a certain disease for a specific individual in accordance with the specific directions by mixing at least two drugs or by dividing one kind of drug into certain dosages according to a specific prescription; (Pharmaceutical Affairs Act Article 2.11).

상의 의약품을 배합하거나 한 가지 의약품을 그대로 일정한 분량으로 나누어서 특정한 용법에 따라 특정인의 특정된 질병을 치료하거나 예방하는 등의 목적으로 사용하도록 약제를 만드는 것을 말한다(약사법 제2조 제11호).

display

A good is displayed if it is in a state that can be seen by the general public, for the purpose of transferring or delivering the good bearing the mark on it or its package. Exhibition, import or export without such purpose shall not qualify as display under the Trademark Act.

전시

'전시'란 다중이 열람할 수 있는 상태에 놓이는 것을 말한다. 상품 또는 상품의 포장에 상표를 표시한 상품을 양도 또는 인도할 목적이 있어야 하고, 이러한 주관적인 의사 없는 전시 · 수출 · 수입행위는 이에 해당하지 아니함.

D

disposition refusing to accept application

In case a patent application does not meet the statutory requirements, and the defect is too significant that it cannot be cured, the KIPO refuses to accept the application and it is deemed that there was no application in the first place (Enforcement Regulation of the Patent Act Article 11(1)).

불수리처분

특허출원서가 법령이 정한 방식에 위반되고 보정조차도 불가능할 정도로 그 위반의 정도가 중대한 경우에는 특허청에 의하여 불수리처분을 받게 되는데 이때는 출원 자체를 없었던 것으로 함(특허법 시행규칙 제11조 제1항).

distinctiveness

A function of a trademark that allows ordinary purchasers or consumers to distinguish the trademark owner's goods from others'.

식별력

자타의 상품을 일반수요자나 소비자로 하여금 식별하게 할 수 있는 상표로서의 기능.

Example Any trademark likely to cause confusion with goods or business of another person remarkably recognized by consumers or to dilute their **distinctiveness** or reputation (Trademark Act Article 34(1)11).

수요자들에게 현저하게 인식되어 있는 타인의 상품이나 영업과 혼동을 일으키게 하거나 그 **식별력** 또는 명성을 손상시킬 염려가 있는 상표는 상표등록을 받을 수 없다(상표법 제34조 제1항 제11호).

distinctness

One of the requirements to be protected under Act on Protection of New Varieties of Plants. The requirements for distinctiveness is provided in Article 18 of the Act. A plant variety shall be deemed distinct if it is clearly distinguishable from any other plant variety, the existence of which is publicly known on the date of filing of the

구별성

식물신품종보호법상 품종보호를 받기 위한 요건 중 하나. 품종보호 출원일 이전까지 일반인에게 알려져 있는 품종과 명확하게 구별되는 품종은 제16조 제2호의 구별성을 갖춘 것으로 본다(식물신품종보호법 제18조 제1항).

application for protection of the plant variety (Act on Protection of New Varieties of Plants Article 18(1)).

distribution (of a publication)

Putting a publication in a state where it can be viewed by unspecified number of people.

(간행물의) 반포

간행물을 불특정다수인이 볼 수 있는 상태에 두는 것.

division

Where there are at least two designated goods the relevant trademark rights may be divided for each of the designated goods.

분할

지정상품이 둘 이상인 경우에 그 권리를 지정상품별로 나누는 것.

divisional application

An applicant who has filed a single patent application for two or more inventions may divide the application into two or more applications within the scope of the features described in the specification or drawings accompanying the initial patent application, within the statutory period (Patent Act Article 52(1)).

분할출원

특허출원인은 둘 이상의 발명을 하나의 특허출원으로 한 경우에는 그 특허출원의 출원서에 최초로 첨부된 명세서 또는 도면에 기재된 사항의 범위에서 법정 기간에 그 일부를 하나 이상의 특허출원으로 분할할 수 있음(특허법 제52조 제1항).

doctrine of equivalents

Even though some elements of the patented invention are not literally identical to the corresponding elements of the infringing subject (see. all-elements rule), infringement may be found if they are equivalent. The requirements for equivalent infringement are: identical principle underlying the solutions, possibility of substitution and obviousness of substitution. Negative requirements relate to principle of excluding publicly known art and file-wrapper estoppel.

균등론

침해대상물의 구성요소의 일부가 특허발명의 대응되는 구성요소와 문언상으로는 동일하지 않더라도('구성요소 완비의 원칙' 참조) 서로 등가관계에 있다면 특허발명의 침해에 해당한다고 보는 이론. 균등침해의 성립요건은 적극적 성립요건으로 ① 과제해결원리 동일성, ② 치환가능성, ③ 치환자명성, 소극적 성립요건으로 ① 공지기술 배제의 원칙, ② 출원경과금반언의 원칙이 있음.

doctrine of foreign equivalents

A doctrine that a foreign word (from a language familiar to an appreciable segment of American consumers) and the English equivalent may be held to be confusingly similar. TMEP § 1207.01(b)(vi).

미 외국어 등가의 원칙

외국어(미국 소비자의 상당수에게 익숙한 언어) 단어와 등가의 영단어는 서로 혼동을 야기할 만큼 유사하다 할 수 있다고 보는 원칙. (미) TMEP § 1207.01(b)(vi).

Example Whether an examining attorney should apply the **doctrine of foreign equivalents** turns upon the significance of the foreign mark to the relevant purchasers, which is

심사관이 **외국어 등가의 원칙**을 적용해야 하는지는 그 외국어 표장이 관련 수요자에 갖는 의의에 따라, 가령 사전, 인터넷,

based on an analysis of the evidence of record, including, for example, dictionary, Internet, and LexisNexis® evidence. If the evidence shows that the relevant English translation is literal and direct, and no contradictory evidence of shades of meaning or other relevant meanings exists, the doctrine generally should be applied by the examining attorney. TMEP § 1207.01(b)(vi)(A).

LexisNexis®의 증거 등을 포함한 기록상 증거를 분석하여 결정한다. 만일 증거에 관련 영문번역이 문자 그대로의 직역으로 나타나며 다른 반대되는 의미나 관련된 의미가 존재한다는 증거가 없다면 일반적으로 외국어 등가의 원칙을 적용해야 한다고 할 수 있다. (미) TMEP § 1207.01(b)(vi)(A).

doctrine of laches

An equitable defense that the plaintiff unreasonably delayed in asserting an infringement claim. If a patentee files suit more than six years after she became (or reasonably should have become) aware of the alleged infringement, a presumption of laches arises and the patentee must present legitimate reasons for the delay. This defense does not bar the plaintiff's action entirely, but prevents the recovery of any damages accrued prior to the filing of the action.

미 **해태(懈怠)**

원고가 침해소송을 제기하기까지 불합리하게 지연하였음을 주장하는 형평법상의 항변. 특허권자가 쟁점이 되는 침해사실을 알았거나 혹은 합리적으로 알았어야 하는 때로부터 6년 이상이 지난 뒤에 소를 제기한다면 해태가 추정되고 특허권자는 지연에 대한 합당한 사유의 존재를 입증하여야 함. 해태로 인해 소 제기 자체가 금지되지는 않으나 소 제기일 이전에 발생한 손해에 대해서는 배상받을 수 없음.

doctrine of legal equivalents

A doctrine under trademark law based on a recognition that a pictorial depiction and equivalent wording are likely to impress the same mental image on purchasers and thus may cause likelihood of confusion.

미 **동일 간주 원칙**

상표법에서, 사진상의 묘사와 등가의 단어가 수요자들에게 동일한 심상을 불러일으켜 혼동을 일으킬 가능성이 있다는 인식에 기반한 원칙.

Example A mark is the **legal equivalent** of a portion of another mark if it creates the same, continuing commercial impression such that the consumer would consider the mark to be the same as the portion of the other mark. TMEP § 1212.02(f)(ii)(B).

수요자들에게 어느 표장과 다른 표장의 일부를 동일한 것으로 간주할 만큼 지속적으로 동일한 상업적 인상을 불러일으킨다면 그 표장은 다른 표장의 일부와 **동일하게 간주된다**. (미) TMEP § 1212.02(f)(ii)(B).

doctrine of progressive encroachment

Progressive encroachment is an offensive countermeasure to the affirmative defense of laches. As a general rule, a plaintiff invoking the doctrine should establish that: (1) during the period of the delay the plaintiff could reasonably conclude that it should not bring suit to challenge the allegedly infringing activity; (2) the defendant materially altered its infringing activities; and (3) suit was not unreasonably delayed after the alteration in infringing activity.

미 **점진적 침해의 원칙**

소 제기의 태만을 근거로 한 적극적 항변에 대한 공격적 대응수단. 점진적 침해를 주장하는 원고는 일반적으로 (1) 지연기간 동안 당해 사건에서 주장하는 침해행위에 대해 소를 제기하지 않은 것이 합리적 결론이었으며 (2) 피고가 그 침해행위의 내용에 중대한 변경을 가하였고 (3) 침해행위에 중대한 변경이 일어난 이후로는 소 제기를 비합

D

(미) Oriental Fin. Grp., Inc. v. Cooperativa de Ahorro y Credito Oriental, 698 F.3d 9, 21 (1st Cir. 2012).

리적으로 지연시키지 아니하였음을 입증하여야 함. Oriental Fin. Grp., Inc. v. Cooperativa de Ahorro y Credito Oriental, 698 F.3d 9, 21 (1st Cir. 2012).

documentary evidence

서증

domestic representative

A person who is domiciled or has his/her place of business in the Republic of Korea, acting as an agent who may take actions relating to IP rights or appeal an administrative decision on behalf of a non-resident.

• manager (법제처)

관리인

재외자의 산업재산권에 관한 대리인으로서, 국내에 주소나 영업소가 있는 자로 재외자를 대리하여 특허권등에 관한 절차를 밟거나 행정청이 한 처분에 대하여 소를 제기할 수 있는 자.

dominant features

Example Despite the aforementioned dissimilarity, it is difficult to say that the extent of dissimilarity is significant enough to extinguish the similarity of the **dominant features** stated above in points ④ and ⑤ (Patent Court Decision, 2014Heo6858, decided April, 2015).

지배적 특징

… 양 디자인 사이에 위와 같은 차이점이 존재하기는 하나, 그 차이의 정도가 양 디자인의 **지배적인 특징**을 나타내는 위 유사점 ④, ⑤로 말미암은 유사성을 상쇄하여 양 디자인이 전체적으로 다른 심미감을 나타낼 정도로는 보기 어렵다(특허법원 2015. 4. 23. 선고 2014허6858 판결 참조).

double entendre

A word or expression capable of more than one interpretation. For trademark purposes, an expression that has a double connotation or significance as applied to the goods or services.

Example Finally, the PTO asserts that Dial-A-Mattress presented no evidence that MATTRESS.COM is a **double entendre** evoking a quality of comfort, and it is not a mnemonic. We agree with the PTO that substantial evidence supported the Board's conclusion that the mark MATTRESS.COM is generic. (미) In re 1800Mattress.com IP, LLC, 586 F.3d 1359, 1362 (Fed. Cir. 2009).

중의적 표현

한 가지 이상의 해석이 가능한 단어나 표현. 상표법에서는 그 상품 또는 서비스에 적용되었을 때 이중의 의미 또는 의의를 갖는 표현을 가리킴.

마지막으로 특허상표청은 Dial-A-Mattress가 MATTRESS.COM이 **중의적 표현**이라는 증거를 제시하지 못하였으며 MATTRESS.COM이 연상기호에 해당하지도 않는다고 주장하였다. 본 법원은 MATTRESS.COM이 보통명칭에 해당한다는 TTAB의 결론이 상당한 증거에 의해 뒷받침되었다는 특허상표청의 주장에 동의한다. In re 1800Mattress.com IP, LLC, 586 F.3d 1359, 1362 (Fed. Cir. 2009).

double patenting

The double patenting doctrine generally prevents a patentee from receiving two patents for the same invention.

중복특허

특허권자가 동일한 발명에 대하여 이중으로 특허를 등록하는 것을 방지하기 위한 원칙.

drawing

A patent application filed under paragraph (1) shall be accompanied by a specification containing the description of the invention and the claims, necessary drawings, and an abstract (Patent Act Article 42(2)).

도면

특허출원서에는 발명의 설명 · 청구범위를 적은 명세서와 필요한 도면 및 요약서를 첨부하여야 한다(특허법 제42조 제2항).

due diligence

To establish a conception date as the date of invention, the inventor must have worked diligently following conception to reduce the invention to practice.

미 지속적 노력

발명의 착상일을 곧 발명일로 하기 위하여는 발명자는 착상으로부터 발명의 구현에 이르기까지 지속적인 노력을 기울였어야 함.

duplicate registrations

Identical registrations on the same register.

중복등록

같은 등록부 상의 동일한 등록.

duration

(Duration of Patent) The term of a patent shall begin on the registration date of the grant of the patent right under Article 87 (1) and last for 20 years from the filing date of the patent application (Patent Act Article 88(1)).

존속기간

(특허권의 존속기간) 특허권의 존속기간은 제87조 제1항에 따라 특허권을 설정등록한 날부터 특허출원일 후 20년이 되는 날까지로 한다(특허법 제88조 제1항).

duty of candor and good faith

Each individual associated with the preparation and prosecution of patent applications or associated with the patent owner in a reexamination proceeding has a duty of candor and good faith in dealing with the Office, which includes a duty to disclose to the Office all information known to that individual to be material to patentability.

미 정직과 신의성실 의무

특허출원 준비 및 심사과정과 연관된 각 사람, 재심사 절차에서 특허권자와 연관된 개인은 특허상표청과의 절차에서 정직과 신의성실의 의무를 지니며 이는 개인이 알고 있는 특허성 결정에 중대한 모든 정보를 특허상표청에 개시할 의무를 포함한다.

duty of confidentiality

An attorney's duty to keep the content of communication with his or her client confidential. Cf. Attorney-client privilege. (US)

비밀유지의무

변호사와 의뢰인 간에 있었던 비밀사항의 소통에 대해 공개를 거부할 변호사의 의무. (미) 비밀유지특권.

duty of disclosure

A duty to disclose to USPTO all information known to

미 개시의무

D

that individual to be material to patentability, owed by each individual associated with the filing and prosecution of a patent application. 37 C.F.R. § 1.56(a).

특허출원 및 심사와 관계된 각 개인이 지는, 특허성에 중대한 모든 정보를 특허상표청에 공개하여야 한다는 의무. (미) 37 C.F.R. § 1.56(a).

duty to state technology used for the invention

In the description of invention in the specification attached to the application, the technology used for the invention shall be stated (Patent Act Article 42(3)2).

배경기술 기재의무

특허출원서에 첨부되는 명세서의 발명의 설명에는 배경기술을 기재하여야 함(특허법 제42조 제3항 제2호).

E

easy-to-create design

A design that may be easily created by a person who has ordinary skills in the art to which the design pertains.

용이하게 창작할 수 있는 디자인

그 디자인이 속하는 분야에서 통상의 지식을 가진 자가 용이하게 창작할 수 있는 디자인.

Example If they are mere commercial and functional modifications without any other aesthetic value seen as a whole, ⋯ , or designs of a low creative level like designs, etc. which are modified, combined or used pursuant to creative or expressive methods frequently used in such design area, design registration will not be granted since a person with ordinary skill in the art to which the design pertains could **easily create** them (Supreme Court Decision, 2008Hu 2800, decided May 13, 2010).

전체적으로 볼 때 다른 미감적 가치가 인정되지 않는 상업적 · 기능적 변형에 불과하거나, 또는 그 디자인 분야에서 흔한 창작수법이나 표현방법에 의해 이를 변경 · 조합하거나 전용하였음에 불과한 디자인 등과 같이 창작수준이 낮은 디자인은 그 디자인이 속하는 분야에서 통상의 지식을 가진 자가 **용이하게 창작할 수 있는** 것이어서 디자인등록을 받을 수 없다(대법원 2010. 5. 13. 선고 2008후2800 판결 참조).

economically relevant relationship

The relationship of the ones that are tied to each other economically.

경제적 견련관계

경제적으로 서로 연결되어 있는 관계.

Example Furthermore, the defendant's registered trademark and the prior used trademarks are similar as they share the English word "Butterfly" as a essential part, and they share an **economically relevant relationship** as the classes of goods for this case and for the prior use trademarks are both used as exercise equipment or as shoes or clothing (Supreme Court Decision, 2010Hu807, decided July 15, 2010).

이 사건 등록상표와 선사용상표들은 공통적으로 '나비'의 뜻을 가진 영어단어 'Butterfly'를 그 요부로 하고 있으므로 서로 유사하고, 이 사건 지정상품들은 선사용상표들의 사용상품들과 같이 운동용으로 사용될 수 있는 것들이거나 신발류 또는 의류의 일종으로서 서로 **경제적 견련관계**도 있다고 할 것이다(대법원 2010. 7. 15. 선고 2010후807 판결 참조).

effect

효력

Example In any of the following cases, the **effect** of a design **right** shall not extend to the goods imported or domestically produced or acquired in good faith after the relevant trial decision became final and conclusive but before a petition filed for an administrative patent retrial is registered:
1. Where an invalidated design right (including a design right that has been finally and conclusively revoked in a trial on a determination to revoke design registration) is restored in the retrial; ··· (Design Protection Act Article 161(1)).

다음 각 호의 어느 하나에 해당하는 경우에 디자인권의 **효력**은 해당 심결이 확정된 후 재심청구 등록 전에 선의로 수입 또는 국내에서 생산하거나 취득한 물품에는 미치지 아니한다.
1. 무효가 된 디자인권(디자인등록취소결정에 대한 심판에 의하여 취소가 확정된 디자인권을 포함한다)이 재심에 의하여 회복된 경우 ··· (디자인보호법 제161조 제1항).

effective filing date

유효출원일

The actual filing date of the patent or the application for the patent, or the filing date of the earliest application for which the patent or application is entitled to a right of priority, as applicable.

경우에 따라, 특허 또는 특허출원의 실제 출원일 또는 우선권을 주장할 수 있는 최초 출원일.

elected office

지정된 사무소

electronic documents

전자문서

A person who initiates a patent-related procedure may convert a patent application and other documents to be filed with the Commissioner of the Korean Intellectual Property Office or the Director General of the Korean Intellectual Property Trial and Appeal Board under this Act, into electronic documents by the method prescribed by Ordinance of the Ministry of Trade, Industry and Energy, and submit them via an information and communications network or by means of any electronic recording medium, such as a portable storage device (Patent Act Article 28-3(1)).

특허에 관한 절차를 밟는 자는 이 법에 따라 특허청장 또는 특허심판원장에게 제출하는 특허출원서, 그 밖의 서류를 산업통상자원부령으로 정하는 방식에 따라 전자문서화하고, 이를 정보통신망을 이용하여 제출하거나 이동식 저장장치 등 전자적 기록매체에 수록하여 제출할 수 있다(특허법 제28조의3 제1항).

electronic signature

전자서명

element

(발명의)구성요소

embodiment

실시례

A manner in which an invention is made, used, practiced, or expressed.

발명이 제작, 사용, 실행되고 표현되는 방식.

employee invention

An invention that an employee, executive officer of a corporation, or public official makes in connection with his/her duties, where it falls within the scope of business of the employer, the corporation, the State, or the competent local government and the activities that have led to the invention fall within the present or past duties of the employee (Invention Promotion Act Article 2.2).

직무발명

종업원, 법인의 임원 또는 공무원이 그 직무에 관하여 발명한 것이 성질상 사용자·법인 또는 국가나 지방자치단체의 업무 범위에 속하고 그 발명을 하게 된 행위가 종업원등의 현재 또는 과거의 직무에 속하는 발명을 말함(발명진흥법 제2조 제2호).

enablement

The requirement that a specification must describe in "full, clear, concise, and exact terms" how to make and use the invention such that any person skilled in the art can do so without undue experimentation.

Example In design patent applications, ornamentality, novelty, nonobviousness, **enablement** and definiteness are necessary prerequisites to the grant of a patent. MPEP § 1504.

실시가능성

명세서가 통상의 기술자가 과도한 실험 없이 발명을 생산하고 실시할 수 있도록 전체적으로 명확하고 간결하며 정확하게 기재되어야 한다는 요건.

디자인특허출원의 특허 허여 필수요건은 장식성, 신규성, 비자명성, **실시가능성**, 명확성이다. (미) MPEP § 1504.

Enforcement Decree of the Trademark Act

상표법 시행령

Enforcement Rule of the Trademark Act

상표법 시행규칙

enhanced damages

가중적 손해배상

entire market value rule

The method that awards damages for infringement based on the amount of the price of the entire product, rather than the parts to which the patent is applied.

미 전체시장가치의 법칙

침해의 손해배상액을 산정할 때 특허가 적용된 부품만이 아닌 전체제품의 가격으로 산정하는 방법.

entrusted judge (법제처)

Judge who has accepted the entrustment from the court for the subject matter. An entrusted judge can investigate evidence in other jurisdiction.

Example Where a court requires, pursuant to the provisions of Article 297, a commissioned judge or an **entrusted judge** to conduct an examination of evidence as to a document,

수탁판사

법원으로부터 특정한 소송행위에 대하여 촉탁을 받은 판사. 다른 관할구역에서의 증거조사도 가능.

법원은 제297조의 규정에 따라 수명법관 또는 **수탁판사**에게 문서에 대한 증거조사를 하게 하는 경우에 그 조서에 적을 사항을 정할 수 있다(민사소송법 제354조

it may determine the matters to be entered in the relevant protocol (Civil Procedure Act Article 354(1)).

제1항).

erroneous grounds of administrative decision

심결의 위법사유

essential part/portion

The part of an industrial property that particularly attracts consumer attention. The portion that distinguishes one's rights from others'.

요부

산업재산권 등에서 수요자의 주의를 끌어 자타권리를 구별하는 부분.

Example The most discernible features of the designs that attract the ordinary observer's attention is to be perceived as the **essential parts**, and the question of similarity depends on whether the comparison of those features provide any aesthetic differences (Patent Court Decision, 2014Heo6858, decided April 23, 2015).

이 경우 디자인을 보는 사람의 주의를 가장 끌기 쉬운 부분을 **요부**로서 파악하고 이것을 관찰하여 심미감에 차이가 생기게 하는지 여부의 관점에서 그 유사 여부를 결정하여야 하며 … (특허법원 2015. 4. 23. 선고 2014허6858 판결 참조).

establishment of authenticity

Establishment of the fact that a submitted documentary evidence was created at the will of the person identified as the author of the document.

진정성립

제출된 서증에 대하여, 문서가 작성명의인의 의사에 의하여 작성되었음을 말함.

Example Whether or not the **authenticity** of a document is **established** is determined at the discretion of the court based on the overall evidence and arguments submitted. While there is no particular limitation, the method of authentication of private document must be credible (Supreme Court Decision, 2009Da10980, decided June 24, 2010).

문서에 대한 **진정성립**의 인정 여부는 법원이 모든 증거자료와 변론 전체의 취지에 터잡아 자유심증에 따라 판단하는 것이고, 사문서의 진정성립에 관한 증명 방법에 관하여는 특별한 제한이 없으나 그 증명 방법은 신빙성이 있어야 하고, … (대법원 2010. 6. 24. 선고 2009다10980 판결 참조).

European Patent Convention

The European Patent Convention is the international agreement establishing the European Patent Organisation, whose main branch is the European Patent Office, as well as the system and underlying law for granting and examination of European Patents.

유럽특허협약(EPC)

유럽특허협약이란, 유럽특허청을 설립하여 유럽에서 특허를 심사하기 위한 시스템과 기본법을 만들기 위한 국제 협약을 말함.

examination

심사

examination of evidence

증거조사

E

examiner

심사관

examiner's amendment

A written confirmation of an amendment made to an application. The examiner assigned to the application will make the amendment after consultation with an applicant or the applicant's attorney. USPTO.

미 심사관 보정

출원에 대한 보정사항의 서면확인. 그 출원의 담당심사관은 출원인 또는 그 대리인과 협의 후에 그 출원을 보정함. (미) USPTO.

Example The examining attorney may issue an **examiner's amendment** whenever the required amendment does not have to be verified by the applicant. For example, in appropriate circumstances, an examiner's amendment may be used to amend the identification of goods/services, enter a disclaimer, add the state of incorporation, or amend from the Principal to the Supplemental Register. TMEP § 707.

심사관은 필요한 보정이 출원인의 확인을 거칠 필요가 없을 때는 언제든지 **심사관보정**으로 그 출원을 보정할 수 있다. 필요한 경우 심사관보정을 통해 상품 또는 서비스의 명칭을 보정하거나 권리불요구사항의 등록, 법인설립현황의 추가, 주등록부에서 보조등록부로의 이전 등을 할 수 있다. (미) TMEP § 707.

exclusion (of a judge)

Disqualifying a judge from discharging his or her authority by law as to a certain case to which he or she has a special relation.

제척

법관이 사건과 특수한 관계에 있는 경우 당해 사건에서 법률상 당연히 배제되는 것.

exclusionary implementation righ

→ See. exclusive license.

독점적 실시권, 배타적 실시권

exclusive license

In case of patents, for example, a right to exclusively exploit the patented invention as granted by the patent owner. Establishment of exclusive license of patent rights requires registration. a patentee may grant an exclusive license of the patent to other persons. an exclusive licensee with the exclusive license shall have the sole right to commercially or industrially execute the patented invention to the extent prescribed at the grant of the license.

전용실시권, 전용(專用) 사용권, 독점적 실시권, 배타적 실시권

가령 특허의 경우, 특허권자로부터 허여받아 특허발명의 실시를 독점할 수 있는 권리. 특허권의 전용실시권의 설정은 등록하여야 한다. 특허권자는 그 특허권에 대하여 타인에게 전용실시권을 설정할 수 있다. 전용실시권을 설정받은 전용실시권자는 그 설정행위로 정한 범위에서 그 특허발명을 업으로서 실시할 권리를 독점한다.

Example … **exclusive licenses** lose validity regardless of whether they are registered or not once the contract establishing such rights is terminated, and further, even if a tacit agreement for restoring the contract with the same

전용사용권은 그 설정계약이 해지되면 등록 여부에 관계없이 그 효력을 상실하며, 종전과 동일한 내용으로 전용사용권설정계약을 부활하는 묵시적 합의가 있었다고 하

terms and conditions existed, one cannot acquire an exclusive right for the use of the Trademark under the Trademark Act unless its establishment is newly registered. Thus, the defendant cannot be viewed as an exclusive license holder as to Trademark 1 and 2 from April 28, 2000 (Supreme Court Decision, 2002Hu703, decided September 13, 2004).

더라도 새로이 설정등록을 하지 않고서는 상표법상의 전용사용권을 취득할 수 없는 것이어서, 2000. 4. 28. 이후에는 피고를 인용상표들에 대한 전용사용권자라고 할 수 없다(대법원 2004. 9. 13. 선고 2002후703 판결 참조).

Example It is true that the Supreme Court's view is that, when the patent application pertains in whole or in part to public knowledge or public use at the time of its filing, a monopolistic, **exclusive license** may not be granted by acknowledging its scope of rights for the mere reason that they are indicated in the claims (Supreme Court Decision, 2012Hu4162, decided March 20, 2014).

다만 대법원은 특허의 일부 또는 전부가 출원 당시 공지공용의 것인 경우까지 청구범위에 기재되어 있다는 이유만으로 권리범위를 인정하여 독점적 · **배타적인 실시권**을 부여할 수는 없으므로 권리범위확인심판에서도 특허무효의 심결 유무에 관계없이 그 권리범위를 부정할 수 있다고 보고 있으나 (대법원 2014. 3. 20. 선고 2012후4162 전원합의체 판결 참조).

executing

As for a product invention, acts of producing, using, assigning, leasing, exporting or importing an article, acts of offer to assign or acts to assign or lease the article; for a process invention, acts to use, assign, lease or import articles manufactured with the process, or to offer to assign or lease the article (Patent Act Article 2).

실시

물건발명의 경우 물품을 생산 · 사용 · 양도 · 대여 · 수출 또는 수입하거나 그 물품을 양도 또는 대여하기 위한 청약행위, 방법발명의 경우 그 방법에 의하여 생산한 물건을 사용 · 양도 · 대여 또는 수입하거나 그 물건의 양도 또는 대여의 청약을 하는 행위 (특허법 제2조).

E

execution of a patented invention for the purpose of research or testing

The effects of a patent shall not extent to the execution of a patented invention for the purpose of research or testing (Patent Act Article 96(1)).

연구 또는 시험을 하기 위한 특허발명의 실시

연구 또는 시험을 하기 위한 특허발명의 실시에 대해서는 특허권의 효력이 미치지 않음(특허법 제96조 제1항).

execution of patented inventions by government

If the Government deems it necessary to non-commercially execute a patented invention due to a national or dire emergency, or for the public interests, it may directly execute the patented invention or authorize any person other than the Government to execute it on its behalf (Patent Act Article 106-2(1)).

정부에 의한 특허발명의 실시

정부는 특허발명이 국가 비상사태, 극도의 긴급상황 또는 공공의 이익을 위하여 비상업적(非商業的)으로 실시할 필요가 있다고 인정하는 경우에는 그 특허발명을 실시하거나 정부 외의 자에게 실시하게 할 수 있다 (특허법 제106조의2 제1항).

exercises due care

The effort made by an ordinarily prudent or reasonable party

상당한 주의

보통의 신중하고 합리적인 당사자가 그 상

to avoid harm to another, taking the circumstances into account. It refers to the level of judgment, care, prudence, determination, and activity that a person would reasonably be expected to do under particular circumstances. The care exercised by an ordinary prudent and reasonable party to avoid inflicting harm to another under the circumstance. The level of judgment, care, prudence, determination, and action that a person would be reasonably expected to exercise under the given circumstances.

황 하에서 타인에게 피해를 입히지 않기 위해 기울이는 노력. 특정한 상황 하에서 합리적으로 취할 것으로 기대되는 판단의 정도, 주의, 신중함, 결단, 행동 등을 가리킴.

Example Where an exclusive licensee or a non-exclusive licensee causes the misunderstanding of the quality of goods or confusion with goods related to another person's business by using a registered trademark or a trademark similar to the registered trademark on the designated goods, or goods similar to the designated goods: Provided, That the foregoing shall not apply where the trademark right holder **pays considerable attention** … (Trademark Act Article 119(1)2).

전용사용권자 또는 통상사용권자가 지정상품 또는 이와 유사한 상품에 등록상표 또는 이와 유사한 상표를 사용함으로써 수요자에게 상품의 품질을 오인하게 하거나 타인의 업무와 관련된 상품과의 혼동을 불러일으키게 한 경우. 다만, 상표권자가 **상당한 주의**를 한 경우는 제외한다(상표법 제119조 제1항 제2호).

exhaustion

소진

Example In case where a trademark owner has assigned goods on which a registered trademark is displayed in Korea, the trademark right is **exhausted** as for the good, and the effect of the trademark right shall not extend to the acts of using, transferring or leasing the good (Supreme Court Decision, 2002Do3445, decided April 11, 2003).

특별한 사정이 없는 한 상표권자 등이 국내에서 등록상표가 표시된 상품을 양도한 경우에는 당해 상품에 대한 상표권은 그 목적을 달성한 것으로서 **소진**되고, 그로써 상표권의 효력은 당해 상품을 사용, 양도 또는 대여한 행위 등에는 미치지 않는다(대법원 2003. 4. 11. 선고 2002도3445 판결 참조).

exhaustion doctrine

Once a patented product is lawfully manufactured and sold, the use or resale by the assignee does not constitute infringement. By the patentee's assignment of the patented product, the patent rights thereto are duly used and exhausted.

권리소진의 원칙

특허품이 적법하게 생산, 판매된 경우에 그 양수인 등이 그 특허제품을 사용하거나 재판매하는 것은 특허침해를 구성하지 아니한다는 원칙으로서, 특허권자가 특허제품을 타인에게 양도함으로써 그 특허권은 정당하게 사용되어 소진되었다는 원칙.

Example When a patentee or licencee of a patented invention of a product or patented invention of method to manufacture a product sells the patented product or product made with the patented manufacturing method, the patent right on that product has achieved its purpose and is exhausted. Also,

물건의 발명 또는 물건을 생산하는 방법의 발명에 대한 특허권자 또는 그 특허권자로부터 허락을 받은 실시권자가 우리나라에서 특허물건 또는 특허방법에 의해 생산한 물건을 양도한 경우에는 당해 물건에 관해

when a patentee of a patented invention of a method sells a product that is only used to execute that method in the territory of Korea, the patent is exhausted with regard to the execution by the buyer or third party that assigned the product from the buyer who use that product to execute the patented method. In light of the patent exhaustion theory above, unless any special circumstances exist, legal theory of **patent exhaustion** applies not only to transfer based on contract but also to transfer in auction procedure (Patent Court Decision, 2008Heo13299, decided December 18, 2009).

서는 특허권이 이미 그 목적을 달성하였으므로 소진된다. 그리고 방법의 발명에 대한 특허권자가 우리나라에서 그 방법의 실시에만 사용하는 물건을 양도한 경우에도 양수인 또는 전득자가 그 물건을 이용하여 해당 방법발명을 실시하는 것과 관련하여서는 특허권이 소진되며, 위에서 본 **특허권 소진**의 근거에 비추어 볼 때 물건의 양도가 계약에 의한 경우뿐만 아니라 경매절차에 의한 경우에도 특별한 사정이 없는 한 특허권 소진의 법리는 적용된다(특허법원 2009. 12. 18. 선고 2008허13299 판결 참조)

exhibit

전시

→ See. display.

ex officio

직권(에 의한)

By the authority of court or administrative trial board, rather than by request of parties.

당사자의 신청이 아닌 법원 또는 심판기관의 권한에 의함.

E

ex officio amendment

직권보정

Amendment of clear error in an application or drawing by the examiner, without request of the applicant.

심사관이 출원서 또는 도면에 적힌 사항이 명백히 잘못된 경우 출원자의 신청에 의하지 아니하고도 그러한 사항을 보정하는 것.

ex officio decisions of mediation

직권조정결정

Example Where parties fail to reach an agreement or a requester's claim is deemed reasonable, the Seed Commission may make an ex officio decision in lieu of mediation (hereinafter referred to as "**ex officio decision of mediation**") and insofar as it does not go against the intent of the request, taking into consideration the interests of the parties and all other circumstances (Act on Protection of New Varieties of Plants Article 123(1)).

종자위원회는 당사자 간에 합의가 이루어지지 아니한 경우 또는 신청인의 주장이 이유 있다고 판단되는 경우에는 당사자들의 이익과 그 밖의 모든 사정을 고려하여 신청 취지에 반하지 아니하는 한도에서 직권으로 조정을 갈음하는 결정(이하 "**직권조정결정**"이라 한다)을 할 수 있다(식물신품종보호법 제123조 제1항).

ex officio examination

직권심사

ex officio hearing

직권심리

An administrative judge may hold hearings about grounds

심판관이 당사자 또는 참가인이 신청하지

a party or an intervenor did not mention in his or her application. In such cases, the administrative judge shall give them an opportunity to state their opinions on such grounds.

아니한 이유에 대해 심리하는 것. 이 경우 심판관은 당사자 또는 참가인에게 그 이유에 대해 진술할 기회를 주어야 함.

expansion-of-trade doctrine

Typically applied in inter partes proceedings where an opposer claims that its priority of use of a mark with respect to its goods/services should be extended to include applicant's goods/services because they are in the natural scope of expansion of opposer's goods/services. TMEP § 1207.01(a)(v).

미 거래확장의 원칙

주로 당사자계 절차에서 적용되는 원칙으로, 출원인의 상품 또는 서비스가 이의신청인의 상품 또는 서비스의 자연적인 확장영역에 속하므로 이의신청인의 그 상품 또는 서비스에 관하여 상표사용에 대한 우선권이 출원인의 상품 또는 서비스에까지 확장된다고 주장하는 것. (미) TMEP § 1207.01 (a)(v).

Example When the identical marks are being used on different lines of goods, and the issue is whether the prior user's line of goods would **normally or reasonably expand to include the other line of goods**, the answer depends on whether the goods "were of such a nature that purchasers would generally expect them to emanate from the same source." J. C. Hall Co. v. Hallmark Cards, Inc., 340 F.2d 960, 963, 52 C.C.P.A. 981, 985 (1965). We think that where the question of normal **expansion of trade** arises between different marks applied to different lines of goods, the differences between the marks must also be considered. J. Wiss & Sons Co. v. W. E. Bassett Co., 462 F.2d 567, 569 (C.C.P.A. 1972).

동일상표가 서로 다른 상품류에 사용되고 선사용자의 상품류가 **일반적 혹은 합리적으로 상대방의 상품류에까지 확장될 것인지**가 쟁점인 사안에서, 그 답은 '수요자가 일반적으로 양 상품이 동일한 출처를 가지는 것으로 생각하는지'에 달려있다. J. C. Hall Co. v. Hallmark Cards, Inc., 340 F.2d 960, 963, 52 C.C.P.A. 981, 985 (1965). 일반적 **거래확장**의 문제가 다른 상품류에 적용된 다른 표장 간에 존재할 경우 양 표장 간의 차이점도 고려되어야 한다. (미) J. Wiss & Sons Co. v. W. E. Bassett Co., 462 F.2d 567, 569 (C.C.P.A. 1972).

ex parte appeals

An appeal from an examiner's final refusal against the application. An applicant may consider a second refusal on the same ground as final for the purpose of appeal.

미 결정계 항소

심사관의 최종거절결정에 대한 항소. 항소를 함에 있어 출원인은 동일한 근거에 의한 2차 거절을 최종거절결정으로 간주할 수 있음.

ex parte prosecution

미 결정계 절차

Example An action taken on a matter arising during the **ex parte prosecution** of an application for registration may, depending on the nature of the matter and the posture of the case, be reviewable only by appeal to the Board, or

출원관련 **결정계 절차** 중 발생한 사항에 대한 결정은 그 사안의 성질이나 사건의 상황에 따라 상표심판항소위원회에 항소를 제기함으로써만 검토 가능한 사안, 특허상표

only by petition to the Director or by either appeal or petition. The following discussion contains general guidelines for determining whether a matter is appealable or petitionable. TMEP § 1201.05.

청장에게 청구함으로써만 검토할 수 있는 사안, 혹은 둘 다를 통해 검토할 수 있는 사안으로 나뉜다. (미) TMEP § 1201.05.

ex parte reexamination

미 결정계 심사

A procedure whereby patentees and third parties can seek reexamination of issued patents.

특허권자 및 제3자가 등록특허의 재심사를 받기 위한 절차.

expedited examination

우선심사

→ See. accelerated examination.

expert witness

전문가 증인, 감정증인

A person whose opinion by virtue of education, training, certification, skills or experience, is accepted by the judge as an expert.

특별한 학식과 경험에 의하여 알게 된 사실을 법정에서 진술하는 증인(민사소송법 제340조). 감정인은 판단을 보고하는 데 반하여 감정증인은 일반증인과 마찬가지로 사실을 진술한다는 점에서 차이가 있음.

Example (**Expert Witness**) Examinations as to the facts known through a special knowledge and experience shall be governed by the provisions relating to the examination of a witness (Civil Procedure Act Article 340).

(**감정증인**) 특별한 학식과 경험에 의하여 알게 된 사실에 관한 신문은 증인신문에 관한 규정을 따른다. 다만, 비디오 등 중계장치 등에 의한 감정증인신문에 관하여는 제339조의3을 준용한다(민사소송법 제340조).

Example If a party files a request for an expert witness, the party shall attach a basic declaration of the **expert witness** that can confirm the expertise and objectivity of the witness. If the request is accepted, the party shall submit a witness statement containing the testimony of the expert witness and a questionnaire for witness examination (Patent Court Guideline of Practice and Procedure of Revocation Action V.3.A).

전문가 증인을 신청할 때에는 증인의 전문성과 객관성을 확인할 수 있는 전문가 증인 기본 사항 확인서를 첨부하여야 하고, 전문가 증인이 채택되면 전문가 증인의 증언이 담긴 증인 진술서와 증인신문사항을 제출하여야 한다(특허법원 심결취소소송 심리매뉴얼 V.3.가).

expert witness statement

전문가 진술서

expiration of duration

존속기간 만료

expiration of trademark registration

상표등록의 만료

Trademark registration becomes no longer active when the

등록권자가 존속기간의 종료 시까지 상표

E

registrant failed to renew the trademark registration by the end of the term.

등록을 갱신하지 못하였을 때 상표등록이 그 효력을 잃는 것.

expire

소멸

→ See. extinguishment.

explanatory documents for evidence

증거설명서

exploitation

실시

→ See. executing.

expropriation

수용

An action based on law acquiring private properties by force for a specific project in public interest.

특정한 공익사업을 위하여 개인의 재산권을 법률에 의하여 강제적으로 취득하는 것을 말함.

extended first-to-file rule

확대된 선출원

The rule that allows a patent examiner to reject an application when the invention for which the patent application is filed is identical to the invention described in the original specification of an earlier-filed patent application, even if the scope of claims of the inventions are not identical.

후출원 발명과 동일한 내용이 선출원 발명의 최초 명세서에 기재되어 있으면, 양발명의 청구범위가 동일하지 않더라도, 심사관은 이를 근거로 후출원 발명을 등록거절할 수 있는 원칙.

extension of duration

존속기간의 연장

Notwithstanding Article 88 (1), the term of a patent on an invention may be extended only once by up to five years to compensate for the period during which the invention cannot be executed, if the invention is specified by Presidential Decree and requires permission, registration, etc. under any other statute (hereinafter referred to as "permission, etc.") to execute patented invention but it takes a long time to undergo necessary tests for validity, safety, etc. for such permission, registration, etc. (Patent Act Article 89(1)).

특허발명을 실시하기 위하여 다른 법령에 따라 허가를 받거나 등록 등을 하여야 하고, 그 허가 또는 등록 등(이하 "허가등"이라 한다)을 위하여 필요한 유효성 · 안전성 등의 시험으로 인하여 장기간이 소요되는 대통령령으로 정하는 발명인 경우에는 제88조 제1항에도 불구하고 그 실시할 수 없었던 기간에 대하여 5년의 기간까지 그 특허권의 존속기간을 한 차례만 연장할 수 있다(특허법 제89조 제1항).

extinguishment

소멸

Example Where a successor of a deceased trademark owner fails to register transfer of the trademark rights within three years after the death of the owner, the trademark rights

상표권자가 사망한 날부터 3년 이내에 상속인이 그 상표권의 이전등록을 하지 아니한 경우에는 상표권자가 사망한 날부터 3

shall be **extinguished** on the day following the date on which three years have passed since the owner's death (Trademark Act Article 106(1)).

년이 되는 날의 다음 날에 상표권이 **소멸**된다(상표법 제106조 제1항).

extinguishment of international registration

국제등록의 소멸

Example The effect of withdrawal or extinguishment under paragraphs (1) and (2) shall occur from the date the relevant **international registration is extinguished** (Trademark Act Article 202(3)).

제1항 및 제2항에 따른 취하 또는 소멸의 효과는 국제상표등록부상 해당 **국제등록이 소멸**된 날부터 발생한다(상표법 제202조 제3항).

extrinsic evidence

미 외적 증거

Evidence used in a Markman hearing, other than intrinsic evidence, such as expert witness testimony, scholarly articles, testimony of the patentee, prior arts not referenced in the application.

마크맨 심리에 사용되는 내적 증거가 아닌 전문가 증언, 학술논문, 특허권자의 증언, 출원에 인용되지 않은 선행기술 등의 증거.

F

failure to function

미 기능(수행)실패

failure to function as a mark, i.e.. as an indicator of the source of the goods or services, identifying and distinguishing them from those of others. TMEP § 1202.17(c).

상표로서의 기능, 즉 자타상품 또는 서비스를 식별하는 출처표시기능 수행에 실패하는 것. (미) TMEP § 1202.17(c).

Example Even if a mark does not directly impart information about goods or services, it may nonetheless **failt of unction** if it conveys an informational message to others. For example, common phrases and slogans that are frequently displayed by many different parties on various goods are not likely to be viewed as source indicators, even if the matter is being used in a non-ornamental manner. TMEP § 1202.17(c)(i)(A).

표장이 그 상품이나 서비스에 대해 직접적으로 정보를 나타내지 않더라도 타인에게 정보를 전달한다면 **상표로서의 기능 수행에는 실패**할 수 있다. 가령 여러 사람들에 의해 다양한 상품에 빈번하게 표시되는 관용어구나 구호는 장식적으로 사용하지 않더라도 출처표시용도로 인식되지 않을 확률이 높다. (미) TMEP § 1202.17(c)(i)(A).

false display

거짓표시

For example, displaying on goods an unregistered mark or a mark for which no application has been filed as if a valid application or registration of the mark exists (Trademark Act Article 233).

가령 등록을 하지 아니한 상표 또는 상표등록출원을 하지 아니한 상표를 등록상표 또는 등록출원상표인 것같이 상품에 표시하는 행위 등(상표법 제233조).

false indication

→ See. false display.

거짓표시

false suggestion of connection

A mark falsely suggests a connection with a person or an institution if: (1) the mark is the same as, or a close approximation of, the name or identity previously used by another person or institution; (2) the mark would be recognized as such, in that it points uniquely and unmistakably to that person or institution; (3) the person or institution named by the mark is not connected with the activities performed by the applicant under the mark; and (4) the fame or reputation of the person or institution is such that, when the mark is used with the applicant's goods or services, a connection with the person or institution would be presumed. Univ. of Notre Dame du Lac v. J.C. Gourmet Food Imps. Co., 703 F.2d 1372, 1375-77, 217 USPQ 505,508-10 (Fed. Cir. 1983); TMEP § 1203.03(c)(i).

미 관계의 허위적 암시

어느 표장이 (1) 타인이나 타 기관이 이전에 사용한 이름 또는 명칭과 동일하거나 이와 유사하고, (2) 독특하고 명백하게 그러한 사람 또는 기관을 나타내는 이름으로 인지되며, (3) 그 표장이 나타내는 사람 또는 기관은 출원인이 그 표장을 사용하여 수행하는 활동과 연관성이 없고, (4) 그 사람 또는 기관이 출원인이 자신의 상품이나 서비스와 관련하여 그 표장을 사용하였을 때 그 사람이나 기관과의 연관성이 추정될 정도의 명성을 지닌 경우, 그 표장은 타인이나 타 기관과의 관계를 허위로 암시하는 것으로 간주됨. (미) Univ. of Notre Dame du Lac v. J.C. Gourmet Food Imps. Co., 703 F.2d 1372, 1375-77, 217 USPQ 505,508-10 (Fed. Cir. 1983); TMEP § 1203.03(c)(i).

fame

→ See. famousness.

저명성

family of marks

A group of marks having a recognizable common characteristic, wherein the marks are composed and used in such a way that the public associates not only the individual marks, but the common characteristic of the family, with the trademark owner. TMEP § 1207.01(d)(xi).

미 가족상표

두드러진 공통의 성질을 공유하여, 그 구성되고 사용되는 방식으로 인해 대중이 개별 상표 뿐 아니라 그 가족상표 내의 공통의 성질까지 상표권자와 관련지어 생각하도록 된 다수의 표장. (미) TMEP § 1207.01(d)(xi).

Example In view of the specific prohibition of Section 2(d) …, the fact that applicant may possess a **family of marks** characterized by the term 'ALD' is of no particular significance herein if the mark for which applicant now seeks registration … is confusingly similar to the previously registered mark … TMEP § 1207.01(d)(xi); In re Ald, Inc., 148 USPQ 520, 521 (TTAB 1965).

2(d)조 하에서 구체적으로 금지하고 있는 사항을 고려하면 출원인이 'ALD'라는 낱말로 나타나는 **가족표장**을 지닐 수 있다는 사실은 출원인이 현재 등록하고자 하는 표장이 선등록상표와 혼동을 일으킬 경우에는 아무런 의미가 없다고 보아야 하고, … (미) TMEP § 1207.01(d)(xi); In re Ald, Inc., 148 USPQ 520, 521 (TTAB 1965).

famousness

Any trademark using his/her own name, title, or trade name, portrait, signature, seal, or well-known pseudonym, stage name, pen name, and the well-known abbreviated title thereof, in accordance with generally accepted business practices (Trademark Act Article 90(1)1). Famousness of a name is determined based on whether the name is widely recognized in the relevant marketplace, judging from the period, manner, type and frequency of use, the scope and practice of trading of goods using the name, among others (Patent Court Decision, 2015Heo7292, decided May 19, 2016).

저명성

저명한 아호, 예명, 필명과 이들의 서명한 약칭을 상거래 관행에 따라 사용하는 상표에는 타 상표권의 효력이 미치지 아니함. (상표법 제90조 제1항 제1호). 이때 타인의 명칭 등이 저명한지는 그 사용기간, 방법, 태양, 사용량 및 거래의 범위와 상품거래의 실정 등을 고려하여 사회통념상 또는 지정상품과 관련한 거래사회에서 타인의 명칭 등이 널리 인식될 수 있는 정도에 이르렀는지 여부에 따라 판단하여야 함(특허법원 2016. 5. 19. 선고 2015허7292 판결 참조).

Example The Trademark in Prior Use 1 and the Service Mark in Prior Use, of the same composition as the name of the group, shall be deemed to have acquired **famousness** by being widely known not only to traders in the industry but also to most of the general public, in connection with the Defendant's goods of "phonorecord albums and music source files" and such services as "singer and musical performances, broadcast appearances, and advertisement endorsements" (Supreme Court Decision, 2013Hu1207, decided October 15, 2015).

이 사건 그룹가수의 명칭과 같은 구성의 선사용상표 1 및 선사용서비스표는 피고의 '음반, 음원' 등의 사용상품 및 '가수공연업, 음악공연업, 방송출연업, 광고모델업' 등의 사용서비스업에 대하여 관계거래자 이외에 일반공중의 대부분에까지 널리 알려지게 됨으로써 **저명성**을 획득하였다고 보아야 하고 … (대법원 2015. 10. 15. 선고 2013후1207 판결 참조).

famous trademark

A famous mark is a mark not only widely known to the consumers of the designated good but also has gained an impression of high quality among the general public due to its superior quality and thus serves as a source indicator for the business. It is therefore distinguished from well-known marks. Whether a trademark is famous is determined by the usage and supply of the mark, the method and period the good is marketed, the broadness of customer basis and course of trade, as well as how widely known it is when objectively viewed under social norms.

저명상표

그 상표가 수요자에게 널리 알려져 있을 뿐 아니라 그 상품이 갖는 품질의 우수성 때문에 상표의 수요자뿐만 아니라 일반대중에게까지 양질감을 획득하고 있어 상품의 출처뿐만 아니라 그 영업주체를 표시하는 힘까지 갖게 된 상표. 따라서 단순한 주지상표와는 구별됨. 저명상표에 해당하는지 여부는, 그 상표의 사용, 공급, 영업활동의 기간, 방법, 태양 및 거래범위 등과 그 거래실정 또는 사회통념상 객관적으로 널리 알려졌느냐의 여부 등이 기준이 됨.

Example In view of pre-use trademarks' foreign and domestic business operation periods, methods and forms, annual sales volumes, popularity through foreign and domestic public authorities and media, etc. revealed by the

선사용상표들의 국내외에서의 영업기간, 방법 및 형태, 연간 매출액, 국내외에서 공적인 기관 및 언론 등을 통하여 알려진 정도 등 제반 사정을 종합하면, 선사용상표들

F

above facts, pre-use trademarks were **famous trademarks** conspicuously known among traders or general consumers around Feb. 28, 2006 when the registered trademark of this case was applied for (Patent Court Decision, 2009Heo6311, decided December 11, 2009).

은 이 사건 등록상표의 출원일인 2006. 2. 28. 무렵에 거래자나 일반 소비자들 사이에서 현저하게 알려진 **저명상표**였다고 봄이 상당하다(특허법원 2009. 12. 11. 선고 2009허6311 판결 참조).

fanciful mark

창작상표

Fanciful marks comprise terms that have been invented for the sole purpose of functioning as a trademark or service mark. Such marks comprise words that are either unknown in the language (e.g., PEPSI, KODAK, EXXON) or are completely out of common usage (e.g., FLIVVER for low-priced vehicle).

상표 또는 서비스표로의 기능만을 위해 만들어진 단어로 된 상표. 그 언어에 없는 말(예: PEPSI, KODAK, EXXON)이거나 보통의 용례를 완전히 벗어난 경우(예: FLIVVER. FLIVVER는 실패, 실수 등의 뜻을 가지며 저가의 승용차를 지정상품으로 하여 사용됨).

feature comparison chart

구성대비표

A chart comparing patented invention and corresponding prior art by elements.

특허발명과 각 선행발명의 대응되는 구성을 대비한 표.

fee

수수료

Example Any person who follows trademark-related procedures shall pay **fees**: Provided, That where an examiner requests a trial to invalidate a trademark pursuant to Articles 117 (1) and 118 (1), he/she shall be exempted from the fees (Trademark Act Article 78(1)).

상표에 관한 절차를 밟는 자는 **수수료**를 내야 한다. 다만, 제117조 제1항 및 제118조 제1항에 따라 심사관이 무효심판을 청구하는 경우에는 수수료를 면제한다(상표법 제78조 제1항).

fee shifting

소송비용청구

The court in exceptional cases may award reasonable attorney fees to the prevailing party. 35 U.S.C. § 285.

법원이 승소자에게 합리적인 변호사비용을 청구할 수 있도록 하는 예외적인 경우. (미) 특허법 제285조.

figurative mark

도형상표

A mark that consists of figures used to identify the source of the good.

상품의 출처를 표시하기 위해 사용하는 도형으로 된 상표.

Example Two **figurative marks** shall be deemed similar when the dominant images created by the appearances of the marks are identical or similar and there is likelihood of confusion and misconception as to the source of the goods among

특히 **도형상표**들에 있어서는 그 외관이 주는 지배적 인상이 동일·유사하여 두 상표를 동일·유사한 상품에 다 같이 사용하는 경우 일반 수요자에게 상품의 출처에 관하

ordinary consumers when the marks are both used on identical or similar goods (Supreme Court Decision, 2015Hu1348, decided July 14, 2016).

여 오인·혼동을 일으킬 염려가 있다면 두 상표는 유사하다고 보아야 한다(대법원 2016. 7. 14. 선고 2015후1348 판결 참조).

file history

출원경과

file wrapper

출원포대

file wrapper estoppel

A patent owner whose application was granted based on the argument that the claims must be reduced or narrowly interpreted, in order to avoid refusal on the ground of publicly known art, shall not be allowed to reclaim his or her rights by the doctrine of equivalents if the rights were so waived in the application.

출원경과 금반언의 원칙

공지기술에 의한 등록거절을 피하기 위한 목적 등으로 청구범위를 감축하거나 또는 좁게 해석하여야 한다고 주장함으로써 특허를 받은 경우, 나중에 출원 중에 포기한 보호범위를 균등론에 의하여 회복하는 것은 허용되지 않는다는 원칙.

Example In order for the invention in quetion to be within the scope of patented invention, the organic composite relationship between each element of the patented invention shall be included in the invention in quetion. However, even if there is a substitution or modification of the element of the invention in quetion, where the substituted element of the invention in quetion is considered equivalent to the corresponding element of the patented invention, then the invention in quetion is still within the scope of the patented invention if the principles of establishing both inventions are the same, the invention in quetion could achieve the same objective and essentially obtain the same effect even though it is due to the substitution and it is self-evident that such substitution is that a person having ordinary skill in the technology (skilled in the technology) could easily have made, unless there are special circumstances such that the technology has been already publicly known or could have easily been invented by those skilled in the technology from the known prior technology or that the substituted element of the invention in quetion and therefore, this substituted element was **purposefully excluded from the scope of the request for a patent during the application procedure** (Supreme Court Decision, 98Hu522, decided August 21, 2001).

확인대상별명이 특허발명의 권리범위에 속한다고 할 수 있기 위하여는 특허발명의 각 구성요소와 구성요소 간의 유기적 결합관계가 확인대상별명에 그대로 포함되어 있어야 할 것이고, 다만 확인대상별명에 구성요소의 치환 내지 변경이 있더라도 양 발명에서 과제의 해결원리가 동일하며, 그러한 치환에 의하더라도 특허발명에서와 같은 목적을 달성할 수 있고 실질적으로 동일한 작용효과를 나타내며, 그와 같이 치환하는 것을 그 발명이 속하는 기술분야에서 통상의 지식을 가진 자가 용이하게 생각해 낼 수 있을 정도로 자명하다면, 확인대상별명이 특허발명의 출원시에 이미 공지된 기술 내지 공지기술로부터 당업자가 용이하게 발명할 수 있었던 기술에 해당하거나 특허발명의 **출원절차를 통하여 확인대상별명의 치환된 구성요소가 청구범위로부터 의식적으로 제외된 것에 해당**하는 등의 특별한 사정이 없는 한, 확인대상별명의 치환된 구성요소는 특허발명의 대응되는 구성요소와 균등관계에 있는 것으로 보아 확인대상별명은 여전히 특허발명의 권리범위에 속한다고 보아야 한다(대법원 2001.8.21, 선고, 98후522, 판결 참조).

F

filing basis

The statutory basis for filing an application for registration of a mark in the United States. An applicant must specify and meet the requirements of one or more bases in a trademark or service mark application. 37 C.F.R. §2.32(a)(5).

미 출원의 기초

미국 내 상표등록출원의 법정 기초. 출원인은 상표 또는 서비스표의 출원을 함에 있어서 최소 1개의 출원의 기초를 명시하고 그에 필요한 요건을 만족하여야 함. (미) 37 C.F.R. §2.32(a)(5).

final (office) action

An Office action that restates all outstanding issues from previous non-final office action(s) and holds these issues final.

최후거절이유통지

이전의 최초 통지부터 계속되는 출원의 거절이유를 다시 나열하고 종국적으로 미해결되었음을 알리는 통지.

final decision

종국판결

final judgment

종국판결

first sale doctrine

→ See. exhaustion doctrine.

권리소진의 원칙

first-to-file rule

1. According to this rule, where at least two patent applications for an identical invention are filed on different dates, only the applicant of the application having the earlier filing date is entitled to a patent on the invention (Patent Act Article 36(1)).
2. The patent regime that grants patent rights to the inventor of the claimed invention with earlier filing date than others.

선출원주의

1. 동일한 발명에 대하여 다른 날에 둘 이상의 특허출원이 있는 경우에는 먼저 특허출원한 자만이 그 발명에 대하여 특허를 받을 수 있다는 원칙(특허법 제36조 제1항)
2. 먼저 출원한 발명자의 특허권을 인정하는 제도. 한국과 마찬가지로 미국도 AIA 이후로는 선출원주의를 따름.

fixed period

The period under paragraph (3) shall be fixed: Provided, That the presiding judge may determine an additional period to the fixed period for those in the area with poor transportation, such as islands and remote rural areas, on his/her own authority, as prescribed by Ordinance of the Ministry of Trade, Industry and Energy (Trademark Act Article 162(4)).

불변기간

심판장은 도서 · 벽지 등 교통이 불편한 지역에 있는 자를 위하여 산업통상자원부령으로 정하는 바에 따라 직권으로 불변기간에 대하여 부가기간을 정할 수 있다(상표법 제162조 제4항).

flavor mark

A mark that provides distinctiveness by taste.

미각상표

미각적인 수단에 의하여 자타상품을 식별하는 표장.

font

A set of characters (including those in the form of numerals, punctuation marks, and symbols) made in a style with common characteristics for recording, marking, or printing (Design Protection Act Article 2(2)).

글자체

기록이나 표시 또는 인쇄 등에 사용하기 위하여 공통적인 특징을 가진 형태로 만들어진 한 벌의 글자꼴(숫자, 문장부호 및 기호 등의 형태를 포함한다)을 의미(디자인보호법 제2조 제2호).

force majeure

Example A "justifiable cause" refers not only to the circumstances where a party is prevented from engaging in his or her business due to illness or **force majeure** events such as act of God, ··· but also to non-use the party shall not be held responsible (Supreme Court Decision, 97Hu3920, decided April 25, 2000).

불가항력

'정당한 이유'라 함은 질병 기타 천재 등의 **불가항력**에 의하여 영업을 할 수 없는 경우뿐만 아니라 ··· 상표권자의 귀책사유로 인하지 아니한 상표 불사용의 경우도 포함된다고 할 것이다(대법원 2000. 4. 25. 선고 97후3920 판결 참조).

forfeiture

→ See. confiscation.

몰수

form

Shape, pattern, color or combination thereof.

Example The term "font" means a set of characters (including those in the **form** of numerals, punctuation marks, and symbols) made in a style with common characteristics for recording, marking, or printing (Design Protection Act Article 2.2).

형태, 모양

형상 · 모양 · 색채 또는 이들의 결합.

"글자체"란 기록이나 표시 또는 인쇄 등에 사용하기 위하여 공통적인 특징을 가진 **형태**로 만들어진 한 벌의 글자꼴(숫자, 문장부호 및 기호 등의 형태를 포함한다)을 말한다(디자인보호법 제2조 제2호).

a form related to a function of the article

Example Even if a form is **related to a function of the article**, it may be a dominant feature of the design if it appeals to the aesthetic sense of purchasers. However, for such a functional element to be a dominant feature of the design, it must attract the attention of the observer or represent the characteristics of the shape in the applied article (Patent Court Decision, 2015Heo3801, decided September 10, 2015).

물품의 기능에 관련된 형태

물품의 기능에 관련된 형태라도 그것이 수요자에게 심미감을 줄 수 있는 부분이라면 디자인의 지배적인 특징으로 판단할 수 있는 것이지만, 그러한 기능적인 요소가 디자인의 지배적인 특징이 되기 위해서는 표현된 물품에서 보는 사람의 주의를 끌 수 있거나 형태적인 특징을 가장 잘 나타낼 수 있어야 한다(특허법원 2015. 9. 10. 선고 2015허3801 판결 참조).

F

FRAND

Fair, Reasonable and Non-Discriminatory. A term that requires the patentee, often a standard and essential patent holder, to grant fair, reasonable and non-discriminatory licenses for the purpose of preventing unfair practices.

FRAND

공정하고 합리적이며 비차별적인. 불공정 행위의 방지를 목적으로 대개 표준필수특허의 특허권자에게 공정하고 합리적이며 비차별적인 실시권을 허여하도록 요구하는 조건.

fraud

Any person who obtains a patent or other rights, registration of an extension, or a trial ruling by fraud or other improper means shall be punished for fraud (Patent Act Article 229).

거짓행위의 죄

거짓 또는 그 밖의 부정행위로 등록, 존속기간 연장등록, 취소신청에 대한 결정 또는 심결을 받는 경우 거짓행위의 죄가 성립함(특허법 제229조).

freely exploited/practiced design

자유실시디자인

freely exploited/practiced invention

A defense that even when an execution of a technology apparently has the same composition with a patented invention or is equivalent with the patented invention, the execution does not constitute infringement of the patent if it is an act merely executing a pre-existing publicly known state-of-the-art technology.

Example The challenged design is merely a **freely exploited** design that can be easily created by a person with ordinary knowledge in the field from prior designs No.2-9, and comparison with the registered design at issue is unnecessary to conclude that it does not fall within the scope of protection of the registered design (Patent Court Decision, 2013Heo 7526, decided March 24, 2017).

자유실시기술

어떤 기술의 실시형태가 외형상 특허발명의 구성과 동일하거나 그 균등의 범주에 속한다 하더라도 그것이 당해 특허발명 이외에 이미 존재하는 공지의 자유기술을 실시하는 것인 때에는 특허발명에 대한 침해를 구성하지 않는다는 항변.

확인대상디자인은 그 디자인이 속하는 분야에서 통상의 지식을 가진 사람이 선행디자인 2~9로부터 쉽게 창작할 수 있는 **자유실시디자인**에 불과하므로, 이 사건 등록디자인과 대비할 필요도 없이 이 사건 등록디자인의 보호범위에 속하지 않는다(특허법원 2017. 3. 24. 선고 2013허7526판결 참조).

free riding

Example Furthermore, if the trademark is already conspicuously known as belonging to a particular source among traders or consumers in Korea and overseas and has accumulated business reputation and customer appeal through years' of continued use, **free riding** on the intangible financial value of the trademark by filing application for

무임승차

나아가 이미 국내 또는 해외의 거래자 또는 수요자간에 특정인의 상표라고 현저하게 인식될 수 있을 정도로 알려져 있고 또 상표권자의 선전, 광고 및 다년간의 지속적인 사용을 통하여 영업상 신용이나 고객흡인력 등의 무형의 재산적 가치(GOODWILL)

a mark that imitates lacks justification under the legal reasoning relating to the previous Trademark Act, Article 9(1)4, … (Patent Court Decision 99Heo31, decided April 15, 1999).

가 축적된 상표를 모방하여 출원함으로써 위 무형의 재산적 가치에 **무임승차**(FREE RIDE)하려는 것도 구 상표법 제9조 제1항 제4호에 관한 법리상 그 사회적 타당성을 결여한 것이고 … (특허법원 1999.04.15 선고 99허31 판결 참조).

functional and commercial modification

Modifications that any person with ordinary knowledge in the industry would be able to make to render the design suitable for the good or the function. Designs that could have been easily created by a person who has ordinary skill in the art (Design Protection Act Article 33(2)).

기능적이고 상업적인 변형

업계에서 통상의 지식을 가진 자라면 누구나 해당 디자인이 그 물품 또는 기능에 맞도록 하기 위하여 가할 수 있을 것이라고 생각되는 정도의 변화를 말함. (유사)용이하게 창작할 수 있는 정도 (디자인보호법 제33조 제2항 참조)

Example … [T]he addition of a support stand on the bottom of the body of the lamp is merely a **functional and commercial modification** that can be made by any skilled persons in the art. … (Patent Court Decision, 98Heo9604, decided March 11, 1999).

스탠드의 몸체 하단에 받침대를 추가하는 정도의 변형은 같은 업계에 종사하는 사람들이 흔히 취할 수 있는 **기능적이고 상업적인 변형**에 불과한 것이므로, … (특허법원 1999.03.11 선고 98허9604판결 참조).

functional claim

A claim in which an element is described in abstract terms such as its function, nature, effect or characteristics rather than in specific terms.

기능식청구항

기능식청구항 중 일부 요소를 구체적 구성으로 기재하지 않고 기능이나 성질, 작용, 특성 등으로 추상화하여 표현한 청구항.

functional form of a product

It is incorrect to immediately label the designs as similar merely based on the ground of similarities in the dominant features, because the significance of such similarities may be undermined if they constitute parts that the product must contain or relate to the fundamental or **functional forms** of the design (Patent Court Decision, 2014Heo6858, decided April 23, 2015).

물품의 기능적 형태

양 디자인의 공통되는 부분이 그 물품으로서 당연히 있어야 할 부분 내지 디자인의 기본적 또는 **기능적인 형태**인 경우에는 그 중요도를 낮게 평가하여야 하므로 이러한 부분들이 유사하다는 사정만으로는 곧바로 양 디자인이 서로 유사하다고 할 수는 없다 (특허법원 2015. 4. 23. 선고 2014허6858판결 참조).

functionality

A feature is functional if it is essential to the use or purpose of the article or if it affects the cost or quality of the article.

기능성

물품의 용도나 목적에 필수적이거나 그 비용 또는 품질에 영향을 미치는 특징.

Example It is incorrect to immediately label the designs similar merely based on the ground of similarities in the

양 디자인의 공통되는 부분이 그 물품으로서 당연히 있어야 할 부분 내지 디자인의

F

dominant features, because the significance of such similarities may be undermined if they constitute parts that the product must contain or relate to the fundamental or **functional** forms of the design (Supreme Court Decision 2012Hu3794 decided April 11, 2013).

기본적 또는 **기능적**인 형태인 경우에는 그 중요도를 낮게 평가하여야 하므로 이러한 부분들이 유사하다는 사정만으로는 곧바로 양 디자인이 서로 유사하다고 할 수는 없다 (대법원 2013. 4. 11. 선고 2012후3794 판결 참조).

fundamental form of a product

물품의 기본적 형태

The shape of an article that is the basis of the design, and is required to perceive and identify the article as such.

디자인의 골격이 되는 기본형태로서 그 형태를 갖춤으로써 그 물품이라고 인식되고 명명될 수 있는 것.

Example However, it is incorrect to immediately label the designs as similar merely based on the ground of similarities in the dominant features, because the significance of such similarities may be undermined if they constitute parts that the product must contain or relate to the fundamental or functional forms of the design (Patent Court Decision, 2014Heo6858, decided April 23, 2015).

다만, 양 디자인의 공통되는 부분이 그 물품으로서 당연히 있어야 할 부분 내지 디자인의 기본적 또는 기능적인 형태인 경우에는 그 중요도를 낮게 평가하여야 하므로 이러한 부분들이 유사하다는 사정만으로는 곧바로 양 디자인이 서로 유사하다고 할 수는 없다(특허법원 2015. 4. 23. 선고 2014허6858판결 참조).

G

general consuming public

일반 수요자

→ See. ordinary consumers.

generally accepted business practices

상거래 관행

Example Where trademark rights (excluding the right to a collective mark with geographical indication) fall under any of the following, trademark rights shall not effect the same: Any trademark using his/her own name, title, or trade name, portrait, signature, seal, or well-known pseudonym, stage name, pen name, and the well-known abbreviated title thereof, in accordance with **generally accepted business practices** (Trademark Act Article 90(1)1).

상표권(지리적 표시 단체표장권은 제외한다)은 다음 각 호의 어느 하나에 해당하는 경우에는 그 효력이 미치지 아니한다. 1. 자기의 성명 · 명칭 또는 상호 · 초상 · 서명 · 인장 또는 저명한 아호 · 예명 · 필명과 이들의 저명한 약칭을 **상거래 관행**에 따라 사용하는 상표 … (상표법 제90조 제1항 제1호).

general succession

일반승계

→ See. assignment.

Example No succession to an application for trademark registration shall take effect unless a report on the change of the applicant is filed, except in cases of inheritance and other **general succession** Trademark Act Article 48(1)).

상표등록출원의 승계는 상속이나 그 밖의 **일반승계**의 경우를 제외하고는 출원인 변경신고를 하지 아니하면 그 효력이 발생하지 아니한다(상표법 제48조 제1항).

generic concepts

상위개념

If a claimed invention is expressed in a generic concept and a cited invention is expressed in a specific concept, the invention in the claims is not novel. "Generic concepts" is defined as concepts integrating matters in the same family or the same genus, or those integrating a plurality of matters with the common characteristic.

출원발명이 상위개념으로 표현되어 있고 인용발명은 하위개념으로 표현되어 있다면, 청구항에 나타난 발명은 신규성이 부정됨. '상위개념'은 동일한 과 또는 속에 속하는 사항을 포괄하는 개념 또는 공통된 성질을 가지는 복수의 사항을 포괄하는 개념으로 정의됨.

Example In order to deny the novelty of the so-called selection invention, which means an invention whose elements are stated in the preceding or already publicized invention as a **generic concept** and entirely or partly consist of a subordinate concept derived from the above generic concept, a preceding invention has disclosed subordinate concepts comprising the selection invention in a concrete manner. The novelty of selective invention is also denied when a person with ordinary knowledge in the technology to which the invention pertains can recognize the existence of selective invention directly from the preceding literature, based on the contents stated in the preceding literature and his common sense in the technology at the time of application, as well as when wordings concerning the selection invention exist in the preceding literature stating the preceding invention (Supreme Court Decision, 2008Hu736, decided October 15, 2009).

선행 또는 공지의 발명에 구성요건이 상위개념으로 기재되어 있고 위 **상위개념**에 포함되는 하위개념만을 구성요건 중의 전부 또는 일부로 하는 이른바 선택발명의 신규성을 부정하기 위해서는 선행발명이 선택발명을 구성하는 하위개념을 구체적으로 개시하고 있어야 하고, 이에는 선행발명을 기재한 선행문헌에 선택발명에 대한 문언적인 기재가 존재하는 경우 외에도 그 발명이 속하는 기술분야에서 통상의 지식을 가진 자가 선행문헌의 기재 내용과 출원시의 기술 상식에 기초하여 선행문헌으로부터 직접적으로 선택발명의 존재를 인식할 수 있는 경우도 포함된다(대법원 2009. 10. 15. 선고 2008후736판결 참조).

G

generic drugs

복제약

A drug made of a newly developed substance is called an original drug. A drug that is made to imitate the original drug and have the same effective substance, formulation, volume, effect and administration method via chemical analysis of the original drug is called a generic drug.

처음 개발된 신물질로 만든 의약품을 오리지널 의약품이라고 하며, 오리지널 의약품의 화학성분 분석을 통해 오리지널 의약품과 동일한 유효성분, 제형, 용량, 효과, 용법 등을 동일하게 복제하여 만든 약을 복제약이라 함.

generic name

Ordinary title, abbreviation or nickname that is actually used and perceived as referring to the good among the ordinary consumers and traders in the relevant marketplace and not perceived as associated with the business of any particular person.

• common name (법제처)

보통명칭

그 지정상품을 취급하는 거래계에서 동종업자 및 일반 수요자 사이에 그 상품을 지칭하는 것으로 실제로 사용되고 인식되어 있는 일반적인 명칭, 약칭, 속칭 등으로서 특정인의 업무에 관련된 상품이라고 인식되지 아니하는 명칭.

genuine goods

A product lawfully manufactured and distributed by the true owner of registered trademark.

Example Based on the foregoing facts, we shall not conclude that there is no difference in quality between the goods manufactured and sold abroad and the goods manufactured and sold by the exclusive licensee in Korea, or that both goods are manufactured and sold by the same source. ⋯ In such cases, parallel import of the so-called **genuine goods** infringes the exclusive license in Korea and therefore is not allowed (Supreme Court Decision, 96Do2191, decided October 10, 1997).

진정상품

진정한 상표권자에 의해 적법하게 제조되어 유통된 상품.

⋯ 사실관계가 이러하다면 국외에서 제조·판매되는 상품과 국내 전용사용권자가 제조·판매하는 상품 사이에 품질상 아무런 차이가 없다거나 그 제조·판매의 출처가 동일한 것이라고 할 수 없고, ⋯ 이러한 경우에는 이른바 **진정상품**의 병행수입이라고 하더라도 국내 전용사용권을 침해하는것으로서 허용되지 않는다고 보아야 할 것이다(대법원 1997. 10. 10. 선고 96도2191 판결 참조).

geographical indication

An indication used to identify goods produced, manufactured, or processed in a specific area in cases where a certain quality, reputation or other characteristic of goods has essentially originated from such specific area (Trademark Act Article 2(1)4).

Example None of the following trademarks shall be registered: ⋯ 9. Any trademark identical or similar to a trademark (excluding a **geographical indication**) widely recognized by consumers as indicating the goods of another person, which is used on goods identical or similar to the goods of another person (Trademark Act Article 34(1)).

지리적 표시

상품의 특정 품질 · 명성 또는 그 밖의 특성이 본질적으로 특정지역에서 비롯된 경우에 그 지역에서 생산 · 제조 또는 가공된 상품임을 나타내는 표시를 말함(상표법 제2조 제1항 제4호).

타인의 상품을 표시하는 것이라고 수요자들에게 널리 인식되어 있는 상표(**지리적 표시**는 제외한다)와 동일 · 유사한 상표로서 그 타인의 상품과 동일 · 유사한 상품에 사용하는 상표는 상표등록을 받을 수 없다(상표법 제34조 제1항 제9호).

geographically deceptively misdescriptive marks

A mark is geographically deceptively misdescriptive if: (1) the primary significance of the mark is a generally known

미 지리적으로 기만적인 허위표시 표장

표장은 (1) 그 주된 의의가 일반적으로 알

geographic location; (2) the goods or services do not originate in the place identified in the mark; (3) purchasers would be likely to believe that the goods or services originate in the geographic place identified in the mark; and (4) the misrepresentation is a material factor in a significant portion of the relevant consumer's decision to buy the goods or use the services. TMEP § 1210.01(b).

려진 지리적 위치에 대한 것이고, (2) 그 상품이나 서비스는 표장에 나타난 장소를 출처로 하지 아니하며, (3) 소비자들은 상품 또는 서비스가 표장에 나타난 장소를 출처로 한다고 믿을 것이라 보여지며, (4) 이러한 허위표시가 해당 분야의 소비자들이 그 상품을 구매하거나 서비스를 사용하기로 결정하는 데에 상당부분 중대한 요소로 작용할 경우 지리적인 기만적 허위표시 표장이라 함. (미) TMEP § 1210.01(b).

Example The primary significance of the mark is the name of a generally-known geographic location, i.e., Normandy, France. A goods/place association exists between cheese and Normandy. Applicant's goods do not or will not originate in or from Normandy. The mark's misrepresentation of the geographic origin of the goods is or would be material to the decision to purchase the goods. Thus, we conclude that NORMANDIE CAMEMBERT is primarily **geographically deceptively misdescriptive** of "cheese," and that applicant's mark accordingly is unregistrable under Trademark Act Section 2(e)(3). In Re Cheezwhse.com, Inc., 85 U.S.P.Q.2d 1917 (TTAB Feb. 1, 2008).

이 사건 표장[NORMANDIE CAMAMBERT]의 주된 의미는 일반적으로 알려진 지리적 위치, 즉 프랑스 노르망디의 명칭에 있다. 치즈와 노르망디 사이에는 상품-장소간 연관성이 존재한다. 출원인의 상품은 노르망디에서 생산되지 않으며 앞으로도 그러할 것이다. 당해 표장의 상품의 지리적 출처에 대한 허위표시는 상품의 구매결정에 중대한 요소로 작용한다. 따라서 NORMANDIE CAMAMBERT 표장은 지정상품인 치즈에 대하여 주로 **지리적으로 기만적인 허위표시 표장**으로, 출원인의 표장은 상표법 2(e)(3)에 따라 등록불가하다. (미) In re Cheezwhse.com, Inc., 85 U.S.P.Q. 2d 1917 (TTAB 2008).

geographically deceptive marks

미 지리적인 기만적 표장

→ See. geographically descriptive marks.

geographically descriptive marks

미 지리적인 기술적 표장

A mark is primarily geographically descriptive if (1) the primary significance of the mark is a generally known geographic location; (2) the goods or services originate in the place identified in the mark; and (3) purchasers would be likely to believe that the goods or services originate in the geographic place identified in the mark. TMEP § 1210.01(a).

표장은 (1) 그 주된 의의가 일반적으로 알려진 지리적 위치에 대한 것이고, (2) 그 상품이나 서비스는 표장에 나타난 장소를 출처로 하며, (3) 소비자들은 상품 또는 서비스가 표장에 나타난 장소를 출처로 한다고 믿을 것이라 보여질 때 주로 지리적인 기술적 표장이라 함. (미) TMEP § 1210.01(a).

good

상품

A tangible and transportable object that repeatedly functions as a subject of transactions; an article that has value for

'반복하여 거래대상이 되는 유체물', '교환가치를 가지고 독립된 상거래의 목적물이

G

exchange and is the subject of independent commercial transaction. The Trademark Act does not define what a "good" is; it shall be determined based on the objective of the Act and trade norms.

되는 물품' 등. 상표법은 상품의 개념에 대하여 규정하고 있지 아니하므로, 이에 해당하는지 여부는 상표법의 목적과 거래사회의 통념을 고려하여 결정하여야 함.

good cause

정당한 이유

A defense to cancellation of trademark based on nonuse.

불사용으로 인한 상표등록취소 등에 대한 항변의 근거.

Example An "**good cause**" includes not only the circumstances where a party is prevented from engaging in his or her business due to illness or reasons of force majure such as acts of God, … but also to non-use the party shall not be held responsible (Supreme Court Decision, 97Hu3920, decided April 25, 2000).

'**정당한 이유**'라 함은 질병 기타 천재 등의 불가항력에 의하여 영업을 할 수 없는 경우뿐만 아니라 상표권자의 귀책사유로 인하지 아니한 상표 불사용의 경우도 포함된다고 할 것이다(대법원 2000. 4. 25. 선고 97후3920 판결 참조).

good faith

선의

good moral

선량한 풍속

Example [T]he Subject Invention is deemed as an invention in breach of the public order and **good moral**s or an invention likely to damage the public hygiene, … (Patent Court Decision, 2016Heo229, decided July 8, 2016).

따라서 이 사건 출원발명은 공공의 질서 또는 **선량한 풍속**을 문란하게 하거나 공중의 위생을 해할 염려가 있는 발명에 해당하므로, … (특허법원 2016. 7. 8. 선고 2016허229 판결 참조).

goods in trade

거래상품

A trademark is used in commerce only when it is applied to goods in trade, i.e. goods commercially sold or transported for use by others.

상표가 거래상 사용되었다고 하기 위해서는 반드시 거래상품, 즉 타인의 사용을 위해 상업적으로 판매 또는 운송되는 물품에 표시되어야만 함.

Example Applicant is engaged not in the sale of reports but solely in the furnishing of financial reporting services to its subscribers, as it likewise is that the reports submitted to its subscribers are merely incidental to and the ultimate result of its services. Such being the case, we are in full agreement with the Examiner that applicant's reports do not constitute **goods in trade**. Application of Shareholders Data Corp., 495 F.2d 1360, 1361 (C.C.P.A. 1974).

출원인이 보고서의 판매가 아닌 가입자를 위한 금융보고 서비스를 업으로 하면, 보고서는 그 서비스의 최종적 결과를 위한 수단으로 서비스 제공과정에서 사용되는 것에 지나지 않는다. 이로 미루어 볼 때 출원인의 보고서는 **거래상품**이 아니라고 본 심사관의 결정은 정당하였다고 볼 수밖에 없다. (미) Application of Shareholders Data Corp., 495 F.2d 1360, 1361 (C.C.P.A. 1974).

goods-place association

상품-장소간 연관성(연계성)

An association between goods and a place is present when consumers identify as a known source of the product.

소비자가 어느 상품의 잘 알려진 출처로 어느 장소를 연상할 때 상품-장소간 연계성이 존재함.

Example If the mark is remote or obscure, the public is unlikely to make a **goods/place or services/place association**. TMEP § 1210.01(b).

표장이 희미하거나 불분명한 경우 공중은 **상품과 장소 또는 서비스와 장소를 연결**지어 생각하지 않을 것이다. (미) TMEP § 1210.01(b).

grace period

미 유예기간

Before the AIA, a one-year grace period before filing is allowed to an inventor during which the inventor can disclose or use the invention without losing its novelty. Under the revised statute, the period is only given to disclosures by the actual inventor but not others, unless disclosure by others is subsequent to disclosure of the actual inventor.

구 특허법 하에서는 1년의 신규성 의제기간이 허락되어 출원 전 1년의 기간 동안 발명을 공지하거나 이용하여도 신규성을 상실하지 아니하였음. 개정 특허법 하에서는 이러한 기간은 진정한 발명자의 공개에만 적용되며 타인의 공개가 있었을 시 신규성이 상실됨. 단 타인의 공개 이전에 진정한 발명자의 공개가 선행되었을 때는 예외로 함.

grade designations

등급표시

Grade designations are used to indicate that a particular product has a certain level of quality within a set range.

등급 지정은 어느 상품이 그 정해진 범위 내에서 특정 수준의 품질을 보유함을 나타내기 위해 사용됨.

ground

(판결) 이유

grounds for appeal

상고/항소 이유

Example (**Grounds for Appeal** to Supreme Court) An appeal to the Supreme Court may be filed only when stating as the grounds therefore that there has been a violation of the Constitution, Acts, administrative decrees, or regulations, which has affected the judgment (Civil Procedure Act Article 423).

(**상고이유**) 상고는 판결에 영향을 미친 헌법 · 법률 · 명령 또는 규칙의 위반이 있다는 것을 이유로 드는 때에만 할 수 있다(민사소송법 제423조).

grounds for invalidation

등록무효사유

Grounds to invalidate a registered intellectual property rights.

산업재산권의 등록이 무효로 되어야 하는

G

Where an administrative trial decision to invalidate a registration becomes final and conclusive, such intellectual property rights shall be deemed never to have existed.

사유. 무효심판 청구에 대한 심결로 결정하며, 확정 시 그 산업재산권은 처음부터 없었던 것으로 간주.

Example Following the Tribunal's decision, the plaintiff filed an appeal in the court below seeking reversal of the decision where the plaintiff alleged Article 5 (2) of the Act is not a valid **ground to invalidate** the registered design at issue because the design was not easily creatable from other comparable designs (Supreme Court Decision, 2010Hu3509, decided March 24, 2011).

…그 심결취소소송인 원심절차에서 원고는 이 사건 심결의 위법사유로서 이 사건 등록디자인이 비교대상디자인 등으로부터 용이하게 창작할 수 있는 디자인에 해당하지 않으므로 같은 법 제5조 제2항 소정의 **등록무효사유**가 존재하지 않는다는 주장만을 하였을 뿐이고,… (대법원 2011. 3. 24. 선고 2010후3509 판결 참조).

grounds of appeal

항소이유

grounds to cancel trademark registration

상표등록취소사유

Grounds to cancel trademark registration as prescribed under Trademark Act Art.119(1), such as abuse or nonuse of trademark or acts causing misconception or confusion by trademark owner.

상표의 부정사용, 불사용, 상표권자의 오인 또는 혼동행위 등 상표법 119조 1항에 규정된 상표 등록의 취소사유.

- grounds to revoke trademark registration (법제처)

group of inventions

일군의 발명

Example A single patent application for **a group of inventions** shall meet the following requirements:
1. The inventions described in the application shall be technologically correlated;
2. The inventions described in the application shall have the same or corresponding technological features. In such case, the technological features shall be those improved than the prior technology in light of the invention at large (Enforcement Decree of Patent Act Article 6).

일군의 발명에 대하여 1특허출원을 하기 위하여는 다음 각호의 요건을 갖추어야 한다.
1. 청구된 발명간에 기술적 상호관련성이 있을 것
2. 청구된 발명들이 동일하거나 상응하는 기술적 특징을 가지고 있을 것. 이 경우 기술적 특징은 발명 전체로 보아 선행기술에 비하여 개선된 것이어야 한다(특허법시행령 제6조).

Guideline of Civil Appellate Practice and Procedure of the Patent Court of Korea

특허법원 침해소송 항소심 심리 매뉴얼

H

hashtag marks | 미 해쉬태그 표장

A mark consisting of or containing the hash symbol (#) or the term HASHTAG. Registrable as a trademark or service mark only if it functions as an identifier of the source of the applicant's goods or services. TMEP § 1202.18.

해쉬 기호(#)나 '해쉬태그'(HASHTAG)라는 단어로 이루어진 표장. 출원인의 상품 또는 서비스의 출처표시 기능을 수행할 때에 한하여 상표 또는 서비스표로 등록할 수 있음. (미) TMEP § 1202.18.

Hague Agreement | 헤이그협정

The Hague Agreement concerning International Registration of Industrial Designs.

산업디자인의 국제등록에 관한 헤이그협정

Example The Hague Agreement allows a design to receive extended protection in the territory of the parties to the Agreement by filing a single application at the WIPO International Bureau.

산업디자인의 국제등록에 관한 헤이그협정 세계지식재산기구(WIPO) 국제사무국에 하나의 국제출원서를 제출하여 여러 체약당사자 영역에서 디자인을 보호받을 수 있도록 한 협정.

~ have economic ties | 경제적 견련관계

hearing | 심리

highly advanced | 고도(高度)의

the term "highly advanced" has been introduced to differentiate "device" under the Utility Model Act from "invention" under the Patent Act.

고도한 것의 의미는 일반적으로 실용신안법상의 고안과 특허법상의 발명을 구분하기 위한 상대적인 개념임.

Example The term "invention" means **highly advanced** creation of a technical idea utilizing the laws of nature (Patent Act Article 2).

"발명"이란 자연법칙을 이용한 기술적 사상의 창작으로서 **고도(高度)한** 것을 말한다(특허법 제2조).

hindsight reconstruction | 사후적 고찰

Example Hindsight reconstruction is an error of determining inventiveness based on whether or not a person skilled in the art can easily create the invention at issue in hindsight assuming that the person already knows the technology disclosed in the specification of the invention (Supreme Court Decision, 2006Hu138, decided August 24, 2007).

어떤 발명의 진보성을 판단함에 있어 그 판단대상이 된 발명의 명세서에 개시되어 있는 기술을 알고 있음을 전제로 하여 사후적으로 통상의 기술자가 그 발명을 용이하게 발명할 수 있는지 판단하는 오류(대법원 2007. 8. 24. 선고 2006후138 판결 참조).

holder of an international registration

국제등록명의인

Example The **holder of an international registration** may renew the duration of an international registration every ten years (Trademark Act Article 173(1)).

국제등록명의인은 국제등록의 존속기간을 10년씩 갱신할 수 있다(상표법 세173조 세1항).

holder of plant variety right

품종보호권자

hologram mark

홀로그램 상표

A trademark that consists of holograms.

홀로그램으로 구성된 상표.

Example The term "mark" means all indications used to identify the source of goods, irrespective of the composition or methods of the expression thereof, which include any sign, letter, figure, sound, smell, three-dimensional shape, **hologram**, movement, color, etc. (Trademark Act Article 2(1)2).

"표장"이란 기호, 문자, 도형, 소리, 냄새, 입체적 형상, **홀로그램** · 동작 또는 색채 등으로서 그 구성이나 표현방식에 상관없이 상품의 출처(출처)를 나타내기 위하여 사용하는 모든 표시를 말한다(상표법 제2조 제1항 제2호).

homonymous geographical indication

동음이의어 지리적 표시

A geographical indication that has the same pronunciation with but refers to a different location from another geographical indication used by another person for the same good (Trademark Act Article 2(1)5).

같은 상품에 대한 지리적 표시가 타인의 지리적 표시와 발음은 같지만 해당 지역이 다른 지리적 표시를 말함(상표법 제2조 제1항 제5호).

house mark

사표(社標)

Marks that identify the manufacturer or seller over a wide variety of goods rather than the goods, which are often themselves identified by a "product mark." House marks are often used in the chemical, pharmaceutical, publishing, and food industries. A product may bear both a productmark and a house mark. TMEP § 1402.03(b).

제품이 '제품표장'에 의해 식별된다면 이와 대비하여 그러한 다양한 제품의 제조업자 또는 판매업자를 식별하는 표장. 주로 화학, 약품, 출판, 식품업계에서 사용된다. 한 제품에 제품상표와 사표 모두를 표시할 수도 있음. (미) TMEP § 1402.03(b).

Example Bose also owns its **house mark** BOSE that frequently accompanies the ACOUSTIC WAVE and WAVE marks. For purposes of this litigation, QSC and the Board accept that the BOSE **house mark** enjoys extensive public recognition and renown and in trademark parlance is therefore "famous." Bose Corp. v. QSC Audio Prod., Inc., 293 F.3d 1367, 1369 (Fed. Cir. 2002)

Bose는 또한 ACOUSTIC WAVE, WAVE 상표와 빈번히 함께 표시되는 BOSE **사표**(社標)의 상표권자이기도 하다. 본 소송의 목적상 QSC와 상표심리위원회 모두 BOSE **사표**는 공중의 인지도가 매우 높으며 상표법상 '저명상표'에 해당함을 인정한다. (미) Bose Corp. v. QSC Audio Prod., Inc., 293 F.3d 1367, 1369 (Fed. Cir. 2002)

I

identical good

Goods identical or deemed identical to the designated good under the norms of the marketplace. The determination is made in an objective manner based on thorough consideration of the characteristics of the goods and course of trade such as the quality, use, form, and usage of the goods, distribution channels, suppliers and consumers.

동일상품

지정상품 그 자체 또는 거래사회의 통념상 이와 동일하게 볼 수 있는 상품. 양 상품의 품질·용도·형상·사용방법·유통경로 및 공급자와 수요자 등 상품의 속성과 거래의 실정을 종합적으로 고려하여 객관적으로 판단함.

Example … The use of the registered trademark at issue on "pearl rings, coral rings," types of jewelery ornaments, is not use the mark on **goods identical** to the designated goods, "pearls and corals" (Supreme Court Decision, 2006Hu2967, decided May 29, 2008).

보석 장신구인 '진주 반지, 산호 반지'에 이 사건 등록상표를 사용한 것은 거래사회의 통념상 이 사건 등록상표의 지정상품인 '진주, 산호'와 **동일성 있는 물품**에 대하여 등록상표를 사용한 것이라고 할 수 없다(대법원 2008. 5. 29. 선고 2006후2967 판결 참조).

identical invention

In judging if two inventions are identical, the actual substance of the two inventions compared shall be examined, rather than the differences as to how they are described, such that even when the two inventions compared fall under the different categories of "invention of a product" and "invention of a process," it shall not be automatically determined that they do not constitute identical inventions (Supreme Court Decision, 2005Hu3017, January 12, 2007).

동일한 발명

두 발명이 서로 동일한 발명인지 여부는 대비되는 두 발명의 실체를 파악하여 따져보아야 할 것이지 표현양식에 따른 차이에 따라 판단할 것은 아니므로, 대비되는 두 발명이 각각 물건의 발명과 방법의 발명으로 서로 발명의 범주가 다르다고 하여 곧바로 동일한 발명이 아니라고 단정할 수 없다(대법원 2007. 1. 12. 선고 2005후3017 판결 참조).

identical trademark

An identical trademark includes not only physically identical one to a registered mark but also those that have modified

동일상표

동일한 상표. 등록된 상표와 물리적으로 동일한 경우뿐 아니라 상표의 동일성을 해치

the registered mark within a degree that does not interfere with the identity and are deemed identical under the trade norms.

지 않을 정도로 변형하여 사용하는 경우, 즉 거래통념상 동일성이 인정되는 형태의 상표까지 포함됨.

Example In light of the purpose of the aforementioned trademark cancellation system by reason of non-use, using a "registered trademark" means using a trademark which is identical to the registered trademark, and does not include similar trademarks; however, "**identical trademark**" may include not just the registered trademark itself, but also trademarks that can be perceived as identical to a registered trademark in terms of trade norms (Supreme Court Decision, 2012Hu2463, decided September 26, 2013).

… 위와 같은 불사용으로 인한 상표등록취소 제도의 취지에 비추어 볼 때, 여기서 '등록상표를 사용'한다고 함은 등록상표와 동일한 상표를 사용한 경우를 말하고 유사상표를 사용한 경우는 포함되지 아니하나, '**동일한 상표**'에는 등록상표 그 자체뿐만 아니라 거래통념상 등록상표와 동일하게 볼 수 있는 형태의 상표도 포함된다고 할 것이다(대법원 2013. 9. 26. 선고 2012후2463 전원합의체 판결 참조).

identification number

고유번호

Example A person specified by Ordinance of the Ministry of Trade, Industry and Energy, who initiate a patent-related procedure, shall apply for issuance of his/her **identification number** to the Commissioner of the Korean Intellectual Property Office or the President of the Korean Intellectual Property Trial and Appeal Board (Patent Act Article 28-2(1)).

특허에 관한 절차를 밟는 자 중 산업통상자원부령으로 정하는 자는 특허청장 또는 특허심판원장에게 자신의 **고유번호**의 부여를 신청하여야 한다(특허법 제28조의2 제1항).

identity of character

인격의 동일성

Example Any person who uses a means indicating the **identity of his/her character**, such as his/her name and trade name, as his/her trademark in accordance with generally accepted business practices, and meets requirements under paragraph (1) 1 shall have the right to continuously use the trademark on goods on which he/she uses the relevant trademark (Trademark Act Article 99(2)).

자기의 성명 · 상호 등 **인격의 동일성**을 표시하는 수단을 상거래 관행에 따라 상표로 사용하는 자로서 제1항 제1호의 요건을 갖춘 자는 해당 상표를 그 사용하는 상품에 대하여 계속 사용할 권리를 가진다(상표법 제99조 제2항).

identity or similarity of designs (shapes)

Identity or similarity of designs is what creates identical or similar aesthetic sense between the shapes (i.e. the configurations, forms, colors or their combination) that constitute the two designs when compared in their appearance.

디자인(형태)의 동일 · 유사성

2개의 디자인을 비교할 때, 그 디자인을 구성하는 형상·모양·색채 또는 이들을 결합한 것, 즉 형태가 외관상 서로 동일·유사한 미감을 일으키게 하는 것.

Example If at least two applications are filed on different dates for registration of an **identical or similar design**, only the first applicant to file an application may have his/her design registered (Design Protection Act Article 46(1)).

동일하거나 유사한 디자인에 대하여 다른 날에 2 이상의 디자인등록출원이 있는 경우에는 먼저 디자인등록출원한 자만이 그 디자인에 관하여 디자인등록을 받을 수 있다(디자인보호법 제46조 제1항).

imitate

모조

Example The following Delivering, selling, forging, **imitating**, or possessing a trademark identical or similar to a registered trademark of another person for the purpose of using or causing a third party to use such trademark on goods identical or similar to the designated goods shall be deemed an infringement of trademark rights (Trademark Act Article 108(1)2).

다음 각 호의 어느 하나에 해당하는 행위는 상표권(지리적 표시 단체표장권은 제외한다) 또는 전용사용권을 침해한 것으로 본다. .2. 타인의 등록상표와 동일 · 유사한 상표를 그 지정상품과 동일 · 유사한 상품에 사용하거나 사용하게 할 목적으로 교부 · 판매 · 위조 · **모조** 또는 소지하는 행위는 상표권 침해에 해당한다(상표법 제108조 제1항 제2호).

immoral or scandalous matter

미 공서양속에 반하는 상표

Example Dictionary definitions alone may be sufficient to establish that a proposed mark comprises **scandalous matter**, where multiple dictionaries, including at least one standard dictionary, all indicate that a word is vulgar, and the applicant's use of the word is limited to the vulgar meaning of the word. TMEP § 1203.01.

최소 하나의 표준사전을 포함한 여러 사전이 모두 어느 단어를 비속어로 표시하고 있고 출원인의 그 단어의 사용이 그 저속한 의미로 한정되어 있다면, 사전적 정의만으로 어떤 제시된 표장이 **공서양속에 반하는 내용**으로 이루어져 있음을 충분히 입증할 수 있다. (미) TMEP § 1203.01.

implementation

실시례

→ See. embodiment.

improvement invention

이용발명, 개량발명

An invention that includes all the components of the patented invention that is being used but adds new components to obtain patentabiltiy. Since Patent Act Article 98 provides that a patent holder who earned his/her patent right by using an earlier-applied patent invention may not execute his/her patent without the permission of the owner of the earlier-applied patent, executing use invention may constitute infringement of the patent used by the use invention.

이용 대상이 되는 특허발명의 구성요소를 모두 그대로 가지고 있으면서 여기에 새로운 구성요소를 부가하여 특허성을 취득한 경우를 말한다. 특허법 제98조는 특허권자가 선출원 특허발명을 이용하여 특허받은 경우에는 선출원 특허권자의 동의를 얻지 아니하고는 자기의 특허발명을 업으로서 실시할 수 없다고 규정함으로써 이용발명에 대하여 규정하고 있으므로, 이용발명의 실시는 이용대상이 되는 특허발명의 침해가 됨.

I

improvement relationship

The subsequent invention in the improvement relationship adds a new technological element to the technical composition of the previous invention, contains all the main substance of the previous invention and applies them as they are. The patented invention as incorporated in the subsequent invention must maintain its consistency as an invention. The relationship is formed not only when the subsequent invention uses an invention identical to the patented invention but also an equivalent one (Supreme Court Decision, 98Hu522, decided August. 21, 2001). The subsequent invention falls within the scope of the previous patented invention.

• use relationship (법제처)

이용관계

이용관계는 후 발명이 선 특허발명의 기술적 구성에 새로운 기술적 요소를 부가하는 것으로서 후 발명이 선 특허발명의 요지를 전부 포함하고 이를 그대로 이용하되, 후 발명 내에 선 특허발명이 발명으로서의 일체성을 유지하는 경우에 성립하는 것이며, 이는 선 특허발명과 동일한 발명뿐만 아니라 균등한 발명을 이용하는 경우도 마찬가지이다(대법원 2001. 8. 21. 선고 98후522 판결 참조). 이용관계에 있는 경우에는 후 발명은 선 특허발명의 권리범위에 속하게 된다.

including

→ See. comprising.

… 을 포함하는 것을 특징으로 하는

in common use

→ See. use in a common manner.

보통으로 사용하다

incomplete invention

Incomplete invention refers to an invention that is not complete enough to be subject to protection of patent.

미완성 발명

미완성 발명은 특허보호의 대상이 될 만한 발명에 이르지 못하였다고 평가되는 경우를 말한다.

Example **Incomplete invention** refers to an invention that is not complete enough to be subject to protection of patent, which includes mere proposal of a problem or idea and not knowing method for materialization, cases in which the purpose of the invention is impossible to achieve because lack of all or part of the means necessary to achieve the purpose, cases in which means to solve technical problems is too remote and cannot be concrete, cases in which the purpose cannot be achieved with only that method, and inventions that cannot be repeated (Patent Court Decision, 2001Heo4722, decided December, 2002).

미완성 발명은 특허보호의 대상이 될 만한 발명에 이르지 못하였다고 평가되는 경우로서, 단순한 과제 또는 착상의 제기에 그치고 그 실현방법을 모르는 것, 발명의 목적을 달성하기 위한 수단의 일부 또는 그 전부가 결여되어 발명의 목적달성이 실제로 불가능한 것, 과제의 해결수단이 막연하여 구체화할 수 없는 것 또는 그 수단만 가지고는 목적을 달성할 수 없는 것, 발명의 빈복재현이 불가능한 것 등을 말한다(특허법원 2002. 10. 10. 선고 2001허4722 판결 참조).

incomplete response (to Office action)

An applicant's response to an Office action that (1) does not address one or more of the requirements or refusals made in the Office action; (2) is unsigned; (3) is signed by an unauthorized person; or (4) is a response to a final action that does not overcome all refusals or satisfy all requirements, when the response period has expired, and the applicant has not timely filed a notice of appeal. Generally, a complete response must be filed within six months from the date of issuance of the Office action to avoid abandonment. 37 C.F.R. § 2.65(a); TMEP § 718.03.

미 (특허상표청 통지에 대한) 불완전한 반박

(1) 특허상표청 통지 중 하나 이상의 거절사항이나 한정요구에 반박하지 않았거나 (2) 서명 누락 (3) 권한 없는 자의 서명 (4) 반박기간이 종료되었을 때 최후 통지에 대한 반박이 모든 거절이유를 해결하지 못하거나 모든 요구사항을 충족하지 못하였고 출원인이 적시에 항소를 신청하지 못하였을 경우 출원인의 특허상표청 통지에 대한 반박은 불완전한 것으로 본다. 일반적으로 출원을 포기하지 않기 위해서는 통지가 발행된 일로부터 6개월 내에 완전한 반박서를 제출하여야 한다. (미) 37 C.F.R. § 2.65(a); TMEP § 718.03.

incontestability

A trademark registration is incontestable if the mark has been in continuous use in commerce for a period of five years after the date of registration. 15 U.S.C. § 1065.

미 불가쟁력

등록일로부터 계속 5년간 거래상 사용되어 왔고 아직도 거래상 사용되고 있는 상품 또는 서비스의 등록표장의 효력을 다툴 수 없음, 즉 불가쟁력을 가지게 됨. (미) 상표법 제 15조

Example Ownership of an **incontestable** registration does not give the applicant a right to register the same mark for different goods or services, even if they are closely related to the goods or services in the incontestable registration. TMEP § 1216.02.

불가쟁력을 지닌 상표의 등록소유권이 있다 하여 출원인이 다른 상품이나 서비스에 대해 동일한 상표를 등록할 수는 없으며 이는 그 상품 또는 서비스가 다툴수없는 등록상표와 긴밀한 연관성이 있다 하더라도 마찬가지이다. (미) TMEP § 1216.02.

incremental profit

The profit a patent owner would have gained by selling additional unit of the patented product prior to the infringing good's entry into the market.

증분이익

침해제품의 시장 진입 이전 시점을 기준으로 특허권자가 특허제품 1대를 추가로 판매함으로써 얻었을 이익.

independent claim

A claim that does not refer back to or depend on another claim.

독립항

특허 청구항 중 다른 청구항을 인용하지 않는 청구항.

Example When claims within the scope of claims under Article 42 (8) of the Act (hereinafter referred to as "claims")

법 제42조 제8항에 따른 청구범위의 청구항(이하 "청구항"이라 한다)을 기재할 때에

are stated, such claims shall be stated in the form of independent claims (hereinafter referred to as "**independent claims**"), but dependent claims may be added to limit or additionally specify such independent claims (hereinafter referred to as "dependent claims"). If it is necessary in such cases, other dependent claims may be added to limit or additionally specify such dependent claims (Enforcement Decree of Patent Act Article 5(1)).

는 독립청구항(이하 "**독립항**"이라 한다)을 기재하여야 하며, 그 독립항을 한정하거나 부가하여 구체화하는 종속청구항(이하 "종속항"이라 한다)을 기재할 수 있다. 이 경우 필요한 때에는 그 종속항을 한정하거나 부가하여 구체화하는 다른 종속항을 기재할 수 있다(특허법시행령 제5조 제1항).

indication

Where a trademark right holder, an exclusive licensee, or a non-exclusive licensee uses a registered trademark, he/she may indicate that the relevant trademark is the registered trademark (Trademark Act Article 222).

표시

상표권자 · 전용사용권자 또는 통상사용권자는 등록상표를 사용할 때에 해당 상표가 등록상표임을 표시할 수 있다(상표법 제222조).

indication of design registration

Indication of the fact that the design embodied in a product, its container or package is registered. A design right-holder or an exclusive or non- exclusive licensee may place a mark indicating design registration on products to which the registered design is applied or containers or packaging materials of such products (Design Protection Act Article 214).

디자인등록표시

물품, 물품의 용기나 포장 등에 그 디자인이 디자인등록을 받은 사실을 표시하는 것. 디자인권자 · 전용실시권자 또는 통상실시권자는 등록디자인에 관한 물품 또는 그 물품의 용기나 포장 등에 디자인등록의 표시를 할 수 있다(디자인보호법 제214조).

indirect infringement

In order to enhance effectiveness of relief in case of future infringement on the patent right, an act may be considered as infringement of a patent right under certain circumstances even where an article having all components of invention is not implemented and only the act prior to that stage is performed, in case the article having all components of invention is highly likely to be implemented (Supreme Court Decision, 2007Hu3356, decided September 10, 2009).

간접침해

발명의 모든 구성요소를 가진 물건을 실시한 것이 아니고 그 전 단계에 있는 행위를 하였더라도 발명의 모든 구성요소를 가진 물건을 실시하게 될 개연성이 큰 경우에는 장래의 특허권 침해에 대한 권리 구제의 실효성을 높이기 위하여 일정한 요건 아래 이를 특허권의 침해로 간주하는 것(대법원 2009. 9. 10. 선고 2007후3356 판결 참조).

Example Conducting either of the following activities commercially or industrially shall be **deemed infringement** of a patent or an exclusive license:

1. If the patent is for the invention of a thing: Producing, selling, leasing, or importing a thing used exclusively for producing such thing or offering to sell or lease such thing;

다음 각 호의 구분에 따른 행위를 업으로서 하는 경우에는 특허권 또는 전용실시권을 **침해한 것으로 본다**.

1. 특허가 물건의 발명인 경우: 그 물건의 생산에만 사용하는 물건을 생산 · 양도 · 대여 또는 수입하거나 그 물건의 양도 또는

2. If the patent is for the invention of a process: Producing, selling, leasing, or importing a thing used exclusively for executing the process or offering to sell or lease such thing (Patent Act Article 127).

대여의 청약을 하는 행위
2. 특허가 방법의 발명인 경우: 그 방법의 실시에만 사용하는 물건을 생산 · 양도 · 대여의 청약을 하는 행위(특허법 제127조).

industrial applicability

One of the requirements for patent registration (Patent Act Article 29(1)). Since the ultimate purpose of patent law is to promote industrial development by facilitating technological development (Patent Act Article 1), an invention must have industrial applicability in order to be patented.

산업상 이용가능성

발명이 특허등록이 되기 위한 요건의 하나(특허법 제29조 제1항 본문). 특허법의 궁극적 목적은 기술발전 촉진을 통한 산업발전 이바지이므로(특허법 제1조), 발명이 특허를 받기 위하여는 산업상 이용가능성이 있어야 함.

industrial usability

Industrial usability of a design means that it can be mass-produced by industrial methods; industrial methods refer to manufacturing a useful product by physically or chemically changing the raw material. Mass-production means repeatedly producing a product in the identical form (Supreme Court Decision, 93Hu1247, decided September 9, 1994).

공업상 이용가능성

디자인의 공업상 이용가능성이란 공업적 방법에 의하여 양산될 수 있는 것을 의미하고, 공업적 방법이란 원자재에 물리적, 화학적 변화를 가하여 유용한 물품을 제조하는 것을 말하며, 양산이라 함은 동일한 형태의 물품을 반복적으로 계속해서 생산함을 뜻한다(대법원 1994. 9. 9. 선고 93후1247 판결 참조.

inequitable conduct

A patent applicant engages in inequitable conduct when he or she breaches the duty to proceed with the patent application in good faith and candor.

불공정행위

특허의 출원인이 정직과 신의성실의 의무를 위반하는 것.

informal applications

Incomplete applications. Applications that do not meet the minimum requirements for receipt of a filing date. TMEP § 202.

Example Sometimes an application under §1 or §44 that does not meet the minimum requirements of 37 C.F.R. §2.21 for receipt of a filing date is erroneously referred to an examining attorney for examination. In this situation, if the examining attorney discovers the error before issuing an action in the case, then the examining attorney should have the **application declared informal**. TMEP § 204.03.

미 방식흠결출원

불완전 출원. 즉 출원일자를 받기에 필요한 최소한의 요건을 만족시키지 못한 출원을 가리킴. (미) TMEP § 202.

출원일자를 받기 위한 37 C.F.R. 2.21조의 최소요건을 충족시키지 못하는 1조나 44조하의 상표출원이 심사를 위해 심사관에게 배정될 때가 있다. 이 경우 해당 사건에 대한 통지를 발행하기 전에 오류를 발견한 심사관은 그 출원을 **방식상 흠결**이 있는 것으로 분류하여야 한다. (미) TMEP § 204.03.

I

information and communication networks

정보통신망

information disclosure statement (IDS)

An IDS shall include patents, publications, U.S. applications, or other information submitted for consideration by the USPTO in a nonprovisional patent application filed under§ 111(a) to comply with applicant's duty to submit information which is material to patentability of the claimed invention.

미 정보공개진술서

출원발명의 특허성 판단에 중요한 정보를 제출할 출원인의 의무를 수행하기 위하여 미 특허법 111(a)조 하에 출원된 정규특허 출원에 대한 특허상표청의 검토를 위하여 제출된 특허, 간행물, 미국내 출원 및 기타 정보를 포함하는 문서.

infringement

An act that interferes with the exclusive rights of a patent, copyright, or trademark owner.

침해

특허나 저작권, 상표권자의 배타적 권리를 침범하는 행위.

infringement by equivalents

균등침해

infringement by inducement

Active inducement of direct infringement. Infringement by inducement requires an intent to induce direct infringement of a patent a third party's direct infringement of the patent.

미 유도 침해

특허의 직접침해를 적극적으로 유도하는 행위. 특허권의 직접침해를 유도하려는 고의와 제3자에 의한 특허권의 직접침해를 요함.

infringing invention

No patentee, exclusive licensee, nor non-exclusive licensee shall commercially or industrially execute any patented invention on which he/she has the right to execute, without permission from the patent holder, the holder of a registered utility model, design, or trademark, if the patented invention uses another person's patented invention or registered utility model or design claimed in an application filed prior to the filing date of the patent application for the patented application, or any similar design or infringes another person's registered design or trademark claimed in an application filed prior to the filing date of the patent application for the patented application (Patent Act Article 98).

저촉발명

특허권자 · 전용실시권자 또는 통상실시권자는 특허발명이 그 특허발명의 특허출원일 전에 출원된 타인의 특허발명 · 등록실용신안 또는 등록디자인이나 그 디자인과 유사한 디자인을 이용하거나 특허권이 그 특허발명의 특허출원일 전에 출원된 타인의 디자인권 또는 상표권과 저촉되는 경우에는 그 특허권자 · 실용신안권자 · 디자인권자 또는 상표권자의 허락을 받지 아니하고는 자기의 특허발명을 업으로서 실시할 수 없다(특허법 제98조).

inherency

An invention is anticipated by inherency and thus lacks novelty when a prior art reference anticipated the invention

내재성

하나의 인용선행기술이 출원발명의 특징을 개시하지 않았다 하더라도 그 개시하지 않

without disclosing a feature of the claimed invention, if the missing characteristic is necessarily present in the single anticipating reference. Schering Corp. v. Geneva Pharms., Inc., 339 F.3d 1373 (Fed. Cir. 2003).

은 특징이 그 선행기술에 필수적으로 존재한다면 출원발명은 내재적으로 예견되어 그 신규성이 부정된다. (미) Schering Corp. v. Geneva Pharms., Inc., 339 F.3d 1373 (Fed. Cir. 2003).

inherent distinctiveness

A suggestive, arbitrary or fanciful mark is inherently distinctive and identifies the source of the product.

고유의 식별력

암시적, 임의적 또는 조어인 표장은 고유의 식별력을 가지고 상품의 출처로서 인식될 수 있다.

Example If a proposed product packaging mark is not **inherently distinctive**, the mark may be registered on either the Principal Register under §2(f), upon proof that the mark has acquired distinctiveness or secondary meaning, or on the Supplemental Register. TMEP § 1202.02(b)(ii).

출원된 포장 상표가 **고유의 식별력**이 없다면 사용에 의한 식별력 또는 2차적 의미의 입증으로 2(f)조 하에 주등록부에 등록하거나 혹은 보조등록부에 등록될 수 있다. (미) TMEP § 1202.02(b)(ii).

inherently compulsory joint litigation

A lawsuit that must be jointly filed by all of the co-owners of rights.

고유필수적 공동소송

공유자 전원이 반드시 공동으로 제기하여야만 하는 소송.

Example A litigant may not be added in the middle of a case which is not so-called "**inherently indispensable co-litigation**." In addition, where more than two claimants jointly seek an adjudication on the invalidation of a patent as to the same patent right and thereafter win the adjudication, the litigation for revocation of such adjudication that a patentee will raise cannot be deemed to be an inherently indispensable co-litigation which shall be raised against all claimants. Thus, in this case, the application for adding a litigant which would cause a change of litigant is unlawful and impermissible (Supreme Court Decision, 2007Hu1510, decided May 28, 2009).

이른바 **고유필수적 공동소송**이 아닌 사건에서 소송 도중에 당사자를 추가하는 것은 허용될 수 없고, 동일한 특허권에 관하여 2인 이상의 자가 공동으로 특허의 무효심판을 청구하여 승소한 경우에 그 특허권자가 제기할 심결취소소송은 심판청구인 전원을 상대로 제기하여야만 하는 고유필수적 공동소송이라고 할 수 없으므로, 위 소송에서 당사자의 변경을 가져오는 당사자추가신청은 명목이 어떻든 간에 부적법하여 허용될 수 없다(대법원 2009. 5. 28. 선고 2007후1510 판결 참조).

• indispensable co-litigation (법제처)

initial examination

미 최초심사

Example If, on **initial examination**, the examining attorney finds the mark in an application for registration on the

최초 심사에서 심사관이 주등록부에 등록하기 위한 출원의 표장이 이의신청을 위해

Principal Register to be in condition for publication for opposition, the examining attorney will approve the application for publication. TMEP § 704.01.

공지될 조건을 갖추었다고 판단하면 그 출원을 공지하도록 허가한다. (미) TMEP § 704.01.

injunction

A patentee or an exclusive licensee may file a complaint to seek injunction against, or prevention of, infringement against a person who infringes, or is likely to infringe, his/her rights. A patentee or an exclusive licensee may also demand the destruction of the means by which the infringement has been committed (including the products obtained by infringement if the relevant invention is a process for manufacturing the products), the removal of the facilities used for infringement, and other measures necessary to prevent infringement (Patent Act Article 126).

금지명령

특허권자 또는 전용실시권자는 자기의 권리를 침해한 자 또는 침해할 우려가 있는 자에 대하여 그 침해의 금지 또는 예방을 청구할 수 있고, 침해행위를 조성한 물건(물건을 생산하는 방법의 발명인 경우에는 침해행위로 생긴 물건을 포함한다)의 폐기, 침해행위에 제공된 설비의 제거, 그 밖에 침해의 예방에 필요한 행위를 청구할 수 있음(특허법 제126조).

inspection

Examination of evidence in litigation procedure in which the judge examines the nature and condition of the subject using his or her own sense. If deemed necessary, the Court may conduct verification procedures either upon a party's request or on an ex officio basis (Guideline of Practice and Procedure of Revocation Action in the Patent Court of Korea, VI.2.A).

검증

법관이 직접 자기의 감각에 의하여 대상의 성질 · 상태를 실험하여 하는 증거조사. 재판부는 필요하다고 인정되는 경우 당사자의 신청에 따라 또는 직권으로 검증절차를 진행할 수 있다(특허법원 심결취소소송 심리매뉴얼 Ⅳ.2가).

Intellectual Property Trial and Appeal Board (IPTAB)

특허심판원

intentionally excluded

→ See. deliberately excluded

의식적 제외

intent to use (ITU)

The assignment of an intent-to-use application to someone who is not the successor to the applicant's businessbefore filing an allegation of use renders the application void, and any resulting registration must be cancelled. TMEP § 501.01(a).

미 사용의사

사용의사에 기반한 출원을 출원인의 영업의 승계인이 아닌 자에게 사용사실주장을 제출하기 전에 양도할 경우 그 출원은 무효로 되고, 그 출원으로 인한 등록은 취소되어야 한다. (미) TMEP § 501.01(a).

intent-to-use applications

application filed based on intent to use.

미 사용의사 출원

사용의사에 기한 출원.

interchangeability

One of requirements of infringement by equivalents. The requirement is met when the invention in question, even if by replacement, achieves the same objective and enables a practically identical effect as the patented invention.

치환가능성

특허 균등침해의 요건의 하나. 균등침해가 성립하기 위해서는 치환에 의하더라도 특허발명에서와 같은 목적을 달성할 수 있고 실질적으로 동일한 작용효과를 나타내야 함.

interested parties

Any interested party may pay patent fees, regardless of the wishes of a person liable to pay the patent fees (Patent Act Article 80(1)).

이해관계인

이해관계인은 특허료를 내야 할 자의 의사와 관계없이 특허료를 낼 수 있다(특허법 제80조 제1항).

interference proceeding (trademark)

A proceeding in which the Board determines which, if any, of the owners of conflicting applications (or of one or more applications and one or more registrations which are in conflict), is entitled to registration. The proceeding is declared by the Office only upon petition to the Director showing extraordinary circumstances therefor, that is, that the party who filed the petition would be unduly prejudiced without an interference. TMBP § 102.02.

미 저촉심사 (상표)

다른 출원 또는 등록과 저촉관계에 놓인 출원인이나 다른 출원과 저촉관계에 놓인 등록권자가 등록을 받을 수 있는지 결정하는 TTAB의 절차. 이는 특허상표청장을 상대로 특수한 상황이 존재함, 즉 저촉심사를 하지 아니하면 청구인이 부당한 피해를 입을 것임을 청구를 통해 입증하여야만 가능함. (미) TMBP § 102.02.

Example **Interference** exists when an application is made for the registration of a mark which so resembles a mark previously registered by another, or for the registration of which another has previously made application, as to be likely when used on or in connection with the goods or services of the applicant to cause confusion or mistake or to deceive. 15 U.S.C. § 1066.

저촉심사관계는 출원인의 상품 또는 서비스와 관련하여 사용될 때에는 혼동, 오인 또는 기만행위가 될 염려가 있을 정도로 타인에 의하여 전에 등록되었거나 타인이 전에 등록출원을 한 표장과 거의 유사한 표장의 등록출원을 한 경우에 존재한다. (미) 상표법 제16조.

interference proceeding (patent)

Replaced by derivation proceeding under the AIA. → See. derivation proceeding.

미 저촉절차 (특허)

개정특허법에 의하여 파생절차로 대체됨. → 파생절차 참조

international applicant

A person seeking international registration of intellectual property rights; citizenship of the Republic of Korea, or domicile or place of business in the Republic of Korea is required.

국제출원인

지재권의 국제등록을 받으려는 출원인. 대한민국 국민이거나 대한민국에 주소 (법인인 경우 영업소의 소재지)를 가진 자여야 함.

International Bureau

WIPO International Bureau, in charge of administrative matters relating to international application and registration of patents, trademarks and designs.

국제사무국

특허, 상표, 디자인 등의 국제출원과 등록에 관한 행정적 업무를 담당하는 WIPO 국제사무국.

• International Secretariat (법제처)

International Classification for Industrial Designs

Classification of goods pursuant to the Locarno Agreement Establishing an International Classification for Industrial Designs.

국제디자인분류

산업디자인의 국제분류 제정을 위한 로카르노협정에 따른 물품 분류.

International Convention for the Protection of New Varieties of Plants

This convention was adopted in Paris on December 2, 1961 and came into force on August 10, 1968. It is also called 'UPOV Convention' since the International Union for the Protection of New Varieties of Plants (UPOV) was established by this convention.

식물 신품종 보호에 관한 국제조약

1961년 12월 2일 파리에서 채택, 1968년 8월 10일 발효됨. 이 조약에 기초하여 형성된 동맹(International Union for the Protection of New Varieties of Plants, UPOV)의 약칭으로 일반적으로 'UPOV 조약'이라고도 함.

International Intellectual Property Training Institute

국제지식재산연수원

International Register

The Register which records international registration of designs under the Hague Agreement or trademarks under the Madrid Protocol.

국제등록부

디자인의 경우 헤이그협정에 의한 국제등록 디자인출원, 상표의 경우 마드리드의정서에 의한 국제등록상표출원의 등록사항이 기록되는 등록부.

international registration

to protect domestically registered patent or other IP rights in the territories of other parties to the treaties. Registration of trademark under the Madrid Protocol or registration of design under the Hague agreement, etc.

국제등록

국내의 산업재산권 등을 여러 체약당사자 영역에서 보호받기 위해 등록하는 것을 의미함. 상표법의 경우 마드리드 의정서, 디자인보호법의 경우 헤이그협정 등.

inter partes reexamination

No requests for inter partes reexamination may be filed on or after September 16, 2012. Under the Leahy-Smith

미 당사자계 재심사

2012년 9월 16일 이후로는 당사자계 재심사를 신청할 수 없음. 미 개정특허법으로

America Invents Act (the AIA), the inter partes reexamination is replaced by the new inter partes review process. MPEP § 2601.

당사자계 재심사는 신설된 당사자계심판절차로 대체됨. (미) MPEP § 2601.

inter partes review

A procedure for third parties to seek invalidation of patents.

미 당사자계 심판

제3자가 특허 등의 무효를 청구할 수 있는 심판절차.

Example An **interpartes review** may not be instituted if, before the date on which the petition for such a review is filed, the petitioner or real party in interest filed a civil action challenging the validity of a claim of the patent. Patent Act, 35 U.S.C. § 315(a)(1).

당사자계 심판 청구일 이전에 청구인 또는 실제 이해관계를 가진 당사자가 특허의 무효를 주장하는 민사소송을 제기하였다면 당사자계 심판을 개시하여서는 아니 된다. (미) 특허법 제315(a)(1)조.

interruption

중단

Example Where trademark-related procedures are **interrupted** or suspended, the running of the relevant period shall be suspended and the entire period shall recommence from the time the resumption of the procedures is notified or such procedures are continued (Trademark Act Article 26).

상표에 관한 절차가 **중단**되거나 중지된 경우에는 그 기간의 진행은 정지되고 그 절차의 수계 통지를 하거나 그 절차를 속행한 때부터 전체 기간이 새로 진행된다(상표법 제26조).

intervening rights

Claims that were modified at reissue, for any reason, are subject to a reliance-type interest (intervening rights). Third parties may rely on the claims of an issued patent.

미 중용권

재발행 시 청구항이 수정되었을 경우 신뢰에 기초한 중용권이 발생함. 제3자는 기존 특허의 청구항에 의지할 수 있음.

intervention

A third party or administrative agency that has an interest in matters at issue joining the lawsuit.

참가

이해관계가 있는 제3자 또는 행정청이 당해 사건에 참가하는 것

intrinsic evidence

Specification, drawings and documents relating to the procedural history of the application, as used for claim construction.

내적 증거

청구범위 해석을 위해 사용되는 그 출원의 명세서, 도면, 출원경과서류.

invalidation

To retroactively void any effect of validly established IP registration due to statutory grounds through trial proceedings.

등록무효, 무효처분

일단 유효하게 성립된 산업재산권등을 일정한 법정사유로 인하여 심판절차에 의해 등록일로 소급하여 그 효력을 상실시키는 것.

invention

발명

Highly advanced creation of a technical idea utilizing the laws of nature.

자연법칙을 이용한 기술적 사상의 창작으로서 고도한 것.

invention at issue

이 사건 발명

invention of a process of manufactoring a thing

물건을 생산하는 방법의 발명

A type of invention recognized by the Patent Act together with 'invention of a thing' and 'invention of a process.'

물건의 발명, 방법의 발명과 함께 특허법상 인정되는 발명의 유형 중 하나.

Example An **invention of a process of manufacturing a thing**: Using, selling, leasing, or importing a thing manufactured by the process or offering to sell or lease such thing, other than the activities specified in item (b) (Patent Act Article 2).

물건을 생산하는 방법의 발명인 경우: 나목의 행위 외에 그 방법에 의하여 생산한 물건을 사용 · 양도 · 대여 또는 수입하거나 그 물건의 양도 또는 대여의 청약을 하는 행위(특허법 제2조).

invention of a thing

물건의 발명

A type of invention recognized by the Patent Act together with 'invention of a process' and 'invention of a process of manufacturing a thing.'

방법의 발명, 물건을 생산하는 방법의 발명과 함께 특허법상 인정되는 발명의 유형 중 하나.

Example An **invention of a thing**: Manufacturing, using, selling, leasing, importing the thing or offering to sell or lease the thing (including displaying a thing for the purpose of sale or lease; hereinafter the same shall apply) (Patent Act Article 2)

물건의 발명인 경우: 그 물건을 생산 · 사용 · 양도 · 대여 또는 수입하거나 그 물건의 양도 또는 대여의 청약(양도 또는 대여를 위한 전시를 포함한다. 이하 같다)을 하는 행위(특허법 제2조).

inventions necessary for national defence

국방상 필요한 발명

If necessary for national defence, the government may prohibit filing a patent application with a foreign patent office or order the inventer etc. to keep the invention confidential. Patent Act Article 41(1). When the invention is necessary for national defence, the government may also refuse to grant patent or expropriate the entitlement to patent (Patent Act Article 41(2)).

정부는 국방상 필요한 경우 외국에 특허출원하는 것을 금지하거나 발명자 등에게 특허출원의 발명을 비밀취급하도록 명할 수 있으며(특허법 제41조 제1항), 특허출원된 발명에 대하여 특허를 허여 하지 않거나 특허를 받을 수 있는 권리를 수용할 수 있음(특허법 제41조 제2항).

inventive step

진보성

One of the requirements for patent registration (Patent Act

특허요건의 하나(특허법 제29조 제2항). 특

Article 29(2)). An invention is not patentable if a person skilled in the art would have come up with the invention at issue based on prior arts before the filing of the application.

허출원 전에 통상의 기술자가 선행발명에 의하여 쉽게 발명할 수 있는 발명에 해당하는 경우 특허를 받을 수 없음.

inventor

발명자

inventor-initiated disclosure

An invention publicly known prior to the filing of a patent application shall not be patented in principle (Patent Act Article 29(1)). However, novelty is not denied if certain requirements are met, such as an exceptional case when the inventor initiated the disclosure (Patent Act Article 30(1)1), or the disclosure was against the inventor's will (Patent Act Article 30(1)2).

자기공지

특허출원 전에 발명이 공개된 경우 원칙적으로 신규성 요건이 부정되어 특허를 받을 수 없으나(특허법 제29조 제1항), 자기공지의 예외에 해당하거나(특허법 제30조 제1항 제1호) 의사에 반한 공지(제30조 제1항 제2호) 등의 경우에는 일정한 요건 하에 신규성이 부정되지 아니함.

inventorship

발명주체

investigation officer

조사관

IPTAB trial

→ See. administrative trial.

심판

irreparable harm

A harm that cannot be corrected by monetary compensation. One of the factors in granting preliminary injunctive relief in case of infringement.

회복할 수 없는 손해

금전적 배상으로 회복할 수 없는 손해. 침해로 인한 잠정적 금지명령 시 판단근거가 되는 요소 중 하나.

issue

The subject matter in dispute between parties, factual or legal.

쟁점

당사자에게 다툼이 있는 사항 즉, 사실상 또는 법률상 쟁점.

issue date

The date that a patent application becomes a patent. The issue date is the date from which patent rights can be exercised.

미 발행일

특허출원이 특허가 되는 날. 발행일은 곧 특허권 행사를 시작할 수 있는 날임.

Jepson type claim

A claim written in Jepson format, divided into the preamble and the body. The preamble may be construed as a limitation on the technical field of the invention, limitation on the product to which the technology of the invention is applied, or exclusion from the sought protection as it is deemed publicly known. The body is the technical characteristics of the claimed invention for which protection is sought in combination with the preamble.

젭슨 타입 청구항

전제부와 특징부로 나뉘어 기재하는 젭슨 타입으로 기재된 청구항. 이 경우 전제부는 발명의 기술분야를 한정하는 경우, 발명의 기술이 적용되는 대상물품을 한정하는 경우, 공지의 기술로 생각하여 권리의 보호범위에서 제외하는 경우 등 여러 가지로 해석이 가능함. 특징부는 전제부와 조합하여 보호하고자 하는 그 발명의 기술적 특징을 가리킴.

joinder of petition for trial

A type of procedure that applies when 2 or more persons file petition for invalidation or confirmation of scope of rights for identical patent or other rights (Patent Act Article 139(1)).

공동심판청구

동일한 권리에 대하여 2인 이상이 무효심판청구 또는 권리범위확인심판청구를 같이 하는 경우 적용될 수 있는 심판청구 형태 (특허법 제139조 제1항).

• joint filing (법제처)

joint applicants

공동출원인

Example An application by **joint applicants** must be verified by all the applicants, since they are individual parties and not a single entity. TMEP § 803.03(d).

공동출원인은 하나의 단체가 아닌 개별당사자이므로 공동출원인에 의한 출원은 모든 출원인에 의해 확인되어야 한다. (미) TMEP § 803.03(d).

joint inventor

The terms 'joint inventor' and 'coinventor' mean any 1 of the individuals who invented the subject matter of a joint invention. If at least two persons jointly make an invention, they are jointly entitled to a patent thereon (Patent Act Article 33(2)).

공동발명자

공동발명자란 공동 발명의 대상을 발명한 자들 중 어느 1인을 의미함. 2명 이상이 공동으로 발명한 경우에는 특허를 받을 수 있는 권리를 공유한다(특허법 제33조 제2항).

joint ownership

IP rights is jointly owned when it is owned by two or more persons. Each owner has the ownership in its entirety.

공유

하나의 산업재산권등에 관한 권리를 2인 이상이 소유하는 형태를 말하며, 권리 전체에 대하여 각각의 지분별로 소유함.

Example (Transfer and **Joint Ownership** of Patents) (3)

(특허권의 이전 및 **공유** 등) ③ 특허권이 공

Except as otherwise agreed in writing, no joint owner of a patent may independently execute the patented invention without the consent of all other joint owners. (4) If a patent is jointly owned, no joint owner of the patent may grant an exclusive or non-exclusive license of the patent, without the consent of all other joint owners (Patent Act Article 99).

유인 경우에는 각 공유자는 계약으로 특별히 약정한 경우를 제외하고는 다른 공유자의 동의를 받지 아니하고 그 특허발명을 자신이 실시할 수 있다. ④ 특허권이 공유인 경우에는 각 공유자는 다른 공유자 모두의 동의를 받아야만 그 특허권에 대하여 전용실시권을 설정하거나 통상실시권을 허락할 수 있다(특허법 제99조).

joint penal provision

양벌규정

Provisions that attach liability to the principal or the corporation for certain unlawful acts of its agent, representative or employee in relation to the business of the principal or the corporation, along with the wrongdoer themselves.

법인의 대표자나 법인 또는 개인의 대리인 · 사용인 기타 종업원이, 업무에 관하여 일정한 위법행위를 하였을 경우에, 현실의 행위자를 처벌하는 이외에도 그 사업주체인 법인 또는 개인도 처벌하는 규정.

joint research agreement

공동연구협약

A written contract, grant, or cooperative agreement entered into by 2 or more persons or entities for the performance of experimental, developmental, or research work in the field of the claimed invention. Patent Act, 35 U.S.C. § 100 (h).

출원발명 분야에서의 실험, 개발, 연구 수행을 위하여 2인 이상 혹은 2개 이상의 단체가 맺는 서면 계약, 지원금, 협력계약. (미) 특허법 100(h)조.

judge sitting by designation

수탁판사

→ See entrusted judge

judge to be in charge

수명법관

→ See. the commissioned judge

judgment

(판결)주문

judicial research officer

조사관

junior party

미 후순위권리자

A party other than the senior party in an interference proceeding. A junior party bears the burden of proof to show that he or she is the first inventor.

저촉심사에서 선순위 권리자가 아닌자. 후순위권리자는 본인이 최초 발명자임을 입증할 책임을 진다.

Jurisdiction

관할

→ See. Personal jurisdiction, subject matter jurisdiction.

jury trial | **배심재판**

Justifiable reason | **정당한 이유**
→ See. good cause.

K

(publicly) known art | **공지기술**
An art or technology already publicly known to a person having ordinary skills in the art.
해당 기술분야에서 통상의 기술자에게 이미 알려져 있는 기술.

Korean Intellectual Property Office (KIPO) | **특허청**

L

lack of sufficient description | **기재불비**
Distinguished from an incomplete invention, in the case of deficiency of description requirement, an invention is complete at the filing but fails to make a description regularly. Claims shall satisfy the requirements: 1. The invention shall be supported by the description; 2. The invention shall be clearly and concisely described (Patent Act Article 42(4)).
특허를 받을 수 없는 불완전한 발명과는 달리, 발명이 완성되었으나 출원시에 기재요건을 만족하지 못한 것. 특허청구항은 1. 발명의 설명에 의하여 뒷받침될 것, 2. 발명이 명확하고 간결하게 적혀 있을 것 등의 기재요건을 갖추어야 한다(특허법 제42조 제4항).

lack of written description | **기재불비**
→ See. lack of sufficient description.

Lanham Act | 미 **미 상표법**

laudatory terms (mark) | 미 **칭송형(稱頌型) 용어(표장)**
Terms that attribute quality or excellence to goods or services. Laudatory terms are merely descriptive under §2(e)(1). TMEP § 1209.03(k).
상품 또는 서비스의 품질이나 우수성을 나타내는 단어. 칭송형 용어는 미 상표법 2(e)(1)조의 단순기술표장으로 분류됨. (미) TMEP § 1209.03(k).

Example **Laudatory marks** that describe the alleged merit of the goods are descriptive because they simply describe the characteristics or quality of the goods in a condensed form. … Accordingly, substantial evidence supports the Board's finding that consumers will immediately regard THE ULTIMATE BIKE RACK as a laudatory descriptive phrase that touts the superiority of Nett Designs' bike racks. In re Nett Designs, Inc., 236 F.3d 1339, 1342 (Fed. Cir. 2001).

상품이 가지고 있는 것으로 주장하는 이점을 묘사하는 **칭송형 표장**은 단순히 압축적으로 그 상품의 성질이나 품질을 묘사하는 것이므로 기술적 표장이다. … 따라서, 소비자들이 즉각적으로 THE ULTIMATE BIKE RACK을 Nett Designs의 자전거 거치대의 우수성을 드러내는 찬사적 및 기술적인 문구로 간주할 것이라는 TTAB의 결정을 뒷받침하는 상당한 증거가 존재한다. In re Nett Designs, Inc., 236 F.3d 1339, 1342 (Fed. Cir. 2001).

law of nature

A requirement for patentable 'invention.' In order to be patentable, an 'invention' shall be highly advanced creation of a technical idea utilizing the laws of nature (Patent Act Article 2.1).

자연법칙

특허의 대상이 되는 '발명'에 해당하기 위한 요건. 특허를 받을 수 있는 '발명'에 해당하기 위하여는 자연법칙을 이용한 기술적 사상의 창작으로서 고도한 것이어야 함(특허법 제2조 제1호).

legal capacity

Capacity to have legal rights or legal obligations.
The capacity to act by oneself so as to bring about changes in one's rights or obligations.

권리능력, 행위능력

법적 권리의무의 주체가 될 수 있는 능력.
자기의 권리 · 의무에 변동이 일어나도록 스스로 행위할 수 있는 능력.

Example Procedures followed by a person who has no **legal capacity** or authority of legal representation, or who has any defect in the delegation of authority necessary to follow trademark-related procedures shall take effect retroactive to the time he/she performed an act if the party whose defect has been rectified or his/her legal representative confirms such procedures (Trademark Act Article 9).

행위능력 또는 법정대리권이 없거나 상표에 관한 절차를 밟는 데 필요한 권한의 위임에 흠이 있는 자가 밟은 절차는 보정(補正)된 당사자나 법정대리인이 추인(追認)하면 행위를 한 때로 소급하여 그 효력이 발생한다(상표법 제9조).

legal fiction as public officials

Example (Executives and Employees of Specialized Agencies, etc. **Deemed Public Officials**) Any current or former executive or employee of a specialized agency designated under Article 58 (1), or an agency for digitization of patent documents shall be deemed a current or former employee of the Korean Intellectual Property Office or the Korean Intellectual Property Trial and Appeal Board for

공무원 의제

(전문기관 등의 임직원에 대한 **공무원 의제**) 제58조 제1항에 따른 전문기관 또는 특허문서 전자화기관의 임직원이거나 임직원이었던 사람은 제226조를 적용하는 경우에는 특허청 소속 직원 또는 직원이었던 사람으로 본다(특허법 제226조의2).

the purposes of adjudicating the offence of divulging secrets or confidential information. (Patent Act Article 226-2).

legal guardian

후견감독인

legally binding force

기속력

A court or administrative agency is bound by a prior decision or action and may not revoke or remand the decision or action.

법원이나 행정기관이 재판이나 처분에 구속되어 이를 취소하거나 변경할 수 없는 효력.

Example Meanwhile, the adjudication on the scope of patent right is a procedure with the limited purpose of confirming whether the cited invention is within the objective scope of the patent right's effectiveness. It is by no means a procedure for confirming or deciding the rights relationship, such as the existence of the right to claim for injunction on infringement or the right to claim damages; nor does its determination carry any **legally binding force** over patent infringement lawsuits or patent invalidation adjudications (Supreme Court Decision 99Da59320, decided January 11, 2002).

한편 특허권의 권리범위확인심판은 확인대상발명이 특허권의 효력이 미치는 객관적인 범위에 속하는지 여부를 확인하는 제한적 목적을 가진 절차일 뿐 침해금지청구권이나 손해배상청구권의 존부와 같은 권리관계까지 확인하거나 확정하는 절차가 아니고, 권리범위확인심판에서의 판단이 특허권침해소송이나 특허무효심판에 **기속력**을 미치는 것도 아니다(대법원 2002. 1. 11. 선고 99다59320 판결 참조).

letter trademark

문자상표

level of obviousness of replacement

치환자명성

One of the requirements of infringement by equivalents. The requirement is met if the replacement is self-evident to the extent that any person of ordinary skill in the pertinent field of technology could have easily conceived it.

특허 균등침해의 요건의 하나. 균등침해가 성립하기 위하여는 그와 같이 치환하는 것을 그 발명이 속하는 분야에서 통상의 지식을 가진 자가 용이하게 생각해 낼 수 있을 정도로 자명해야 한다는 것.

Example An invention in question falls under the scope of the patent right of a patented invention only when each element and the whole combination of its components as specified within the scope of the patent claim for the patented invention are intact within the invention in question. Even in cases where an invention in question contains portions which replace or substitute elements included in the scope of a patent claim for a patented invention, if both inventions share the same solution principle, if such a replacement still makes it possible to achieve the goal of the patented

확인대상발명이 특허발명의 권리범위에 속한다고 할 수 있기 위해서는 특허발명의 청구범위에 기재된 각 구성요소와 그 구성요소 간의 유기적 결합관계가 확인대상발명에 그대로 포함되어 있어야 한다. 한편, 확인대상발명에서 특허발명의 청구범위에 기재된 구성 중 치환 내지 변경된 부분이 있는 경우에도, 양 발명에서 과제의 해결원리가 동일하고, 그러한 치환에 의하더라도 특허발명에서와 같은 목적을 달성할 수 있고 실질적으로 동일한 작용효과를 나타내며,

invention and enables an identical effect on an actual level, and **if this replacement is self-evident to the extent that any person of ordinary skill in the pertinent field of technology could have easily conceived it**, then the invention in question must be seen as **equivalent** in whole to the elements specified in the scope of the patent claim for a patented invention (Supreme Court Decision, 2010Hu296, decided May 27, 2010).

그와 같이 치환하는 것이 그 발명이 속하는 기술분야에서 통상의 지식을 가진 사람이라면 누구나 용이하게 생각해 낼 수 있는 정도로 자명하다면 확인대상발명은 전체적으로 특허발명의 청구범위에 기재된 구성과 균등한 것으로서 여전히 특허발명의 권리범위에 속한다고 보아야 한다(대법원 2010. 5. 27. 선고 2010후296 판결 참조).

license

실시권

Right to execute an industrial property right. A license may either be exclusive or non-exclusive.

산업재산권을 실시할 수 있는 권리. 전용실시권과 통상실시권으로 구분됨.

Example A patentee may grant a non-exclusive **license** of the patent to others (Patent Act Article 102(1).

특허권자는 그 특허권에 대하여 타인에게 통상**실시권**을 허락할 수 있다(특허법 제102조 제1항).

likelihood of confusion

혼동가능성

a statutory basis (Trademark Act Section 2(d), 15 U.S.C. Section 1052(d), TMEP § §1207 et seq.) for refusing registration of a trademark or service mark because it is likely to conflict with a mark or marks already registered or pending before the USPTO. USPTO.

법률에 규정된 상표나 서비스표의 등록거절이유. 이미 등록되었거나 특허상표청에 계류중인 상표와 혼동을 일으킬 가능성이 있으므로 거절하는 것.(미)

Example The test of **likelihood of confusion** is not whether the marks can be distinguished when subjected to a side-by-side comparison, but whether the marks are sufficiently similar that there is a **likelihood of confusion** as to the source of the goods or services. TMEP § 1207.01(b).

혼동가능성의 판단은 그 표장이 대비적 관찰을 하였을 때 식별가능한지가 아닌 그 상품 또는 서비스의 출처에 있어 **혼동을 일으킬 수 있을 만큼** 충분히 유사하다 할 것인지를 기준으로 한다. (미) TMEP § 1207.01(b).

Example 1. In the case of a mark combining a dimensional shape with a device or word, if the dimensional shape lacks distinctiveness but the word is distinctive, the non-distinctive dimensional shape cannot function as a source identifier, and thus, there is no **likelihood of confusion** arising with respect to the goods having a similar dimensional shape. It appears that the consumers can easily recognize whose goods the mark identifies by the distinctive word (Patent Court Decision, 2014Heo2344, decided on September 19, 2014).

1. 입체적 형상과 기호 · 문자 등이 결합된 상표에서 입체적 형상에는 식별력이 없고 문자 등에 식별력 있는 경우, 식별력이 없는 입체적 형상은 출처표시기능을 할 수 없으므로, 그와 유사한 입체적 형상의 상품간의 관계에서 출처의 **혼동 우려**가 없다. 수요자들은 식별력이 있는 문자 등으로부터 누구의 업무에 관련된 상품을 표시하는 것인가를 어렵지 않게 인식할 수 있을 것으로 보인다(특허법원 2014. 9. 19. 선고 2014허2344)

linking claim

미 연결청구항

Linking claims and the inventions they link together are usually either all directed to products or all directed to processes (i.e., a product claim linking properly divisible product inventions, or a process claim linking properly divisible process inventions). MPEP § 809.

연결청구항과 그 청구항이 연결하는 발명들은 대개 제품만에 대한 것이거나 방법만에 대한 것(즉 분할 가능한 제품발명을 연결한 제품 청구항 또는 분할가능한 방법발명을 연결한 방법 청구항)이다. (미) MPEP § 809.

liquidation

청산

literal infringement

문언침해

The most basic type of infringement, which is established when, literally interpreted, the accused device uses all elements of the patented invention.

청구범위의 문언해석에 의하여 당해 특허의 구성요소를 모두 사용하는 경우에 성립하는 침해로서, 가장 기본적인 침해유형.

literal interpretation

문언해석

A patent claim shall be interpreted based on the general, objective meaning of the expression of the word in the claim, and how persons skilled in the art would interpret the word. The protection scope of a patented invention is decided by what is written in the claim, therefore a matter included in detailed description or drawing is excluded from protection if it is not disclosed in the claim.

청구범위를 해석함에 있어서 청구범위에 표현된 문언이 일반적, 객관적으로 어떠한 의미를 나타내는지 해당 기술분야의 통상의 기술자를 기준으로 해석한다는 것. 특허발명은 청구범위에 '기재된' 사항에 의하여 보호범위가 결정되므로 발명의 설명이나 도면에 나타난 것이라도 청구범위에 기재되지 않은 사항은 원칙적으로 보호범위에서 제외됨.

Locarno Agreement

로카르노협정

Locarno Agreement Establishing an International Classification for Industrial Designs. The Locarno Agreement establishes a classification for industrial designs (the Locarno Classification). The competent offices of the Contracting States must indicate in official documents reflecting the deposit or registration of industrial designs the numbers of the classes and subclasses of the Classification to which the goods incorporating the designs belong. WIPO.

디자인의 국제분류에 관한 로카르노협정. 산업디자인 분류법인 로카르노 분류체계를 정립함. 회원국의 산업디자인 담당기관은 각 디자인의 기탁 또는 등록에 관련된 공문서에 로카르노분류 하에서 그 상품이 속하는 분류 및 세분류의 번호를 표시하여야 함. WIPO.

long-felt need

장기간의 필요성

Long-felt need is established when an art recognized problem existed in the art for a long period of time without solution.

그 발명이 속하는 기술 분야에서 오랫동안 그 과제의 존재를 인지하고 있었으나 해결하지 못한 경우 장기간의 필요성이 인정됨.

lost profit

The profit that an infringed party would have made had it not been for the infringement.

일실이익

침해가 없었더라면 그로 인한 피해를 입은 당사자가 얻을 수 있었을 이익.

M

machine-or-transformation test

A test on patent eligibility that requires a claim to a process invention to be implemented by a particular machine in a non-conventional and non-trivial manner or transforms an article from one state to another.

미 장치-변환 테스트

방법발명에 대한 청구항의 내용이 특정한 기계에 전형적이거나 사소하지 않은 방식으로 구현되었거나 물품의 상태를 변형시키는 것일 때 특허적격성을 지닌다고 보는 판단기준.

Madrid Agreement Concerning the International Registration of Marks

The Madrid Agreement governs the Madrid System along with the Madrid Protocol. The Madrid System allows trademark owners to file a single application with the International Bureau (through the office of the home country), in one language (English, French or Spanish) and paying one set of fees for international registration and enjoy protection of their rights in each of the designated contracting parties. WIPO.

상표의 국제등록에 관한 마드리드 협정

마드리드협정은 마드리드의정서와 함께 마드리드시스템을 주관함. 마드리드시스템 하에서 상표권자는 자국의 상표청을 통해 국제사무국에 일괄적으로 수수료를 지불하고 하나의 언어(영어 또는 프랑스어, 스페인어)로 된 단일한 출원을 신청함으로써 국제등록을 통해 지정한 회원국 각각에서 그 상표를 보호받을 수 있음.

Madrid Agreement for the Repression of False or Deceptive Indications of Source on Goods

According to this Agreement, all goods bearing a false or deceptive indication of source, by which one of the Contracting States, or a place situated therein, is directly or indirectly indicated as being the country or place of origin, must be seized on importation, or such importation must be prohibited, or other actions and sanctions must be applied in connection with such importation. WIPO.

상품의 허위 또는 기만표시 억제를 위한 마드리드협정

허위로 혹은 기만적으로 회원국이나 그 회원국 내의 장소를 원산국이나 원산지로 출처를 표시하는 상품은 수입시 압류하거나 수입을 금지하거나 기타 수입과 관련한 조치 및 제재를 받도록 하는 협정. WIPO.

Madrid Protocol

The "Protocol Relating to the Madrid Agreement Concerning the International Registration of Marks" (Madrid Protocol).

마드리드 의정서

표장의 국제등록에 관한 마드리드협정에 대한 의정서. 상표권자로 하여금 '국제출원'

An international treaty that allows a trademark owner to seek registration in any of the countries that have joined the Madrid Protocol by filing a single application, called an "international application."

이라 불리는 단일출원을 함으로써 마드리드 의정서에 가입한 체약국 어디에서나 그 상표를 등록할 수 있도록 하는 조약.

maintenance fees

등록유지료

malpractice

배임행위

Manual of Patent Examining Procedure (MPEP)

미 특허심사지침

manufacture

제조물

Example Whoever invents or discovers any new and useful process, machine, **manufacture**, or composition of matter, or any new and useful improvement thereof, may obtain a patent therefor, subject to the conditions and requirements of this title. Patent Act, 35 U.S.C. § 101.

새롭고 유용한 방법, 기계장치, **제조물**, 조성물, 또는 이들에 대한 새롭고 유용한 개량을 한 자는 법정 조건 및 요건이 적용되는 경우를 예외로 하고 누구든지 특허를 받을 수 있다. (미) 특허법 101조.

mark

All indications used to identify the source of goods, irrespective of the composition or methods of the expression thereof, which include any sign, letter, figure, sound, smell, three-dimensional shape, hologram, movement, color, etc. (Trademark Act Article 2(1)2).

표장

기호, 문자, 도형, 소리, 냄새, 입체적 형상, 홀로그램 · 동작 또는 색채 등으로서 그 구성이나 표현방식에 상관없이 상품의 출처(출처)를 나타내기 위하여 사용하는 모든 표시(상표법 제2조 제1항 제2호).

marketplace

A marketplace in which goods or services are traded.

거래사회

상품, 서비스 등의 거래가 발생하는 시장을 의미함.

Example There is no evidence that the mark at issue as a whole is commonly used in slogans or advertising phrases in the **marketplace**, nor is there any data that ordinary consumers would perceive as such (Patent Court Decision, 2015Heo3993, decided February 3, 2016).

이 사건 출원상표 · 서비스표가 전체로서 **거래사회**에서 흔히 구호나 광고 문안으로 사용되는 점에 대한 증거가 없고, 일반 수요자가 그와 같이 인식하리라고 볼만한 자료도 없다(특허법원 2016.2.3 선고 2015허3993판결 참조).

- trading society (법제처)

marking of protected plant variety

The holder of a plant variety right, exclusive license holder or non-exclusive license holder may label the relevant plant variety as a protected plant variety (Act on Protection of New Varieties of Plants Article 88).

보호품종의 표시

품종보호권자 · 전용실시권자 또는 통상실시권자는 해당 품종이 보호품종임을 표시할 수 있다(식물신품종보호법 제88조).

Markman hearing

A district-court level pretrial hearing held for the purpose of claim construction based on intrinsic and extrinsic evidence. Also known as a claim construction hearing.

미 마크맨 심리

1심 단계에서 내적 증거 및 외부증거를 고려하여 청구항을 해석하기 위한 변론전 심리. 청구항 해석 심리라고도 함.

M

Markush type claim

A Markush-type claim recites alternatives in a format such as "selected from the group consisting of A, B and C." Ex parte Markush, 1925 C.D. 126 (Comm'r Pat. 1925).

마쿠쉬 청구항

마쿠쉬 청구항이란 대안적인 형태로서 'A, B, C로 구성된 그룹에서 선택된'과 같은 형태를 의미함. (미) Ex parte Markush, 1925 C.D. 126 (Comm'r Pat. 1925).

Example The members of the Markush group (A, B, and C in the example above) ordinarily must belong to a recognized physical or chemical class or to an art-recognized class. However, when the Markush group occurs in a claim reciting a process or a combination (not a single compound), it is sufficient if the members of the group are disclosed in the specification to possess at least one property in common which is mainly responsible for their function in the claimed relationship, and it is clear from their very nature or from the prior art that all of them possess this property. MPEP § 2173.05(h).

마쿠쉬 그룹(위 예의 A. B, C)는 일반적으로 알려진 물리적 또는 화학적 집단 또는 기술집단에 속해야 한다. 그러나 마쿠쉬 그룹이 방법항이나 조성물 발명 청구항에 사용되는 경우에는(즉, 단일한 화합물로 구성되지 않은 경우에는), 그 그룹의 구성원들이 청구된 관계에서의 기능을 하기 위한 적어도 하나의 기능을 보유하는 것으로 명세서에 개시되어 있고, 그것들의 성질 또는 선행기술에 비추어 구성원 모두가 그 성질을 갖고 있음이 명백하면 충분하다. (미) MPEP 2173.05(h).

material alteration

요지의 변경

Example As a general rule, the addition of any element that would require a further search will constitute a **material alteration**. However, while the question of whether a new search would be required is a factor to be considered in deciding whether an amendment would materially alter a mark, it is not necessarily the determining factor. TMEP § 807.14.

일반적으로 추가 검색이 필요한 구성요소의 부가는 **요지의 변경**에 해당한다. 그러나 새로운 검색이 필요한지가 중대한 변경의 존부 결정에 고려해야 할 요소이기는 하나 반드시 결정적 요소인 것은 아니다. (미) TMEP § 807.14.

means plus function claim
→ See. functional claim.

기능식청구항

means to solve the problem
→ See. solution principles.

과제해결원리

mediation

조정

mediation judge
In principle, the mediation judge shall be in charge of cases referred to an early mediation proceeding. Upon discussions with the parties, the mediation judge may conduct mediation proceedings at suitable locations other than the Court (Guideline of Civil Practice and Procedure of the Patent Court of Korea, VI.1.B).

조정전담판사
조기조정 절차에 회부된 사건은 원칙적으로 조정전담판사가 담당한다. 조정담당판사는 당사자와 협의하여 법원 외의 적당한 장소에서 조정절차를 진행할 수 있다(특허법원 침해소송 항소심 심리매뉴얼 VI.1.나).

medical practice

Example Meanwhile, inventions concerning **medical practices**, such as diagnosis, alleviation, therapy, and treatment of human disease, are excluded from patentability (Supreme Court Decision, 90Hu250, decided Mar. 12, 1991).

의료행위

한편, 사람의 질병을 진단 · 경감 · 치료 · 처치하고 예방하거나 건강을 증진하는 등의 **의료행위**에 관한 발명은 특허의 대상에서 제외되므로 … (대법원 1991. 3. 12. 선고 90후250 판결 참조).

medical usage

의약용도

merely descriptive mark
A mark is considered merely descriptive if it describes an ingredient, quality, characteristic, function, feature, purpose or use of the specified goods or services.

Example If a mark consists of a merely descriptive universal symbol and other descriptive, generic, or otherwise non-source-indicating matter, then the mark is **merely descriptive** in its entirety and the examining attorney must issue a refusal under §2(e)(1). TMEP § 1202.17(d)(i).

미 단순 기술표장
특정 상품이나 서비스의 성분이나 품질, 성격, 기능, 특성, 목적이나 용도를 설명하는 표장은 단순기술표장으로 봄.

단순히 기술적인 보편적 기호와 다른 기술적이거나 보통명칭, 기타 출처표시기능이 없는 사항으로 구성된 표장은 전체적으로 **단순기술표장**에 해당하고 심사관은 이에 대해 상표법 2(e)(1)에 따라 거절결정을 하여야 한다. (미) TMEP § 1202.17(d)(i).

method claim
→ See. process claim.

방법청구항

Ministry of Food and Drug Safety

식품의약품안전처

misappropriation

The act of using registered IP rights without lawful authority to do so.

도용

타인의 산업재산권등을 무단으로 사용하는 행위.

Example Any employee of the Korean Intellectual Property Office or the Intellectual Property Trial and Appeal Board that divulges or misappropriates confidential information which becomes known to him/her about a design claimed in a pending application for design registration (including designs claimed in a pending application for international design registration, for which a request for deferment has been filed under Article 11 of the Hague Agreement) in the course of performing his/her duties shall be punished by imprisonment with labor for not more than five years or by a fine not exceeding 50 million won (Design Protection Act Article 225(1)).

특허청 또는 특허심판원 직원이나 그 직원으로 재직하였던 사람이 디자인등록출원 중인 디자인(헤이그협정 제11조에 따라 연기 신청된 국제디자인등록출원 중인 디자인을 포함한다)에 관하여 직무상 알게 된 비밀을 누설하거나 **도용**한 경우에는 5년 이하의 징역 또는 5천만원 이하의 벌금에 처한다(디자인보호법 제225조 제1항).

mistake and confusion as to the source

When a trademark owner or licensee changes, modifies, limits or expands a part or parts of the registered trademark and thereby causing misconception or confusion with other person's trademark.

출처의 오인(혼동)

사용권자가 등록상표 구성의 일부를 변경, 가감, 축소, 확대하여 변형 사용함으로써 타인이 사용하는 상표와 오인 또는 혼동을 일으키는 경우를 의미함.

Example When a trademark owner uses a prior used trademark that is same or similar to a subject trademark while being fully aware of the latter's existence - which will likely result in **mistake or confusion** - and thus had the intent of trademark abuse. Additionally, if the subject trademark is widely recognized and well-known, it is assumed that the aforementioned intent existed; provided that there were no unique circumstances, such as the trademark owner being unaware of the subject trademark or the products it marks (Supreme Court Decision, 2012Hu2227, decided October 11, 2012).

상표권자가 **오인·혼동**을 일으킬 만한 대상상표의 존재를 알면서 그 대상상표와 동일·유사한 실사용상표를 사용하면 상표부정사용의 고의가 있다 할 것이고, 특히 그 대상상표가 주지·저명 상표인 경우에는 그 대상상표나 그 표장상품의 존재를 인식하지 못하였다는 등의 특별한 사정이 없는 한 고의의 존재를 추정할 수 있다(대법원 2012. 10. 11. 선고 2012후2227판결 참조).

mistake as to the quality of goods

품질오인

Example Notwithstanding Article 33, none of the following trademarks shall be registered: … 12. Any trademark which

제33조에도 불구하고 다음 각 호의 어느 하나에 해당하는 상표에 대해서는 상표등록

M

is likely to **mislead** consumers about the **quality** of goods or deceive consumers (Trademark Act Article 34(1)).

을 받을 수 없다. … 12. 상품의 **품질을 오인**하게 하거나 수요자를 기만할 염려가 있는 상표(상표법 제34조 제1항).

• mislead consumers about the quality of goods (법제처)

model designations

Model designations appear in connection with a wide variety of products to identify a specific style, type, or design of a product within a particular line of goods, or to distinguish between different types of automobile parts within a single product line. TMEP § 1202.16.

미 모델 표시

모델 표시는 다양한 상품에 대해 특정한 스타일이나 타입, 특정 제품라인 내의 상품의 디자인을 특정하기 위해서나 동일한 생산라인의 다른 자동차 부품 타입을 구별하기 위해 사용됨. (미) TMEP § 1202.16.

modification of the application

Making procedural modification to an application while maintaining the identity of the applicant or the substance. E.g. modifying a patent application into a utility model application.

출원변경

출원의 주체나 내용의 동일성을 유지하면서 출원의 형식만을 변경하는 것. 예를 들어 특허출원을 실용신안등록출원으로 변경하는 것.

motion for judgment as a matter of law (JMOL)

A party's request that the court enter a judgment in its favor before the case is submitted to the jury or after a contrary jury verdict on the ground that there is no legally sufficient evidence on which a jury could find for the other party.

미 법적판결신청

배심원의 숙고 이전 혹은 신청인이 패소하여야 한다고 본 배심원 평결 이후 상대방에게 승소평결을 내릴 만큼 법적으로 충분한 증거가 없었음을 근거로 재판부가 승소판결을 내려줄 것을 요청하는 당사자 신청.

motion for transfer

A motion to transfer the case to another district.

이송신청

사건을 다른 재판지로 이송하기 위한 신청.

motion marks

Marks that include a repetitive motion of short duration, i.e. motion, as a feature. TMEP § 807.11.

동작상표

짧은 시간 사이에 반복되는 동작을 그 표장의 특성으로 포함하고 있는 상표.

Example To show that a **motion mark** actually identifies and distinguishes the goods/services and indicates their source, an applicant must submit a specimen that depicts the motion sufficiently to show how the mark is used on or in connection with the goods/services, and that matches the required description of the mark. TMEP § 904.03(l).

동작상표가 실제로 상품을 특정, 식별하며 출처를 표시함을 입증하기 위해 출원인은 그 표장이 상품 또는 서비스에 혹은 그와 관련하여 어떻게 사용되는지를 나타내기에 충분하게 그 동작을 묘사하고 표장에 필요한 설명에 일치하는 견본을 제출하여야 한다. (미) TMEP § 904.03(1)

motion to dismiss

Formal request for the court to dismiss a case for various reasons, such as lack of jurisdiction or settlement between the parties.

소각하 신청

당사자 합의나 재판관할 부재 등 여러 가지 이유로 법원에 정식으로 소를 각하할 것을 요청하는 것.

motion to stay

A motion for the court order to temporarily stop the proceeding.

절차 중지 신청

일시적으로 절차를 중지하는 법원의 명령을 구하는 신청.

motto

The trademark/service mark at issue is recognized as having the meaning of "designed to make difference", "distinguished design", "devised (planned) to make difference" when used in relation to the designated good or service. Hence, even if it is not a mark that indicates the quality or benefit of the designated good or service, general consumers would likely recognize the trademark/service mark at issue not as a particular person's trademark but as a slogan, motto or advertisement phrase that may be commonly used (Patent Court Decision, 2012Heo10129, decided March 14, 2013).

표어

이 사건 출원상표/서비스표는 그 지정상품/서비스업과 관련하여 '차이를 만들기 위하여 디자인(고안, 계획) 된', '차별화 된 디자인', '차별화를 시키기 위하여 고안된(계획된)' 등의 의미로 인식되므로, 설령 지정상품/서비스업의 품질, 효능 등을 표시하는 표장에 해당되지 않는다고 하더라도, 일반 수요자로서는 이를 특정인의 상표로 인식한다기보다는 흔히 쓰일 수 있는 구호 또는 표어나 광고문안 정도로 인식할 것으로 보여진다(특허법원 2013. 3. 14. 선고 2012허10129 판결 참조).

multiple-class application

An application to register the same mark for goods, services, and/or a collective membership organization in multiple classes in a single application.

다류(多類)출원(제도)

동일한 표장을 하나의 출원을 통해 여러 분류 하의 상품, 서비스, 단체 또는 그 모두에 대해 등록하고자 하는 출원.

multiple dependent claim

A dependent claim that further limits and refers back in the alternative to more than one preceding independent or dependent claim.

다중종속항

앞에 기재된 하나 이상의 독립항 또는 종속항을 선택적으로 인용하고 이를 한정하는 종속항.

multiple-design application

Applying for multiple designs of the same classification, not exceeding one hundred, in a single application. Each design must be separately described (Design Protection Act Article 41).

복수디자인등록출원

물품류 구분에서 같은 물품류에 속하는 물품에 대해 100 이내의 디자인을 1디자인등록출원으로 출원하는 것. 1 디자인마다 분리하여 표현하여야 함(디자인보호법 제41조).

M

Example An applicant for design registration may request that the design be kept secret for a prescribed period of up to three years from the date of registration for establishment of the design right. It may be also requested to keep confidential all or some of designs claimed in an **application for multiple designs registration** (Design Protection Act Article 43(1)).

디자인등록출원인은 디자인권의 설정등록일부터 3년 이내의 기간을 정하여 그 디자인을 비밀로 할 것을 청구할 수 있다. 이 경우 **복수디자인등록출원**된 디자인에 대하여는 출원된 디자인의 전부 또는 일부에 대하여 청구할 수 있다(디자인보호법 제43조 제1항).

mutilation of mark

When the representation on a drawing of a mark does not constitute a complete mark so as to conclude essential and integral subject matter is missing from the drawing. TMEP § 807.12(d).

표장의 훼손

표장의 도면에 나타난 표시가 완전한 표장을 보여준다 할 수 없어 필수적이고 완전한 대상이 도면에서 누락되었다고 하여야 할 경우. (미) TMEP § 807.12(d).

Example In re Schecter Bros. Modular Corp.,182 USPQ 694 (TTAB 1974) (where specimens show mark consisting in part of "RAINAIRE" together with its shadow image, it is not a **mutilation of mark** to delete shadow image from drawing since "RAINAIRE" creates the essential impression); … TMEP § 807.12(d).

In re Schecter Bros. Modular Corp.,182 USPQ 694 (TTAB 1974)(표장의 일부가 "RAINAIRE"과 그 그림자 이미지인 것으로 견본에 보여지는 경우, "RAINAIRE"가 그 표장의 필수적인 인상을 만들어내는 것이어서 도면에서 그림자 이미지를 삭제한 것은 **표장의 훼손**이라 볼 수 없다고 본 사례)

N

national stage application

An application that has entered the national phase of the Patent Cooperation Treaty by the fulfillment of certain requirements in a national patent office.

국내단계출원

국내 특허관청의 요건을 충족시킴으로써 특허협력조약의 국내단계에 이른 출원.

Example For **national stage applications** under Patent Act, 35 U.S.C. § 371, the claim for priority must be made withinthe time limit set forth in the PCT and the Regulations underthe PCT. MPEP § 214.3.

미 특허법 371조 하의 **국내단계출원**의 우선권 주장은 특허협력조약에 명시된 기한 및 규정에 따라 하여야 한다. (미) MPEP § 214.3.

negative dictionary evidence

Evidence that a term is absent from dictionaries or atlases.

미 사전상 부재 증거

어느 단어가 사전이나 지도에 없다는 증거.

Example **Negative dictionary evidence** may demonstrate the

사전상 부재 증거는 그 단어에 성(姓)이 아

lack of non-surname significance of a term. TMEP § 1211.02(b)(vi).

닌 다른 의미가 없음을 입증할 수 있다. (미) TMEP § 1211.02(b)(vi).

new matter

Subject matter which has no antecedent basis in the original specification, drawings or claim. An amendment to the claim which introduces new matter shall be rejected.

신규사항

최초의 명세서, 도면 또는 청구범위에서 선행 근거가 없는 대상. 신규사항을 도입하는 청구범위에 대한 보정은 거절되어야 함.

Nice Agreement

The Nice Agreement Concerning the International Classification of Goods and Services for the Purposes of the Registration of Marks, effective January 1, 2002. The aim of the Trademark Law Treaty (TLT) is to standardize and streamline national and regional trademark registration procedures. The great majority of the provisions of the TLT concern the procedure before a trademark office which can be divided into three main phases: application for registration; changes after registration; and renewal.

니스협정

2002년 1월 1일 발효된 표장의 등록을 위한 상품 및 서비스의 국제분류에 관한 니스 협정. 상표 및 서비스표 등록을 위한 상품 및 서비스의 분류체계인 니스국제상품분류표를 정립함. 회원국의 상표청은 각 상표등록에 관련된 공문서 및 공지에 니스분류표 하에서 그 상품 또는 서비스가 속하는 상품류 또는 서비스류의 번호를 표시하여야 함.

N

non bis in idem

일사부재리

Example **(Non Bis In Idem)** If a trial ruling rendered under this Act becomes final and conclusive, no person may demand re-trial, based on the same facts and evidence: Provided, That the foregoing shall not apply where the final and conclusive trial ruling is a rejection (Patent Act Article 163).

(일사부재리) 이 법에 따른 심판의 심결이 확정되었을 때에는 그 사건에 대해서는 누구든지 동일 사실 및 동일 증거에 의하여 다시 심판을 청구할 수 없다. 다만, 확정된 심결이 각하심결인 경우에는 그러하지 아니하다(특허법 제163조).

non-distinctive mark

A mark that is not overall, unsuitable for trademark registration because it lacks distinctiveness or it is improper to grant exclusive right to a particular person for the sake of public interest.

식별력이 없는 표장

전체적으로 보아서 자타상품의 식별력이 없거나 공익상 특정인에게 독점시키는 것이 적당하지 아니한 표장.

Example The proposed mark at issue is not perceived as a slogan or advertising phrase that may be commonly used in the marketplace, and it cannot be stated that a grant of exclusive rights of the mark to a particular person is inappropriate for the sake of public interest; … and thus does not have any grounds to conclude that the mark falls

… 이 사건 출원상표는 거래계에서 흔히 쓰일 수 있는 구호나 광고문안 정도로 인식되는 표장이 아니고, 공익상 특정인에게 독점시키는 것이 적합하지 않은 경우에도 해당하지 않으며 … '기타 **식별력이 없는 표장**'의 구체적인 인정 사유들 중 어디에도 해당

under the category of "other **non-distinctive marks**" (Patent Court Decision, 2016Heo8322, decided April 14, 2017).

하지 않는다(특허법원 2017.04.14. 선고 2016허8322 판결 참조).

non-exclusive license

By granting a non-exclusive license, a right holder keeps his or her right to use the registered right along with the licensee.

통상실시권, 통상사용권

등록권리에 대한 자신의 사용권을 유지하면서 다른 사람에게도 사용하도록 허락하는 것.

Example A patentee may grant a **non-exclusive license** of the patent to others (Patent Act Article 102(1)).

특허권자는 그 특허권에 대하여 타인에게 **통상실시권**을 허락할 수 있다(특허법 제102조 제1항).

non-exclusive licenses after expiration of design rights

If a design right claimed in an application filed on or before the filing date of a patent application and registered accordingly conflicts with the patent, the holder of the design right at the expiration of the term of the design right shall have a non-exclusive license of the patent within the scope of the design right or a non-exclusive license of the exclusive license that exists on the patent at the expiration of the term of the design right, within the scope of the design right (Patent Act Article 105(1)).

디자인권 존속기간 만료 후의 통상실시권

특허출원일 전 또는 특허출원일과 같은 날에 출원되어 등록된 디자인권이 그 특허권과 저촉되는 경우 그 디자인권의 존속기간이 만료될 때에는 그 디자인권자는 그 디자인권의 범위에서 그 특허권에 대하여 통상실시권을 가지거나 그 디자인권의 존속기간 만료 당시 존재하는 그 특허권의 전용실시권에 대하여 통상실시권을 가짐(특허법 제105조 제1항).

non-exclusive licenses based on prior use

A person may obtain nonexclusive license to practice a patented invention if he or she was commercially practicing or preparing to commercially practice the invention at the time of the filing of the application, provided that he or she created the invention or learned of the invention from the inventor, without knowledge of the patent application, and that the nonexclusive license is limited to the commercial scope the person is practicing or preparing to practice the invention.

선사용에 의한 통상실시권

특허출원 시에 그 특허출원된 발명의 내용을 알지 못하고 그 발명을 하거나 그 발명을 한 사람으로부터 알게 되어 국내에서 그 발명의 실시사업을 하거나 이를 준비하고 있는 자는 그 실시하거나 준비하고 있는 발명 및 사업목적의 범위에서 그 특허출원된 발명의 특허권에 대하여 통상실시권을 가짐.

non-exclusive license for prior users of patent reinstated through retrial

A person who executes, or prepares to execute, the relevant patent commercially or industrially, in good faith, in the Republic of Korea after the relevant trial ruling becomes

재심에 의하여 회복한 특허권에 대한 선사용권자의 통상실시권

특허취소결정 또는 심결이 확정된 후 재심청구 등록 전에 국내에서 선의로 그 발명의 실시사업을 하고 있는 자 또는 그 사업을

final and conclusive, but before the petition filed for retrial is registered shall be granted a non-exclusive license of the patent within the scope of subject matter of the patented invention that the person executes or prepares to execute, or the objectives of the business (Patent Act Article 182).

준비하고 있는 자는 실시하고 있거나 준비하고 있는 발명 및 사업목적의 범위에서 그 특허권에 관하여 통상실시권을 가진다(특허법 제182조).

non-final office action

최초거절이유통지

An Office action letter that raises new issues in the initial phase of the examination process. Applicants must respond to non-final Office action letters within a given time to avoid abandonment of the application.

새로운 흠결사항에 대한 특허청의 통지로 주로 심사 초기단계에 해당함. 출원인은 출원이 포기되는 것을 막기 위해 그 통지에 대해 정해진 기간 이내에 반박하여야 함.

non-obviousness

미 비자명성

→ See. inventive step.

non-patent literature

비특허문헌

Documents and publications that are not patents or published patent applications but are cited as references for being relevant in a patent prosecution.

특허 또는 공개된 특허출원은 아니나 특허 심사절차에서 관련성이 있는 인용문헌으로 인용된 문서 또는 간행물.

Example When determining the field of search, three reference sources must be considered, domestic patents (including patent application publications), foreign patent documents, and **non-patent literature** (NPL). MPEP § 904.02.

검색분야 결정시에는 국내특허(출원공개를 포함한다), 해외특허문헌, **비특허문헌**의 3가지 인용출처를 검토하여야 한다. (미) MPEP § 904.02.

non-practicing entity (NPE)

특허관리전문사업자 (NPE)

A business entity engaging in business activities to make profits by exercising a patent over patent licensees, etc., rather than manufacturing or selling products or providing services by applying the patented technology.

특허기술을 이용한 상품의 제조 또는 판매, 서비스 공급 등은 하지 아니하면서도 특허를 실시하는 자 등에 대한 특허권의 행사를 통하여 수익을 창출하는 것을 사업활동으로 하는 사업자를 말함.

non-provisional application

미 정규출원

The "regular" type of patent applications, as distinguished from provisional applications.

가출원과 구분되는, '일반적' 의미의 특허출원.

non-resident

재외자

A person who is not domiciled or does not have his/her place of business in the Republic of Korea.

국내에 주소나 영업소가 없는 자.

Example No **non-resident** foreigner shall be entitled to enjoy trademark rights or the rights relating to the trademark, except in any of the following cases: 1. Where a state to which such foreigner is a citizen recognizes trademark rights or the rights relating to the trademark owned by a citizen of the Republic of Korea on the same conditions as those of its citizen; … (Trademark Act Article 27(1)).	**재외자**인 외국인은 다음 각 호의 어느 하나에 해당하는 경우를 제외하고는 상표권 또는 상표에 관한 권리를 누릴 수 없다. 1. 그 외국인이 속하는 국가에서 대한민국 국민에 대하여 그 국민과 같은 조건으로 상표권 또는 상표에 관한 권리를 인정하는 경우 … (상표법 제27조 제1호).
nonstatutory subject matter	**미 부등록대상**
Example The claim is rejected under 35 U.S.C. 171 as directed to **nonstatutory subject matter** because the design is not shown embodied in or applied to an article. MPEP § 1504.01.	디지인이 물품에 회체되기나 적용된 것이 아니므로, 청구범위는 35 U.S.C. 171에 따라 **부등록대상**인 것으로 되어 거절된다. (미) MPEP § 1504.01.
non-traditional mark	**비전형상표**
Trademarks can be classified into traditional and non-traditional marks. The latter may be distinctive only if it is distinctive by itself or has acquired distinctiveness by use.	상표는 전형상표와 비전형상표로 구분되고, 비전형상표는 그 자체가 식별력을 갖추거나 사용에 의하여 식별력을 취득하여야만 식별력이 인정된다.
non-use cancellation	**불사용취소**
When a registered trademark was not used on the designated goods in the Republic of Korea for at least three consecutive years. Grounds for trademark cancellation (Trademark Act Article 119(1)3).	등록상표를 그 지정상품에 대하여 3년 이상 국내에서 사용하고 있지 아니한 경우. 상표등록취소의 사유가 됨(상표법 119조 1항 제3호).
Example The temporariness of the use of the above leaflet does not necessarily mean that such use was only for the purpose of avoiding a **non-use cancellation** (Patent Court Decision, 2016Heo2904, decided December 29, 2016).	위 전단지가 일시적으로 사용되었다고 해서 이를 **불사용 취소**를 면탈하기 위한 형식적인 사용에 불과하다고 단정할 수는 없으며, … (특허법원 2016.12.29 선고 2016허2904판결 참조).
non-visual marks	**비시각적 상표**
A trademark consists solely of a sound (e.g., music or words and music), a scent, or other completely non-visual matter.	소리(음악, 또는 단어와 음악), 냄새, 기타 완전히 비시각적인 사항으로만 된 상표.
notice of action	**처분통지서**
Where the Commissioner of the Korean Intellectual Property Office or the Director General of the Intellectual Property	특허청장 또는 특허심판원장은 무효처분 또는 무효처분의 취소처분을 할 경우에는

Trial and Appeal Board invalidates procedures or revokes the invalidation he/she shall serve a notice of his/her action on a person ordered to make an amendment (Trademark Act Article 18; Design Protection Act Article 18).

그 보정명령을 받은 자에게 처분통지서를 송달하여야 한다(상표법 제18조, 디자인보호법 제18조).

notice of allowability

미 등록가능통지

Example In all instances, both before and after final rejection, in which an application is placed in condition for allowance, applicant should be notified promptly of allowability of the claims by a **Notice of Allowability**. PTOL-37. MPEP §1302.03.

최종거절결정 전후로 출원이 등록허여를 위한 요건을 만족하는 모든 경우, 출원인에게 **등록가능통지** 양식 PTOL-37로 이를 신속히 통지하여야 한다. (미) MPEP § 1302.03.

notice of allowance

미 등록결정통지

A notification to the applicant that she/he is entitled to a patent or other rights under the law. In trademark law, Notices of allowance are only issued for applications that have been filed based on "intent to use" and does not mean that the mark has registered yet. USPTO.

출원인에게 법에 따른 특허권등을 소유할 자격이 있음을 알리는 내용의 통지. 미 상표법 상 등록결정통지는 사용의사에 기한 출원에 대해서만 발행되며, 아직 상표가 등록되었다는 의미는 아님. (미) USPTO.

Example If, on examination, it appears that the applicant is entitled to a patent under the law, a **notice of allowance** will besent to the applicant at the correspondence address indicated in § 1.33. 37 C.F.R. § 1.311.

심사결과 출원인이 법에 따라 특허권을 허여받을 자격이 있는 것으로 나타날 경우 1.33에 따른 주소로 **등록결정통지**를 발송하게 된다. 37 C.F.R. § 1.311.

notice of grounds for rejection/refusal

거절이유통지

When an applicant of patent or other IP rights fails to meet the requirements for patent registration or there are other grounds to reject the application, the patent examiner should reject the application (Patent Act Article 63).

특허등의 출원인이 특허출원을 한 발명이 특허요건을 갖추지 못하는 등 거절사유에 해당하는 경우 특허심사관은 특허등록을 거절해야 하는데, 이 때 심사관은 출원인에게 거절이유를 통지하고 일정기간 내에 의견제출을 할 기회를 부여하여야 함(특허법 제63조).

novelty

신규성

One of the requirements for patent registration. In order to be patentable, an invention shall not be publicly known or executed in the Republic of Korea or in a foreign country prior to the filing of a patent application.

특허요건의 하나. 특허를 받을 수 있는 발명이기 위해서는 특허 출원 전에 국내 또는 국외에서 공지되었거나 공연히 실시된 발명 등에 해당하지 아니하여야 함.

numerical limitation invention

수치한정발명

Inventions that use numerical values to express the scope of its elements (e.g., temperature, mix ratio) is called numerical limitation invention. In order for a numerical limitation invention to have novelty or an inventive step, the numerical limit must yield significant effect. The significance of this effect is called critical significance.

발명의 구성요건 중 예컨대 온도나 배합비율과 같이 일정한 범위를 가지는 구성요소에 관하여 수치를 한정한 발명을 수치한정발명이라 함. 이때 수치한정발명에 신규성 또는 진보성이 인정되기 위하여는 한정된 수치범위 내외에서 현저한 작용효과가 있어야 하는데, 이러한 현저한 작용효과를 임계적 의의라 지칭함.

Example In the case of a patented invention which uses specific numerical values to express the scope of elements for an invention already publicly known at the time of application, if there is a difference only in the **numerical limitation** while the object and functional effects of the patented invention are in line with those of publicly known inventions, and if no substantial difference in functional effect occurs within the limited numerical range, the patented invention lacks the requisite “inventive step” since it is no more than a simple numerical limitation that a person having ordinary skill in the art can properly derive through ordinary and repetitive experiments (Supreme Court Decision, 2008Hu4998, decided August 19, 2010).

특허등록된 발명이 그 출원 전에 공지된 발명이 가지는 구성요소의 범위를 수치로써 한정하여 표현한 경우에 있어, 그 특허발명의 과제 및 효과가 공지된 발명의 연장선상에 있고 **수치한정**의 유무에서만 차이가 있는 경우에는 그 한정된 수치범위 내외에서 현저한 효과의 차이가 생기지 않는다면 그 특허발명은 그 기술분야에서 통상의 기술자가 통상적이고 반복적인 실험을 통하여 적절히 선택할 수 있는 정도의 단순한 수치한정에 불과하여 진보성이 부정된다(대법원 2010. 8. 19. 선고 2008후4998 판결 참조).

O

oath

선서

objective creativity

객관적 창작성

The objective creativity is required for design registration. It does not mean that a design should be unique without any similarity to all past or present designs but is present if aesthetic creation is based on the past or the existing design, combined with artistic creation providing a new aesthetic sense, such that as a whole there can be recognizable aesthetic value that is different from the prior design (Supreme Court Decision, 2005Hu2922, decided July 28, 2006).

디자인 등록을 받기 위해서는 객관적 창작성이 요구됨. 객관적 창작성은 과거 또는 현존의 모든 것과 유사하지 아니한 독특함만을 말하는 것이 아니고, 과거 및 현존의 것을 기초로 하여 거기에 새로운 미감을 주는 미적 창작이 결합되어 그 전체에서 종전의 디자인과는 다른 미감적 가치가 인정되는 정도면 족하다(대법원 2006. 7. 28. 선고 2005후2922 판결 등 참조).

objective observation

In determining similarity of trademarks, observing whether an ordinary person encountering the good, i.e. an ordinary person in the marketplace who purchases or trades the good, would be misled or confused as to the source of the good when exercising ordinary care.

객관적 관찰

상표의 유사 여부를 판단할 때 그 상품에 직접 접촉하는 일반인들, 즉 당해 상품의 일반적인 거래자가 그런 종류의 물품을 구입하거나 거래할 경우에 기울이는 통상의 주의력을 기준으로 삼아 관찰 시 출처의 오인, 혼동의 우려가 있는지 판단하는 것.

Example Determination on similarity between trademarks is to be based on whether there are concerns for ordinary consumers to misperceive or confuse the origin of the designated goods in transactions from the perspective of their intuitive perception of the trademark, grounded in an **objective**, overall **observation** of the appearance, name, and conception of the trademark by recollection (Supreme Court Decision, 2011Hu3698, decided March 20, 2014).

상표의 유사 여부는 외관, 호칭 및 관념을 **객관적**, 전체적, 이격적으로 **관찰**하여 지정상품의 거래에서 일반 수요자들이 상표에 대하여 느끼는 직관적 인식을 기준으로 상품의 출처에 관하여 오인 · 혼동을 일으키게 할 우려가 있는지에 따라 판단하여야 한다(대법원 2014. 3. 20. 선고 2011후3698 전원합의체 판결 참조).

obviousness-type double patenting (ODP)

→ See. double patenting.

미 자명식 중복특허

obvious to try

A standard to determine non-obviousness as provided in the KSR case, 550 U.S. 398 (2007) → See. TSM; common sense selection.

시도의 자명성

KSR 판례에서 제시된 비자명성 판단 기준. → TSM기준 (교시, 암시, 동기) 및 상식적 선택 참조.

OEM (original equipment manufacturing)

Manufacturing products under a trademark requested by the client company instead of the manufacturer's own.

주문자상표 부착방식 (OEM)

자신의 상표가 아니라 주문자가 요구하는 상표로 상품을 생산하여 주는 주문자상표 부착생산 방식.

offense of divulging secrets or confidential information

비밀누설죄

Example Any employee of the Korean Intellectual Property Office or the Intellectual Property Trial and Appeal Board that **divulges or misappropriates confidential information** which becomes known to him/her about a design claimed in a pending application for design registration (including designs claimed in a pending application for international design registration, for which a request for deferment has

특허청 또는 특허심판원 직원이나 그 직원으로 재직하였던 사람이 디자인등록출원 중인 디자인(헤이그협정 제11조에 따라 연기 신청된 국제디자인등록출원 중인 디자인을 포함한다)에 관하여 직무상 알게 된 **비밀을 누설**하거나 도용한 경우에는 5년 이하의 징역 또는 5천만원 이하의 벌금에

been filed under Article 11 of the Hague Agreement) in the course of performing his/her duties shall be punished by imprisonment with labor for not more than five years or by a fine not exceeding 50 million won (Design Protection Act Article 225, Patent Act Article 226, etc.).

처한다(디자인보호법 제225조 제1항, 특허법 제226조 등).

offense of false marking

허위표시죄

Any person who commit marking "patented" or any similar misleading word on any unpatented thing shall be punished for offense of false marking (Patent Act Article 228).

특허된 것이 아닌 물건에 특허표시 또는 이와 혼동하기 쉬운 표시를 하는 경우 허위표시죄로 처벌된다(특허법 제228조).

Office action

미 (최초)거절이유통지

An examining attorney sends an Office action to notify an applicant about issues with his or her application. This type of action will include the reason why registration is being refused or what requirements must be satisfied. There are several types of Office actions: examiner's amendments, priority actions, non-final Office actions, final Office actions, and suspension inquiry letters. USPTO.

심사관이 거절이유통지를 하는 것은 출원인에게 출원의 문제점에 대해 고지하기 위함이다. 여기에는 등록거절이유 또는 필요요건 등이 기재된다. 거절이유통지에는 크게 심사관보정, 우선조치, 최초거절이유통지, 최후거절이유통지, 외국등록중상태여부를 묻는통지 등이 있음. (미) USPTO.

Example The examining attorney's **first Office action** must be complete, so the applicant will be advised of all requirements for amendment and all grounds for refusal, with the exception of use-related issues that are considered for the first time in the examination of an amendment to allege use under 15 U.S.C. §1051(c) or a statement of use under 15 U.S.C. §1051(d) in an intent-to-use application. TMEP § 704.01.

심사관의 **최초거절이유통지**는 출원인에게 모든 보정요구사항 및 거절이유를 고지할 수 있도록 완전성을 갖추어야 한다. 단 사용주장보정, 또는 사용의사 기반 출원에서 사용사실의 진술에 대한 심사에서 최초로 고려하는 사용 관련 쟁점은 예외로 한다. (미) TMEP § 704.01.

Official Reports on Plant Variety Protection

품종보호공보

olfactory marks

후각상표, 냄새상표

→ See. scent mark.

one design for one application

1디자인 1디자인등록 출원

The principle that one application is allowed to display one design embodied in one article.

하나의 출원에는 하나의 디자인만을 표시하여야 하는 원칙.

- doctrine of one-design for one-registration application (법제처)

ongoing royalty — **계속적 실시료**

Royalty paid to the patent owner for the infringer's future use of the patent, either via negotiation or by court order, as opposed to royalties awarded for the past infringement.

협상을 통해 또는 법원 명령으로 침해자의 특허의 향후 사용에 대하여 특허권자에게 지급하는 실시료. 과거 침해에 대해 지급하는 실시료와 구분됨.

opinion counsel — **자문변호사**

opportunity to submit arguments — **의견제출기회의 부여**

Example When an examiner intends to determine to reject a patent application, he/she shall notify the applicant of the grounds for rejection and provide the applicant with an **opportunity to submit written arguments** within a specified period.

심사관은 특허거절결정을 하려는 경우 특허출원인에게 거절이유를 통지하고, 기간을 정하여 **의견서를 제출할 수 있는 기회**를 주어야 한다(특허법 제63조 제1항).

opposition — **이의신청**

Any person can file for opposition to the Commissioner of KIPO within two months of the publication of an application if there is a reason to believe that registration should be denied.

등록거절이유 등이 있는 경우 누구든지 출원공고일부터 2개월 내에 특허청장에게 이의신청을 할 수 있다.

oral argument — **변론**

→ See. pleading.

oral hearing — **구술심리**

order — **(판결)주문**

order to make an amendment — **보정명령**

Example When a person **ordered to make an amendment** under Article 46 fails to do so within a specified period, the Commissioner of the Korean Intellectual Property Office or the Director General of the Korean Intellectual Property Trial and Appeal Board may invalidate the patent-related procedure (Patent Act Article 16(1)).

특허청장 또는 특허심판원장은 제46조에 따른 **보정명령**을 받은 자가 지정된 기간에 그 보정을 하지 아니하면 특허에 관한 절차를 무효로 할 수 있다(특허법 제16조 제1항).

O

order to maintain confidentiality

If a party establishes a prima facie case of the party's trade secret on any of the following grounds in legal proceedings on infringement of a patent or exclusive license, the court may, upon the party's request, order the other party (if the party is a corporation, its representative), the person who represents the other party in the legal proceedings, or any other person who becomes aware of the trade secret in the course of the legal proceedings not to use the trade secret for any purpose other than to proceed in the legal proceedings, and not to disclose the trade secret to any person other than the persons in receipt of the order under this paragraph in connection with the trade secret.

비밀유지명령

법원은 특허권 또는 전용실시권의 침해에 관한 소송에서 그 당사자가 보유한 영업비밀에 대하여 다음 각 호의 사유를 모두 소명한 경우에는 그 당사자의 신청에 따라 결정으로 다른 당사자(법인인 경우에는 그 대표자), 당사자를 위하여 소송을 대리하는 자, 그 밖에 그 소송으로 인하여 영업비밀을 알게 된 자에게 그 영업비밀을 그 소송의 계속적인 수행 외의 목적으로 사용하거나 그 영업비밀에 관계된 이 항에 따른 명령을 받은 자 외의 자에게 공개하지 아니할 것을 명할 수 있음.

order to produce documents

Upon receipt of a request from either party to legal proceedings on infringement of a patent or exclusive license, the court may order the other party to submit documents necessary to assess losses caused by the relevant infringement. Upon receipt of a request from either party to legal proceedings on infringement of a patent or exclusive license, the court may order the other party to submit documents necessary for assessing losses caused by the relevant infringement: Provided, That the foregoing shall not apply where the person possessing the documents has a reasonable ground to refuse to submit them (Patent Act Article 132).

• order to submit documents (법제처)

자료제출명령

소송에서 법원이 당사자의 신청에 의하여 상대방 당사자에게 해당 침해의 증명 또는 침해로 인한 손해액의 산정에 필요한 자료를 제출하도록 하는 명령. 법원은 특허권 또는 전용실시권 침해소송에서 당사자의 신청에 의하여 상대방 당사자에게 해당 침해의 증명 또는 침해로 인한 손해액의 산정에 필요한 자료의 제출을 명할 수 있다. 다만, 그 자료의 소지자가 그 자료의 제출을 거절할 정당한 이유가 있으면 그러하지 아니하다(특허법 제132조 제1항).

order to supplement an application

Where the purpose for which an applicant intends to obtain IP rights registration is not clearly indicated, the Commissioner of the Korean Intellectual Property Office shall order the person to supplement the application in due time.

(절차)보완명령

등록을 받으려는 취지가 명확하게 표시되지 아니하는 등의 경우에 특허청장이 등록을 받으려는 자에게 적절한 기간을 정하여 보완할 것을 명하는 것.

Example Where a person **ordered to supplement an application** under paragraph (2) supplements this application for trademark registration, he/she shall submit a document concerning the complement of procedures (hereafter in this

제2항에 따른 **보완명령**을 받은 자가 상표등록출원을 보완하는 경우에는 절차보완에 관한 서면(이하 이 조에서 "절차보완서"라 한다)을 제출하여야 한다(상표법 제37조 제

Article, referred to as "document concerning the complement of procedures") (Trademark Act Article 37(3).

3항).

ordinary consumers

일반 수요자

Example Even if the trademark owner or licensee uses a trademark which omits either the English letters or their transliteration in Korean, denying the identicalness of the trademarks will result in destroying the trust of **general ordinary consumers** or traders, since general consumers or traders will recognize that the trademark shares the same name and concept as the above trademark, and their trust will be based on such understanding (Supreme Court Decision, 2012Hu2463, decided September 26, 2013).

상표권자 또는 사용권자가 위 등록상표에서 영문자나 그 한글 음역 중 어느 한 부분이 생략된 형태의 상표를 사용하더라도, **일반수요자**나 거래자에게는 위 등록상표와 동일하게 호칭·관념되는 같은 상표가 사용된다고 인식되어 그에 대한 신뢰가 형성될 것이므로, 그 상표들 사이의 동일성을 부정한다면 일반 수요자나 거래자의 신뢰를 깨뜨리는 결과가 초래된다 (대법원 2013. 9. 26. 선고 2012후2463 전원합의체 판결 참조).

ordinary course of business

통상의 거래

ordinary observer

통상의 관찰자

Example In determining the question of similarity of the designs in contention, a judge or an examiner is not to compare individual features that comprise the designs separately, but rather must consider whether an **ordinary observer** is able to identify differing aesthetic features by comparing and contrasting each designs' over all appearance (Patent Court Decision, 2014Heo6858, decided April 23, 2015).

디자인의 유사 여부는 이를 구성하는 각 요소를 분리하여 개별적으로 대비할 것이 아니라 그 외관을 전체적으로 대비 관찰하여, **보는 사람(통상의 관찰자)**으로 하여금 상이한심미감을느끼게하는지의여부에따라판단하여야하고,… (특허법원 2015. 4. 23. 선고 2014허6858 판결 참조).

original application

미 최초 출원

Example While the filing of the **original application** theoretically constituted a constructive reduction to practice at the time, the subsequent abandonment of that application also resulted in an abandonment of the benefit of that filing as a constructive reduction to practice. The filing of the original application is, however, evidence of conception of the invention. In re Costello, 717 F.2d 1346 (Fed. Cir. 1983).

최초출원신청으로 이론적으로는 그 시점에 발명이 구현된 것으로 간주하여야 하나, 해당 출원을 이후 포기함으로써 그 효과 또한 포기한 것이다. 그러나 최초출원신청은 발명의 착상에 대한 증거가 된다. In re Costello, 717 F.2d 1346, 1350 (Fed. Cir. 1983).

original claim

최초 청구항

O

original patent owner (right holder)

Where patent rights registered after filing an application for the patent before the filing date of a trademark application or on the same date as the filing of a trademark application is in conflict with such trademark right, and the duration of the patent rights expires, the original patent right holder shall have the right to use a trademark identical or similar to such registered trademark on goods identical or similar to designated goods of the registered trademark to the extent of the original patent rights (Trademark Act Article 98(1)).

원특허권자

상표등록출원일 전 또는 상표등록출원일과 동일한 날에 출원되어 등록된 특허권이 그 상표권과 저촉되는 경우 그 특허권의 존속기간이 만료되는 때에는 그 원특허권자는 원특허권의 범위에서 그 등록상표의 지정상품과 동일·유사한 상품에 대하여 그 등록상표와 동일·유사한 상표를 사용할 권리를 가진다(상표법 제98조 제1항).

original patent right holder

→ See. original patent owner.

원특허권자

ornamentality

Articles of manufacture may possess both functional and ornamental characteristics. A design right only concerns the ornamental aspects of the design.

장식성

물품은 기능성과 장식성을 모두 갖출 수 있는데, 디자인권은 오로지 그 디자인의 장식적 측면과 관련이 있음.

Example [A] design patent only protects the **ornamental aspects** of the design. Because the presence of a tailshaft and fins has been shown to be necessary to have a ball with similar aerodynamic stability to OddzOn's commercial embodiment, such general features are functional and thus not protectable as such. OddzOn Prod., Inc. v. Just Toys, Inc., 122 F.3d 1396, 1404 (Fed. Cir. 1997).

디자인특허는 그 디자인의 **장식적 측면**만을 보호하는 것이다. OddzOn의 특허 구현제품과 같은 공기역학적 안정성을 갖기 위해서는 프로펠러축과 지느러미부분이 필수적임이 입증되었으므로 이러한 일반적 특성은 기능적이며 따라서 디자인으로서 보호될 수 없다. (미) OddzOn Prod., Inc. v. Just Toys, Inc., 122 F.3d 1396, 1404 (Fed. Cir. 1997).

ornamental matter

Subject matter that is merely a decorative feature. A mere ornamentation does not distinguish the applicant's goods and thus does not function as a trademark.

장식

장식적 특성만을 지닌 대상. 장식은 자타상품 식별력이 없어 상표로서 기능하지 아니함.

Example **Ornamental matter** that is neither inherently distinctive nor a secondary source indicator may be registered on the Principal Register under §2(f), if the applicant establishes that the subject matter has acquired distinctiveness as a mark in relation to the goods. TMEP § 1202.03(2).

본질적인 식별력도 2차적 출처표시기능도 없는 **장식**도 출원인이 그 대상이 지정상품에 관련하여 식별력을 취득하였음을 입증할 경우 미 상표법 2(f)조에 따라 주등록부에 등록될 수 있다. (미) TMEP § 1202.03(2).

ornamentation

장식

→ See. ornamental matter.

overrule

각하, 기각

→ See. dismissal.

P

panel of administrative judges

심판관합의체

An administrative trial shall be conducted by a panel consisting of three or five administrative judges. A consensus shall be reached by a majority decision and shall not be disclosed.

심판은 3인 또는 5인의 심판관의 합의체가 행하며 합의는 심판관 중 과반수에 의하여 결정함. 심판의 합의는 공개하지 아니함.

- panel for trial (법제처)

parallel import

병행수입

A non-counterfeit product imported from another country without permission of the intellectual property owner.

산업재산권자의 허락없이 모조품이 아닌 제품을 다른 나라로부터 수입하는 것.

Example By itself, **parallel import** is neither illegal nor unlawful and does not constitute infringement of trademark rights, as held by the lower court. Therefore, there is no doubt that sale of goods by parallel importers with the trademark owner's mark affixed to the good is permissible (Supreme Court Decision, 99Da42322, decided September 24, 2002).

병행 수입 그 자체는 위법성이 없는 정당한 행위로서 상표권 침해 등을 구성하지 아니함은 원심의 판단과 같으므로 병행수입업자가 상표권자의 상표가 부착된 상태에서 상품을 판매하는 행위는 당연히 허용될 것인바, … (대법원 2002. 9. 24. 선고 99다42322 판결 참조).

parameter invention

파라미터 발명

A parameter invention is an invention in which an applicant arbitrary creates a certain parameter which is not standard or commonly used in physics or chemistry, parameterizes it arithmetically by using the correlation among plural parameters, and employs it as a part of essential elements of the invention.

파라미터 발명은 물리, 화학 분야에서 표준적이거나 흔하게 사용되지 않는 특성값을 창출하고 복수의 특성값 간 상관관계를 이용하여 산술적으로 파라미터화하여 이를 발명의 필수적 구성요소의 일부로 하는 발명을 말함.

parent application

모출원(母出願)

the Paris Convention for the Protection of Industrial Property (the Paris Convention)

The Paris Convention. It is intended to protect patents, utility models, industrial designs, trademarks, service marks, trade names, indications of source or appellations of origin, and to repress unfair competition.

산업재산권의 보호를 위한 파리 협약

파리협약. 특허, 실용신안, 디자인, 상표, 서비스표, 상호, 원산지표시 또는 원산지명칭의 보호 및 부당경쟁의 방지를 목적으로 함.

partial abandonment (of application)

Abandonment of application only as to particular goods or services that are subject to a refusal or other decisions.

Example **Partial abandonment** applies only if the Office action expressly states that a refusal or requirement is limited to only certain goods/services/class(es). TMEP § 718.02(a).

(출원의) 일부포기

거절결정 대상이 되는 특정 상품 또는 서비스에 대해서만 출원을 포기하는 것.

출원의 일부 포기는 특허상표청의 통지에 거절결정이나 한정요구가 특정 상품 또는 서비스, 분류에만 제한되어 있음이 명시되어 있을 때에만 가능하다. (미) TMEP § 718.02(a).

partial design

A design applied to a part of an article.

Example The proposed design at issue, applied as a **partial design** on the subject article of a cellular phone cover, to be granted protection limited to Drawing 2 part in the upper side of the article and Drawing 3 projected at the back bottom, exclusive of the main body of the cover, described in gray color in the perspective view in [Drawing 1], … (Supreme Court Decision, 2012Hu3343, decided February 15, 2013).

부분디자인

물품의 부분에 대한 디자인.

휴대폰 케이스를 대상물품으로 하여 우측 [그림 1]과 같은 사시도에서 회색으로 표현된 케이스 본체 부분을 제외한 나머지 부분, 즉 대상물품 상부의 [그림 2] 부분과 하단 뒷면에 돌출된 [그림 3] 부분만을 보호받고자 **부분디자인**으로 출원된 이 사건 출원 디자인은 … (대법원 2013. 2. 15. 선고 2012후3343 판결 참조).

partial examination

A design is registered if an application successfully passes an examination as to whether it meets only some of the requirements for design registration (Design Protection Act Article 2.6). If a written opposition to registration of a partially-examined design is withdrawn, the written opposition shall be deemed to have never existed (Design Protection Act Article 75(2)).

일부심사등록

디자인등록출원이 디자인등록요건 중 일부만을 갖추고 있는지를 심사하여 등록하는 것(디자인보호법 제2조 제6호). 디자인 일부심사등록 이의신청을 취하하면 그 이의신청은 처음부터 없었던 것으로 본다(디자인보호법 제75조 제2항).

particularly point out the invention

A requirement to grant patent that claims must specify and identify the distinct scope of the invention, used as a standard

발명을 특정하여 지칭함

발명의 범위가 구별되도록 청구범위에 이를 특정하여 지칭하고 정의하여야 한다는

to determine whether the claims are sufficiently clear.

특허 허여의 요건. 청구범위의 명확성 판단을 위한 기준으로 사용됨.

parts

A part of an article. A part is also an article, eligible for design protection if the part may be separated for replacement and can be an independent subject of transaction.

부품

물품 전체의 일부. 그 부분만을 따로 분리하여 교체할 수 있고(호환가능성), 또 분리된 부분만으로 독립된 거래의 대상(독립거래가능성)이 된다면 디자인 보호의 대상이 되는 물품으로 봄.

patentability

→ See. requirements for patent registration.

특허요건

patentable subject matter

In general, any new and useful process, machine, manufacture, or composition of matter, or any new and useful improvement thereof, subject to the conditions and requirements under the law. 35 U.S.C. § 101.

미 특허 대상

일반적으로 새롭고 유용한 방법, 기계장치, 제조물, 조성물, 또는 이들에 대한 새롭고 유용한 개량은 법에 의한 조건이나 요건이 적용되는 경우를 예외로 하고 무엇이든 특허 대상이 된다. (미) 특허법 101조.

patent administrator

No person with no domicile or place of business in the Republic of Korea (hereinafter referred to as "overseas resident") shall initiate any patent-related procedure or file legal proceedings against a disposition made by an administrative authority under this Act or an order issued under this Act, unless he/she is represented by an agent with respect to his/her patent, who has a domicile or place of business in the Republic of Korea (hereinafter referred to as "patent administrator"), except where the overseas resident (or the representative if the overseas resident is a corporation) sojourns in the Republic of Korea (Patent Act Article 5(1)).

특허관리인

국내에 주소 또는 영업소가 없는 자(이하 "재외자"라 한다)는 재외자(법인의 경우에는 그 대표자)가 국내에 체류하는 경우를 제외하고는 그 재외자의 특허에 관한 대리인으로서 국내에 주소 또는 영업소가 있는 자(이하 "특허관리인"이라 한다)에 의해서만 특허에 관한 절차를 밟거나 이 법 또는 이 법에 따른 명령에 따라 행정청이 한 처분에 대하여 소를 제기할 수 있다(특허법 제5조 제1항).

patent agent

Those who are authorized to represent others in patent application and prosecution by passing USPTO's patent bar.

미 특허대리인

USPTO의 변리사시험(patent bar)을 통과하여 특허의 출원 및 심사과정에서 타인을 대리할 자격을 가진 자.

patent attorney

Those who are authorized to represent others in patent

미 특허변호사

USPTO의 변리사시험(patent bar exam) 및

P

application, prosecution and litigation in court by passing USPTO's patent bar and a state bar exam in the U.S.

해당 주의 변호사 시험(bar exam)을 통과하여 특허의 출원 및 심사과정뿐만 아니라 소송에서까지 타인을 대리할 자격을 가진 자.

Patent Cooperation Treaty (PCT)

특허협력조약 (PCT)

According to this treaty, a patent applicant who is planning to apply patent registration in several foreign countries may file a single application in a prescribed form designating the countries he/she is willing to have the patent registered, then it is deemed that the applicant filed application in the designated countries on the date he/she filed international application.

외국의 여러나라에 동일한 발명에 대한 특허를 받고자 하는 출원인이 소정의 방식에 따라 지정국을 표시하여 하나의 국제출원을 수리관청에 제출하면 각 지정국에 위 국제출원일에 정규의 출원이 있었던 것으로 효력을 인정받는 것을 특징으로 하는 조약.

patent-drug approval linkage

허가-특허 연계제도

→ See. patent linkage system.

patented invention

특허발명

Invention for which a patent has been granted.

특허를 받은 발명.

patentee

특허권자

A patent owner. Patentees include not only the one to whom the patent was issued but also the successors in title to the patentee.

특허권의 소유권자. 특허권자는 특허가 발행된 자뿐 아니라 그 권원의 승계자를 포함한다.

patent examiner

특허심사관

KIPO examiners who review applications for patent and other industrial rights.

특허청에 소속되어 특허 등 산업재산권의 출원을 심사하는 자

patent fee

특허료

A person who intends to register the establishment of patent rights shall pay patent fees for three years from the date he or she intends to register the patent rights (Patent Act Article 79).

특허권의 설정등록을 받으려는 자는 설정등록을 받으려는 날로부터 3년분의 특허료를 내야 한다(특허법 제79조).

patent gazette

특허공보

patent holder

특허권자

→ See. patentee.

patent holdup

특허억류

An opportunistic move by a patentee, whose patented

특허권자의 특허기술이 표준필수특허가 됨

technology is an SEP, to demand royalties exceeding the value of the patent itself. As a preventive measure, patentees are often required to make FRAND commitment.

에 따라 기회주의적으로 그 특허의 가치 자체를 상회하는 실시료를 요구하는 것. 이를 방지하기 위해 보통 FRAND 확약을 요구한다.

patent infringement

Execution of a patent in the absence of a permission by the patent owner or an exclusive licensee against their will.

특허침해

특허권자 또는 전용실시권자의 허락 없이 권리자의 의사에 반하여 특허를 실시하는 것.

patent linkage system

Under the system, a generic drug company that files application with the Korean Ministry of Food and Drug Safety ("MFDS") to sell a certain generic drug, using a pharmaceutical patent listed on the patent list managed by the MFDS must give notice to the patent holder of the above patent within 45 days of the application. After the patent holder receives the notice, it is entitled to request MFDS to prohibit the sale of the generic drug for up to 9 months, after filing suit against the generic drug company for infringement.

허가-특허 연계제도

복제약 제조사가 식품의약품안전처에서 관리하는 등재목록에 등재된 특허를 이용하여 복제약을 제조 · 판매하기 위해 품목허가신청을 하는 경우 45일 내에 해당 특허의 특허권자에게 품목허가신청 사실을 통지하도록 강제하고, 통지를 받은 특허권자는 복제약 제조사를 상대로 침해금지소송을 제기하면서 통지받은 날로부터 9개월 간 판매금지신청을 할 수 있게 하는 제도.

patent marking

A patentee or exclusive or non-exclusive licensee may mark his/her products as patented in any of the following relevant manners: 1. If the patent is for the invention of a thing: The patent shall be marked on the thing; 2. If the patent is for the invention of a process for manufacturing a thing: The patent shall be marked on the thing manufactured by the process; 3. If it is impossible to mark the patent on a thing: The patent shall be marked on the containers or packaging of the thing (Patent Act Article 223).

특허표시

특허권자, 전용실시권자 또는 통상실시권자는 다음 각 호의 구분에 따른 방법으로 특허표시를 할 수 있다. 1. 물건의 특허발명의 경우: 그 물건에 특허표시 2. 물건을 생산하는 방법의 특허발명의 경우: 그 방법에 따라 생산된 물건에 특허표시 3. 물건에 특허표시를 할 수 없는 경우: 그 물건의 용기 또는 포장에 특허표시 (특허법 제223조 제1항).

patent pool

A patent pool put together multiple patents that are essential to manufacture a particular product, for example, and allows its member companies to cross-license their patented technologies that belong to the pool, which lowers the burden of individually obtaining licenses for each patent in the pool.

특허풀

특정 제품의 생산 등에 필요한 다수의 특허를 하나의 풀(pool)로 묶어 그 소속 기업들 간 크로스 라이센싱 등을 통해 각 기술마다 개별적으로 실시권을 얻을 때 발생하는 부담을 줄이는 등의 기능을 수행함.

patent register

특허원부

patent registration certificate

특허증

patent right

A patent shall take effect when the grant of the patent is registered (Patent Act Article 87(1)).

특허권

특허권은 설정등록에 의하여 발생한다(특허법 제87조 제1항).

Patent Trial and Appeal Board

미 미국 특허심판원

pattern

모양

Example The term "design" means a shape, **pattern**, or color of an article which invokes a sense of beauty through visual perception (Design Protection Act Article 2.1).

디자인이란 형상 · **모양** · 색채 또는 이들을 결합한 것으로서 시각을 통하여 미감(미감)을 일으키게 하는 것을 말한다(디자인보호법 제2조 제1호).

payment of remainder

To pay off any unpaid balance of registration fee.

등록료의 보전

등록료의 일부를 납부하지 아니하여 부족한 부분을 보태어 채우는 것.

pending application

An application is pending until it registers or abandons. Pending applications include applications that have been approved for publication or for registration on the Supplemental Register, applications in the Intent-to-Use ("ITU")/Divisional Unit, and revived or reinstated applications. TMEP § 702.03(a).

미 계류출원

출원은 등록되거나 포기되기까지는 계류중인 것으로 본다. 공고 승인된 출원이나 보조등록부 등록이 승인된 출원, 사용의사에 기한 출원, 복권 또는 회복된 출원의 경우가 모두 계류 중 출원에 해당함. (미) TMEP § 702.03(a).

Example The letter of protest procedure applies only to **pending applications** and is intended to aid in examination without causing undue delay and without compromising the integrity and objectivity of the ex parte examination process. TMEP § 1715.

항의서 절차는 **계류중인 출원**에 대해서만 밟을 수 있으며 불필요한 지연을 야기하거나 결정계 심사절차의 위상과 객관성을 해하지 아니하고 심사를 지원하는 데에 그 의의가 있다. (미) TMEP § 1715.

peripheral claiming

A regime in which an applicant delineates the precise boundaries of the claimed area of exclusivity, in contrast to central claiming in which the applicant defines the claim directly.

주변한정주의

출원인이 청구항을 직접 정의하는 중심한정주의의 반대개념으로, 배타적 권리를 주장하는 정확한 경계를 표시하게 하는 주의.

permanent injunction

An injunction granted after a final hearing on the merits.

미 (영구)금지명령

본안에 대한 최종공판 이후에 내려진 금지명령.

personal jurisdiction

A court's power to make decisions over parties.

인적관할

법원이 소송 당사자에 대해 판결을 내릴 권한.

person having ordinary skills in the art

A hypothetical person that possesses the technological common sense at the time of the patent application, who can utilize ordinary means and ability for research and development with ease, collect all the information in the state of the art at the time of the application and make it his/her own, and process the knowledge in the technological field relevant to the technical problem of the invention.

통상의 기술자

출원시에 당해 기술분야의 기술상식을 보유하고 있고, 연구개발을 위하여 통상의 수단 및 능력을 자유롭게 구사할 수 있으며, 출원시의 기술수준에 있는 모든 것을 입수하여 자신의 지식으로 할 수 있고, 발명의 과제와 관련되는 기술분야의 지식을 자신의 지식으로 할 수 있는 가상의 인물.

perspective view

Perspective views are suggested and may be submitted to clearly show the appearance of three dimensional designs. If a perspective view is submitted, the surfaces shown would normally not be required to be illustrated in other views if these surfaces are clearly understood and fully disclosed in the perspective. MPEP § 1503.02.

사시도

사시도는 3차원 디자인의 외관을 명확하게 도시하기 위하여 추천되는 것이고 제출될 수 있다. 사시도가 제출되는 경우에는, 표면이 사시도에서 명확하게 이해되고 완전히 도시된 경우 일반적으로 이들 표면은 다른 도면에서는 도시될 필요가 없다. (미) MPEP § 1503.02.

P

petition

소장, 청구

petitionee

피청구인

petitioner

청구인

petition (request) for an injunction against infringement

An owner of patent or other rights, or an exclusive licensee thereof, may seek an injunction for prohibition or prevention of infringement against a person who infringes or is likely to infringe on his/her rights.

침해금지청구권

특허권 등의 소유권자 또는 전용실시권자는 자기의 권리를 침해한 자 또는 침해할 우려가 있는 자에 대하여 그 침해의 금지 또는 예방을 청구할 수 있음.

petition for correction

정정청구

petition for patent cancellation

In any of the following cases, Any person may file a petition for the cancellation to the Director General of the Intellectual Property Trial and Appeal Board, if six month have not passed since the date when the registration of the patent is published after the grant of the patent is registered (Patent Act Article 132-2(1)).

특허취소신청

누구든지 특허권의 설정등록일부터 등록공고일 후 6개월이 되는 날까지 그 특허가 다음 각 호의 어느 하나에 해당하는 경우에는 특허심판원장에게 특허취소신청을 할 수 있다(특허법 제132조의2 제1항).

petition for (administrative) trial

심판청구

petition of appeal

항소장

petition to revive an application

When an applicant failed to respond to Office action within the given period and the application was abandoned as a result, the applicant may file a petition to revive the application if the delay was unintentional.

(포기된 출원의) 권리회복청구

출원인이 거절이유통지에 기한 내에 답변을 제출하지 않아 출원이 포기되었으나 그 지연이 의도치 않은 것이었을 경우 포기된 출원에 대한 권리를 회복하기 위한 청구를 할 수 있음.

phantom elements

A word, alpha-numeric designation, or other component that is subject to change an applicant seeks to register as part of the mark. Examples include marks incorporating a date (usually a year), a geographic location, or a model number that is subject to change. TMEP § 1214.

미 가변요소

출원인이 상표의 일부로 등록하고자 하는 추후 변경 가능한 단어나 영숫자, 기타 구성부분. 가령 연도 등 날짜를 포함한 표장, 변경될 수 있는 지리적 위치나 모델 번호를 포함한 표장 등에 나타남. (미) TMEP §1214.

Example … Otherwise, if it is clear that the applicant is seeking registration of a "**phantom mark**" (e.g., if the application includes a statement that "the blank line represents matter that is subject to change") that would not provide adequate constructive notice of the nature of the mark and that precludes a thorough and effective search for conflicting marks, the examining attorney should issue a refusal of registration … on the ground that the application seeks registration of more than one mark. TMEP § 1214.03.

반대로 출원인이 표장의 성격에 대한 실질적이고 적절한 공지를 제시하지 않으면서 저촉표장에 대한 포괄적이고 효과적인 검색을 방해하는 **가변요소**의 등록을 하고자 함이 명백할 경우 (예: 출원에 '빈 칸은 앞으로 변경될 수 있는 부분이다'라고 기재된 경우) 심사관은 하나 이상의 표장에 대한 등록을 하고자 함을 들어 등록거절결정을 하여야 한다. (미) TMEP § 1214.03.

phonetic similarity

호칭유사

Similarity in pronunciation of marks that causes misconception or confusion between the marks among ordinary purchasers. Such marks are similar if there is likelihood of confusion as to the source of the goods.

일반 거래자들이 대비되는 상표를 부르는 호칭이 서로 동일·유사하게 들림으로써 상표를 오인·혼동하는 것인데 그로 인하여 당해 상품의 출처에 대하여 혼동을 일으킬 염려가 있는 경우 상표 유사로 판단될 수 있음.

Example While the cited mark is written as "한라" in Korean, it is called as "HALLA", which is **phonetically similar** ⋯ (Supreme Court Decision, 82Hu62, decided September 11, 1984).

인용상표도 그 한글표기는 비록 "한라"라고 표시되어 있으나⋯ "할라"로 **호칭되어 유사하며**⋯ (대법원 1984. 9. 11. 선고 82후62 판결 참조).

place of business

영업소

Example No person with no domicile or **place of business** in the Republic of Korea (hereinafter referred to as "overseas resident") shall initiate any patent-related procedure or file legal proceedings against a disposition made by an administrative authority under this Act or an order issued under this Act, unless he/she is represented by an agent with respect to his/her patent, who has a domicile or place of business in the Republic of Korea (hereinafter referred to as "patent administrator"), except where the overseas resident (or the representative if the overseas resident is a corporation) sojourns in the Republic of Korea (Patent Act Article 5(1)).

국내에 주소 또는 **영업소**가 없는 자(이하 "재외자"라 한다)는 재외자(법인의 경우에는 그 대표자)가 국내에 체류하는 경우를 제외하고는 그 재외자의 특허에 관한 대리인으로서 국내에 주소 또는 영업소가 있는 자(이하 "특허관리인"이라 한다)에 의해서만 특허에 관한 절차를 밟거나 이 법 또는 이 법에 따른 명령에 따라 행정청이 한 처분에 대하여 소(訴)를 제기할 수 있다 (특허법 제5조 제1항).

place of origin

원산지

Example The term "certification mark" means a mark used by a person who commercially certifies and manages the quality, **place of origin**, methods of production, or other characteristics of goods to certify that goods of others meet quality criteria, the **place of origin**, methods of production, or other characteristics; ⋯ (Trademark Act Article 2(1)7).

"증명표장"이란 상품의 품질, **원산지**, 생산 방법 또는 그 밖의 특성을 증명하고 관리하는 것을 업(業)으로 하는 자가 타인의 상품에 대하여 그 상품이 품질, **원산지**, 생산방법 또는 그 밖의 특성을 충족한다는 것을 증명하는 데 사용하는 표장을 말한다(상표법 제2조 제1항 제7호).

place of production

산지(産地)

The geographical name of the region that produces the designated good.

지정상품이 생산되는 지역의 지리적 명칭

P

plain meaning

The ordinary and customary meaning given to a term by those of ordinary skill in the art at the time of the invention. MPEP § 2111.01.

문언적 의미

발명 당시 그 발명이 속하는 기술 분야의 통상의 기술자가 그 용어에 부여한 일반적이고 관용적인 의미. (미) MPEP § 2111.01.

plaintiff's demand

The conclusion of the plaintiff's action, i.e. the social and economic objective the plaintiff seeks to achieve by filing the action. Any person who intends to request a trial shall state a relief demanded in the suit and any grounds therefor.

청구의 취지

소로써 달성하려는 사회경제적 목적, 소의 결론. 심판을 청구하려는 자는 심판청구서에 반드시 청구의 취지 및 그 이유를 기재하여야 함.

plaintiff's exhibit

Evidence submitted to the court by the plaintiff. Cf. Evidence submitted by the defendant is called defendant's exhibit.

갑호증

원고가 법원에 제출하는 증거. 피고가 제출하는 증거는 을호증이라고 함.

plant patents

Example Whoever invents or discovers and asexually reproduces any distinct and new variety of plant, including cultivated sports, mutants, hybrids, and newly found seedlings, other than a tuber propagated plant or a plant found in an uncultivated state, may obtain a patent therefor … Patent Act, 35 U.S.C. § 161.

식물특허

덩이줄기식물(tuber propagated plant)나 야생식물을 제외한 배양된 변종, 돌연변이, 교잡종, 새로 발견된 묘목, 무성생식이 가능한 식물의 독특하고 새로운 품종을 발명 또는 발견한 자는 그에 대한 특허를 받을 수 있다. (미) 특허법 제161조.

Plant Varieties Protection Act

A U.S. statute on plant varieties protection. The Act gives breeders up to 25 years of exclusive control over new plant varieties. The rights granted under the Act should not be confused with plant patents, which are limited to asexually reproduced plants.

미 식물품종보호법

식물품종의 보호에 대한 미국 법명. 본 법은 육성자에게 최장 25년 간 새로운 식물종에 대한 독점적 통제권을 줌. 특허권과 유사한 권리가 주어지는 것이지만 식물특허는 무성생식 식물에만 적용된다는 점에서 차이가 있음.

plant variety

Example The term "**plant variety**" means a plant grouping within a single botanical taxon of the lowest known rank, which, irrespective of whether the conditions for the grant of a plant variety right under Article 12 are fully met, can be defined by the expression of the characteristics resulting from a given genotype or combination of genotypes

품종

"**품종**"이란 식물학에서 통용되는 최저분류 단위의 식물군으로서 제16조에 따른 품종보호 요건을 갖추었는지와 관계없이 유전적으로 나타나는 특성 중 한 가지 이상의 특성이 다른 식물군과 구별되고 변함없이 증식될 수 있는 것을 말한다(식물신품종보

distinguished from any other plant grouping, by the expression of at least one of the said characteristics, and considered as units with regard to its suitability for being propagated unchanged (Act on Protection of New Varieties of Plants Article 2.2).

호법 제2조 제2호).

plant variety protection tribunal

품종보호심판위원회

A Plant Variety Tribunal (hereinafter referred to as the "Tribunal") shall be established within the Ministry of Agriculture, Food and Rural Affairs to take charge of adjudication and re-adjudication on plant variety protection (Act on Protection of New Varieties of Plants Article 90(1)).

① 품종보호에 관한 심판과 재심을 관장하기 위하여 농림축산식품부에 품종보호심판위원회(이하 "심판위원회"라 한다)를 둔다(식물신품종보호법 제90조 제1항).

plant variety right

품종보호권

pleading

변론

Actions of parties of a litigation arguing, demonstrating, offending and defending at the court under the instruction of the presiding judge by oneself or through its legal counsel.

당사자가 직접 또는 소송대리인을 통해 법정에서 재판장의 지휘 하에 주장과 입증, 공격과 방어를 하는 행위.

pledge

질권

Example Establishment, transfer (excluding transfer by inheritance or other general succession), amendment, extinguishment by abandonment or restrictions on disposition of a **pledge**, the object of which is to acquire the exclusive license or the non-exclusive license (Trademark Act Article 100(1)2, Patent Act Article 121).

전용사용권 또는 통상사용권을 목적으로 하는 **질권**의 설정 · 이전(상속이나 그 밖의 일반승계에 의한 경우는 제외한다) · 변경 · 포기에 의한 소멸 또는 처분의 제한은 등록하지 아니하면 제3자에 대항할 수 없다(상표법 제100조 제2항, 특허법 제121조).

positional mark

위치상표

A mark which is a consistent image or shape formed by an individual sign, letter, figure, or the combination thereof and distinguishes the designated good from other product by being attached to a certain location of the product, location of the product.

기호 · 문자 · 도형 각각 또는 그 결합이 일정한 형상이나 모양을 이루고, 이러한 일정한 형상이나 모양이 지정상품의 특정 위치에 부착되는 것에 의하여 자타상품을 식별하게 되는 표장.

Example A **position mark** requires space for labeling in order to explain where an image or shape is specifically located on the designated product (Supreme Court Decision, 2010Hu2339, decided December 20, 2012).

위치상표에서는 지정상품에 일정한 형상이나 모양 등이 부착되는 특정 위치를 설명하기 위하여 지정상품의 형상을 표시하는 부분을 필요로 하게 된다(대법원 2012. 12. 20. 선고 2010후2339 전원합의체 판결 참조).

post grant review

Under this new procedure added by the AIA, third parties may file a petition seeking to cancel one or more patent claims within nine months of a patent's issue or reissue date.

Example If more than one petition for a **post-grant review** under this chapter is properly filed against the same patent and the Director determines that more than one of these petitions warrants the institution of a post-grant review under section 324, the Director may consolidate such reviews into a single post-grant review. Patent Act, 35 U.S.C. § 325(c).

미 등록후재심사

개정 특허법에 신설된 절차로, 이에 따라 제3자가 특허의 발행 또는 재발행일로부터 9개월 내에 하나 또는 복수의 특허를 취소할 것을 청구할 수 있음.

복수의 **등록후재심사**를 이 장 하에 동일한 특허에 대하여 청구하였고 그 중 복수의 청구가 324조 하에 등록후재심사의 대상이 될 자격이 있다고 판단할 경우 특허상표청장은 각 청구를 단일한 등록후재심사 사건으로 병합할 수 있다. (미) 특허법 제325(c)조.

preamble

The introductory statement of the claim.

Example Drafting a claim in Jepson format … is taken as an implied admission that the subject matter of the **preamble** is the prior art work of another. MPEP § 2129.

전제부

청구항의 서두.

젭슨 형식 청구항 작성은 **전제부**의 대상이 타인의 선행기술임을 암묵적으로 인정하는 것으로 간주된다. (미) MPEP § 2129.

preceding invention

→ See. prior art.

선행고안

predictability

The ability of one skilled in the art to extrapolate the disclosed or known results to the claimed invention. If one skilled in the art can readily anticipate the effect of a change within the subject matter to which the claimed invention pertains, then there is predictability in the art.

예측가능성

통상의 기술자가 출원발명의 공개 또는 공지된 결과를 추정할 가능성. 통상의 기술자가 선행기술로부터 출원발명의 대상의 변화로 인한 효과를 쉽게 예견할 수 있다면 예측가능성이 있다고 본다.

preferred embodiment

How the inventor sets forth the best mode for carrying out the claimed invention in the application.

바람직한 구현례

발명자가 제시하는 출원의 출원발명을 수행하는 최적의 실시례.

preliminary amendment

An amendment that is received in the Office on or before the mail date of the first Office action under § 1.104. 37 C.F.R. § 1.115(a).

미 예비보정

1.104조 하 최초거절사유통지의 발송일 혹은 그 이전에 특허상표청에 도달한 보정. 37 C.F.R. § 1.115(a).

preliminary injunction

A temporary injunction issued before or during trial to prevent an irreparable harm from occurring before the court has a chance to decide the case.

가처분

재판 전 혹은 도중에 법원이 사건을 판단하기 전에 회복할 수 없는 피해가 발생하는 것을 막기 위한 일시적인 금지명령.

- provisional disposition (법제처)

preparatory order

Example An order issued to the appellant to submit a brief stating the ground of appeal immediately upon submission of a notice of appeal with insufficient statement of appeal. (Guidelines of Civil Appelate Practice and Procedure of Patent Court of Korea 2. B)

준비명령

항소장에 항소이유 기재가 충분하지 아니한 경우 항소사건이 접수된 직후 항소인에게 항소이유가 기재된 준비서면 제출을 명한다(특허법원 침해소송 항소심 심리메뉴얼 2. 나.).

preparatory order for hearing

An order issued by the presiding judge to the parties to prepare for the pleading.

변론준비명령

재판장이 당사자에게 변론준비를 하도록 하는 명령

preponderance of evidence

A standard of proof applied to determine whether a party has met his or her burden of proof. The greater weight of the evidence that is sufficient to incline a fair and impartial mind to one side on the issue.

미 증거의 우위성

소송당사자가 그 입증책임을 충족시켰는지를 판단하기 위한 입증기준. 공정하고 중립적인 사람이 소송의 쟁점에 대하여 어느 한 쪽으로 마음을 정할 수 있을 만큼 증거의 비중이 기울어졌다고 보는 것.

preservation of evidence

Collecting particular evidence prior to or during continuation of a litigation for factfinding in the main proceeding (Civil Procedure Act Article 375).

증거보전

소송계속 전 또는 소송계속 중에 특정의 증거를 미리 조사해 두었다가 본안소송에서 사실을 인정하는 데 사용하기 위한 증거조사방법(민사소송법 제375조).

presumption of (the amount of) damages

If the infringer has sold the infringing products to third parties, the amount of loss may be calculated by multiplying the quantity of products so sold by the profit per unit of the products that the patentee or the exclusive licensee could have sold, but for the infringement (Patent Act Article 128).

손해액 추정

손해배상을 청구하는 경우 그 권리를 침해한 자가 그 침해행위를 하게 한 물건을 양도하였을 때에는 그 물건의 양도수량에 특허권자 또는 전용실시권자가 그 침해행위가 없었다면 판매할 수 있었던 물건의 단위수량당 이익액을 곱한 금액을 특허권자 또는 전용실시권자가 입은 손해액으로 할 수 있다(특허법 제128조).

P

presumption of manufacturing process

Where a patent has been granted for inventing a manufacturing process of a thing, any product identical to the thing shall be deemed manufactured by the patented process (Patent Act Article 129).

생산방법의 추정

물건을 생산하는 방법의 발명에 관하여 특허가 된 경우에 그 물건과 동일한 물건은 그 특허된 방법에 의하여 생산된 것으로 추정한다(특허법 제129조).

presumption of negligence

Example A person who infringes a patent or exclusive license of any third person shall be presumed negligent regarding such infringement (Patent Act Article 130).

과실의 추정

타인의 특허권 또는 전용실시권을 침해한 자는 그 침해행위에 대하여 과실이 있는 것으로 추정한다(특허법 제130조).

pretrial hearing

A date set up by the presiding judge when it is necessary to organize the arguments and evidences.

- preperatory hearing (법제처)

변론준비기일

변론기일 전에 주장과 증거의 정리를 위해 필요한 경우 재판장에 의해 열리는 기일.

previously registered mark

→ See. prior-registered mark.

선등록상표

price erosion

A harm caused by acts of infringement when the patent owner is forced to sell its product at a lower price than it could have sold in the absence of the infringing acts.

가격침식

침해행위로 인하여 그 행위가 없었을 경우 특허권자가 제품을 판매하였을 가격보다 더 낮은 가격에 제품을 판매하게 되어 손해를 입는 경우.

prima facie case

If the examiner does not produce a prima facie case, the applicant is under no obligation to submit secondary evidence to show nonobviousness. If, however, the examiner does produce a prima facie case, the burden of coming forward with evidence or arguments shifts to the applicant who may submit additional evidence of nonobviousness, such as comparative test data showing that the claimed invention possesses improved properties not expected by the prior art. MPEP § 2142.

미 일응의 유리한 사건

심사관이 일응의 유리한 사건을 제시하지 못하면 출원인은 비자명성 입증을 위해 2차적 증거를 제출할 어떠한 의무도 없다. 반면 심사관이 일응의 유리한 사건을 제시하였다면 증거 또는 주장을 제시할 책임은 출원인에게로 전환되는데, 출원인은 출원발명이 선행기술에서 예측할 수 없는 개선된 특성을 지니고 있음을 나타내는 비교실험데이터 등 비자명성에 대한 추가적인 증거를 제시할 수 있다. (미) MPEP § 2142.

prima facie obviousness

Example Once the factual inquiries mandated under Graham v. John DeereCo., 383 U. S. 1, 148 USPQ 459 (1966), have been made, the examiner must determine whether they support a conclusion of **prima facie obviousness**. To establish **prima facie obviousness**, all the claim limitations must be taught or suggested by the prior art. MPEP § 1504.03.II.

미 일응의 자명성

Graham v. John Deere Co., 383 U.S. 1, 148 USPQ 459 (1966) 판례에 따른 사실조사가 수행된 후에는, 심사관은 이들이 **일응의 자명성**이라는 결론을 뒷받침 하는지 판단하여야 한다. **일응의 자명성**이 성립하기 위하여는, 모든 청구범위 한정이 공지디자인에서 교시되거나 암시되어야 한다. (미) MPEP § 1504.03.II.

(A mark that is) Primarily merely a surname

When the primary significance of the mark as a whole to the purchasing public is merely a surname.

미 주로 단지 성(姓)만으로 구성된 표장

일반 수요자가 보기에 전체적으로 그 표장이 주로 성만을 나타내는 경우.

Example The question of whether a word sought to be registered is **primarily merely a surname** within the meaning of the statute can be resolved only on a case by case basis. Even though a mark may have been adopted because it is the surname of one connected with the business, it may not be primarily merely a surname under the statute because it is also a word having ordinary language meaning. The language meaning is likely to be the primary meaning to the public. In re Etablissements Darty Et Fils, 759 F.2d 15, 17 (Fed. Cir. 1985).

상표로 등록하고자 하는 단어가 상표법상 **주로 단지 성만으로 구성**되었는지는 각각의 사례에 따라서만 판단할 수 있을 것이다. 영업과 관련이 있는 자의 성을 따라 정한 상표라 하더라도 일반적인 의미도 가지는 단어라면 상표법상 주로 단지 성만으로 된 상표에 해당하지 않는 것도 가능하다. 공중에게는 일반적 의미가 주된 의미일 가능성이 높기 때문이다. In re Etablissements Darty Et Fils, 759 F.2d 15, 17 (Fed. Cir. 1985).

primary references

Example Therefore, in order to support a holding of obviousness, a **primary reference** must be more than a design concept; it must have an appearance substantially the same as the claimed design. MPEP § 1504.03.

주인용문헌

자명성의 판단을 뒷받침하기 위해서는 **주인용문헌**에 디자인 관념 이상의 것이 있어야 하며, 주장하는 디자인과 실질적으로 동일한 외관이 나타나야 한다. (미) MPEP § 1504.03.

principal design

The principle design in a pending application or registration that is compared with related design to determine similarity (Design Protection Act Article 35).

기본디자인

자기의 등록디자인 또는 디자인등록출원한 디자인으로서, 관련디자인과 대비하여 유사의 판단기준이 되는 이미 등록되었거나 등록출원한 디자인(디자인보호법 제35조 참조).

P

Principal Register

Primary trademark register of the USPTO. When a mark has been registered on the Principal Register, the mark is entitled to all the rights provided by the Trademark Act. USPTO.

미 주등록부

특허상표청의 주된 상표등록부. 주등록부에 등록된 상표는 상표법 하의 모든 권리를 가짐. (미) USPTO.

principle of general reliance

→ See. principle of trust protection.

신뢰보호의 원칙

principle of individual representation

Where there are more than one legal representative for the same party in a lawsuit, each shall be the representative of the party.

개별대리의 원칙

같은 당사자에 대하여 여러 사람의 소송대리인이 있을 때에는 대리인 각자가 당사자를 대리하는 것.

principle of registration

The principle that one shall be entitled to IP rights, whether or not the IP rights is actually used, by registration.

등록주의

사용 여부와 관계없이 등록에 의하여 권리를 인정하는 주의.

principle of trust protection

The principle that a citizen's trust on a government agency's public expression of its opinion should be protected, when the citizen acted in reliance of the trust and such trust deserves protection.

Example However, it cannot be said that the final rejection on the Subject Invention is illegal due to violation of the **principle of trust protection** on the following grounds (Patent Court Decision, 2016Heo229, decided July 8, 2016).

신뢰보호의 원칙

신뢰보호원칙이란 행정청의 공적견해표명에 대한 보호가치 있는 신뢰를 가진 국민이 그 신뢰에 기초하여 어떠한 행위를 하였을 때, 위 신뢰는 보호되어야 한다는 원칙.

그러나 다음과 같은 이유로 이 사건 출원발명에 대한 거절결정이 **신뢰보호원칙**에 위배되어 위법하다고 할 수 없다(특허법원 2016. 7. 8. 선고 2016허229 판결 참조).

principle to exclude publicly known art

One of the negative requirements of the doctrine of equivalents. According to this principle, an invention does not constitute patent infringement if the technology has been already publicly known or could have easily been invented by those skilled in the technology from the known prior technology (Supreme Court Decision, 98Hu522, decided August 21, 2001).

공지기술 배제의 원칙

특허 균등침해의 소극적 성립요건 중 하나. 특허발명과 구분되는 확인대상발명이 공지의 기술에 해당하거나 공지의 기술로부터 진보성이 없는 경우에는 특허침해에 해당하지 아니한다는 원칙(대법원 2001. 8. 21. 선고 98후522 판결 참조).

prior art

Technology or invention that are published or publicly known at the time of the patent application. It is used as a basis to determine novelty or inventive step of an invention. Prior art is referred to as "prior art" in litigation but as "cited invention" in KIPO's examination process.

선행발명

특허출원 당시 공지되었거나 공연히 실시된 기술 또는 발명. 특허의 신규성 또는 진보성 판단 기준이 됨.

prior art exceptions

If an invention has been laid open by a person entitled to a patent or contrary to the will of the person entitled to a patent, a patent application filed within 12 months from the relevant date shall not be deemed to be publicly known or practiced (Patent Act Article 30(1)).

공지의 예외

특허를 받을 수 있는 권리를 가진자의 발명이 그에 의하여 또는 그 의사에반 하여 공지 또는 공연 실시된 경우 그로부터 12개월 이내에 특허출원을 하면 공지 등이 되지 아니한 발명으로 본다(특허법 제30조 제1항 참조).

prior design

→ See. prior art.

선행디자인

prior invention

→ See. prior art.

선행기술

priority action

An examining attorney sends a priority action after having consulted with the applicant regarding problems with the application, to confirm in writing what was discussed. This type of action will include reasons why registration is being refused and/or how to satisfy certain application requirements.

선행조치

심사관은 출원인과 출원의 문제점을 의논한 뒤 그 의견교환과정을 서면으로 확인하는 목적으로 선행조치를 발송함. 여기에는 거절이유나 특정 출원요건의 충족 방법 등이 포함된다.

priority claim

→ See. claim of priority.

우선권 주장

prior-registered mark

선등록상표

Example It does not appear that consumers of the designated goods were mistaken or confused between the mark at issue and the **prior-registered** trademark (Patent Court Decision, 2015Heo5432, decided December 18, 2015).

지정상품에 관하여 그 수요자들이 이 사건 등록상표와 **선등록상표**를 오인 · 혼동한 사례는 보이지 않는다(특허법원 2015. 12. 18. 선고 2015허5432 판결 참조).

P

problem to be solved

기술적 과제

Example The invention in Claim 1 is different from the Prior Art in that specific **technical problems** of these two inventions are different, and the principle or the method made for solving the problems is not inherent in the Prior Art nor easily conceived from the Prior Art (or related arts other than the Prior Art), and as a result, the objective of the invention in Claim 1 is distinct (Patent Court Decision, 2006Heo6009, decided April 6, 2007).

이 사건 제1항 발명은 비교대상발명과는 구체적인 **기술적 과제**가 상이하고, 이를 해결하고자 착안한 원리 내지 방법이 비교대상발명에 내재되어 있거나 비교대상발명으로부터(비교대상발명 이외의 종래기술을 포함하더라도) 용이하게 도출되지도 아니하므로, 목적의 특이성이 인정된다(특허법원 2007. 4. 6. 선고 2006허6099 판결).

process claim

방법청구항

A claim covering a way of doing something, typically conveyed as a series of steps.

무언가를 실행하는 방법에 대한 청구로, 주로 일련의 단계로 설명된다.

process invention

방법발명

A type of invention recognized by the Patent Act together with 'invention of a thing' and 'invention of a process of manufacturing a thing.'.

물건의 발명, 물건을 생산하는 방법의 발명과 함께 특허법상 인정되는 발명의 유형 중 하나.

product by process claim

제법(製法) 한정 물건발명

A claim for a product invention that describes its manufacturing process. A product-by-process claim raises the issue of whether the technological characteristics of the process should be taken into consideration or only the final product must be assessed in determining non-obviousness.

물건의 발명임에도 그 청구범위에 그 물건의 제조방법이 기재되는 경우로서, 그 제조방법의 기술적 특징을 고려하여 진보성을 판단할 것인가 아니면 최종산물인 물건만을 기준으로 진보성을 판단할 것인가 문제가 있음.

product design

제품디자인

Example A mark that consists of **product design** trade dress is never inherently distinctive and is not registrable on the Principal Register unless the applicant establishes that the mark has acquired distinctiveness under §2(f). TMEP § 1202.02(b)(i).

제품디자인 트레이드 드레스로 구성된 표장은 결코 본질적인 식별력이 있다 할 수 없으며 출원인이 미 상표법 2(f)조에 따라 그 표장이 식별력을 취득하였음을 입증하지 아니하면 주등록부에 등록될 수 없다. (미) TMEP § 1202.02(b)(i).

product packaging

제품포장

Example If a proposed **product packaging** mark is not inherently distinctive, the mark may be registered on either

제품포장에 대한 출원표장에 본질적인 식별력이 없을 경우 그 표장은 미 상표법 2(f)

the Principal Register under §2(f), upon proof that the mark has acquired distinctiveness or secondary meaning, or on the Supplemental Register. TMEP § 1202.02(b)(ii).

조에 따라 사용에 의한 식별력 또는 2차적 의미를 입증함으로써 주등록부에 등록되거나 보조등록부에 등록될 수 있다. (미) TMEP § 1202.02(b)(ii).

pro-se application

Applications filed by an independent inventor who has elected to file the application by on his or her own without the services of a licensed representative.

본인출원

대리인 자격을 보유한 대리인의 도움을 받지 아니하고 직접 출원을 제출하기로 한 독립된 발명자의 출원.

prosecution

The entire process for the application in the KIPO.

(심사) 절차

출원에 대한 특허청의 일련의 심사절차.

prosecution history

출원경과

prosecution history estoppel

→ See. file wrapper estoppel.

출원경과 금반언의 원칙

protected plant variety

A plant variety for which a plant variety right is granted as it meets requirements for plant variety protection under the Act on Protection of New Varieties of Plants.

보호품종

식물신품종보호법상 품종보호 요건을 갖추어 품종보호권이 주어진 품종.

protective order

→ See. order to maintain confidentiality.

비밀유지명령

provisional application[1]

A patent application under 35 U.S.C. § 111(b) that provides the means to establish an early effective filing date in a nonprovisional patent application. It allows filing without a formal patent claim, oath or declaration, or any information disclosure (prior art) statement. A provisional application automatically becomes abandoned after one year. USPTO.

미 가출원

미 특허법 제 111(b)조에 따라 정규특허출원에 유효한 조기 출원일자를 부여하기 위한 출원. 공식적인 청구항이나 선서나 선언, 선행기술 등의 정보 공개 없이 신청할 수 있다. 가출원은 1년 경과시 자동으로 포기처리됨. (미) USPTO.

provisional application[2]

A temporary application mainly submitted to secure a filing date, containing explanation as to the invention but without claims.

청구범위 제출유예제도

출원일 확보 등을 위하여 특허출원서에 청구범위를 생략한 채 발명의 설명만을 기재하여 임시로 제출한 출원.

provisional execution

Provisional execution refers to a compulsory execution on a judgment that is not final or not complete. Provisional execution is commenced when there is an approval thereof by the court accompanied with the subject judgment (Civil Execution Act Article 24, 56.2).

가집행

가집행이란 가집행선고가 있는 미확정의 종국판결 또는 가집행선고가 있는 재판에 의하여 행해지는 강제집행을 말함(민사집행법 제24조, 제56조 제2호).

provisional seizure

Provisional seizure refers to the attachment to deprive the right to dispose of properties of the debtor to preserve any future execution based on monetary claims until the court renders a judgment on the merit (Civil Execution Act Article 276).

가압류

가압류란 금전 또는 금전으로 환산할 수 있는 채권에 대한 강제집행을 보전하기 위한 조치로서, 본안판결 선고 시까지 미리 일반 담보가 되는 채무자의 재산을 압류하여 현상을 보전하고, 그 변경을 금지하는 절차를 말함(민사집행법 276조).

provision of information about patent applications

Example Any person may provide the Commissioner of the Korean Intellectual Property Office with information that a patent application is ineligible for a patent as it falls under a ground for rejection, along with evidentiary documents: Provided, That the foregoing shall not apply where the patent application fails to meet any of the requirements prescribed under Articles 42 (3) 2 and (8) and Article 45 (Patent Act Article 63-2).

특허출원에 대한 정보제공

특허출원에 관하여 누구든지 그 특허출원이 거절이유에 해당하여 특허될 수 없다는 취지의 정보를 증거와 함께 특허청장에게 제공할 수 있다. 다만, 제42조 제3항 제2호, 같은 조 제8항 및 제45조에 따른 요건을 갖추지 아니한 경우에는 그러하지 아니하다(특허법 제63조의2).

pseudo mark

A way of locating a word mark that is comprised of an alternative or intentionally corrupted spelling of an English word. The pseudo mark search locates spellings that are very similar or phonetically equivalent to the word mark. USPTO.

미 유사표장

대안적 또는 의도적으로 바꾼 스펠링으로 된 문자표장을 검색하기 위해 사용. 유사표장검색으로 해당 문자표장과 매우 유사하거나 발음상 동등한 스펠링을 찾을 수 있음. (미) USPTO.

pseudonym

A name that a person (such as a writer) uses instead of his or her real name.

아호

작가 등이 본래의 이름 외에 사용하는 이름.

Example Where trademark rights (excluding the right to a collective mark with geographical indication) fall under

상표권(지리적 표시 단체표장권은 제외한다)은 다음 각 호의 어느 하나에 해당하는

any of the following, trademark rights shall not effect the same:
1. Any trademark using his/her own name, title, or trade name, portrait, signature, seal, or well-known **pseudonym**, stage name, pen name, and the well-known abbreviated title thereof, in accordance with generally accepted business practices; ··· (Trademark Act Article 90(1)1).

경우에는 그 효력이 미치지 아니한다.
1. 자기의 성명 · 명칭 또는 상호 · 초상 · 서명 · 인장 또는 저명한 **아호** · 예명 · 필명과 이들의 저명한 약칭을 상거래 관행에 따라 사용하는 상표 ··· (상표법 제90조 제1항).

publication

Documents, drawings or photographs printed or copied either mechanically, chemically or electromagnetically (Supreme Court Decision, 92Hu377, decided October 27, 1992). The most representative type of 'publication' would be official gazettes of patents. Books, journals, catalogs, micro films, computer disk, CD-ROMs, electric films and any kind of media also fall under 'publication'.

간행물

공개를 목적으로 인쇄 기타의 기계적, 화학적 또는 전자기적 방법으로 복제된 문서, 도화, 사진 등(대법원 1992. 10. 27. 선고 92후377 판결 참조). 특허공보가 가장 대표적인 간행물이고 그 밖에 서적, 논문, 제품의 카탈로그 등을 포함하며 마이크로필름, 컴퓨터 디스크, CD-ROM, 자기필름 등 현재 개발되어 있거나 향후 개발될 매체들 모두 포함.

publication contrary to the will of the person entitled to a patent

In order to be patentable, an invention shall not be publicly known prior to the filing of a patent application. However, when the invention became publicly known against the will of the person entitled to the patent, the inventions may not be deemed as publicly known under certain circumstances.

의사에 반한 공지

특허출원 전에 발명이 공개된 경우 원칙적으로 신규성 요건이 부정되어 특허를 받을 수 없으나, 특허법은 출원전 공개가 의사에 반한 공지인 경우 일정한 요건 하에 신규성이 부정되지 않도록 예외를 두고 있음.

publication of patent applications

The Commissioner of the Korean Intellectual Property Office shall publish a patent application in the Patent Gazette to lay it open, after the lapse of one year and six months from the filing date of the patent application (Patent Act Article 64(1)).

출원공개

특허청장은 특허출원일로부터 1년 6개월이 지난 후 또는 그 전이라도 특허출원인이 신청한 경우에는 그 특허출원에 관하여 특허공보에 게재하여 출원공개를 하여야 한다(특허법 제64조 제1항).

• laying-open of applications (법제처)

publication of the application

출원공고

Example Where an examiner fails to discover any grounds for rejection of an application for trademark registration,

심사관은 상표등록출원에 대하여 거절이유를 발견할 수 없는 경우에는 **출원공고**결정

P

he/she shall decide to **publish such application**: … (Trademark Act Article 57(1)).

을 하여야 한다. … (상표법 제57조 제1항).

public known

→ See. (publicly) known art.

공지

publicly known design

A design is publicly known if it is in a state that may be known to unspecified number of people, which does not require actual recognition by such.

공지된 디자인

반드시 불특정 다수인에게 인식되었을 필요는 없더라도 적어도 불특정 다수인이 인식할 수 있는 상태에 놓여 있는 디자인.

publicly known invention

Publicly known invention refers to an invention when the content of the invention is left in a situation that many non-specified people can perceive (e.g., when someone distributes drawings and samples of an invention to construction practitioners without imposing any confidential duty) (Supreme Court Decisions, 92Hu377, decided December 27, 1992, 95Hu19, decided June 14, 1996).

공지된 발명

'공지된 발명'이라 함은 아무런 비밀유지의무의 부과 없이 공사 실무자들에게 발명의 도면과 샘플을 제공하는 경우와 같이 발명의 내용이 불특정 다수인이 인식할 수 있는 상태에 놓인 것을 말함(대법원 1992. 10. 27. 선고 92후377 판결, 대법원 1996. 6. 14. 선고 95후19 판결 등 참조).

publicly practiced design

A design publicly known or practiced in a state that unspecified number of people may know about the design.

공연히 실시된 디자인

디자인의 내용이 공연히 알려진 또는 불특정 다수인이 알 수 있는 상태에서 실시된 디자인.

Example "**A publicly practiced design**" refers to a design of which content is publicly known or which has been practiced in a state where unspecified number of people may know about the design. If a good in identical shape of the design was supplied to a merchant in the industry prior to the application date, the design is revealed to the general public and may be simulated. Thus the design lost its novelty or secrecy and is publicly known (Supreme Court Decision, 2000Hu3012, decided December 22, 2000).

… '**공연히 실시된 의장(디자인)**'이라 함은 의장의 내용이 공연히 알려진 또는 불특정 다수인이 알 수 있는 상태에서 실시된 의장을 말하는 것이며, 당해 의장과 동일한 형상 모양의 물품을 그 출원일 이전에 동종업자에게 납품한 사실이 있다면 그 의장은 일반사람의 눈에 띔으로써 바로 알려져 모방할 수 있는 것이므로 그의 신규성 내지 비밀성을 잃어 공지로 된다고 할 것이다(대법원 2000. 12. 22. 선고 2000후3012 판결 참조).

publicly practiced invention

"A publicly worked invention" means an invention which has been worked under the conditions where the contents

공연히 실시된 발명

공연히 실시된 발명은 국내나 국외에서 그 발명이 공연히 알려진 상태 또는 공연히 알

of the invention are to be publicly known or can potentially be publicly known in the Republic of Korea or a foreign country (Patent Court Decision, 98Heo4449, decied January 14, 1999)

려질 수 있는 상태에서 실시되고 있는 것을 의미함(특허법원 1999.1.14. 선고 98허4449 판결 참조).

Example **An invention publicly known or executed** in the Republic of Korea or in a foreign country prior to the filing of a patent application is not patentable (Patent Act Article 29(1)).

특허출원 전에 국내 또는 국외에서 공지(公知)되었거나 **공연(公然)히 실시된 발명**은 특허를 받을 수 없다(특허법 제29조 제1항).

• publicly executed (법제처)

public notice in lieu of service

공시송달

Where it is impossible to serve a party because the address or the place of business of the party cannot be identified, service may be done by publication on the court bulletin board of the fact that the party may retrieve the document from the court at any time.

당사자의 송달장소가 불명하여 통상의 송달방법에 의해서는 송달을 실시할 수 없게 되었을 때, 법원에서 송달한 서류를 보관해 두고 송달을 받을 자가 나타나면 언제든지 그것을 그 자에게 교부한다는 것을 법원게시장에 게시함으로써 행하는 송달방법.

• service by publication (법제처)

public order

공공의 질서

public practiced

공용

→ See. publicly practiced invention.

punitive damages

미 징벌적 손해배상

An infringer may be liable for punitive damages up to three times of the amount found in case of willful infringement. Willfulness is now determined by subjective knowledge of the infringer instead of objective recklessness. In addition, the burden of proof is now easier to satisfy, as the applicable standard has changed to preponderance of evidence from clear and convincing evidence. Halo Elecs., Inc. v. Pulse Elecs., Inc., 136 S. Ct. 1923, 1927, 195 L. Ed. 2d 278 (2016).

고의침해 시 침해자에게 인정된 손해의 최대 3배까지 증액하여 배상하도록 함. Halo 미 대법원 판결 이후 침해의 고의는 더 이상 객관적인 무모함(recklessness)이 아닌 침해자의 주관적 인지에 따라 결정되며, 그 입증책임 기준도 '명백하고 확실한 증거(clear and convincing evidence)'에서 '증거의 우월성(preponderance of evidence)'으로 완화되었다. (미) Halo Elecs., Inc. v. Pulse Elecs., Inc., 136 S. Ct. 1923, 1927, 195 L. Ed. 2d 278 (2016)

purport of claim

청구의 취지

→ See. plaintiff's demand.

purport of evidence

입증취지

Q

quality assurance

품질보증기능

A function of trademark, which is to assure consumers to expect that goods with the trademark to all show identical performance and quality.

수요자로 하여금 그 상표가 부착된 상품은 동일한 성능과 품질을 가지고 있다고 기대할 수 있도록 하는 상표의 기능.

Example Given that a trademark's main functions boil down to source indication that the goods to which the mark is affixed come from a particular business, along with **quality assurance**··· (Supreme Court Decision, 99Da42322, decided September 24, 2002).

상표는 기본적으로 당해 상표가 부착된 상품의 출처가 특정한 영업주체임을 나타내는 상품출처표시기능과 이에 수반되는 **품질보증기능**이 주된 기능이라는 점 등에 비추어 볼 때, ··· (대법원 2002. 9. 24. 선고 99다42322 판결 참조).

quasi-compulsory joint litigation

유사필수적 공동소송

A form of joint litigation by certain parties who are not necessarily required to jointly pursue the litigation in the first place but requested joinder and who shall now be subject to a uniform disposition.

특정 당사자들이 반드시 공동으로 소송을 수행할 필요는 없으나 합일확정이 요청되어 승패를 일률적으로 하여야 할 공동소송 형태.

Example Even if the plaintiff's claim to invalidate the registration through intervention has substantive merits as a claim for a new trial and therefore is a quasi-compulsory joint litigation to that of ooo's petition, the decision to dismiss the petition is already confirmed and its lawfulness can no longer be disputed. As such, it may not be an issue in the present proceeding to revoke the administrative decision (Patent Court Decision, 2015Heo8424, decided June 10, 2016).

원고의 이 사건 당사자참가신청을 통한 등록무효 심판청구가 새로운 심판청구로서의 실질을 갖고 있고 그에 따라 ooo의 이 사건 심판청구와 유사필수적 공동심판관계에 놓이게 된다 하더라도, 그 신청서를 각하한 이 사건 결정이 이미 확정되어 그 위법성을 더 이상 다툴 수 없는 이상, 이 사건 심결취소소송에서도 이를 다툴 수 없는 것은 마찬가지이다(특허법원 2016.06.10 선고 2015허8424판결 참조).

questionnaire for examination

증인신문사항

The Court may issue a preparatory order for examination

전문가증인의 신문을 위해 필요한 사항(전

of an expert witness (e.g. deadlines for submission of affidavit and a questionnaire for the direct examination, limitation of the time for examination, and deadlines for submission of arguments and evidence for impeaching the credibility of the expert witness testimony) (Patent Court Guideline of Civil Practice and Procedure, VI.2.B).

문가증인 진술서 및 증인신문사항의 제출기한, 증인신문시간의 제한, 전문가증인의 증언의 신빙성을 탄핵하는 주장 및 증거의 제출기한 등)에 대해서는 준비명령을 할 수 있다(특허법원 침해소송 항소심 심리매뉴얼 VI.2.나).

R

range of similarity

The scope of similarity applied in determining the similarity of trademarks or designs. It may be broad or narrow depending on the particular course of trade.

유사의 폭

상표 또는 디자인의 유사성 판단에 있어 적용되는 상표 또는 디자인의 유사 범위. 구체적인 거래실정에 따라 좁아질 수도, 넓어질 수도 있음.

Example In case of a motif created or adopted for the first time by the registered design, use of the same motive would create the identical aesthetic feel. Therefore, the **range of similarity** of both designs should be viewed as broad (Patent Court Decision, 2007Heo8559, decided September 11, 2008).

등록디자인에 의하여 비로소 창작되거나 채택된 모티브인 경우 모티브의 동일성만으로도 동일한 심미감을 형성할 것이므로 양 디자인의 **유사의 폭**은 넓게 보아야 할 것인바, … (특허법원 2008. 9. 11. 선고 2007허8559 판결 참조).

ratify

Procedures followed by a person who has no legal capacity or authority of legal representation, or who has any defect in the delegation of authority shall take effect retroactive to the time he/she performed an act if the party whose defect has been rectified or his/her legal representative confirms such procedures.

추인

행위능력 또는 법정대리권이 없거나 필요한 권한의 위임에 흠이 있는 자가 밟은 절차는 보정(補正)된 당사자나 법정대리인이 추인하면 행위를 한 때로 소급하여 그 효력이 발생한다.

reason

(판결) 이유

reasonable diligence

→ See. due diligence.

미 합리적인 노력

Example The work relied upon to show **reasonable diligence** must be directly related to the reduction to practice of the invention in issue. MPEP § 2138.06.

합리적인 노력을 입증하기 위해 근거로 든 노력은 해당 사건의 발명의 구현과 직접적으로 연관되어야 한다. (미) MPEP § 2138.06.

reasonable royalty

The amount that a person, desiring to manufacture, use, or sell a patented article, as a business proposition, would be willing to pay as a royalty and yet be able to make, use, or sell the patented article, in the market, at a reasonable profit. Trans-World Mfg. Corp. v. Al Nyman & Sons, Inc., 750 F.2d 1552, 1568 (Fed. Cir. 1984).

합리적인 실시료

특허대상인 물품을 업으로 생산, 사용, 판매하고자 하는 자가 지불할 의향이 있으며 지불하고도 그 물품의 생산, 사용, 판매로 시장에서 합리적인 이익을 얻을 수 있을 정도의 금액. (미) Trans-World Mfg. Corp. v. Al Nyman & Sons, Inc., 750 F.2d 1552, 1568 (Fed. Cir. 1984)

Example The right under paragraph (1) to obtain a **reasonable royalty** shall be available only in an action brought not later than 6 years after the patent is issued. 35 U.S.C. § 154(d)(3).

제(1)항에 따라 **합리적인 실시료**를 받을 권리는 특허등록 이후 6년 이내에 제기된 소에 따라서만 인정될 수 있다. (미) 특허법 154(d)(3)조.

rebuttal evidence

Submitted by the applicant in response to an Office action to avoid rejection. Rebuttal evidence regarding a patent application, for example, may include evidence of secondary considerations, such as commercial success long felt but unsolved needs, [and] failure of others (Graham v. John Deere Co.), and may also include evidence of unexpected results. MPEP § 2141.01.

반박증거

출원인이 거절결정을 막기 위해 특허상표청의 통지에 대해 제출함. 가령 특허출원에 대한 반박증거에는 상업적 성공, 오래 되었으나 해결되지 않은 필요, 타인의 실패 등 2차적 고려사항(Graham v. John Deere Co. 판례 참조)과 예상치 못한 결과에 대한 증거가 포함될 수 있음. (미) MPEP § 2141.01.

recover (an application)

Reinstating the effectiveness of application, for example by paying outstanding balance of registration fee.

출원의 회복

등록료의 보전 등으로 출원의 효력을 회복하는 것.

Example Where an application for trademark registration, an application for registration of additional designated goods or a bundle of trademark rights (···) has been recovered pursuant to paragraph (2), such application for trademark registration, etc. shall not effect an act of using a trademark identical or similar to such trademark on goods identical or similar to such designated goods before the application for trademark registration, etc. is recovered after the period for payment under Article 72 (3) or 74 expires (Trademark Act Article 77(3)).

제2항에 따라 상표등록출원, 지정상품추가등록출원 또는 상표권(···)이 회복된 경우에는 그 상표등록출원등의 효력은 제72조 제3항 또는 제74조에 따른 납부기간이 지난 후 상표등록출원등이 회복되기 전에 그 상표와 동일 · 유사한 상표를 그 지정상품과 동일 · 유사한 상품에 사용한 행위에는 미치지 아니한다(상표법 제77조 제3항).

rectification of clerical errors

To correct ambiguity or errors in the specification and

오기정정

출원발명 또는 특허발명의 명세서, 도면의

drawings of a patent or an application.

오류나 불분명한 기재를 정정하는 것.

Example The purport of Articles 133-2 and 136(3) of the former Patent Act (amended by Act No. 9381, Jan. 30, 2009) is to: enable the patent-holder as the respondent in a patent invalidation trial to petition for correction in the invalidation trial procedure without having to file for a separate trial for correction; prohibit any substantial extension of, or amendment to, the claims; but allow for a reduction in the number of claims, **rectification of clerical errors**, and clarification of ambiguous indications, to the extent they are not likely to infringe on third party rights (Supreme Court Decision, decided November 25, 2016).

구 특허법 제133조의2, 제136조 제3항의 규정 취지는 무효심판의 피청구인이 된 특허권자에게 별도의 정정심판을 청구하지 않더라도 무효심판절차 내에서 정정청구를 할 수 있게 해주되, 청구범위를 실질적으로 확장하거나 변경하는 것은 허용하지 아니하고, 제3자의 권리를 침해할 우려가 없는 범위 내에서의 청구범위의 감축이나 **오기를 정정**하고 기재상의 불비를 해소하여 바르게 하는 오류의 정정은 허용하는 데 있다 (대법원 2016. 11. 25. 선고 2014후2184 판결 참조).

recusal

회피

To voluntarily avoid discharging authority on cases when a judge believes there is a reason to be excluded or avoided.

법관 스스로 제척 또는 기피의 원인이 있다고 인정한 때에 직무의 집행을 피하는 것.

- avoidance (법제처)

reduction to practice

(발명의)완성, (발명의)구체화

Starting with conception, an invention is complete when it is reduced to practice. Reduction to practice may be actual such as constructing a physical embodiment of the invention, or constructive by filing a patent application that satisfies the disclosure requirements.

발명은 착상으로 시작되어 구현으로 완성된다. 발명의 구현은 발명의 물리적 형상을 만들어 내는 것과 같이 실제적일 수도 있으며, 개시요건을 만족시키는 특허출원을 제기함으로써 의제적으로 할 수도 있음.

reexamination

재심사

A patent applicant may file a request to re-examine his/her patent application (hereinafter referred to as "re-examination") after amending the specification or drawings of the patent application within 30 days (referring to an extension, if the period is extended under Article 15 (1)) after receipt of a certified copy of the decision to reject the patent application (Patent Act Article 67-2(1)).

특허출원인은 그 특허출원에 관하여 특허거절결정등본을 송달받은 날부터 30일 이내에 그 특허출원의 명세서 또는 도면을 보정하여 해당 특허출원에 관한 재심사(이하 "재심사"라 한다)를 청구할 수 있다(특허법 제67조의2 제1항).

reference provisions

참조 조문

(cited) references

인용문헌

Documents cited as relevant in a patent prosecution.

특허심사절차에서 관련성이 있는 것으로

R

References may be categorized into: domestic patents and patent application publications; foreign patents; and non-patent literature.

인용된 문헌. 크게 국내특허, 특허출원공고, 해외특허, 비특허문헌으로 나눌 수 있음.

Example The question in design cases is not whether the **references** sought to be combined are in analogous arts in the mechanical sense, but whether they are so related that the appearance of certain ornamental features in one would suggest the application of those features to the other. In re Glavas, 230 F.2d 447, 450, 109 USPQ 50, 52 (CCPA 1956).

디자인 사례에서의 쟁점은 결합하고자 하는 **인용문헌**이 기계적으로 유사한 기술분야에 속하는지가 아닌 한 디자인의 특정한 장식적 특징이 그 외관상 다른 디자인에 적용된 것으로 암시할 만큼 서로 연관되어 있는가이다. In re Glavas, 230 F.2d 447, 450, 109 USPQ 50, 52 (CCPA 1956).

refusal

거절결정

→ See. rejection.

regarding as confession/admission

자백간주

When a party has failed to evidently contest at his/her pleading the facts alleged by the other party, he/she shall be deemed to have confessed such facts: Provided, That the same shall not apply where it is deemed that a contest has been made against such facts, in view of the purports of entire pleadings (Civil Procedure Act Article 150(1)).

당사자가 변론에서 상대방이 주장하는 사실을 명백히 다투지 아니한 때에는 그 사실을 자백한 것으로 본다. 다만, 변론 전체의 취지로 보아 그 사실에 대하여 다툰 것으로 인정되는 경우에는 그러하지 아니하다(민사소송법 제150조 제1항).

(patent) register

특허등록원부

A book in the KIPO that is used to enter the grant, expiration, reinstatement of patents or other rights, restrictions on the disposal and the extension of terms, etc.

특허청에 있는, 특허권 등의 설정, 이전, 소멸, 회복, 처분의 제한 또는 존속기간의 연장 등을 등록하는 장부.

registered trademark

등록상표

A trademark owner or applicant may add designated goods in the registration or application. In such cases, the expiration date of the trademark on the subsequently added designated goods shall be the expiration date of the registered trademark (Trademark Act Article 86(1)).

상표권자 또는 출원인은 등록상표 또는 상표등록출원의 지정상품을 추가하여 상표등록을 받을 수 있다. 이 경우 추가등록된 지정상품에 대한 상표권의 존속기간 만료일은 그 등록상표권의 존속기간 만료일로 한다(상표법 제86조 제1항).

registered utility model

등록실용신안

A device for which a utility model has been granted.

실용신안등록을 받은 고안.

registration date

등록일

registration fee

등록료

Fee to establish patent or other IP rights, to renew their terms or add designated goods.

특허권등의 설정등록, 존속기간갱신등록, 지정상품추가등록 등을 받기 위해 납부하는 금액.

Example A person granted a design right registered under Article 90 (1) shall pay a design registration fee (hereinafter referred to as "**registration fee**") for three years from the date the grant of the right is registered, and the owner of a design right shall pay a registration fee for one year thereafter on or before each anniversary of the registration date of the grant of the relevant right (Design Protection Act Article 79(1)).

제90조 제1항에 따른 디자인권의 설정등록을 받으려는 자는 설정등록을 받으려는 날부터 3년분의 디자인등록료(이하 "**등록료**"라 한다)를 내야 하며, 디자인권자는 그 다음 해부터의 등록료를 그 권리의 설정등록일에 해당하는 날을 기준으로 매년 1년분씩 내야 한다(디자인보호법 제79조 제1항).

registration for establishment of rights

설정등록

In countries that adopt the principle of registration such as the Republic of Korea, intellectual property rights arise from registration. Registration to give rise to such rights is referred to as registration for establishment of rights.

등록주의를 채택하고 있는 한국 등의 나라에서 산업재산권은 등록에 의해 권리가 발생하며, 권리를 발생시키기 위한 등록을 설정등록이라 함.

Example Trademark rights shall come into existence by obtaining trademark registration and **establishing** trademark rights (Trademark Act Article 82(1)).

상표권은 **설정등록**에 의하여 발생한다(상표법 제82조 제1항).

- registration of grant of design rights (법제처)

registration of additional designated goods

지정상품추가등록

A trademark right holder or an applicant may obtain trademark registration by adding designated goods to the registered trademark or to the application for trademark registration (Trademark Act Article 86(1)).

상표권자 또는 출원인은 등록상표 또는 상표등록출원의 지정상품을 추가하여 상표등록을 받을 수 있다(상표법 제86조 제1항).

reinstate (an application)

출원의 회복

→ See. recover.

reissue application

미 재발행출원

Whenever any patent is, through error, deemed wholly or partly inoperative or invalid, by reason of a defective specification or drawing, or by reason of the patentee claiming more or less than he had a right to claim in the patent,

특허의 결함 있는 명세서나 도면, 혹은 청구가능한 범위보다 넓거나 좁게 청구하였을 경우와 같은 오류로 인하여 특허가 그 전체 또는 부분이 작용이 불가능하거나 무

R

the Director shall, on the surrender of such patent and the payment of the fee required by law, reissue the patent for the invention disclosed in the original patent, and in accordance with a new and amended application, for the unexpired part of the term of the original patent. No new matter shall be introduced into the application for reissue. In practice, surrender is automatic upon the grant of the reissue patent and no physical surrender is required. MPEP § 1416.

효로 간주되었을 때 특허권자가 그 특허를 포기(surrender)하고 법에 정한 수수료를 납부하면 특허상표청장은 원출원에 개시된 발명에 대하여 그 특허를 재발행하여야 하며 이는 신규 또는 보정된 출원과 일관되고 원 특허의 잔존기간 동안 유효하다. 재발행출원에는 신규사항이 포함되어서는 아니된다. 단 실무적으로는 특허의 재발행으로 자동적으로 원 특허는 포기된 것으로 보며 물리적으로 문서를 제출할 필요는 없다. (미) MPEP § 1416.

reject

거절결정

→ See. rejection.

rejection

거절결정

An examiner's decision to refuse to register intellectual property rights when the application therefor fails to meet the requirements for registration.

출원된 산업재산권이 등록요건에 맞지 아니하는 경우 심사관이 등록거절결정을 내리는 것을 말함.

Example The claim on appeal is that the mark "BLU-109" is registered in many foreign countries and many names of weapons are registered in Korea as trademarks for weapons as designated goods, and thus the **decision to refuse** the application was unlawful. However, whether or not a trademark is a common name for the designated good must be determined based on the course of trade of the good in the country (Supreme Court Decision, 2003Hu595, decided June 13, 2003).

상고이유의 주장은, "BLU-109" 라는 표장에 관하여 해외의 여러 나라에서 상표등록을 받았을 뿐만 아니라 많은 무기류의 명칭이 무기류를 지정상품으로 하여 우리나라에서 상표등록이 되었으므로 이 사건 출원상표의 출원에 대한 **거절결정**은 부당하다는 것이나, 어느 상표가 지정상품의 보통명칭이 되었는지 여부는 그 나라에 있어서 당해 상품의 거래실정에 따라 결정하여야 하므로… (대법원 2003.06.13 선고 2003후595 판결 참조).

Example An examiner shall **determine to reject** a patent application if the patent application falls under any of the following grounds for rejection (hereinafter referred to as "grounds for rejection"). 1. If an invention is unpatentable under any provision of Articles 25, 29, 32, 36 (1) through (3), and 44; … (Patent Act Article 62.1).

특허출원이 다음 각 호의 어느 하나의 거절이유(이하 "거절이유"라 한다)에 해당하는 경우에는 **특허거절결정**을 하여야 한다. 1. 제25조 · 제29조 · 제32조 · 제36조 제1항부터 제3항까지 또는 제44조에 따라 특허를 받을 수 없는 경우… (특허법 제62조 제1호).

- determination to reject applications for design registration (법제처)

related companies
관계회사

When a mark is used by a related company, use of the mark inures to the benefit of the party who controls the nature and quality of the goods or services. TMEP § 1201.03.

관계회사가 표장을 사용할 경우 그 사용효과는 그 상품이나 서비스의 성질 또는 품질을 통제하는 당사자에게 귀속된다. (미) TMEP § 1201.03.

related design
관련디자인

A related design is a design that is only similar to the principal design and not to others' designs applied, registered or publicly known prior to the application date of the related design.

기본디자인과만 유사한 디자인으로 그 출원일보다 선행하는 타인의 디자인(출원디자인, 등록디자인, 공지디자인)과 유사하지 않은 것.

Example A right to have a design registered is transferable: Provided, That a right to have a principal design registered and a right to have **related designs** registered shall be transferred together (Design Protection Act Article 54(1)).

디자인등록을 받을 수 있는 권리는 이전할 수 있다. 다만, 기본디자인등록을 받을 수 있는 권리와 **관련디자인**등록을 받을 수 있는 권리는 함께 이전하여야 한다(디자인보호법 제54조 제1항).

relatedness (of the goods or services)
(물품과 서비스의)연관성

A factor in finding likelihood of confusion. The test is not whether the goods or services are related; it must be determined whether the public would confuse the source of the goods or services.

혼동가능성의 결정 요소 중 하나. 물품/서비스가 혼동될 수 있는지가 아닌, 공중이 그 출처를 혼동할 것인지가 기준임. (미) TMEP § 1207.01(a)(i).

Example **Relatedness** would generally be recognized when the services clearly include or encompass the goods in the identification, such as when the services are "brew pubs" and the goods are "beer" … TMEP § 1207.01(a)(ii).

서비스가 명칭에 나타난 상품을 명백히 포함한다면 일반적으로 **연관성**이 있다 할 것이다. 가령 '맥주 제조 및 판매' 서비스와 '맥주'라는 상품 등이 이에 해당한다. (미) TMEP § 1207.01(a)(ii).

relevant art
유사한 (기술)분야

→ See. analogous art.

relief
권리구제

relief demanded
청구의 취지

→ See. plaintiff's demand.

relinquishment
(지정상품의) 포기

Where trademark rights, exclusive license, non-exclusive

해당 지정상품에 대한 상표권의 포기. 상표

R

license, or pledge is relinquished, the trademark rights, exclusive license, non-exclusive license, or pledge shall be extinguished henceforth (Trademark Act Article 103).

권, 전용사용권, 통상사용권, 질권 등을 포기하였을 경우 그 해당 권리는 그때부터 소멸된다(상표법 제103조).

remand

Appellate court sending back the case to the inferior court for additional hearings.

환송

상급심 법원이 재심리를 위해 사건을 하급심 법원으로 돌려보냄.

Example Judgment of the lower court is reversed, and the cases is **remanded** to the Patent Court of Korea (Supreme Court Decision, 2014Hu2184, decided November 25, 2016).

원심판결을 파기하고, 사건을 특허법원에 **환송**한다(대법원 2016.11.25. 선고 2014후2184판결 참조).

remedies

Measures to make a harmed party whole again when his or her rights are infringed. E.g. Monetary damages or injunction.

구제책

권리가 침해되었을 때 그로 인한 피해를 보전하여 주기 위한 방법. 금전적 손해배상이나 금지명령 등이 있다.

renewal of duration

The duration of trademark rights may be renewed for another ten years by filing an application to register the renewal of the duration (Trademark Act Article 83(2)).

존속기간 갱신

상표권의 존속기간은 존속기간 갱신등록신청에 의하여 10년씩 갱신할 수 있다(상표법 제83조 제2항).

repeating pattern marks

A mark composed of a single repeated element or a repeated combination of designs, numbers, letters, or other characters, forming a pattern that is displayed on the surface of goods, on product packaging, or on materials associated with the advertising or provision of services. TMEP § 1202.19.

반복패턴표장

디자인, 숫자, 글자, 기타 다른 문자의 반복되는 단일한 구성요소 또는 반복적 조합으로, 제품 포장이나 상품의 표면, 서비스의 광고나 제공과 관련된 물건에 패턴으로 나타나는 표장. (미) TMEP § 1202.19.

Example The impression created by a **repeating pattern** may change depending on a number of factors, including the nature of the pattern and the item it appears on, the particular placement of the pattern on the item, and the size and scale of the elements in the pattern as applied. Thus, in most cases, to accurately depict the mark, a drawing showing the particular manner of display and placement of the **repeating pattern** is necessary. TMEP § 1202.19(a).

반복패턴으로 형성된 인상은 가령 그 패턴이나 패턴이 사용되는 물품의 성질, 그 물품에서 패턴이 사용된 위치, 사용시 패턴의 구성요소의 크기나 범위 등 여러 요소에 의해 변할 수 있다. 따라서 대부분의 경우 표장을 정확히 묘사하기 위해서는 **반복패턴**의 특정한 표시방법이나 위치가 도면에 반드시 나타나야 할 것이다. (미) TMEP § 1202.19(a).

replacement

치환

Example An invention in question falls under the scope of the patent right of a patented invention only when each element and the whole combination of its components as specified within the scope of the patent claim for the patented invention are intact within the invention in question. Even in cases where an invention in question contains portions which **replace** or substitute elements included in the scope of a patent claim for a patented invention, if both inventions share the same solution principle, if such a replacement still makes it possible to achieve the goal of the patented invention and enables an identical effect on an actual level, and if this replacement is self-evident to the extent that any person of ordinary skill in the pertinent field of technology could have easily conceived it, then the invention in question must be seen as equivalent in whole to the elements specified in the scope of the patent claim for a patented invention (Supreme Court Decision, 2010Hu296, decided May 27, 2010).

확인대상발명이 특허발명의 권리범위에 속한다고 할 수 있기 위해서는 특허발명의 청구범위에 기재된 각 구성요소와 그 구성요소 간의 유기적 결합관계가 확인대상발명에 그대로 포함되어 있어야 한다. 한편, 확인대상발명에서 특허발명의 청구범위에 기재된 구성 중 **치환** 내지 변경된 부분이 있는 경우에도, 양 발명에서 과제의 해결원리가 동일하고, 그러한 치환에 의하더라도 특허발명에서와 같은 목적을 달성할 수 있고 실질적으로 동일한 작용효과를 나타내며, 그와 같이 치환하는 것이 그 발명이 속하는 기술분야에서 통상의 지식을 가진 사람이라면 누구나 용이하게 생각해 낼 수 있는 정도로 자명하다면 확인대상발명은 전체적으로 특허발명의 청구범위에 기재된 구성과 균등한 것으로서 여전히 특허발명의 권리범위에 속한다고 보아야 한다(대법원 2010.5.27, 선고, 2010후296, 판결 참조).

reply brief

답변서

Where a defendant contests the claim of a plaintiff, he/she shall submit a written defence within 30 days from the date of receiving a service of a duplicate of the written complaint (Civil Procedure Act Article 256(1)).

피고가 원고의 청구를 다투는 경우에는 소장의 부본을 송달받은 날부터 30일 이내에 답변서를 제출하여야 한다(민사소송법 제256조 제1항).

representation of mark

표장의 표시

A clear depiction of the mark an applicant seeks to register. Every application must include a representation of the mark.

출원인이 등록하고자 하는 표장의 명확한 묘사. 모든 출원에는 상표가 표현되어야 함.

Example If the mark is otherwise merely descriptive or primarily geographically descriptive, and the design replacing a letter is an accurate pictorial **representation** of generic, merely descriptive, or geographically descriptive matter, the examining attorney must require the applicant to amend to the Supplemental Register or seek registration on the Principal Register under Trademark Act §2(f). The applicant must disclaim any generic wording or any accurate

단순히 기술적이거나 주로 지리적으로 기술적인 표장으로 문자를 대체하는 디자인이 보통의 사항이나 단순히 기술적 혹은 지리적으로 기술적인 사항의 정확한 사진적 **표현**에 해당한다면 심사관은 출원인에게 보조등록부 등록 또는 2(f)조 하에 주등록부 등록을 위해 보정하도록 하여야 한다. 또한 출원인은 보통명칭으로의 단어사용이나 보통의 사항에 대한 정확한 사진적 **표현**

R

pictorial **representation** of generic matter. TMEP § 1213.05(g)(iii).

에 해당하는 모든 부분에 대한 권리를 포기하여야 한다. (미) TMEP § 1213.05(g)(iii).

representative

대리인

request for continued examination

A request filed in an application in which prosecution is closed (e.g., the application is under final rejection or a notice of allowance) that is filed to reopen prosecution and continue examination of the application.

미 계속심사청구

최종 거절결정 되었거나 허여통지를 받은 경우 등 심사절차가 종결된 출원에 대해 청구된 심사절차를 재개하고 심사를 계속할 것에 대하여 요청하는 것.

request for examinations of applications

출원심사청구

request to reinstate an application

출원의 회복요청

request to restore filing date

출원일자의 회복

Example If an applicant believes that the USPTO committed an error in denying the application a filing date, the applicant may submit a **request to restore the filing date**. TMEP § 204.02.

출원일자 발급 거부가 특허상표청의 실수로 인한 것이라 보는 출원인은 그 **출원일자의 회복**요청을 할 수 있다. (미) TMEP § 204.02.

requests for examinations (of Patent Applications)

A patent application shall be examined only upon receipt of a request for examination. Any person may file a request for examination of a patent application with the Commissioner of the Korean Intellectual Property Office within five years from the filing date of the patent application (Patent Act Article 59).

심사청구

특허출원에 대하여 심사청구가 있을 때에만 이를 심사한다. 누구든지 특허출원에 대하여 특허출원일부터 5년 이내에 특허청장에게 출원심사의 청구를 할 수 있다(특허법 제59조).

requirements for patent registration

The requirements an invention must meet to be patented. Novelty, inventiveness and industrial applicability.

특허요건

발명이 특허로 등록되기 위한 요건. 신규성, 진보성, 산업상 이용가능성.

reserved trademark

A trademark registered for the purpose of preserving it earlier than the applicant's competitor and using it in the unforeseeable future.

저장상표

경쟁사에 대하여 선점을 위해 불확정한 미래에 사용할 목적으로 등록을 받은 상표.

Example Under the Trademark Act, Article 73(1)3, a registered trademark may be cancelled if on the ground that none of the trademark owner, exclusive or non-exclusive licensee used the trademark, without just cause, for three consecutive years or more prior to the date the cancellation action was filed. This is to cancel registration of a **reserved trademark** with no intent to use by extinguishing registration of such an unused mark (Patent Court Decision, 2011 Heo5946, decided October 26, 2011).

상표법 제73조 제1항 제3호는 상표권자 · 전용사용권자 또는 통상사용권자중 어느 누구도 정당한 이유 없이 등록상표를 그 지정상품에 대하여 취소심판청구일전 계속하여 3년 이상 국내에서 사용하고 있지 아니한 경우를 상표등록의 취소사유로 규정하고 있는바, 이는 사용되지 아니하는 상표의 등록을 말소시킴으로써 사용의사가 없는 **저장상표**를 등록취소 시키고 , … (특허법원 2011. 10. 26. 선고 2011허5946 참조).

res judicata
기판력

The requirements an invention must meet to be patented. Novelity, industrial applicability, non-obviousness.

청구배제효. 이미 그 이유에 대해 판단한 사항을 다시 소송할 수 없다는 원칙.

respondent
피청구인

response brief
답변서

→ See. reply brief.

restriction
한정

retrial
재심

Any party may file a petition for retrial against the final and conclusive trial ruling (Patent Act Article 178(1)).

당사자는 확정된 특허취소결정 또는 확정된 심결에 대하여 재심을 청구할 수 있다(특허법 제178조 제1항).

retroactive
소급

Example Procedures followed by a person who has no legal capacity or authority of legal representation, or who has any defect in the delegation of authority necessary to follow trademark-related procedures shall take effect **retroactive** to the time he/she performed an act if the party whose defect has been rectified or his/her legal representative confirms such procedures (Trademark Act Article 9).

행위능력 또는 법정대리권이 없거나 상표에 관한 절차를 밟는 데 필요한 권한의 위임에 흠이 있는 자가 밟은 절차는 보정(補正)된 당사자나 법정대리인이 추인(追認)하면 행위를 한 때로 **소급**하여 그 효력이 발생한다(상표법 제9조).

return
반려

Example In case the recipient of the order to supplement

상표등록출원에 대한 보완명령을 받은 자

R

the application fails to comply within the designated period, the application documents shall be **returned** (Enforcement Rule of the Trademark Act, Article. 25(6)).

가 지정기간 내에 보완하지 아니한 경우 출원서류를 **반려**한다(상표법 시행규칙 제25조 제6항).

reverse (judgment)

(판결의) 파기

Example Judgment of the lower court is **reversed**, and the cases is remanded to the Patent Court of Korea (Supreme Court Decision, 2014Hu2184, decided November 25, 2016).

원심판결을 **파기**하고, 사건을 특허법원에 환송한다(대법원 2016. 11. 25. 선고 2014후2184 판결 참조)

reverse confusion

역혼동

Reverse confusion is created where a mark put to use in commerce earlier has not gained fame while another mark that entered the market later became well known or famous, causing confusion that the former may belong to the source of the latter.

선발사용자의 상표는 무명의 존재인데, 후발사용자의 상표가 주지 또는 저명해져서 선발사용자의 상표가 오히려 후발사용자의 그것이 아닌가 하는 혼동을 초래하는 경우.

Example Even if the defendant's mark became well-known later, the act created **reverse confusion** and was illegal (Seoul High Court Decision, 2013Na6058, decided August 29, 2013).

설령 피고 표장이 뒤늦게 주지성을 획득하였다고 하더라도, 피고의 행위는 이른바 **역혼동**에 해당하여 위법하다(서울고등법원 2013.08.29 선고 2013나6058 참조).

revocation

각하, 기각

→ See. dismissal.

revocation action of administrative decision

심결취소소송

Actions filed to seek revocation of the administrative decisions of KIPO (IPTAB) regarding KIPO examiner's rejection on the application, decisions from invalidation trials, or confirmation of the scope of rights and etc. Revocation of administrative action involves a two-tiered trial system, with the Patent Court being the sole court of first instance.

특허권, 실용신안권, 디자인권, 상표권에 관한 거절결정, 무효심판, 권리범위확인심판에 대한 심결 등에 대하여 그 취소를 구하는 소송. 심결취소소송은 2심제 구조를 취하며 1심은 특허법원이 전속 관할함.

revocation of decision

결정의 취소

Where the court deems a pleading in a lawsuit is well-grounded, it shall revoke the relevant decision of the examiner or administrative judge by judgment.

법원은 소가 제기된 경우에 그 청구가 이유있다고 인정할 경우에는 판결로써 해당 심결 또는 결정을 취소함.

revocation of invalidation

무효처분의 취소

Example When the Commissioner of the Korean Intellectual Property Office or the Director General of the Intellectual Property Trial and Appeal Board invalidates a procedure under paragraph (1) or **revokes the invalidation** of the proceeding under the body of paragraph (2), he/she shall give notice of the disposition to the person ordered to amend the procedure (Design Protection Act Article 18(3)).

특허청장 또는 특허심판원장은 제1항에 따른 무효처분 또는 제2항 본문에 따른 **무효처분의 취소**처분을 할 때에는 그 보정명령을 받은 자에게 처분통지서를 송달하여야 한다(디자인보호법 제18조 제3항).

right to request an indication to avoid confusion

The right of a trademark owner or exclusive licensee to request a prior user to mark his or her goods to avoid misconception or confusion of source between the goods.

혼동 방지 표시 청구권

선사용자에게 자기의 상품과 선사용자의 상품간의 출처의 오인이나 혼동을 방지할 수 있는 적당한 표시를 할 것을 청구할 수 있는 상표권자나 전용사용권자의 권리.

Example An trademark owner or exclusive licensee of a trademark may request a party who has the right to use the mark under paragraph (1) to make an **indication on the good necessary to avoid misconception or confusion** as to the source of the goods of both parties (Trademark Act Article 99(3)).

상표권자나 전용사용권자는 제1항에 따라 상표를 사용할 권리를 가지는 자에게 그 자의 상품과 자기의 상품 간에 출처의 오인이나 **혼동을 방지하는데 필요한 표시를 할 것을 청구**할 수 있다(상표법 제99조 제3항).

royalty base

Product or service to determine reasonable royalty. Downstream retail price is often used.

실시료 기초

합리적 실시료 또는 FRAND 실시료 산정 시의 기준이 되는 제품이나 서비스. 주로 하위시장 제품의 소매가를 활용함.

royalty stacking

A problem that occurs in case of a single product infringing multiple patents as the multiple royalty burdens are likely to be excessive.

실시료 과적

단일제품이 복수의 특허를 침해할 경우 발생하는, 복수의 실시료 책정으로 과도한 부담이 주어지는 경우.

rule of thumb

A principle based on experience in society or concept used as a trade norm.

경험법칙

사회생활에 있어서의 경험법칙 또는 거래상의 관념.

running royalty

The royalty incurred based on the number of units manufactured or sold, as opposed to lump sum.

경상실시료

일시불이 아닌 제조 또는 판매 단위당 발생하는 실시료.

S

scandalous matter

미 저속한 사항

→ See. immoral or scandalous matter.

scent mark

냄새상표

A mark that consists of scent used to identify the source of the good.

상품의 출처를 표시하기 위해 사용하는 냄새로 된 상표.

scope of protection of patent

특허권의 효력범위

The scope of protection of a patented invention shall be determined by the descriptions of the claims (Patent Act Article 97).

특허발명의 보호범위는 청구범위에 적혀 있는 사항에 의하여 정하여진다(특허법 제97조).

secondary considerations

2차적 고려요소

Objective evidence regarding inventive step, such as commercial success, expert testimony, copying of the design by others, etc.

비자명성에 대한 객관적인 증거. 2차적 고려에 대한 예로는, 상업적 성공, 전문가 증언, 및 타인에 의한 디자인의 복제가 있음.

Example **<u>Secondary considerations</u>**, such as commercial success and copying of the design by others, are relevant to the evaluation of obviousness of a design claim. Evidence of nonobviousness may be present at the time a prima facie case of obviousness is evaluated or it may be presented in rebuttal of a prior obviousness rejection. MPEP § 1504.03.I.D.

상업적 성공 및 타인에 의한 디자인의 복제와 같은 **<u>2차적 고려요소</u>**도 디자인 청구 범위의 자명성의 평가에 관련될 수 있다. 비자명성의 증거는 자명성에 관한 일응의 증명이 평가될 때에 제출될 수 있으며, 이전의 자명성 거절에 대한 반박에서 제출될 수 있다. (미) MPEP § 1504.03.I.D.

secondary meaning

2차적 의미

Secondary meaning is created when the word used as a trademark are used on a particular good for a long period of time so as to the public would associate the word as indicating the source of the good.

상표로 선택된 단어가 특정 상품에 장기간 사용됨으로써 특정 상품의 출처를 나타내는 것으로 일반인에게 알려지게 되는 것.

Example Nothing, …, demands the conclusion that every category of mark necessarily includes some marks "by which the goods of the applicant may be distinguished from the goods of others" without secondary meaning— that in every category some marks are inherently distinctive. … In Qualitex, … [w]e held that a color could be protected as a trademark, but only upon a showing of **<u>secondary meaning</u>**.

제2조의 어디에서도 상표가 모든 분류에 2차적 의미 없이 '출원인의 지정상품이 타인의 상품과 식별되는' 상표를 반드시 포함하여야 한다, 즉 모든 분류에 본질적인 식별력을 지닌 상표를 포함하여야 한다고 요하고 있지 아니하다. … Qualitex 판례에서 … 본 법원은 색채를 상표로 보호가능하다고

Wal-Mart Stores, Inc. v. Samara Bros., 529 U.S. 205, 211-12 (2000).

판시하였으나, 단 **2차적 의미**를 입증하였을 때에만 그러하다고 하였다. Wal-Mart Stores, Inc. v. Samara Bros., 529 U.S. 205, 211-12 (2000).

secondary references

2차적 인용문헌

Example A rejection under 35 U.S.C. § 103 would be appropriate if a designer of ordinary skill would have been motivated to modify a primary reference by deleting features thereof or by interchanging with or adding features from pertinent secondary references. In order for **secondary references** to be considered, there must be some suggestion in the prior art to modify the basic design with features from the **secondary references**. MPEP § 1504.03.II.A.

통상의 지식을 가진 디자이너의 관점에서 그 특징을 삭제하거나, 관련된 이차적 인용문헌에서의 특징으로 치환하거나 이를 추가함으로써 1차적 인용문헌을 변형하는 것에 대한 동기가 있었을 것이라면, 35 U.S.C. 103(a)조에 따른 거절은 적절한 것이다. **2차적 인용문헌**이 고려되기 위하여는, **2차적 인용문헌**에서의 특징을 사용하여 기본적인 디자인을 변형하는 것에 대한 암시가 공지디자인에 존재하여야 한다. (미) MPEP § 1504.03.II.A.

second examination

미 2차 심사

Examination of the statement of use. To be distinguished with reconsideration. TMEP § 1109.07.

사용진술서의 심사. 재심사와 구분하여야 함. (미) TMEP § 1109.07.

Example Where a significant length of time has elapsed since the initial examination, a mark may have become descriptive or even generic with respect to the goods/services. In such a case, since the evidence of the descriptive or generic use would not have been available during initial examination, the requirement or refusal must be issued during **second examination**. TMEP § 1102.01.

최초심사 이후 상당한 시간이 지났을 경우 그 표장은 지정상품 또는 서비스와 관련하여 기술적 표장 또는 보통명칭이 되었을 수도 있다. 이 경우 최초심사에서는 기술적 표장 또는 보통명칭으로서의 사용에 대한 증거를 제출할 수 없었으므로 **2차 심사**에서 요청을 하거나 또는 거절결정을 하여야 한다. (미) TMEP § 1102.01.

secret design

비밀디자인

An applicant for design registration may request that the design be kept secret for a prescribed period of up to three years from the date of registration for establishment of the design right (Design Protection Act Article 43(1)).

디자인등록출원인의 청구에 의하여 설정등록일로부터 3년 이내의 지정기간 동안 공개되지 않는 디자인(디자인보호법 제43조 제1항).

sectional view

단면도

Example Where the exact contour or configuration of the

청구된 디자인의 바깥 표면의 정확한 윤곽

exterior surface of a claimed design is not apparent from the views of the drawing, and no attempt is made to illustrate features of internal construction, a **sectional view** may be included to clarify the shape of said design. MPEP 1503.02.

이나 구성이 도면의 도로부터 명백하지 않고, 내부 구조의 특징을 표현하려는 시도가 아닌 경우에는, 그 디자인의 형상을 명확하게 하기 위하여 **단면도**가 포함될 수 있다. (미) MPEP 1503.02.

seed

종자

Example The **seed** as defined in subparagraph 1 of Article 2 of the Seed Industry Act as well as the seed of aquatic plants defined in subparagraph 3 of Article 2 of the Fisheries Seed Industry Promotion Act (Act on New Varieties of Plants Article 2.1).

종자산업법」 제2조 제1호에 따른 **종자** 및 「수산종자산업육성법」 제2조 제3호에 따른 수산식물종자를 말한다(식물신품종보호법 제2조 제1호).

Seed Industry Act

종자산업법

selection invention

선택발명

"A selection invention" is an invention which comprises indispensible elements with a more specific concept selected from a generic concept disclosed in a cited invention, wherein the specific concept is not directly disclosed in the cited invention.

선택발명은 인용발명에는 상위개념으로 표현되어 있으나 청구항에 기재된 발명은 하위개념으로 표현된 발명으로, 인용발명에는 직접적으로 개시되어 있지 아니한 사항을 발명의 필수 구성요소의 일부로 하여 선택한 발명을 의미함

Example In order to deny the novelty of the so-called **selection invention**, which means an invention whose elements are stated in the preceding or already publicized invention as a generic concept and entirely or partly consist of a subordinate concept derived from the above generic concept, a preceding invention has disclosed subordinate concepts comprising the selection invention in a concrete manner. The novelty of selective invention is also denied when a person with ordinary knowledge in the technology to which the invention pertains can recognize the existence of selective invention directly from the preceding literature, based on the contents stated in the preceding literature and his common sense in the technology at the time of application, as well as when wordings concerning the selection invention exist in the preceding literature stating the preceding invention (Supreme Court Decision, 2008Hu736, decided October 15, 2009).

선행 또는 공지의 발명에 구성요건이 상위개념으로 기재되어 있고 위 상위개념에 포함되는 하위개념만을 구성요건 중의 전부 또는 일부로 하는 이른바 **선택발명**의 신규성을 부정하기 위해서는 선행발명이 선택발명을 구성하는 하위개념을 구체적으로 개시하고 있어야 하고, 이에는 선행발명을 기재한 선행문헌에 선택발명에 대한 문언적인 기재가 존재하는 경우 외에도 그 발명이 속하는 기술분야에서 통상의 지식을 가진 자가 선행문헌의 기재 내용과 출원시의 기술 상식에 기초하여 선행문헌으로부터 직접적으로 선택발명의 존재를 인식할 수 있는 경우도 포함된다(대법원 2009. 10. 15. 선고 2008후736 판결 참조).

senior party
The applicant or inventor of an earlier-filed patent application in an interference proceeding. → See. interference proceeding.

선순위권리자
저촉심사에서 선출원의 출원인 혹은 발명자를 가리킴. → 저촉심사 참조.

sensory mark
A mark that appeals to one or more of the five senses of human, consisting of color, three-dimensional shape, smell, sound, motion or trade dress.

오감상표
오감에 호소하는 색채나, 입체적인 형상, 냄새, 동작, 소리, 트레이드레스 등으로 구성된 상표.

separation

(변론의) 분리

Example A court may order a limitation, **separation** or combination of pleadings, or may cancel such order (Civil Procedure Act Article 141).

법원은 변론의 제한 · **분리** 또는 병합을 명하거나, 그 명령을 취소할 수 있다(민사소송법 제141조).

serial number (of application)

(출원의) 일련번호

service

송달

Example (**Service** of Documents) Matters necessary for the procedure for service of documents, etc. specified in this Act shall be prescribed by Presidential Decree (Patent Act Article 218).

(서류의 **송달**) 이 법에 규정된 서류의 송달 절차 등에 관하여 필요한 사항은 대통령령으로 정한다(특허법 제218조).

service mark
A word, name, symbol or device that is to indicate the source of the services and to distinguish them from the services of others. A service mark is the same as a trademark except that it identifies and distinguishes the source of a service rather than a product. The terms "trademark" and "mark" are often used to refer to both trademarks and service marks.

서비스표
서비스의 출처를 표시하고 자타서비스를 식별하기 위한 단어, 명칭, 기호, 고안. 서비스표는 상품이 아닌 서비스를 특정하고 출처를 식별한다는 점 외에는 상표와 동일함. '상표'나 '표장'이 상표와 서비스표를 모두 가리키기도 함.

a set of articles
Where two or more articles are used as one set.

한 벌의 물품
둘 이상의 물품이 짝을 이루는 경우.

Example Where at least two articles are used together as **a set of articles**, a design for the set of products may be registered as one design, if the design for **the set of articles** is unitary (Design Protection Act Article 42(1)).

한 벌의 물품으로 동시에 사용되는 경우 그 **한 벌의 물품**의 디자인이 한 벌 전체로서 통일성이 있을 때에는 1디자인으로 디자인등록을 받을 수 있다(디자인보호법 제42조 제1항).

S

settlement

화해

shape

형상

The contours of an article. All designs have shapes.

물품의 윤곽. 모든 디자인은 형상을 수반함.

Example The term "design" means a **shape**, pattern, or color of an article [including parts of an article (excluding those defined under Article 42) and fonts; the same shall apply hereinafter], which invokes a sense of beauty through visual perception; (Design Protection Act Article 2.1).

"디자인"이란 물품[물품의 부분(제42조는 제외한다) 및 글자체를 포함한다. 이하 같다]의 **형상**·모양·색채 또는 이들을 결합한 것으로서 시각을 통하여 미감(美感)을 일으키게 하는 것을 말한다(디자인보호법 제2조 제1호).

a shape essential for a function of the relevant article

물품의 기능을 확보하는 데 불가결한 형상

A shape necessitated by the article's function. It is unsubstitutable or, even if physically substitutable, such substitution would be exceptional in the field. A design that solely consists of a shape essential to a function of the article (Design Protection Act Article 34).

물품의 기능을 확보하기 위해 필연적으로 결정되어 버린 형상으로서 대체가능성이 없는 것뿐만 아니라 물리적으로 대체가능성이 있다고 하더라도 그 분야에서 그러한 형상의 변화를 추구하는 것이 예외적인 경우. 물품의 기능을 확보하는 데에 불가결한 형상만으로 된 디자인은 디자인등록을 받을 수 없다(디자인보호법 제34조).

significant effect

현저한 효과

Example To sum the above explanations, Claim 1 of the patented invention has a clear difference from Prior Art 1 in terms of part or the structure, and PHOSITA cannot easily overcome the difference with Prior Arts 1, 2 or common general knowlege, and Claim 1 has a **significant effect**. Thus, it is considered that its inventive step is not rejected (Patent Court Decision, 2015Heo666, decided May 27, 2016).

이상에서 살핀 바를 종합하면, 이 사건 등록고안 중 청구항 1은 그 일부 구성에서 선행고안1과 분명한 차이가 있고, 통상의 기술자가 선행고안 1, 2 또는 주지관용기술에 의하여 그와 같은 차이를 극히 쉽게 극복할 수 없으며, 그로 인한 **작용효과 역시 현저**하므로, 그 진보성이 부정되지 않는다고 보아야 한다(특허법원 2016.05.27 선고 2015허666판결 참조).

similar goods

유사상품

Goods with overlapping usage, consumers and course of dealing.

용도, 수요자, 거래형태 등이 중첩되는 상품.

Example Since the two goods have significantly different

양 상품의 품질, 형상, 용도가 전혀 다르고,

quality, [shape] and use and their range of production, sales or consumer pool seldom overlap, **the two goods are not similar** under trade norms (Patent Court Decision, 2009Heo6311, decided December 11, 2009).

그 생산 부문, 판매 부문, 수요자의 범위 역시 중첩된다고 보기 어려우므로, **양 상품은 거래통념상 유사하지 않다**고 할 것이다(특허법원 2009. 12. 11. 선고 2009허6311 판결 참조).

similarity in appearance

외관유사

Two marks are similar in appearance when visible comparison of their appearance, such as the word, figure, symbol, dimensional shape and color, indicate that they are likely to create confusion when used as identifiers of goods.

대비되는 두 개의 상표에 표시된 문자·도형·기호·입체적 형상·색채 등 상표의 외관상의 형상을 시각에 호소하여 관찰하였을 경우 그들이 상품의 식별표지로서 서로 혼동되기 쉬운 것을 말함.

Example The registered trademark here consists only of a diagram in the shape of a black anchor and cable twined around it, while the shoulder emblem incorporates an anchor-shaped diagram positioned directly above the center of a pentagon, with lines on the bottom representing the grade of a cadet. On the whole, the registered trademark and the shoulder emblem are not **similar in appearance** (Supreme Court Decision, 2008Hu4721, decided July 29, 2010).

이 사건 등록상표는 닻줄을 휘감은 검은색의 닻 모양의 도형만으로 구성되어 있는 반면 이 사건 견장은 오각형 도형의 중앙 바로 윗 부분에 닻줄이 없는 닻 모양의 도형과 오각형 도형의 아랫 부분에 학년을 표시하는 띠 형상의 선 등을 포함하고 있는 차이가 있어서, 전체적으로 관찰하여 볼 때 이 사건 등록상표와 이 사건 견장은 그 **외관이 유사**하지 아니하다(대법원 2010. 7. 29. 선고 2008후4721 판결 참조).

similarity in concept

관념의 유사

Similarity of two trademarks in concept exists when the meanings of the two marks are so identical or confusing that consumers are likely to instinctively believe that the goods with the marks are from the same manufacturer or seller.

2개의 상표가 가진 의미가 같거나 혼동되기 쉽기 때문에 이들 상표를 붙인 상품이 동일한 제조업자, 판매업자에 의하여 제조 판매하는 상품으로 직감하게 될 염려가 있는 경우.

Example While the two trademarks are different in appearance and sound, such difference does not overcome the **similarity in concept**. Therefore, if the conceptually similar marks are both used on identical or similar designated goods, it may cause misconception or confusion to ordinary consumers or traders as to the source of the good, … (Supreme Court Decision, 2011Hu3322, decided January 16, 2013).

양 상표는 외관 및 호칭에 차이가 있기는 하지만 **관념의 유사**를 압도할 정도에까지 이르렀다고 할 수 없으므로, 관념이 유사한 양 상표를 동일·유사한 지정상품에 함께 사용할 경우 일반 수요자나 거래자로 하여금 상품의 출처에 관하여 오인·혼동을 일으키게 할 염려가 있고, … (대법원 2013. 1. 16. 선고 2011후3322 판결 참조).

similar mark

유사상표

A mark that is not identical with but similar to the registered

등록상표와 동일한 것은 아니나 외관, 호칭,

S

trademark in appearance, sound and concept, and therefore likely to cause confusion of source of goods under trade norms.

관념의 면에서 유사하여 이를 동일, 유사 상품에 사용할 경우 거래통념상 상품 출처의 혼동을 일으킬 염려가 있는 상표.

Example If a trademark, when compared in composition and conception, is easily associated with others' well-known trademark or goods, or recognized as having close relation with others' trademark or goods, which can cause misconception and confusion about the origin of goods, the registration cannot be granted, even though those trademarks are not **similar** (Patent Court Decision, 2009Heo6311, decided December 11, 2009).

또한, 저명상표의 경우 상표 자체로서는 **유사상표**라고 할 수 없는 상표라도 양 상표의 구성이나 관념 등을 비교하여 그 상표에서 타인의 저명상표 또는 상품 등이 용이하게 연상되거나 타인의 상표 또는 상품 등과 밀접한 관련성이 있는 것으로 인정되어 상품의 출처에 오인·혼동을 일으키는 경우에는 등록될 수 없다(특허법원 2009. 12. 11. 선고 2009허6311 판결 참조).

simple and common mark

간단하고 흔히 있는 표장

A ground for non-registration. A mark may be found simple and common based on its distinctiveness, course of trade and whether exclusive use of the mark may be granted.

상표부등록 사유. 해당 여부는 자타상품에 대한 식별력, 거래의 실정, 그 표장에 대한 독점적 사용이 허용되어도 좋은가 등의 사정을 참작하여 판단함.

Example As it is sufficient for consumers to distinguish the goods as to their relevant businesses, the mark at issue, when looked at its entirety, is not considered to be **simple and common** (Supreme Court Decision, 2003Hu2942, decided November 26, 2004).

… 이로써 수요자가 누구의 업무에 관련된 상품을 표시하는 것인가를 식별하기에 충분하므로, 이 사건 출원상표는 전체로서 관찰할 때 **간단하고 흔히 있는 표장**만으로 된 상표라고 보기 어렵다(대법원 2004. 11. 26. 선고 2003후2942 판결 참조).

- simple and readily available mark (법제처)

simulation

모방

claim directed to a design for an article which simulates a well known or naturally occurring object or person should be rejected as nonstatutory subject matter in that the claimed design lacks originality.

물품을 대상으로 한 디자인에 관한 청구범위가 잘 알려지거나 자연적으로 발생되는 물건이나 사람을 모방한 경우, 이는 청구된 디자인이 독창성이 부족하여 등록을 받을 수 없다.

single/single-class application

단류(單類)출원

An application in which the designated goods or services all fall into a single category in the classification schedule.

분류표에서 하나의 분류에 속하는 상품이나 서비스에 대해서만 등록하고자 하는 출원.

slogan

구호

Example There is also no evidence that the mark at issue as a whole is commonly used in **slogans** or advertising phrases in the marketplace, nor is there any data that ordinary consumers would perceive as such (Patent Court Decision, 2015Heo3993, decided February 3, 2016).

또한 이 사건 출원상표 · 서비스표가 전체로서 거래사회에서 흔히 **구호**나 광고문안으로 사용되는 점에 대한 증거가 없고, 일반 수요자가 그와 같이 인식하리라고 볼만한 자료도 없다(특허법원 2016.2.3 선고 2015허3993판결 참조).

solution principles

과제해결원리

Identity of the principle underlying the solutions of the problems is one of the requirements for infringement by equivalents. Infringement by equivalents is established when two inventions have the same technical idea or principle.

과제해결원리의 동일성은 특허 균등침해의 적극적 성립요건 중 하나. 균등침해가 성립하기 위하여는 양 발명의 기술적 사상 내지 과제의 해결원리가 동일하여야 함. → 균등론 참조

Example If a patented invention and invention in question share the identical **solution principles**, this means that the element replaced within the invention in question is an inessential part of the patented invention and that the invention in question assumes the characteristic elements of the patented invention. Therefore, in order to grasp the characteristic elements of the patented invention, the detailed descriptions within the specifications and prior art existing at the time of application must be taken into consideration to investigate the solution principle upon which the patented invention establishes a unique solution that is unique to the problem when compared to prior art (Supreme Court Decision, 2010Hu296, decided May 27, 2010).

특허발명과 확인대상발명의 양 발명에서 **과제의 해결원리**가 동일하다는 것은 확인대상발명에서 치환된 구성이 특허발명의 비본질적인 부분이어서 확인대상발명이 특허발명의 특징적 구성을 가지는 것을 의미하는바, 특허발명의 특징적 구성을 파악하기 위하여는 명세서 중 발명의 상세한 설명의 기재와 출원 당시의 공지기술 등을 참작하여 선행기술과 대비하여 볼 때 특허발명에 특유한 해결수단이 기초하고 있는 과제의 해결원리가 무엇인가를 실질적으로 탐구하여야 한다(대법원 2010. 5. 27. 선고 2010후296 판결 참조).

sound mark

소리상표

A mark that solely consists of sound.

소리만으로 된 상표

Example **Sound marks** function as source indicators when they "assume a definitive shape or arrangement" and "create in the hearer's mind an association of the sound" with a good or service. In re Gen. Electric Broad. Co.,199 USPQ 560, 563 (TTAB 1978).

소리상표는 듣는 이에게 '특정한 형태나 상태를 떠올리게 하고' 그 '상품이나 서비스와 소리 사이에 연관성을 형성'할 경우 출처표시기능을 한다. In re Gen. Electric Broad. Co.,199 USPQ 560, 563 (TTAB 1978).

source

출처

Example Where at least two registered collective marks with

둘 이상의 지리적 표시 등록단체표장이 서

geographical indication correspond to a mutually homonymous geographical indication, each collective mark right holder and its members shall use a mark that prevents consumers from being confused about the geographical **source** along with its registered collective mark (Trademark Act Article 223).

로 동음이의어 지리적 표시에 해당하는 경우 각 단체표장권자와 그 소속 단체원은 지리적 **출처**에 대하여 수요자가 혼동하지 아니하도록 하는 표시를 등록단체표장과 함께 사용하여야 한다(상표법 제223조).

source indicator (indication)

출처표시기능

A function of trademark; indicating to consumers that goods that use the same trademark are produced by the same source and sold through the same channel.

동일한 상표가 사용된 상품은 동일한 출처(source)에서 생산되어 동일한 판로(channel)를 거쳐 판매된다는 것을 수요자에게 나타내는 상표의 기능.

Example Given that a trademark's main functions boil down to **source indication** that the goods to which the mark is affixed come from a particular business, along with quality assurance··· (Supreme Court Decision, 99Da42322, decided September 24, 2002).

상표는 기본적으로 당해 상표가 부착된 상품의 출처가 특정한 영업주체임을 나타내는 상품**출처표시기능**과 이에 수반되는 품질보증기능이 주된 기능이라는 점 등에 비추어 볼 때, ··· (대법원 2002. 9. 24. 선고 99다42322 판결 참조).

special applications

미 우선심사신청 출원

Applications that receive expedited examination when certain requirements are met, e.g. the invention will materially contribute to the development of energy resources; or the trademark registration was inadvertently cancelled or expired.

특정 요건을 만족하여 우선심사의 대상이 된 출원. 에너지원 개발에 중대한 기여를 할 발명이거나 잘못 취소되거나 만료된 상표등록의 대상인 경우 등이 있음.

specialized trademark institution

상표전문기관

A specialized institution that performs trademark search and/or classification of goods upon designation by the Commissioner of the Korean Intellectual Property Office (Trademark Act Article 51).

특허청장의 지정에 따라 상표검색, 상품분류 등을 수행하는 전문기관(상표법 제51조 참조).

species

하위개념

→ See. subordinate concept.

specification

명세서

A document that includes detailed explanation of the invention, patent claims, etc. When filing patent application, specification shall be attached to the written application.

특허발명의 발명의 설명, 청구범위 등이 상세하게 기재된 서면. 특허출원시 출원서에 첨부하여 제출하여야 하며 특허법상 요건

Specification shall meet the specificity required by the relevant provisions of the Patent Act.

에 따라 구체적으로 명확하게 적어야 함.

specimen

A sample taken as an example of the whole material or design, etc.

견본

제품, 디자인 등의 전체를 대표하여 본보기가 되는 것.

Example The scope of protection of a registered design shall be defined by the design represented in the content of the written application as well as the drawing, picture, **specimen** and description of the design in the drawing, attached to the application (Design Protection Act Article 93).

등록디자인의 보호범위는 디자인등록출원서의 기재사항 및 그 출원서에 첨부된 도면 · 사진 또는 **견본**과 도면에 적힌 디자인의 설명에 따라 표현된 디자인에 의하여 정하여 진다(디자인보호법 제93조).

stability

One of the requirements for protection of plant varieties under the Act on the Protection of New Varieties. A plant variety shall be deemed stable if its relevant characteristics remain unchanged after repeated propagation (at the end of each cycle of propagation in the case of a particular cycle of propagation, such as a first filial generation hybrid) (Act on the Protection of New Varieties Article 20).

안정성

식물신품종보호법상 품종보호를 받기 위한 요건의 하나. 품종의 본질적 특성이 반복적으로 증식된 후(1대 잡종 등과 같이 특정한 증식주기를 가지고 있는 경우에는 매 증식주기 종료 후를 말한다)에도 그 품종의 본질적 특성이 변하지 아니하는 경우에는 그 품종은 안정성을 갖춘 것으로 본다(식물신품종 보호법 제20조).

standard character drawings

Formerly "typed" drawing. Standard character drawing refers to those that applicants who seek to register a mark without any claim as to the manner of display submit. The drawing must show the mark in black on a white background and comply with the requirements of 37 C.F.R. § 2.52(a). TMEP §§ 807.03; 807.03(a).

미 표준도면

구 typed drawing. 그 제출된 표현방식에 대해 특별한 주장을 하지 아니하는 표장에 사용되는 도면을 가리킨다. 이 경우 도면은 반드시 흰색 바탕에 검은색으로 표장을 나타내야 하며 37 C.F.R.§ 2.52(a)조의 요건을 만족시켜야 함. (미) TMEP §§ 807.03; 807.03(a).

Example A **standard character drawing** cannot be amended to a special form drawing containing a design element, color, or a claim to a distinctive style or size of lettering, unless the examining attorney determinesthat the amendment is not material. 37 C.F.R. §2.72; TMEP § 807.03(d).

표준도면은 디자인 요소, 색채, 문자의 특별한 스타일이나 크기에 대한 주장을 포함하는 특수양식도면으로 보정될 수 없다. 단 심사관이 그 보정이 중대한 변경이 아니라고 결정하는 경우에는 그렇지 아니하다. 37 C.F.R. §2.72; (미) TMEP § 807.03(d).

S

standard essential patents (SEP)

A patent for a technology which is essential to manufacture products or provide services in compliance with a standard set by a Standard Setting Organization.

표준필수특허 (SEP)

표준화기구가 지정한 표준을 준수하여 제품을 생산 또는 서비스를 제공하는 데에 필수적인 기술에 대한 특허.

standard setting organization (SSO)

Organizations that promote setting standards and engage in other standardization-related activities. SSOs generally require their members to grant license under FRAND terms.

표준화기구

표준의 설정을 추진하는 등 기타 표준화 활동을 수행하는 단체 및 기구. 일반적으로 소속 회원들이 FRAND 조건에 따라 실시권을 허락할 것을 요구함. → FRAND 참조.

stare decisis

To stand by decided cases; to uphold precedents; to maintain former adjudications.

미 선례 구속의 원칙

이미 결정된 판례를 따름. 선례를 지킴. 기존 판결을 유지함.

Example A prior adjudication against an applicant may be dispositive of a later application for registration of the same mark on the basis of the same facts and issues, under the doctrine of res judicata, collateral estoppel, or **staredecisis**. TMEP § 1217.

기판력, 부수적 금반언, **선례구속의 원칙**에 따라 출원인이 패한 기존의 결정은 동일한 사실관계와 쟁점에 기초하여 동일한 표장을 등록하고자 하는 이후의 출원에 대해서도 구속력을 지닐 수 있다. (미) TMEP § 1217.

statement (법제처)

The scope of protection of registered trademarks shall be determined by a trademark and statement in an application for trademark registration (Trademark Act Article 91(1)).

기재사항

등록상표의 보호범위는 상표등록출원서에 적은 상표 및 기재사항에 따라 정해진다(상표법 제91조 제1항).

statement of use

A sworn statement signed by the applicant or a person authorized to sign on behalf of the applicant attesting to use of the mark in commerce. USPTO.

미 사용진술서

상표의 거래상 사용에 대해 증언하는 출원인 또는 출원인을 대신하여 서명할 권한이 있는 자가 서명하고 선서한 문서. (미) USPTO.

state of the art

기술 수준

Example Thus, the examiner may require that an applicant requesting an interview before the first Office action provide a paper that includes a general statement of the **state of the art** at the time of the invention, and an identification of no more than three (3) references believed to be the "closest" prior art and an explanation as to how the broadest

심사관은 최초거절결정 이전에 인터뷰를 신청하는 출원인에 대하여 발명 당시의 **기술수준**에 대한 일반적 진술과 가장 밀접한 것으로 생각되는 최소 3개의 인용문헌, 그리고 청구항을 가장 폭넓게 해석하였을 때 이 인용문헌과 발명이 어떻게 구별되는지

claim distinguishes over such references. MPEP § 713.02.

를 설명한 문서를 제출하도록 요구할 수 있다. (미) MPEP § 713.02.

statute of repose

The period within which parties can file actions for (administrative) trial, often limited to promote legal stability of rights and protect business reputation.

제척기간

권리의 법적 안정성 확보나 업무상의 신용 보호 등을 위하여 심판을 청구(소송을 제기)할 수 있도록 한정된 기간.

statutory bar

Example Where the reference publication date is more than 1 year prior to applicant's or patent owner's effective filing date. Such a reference is a "**statutory bar**" under pre-AIA Patent Act, 35 U.S.C. § 102(b) as referenced in 37 C.F.R. § § 1.131(a)(2). MPEP § 715.

미 법정제한요건

인용문헌의 공개일이 출원인 또는 특허권자의 유효출원일보다 1년 이상 앞서는 경우. 이러한 인용문헌은 37 C.F.R. § 1.131(a)(2)에 인용된 구 특허법 102(b)조 하의 **법정제한요건**에 해당한다. (미) MPEP § 715.

statutory damages

Damages a plaintiff in an infringement suit may recover without meeting any burden of proof pursuant to applicable statutory law prescribing the amount of damages.

Example For a trademark owner to seek damages hereunder, the owner must have used the registered mark at issue at the time of the infringement, the mark used by the infringer must be identical or deemed to have identicality with the owner's mark. In the absence of identicality, the owner must prove the damages as in other cases and shall not be entitled to seek **statutory damages** as prescribed in the foregoing (Supreme Court Decision, 2014Da59712, decided September 30, 2016).

• legal damages (법제처)

법정손해배상

산업재산권을 침해 당한경우 원고가 입증하지 않더라도 법률에 근거하여 받을 수 있는 손해의 배상액.

상표권자가 이 규정에 의한 손해배상을 청구하려면, 상표권 침해 당시 해당 등록상표를 상표권자가 실제 사용하고 있었어야 하고, 침해자가 사용한 상표가 상표권자의 등록상표와 같거나 동일성이 있어야 하며, 동일성 요건을 갖추지 못한 경우에는 통상의 방법으로 손해를 증명하여 배상을 청구하여야지 위 규정에서 정한 **법정손해배상**을 청구할 수는 없고, … (대법원 2016. 9. 30. 선고 2014다59712판결 참조)

statutory disclaimer

There are two types of disclaimers under § 253: statutory disclaimers and terminal disclaimers. A patentee may make a statutory disclaimer of any complete claim, stating therein the extent of his or her interest in such patent. A patentee may make a terminal disclaimer to disclaim or dedicate to the public the remaining time of the term of the patent granted.

미 법정 포기

미 특허법 253조 하의 포기는 법정 포기와 존속기간 포기의 두 종류로 나뉨. 특허권자는 어떠한 청구항에 대하여도 그 특허에 대한 본인의 이해관계의 범위를 진술한 법정 포기를 할 수 있음. 또한 존속기간 포기를 통해 그 특허의 잔존특허기간을 포기하거나 공중에 이를 개방할 수 있도록 함.

S

statutory period

미 법정기간

Example Extensions of the **statutory period** under Patent Act, 35 U.S.C. § 133 may be obtained under 37 C.F.R. § § 1.136, provided the extension does not go beyond the 6-month statutory period from the date of the Office action (Patent Act, 35 U.S.C. § 133). MPEP § 710.02(d).

미 특허법 133조 하의 **법정기간**은 37 C.F.R. § 1.136조에 따라 연장될 수 있는데, 단 거절이유통지일로부터 6개월의 법정기간을 초과할 수 없다. (미) MPEP § 710.02(d).

stylized

미 양식화

Example If generic wording is **stylized** to create a display or design that is not inherently distinctive, but is nonetheless capable of functioning as a mark, the mark may be registered on the Supplemental Register with a disclaimer of the generic wording. TMEP § 1209.03(w).

보통명칭에 본질적인 식별력은 없으나 상표로서 기능할 수 있는 표현 또는 디자인을 형성하도록 **양식화** 되었을 경우 그 표장은 보통명칭에 대한 권리불요구를 포함하여 보조등록부에 등록될 수 있다. (미) TMEP § 1209.03(w).

subject invention

이 사건 발명

subject matter

미 발명대상

Example The specification shall conclude with one or more claims particularly pointing out and distinctly claiming the **subject matter** which the inventor or a joint inventor regards as the invention. 35 U.S.C. § 112(b).

명세서는 그 발명자 또는 공동발명자가 발명으로 간주하는 **발명대상**을 특정하게 지칭하고 구별되도록 청구하는 하나 이상의 청구항으로 끝을 맺어야 한다. (미) 특허법 제112(b)조.

subject matter jurisdiction

미 사물관할

A court's authority to make decisions over a particular subject matter.

특정 대상에 관한 결정을 내릴 그 법원의 권한.

submarine patent

미 잠수함 특허

Submarine patents are those used by an applicant who waits to enforce patent rights until a third party uses the invention not knowing the existence of the pending application, abusing the continuation application process. In response, an affected party can argue procedural laches.

출원인이 계속출원제도를 악용하여 특허심사를 지연시킴으로써 타인이 자신의 특허의 존재를 모르고 사용할 때 등록하여 권리를 행사하는 경우. '특허심사절차에서의 태만'을 들어 항변할 수 있음.

subordinate concept

하위개념

Example In order to deny the novelty of the so-called

선행 또는 공지의 발명에 구성요건이 상위

selection invention, which means an invention whose elements are stated in the preceding or already publicized invention as a generic concept and entirely or partly consist of a subordinate concept derived from the above generic concept, a preceding invention has disclosed **subordinate concept**s comprising the selection invention in a concrete manner. The novelty of selective invention is also denied when a person with ordinary knowledge in the technology to which the invention pertains can recognize the existence of selective invention directly from the preceding literature, based on the contents stated in the preceding literature and his common sense in the technology at the time of application, as well as when wordings concerning the selection invention exist in the preceding literature stating the preceding invention (Supreme Court Decision, 2008Hu736, decided October 15, 2009).

개념으로 기재되어 있고 위 상위개념에 포함되는 **하위개념**만을 구성요건 중의 전부 또는 일부로 하는 이른바 선택발명의 신규성을 부정하기 위해서는 선행발명이 선택발명을 구성하는 하위개념을 구체적으로 개시하고 있어야 하고, 이에는 선행발명을 기재한 선행문헌에 선택발명에 대한 문언적인 기재가 존재하는 경우 외에도 그 발명이 속하는 기술분야에서 통상의 지식을 가진 자가 선행문헌의 기재 내용과 출원시의 기술 상식에 기초하여 선행문헌으로부터 직접적으로 선택발명의 존재를 인식할 수 있는 경우도 포함된다(대법원 2009. 10. 15. 선고 2008후736 판결 참조).

subpoenas to witnesses

A writ to summon a witness to appear in a court proceeding.

증인소환장

증인에 대한 재판출석요청.

subrogation

A pledge may also be exercised against money or other things which the pledger is entitled to receive by reason of the loss, damage or expropriation of the pledged article. In such case, an attachment must be levied thereon prior to their payment or delivery (Civil Act Article 342).

물상대위

담보권자가 담보목적물의 멸실, 훼손, 공용징수 등으로 인하여 담보설정자가 받을 금전 기타 물건에 대하여 담보권을 행사하는 것(민법 제342조)

subsequent completion

If a person who has initiated a patent-related procedure fails to complete the procedure within either of the following periods due to a cause not attributable to him/her, he/she may subsequently complete the procedure within 2 months after the cause ceases to exist: Provided, That the foregoing shall not apply where one year has passed since the expiration of the specified period (Patent Act Article 17).

추후보완

특허에 관한 절차를 밟은 자가 책임질 수 없는 사유로 다음 각 호의 어느 하나에 해당하는 기간을 지키지 못한 경우에는 그 사유가 소멸한 날부터 2개월 이내에 지키지 못한 절차를 추후 보완할 수 있다. 다만, 그 기간의 만료일부터 1년이 지났을 때에는 그러하지 아니하다(특허법 제17조).

S

subsequent designation

Designating a country for trademark protection subsequent to the international registration when the protection was unavailable at the time the international application was filed

사후지정

국제출원할 당시에는 마드리드 의정서 체약국이 아니었던 국가, 보호가 불필요하여 지정하지 않았던 국가, 거절·무효·포기 등

because the country was not a party to the Madrid Protocol or protection in the territory of the country was unnecessary at the time of filing, or protection was denied by refusal, invalidation or abandonment but such circumstances have changed.

으로 보호되지 않았으나 현재는 해당 사유가 해소된 국가에 대해서 국제등록 후 신청하여 상표에 대한 보호를 받는 것.

substance[1]

요지

The substantive content made in the initial application.

최초 출원서에 기재되어 있는 실질적 내용

Example An applicant for design registration may amend any statement made in the application, drawing attached to the application, statement in the drawing, picture or specimen, to the extent that the **substance** of the initial application remains unchanged (Design Protection Act Article 48(1)).

디자인등록출원인은 최초의 디자인등록출원의 **요지**를 변경하지 아니하는 범위에서 디자인등록출원서의 기재사항, 디자인등록출원서에 첨부한 도면, 도면의 기재사항이나 사진 또는 견본을 보정할 수 있다(디자인보호법 제48조 제1항).

- gist (법제처)

substance[2]

실체

Example The **substance** of the two inventions compared shall be examined, rather than the differences as to how they are described, such that even when the two inventions compared fall under the different categories of "invention of a product" and "invention of a process," it shall not be automatically determined that they do not constitute identical inventions (Supreme Court Decision, 2005Hu3017, decided January 12, 2007).

두 발명이 서로 동일한 발명인지 여부는 대비되는 두 발명의 **실체**를 파악하여 따져보아야 할 것이지 표현양식에 따른 차이에 따라 판단할 것은 아니므로, 대비되는 두 발명이 각각 물건의 발명과 방법의 발명으로 서로 발명의 범주가 다르다고 하여 곧바로 동일한 발명이 아니라고 단정할 수 없다(대법원 2007. 1. 12. 선고 2005후3017 판결 참조).

substantial amendment to (the claims)

(청구범위의) 실질적 변경

Example The purport of Articles 133-2 and 136(3) of the former Patent Act (amended by Act No. 9381, Jan. 30, 2009) is to: (a) enable the patent-holder as the respondent in a patent invalidation trial to petition for correction in the invalidation trial procedure without having to file for a separate trial for correction; (b) prohibit any **substantial extension of, or amendment to, the claims**; but (c) allow for a reduction in the number of claims, rectification of

구 특허법 제133조의2, 제136조 제3항의 규정 취지는 무효심판의 피청구인이 된 특허권자에게 별도의 정정심판을 청구하지 않더라도 무효심판절차 내에서 정정청구를 할 수 있게 해주되, **청구범위를 실질적으로 확장하거나 변경**하는 것은 허용하지 아니하고, 제3자의 권리를 침해할 우려가 없는 범위 내에서의 청구범위의 감축이나 오기

clerical errors, and clarification of ambiguous indications, to the extent they are not likely to infringe on third party rights (Supreme Court Decision, 2014Hu2184, decided November 25, 2016).

를 정정하고 기재상의 불비를 해소하여 바르게 하는 오류의 정정은 허용하는 데 있다(대법원 2016. 11. 25. 선고 2014후2184 판결 참조).

substantial new question of patentability (SNQP)

The requirement for reexamination that there must be a substantial new question of patentability that affects all claims raised in the request for reexamination.

미 특허성에 대한 실질적인 새로운 문제 (SNQP)

재심사를 청구한 각 청구항에 영향을 미치는 특허성에 관한 실질적인 새로운 문제가 있어야 한다는 재심사 개시를 위한 요건.

substantive refusal

A refusal based on substantive reasons such as likelihood of confusion or lack of distinctiveness.

실체적 거절

식별력의 부재 또는 혼동가능성 등 실체적 사유에 근거한 거절결정.

substitutability

The possibility a part of an article can be separated and replaced.

호환가능성

어느 물건의 일부인 부품을 그 부분만을 따로 분리하여 교체할 수 있는 가능성.

Example For such an article to be registered as a design, it shall be a subject matter of an independent dealing in its ordinary state. In case of a component to another article, it must also be substitutable. However, it is not to say that there must be actual trading of the component in the marketplace and substituted by other articles; merely the possibility of independent trading and **substituabiliy** shall suffice (Supreme Court Decision, 98Hu2900, decided December 4, 1998).

이러한 물품이 의장등록의 대상이 되기 위해서는 통상의 상태에서 독립된 거래의 대상이 되어야 하고, 그것이 부품인 경우에는 다시 호환성을 가져야 하나, 이는 반드시 실제 거래사회에서 현실적으로 거래되고 다른 물품과 호환될 것을 요하는 것은 아니고, 그러한 독립된 거래의 대상 및 **호환의 가능성**만 있으면 의장등록의 대상이 된다고 할 것이다(대법원 1998.12.4.선고 98후2900 판결 참조.

substitute application

An application that is, in essence, a duplicate of a prior application by the same applicant abandoned before the filing of the substitute application. A substitute application does not obtain the benefit of the filing date of the prior application.

미 대체출원

출원인이 현 출원을 신청하기 전에 포기한 이전 출원과 사실상 동일한 출원. 대체출원으로는 이전 출원의 출원일을 인정받을 수 없음.

substitution

치환

succession

승계

S

Example The effects of a procedure taken with respect to a patent or any other right in a patent shall extend to the successor to the patent or the right in the patent (Patent Act Article 18).

특허권 또는 특허에 관한 권리에 관하여 밟은 절차의 효력은 그 특허권 또는 특허에 관한 권리의 **승계**인에게 미친다(특허법 제18조).

suggestive mark

암시적 표장

A mark that, when applied to the goods or services at issue, requires imagination, thought or perception to reach a conclusion as to the nature of those goods or services.

해당 상품이나 서비스에 사용되었을 때 그 성질을 추측하기 위해서 상상력, 사고력, 지각력을 요하는 표장.

Example Generally, coined marks are considered more distinctive than **suggestive**, descriptive or generic marks (Patent Court Decision, 2013Heo5445, decided November 22, 2013).

… 일반적으로 조어상표의 식별력은 **암시적 상표**, 기술적 상표, 보통명칭 상표 등에 비해 높게 평가된다(특허법원 2013. 11. 22. 선고 2013허5445 판결 참조).

summary judgment

미 약식판결

A judgment granted upon a motion that shows there is no genuine dispute as to any material fact and the movant is entitled to a favorable judgment as a matter of law. F.R.C.P. § 56(a).

사실심리 없는 판결은 중대한 사실에 대한 진정한 쟁점이 부재하며 신청인이 법에 따라 승소할 권리가 있음을 신청(motion)을 통해 보임으로써 얻어내는 판결. F.R.C.P. § 56(a).

summary of invention

발명의 요지

The essence of a claimed invention that must be identified to determine patentability. A separate section in the specification as for U.S. applications.

특허성 판단을 위하여 파악하여야 할 발명의 핵심적 내용. 미국출원의 경우 명세서의 별도의 항목.

Example A brief **summary of the invention** indicating its nature and substance, which may include a statement of the object of the invention, should precede the detailed description. Such summary should, when set forth, be commensurate with the invention as claimed and any object recited should be that of the invention as claimed. 37 C.F.R. § § 1.73.

발명의 상세한 설명에 앞서 발명의 목적 등을 포함한 발명의 속성과 내용을 표시한 간략한 **발명의 요지**를 기재하여야 한다. 발명의 요지를 기재할 때는 출원발명에 부합하도록 하여야 하며 요지에 설명한 목적은 청구된 발명의 목적이어야 한다. 37 C.F.R. § 1.73.

supplementation

추후보완

→ See. subsequent completion.

supplemental examination
A new proceeding introduced by AIA that allows patentees to request the USPTO to consider or correct information believed to be relevant to the patent. 35 U.S.C. § 257(a).

미 보충심사
특허등록 이후에도 특허권자가 특허상표청에 특허와 관련 있는 정보를 고려 또는 정정하도록 요청할 수 있도록 하는 개정 특허법으로 신설된 제도. (미) 특허법 제257(a)조.

supplemental portion
Ancillary part. A part that does not affect the similarity or dissimilarity of a mark.

부기적 부분
부수적 부분. 상표 유사 판단에 영향을 미치지 않음.

Example Where an amendment made under paragraph (1) falls under any of the following, the substance of the relevant application for trademark registration shall be deemed unchanged: … 4. Omission of **supplemental portion** of the trademark (Trademark Act Article 40(2)4).

상표의 **부기적인 부분**의 삭제는 상표등록출원의 요지를 변경하지 아니하는 것으로 본다(상표법 제40조 제2항 제4호).

Supplemental register
Secondary trademark register for the USPTO. It allows for registration of certain marks that are not eligible for registration on the Principal Register, but are capable of distinguishing an applicant's goods or services. Marks registered on the Supplemental Register receive protection from conflicting marks and other protections, but are excluded from receiving the advantages of certain sections of the Trademark Act of 1946. USPTO.

미 보조등록부
특허상표청의 부차적 상표등록부. 주등록부에는 등록될 수 없으나 출원인의 상품이나 서비스를 식별할 수는 있는 상표를 등록한다. 보조등록부에 등록된 상표는 저촉표장으로부터 보호되는 등 다양한 보호를 받으나 상표법의 일부 혜택으로부터 제외됨. (미) USPTO.

supplementary participant

보조참가인

Supplementary Intervention
Any third party interested in the result of a lawsuit may intervene in the lawsuit pending before the court in order to assist either party: Provided, That the same shall not apply where it may retard the litigation procedures significantly (Civil Procedure Act Article 71).

보조참가
소송결과에 이해관계가 있는 제3자는 한 쪽 당사자를 돕기 위하여 법원에 계속중인 소송에 참가할 수 있다. 다만, 소송절차를 현저하게 지연시키는 경우에는 그러하지 아니하다(민사소송법 제71조).

superordinate concept
→ See. generic concepts.

상위개념

S

surcharge

An administrative punishment that involves forfeiture of money.

• fine for negligence (법제처)

과태료

금전의 징수를 내용으로 하는 행정벌.

surface ornamentation

Example The inventive novelty or unobviousness resides in the ornamental shape or configuration of the article in which the design is embodied or the **surface ornamentation** which is applied to or embodied in the design. MPEP § 1504.

표면 장식

발명적 신규성 또는 비자명성은 디자인이 화체된 물품 또는 디자인에 적용되거나 화체된 **표면 장식**의 장식적인 형상이나 구성에 있다. (미) MPEP § 1504.

surface treatment

Any indicia, contrasting color or materials, graphic representations, or other ornamentation applied to the article. Surface treatment must be applied to or embodied in an article of manufacture. Surface treatment, per se (i.e., not applied to or embodied in a specific article of manufacture), is not proper subject matter for a design patent under 35 U.S.C. 171. MPEP § 1503.02.IV.

미 표면 처리

물품에 적용된 여하한 표시, 대조적인 색채나 재질, 그래픽 표현물, 또는 다른 장식. 표면 처리는 물품에 적용되거나 화체된 것이어야 함. 표면 처리는, 그 자체로는 (즉, 특정한 물품에 적용되거나 화체되지 않은 상태로는) 35 U.S.C. § 171에 따른 디자인특허의 올바른 대상이 아님. (미) MPEP § 1503.02.IV.

surrender

To be distinguished from abandonment of application. A patent or trademark is surrendered for the purpose of reissue or cancellation of registration.

Example Upon application of the owner the Director may permit any registration to be **surrendered** for cancellation, and upon cancellation appropriate entry shall be made in the records of the United States Patent and Trademark Office. … 15 U.S.C. § 1057(e).

미 포기

출원의 포기와 다른 미국 특유의 제도. 특허 또는 상표의 재발행 또는 등록취소를 목적으로 함.

상표권자의 신청에 따라 특허상표청장은 어느 상표등록이든지 취소를 위하여 **포기**하도록 할 수 있다. 상표등록이 취소되면 그에 따라 필요한 사항이 특허상표청에 기록되어야 한다. (미) 상표법 제1057(e)조.

suspension

Where the Commissioner of the Korean Intellectual Property Office or an examiner is unable to perform any of his/her duties due to a natural disaster or other extenuating circumstances, procedures pending in the Korean Intellectual

중지

특허청장 또는 심판관이 천재지변이나 그 밖의 불가피한 사유로 그 직무를 수행할 수 없는 경우에는 특허청 또는 특허심판원에 계속 중인 절차는 그 사유가 없어질 때까지

Property Office or the Intellectual Property Trial and Appeal Board shall be suspended until such circumstance ceases to exist (Trademark Act Article 25(1)).

중지된다(상표법 제25조 제1항).

suspension of action by office

미 심사의 보류

Suspending action by the Patent and Trademark Office for a reasonable time for good and sufficient cause. The term "suspension of action" means suspending action by the examining attorney. It does not mean suspending or extending an applicant's time to respond. 37 C.F.R. §2.67; TMEP § 716.

특허상표청의 절차를 정당하고 충분한 사유에 따라 합리적인 기간 동안 중지함. '절차의 중지'란 심사관이 이를 중지함을 가리키며, 출원인이 답변할 시간을 중지시키거나 연장함을 뜻하지 아니함. 37 C.F.R. §2.67; (미) TMEP § 716.

swatch-type drawing

참고도면

Example These **swatch-type drawings** usually will not adequately depict the nature of the mark for which registration is sought, because the impression created by a repeating pattern may change depending on the nature of the pattern, the type of item on which the pattern appears, the particular placement of the pattern on that item, and the size and scale of the elements in the pattern as applied. TMEP § 1202.19(a)(iii).

패턴의 특성이나 패턴이 표시되는 물품의 종류, 물품에서 패턴이 차지하는 특정한 위치, 적용 시 패턴에서 그 구성요소가 갖는 크기나 범위에 따라 반복패턴이 주는 인상이 달라질 수 있으므로, **참고도면**은 보통 등록하고자 하는 표장의 성질을 적절히 묘사하지 못할 것이다. (미) TMEP § 1202.19 (a)(iii).

T

takeover

수계

- resumption (법제처)

tarnishment

미 손상

Example Noting that petitioners did not challenge Victoria's Secret's claim that its mark is "famous," the only question it had to decide was whether petitioners' use of their mark diluted the quality of respondents' mark. Reasoning from the premise that dilution "corrodes" a trademark either by " 'blurring its product identification or by damaging positive

Victoria's Secret 측의 상표가 저명성을 갖추었다는 주장에 대해서는 청구인들도 다투지 아니하므로, 원심에서 남은 쟁점은 청구인의 상표의 사용이 피청구인의 상표의 품질을 희석시켰는가 하는 것이다. 원심은 상표희석은 '제품 특정기능의 약화 또는 상표

associations that have attached to it,' " the court first found the two marks to be sufficiently similar to cause dilution, and then found "that Defendants' mark dilutes Plaintiffs' mark because of its **tarnishing** effect upon the Victoria's Secret mark." Moseley v. V Secret Catalogue, Inc., 537 U.S. 418, 425 (2003).

와 제품간의 긍정적 연관성을 손상시킴으로써' 상표를 '침식'시킨다는 전제에서 출발하여, 우선 양 상표는 희석을 야기할 만큼 충분히 유사하다고 판단하고, '피고의 상표가 Victoria's Secret 상표에 미치는 **손상**의 효과를 고려할 때 원고의 상표를 희석시킨다고 보아야 한다'고 판시하였다. (미) Moseley v. V Secret Catalogue, Inc., 537 U.S. 418, 425 (2003).

teaching, suggestion and motivation (TSM)

An obviousness test that provides teaching, suggestion or motivation to combine the prior arts by a person having ordinary skills in the art found in the prior arts renders the invention unpatentable. Limited by "common sense selection" test in KSR v. Teleflex, 550 U.S. 398 (2007). → See. common sense selection; obvious to try.

TSM기준 (교시, 암시, 동기)

선행기술에 통상의 기술자로 하여금 그 선행기술을 결합하도록 하는 교시, 암시, 동기가 있었을 경우 그 발명은 특허를 받을 수 없다고 하는 자명성에 대한 테스트. KSR 판례의 '상식적 선택' 기준에 의하여 제한됨. → 상식적 선택 및 시도의 자명성 참조.

technical advisors

Professional examiners are those who have the expertise to submit a report stating explanation or opinion, or provide explanation or opinion in court in litigations that require specialized knowledge on the matter (Civil Procedure Act Article 164-2(2)).

Example In order to clarify litigation relations or to smoothly proceed with litigation procedures, the court may designate **professional examiners** ex officio or upon application of parties and have them participate in the litigation procedures (Civil Procedure Act Article 164-2(1)).

• professional examiners (법제처)

전문심리위원

전문적인 지식을 필요로 하는 소송절차에서 설명 또는 의견을 기재한 서면을 제출하거나 기일에 출석하여 설명이나 의견을 진술할 수 있는 전문성을 갖춘 자(민사소송법 제164조의2 제2항).

법원은 소송관계를 분명하게 하거나 소송절차를 원활하게 진행하기 위하여 직권 또는 당사자의 신청에 따른 결정으로 **전문심리위원**을 지정하여 소송절차에 참여하게 할 수 있다(민사소송법 제164조의2 제1항).

(judicial) technical examiners

기술심리관

technical explanatory session

The court may hold a technical explanatory session by the parties before the oral hearing to examine the technical issues.

기술설명회

법원은 기술적 쟁점을 심리하기 위해 변론기일에 앞서 당사자에 의한 기술설명회를 개최할 수 있다.

Example In a video conference for case management, the following matters may be discussed and a preparatory order (scheduling order) may be issued based on the results of the discussion. [See. Attachment 7] ⑤ Whether to hold a **technical explanatory session** by the parties (Guideline of Practice and Procedure of Revocation Action in the Patent Court of Korea, III.3.C).

사건관리 화상회의에서는 아래 사항을 협의할 수 있고, 협의된 내용에 대하여는 [첨부 7]의 준비명령을 할 수 있다. … ⑤ 당사자에 의한 **기술설명회**의 실시 여부(특허법원 심결취소소송 심리매뉴얼 III.3.다).

technological common sense

기술상식

A well-known general knowledge in the technical field.

해당 기술분야에서 널리 알려진 일반적인 지식.

Example Thus, it is reasonable to interpret a patent nullity ground under Article 157-20 of the former Patent Act as "where items stated in the patent application translation were absent in the items stated in the international patent application specification, etc." Further, items stated in the international patent application specification, etc., refer to those explicitly stated in the international patent application specification, etc., or otherwise, items which a person having ordinary knowledge in the art to which the invention pertains would understand the items in the patent application translation to be the same as those in the international patent application specification, etc., in light of **technological common sense** at the time of patent application (Supreme Court Decision, 2011Hu767, decided April 30, 2014).

따라서 구 특허법 제157조의20에서 정하는 국제특허출원의 특허에 대한 무효사유는 '출원번역문에 기재된 사항이 국제출원명세서 등에 기재된 사항의 범위 내에 없는 경우'를 의미한다. 또한 여기서 국제출원명세서 등에 기재된 사항이란, 국제출원명세서 등에 명시적으로 기재되어 있는 사항이거나 또는 명시적인 기재가 없더라도 발명이 속하는 기술분야에서 통상의 지식을 가진 자라면 출원 시의 **기술상식**에 비추어 보아 출원번역문에 기재되어 있는 사항이 국제출원명세서 등에 기재되어 있는 것과 마찬가지라고 이해할 수 있는 사항이어야 한다(대법원 2014. 4. 30. 선고 2011후767 판결 참조).

term

존속기간

term of patent

특허권의 존속기간

Example The **term of a patent** shall begin on the registration date of the grant of the patent right under Article 87 (1) and last for 20 years from the filing date of the patent application (Patent Act Article 88(1)).

특허권의 존속기간은 제87조 제1항에 따라 특허권을 설정등록한 날부터 특허출원일 후 20년이 되는 날까지로 한다(특허법 제88조 제1항).

term of utility model right

실용신안권의 존속기간

The term of a utility model right shall commence on the registration date of the establishment of the utility model

실용신안권의 존속기간은 제21조 제1항에 따라 실용신안권을 설정등록한 날부터 실

T

right under Article 21 (1), and shall expire on the tenth anniversary of the filing date of the application for the utility model registration (Utility Model Act Article 22(1)).

용신안등록출원일 후 10년이 되는 날까지로 한다(실용신안법 제22조 제1항).

territorial principle

The principle that application of a country's laws is limited to the territory of the country. Industrial property laws are subject to the territorial principle. Therefore, an industrial property right acknowledged in a certain country under its system is effective only in the territory of that country and does not have effect outside the territory.

속지주의

국가의 영토를 기준으로 하여 그 영토 내에서 법을 적용하는 원칙. 산업재산권법에는 속지주의 원칙이 적용되며, 따라서 어느 한 국가의 산업재산제도에 따라 인정되는 특정 산업재산권의 효력은 그 나라 영토 내에만 미치고 영토 밖에서는 미치지 않음.

three-dimensional shape

In the case of a mark combining a dimensional shape with a device or word, if the dimensional shape lacks distinctiveness but the word is distinctive, the non-distinctive dimensional shape cannot function as a source identifier, and thus, there is no likelihood of confusion arising with respect to the goods having a similar dimensional shape (Patent Court Decision, 2014Heo2344, decided September 19, 2014).

입체적 형상

입체적 형상과 기호 · 문자 등이 결합된 상표에서 입체적 형상에는 식별력이 없고 문자 등에 식별력 있는 경우, 식별력이 없는 입체적 형상은 출처표시기능을 할 수 없으므로, 그와 유사한 입체적 형상의 상품간의 관계에서 출처의 혼동 우려가 없다(특허법원 2014. 9. 19. 선고 2014허2344 판결 참조).

- dimensional shape (법제처)

three-dimensional trademark

A mark that consists of a three-dimensional shape.

Example A 3D mark does not necessarily have to be a **trademark** consisting of a **dimensional** shape alone. A mark combining a dimensional shape with a word should also surely be granted trademark registration (Patent Court Decision, 2014Heo2344, decided September 19, 2014).

입체상표

3차원의 입체적 형상으로 구성된 상표.

입체상표는 입체적 형상만으로 된 상표여야 하는 것은 아니다. 입체적 형상과 문자가 결합된 상표도 그 자체로서 상표등록 받을 수 있어야 한다(특허법원 2014. 9. 19. 선고 2014허2344 판결 참조).

title

A trademark shall not be effective when it uses his or her own name, title, or trade name, portrait, signature, seal, or well-known pseudonym, stage name, pen name, and the well-known abbreviated title thereof, in accordance with generally accepted business practices (Trademark Act Article 90(1)1).

명칭

상표권은 자기의 성명 · 명칭 또는 상호 · 초상 · 서명 · 인장 또는 저명한 아호 · 예명 · 필명과 이들의 저명한 약칭을 상거래 관행에 따라 사용하는 상표에는 효력이 미치지 아니한다(상표법 제90조 제1항 1).

title (of a book, etc.)

As long as a title of a book is not commonly used and does not directly indicate the content of the work of art, it is distinctive and works as a source identifier when used as a mark for books or films (Supreme Court Decision, 95Da3381, decided September 26, 1995).

제호

서적의 제호는 그것이 보통 일반적으로 사용되는 것이 아니고 그 저작물의 내용을 직접 표시하는 것이 아닌 한은 서적이나 필름 등의 상표로서 사용되는 경우에는 다른 상품과 식별하는 능력이 있고 출처표시로서의 기능도 있다고 할 것이나, … (대법원 1995. 9. 26. 선고 95다3381 판결 참조).

title of invention

Example The **title of the invention** may not exceed 500 characters in length and must be as short and specific as possible. 37 C.F.R. § 1.72(a).

발명의 명칭

발명의 명칭은 500자를 넘지 않아야 하며 최대한 짧고 구체적이어야 한다. 37 C.F.R. § 1.72(a).

token use

Use of a mark solely for the purpose of reserving rights in the mark.

Example Thus, neither promotional use of the mark on goods in a different course of trade nor mere **token use** constitute "use" under the Lanham Act. Emergency One, Inc. v. Am. FireEagle, Ltd., 228 F.3d 531, 536 (4th Cir. 2000)

명목상의 사용

상표에 대한 권리를 확보해 두기 위한 목적으로만 상표를 사용하는 것.

따라서, 다른 종류의 거래에서 판촉목적으로 상품에 상표를 사용한 것이나 단순한 **명목상의 사용**은 랜햄법 상 '사용'에 해당하지 아니한다. (미) Emergency One, Inc. v. Am. FireEagle, Ltd., 228 F.3d 531, 536 (4th Cir. 2000).

trade dress

A product's design, product packaging, color, or other distinguishing nonfunctional element of appearance.

Example In general terms, **trade dress** is functional, and cannot serve as a trademark, if a feature of that trade dress is "essential to the use or purpose of the article or if it affects the cost or quality of the article." QualitexCo. v. Jacobson Prods. Co., 514 U.S. 159, 165 (1995); TMEP § 1202.02(a).

트레이드 드레스

제품디자인이나 제품포장, 색채, 외관상의 식별력 있는 비기능적 구성요소.

일반적으로 **트레이드 드레스**는 그 특성이 물건의 용도나 목적에 필수적이거나 그 비용 또는 품질에 영향을 미칠 경우 기능적이며 상표로 사용할 수 없다. QualitexCo. v. Jacobson Prods. Co., 514 U.S. 159, 165 (1995); (미) TMEP § 1202.02(a).

trademark

Example A mark used to distinguish goods (including services or goods related to the provision of services except

상표

'상품을 생산, 가공, 증명, 판매하는 것을 업으로 영위하는 자'가 사용하는 표장 (상

T

goods on which a geographical indication is used; hereinafter the same shall apply) of one business from those of others (Trademark Act Article 2(1)1).

표법 제2조 제1항 제1호).

trademark abuse

When use of a registered or similar mark on a designated or similar good, creating misconception of quality of the good or confusion with a good associated with other person's business. Grounds for cancellation of a trademark (Trademark Act Article 119(1)5).

부정사용

지정상품 또는 이와 유사한 상품에 등록상표 또는 이와 유사한 상표를 사용함으로써 수요자에게 상품의 품질을 오인하게 하거나 타인의 업무와 관련된 상품과의 혼동을 불러일으키게 한 경우. 상표등록취소심판 청구의 근거가 됨(상표법 제119조 제1항 제5호).

Example Therefore, the judgment below was correct; and contrary to the arguments in the grounds of appeal, there was no error of law on the intent element for **trademark abuse** (Supreme Court Decision, 2012Hu2227, decided October 11, 2012).

… 따라서 같은 취지의 원심판단은 정당하고, 거기에 상고이유의 주장과 같은 상표 **부정사용**의 고의에 관한 법리오해 등의 위법이 없다(대법원 2012. 10. 11. 선고 2012후2227 판결 참조).

Trademark Act

상표법

Trademark Manual of Examining Procedure (TMEP)

A reference work on the practices and procedures relative to prosecution of applications to register marks in the USPTO. It contains guidelines for USPTO examining attorneys, trademark applicants and owners, and attorneys and representatives for trademark applicants and owners. USPTO.

미 상표심사기준

미 특허상표청의 상표등록출원의 처리실무 및 절차에 대한 참고자료. 특허상표청 심사관, 상표출원인, 상표권자, 출원인 및 상표권자의 변호사와 대리인을 위한 지침을 제시함. (미) USPTO.

Trademark Official Gazette (TMOG)

상표공보

Trademark Owner

A person who has the ownership of the registered trademark. The owner of a trademark has exclusive rights to use the mark on the designated goods.

• trademark right holder (법제처)

상표권자

등록상표에 대한 상표권을 가진 자. 등록상표를 그 지정상품에 사용할 권리를 독점함.

Trademark Register
The register is managed by the KIPO and keeps record of the establishment, transfer, amendment, extinguishment of trademark rights, exclusive or non-exclusive licenses among others (Trademark Act Article 80).

상표등록원부
등록상표에 대한 상표권, 전용사용권, 통상사용권의 설정, 이전, 변경, 소멸 등의 사항을 기록하는 장부로서 특허청에서 관리함(상표법 제80조).

Trademark Registration Treaty (TRT)
Under TRT, a trademark owner may enjoy the same rights as trademark owners in each of the member states to the Treaty by registering the mark with the International Bureau in Geneva.

상표등록조약
본 조약에 따라 상표의 소유자는 제네바의 국제사무국에 국제등록을 함으로써 본 조약의 동맹국에 각각 자기의 상표를 등록시킨 것과 동일한 권리를 향유할 수 있음.

Trademark Trial and Appeal Board (TTAB)

미 상표심판항소위원회

trade name
Any name used by a person to identify his or her business or occupation.

상호
본인의 사업이나 직업등을 나타내기 위해 사용하는 명칭.

trade norms
Common ideas socially accepted in the marketplace.

거래통념
일반적으로 거래시장에서 널리 통하는 개념.

Example Therefore, the use of the actually used mark shall constitute a use of a mark deemed identical to the registered mark under the **trade norms** (Supreme Court Decision, 2012Hu2463, decided September 26, 2013).

그렇다면 실사용상표의 사용은 **거래통념**상 이 사건 등록상표와 동일하게 볼 수 있는 형태의 상표 사용에 해당한다고 봄이 타당하다(대법원 2013. 9. 26. 선고 2012후2463 전원합의체 판결 참조).

trade secret
The term "trade secret" means information, including a production method, sale method, useful technical or business information for business activities, that is not known publicly, is the subject of reasonable efforts to maintain its secrecy, and has independent economic value (Unfair Competition Prevention and Trade Secret Protection Act 2(2)).

영업비밀
영업비밀이란 공공연히 알려져 있지 아니하고 독립된 경제적 가치를 가지는 것으로서, 합리적인 노력에 의하여 비밀로 유지된 생산방법, 판매방법, 그밖에 영업활동에 유용한 기술상 또는 경영상의 정보를 말한다(부정경쟁방지 및 영업비밀보호에 관한 법률 제2조 제2호).

Example In some circumstances, it may be possible to submit the information in such a manner that legitimate **trade secrets**,

정보제출시 경우에 따라 관련 정보의 중요하지 않은 부분을 적절히 삭제하는 등의 방

T

etc., will not be disclosed, e.g., by appropriate deletions of nonmaterial portions of the information. MPEP § 724.

법을 통해 정당한 **영업비밀**이 공개되지 않도록 할 수 있다. (미) MPEP § 724.

transfer

A patent is transferable (Patent Act Article 99(1)).

이전(移轉)

특허권은 이전할 수 있다 (특허법 제99조 제1항).

transition

The transitional phrases such as "comprising", "consisting essentially of" and "consisting of" used in patent claims.

연결부

특허청구항 중 '…로 구성되는 것을 특징으로 하는', '본질적으로 …로 이루어지는', '…로 포함되는 것을 특징으로 하는'과 같은 용어를 이름.

transitional measure

The measures and provisions prescribing the measures that are applicable in transition period from an old act to a new one in case of enactment, abolishment or amendment.

경과조치

법령의 제정 · 개폐가 있는 경우 구법에서 신법으로 이행하는 데 따르는 여러 가지 조치 또는 이에 대한 규정.

Example … where the provision of the Trademark Act concerning trademark registration requirements is amended, with no separate **transitional provision** in its addendum, the former provision should apply to adjudication and litigation concerning a trademark registered prior to the amendment, in order to maintain the stability/order of the Trademark Act established under the former provision (Supreme Court Decision, 2010Hu456, decided July 22, 2010).

상표등록요건에 관한 상표법의 규정이 개정되면서 그 부칙에서 개정 규정과 관련하여 별도의 **경과규정**을 두지 아니하는 경우에는 특별한 사정이 없는 한 그 개정 전에 출원하여 등록된 상표에 대한 심판 및 소송에 대하여는 종전의 규정에 의하여 형성된 상표법 질서의 안정을 손상시키지 않도록 하기 위하여 원칙적으로 종전의 규정이 적용되어야 하고 … (특허법원 2016.02.03 선고 2010후456판결 참조).

transitional provision

→ See. transitional measure.

경과규정

transliteration

To change foreign letters into corresponding characters of another language based on pronunciation.

음역

외국어의 음을 대응되는 알파벳 또는 언어로 변경하여 표시하는 것.

Example Similarly, an application for a mark that comprises non-Latin characters must include a **transliteration** of those characters, and either an English translation or a statement that this portion of the mark has no meaning in English. 37 C.F.R. §2.32(a)(10).

마찬가지로, 비라틴문자를 포함하는 상표의 출원은 반드시 그 문자의 **음역**과 함께 영어 번역문이나 상표의 해당 부분은 영어로 아무 의미를 갖지 않음을 진술하는 내용을 포함하여야 한다. (미) 37 C.F.R. §2.32(a)(10).

traverse

반박

Example When any claim of an application or a patent under reexamination is rejected or objected to, any evidence submitted to **traverse** the rejection or objection on a basis not otherwise provided for must be by way of an oath or declaration under this section. MPEP § 1.132.

출원의 청구항이나 재심사대상 특허가 거절 또는 이의신청의 대상이 되었을 때에는 그 거절 또는 이의신청을 **반박**하기 위해 제출하는 증거는 그 근거가 별도로 명시되지 아니하였을 경우 이 조항에 따라 선서 또는 선언서와 함께 제출되어야 한다. (미) MPEP § 1.132.

trial against rejection

A type of revocation action filed with the Patent Court by a patent applicant requesting revocation of a rejection decision of IPTAB.

거절결정 불복소송

심결취소소송의 하나로, 거절결정 불복심판의 당사자가 해당 심판결정(거절결정)에 불복하여 특허법원에 제기하는 소송. 거절결정불복심판의 항소심.

trial date

The date the trial is held at court.

변론기일

법정에서 변론이 열리는 기일.

trial for corrections

In any of the following cases, a patentee may file a petition for trial to correct the specification or drawings of his/her patented invention: Provided, That the foregoing shall not apply where a trial to invalidate a patent or to invalidate a correction is pending in the Korean Intellectual Property Trial and Appeal Board:
1. Where he/she intends to reduce the number of claims;
2. Where he/she intends to rectify a clerical error;
3. Where he/she intends to clarify an ambiguous description (Patent Act Article 136(1)).

정정심판

특허권자는 다음 각 호의 어느 하나에 해당하는 경우에는 특허발명의 명세서 또는 도면에 대하여 정정심판을 청구할 수 있다.
1. 청구범위를 감축하는 경우, 2. 잘못 기재된 사항을 정정하는 경우, 3. 분명하지 아니하게 기재된 사항을 명확하게 하는 경우 (특허법 제136조 제1항).

trial for grant of non-exelusive licenses

In case a patented invention uses or interferes with an earlier-filed patented invention, the patent owner of the later-filed invention infringes the rights of the earlier-filed patent if he or she exploits the invention without permission of the earlier-filed patent's owner. However, the permission may be granted via administrative trial if necessary if the owner of earlier-filed patent refuses to grant license without just cause.

통상실시권 허락의 심판

특허출원을 한 자가 선출원 특허발명 등을 이용하는 관계에 있거나 저촉 관계에 있는 경우, 후출원 특허권자가 선출원자의 허락 없이 후출원 특허발명을 실시하면 선출원자의 권리를 침해하게 되지만, 특허법은 선출원자가 정당한 이유 없이 실시허락을 하지 않는 경우 후출원자가 필요한 범위 내에서 심판을 통해 실시권 허락을 받도록 함.

T

trial minutes

변론조서

→ See. trial record.

trial on invalidation

무효심판

→ See. trial on invalidity (of patents).

trial on invalidity (of patents)

무효심판

An action filed with the IPTAB by interested persons in order to invalidate the IP rights registration.

이해관계자들이 권리자를 상대로 등록된 권리의 무효를 구하기 위하여 특허심판원에 제기하는 심판.

Example In any of the following cases, an interested party or examiner may file a petition for trial to seek invalidation of a patent. In such cases, when the claim contains at least two claims, a petition for trial for invalidation may be filed for each claim: Provided, That any person may file a petition for trial for invalidation on any of the following grounds (excluding the ground specified in subparagraph 2), if three months have not passed since the date when the registration of the patent is published after the grant of the patent is registered (Patent Act Article 133(1)).

이해관계인(제2호 본문의 경우에는 특허를 받을 수 있는 권리를 가진 자만 해당한다) 또는 심사관은 특허가 다음 각 호의 어느 하나에 해당하는 경우에는 무효심판을 청구할 수 있다. 이 경우 청구범위의 청구항이 둘 이상인 경우에는 청구항마다 청구할 수 있다(특허법 제133조 제1항).

trial record

변론조서

Official transcript in which the process and content of the pleading at the court proceeding on the trail date is recorded.

변론기일의 재판 진행사항과 내용이 기록된 공식문서.

- protocol of pleadings (법제처)

trial to cancel trademark registration

상표등록취소심판

Administrative trial proceeding held pursuant to the petition to cancel a trademark registration. A proceeding held based on the Trademark Act Art.119(1)4 and (1)6 shall be filed by interested parties. Proceedings based on all the other grounds under Art.119(1) may be requested by anyone (Trademark Act Article 119(5)).

상표등록취소의 청구에 따른 심판. 상표법 119조 1항 4호 및 6호에 해당하는 사유에 근거한 취소심판은 이해관계인이, 그 외의 119조 1항의 사유에 근거한 취소심판은 누구든지 청구할 수 있음(상표법 119조 5항).

Example Where a registered trademark falls under any of the followings, a **trial to revoke[cancel] the trademark registration** may be requested:

등록상표가 다음 각 호의 어느 하나에 해당하는 경우에는 그 **상표등록의 취소심판**을 청구할 수 있다.

Where a trademark right holder causes the misunderstanding of the quality of goods or confusion with goods related to another person's business among consumers by wilfully using a trademark similar to the registered trademark on the designated goods, or using the registered trademark or a similar trademark on goods similar to the designated goods (Trademark Act Article 119(1)1).

1. 상표권자가 고의로 지정상품에 등록상표와 유사한 상표를 사용하거나 지정상품과 유사한 상품에 등록상표 또는 이와 유사한 상표를 사용함으로써 수요자에게 상품의 품질을 오인하게 하거나 타인의 업무와 관련된 상품과 혼동을 불러일으키게 한 경우 … (상표법 제119조 제1항 제1호).

(administrative) trial to confirm scope of rights

An administrative proceeding filed with IPTAB by a patent holder requesting IPTAB to confirm that the opponent's execution of certain technique falls within the scope of patent holder's registered patent (affirmative scope of rights trial), or by a person executing certain technology seeking to confirm that his or her execution does not fall within the scope of the other party's registered patent rights (defensive scope of rights trial).

• trials to confirm scope of rights (법제처)

권리범위확인심판

특허심판원 심판으로서 특허권자가 청구인이 되어 어떤 기술실시가 특허등록된 발명의 청구범위에 포함됨을 확인하여 달라는 내용의 적극적 권리확인심판과 이해관계인이 자신의 기술실시가 특허등록된 발명의 청구범위에 포함되지 않음을 확인하여 달라는 소극적 권리확인심판이 있음(특허법 제135조, 상표법 제121조, 디자인보호법 제122조).

TRIPs (Trade-Related Intellectual Property portions of General Agreement on Tariffs and Trade)

The areas of intellectual property that it covers are: copyright and related rights; trademarks including service marks; geographical indications including appellations of origin; industrial designs; patents including the protection of new varieties of plants; the layout-designs of integrated circuits; and undisclosed information including trade secrets and test data. The basic obligation on each Member country is to accord the treatment in regard to the protection of intellectual property provided for under the Agreement to the persons of other Members. WTO.

무역관련 지적재산권에 관한 협정

보호대상 지식재산권은 저작권 및 저작인접권, 서비스표를 포함한 상표, 원산지명칭을 포함한 지리적 표시, 산업디자인, 식물품종보호를 포함한 특허, 집적회로 배치설계, 영업비밀과 테스트 데이터 등의 비공개정보 등이 있다. 회원국은 조약에 따른 지식재산권 보호에 있어 자국민과 타 회원국의 국민을 동등하게 대우하여야 함. WTO.

U

undue experimentation

Enablement requires that the specification teach those in

미 과도한 실험

발명이 실시가능하려면 명세서에 교시된

the art to make and use the invention without undue experimentation. Factors to determine whether a disclosure would require undue experiment include (1) the quantity of experimentation necessary, (2) the amount of direction or guidance presented, (3) the presence or absence of working examples, (4) the nature of the invention, (5) the state of the prior art, (6) the relative skill of those in the art, (7) the predictability or unpredictability of the art, and (8) the breadth of the claims. In re Wands, 858 F.2d 731, 737 (Fed. Cir. 1988)

내용에 따라 통상의 기술자가 과도한 실험 없이 그 발명을 생산하고 사용할 수 있어야 한다. 개시된 내용이 과도한 실험을 요하는지를 결정하기 위해서는 (1) 필요한 실험의 양, (2) 제시된 지침이나 지시의 양, (3) 유효사례의 존부, (4) 발명의 속성, (5) 선행기술수준, (6) 통상의 기술자의 기술수준, (7) 해당 기술분야의 예측가능성 정도, (8) 청구항의 범위가 얼마나 넓은지 등을 고려하여야 한다. (미) In re Wands, 858 F.2d 731, 737 (Fed. Cir. 1988)

unentitled person

A person who is neither the creator/inventor of IP rights nor a legitimate successor to such right.

무권리자

특허권등의 권리자가 아닌 자로서, 창작자나 발명가 또는 권리의 승계인이 아닌 자.

unfair competition

An act of causing confusion with another person's goods by using marks identical or similar to, another person's name, trade name, trademark, or container or package of goods, or any other mark indicating another person's goods, which is widely known in the Republic of Korea; or by selling, distributing, importing, or exporting goods bearing such marks (Unfair Competition Prevention Act, Art.2.1)

부정경쟁

국내에 널리 인식된 타인의 성명, 상호, 상표, 상품의 용기 · 포장, 그 밖에 타인의 상품임을 표시한 표지와 동일하거나 유사한 것을 사용하거나 이러한 것을 사용한 상품을 판매 · 반포 또는 수입 · 수출하여 타인의 상품과 혼동하게 하는 행위 등(부정경쟁방지법 제2조 제1호).

Unfair Competition Prevention and Trade Secret Protection Act

The purpose of this Act is to maintain orderly trade by preventing acts of unfair competition such as improper use of domestically well-known trademarks and trade names, and by preventing infringement of trade secrets.

부정경쟁방지 및 영업비밀보호에 관한 법률

국내에 널리 알려진 타인의 상표 · 상호(商號) 등을 부정하게 사용하는 등의 부정경쟁행위와 타인의 영업비밀을 침해하는 행위를 방지하여 건전한 거래질서를 유지함을 목적으로 하는 법률.

uniformity

One of the requirements to be protected under the Act on Protection of New Varieties of Plants. A plant variety shall be deemed uniform if, subject to the variation that may be expected from the particular features of its propagation, it is sufficiently uniform in its relevant characteristics (Act on Protection of New Varieties of Plants Article 19).

균일성

식물신품종보호법상 품종보호를 받기 위한 요건 중 하나. 품종의 본질적 특성이 그 품종의 번식방법상 예상되는 변이를 고려한 상태에서 충분히 균일한 경우에는 그 품종은 균일성을 갖춘 것으로 본다(식물신품종보호법 제19조).

unity of invention

The requirement that an international application shall relate to one invention only or to a group of inventions so linked as to form a single general inventive concept. PCT Rule 13.1.

발명의 단일성

국제출원이 하나의 발명 또는 단일한 일반적 발명의 관념을 이룬다고 할 만큼 연결된 다수의 발명만을 대상으로 하여야 한다는 요건. PCT Rule 13.1.

unjust enrichment

An injured party may seek to recover benefits from a person who is enriched with the benefit from the injured party's property or labor without legal ground.

부당이득

타인이 법률상 원인 없이 자기의 재산 또는 노무로 인하여 이익을 얻은 경우에 그로 인하여 손해를 입은 자가 그 타인을 상대로 위 이익의 반환을 청구할 수 있음.

use as a trademark

To state a mark is used, the use must be a "use as a mark," in contrast to use as a design or use merely as a trade name.

상표적 사용

상표의 사용에 해당하기 위해서는 그 사용이 반드시 '상표적 사용'이어야 함. 디자인적 사용, 순수한 상호로서만의 사용 등과 대비되는 개념.

use-based application

An application for trademark registration based on use of the mark in commerce. USPTO.

미 사용기반출원

거래상 상표의 사용에 기반한 상표등록출원. (미) USPTO.

Example Coach Services, Inc. ("CSI") appeals from the final decision of the Trademark Trial and Appeal Board ("the Board") dismissing its opposition to Triumph Learning, LLC's ("Triumph") **use-based applications** to register the mark COACH for educational materials used to prepare students for standardized tests. Coach Servs., Inc. v. Triumph Learning LLC, 668 F.3d 1356, 1360 (Fed. Cir. 2012).

CSI는 표장 'COACH'를 학생용 표준능력시험 대비 교재에 대하여 등록하고자 하는 Triumph의 **사용기반출원**에 대한 이의신청을 기각하기로 하는 상표심판항소위원회의 최종결정에 대한 항소를 제기하였다. Coach Servs., Inc. v. Triumph Learning LLC, 668 F.3d 1356, 1360 (Fed. Cir. 2012).

use in a common manner

보통으로 사용하다

Example Trademark registration may be obtained, excluding the following trademarks:
1. A trademark consisting solely of a mark indicating, **in a common manner**, the common name of the goods;
5. A trademark consisting solely of a mark indicating a common surname or name according to the method **in common use** (Trademark Act Article 33(1)).

다음 각 호의 어느 하나에 해당하는 상표를 제외하고는 상표등록을 받을 수 있다.
1. 그 상품의 보통명칭을 **보통으로 사용하는** 방법으로 표시한 표장만으로 된 상표
5. 흔히 있는 성(姓) 또는 명칭을 **보통으로 사용하는** 방법으로 표시한 표장만으로 된 상표(상표법 제33조 제1항).

use in commerce

(상표의) 거래상의 사용

→ See. use of the mark in commerce.

use invention

용도발명

An invention offering a new use based on the discovery of an unknown feature of a specific effect.

미지의 속성의 발견에 기초하여 어떠한 효능을 발휘하는 새로운 용도를 제공하는 발명을 의미함.

Example **Invention of pharmaceutical use** means an invention offering a new use in which the pharmaceutical substance demonstrates efficacy as a medicine based on the discovery of an unknown feature of a specific pharmacological effect. Meanwhile, as a pharmaceutical substance has diverse features, even when the pharmaceutical substance itself is known, in many instances its concrete pharmacological effect is only revealed by undergoing a multi-faceted experiment. Also, developing a new use based on pharmacological effect demands cost and effort over a prolonged period of clinical trials. In this regard, it is necessary to protect and encourage such development of use by means of patent (Supreme Court Decision, 2014Hu768, decided May 21, 2015).

의약용도발명이란 의약물질이 가지는 특정의 약리효과라는 미지의 속성의 발견에 기초하여 의약으로서의 효능을 발휘하는 새로운 용도를 제공하는 발명을 의미한다. 그런데 의약물질은 다양한 속성을 가지고 있으므로, 의약물질 자체가 알려져 있더라도 그 구체적인 약리효과는 다각도의 시험을 거쳐야 비로소 밝혀지는 경우가 많고, 약리효과에 기초한 새로운 용도를 개발하기 위하여는 오랜 기간의 임상시험에 따른 비용과 노력이 소요되는 점에서, 이와 같은 용도의 개발을 특허로써 보호하여 장려할 필요가 있다(대법원 2015. 5. 21. 선고 2014후768 전원합의체판결 참조).

use of a trademark

상표의 사용

Displaying a trademark on goods or packages of goods; transferring or delivering goods or packages of goods on which a trademark is displayed, or exhibiting, exporting, or importing such goods for the purpose of transfer or delivery; displaying a trademark on advertisements for goods, price tags, transaction documents, or other means, and exhibiting or giving wide publicity to the trademark (Trademark Act Article 2(1)11).

상품 또는 상품의 포장에 상표를 표시하는 행위, 상품 또는 상품의 포장에 상표를 표시한 것을 양도 또는 인도하거나 양도 또는 인도할 목적으로 전시 · 수출 또는 수입하는 행위, 상품에 관한 광고 · 정가표(定價票) · 거래서류, 그 밖의 수단에 상표를 표시하고 전시하거나 널리 알리는 행위 (상표법 제2조 제1항 제11호).

Example In light of the purpose of the aforementioned trademark cancellation system by reason of non-use, **using a "registered trademark"** means using a trademark which is identical to the registered trademark, and does not include similar trademarks; however, "identical trademark" may include not just the registered trademark itself, but also trademarks that can be perceived as identical to a registered

… 위와 같은 불사용으로 인한 상표등록취소 제도의 취지에 비추어 볼 때, 여기서 '**등록상표를 사용**'한다고함은등록상표와동일한상표를사용한경우를말하고유사상표를사용한경우는포함되지아니하나, '동일한 상표'에는 등록상표 그 자체뿐만 아니라 거래통념상 등록상표와 동일하게 볼 수 있는 형

trademark in terms of trade norms (Supreme Court Decision, 2012Hu2463, decided September 26, 2013).

태의 상표도 포함된다고 할 것이다(대법원 2013. 9. 26. 선고 2012후2463 전원합의체 판결 참조).

use of mark as a trade name

미 상호로서의 사용

Example If the examining attorney determines that matter for which registration is requested **is merely a trade name**, registration must be refused both on the Principal Register and on the Supplemental Register. TMEP § 1202.01.

심사관은 상표로 등록하고자 하는 사항이 **상호로서의 사용에 그친다**고 판단할 경우 주등록부와 보조등록부 등록을 모두 거절하여야 한다. (미) TMEP § 1202.01.

use of the mark in commerce

미 (상표의) 거래상의 사용

Bona fide use of a mark in the ordinary course of trade.

통상의 거래에서의 진실한 상표의 사용.

Example (1) For a trademark or service mark, **use of the mark in commerce** by an applicant, owner, or holder on or in connection with the goods or services specified in a U.S. application, amendment to allege use, statement of use, or affidavit or declaration of use or excusable nonuse; (2) For a collective trademark or collective service mark, **use of the mark in commerce** by members on or in connection with the goods or services specified in a U.S. application, amendment to allege use, statement of use, or affidavit or declaration of use or excusable nonuse; … 37 C.F.R. §2.2(k).

(1) 상표나 서비스표에 있어 출원인, 상표권자 또는 등록권자, 국제등록의 명의인이 미국내 출원, 사용사실주장의 보정, 사용사실진술, 계속사용 또는 정당한 이유에 의한 불사용에 대한 선언서나 선서서에서 특정한 상품 또는 서비스에 또는 그와 관련하여 **거래상 상표를 사용**하는 것, (2) 단체상표나 단체서비스표에 있어, 그 단체의 구성원이 미국내 출원, 사용사실주장의 보정, 사용사실진술, 계속사용 또는 정당한 이유에 의한 불사용에 대한 선언서나 선서서에서 특정한 상품 또는 서비스에 또는 그와 관련하여 **거래상 상표를 사용**하는 것, … 37 C.F.R. §2.2(k).

utility

실용성

To be patentable, an invention must have specific, substantial, and credible utility.

어떤 발명이 특허성을 갖추기 위해서는 구체적이고 실질적이며 믿을만한 실용성이 있어야 한다.

utility model

고안

Subject of registration under the Utility Model Act. Creation of technical ideas applying the law of nature. Such creations that are highly advanced are inventions that may be patented under the Patent Act (Utility Model Act Article 2).

실용신안법상 실용신안 등록의 대상. 자연법칙을 이용한 기술적 사상의 창작. 그 중 고도한 것은 특허법상 등록의 대상인 발명에 해당하게 됨(실용신안법 제2조).

- device (법제처)

Utility Model Gazette — **실용신안공보**

V

venue — **재판적**

The proper or possible place for the trial of a case.

사건의 재판에 적절하거나 재판이 가능한 장소.

verification — **검증**

→ See. inspection.

verified statement — 미 **확인진술서**

a statement that is sworn to, made under oath or in an affidavit, or supported by a declaration and signed. 37 C.F.R. § 2.2(n)

선서서 또는 선서를 통해 서약하였거나 선언서로 보완하고 서명한 진술서. 37 C.F.R. § 2.2(n)

Example In a trademark or service mark application based on …, the applicant must submit a **verified statement** that the applicant has a bona fide intention to use the mark incommerce. If the verified statement is not filed with the initial application, the **verified statement** must also allege that the applicant had a bona fide intention to use the mark in commerce as of the application filing date. TMEP § 806.01(b).

…에 따른 상표나 서비스표의 출원에서 출원인은 그 상표를 거래상 사용하고자 하는 진실한 의도를 가지고 있음에 대한 **확인진술서**를 제출하여야 한다. **확인진술서**가 최초 출원시 함께 제출되지 않았을 경우에는 여기에 출원인이 출원일자에 상표를 거래상 사용하고자 하는 진실한 의도를 가지고 있었음을 주장하여야 한다. (미) TMEP § 806.01(b).

video conference for case management — **사건관리 화상회의**

After hearing opinions of the parties, the presiding judge may discuss procedural matters of the case with the parties simultaneously through video and audio communication means.

재판장은 당사자의 의견을 들어 양쪽 당사자와 영상·음성의 송수신에 의하여 동시에 통화를 할 수 있는 방법으로 절차 진행에 관한 사항을 협의할 수 있다.

Vienna Agreement — **비엔나협정**

The Vienna Agreement Establishing an International Classification of the Figurative Elements of Marks

도형상표의 국제분류설정에 관한 비엔나협정

visual similarity — **시각적 유사성**

Example When the marks at issue are both design marks, the similarity of the marks must be decided primarily on the basis of **visual similarity**. In this situation, consideration must be given to the fact that the marks usually will not be viewed side-by-side in the marketplace and a purchaser's recollection of design marks is often of a general, rather than specific, nature; thus the marks may be confusingly similar despite differences between them. TMEP § 1207.01(c).

쟁점의 대상이 둘 다 디자인표장이라면 표장의 유사성은 주로 **시각적 유사성**을 바탕으로 결정되어야 한다. 이 경우 표장이 대부분의 경우 거래사회에서 그 구체적인 성질보다는 일반적인 성질에 대해 이격적으로 관찰하는 경우가 대비관찰보다 흔하다는 사실을 염두에 두어야 한다. 따라서 양 표장 간의 차이에도 불구하고 혼동을 일으킬 만한 유사성이 존재할 수 있다.

(claim) vitiation

An accused device cannot be infringing if it would effectively vitiate (or eliminate) any claim limitation. A natural conclusion from all-elements rule.

미 (청구항) 무효화

침해가 의심되는 고안이 청구항의 한정사항을 무효화 또는 제거한다면 침해물이라 할 수 없음. 구성요소 완비의 법칙에 의한 필연적 결과.

W

waiver of confidentiality

미 비밀유지권 포기

Example A CPA (Continued Prosecution Applications) is construed to include a **waiver of confidentiality** by the applicant under Patent Act, 35 U.S.C. § 122 to the extent that … 37 C.F.R. § § 1.53(d)(6).

계속심사출원은 다음의 범위 내에서 특허법 제122조 하의 출원인의 **비밀을 유지 받을 권리에 대한 포기**가 포함된 것으로 본다. 37 C.F.R. § § 1.53(d)(6)

well-known and commonly used art

주지관용기술

Example 2. As to the ground of appeal on whether the challenged invention is the state-of-the-art technology
A. On the grounds as laid out below, the lower court determined that the challenged invention is not subsumed in the scope of the right of the instant Patented Invention (patent registration number omitted) Claim 1 (hereinafter "Invention Claim 1"), titled, "low dosage entecavir tablet and its uses," without even having to contrast the two, since it constitutes the state-of-the-art technology that a person of ordinary skill in the art (hereinafter "a person with ordinary

가. 원심은, 아래와 같은 이유를 들어, 확인대상발명은 그 발명이 속하는 기술분야에서 통상의 지식을 가진 사람(이하 '통상의 기술자'라 한다)이 그 판시 비교대상발명들과 **주지관용기술**로부터 용이하게 실시할 수 있는 자유실시기술에 해당하므로, 명칭을 '저용량의 엔테카비르 제제 및 그의 용도'로 하는 이 사건 특허발명(특허등록번호 생략)의 청구범위 제1항(이하 '이 사건 제1항 발명'이라 한다)과 대비할 필요 없이 그

skill") can easily implement based on the cited inventions and **well known and commonly usedart** (Supreme Court Decision, 2014Hu768, decided May 21, 2015).

권리범위에 속하지 아니한다고 판단하였다(대법원 2015. 5. 21. 선고 2014후768 전원합의체판결 참조).

well-known and famous trademark

주지저명상표

Example When a trademark owner uses a prior used trademark that is same or similar to a subject trademark while being fully aware of the latter's existence - which will likely result in misconception or confusion - and thus had the intent of trademark abuse. Additionally, if the subject trademark is **well-known and famous,** it is assumed that the aforementioned intent existed; provided that there were no unique circumstances, such as the trademark owner being unaware of the subject trademark or the products it marks (Supreme Court Decision, 2012Hu2227, decided October 11, 2012).

상표권자가 오인·혼동을 일으킬 만한 대상상표의 존재를 알면서 그 대상상표와 동일·유사한 실사용상표를 사용하면 상표부정사용의 고의가 있다 할 것이고, 특히 그 대상상표가 **주지·저명 상표인 경우에는** 그 대상상표나 그 표장상품의 존재를 인식하지 못하였다는 등의 특별한 사정이 없는 한 고의의 존재를 추정할 수 있다(대법원 2012. 10. 11. 선고 2012후2227 판결 참조).

well-known art

주지기술

A "well-known art" means a technology generally known in the relevant technical field, e.g., those appeared in many prior art documents, those widely known throughout the industry, or those well-known to the extent that there is no need to present examples.

그 기술에 관해 상당히 다수의 문헌이 존재하거나, 또는 업계에 알려져 있거나, 혹은 예시할 필요가 없을 정도로 잘 알려진 기술과 같이 그 기술분야에서 일반적으로 알려진 기술.

well-known design

주지디자인

A design that adopts or appropriates well-known shape or pattern, or a design with immaterial change from such well-known shape or pattern that a person with ordinary knowledge in the field would be able to make to apply the design to the article.

주지의 형상이나 모양을 거의 그대로 이용하거나 전용하여 물품에 표현하였거나 이들을 물품에 이용 또는 전용함에 있어서 그 디자인이 속하는 분야에서 통상의 지식을 가진 자라면 누구나 그 디자인이 그 물품에 맞도록 하기 위하여 가할 수 있을 정도의 변화에 지나지 아니한 디자인.

Example … Therefore, the registered design at issue may be easily created by an ordinary designer based on granite pattern in nature, a **well-known design** (Patent Court Decision, 2014Heo447, decided April 11, 2014).

… 따라서 이 사건 등록디자인은 통상의 디자이너가 **주지디자인**인 자연물로서의 화강암 무늬 등에 의하여 용이하게 창작할 수 있는 디자인에 해당한다(특허법원 2014. 4. 11. 선고 2014허447 판결 참조).

well-known geographical terms

A trademark consisting solely of a conspicuous geographical name, the abbreviation thereof, or a map may not be obtained trademark registration (Trademark Act Article 33(1)4).

현저한 지리적 명칭

현저한 지리적 명칭이나 그 약어 또는 지도만으로 된 상표는 상표등록을 받을 수 없다(상표법 제33조 제1항 제4호).

Example In determining similarity of trademarks under the old Trademark Act, the part of a trademark that constitutes **conspicuous geographical name** cannot be an essential part that distinguishes one's product from another's, regardless of whether the trademark is conspicuously recognized as belonging to a specified person by consumers as a result of usage (Supreme Court Decision, 2004Hu1175, decided January 26, 2006).

구 상표법 하에서의 상표의 유사여부를 판단함에 있어서는 상표의 구성 중 **현저한 지리적 명칭**에 해당하는 부분은 사용의 결과 수요자 간에 특정인의 상표로 현저하게 인식되어 있는지의 여부에 관계없이 자타상품을 식별할 수 있는 요부가 된다고 할 수 없다(대법원 2006. 1. 26. 선고 2004후1175 판결 참조).

- conspicuous geographical name (법제처)

well-known pattern

A widely known shape in the country that may be identified by name, such as droplet shape or checkered shape.

주지모양

한 국가 내에서 널리 알려진 모양. 물방울 모양이나 체크모양 등과 같이 명칭으로써 그 모양을 특정할 수 있는 것.

Example The Subject Design is just a simple transformation of the pattern on the turtlebacks or giraffes which is a domestically **well known** figure or **shape**, … (Patent Court Decision, 2015Heo8370, decided March 31, 2016).

이 사건 등록디자인은 국내에서 널리 알려진 **주지**의 형상, **모양**인 기린무늬, 거북등무늬 등을 단순 변형한 것으로서, … (특허법원 2016.03.31 선고 2015허8370 판결 참조).

well-known trademark

A mark conspicuously perceived among purchasers as indicating goods of another person. To prevent another person's trademark from being registered on the ground that it is well-known, widespread recognition among purchasers or traders that the mark is used by a particular source must be shown. More specifically, a prima facie case may be established based on the usage and supply of the mark, the method and period the good is marketed, the broadness of customer basis and course of trade, as well as how widely known it is when objectively viewed under social norms (Supreme Court Decision, 93Hu268, decided January 25, 1994).

주지상표

타인의 상품을 표시하는 것이라고 수요자 간에 현저하게 인식되어 있는 상표. 주지상표로서 타인의 상표등록을 배제하려면 그 상표가 특정인의 상품에 사용되는 것임이 수요자 또는 거래자간에 널리 인식되어 있을 것이 필요하고, 구체적으로 그 상표가 주지인가의 여부는 그 사용, 공급, 영업활동의 기간, 방법, 태양, 사용량, 거래범위 등과 거래실정이나 사회통념상 객관적으로 널리 알려졌느냐의 여부가 일응의 기준이 된다고 할 것이다(대법원 1994. 1. 25. 선고 93후268 판결 참조).

willful

고의

→ See. willful infringement.

willful infringement

고의침해

Example A trademark right holder or an exclusive licensee may claim damages he/she has incurred against a person who has **willfully** or negligently **infringed** his/her trademark rights or exclusive license (Trademark Act Article 109).

상표권자 또는 전용사용권자는 자기의 상표권 또는 전용사용권을 **고의** 또는 과실로 침해한 자에 대하여 그 침해에 의하여 자기가 받은 손해의 배상을 청구할 수 있다(상표법 제109조).

willing licensee

실시의사가 있는 자

An implementer of a patent who is willing to negotiate a binding license agreement with a willing licensor. A concept used to determine reasonably royalty or FRAND royalty as a party to a hypothetical negotiation to ascertain the royalty just before the infringing acts began.

특허의 실시자로서 협상의 용의가 있는 특허권자와 구속력 있는 실시권계약을 협상할 용의가 있는 자. 합리적 실시료 또는 FRAND 실시료 결정 시 사용되는, 침해행위 시작 직전 시점에 가상의 협상을 하고자 하는 당사자의 개념.

windup

청산

withdrawal (of request for administrative trial)

(심판청구의) 취하

A petitioner's act of withdrawing an already filed request. Withdrawal renders the petition as if it was never filed in the first place. A petition for trial may be voluntarily withdrawn before a trial ruling becomes final and conclusive: Provided, That once the defendant has submitted a response, his/her consent shall be obtained to withdraw such petition (Patent Act Article 161(1)).

심사청구인이 해당 심사청구를 철회하는 등의 의사표시로서 이를 취하하면 처음부터 심판청구가 없었던 것으로 됨. 심판청구는 심결이 확정될 때까지 취하할 수 있다. 다만, 답변서가 제출된 후에는 상대방의 동의를 받아야 한다(특허법 제161조 제1항).

without merit

이유 없다

Example The Plaintiff's petition is well grounded and therefore shall be granted.
The Plaintiff's petition is **without merit** and therefore dismissed.

원고의 청구는 이유 있으므로 이를 인용한다.
원고의 청구는 **이유 없으므로** 이를 기각한다.

word mark

문자상표

A mark that comprises of letters, such as Korean, Chinese, Roman characters, other foreign languages or numbers.

한글·한자·로마자·외국어·숫자 등의 문자로 구성된 상표.

Example "APP STORE," the trademark of this case, is a **letter trademark** combining "APP," abbreviation of "Application" which means "application, application program, etc.," and "STORE," meaning "department store, store, storage, etc.," … (Patent Court Decision, 2013Heo 9126, decided May 8, 2014).

이 사건 출원상표 'APP STORE'는 "적용, 응용, 응용 프로그램" 등의 의미가 있는 'Application'의 약어인 'APP'과 "백화점, 가게, 저장(소)" 등의 의미가 있는 'STORE'가 결합하여 구성된 **문자상표**로서, … (특허법원 2014. 5. 8. 선고 2013허9126 판결 참조).

writ of certiorari

미 이송명령

written argument

의견서

written defense

→ See. reply brief.

답변서

written description requirement

The written description requirement implements the principle that a patent must describe the technology that is sought to be patented. → See. lack of sufficient description.

발명의 기재 요건

특허는 그 특허를 받고자 하는 기술을 설명하여야 한다는 원칙을 반영. → 기재불비 참조.

Example To satisfy the **written description requirement**, a patent specification must describe the claimed invention in sufficient detail that one skilled in the art can reasonably conclude that the inventor had possession of the claimed invention. MPEP § 2163.

발명의 기재요건 충족을 위해 특허명세서에는 발명자가 그 출원발명을 소유하고 있는 것으로 통상의 기술자가 합리적으로 결론지을 수 있을 만큼 충분히 상세하게 기재되어야 한다. (미) MPEP § 2163.

written hearing

To hear and determine the merits of a petition/trial solely based on written documents.

서면심리

서면만으로 신청/청구의 당부를 심리하는 것.

Example A **hearing** in a trial shall be either oral **on paper**: Provided, That where a party applies for an oral hearing, the oral hearing shall beheld except where it is deemed that a decision may be made only by a paper hearing (Trademark Act Article 141(1)).

심판은 구술심리 또는 서면심리로 한다. 다만, 당사자가 구술심리를 신청한 경우에는 서면심리만으로 결정할 수 있다고 인정되는 경우 외에는 구술심리를 하여야 한다 (상표법 제141조 제1항).

- paper hearing (법제처)

대한민국법원

2017

지식재산 법률용어사전

Korean-English Intellectual Property Law Dictionary

Korean-English
Intellectual Property
Law Dictionary

부 록

2017

지식재산 법률용어사전

Korean-English
Intellectual Property
Law Dictionary

1.

특허법원 침해소송 항소심 심리 매뉴얼

특허법원 침해소송 항소심 심리 매뉴얼

2016. 3. 16. 제정

I. 제정 취지

특허권 등에 관한 민사 항소심 사건 중 쟁점이 복잡한 사건에서의 절차 협의, 주장·항변의 제출기한 지정, 쟁점별 집중 심리 등을 규정하여 신속하고 효율적인 절차 진행이 가능하게 하고, 특허소송의 성격에 맞는 변론절차의 진행방법 및 증거의 신청·조사방법 등을 규정하고 공개함으로써 사건관계인에게 예측가능성을 부여하며, 충실한 소송 준비가 가능하게 한다.

II. 사건의 접수 및 준비명령

1. 항소인에 대한 준비명령

가. 항소장에 항소이유 기재가 충분하지 아니한 경우 항소사건이 접수된 직후 항소인에게 항소이유가 기재된 준비서면 제출에 대한 준비명령을 발령한다(첨부1 항소인 준비명령 참고).

나. 항소인은 준비명령 수령 후 3주 이내에 다음 사항을 포함하는 준비서면을 제출하여야 한다.

① 1심 판결 중 사실을 잘못 인정한 부분 또는 법리를 잘못 적용한 부분

② 1심에서의 항소인과 피항소인의 사실상·법률상 주장의 요지, 피항소인의 주장 중 다툼 없는 사실

③ 1심에서 제출한 증거의 요지와 그 입증취지

④ 항소심에서 새롭게 주장하는 사항, 항소심에서 새롭게 신청하는 증거와 그 입증취지, 위 주장 및 증거를 1심에서 제출하지 못한 이유

⑤ 관련 사건의 표시[동일한 특허·실용신안·상표·디자인에 대해 특허심판원 또는 법원에 계속 중인 사건은 모두 관련 사건으로 봄(정정심판청구사건 및 정정청구 포함). 정당한 이유 없이 이를 기재하지 않은 경우 소송절차 진행에서 고려하지 아니할 수 있음].

⑥ 조정·화해 희망 여부

2. 피항소인에 대한 준비명령

가. 피항소인은 항소인의 항소이유를 기재한 준비서면을 송달받은 후로부터 3주 이내에 다음 사항을 포함하는 반박 준비서면을 제출하여야 한다.

① 항소인의 주장에 대한 답변, 항소인의 주장 중 다툼 없는 부분

② 1심에서 제출한 증거의 요지와 그 입증취지

③ 항소심에서 새롭게 주장하는 사항, 항소심에서 새롭게 신청하는 증거와 그 입증취지, 위 주장 및 증거를 1심에서 제출하지 못한 이유

④ 관련 사건의 표시[동일한 특허·실용신안·상표·디자인에 대해 특허심판원 또는 법원에 계속 중인 사건은 모두 관련 사건으로 봄(정정심판청구사건 및 정정청구 포함)]. 정당한 이유 없이 이를 기재하지 않은 경우 소송절차 진행에서 고려하지 아니할 수 있음].

⑤ 조정·화해 희망 여부

나. 피항소인이 답변서를 제출하지 아니하거나 답변서(또는 최초 준비서면)에 항소이유에 대한 답변의 기재가 충분하지 아니한 경우, 피항소인에게 답변의 취지가 구체적으로 기재된 준비서면 제출에 대한 준비명령을 할 수 있다(첨부2 피항소인 준비명령 참조).

3. 새로운 주장·증거의 제출 시 유의사항

1심에서 변론준비기일을 진행하거나 주장의 제출기한을 정한 경우, 1심 변론준비기일의 종결 시까지 또는 제출기한까지 제출되지 아니한 주장을 새로이 추가·변경하거나 추가·변경된 주장에 대한 증거를 제출하기 위해서는 정당한 사유로 그 기간 내에 제출하지 못하였음을 구체적으로 소명하여야 하고, 그 제출로 인하여 소송을 현저히 지연시키지 않는 경우여야 한다.

III. 사건 분류 및 변론의 준비

1. 사건 분류

항소이유가 기재된 준비서면이 제출되면, 재판장은 위 준비서면과 항소기록을 토대로 심리계획 수립이 필요한 사건인지 여부를 검토하여, 바로 변론기일을 지정할 사건, 절차 협의 등이 필요하거나 변론준비기일 지정이 필요한 사건, 조기 조정절차에 회부할 사건을 분류한다.

2. 변론준비명령

바로 변론기일을 지정하는 사건에 대하여, 충실한 심리를 위해 항소인 및 피항소인에게, 주장 및 증거의 제출기한, 전문가증인 등 시일을 요하는 증거의 신청 기한 등을 정한 준비명령을 할 수 있다(첨부3 변론준비명령 참조).

3. 사건관리를 위한 화상회의

가. 재판장은 당사자의 의견을 들어 양쪽 당사자와 영상·음성의 송수신에 의하여 동시에 통화를 할 수 있는 방법(이하 '사건관리 화상회의'라고 한다)으로 절차 진행에 관한 사항을 협의할 수 있다. 재판장은 합의부원을 수명법관으로 지정하여 위 절차를 담당하게 할 수 있다.

나. 사건관리 화상회의를 개최하기로 한 사건에 대해서는 항소인과 피항

소인에게 화상회의 개최사실을 통지하고, 그에 관한 준비명령을 할 수 있다(첨부4 사건관리 화상회의 준비명령 참조).

다. 사건관리 화상회의에서는 다음과 같은 사항을 협의할 수 있다.

① 변론기일 일자 및 횟수, 각 기일별 변론 쟁점

② 주장 및 증거의 제출기한(종합준비서면의 제출기한, 전문가 진술서 제출기한, 준비서면의 제출횟수 및 분량 포함)

③ 전문가증인 등 시일을 요하는 증거의 신청 여부 및 기한

④ 당사자에 의한 기술설명회 실시 여부

⑤ 조정절차 회부 여부

⑥ 쟁점 확인 및 정리

라. 사건관리 화상회의에서 협의된 내용에 대해서는 준비명령을 할 수 있다(첨부5 절차에 관한 준비명령 참조).

마. 전항의 준비명령에서 종합준비서면의 제출을 명한 경우, 항소인은 사건관리 화상회의 후 3주 이내(또는 준비명령에서 정한 기한)에 종합준비서면을 제출하고, 피항소인은 항소인의 종합준비서면이 제출된 날로부터 3주 이내(또는 준비명령에서 정한 기한)에 종합준비서면을 제출한다.

바. 종합준비서면에는 모든 주장(1심에서 한 주장 중 철회하지 아니하는 주장 포함)을 기재하고, 그에 대한 주된 증거를 제출하여야 한다. 다만 변론기일을 쟁점별로 운영하는 등의 이유로 라.항의 준비명령에서 특정 쟁점에 대해서 종합준비서면의 제출을 명한 경우에는 특정 쟁점에 대한 모든 주장을 기재하여야 한다. 기 제출된 준비서면과 동일한 내용에 대해서는 해당 부분을 인용할 수 있다.

사. 준비명령에서 정한 주장 및 증거의 제출·신청 기한 이후 주장을 추가·변경하거나 추가·변경된 주장에 대한 증거를 제출·신청하기 위해서는 정당한 사유로 위 기간 이내에 제출·신청하지 못하였음을 소명하여야 한다[예를 들어, 청구원인이나 항변에 해당하는 주장, 신규성·진보성에 관한 주장이나 자유실시기술 항변에 있어서 가장 근접한 선행발명(이하, '주선행발명'이라 한다)을 변경하거나 선행발명 및 그 결합

관계를 추가·변경하는 주장, 적용법조를 달리하는 명세서 기재불비 주장, 1심에서 인정한 사실·법적 판단에 반하는 주장 등의 추가·변경].

4. 변론준비기일

가. 주장 및 증거를 정리하거나 기술설명회를 개최하기 위하여 필요한 경우 변론준비기일을 열어 당사자를 출석하게 할 수 있다.

나. 변론준비기일이 종결된 이후에 주장을 추가·변경하거나 추가·변경된 주장에 대한 증거를 제출하기 위해서는 정당한 사유로 변론준비기일 종결 이전에 제출하지 못하였음을 소명하여야 한다.

IV. 변론기일

1. 변론기일의 운영

가. 항소인, 피항소인 순서로 각 15분간 구두로 변론한다. 수인의 소송대리인이 선임된 경우에도 위 시간 내에 변론하여야 한다. 변론시간은 재판장이 필요하다고 판단하는 경우 연장 또는 단축할 수 있다.

나. 구두 변론을 위한 변론자료 등은 변론기일 1주일 전까지 제출하여야 한다.

다. 당사자는 필요한 경우 사건과 직접적으로 관련된 제품(특허실시제품, 침해제품 등)을 지참하여야 한다. 재판장은 당사자에게 제품에 대한 설명 또는 시연을 요구할 수 있다.

2. 변론기일을 쟁점별로 집중 심리하는 경우

가. 법원은 다음과 같은 사건에서 필요한 경우 당사자와 협의하여 변론기일을 쟁점별로 운영할 수 있다.

① 수 개의 청구가 병합되어 있거나 쟁점이 여러 개여서 청구별·쟁

점별로 집중 심리를 할 필요가 있는 사건[1)]

② 청구항 해석이 다투어지고, 그 해석에 따라 나머지 쟁점에 대한 주장이 달라질 수 있어 청구항 해석에 대한 심리가 선행되어야 하는 사건[2)]

③ 기타 쟁점별 집중 심리가 필요한 사건

나. 각 변론기일에서는 각 변론기일에 심리하기로 한 쟁점에 한하여 심리한다.

다. 법원은 변론기일 이후 심리를 마친 쟁점에 대해 구두 또는 서면으로 견해를 밝힐 수 있다. 위 견해는 이후 변경될 수 있다. 재판부는 당사자에게 위 견해를 토대로 나머지 쟁점 등에 대한 변론을 준비할 것을 명할 수 있다(첨부6 청구항 해석 및 변론준비명령 참조).

3. 침해소송과 심결취소소송의 심리

가. 동일한 특허·실용신안·상표·디자인에 관한 침해소송과 심결취소소송이 함께 제기되었고, 양 사건의 당사자 및 소송대리인이 동일한 경우 등 필요하다고 인정되는 경우, 양 사건을 병행하여 심리할 수 있다.[3)]

---

1) <운영례> 침해와 손해액이 쟁점인 경우
① 사건관리 화상회의에서 침해와 손해에 대해 쟁점을 분리하여 진행하기로 협의하고, 침해 쟁점에 관하여 주장 및 증거의 제출기한을 설정 → 1회 변론기일에서 침해 여부에 대해 심리 → 법원은 침해에 대해 구두 또는 서면으로 견해를 밝힐 수 있음
② 침해가 일응 인정되는 경우 변론준비절차에서 손해액에 대한 주장 및 증거의 제출기한, 증거조사절차 및 방법 등에 대해 협의 침해가 명확하지 않은 경우 변론준비절차에서 미진한 부분을 2회 변론기일에서 추가 심리하기로 협의
③ 2회 변론기일에서 변론준비절차에서 협의한 쟁점에 대해 심리 → 판결선고

2) <운영례> 청구항 해석이 문제되는 경우
① 사건관리 화상회의에서 청구항 해석에 대해 먼저 진행하기로 협의하고, 청구항 해석을 비롯한 각 쟁점에 관하여 주장 및 증거의 제출기한을 설정 → 1회 변론기일에서 쟁점 청구항의 해석에 대해 심리
② 법원은 구두 또는 서면으로 청구항 해석에 대한 견해를 밝히고, 이를 토대로 나머지 쟁점에 대한 변론을 준비할 것을 명함
③ 2회 변론기일에서 나머지 쟁점에 대해 심리 → 판결선고

3) <운영례> 침해소송과 등록무효심판 심결취소소송을 병행하여 심리하는 경우

나. 침해소송과 심결취소소송에서의 관련 주장을 정리할 필요가 있는 등의 경우에는 변론준비절차를 병행하여 진행할 수 있다.

V. 증거의 신청 및 조사 등

1. 증거의 신청 및 채부

가. 항소심에서 새로운 증거를 신청하는 경우, 신청인은 1심에서 이를 제출하지 못한 이유를 구체적으로 소명하여야 한다. 법원은 재판절차의 지연으로 일방 당사자에게 큰 손해가 예상되는지 여부, 신속한 절차 진행이 필요한지 여부 등의 사정을 고려하여 그 채택 여부를 결정한다.

나. 1심에서 채택되어 조사된 증거와 입증취지가 동일·유사한 증거를 신청하는 경우(예시: 1심에서 손해액을 감정한 경우 그 감정액을 탄핵하기 위한 별도의 감정신청), 신청인은 그 필요성을 구체적으로 소명하여야 한다.

다. 1심에서 신청하였으나 채택되지 아니한 증거, 1심에서 철회한 증거를 재신청하는 경우, 신청인은 그 필요성을 구체적으로 소명하여야 한다.

라. 증거조사절차의 협의를 위해 필요한 경우 변론준비절차에 회부할 수 있다. 재판장은 당사자의 의견을 들어 III.3.가.항의 화상회의의 방법으로 절차 진행에 관한 사항을 협의할 수 있고, 필요한 경우 그에 관한 준비명령을 할 수 있다(첨부7 증거조사를 위한 화상회의 준비명령).

---

① 1회 변론기일에서 무효(및 침해) 쟁점에 대해 심리 → 심결취소소송에 대해서는 변론을 종결하거나 추정

② 무효가 인정되지 않는 경우, 법원은 이에 대해 견해를 밝히고(이와 함께 심결취소소송에 대하여 먼저 판결을 선고할 수 있음), 변론준비절차에서 침해소송의 나머지 쟁점에 대하여 협의 → 2회 변론기일 → 판결 선고 무효가 인정되는 경우, 법원은 이에 대해 견해를 밝힘(이와 함께 심결취소소송에 대하여 판결을 선고할 수 있음) → 2회 변론기일 → 판결 선고

2. 전문가증인

가. 전문가증인을 신청할 때에는 증인의 전문성과 객관성을 확인할 수 있는 기본 진술서를 첨부하여야 한다(첨부8 전문가증인 기본진술서 참조).

나. 전문가증인의 신문을 위해 필요한 사항(전문가증인 진술서 및 증인신문사항의 제출기한, 증인신문시간의 제한, 전문가증인의 증언의 신빙성을 탄핵하는 주장 및 증거의 제출기한 등)에 대해서는 준비명령을 할 수 있다(첨부9 전문가증인신문을 위한 변론준비명령).

다. 주신문은 전문가증인 진술서의 범위 내에서 하여야 한다. 전문가증인에게 주신문에서 제시하거나 인용하는 모든 자료는 증인신문기일 전에 증거로 제출되어야 한다.

라. 전문가증인이 외국인인 경우 당사자는 각 주신문과 반대신문을 위한 통역을 대동할 수 있다. 통역을 대동하지 못하는 경우 증인신문기일 4주 전까지 재판부에 이를 알리고 통역인 지정신청을 하여야 한다.

3. 서류(자료)제출명령4)

가. 법원은 당사자의 신청에 따라 상대방 당사자에 대하여 침해의 증명에 필요한 서류 또는 자료, 침해행위로 인한 손해액의 계산에 필요한 서류 또는 자료(회계장부, 매출 관련 장부, 경비 지출 관련 장부, 계약서, 세금계산서, 세금신고서, 은행거래내역 등)의 제출을 명할 수 있다(전자문서를 포함한다). 법원은 서류(자료)가 제출되지 않음으로 인해 신청인이 받은 불이익과 서류(자료)의 공개로 인해 상대방 당사자가 받는 불이익을 비교 형량하여 제출 서류(자료)의 종류와 범위를 정할 수 있다. 제출 대상 서류가 민감한 개인정보를 포함하고 있거나 침해의 증명, 손해액의 계산과 관계없는 정보를 포함하는 등 정당한 이유가 있는 경우 법원은 상대방 당사자의 신청에 따라 해당 부분을 삭제한 서류의 제출을 허가할 수 있다.

---

4) 자료제출명령에 대한 부분은 2016. 3. 3. 국회 본회의를 통과한 개정 특허법의 시행일부터 시행된다.

나. 법원은 필요한 경우 당사자의 신청에 따라 신청의 대상이 되는 서류(자료)의 취지나 그 서류(자료)로 증명할 사실을 개괄적으로 표시하여 상대방 당사자에게 신청내용과 관련하여 가지고 있는 서류(자료)의 표시와 취지를 적어 내도록 명할 수 있다.

다. 서류(자료)의 소지 여부가 다투어지는 등 필요한 경우, 서류(자료)제출명령을 하기에 앞서 당사자신문 또는 증인신문을 할 수 있다.

라. 법원은 상대방 당사자가 서류(자료)의 제출을 거부하는 경우 제출 거부에 정당한 사유가 있는지 여부를 판단하기 위해 해당 서류(자료)의 제시를 요구할 수 있다.

마. 법원은 제출 대상 서류(자료)에 영업비밀이 포함된 경우 상대방 당사자의 신청에 따라 결정으로 당사자 또는 그 대리인 등에게 해당 서류에 기재된 사항에 대해 비밀을 유지할 것을 명할 수 있다.

4. 감정

가. 1심에서 손해액을 산정하기 위해 감정이 실시되지 아니한 경우, 통상의 실시료나 특허발명의 기여분 등을 정하기 위해 감정이 필요한 경우, 기타 필요하다고 인정되는 경우, 이에 대한 감정을 실시할 수 있다.

나. 당사자는 감정인에게 손해액의 감정에 필요한 사항을 설명하여야 한다.

5. 전문심리위원

가. 법원은 필요하다고 인정되는 경우 당사자의 의견을 들어 1인 또는 수인의 전문심리위원을 지정한다.

나. 전문심리위원의 사건 파악 등을 위해 필요한 경우 변론준비기일을 열 수 있다. 전문심리위원은 기일에 재판장의 허가를 받아 당사자 등에게 직접 질문할 수 있다. 당사자는 전문심리위원의 질문에 대해 추가로 답변할 필요가 있는 경우 재판장이 정한 기한까지 법원에 서면으로 제출하여야 한다.

6. 손해액에 관한 주장 및 증거의 제출

가. 손해배상의 피청구인은 청구인의 주장에 대해 구체적으로 답변하고, 청구인의 주장이 사실과 다른 경우 제품의 실제 판매기간, 판매수량, 판매단가, 판매액, 제조원가, 이익률 등을 밝혀야 한다.

나. 회계장부 또는 매출이나 경비 지출 등을 기재한 회계·재무 관련 장부 등을 제출하는 경우에는 그 문서가 원본 또는 원본과 동일한 사본으로 수정·삭제·누락되지 아니한 것임을 확인하는 작성주체(회사인 경우 대표이사 및 회계담당이사)의 확인서를 첨부하여야 한다. 상대방이 회계장부의 진위에 대해 합리적인 의문을 제기하는 경우 장부 작성의 기초가 되는 서류(은행 또는 재무 서류 등)를 추가로 제출하여야 한다.

Ⅵ. 조정

1. 조기조정

가. 재판장은 항소사건이 접수된 직후 또는 적절한 시기에 사건의 조정 적합 여부를 판단하여 조기조정 절차에 회부할 수 있다.

나. 조기조정 절차에 회부된 사건은 원칙적으로 조정전담판사가 담당한다. 조정담당판사는 당사자와 협의하여 법원 외의 적당한 장소에서 조정 절차를 진행할 수 있다.

2. 변론기일 이후의 조정

재판장은 1회 변론기일 이후에도 필요한 경우 사건을 조정 절차에 회부하여 특허법원 조정위원회 등으로 하여금 조정을 하게 할 수 있다.

VII. 제출서류의 작성방법

1. 준비서면

가. 준비서면의 기재

① 20페이지 이상의 준비서면을 제출하는 경우에는 서두에 목차를 기재한다.

② 주장을 뒷받침하는 증거가 제출된 경우 해당 부분에 증거번호를 표시한다.

③ 기술용어에 대해서는 각주로 용어의 정의를 기재하고, 그 출처를 명시한다.

④ 종합준비서면은 서두에 이 사건 소송에서 주장하는 모든 공격·방어방법과 주요 증거(선행발명 포함)의 내용을 요약하여 기재한다.

⑤ 종합준비서면을 제외한 나머지 준비서면에는 이미 주장한 내용을 반복하여 기재하지 않는다. 필요한 경우 종합준비서면의 해당 부분을 인용하여 기재한다.

나. 진보성에 대한 주장

① 선행발명과의 구체적인 결합관계, 결합이 쉬운 이유를 명시한다. 명시되지 않은 주장에 대해서는 주장하지 아니한 것으로 볼 수 있으므로 유의한다.

예시) 선행발명 1 내지 3에 의하여 진보성이 부정된다(×).
주선행발명인 선행발명 1에 선행발명 2의 ○○ 구성을 부가(또는 선행발명 1의 구성 2를 선행발명 2의 ○○구성으로 대체)하면 특허발명이 도출되고, 선행발명 1에 그와 같은 결합에 대한 시사가 있어 통상의 기술자가 그러한 결합을 쉽게 생각해낼 수 있으므로 특허발명의 진보성이 부정된다(○).

② 특허발명과 각 선행발명의 대응되는 구성을 대비한 구성대비표를 제출한다.

③ 선행발명은 그 구성을 구체적으로 특정한다. 하나의 문서에 수 개의

발명이 포함되어 있는 경우 그중 어떤 것을 선행발명으로 주장하는 것인지 명확히 한다.

④ 통상의 기술자가 누구인지와 그 기술수준을 구체적으로 기재한다.

⑤ 자유실시기술항변에 있어서도 위 각 항에서 기재한 바와 같다.

다. 명세서 기재불비에 대한 주장은 적용법조를 명시한다.

라. 침해에 대한 주장

① 침해 제품·방법은 집행기관이 별도의 판단없이 식별할 수 있도록 구체적·개별적·사실적으로 특정한다(예시: 상품명, 제품의 형식번호를 기재하고, 도면이나 사진을 첨부함).

② 침해 제품·방법에 대해서는 특허발명과 대비할 수 있도록 구체적으로 주장하되, 상대방이 실시하는 제품·방법과 사실적 관점에서 동일하게 기재한다.

③ 특허발명과 침해 제품·방법의 대응되는 구성을 대비한 구성대비표를 제출한다.

마. 손해액에 관한 주장

① 손해액에 관한 원고의 주장은, 적용법조를 명시하고, 각 요건사실에 대한 주장에 관련되는 증거번호를 표시한다.

② 손해액에 관한 피고의 답변은 원고 주장 사실에 대한 구체적인 반박을 포함한다(구체적으로 부인하지 않은 사실에 대해서는 다툼이 없는 것으로 볼 수 있으므로 유의한다). 특히 원고가 특허법 제128조 제1항에 기해 손해액을 주장하는 경우 원고 주장의 양도수량을 부인하는 답변에는 실제 양도수량을 기재한다. 원고가 동조 제3항에 기해 손해액을 주장하는 경우 원고 주장의 이익액을 부인하는 답변에는 실제 이익액과 그 산정의 근거가 되는 매출액, 경비, 이익률 등을 기재한다.

2. 증거설명서

가. 각 증거와 이를 통한 입증취지를 간략히 기재한다.

나. 신규성, 진보성, 자유실시기술 주장에 대한 증거를 제출하는 경우, 선행발명으로 제출하는 것인지, 주지관용기술의 증거로 제출하는 것인지 명확히 한다.

3. 서증

가. 외국어로 된 서증은 번역문이 첨부되어야 하고, 주된 증거(선행발명 등)에 대해서는 전문 번역문을 첨부한다. 기계번역(자동번역)으로 제출하여서는 안 된다.

나. 서증명은 문서의 제목이 있는 경우에는 그 제목을 표시하고, 제목이 없는 경우에는 문서의 내용을 요약하여 기재한다[예시: "○○회사의 상품 카탈로그(2006. 1. 2. 발행)"]. 선행발명으로 제출하는 증거는 서증명에 이를 명시한다[예시: "(선행발명 1) 등록특허공보 제0012345호"].

다. 한 개의 서증에는 한 개의 증거만이 포함되어야 한다[예시: 상표사건에서 수개의 블로그 게시글은 각각 별개의 서증으로 제출하여야 한다. 다만 관련되는 내용인 경우 가지번호로 표시한다(갑 제2호증의 1, 갑 제2호증의 2 등)].

[첨부 1]

특 허 법 원

제 21 부

준비명령(항소이유서)

사　　　건　　2016나100001
원고(항소인)　　○○○ 귀하

귀하의 항소에 따라 위 사건의 소송기록이 이 법원에 접수되었습니다. 항소인은 항소이유를 구체적으로 기재한 준비서면과 필요한 증거를 제출하시기 바랍니다.

제출기한: 2016. ○. ○.

준 비 사 항

1. 항소인은 다음 사항을 포함한 준비서면을 제출하시기 바랍니다.
   ① 1심 판결 중 사실을 잘못 인정한 부분 또는 법리를 잘못 적용한 부분
   ② 1심에서의 항소인과 피항소인의 사실상·법률상 주장의 요지, 피항소인의 주장 중 다툼 없는 부분
   ③ 1심에서 제출한 증거의 요지와 그 입증취지
   ④ 항소심에서 새롭게 주장하는 사항, 항소심에서 새롭게 신청하는 증거와 그 입증취지, 위 주장 및 증거를 1심에서 제출하지 못한 이유
   ⑤ 관련 사건의 표시[동일한 특허·실용신안·상표·디자인에 대해 특허심판원 또는 법원에 계속 중인 사건은 모두 관련 사건으로 봄(정정심판청구사건 및 정정청구 포함). 정당한 이유 없이 이를 기재하지 않은 경우 소송절차 진행에서 고려하지 아니할 수 있음].
   ⑥ 조정·화해 희망 여부

2. 1심에서 변론준비기일을 진행하거나 주장의 제출기한을 정한 경우, 1심 변론준비기일의 종결 시까지 또는 제출기한까지 제출되지 아니한 주장을 새로이 추가·변경하거나 추가·변경된 주장에 대한 증거를 제출하기 위해서는 정당한 사유로 그 기간 내에 제출하지 못하였음을 구체적으로 소명하여야 합니다.

3. 특허법원에서는 '특허 등 침해소송 항소심 심리 매뉴얼'을 정하고 있습니다. 구체적인 내용은 홈페이지(http://patent.scourt.go.kr)를 참조하여 주십시오. 신속하고 효율적이며 충실한 재판 진행을 위해 위 매뉴얼의 내용을 숙지하고 이에 따라 주시기 바랍니다. <u>특히, 준비서면은 위 매뉴얼의 '제출서류의 작성방법'에 따라 작성하고, 증거는 '증거의 신청' 방법에 따라 신청해 주시기 바랍니다.</u>

4. 위와 같은 사항을 준수하지 않은 주장 및 증거신청의 경우 재판부는 민사소송법 제149조를 엄격히 적용할 예정입니다.

[첨부 2]

특 허 법 원

제 21 부

준비명령(답변서)

사　　　건　　2016나100001
피고(피항소인)　○○○ 귀하

피항소인은 답변의 내용을 구체적으로 기재한 준비서면과 필요한 증거를 제출하시기 바랍니다.

제출기한: 2016. ○. ○.

준 비 사 항

1. 피항소인은 다음 사항을 포함한 답변서를 제출하시기 바랍니다.
   ① 항소인의 주장에 대한 답변, 항소인의 주장 중 다툼 없는 부분
   ② 1심에서 제출한 증거의 요지와 그 입증취지
   ③ 항소심에서 새롭게 주장하는 사항, 항소심에서 새롭게 신청하는 증거와 그 입증취지, 위 주장 및 증거를 1심에서 제출하지 못한 이유
   ④ 상대방이 제출한 서증에 대한 인부서
   ⑤ 관련 사건의 표시[동일한 특허·실용신안·상표·디자인에 대해 특허심판원 또는 법원에 계속 중인 사건은 모두 관련 사건으로 봄(정정심판청구사건 및 정정청구 포함)]. 정당한 이유 없이 이를 기재하지 않은 경우 소송절차 진행에서 고려하지 아니할 수 있음].
   ⑥ 조정·화해 희망 여부

2. 1심에서 변론준비기일을 진행하거나 주장의 제출기한을 정한 경우, 1심 변론준비기일의 종결 시까지 또는 제출기한까지 제출되지 아니한 주장

을 새로이 추가·변경하거나 추가·변경된 주장에 대한 증거를 제출하기 위해서는 정당한 사유로 그 기간 내에 제출하지 못하였음을 구체적으로 소명하여야 합니다.

3. 특허법원에서는 '특허 등 침해소송 항소심 심리 매뉴얼'을 정하고 있습니다. 구체적인 내용은 홈페이지(http://patent.scourt.go.kr)를 참조하여 주십시오. 신속하고 효율적이며 충실한 재판 진행을 위해 위 매뉴얼의 내용을 숙지하고 이에 따라 주시기 바랍니다. <u>특히, 준비서면은 위 매뉴얼의 '제출서류의 작성방법'에 따라 작성하고, 증거는 '증거의 신청' 방법에 따라 신청해 주시기 바랍니다.</u>

4. 위와 같은 사항을 준수하지 않은 주장 및 증거신청의 경우 재판부는 민사소송법 제149조를 엄격히 적용할 예정입니다.

[첨부 3]

특 허 법 원

제 21 부

기일지정 및 변론준비명령

사　　　건　　2016나100001
원고(항소인)　　○○○ 귀하
피고(피항소인)　○○○ 귀하

당사자의 주장을 명확하게 하고, 충실한 심리를 위해 다음 사항에 대해 준비를 명합니다.

다　　음

1. 1회 변론기일을 **2016. ○. ○. ○시** 특허법원 ○○호 법정으로 지정한다.

2. 원고(항소인)는 **2016. ○. ○.까지** 모든 주장 및 그에 대한 주된 증거를 제출·신청하여야 한다.

3. 피고(피항소인)는 **2016. ○. ○.까지** 모든 주장 및 그에 대한 주된 증거를 제출·신청하여야 한다.

4. 증인신청, 감정신청 등 시일을 요하는 증거의 신청은 **2016. ○. ○.까지** 서면으로 신청하여야 한다.

5. 유의사항

   가. 변론기일 변경 신청, 주장 및 증거의 제출·신청기한 연장신청은 기한이 도래하기 1주 전까지 정당한 사유를 소명하여 서면으로 신청하여야 합니다.

나. 주장 및 증거의 제출·신청 기한 이후 주장을 추가·변경하거나 추가·변경된 주장에 대한 증거를 제출·신청하기 위해서는 정당한 사유로 위 기간 이내에 제출하지 못하였음을 소명하여야 합니다(예를 들어, 청구원인이나 항변에 해당하는 주장, 신규성·진보성에 관한 주장이나 자유실시기술 항변에 있어서 주선행발명을 변경하거나 선행발명 및 그 결합관계를 추가·변경하는 주장, 적용법조를 달리하는 명세서 기재불비 주장, 1심에서 인정한 사실·법적 판단에 반하는 주장, 적용법조를 달리하는 손해액에 대한 주장 등의 추가·변경). 정당한 사유가 소명되지 아니하는 경우 재판부는 민사소송법 제149조를 엄격히 적용할 예정입니다.

다. 변론기일에는 항소인, 피항소인 순서로 각 15분간 구두로 변론합니다. 구두 변론을 위한 변론자료 등은 변론기일 1주 전까지 제출하여야 합니다.

라. 변론기일에는 필요한 경우 사건과 직접적으로 관련된 제품(특허실시제품, 침해제품 등)을 지참합니다.

마. 특허법원에서는 '특허 등 침해소송 항소심 심리 매뉴얼'을 정하고 있습니다. 구체적인 내용은 홈페이지(http://patent.scourt.go.kr)를 참조하여 주십시오. 신속하고 효율적이며 충실한 재판 진행을 위해 위 매뉴얼의 내용을 숙지하고 이에 따라 주시기 바랍니다. 특히, 준비서면은 위 매뉴얼의 '제출서류의 작성방법'에 따라 작성하고, 증거는 '증거의 신청' 방법에 따라 신청해 주시기 바랍니다.

[첨부 4]

특 허 법 원

제 21 부

사건관리 화상회의 준비명령

사　　　건　　2016나100001
원고(항소인)　　○○○ 귀하
피고(피항소인)　○○○ 귀하

당사자의 주장을 명확하게 하고, 충실한 심리를 위해 아래 준비사항에 대해 준비를 명합니다.

준 비 사 항

1. 사건관리 화상회의 일정
   사건관리 화상회의를 **2016. ○. ○. ○시**에 영상통화(원격영상증언시스템, vidyo) 방식으로 진행합니다.[5] 회의 시작 5분 전까지 원격영상증언시스템(vidyo)에 접속하고, 영상 및 스피커, 마이크 상태 점검을 마쳐주시기 바랍니다.

2. 사건관리 화상회의의 내용
   사건관리 화상회의에서는 아래의 내용 및 일정에 대해 협의할 예정입니다. 이후의 재판절차는 협의된 내용 및 일정에 따라 진행되므로, 미리 주장 및 증거방법을 준비하시기 바랍니다(민사소송법 제147조 참조). 효율적인 회의 진행을 위해 상대방 대리인과 아래 사항에 대해 미리 협의하시기 바랍니다.

---

5) 화상회의를 위해서는 원격영상증언시스템(vidyo) 프로그램의 설치(위 프로그램은 http://vc.scourt.go.kr URL 접속하여 다운받을 수 있습니다), 웹카메라(화상 카메라), 헤드셋(스피커, 마이크) 등의 장치가 필요합니다.

① 변론기일 일자 및 횟수, 각 기일별 변론 쟁점

② 주장 및 증거의 제출기한(종합준비서면의 제출기한, 전문가 진술서 제출기한, 준비서면의 제출횟수 및 분량 포함)

③ 전문가증인 등 시일을 요하는 증거의 신청 여부 및 기한

④ 당사자에 의한 기술설명회 실시 여부

⑤ 조정절차 회부 여부

⑥ 쟁점 확인 및 정리

3. 유의사항

가. 원활한 절차 진행을 위해 본 사건에서 다투는 사실·법적 쟁점을 회의 7일 전까지 제출합니다. 특히 청구항 해석에 대해 다툼이 있는 경우 해당 청구항, 용어(구, 절 포함) 및 그에 대해 주장하는 해석을 제출합니다.

나. <u>준비명령에서 주장 및 증거의 제출기한을 정한 경우 그 기한을 위반하여 주장 및 증거를 제출하고자 하는 당사자는 정당한 이유로 위 기간 이내에 제출하지 못하였음을 소명하여야 하고, 정당한 이유가 소명되지 아니한 주장 및 증거는 민사소송법 제147조 제2항, 제149조에 의하여 각하될 수 있습니다.</u>

다. 특허발명 무효사유에 관한 주장은 다음과 같은 사항을 포함하여야 하며, 최종 기한 이후에 아래 사항에 대한 주장을 추가·변경하기 위해서는 정당한 사유가 있음을 소명하여야 합니다.

① 통상의 기술자의 기술수준(학력, 자격, 종사기간 등)

② 선행발명: 주선행발명을 추가·변경하거나 수 개의 선행발명을 결합함에 있어서 구체적인 결합관계를 달리하는 경우(진보성 부정 주장의 예시: 주선행발명인 선행발명 1의 구성 2를 선행발명 2의 ○○구성으로 대체하면 특허발명이 도출되고, 선행발명 1에 그와 같은 결합에 대한 시사가 있어 통상의 기술자가 그러한 결합을 쉽게 생각해낼 수 있으므로 특허발명의 진보성이 부정된다)

라. 특허법원에서는 '특허 등 침해소송 항소심 심리 매뉴얼'을 정하고 있습니다. 구체적인 내용은 홈페이지(http://patent.scourt.go.kr)를 참조하여 주십시오. 신속하고 효율적이며 충실한 재판 진행을 위해 위 매뉴얼의 내용을 숙지하고 이에 따라 주시기 바랍니다. 특히, 준비서면은 위 매뉴얼의 '제출서류의 작성방법'에 따라 작성하고, 증거는 '증거의 신청' 방법에 따라 신청해 주시기 바랍니다.

[첨부 5]

특 허 법 원

제 21 부

기일지정 및 절차에 관한 준비명령

사 건 2016나100001
원고(항소인) ○○○ 귀하
피고(피항소인) ○○○ 귀하

위 사건에 관하여 2016. ○. ○. 사건관리 화상회의에서 협의한 내용에 기초하여 주장·증거제출기한과 변론기일 등을 다음과 같이 지정한다.

다 음

1. 원고(항소인) 종합준비서면의 제출기한은 **2016. ○. ○.까지**로 한다. 종합준비서면에는 3.가.항 기재 쟁점에 관한 모든 주장을 기재하고, 그에 대한 주된 증거를 제출하여야 한다. 본 서면 제출 이후 주장을 추가·변경하거나 추가·변경된 주장에 대한 증거를 제출하기 위해서는 정당한 이유로 위 기간 이내에 제출하지 못하였음을 소명하여야 한다(예를 들어, 청구원인이나 항변에 해당하는 주장, 신규성·진보성에 관한 주장이나 자유실시기술 항변에 있어서 주선행발명을 변경하거나 선행발명 및 그 결합관계를 추가·변경하는 주장, 적용법조를 달리하는 명세서 기재불비 주장, 1심에서 인정한 사실·법적 판단에 반하는 주장 등의 추가·변경).

2. 피고(피항소인) 종합준비서면의 제출기한은 **2016. ○. ○.까지**로 한다. 종합준비서면에는 3.가.항 기재 쟁점에 관한 모든 주장을 기재하고, 그에 대한 주된 증거를 제출하여야 한다. 본 서면 제출 이후 주장을 추가·변경하거나 추가·변경된 주장에 대한 증거를 제출하기 위해서는 정당

한 이유로 위 기간 이내에 제출하지 못하였음을 소명하여야 한다.

3. 1회 변론기일을 **<u>2016. ○. ○. ○시</u>** 특허법원 ○○호 법정으로 지정한다.
   가. 1회 변론기일에서 논의할 쟁점은 특허 제1234567호 청구항 제1항 발명의 무효 여부와 피고 제품이 위 특허발명의 권리범위에 속하는지 여부이다.
   나. 변론기일에는 원고(항소인), 피고(피항소인) 순서로 각 15분간 구두로 변론한다.
   다. 구두 변론을 위한 변론자료 등은 변론기일 1주일 전까지 제출하여야 한다.

4. 3.가.항 기재 쟁점에 관한 전문가증인의 신청 기한은 **<u>2016. ○. ○.</u>**까지로 한다. 전문가증인 신청서에는 전문가증인의 전문성과 객관성을 확인할 수 있는 기본 진술서[특허법원 홈페이지(http://patent.scourt.go.kr) 참조]를 첨부하여야 한다.

   ※ 전문가증인이 채택되고, 1회 변론기일에서 증인신문을 함께 할 필요가 있는 경우 협의 하에 1회 변론기일을 변경할 수 있습니다.

[첨부 6]

특 허 법 원

제 21 부

청구항 해석 및 변론준비명령

사　　　건　　2016나100001
원고(항소인)　　○○○ 귀하
피고(피항소인)　○○○ 귀하

당사자들의 현재까지의 주장과 증거를 종합하여, 이 사건 특허발명의 청구항 중 해석에 다툼이 있는 주요 용어에 관하여 다음과 같이 해석합니다. 따라서 당사자들은 아래 해석에 기초하여 변론을 준비하여 주시기 바랍니다.

다 음

1. 이 사건 특허발명의 청구항
【 청구항 】 (중략) (이하 '이 사건 제1항 발명'이라 한다)

2. 이 사건 제1항 발명의 주요 용어에 대한 해석
가. ○○○
살피건대, (중략) 으로 봄이 타당하다.

(이하 생략)

[첨부 7]

특 허 법 원

제 21 부

화상회의 준비명령

사 건 2016나100001
원고(항소인) ○○○ 귀하
피고(피항소인) ○○○ 귀하

당사자의 주장을 명확하게 하고, 충실한 심리를 위해 아래 준비사항에 대해 준비를 명합니다.

준 비 사 항

1. 화상회의 일정
   증거조사 일정 등 협의를 위한 화상회의를 **2016. ○. ○. ○시**에 영상통화(원격영상증언시스템, vidyo) 방식으로 진행합니다.[6] 회의 시작 5분 전까지 원격영상증언시스템(vidyo)에 접속하고, 영상 및 스피커, 마이크 상태 점검을 마쳐주시기 바랍니다.

2. 원고(항소인)는 **2016. ○. ○.까지** 손해액에 관한 모든 주장 및 그에 대한 입증계획을 제출하여야 한다.

3. 원고(항소인)는 손해액 산정의 요건사실에 관하여 피고(피항소인)에 대하여 석명을 구하는 사항, 손해액 산정을 위해 피고(피항소인)로부터 제출받아야 하는 서류(자료)가 있는 경우 **2016. ○. ○.까지** 이를 구체

6) 화상회의를 위해서는 원격영상증언시스템(vidyo) 프로그램의 설치(위 프로그램은 http://vc.scourt.go.kr URL 접속하여 다운받을 수 있습니다), 웹카메라(화상 카메라), 헤드셋(스피커, 마이크) 등의 장치가 필요합니다.

적으로 기재하여 서면으로 제출하여야 한다.

4. 피고(피항소인)는 **2016. ○. ○.까지** 다음 사항을 포함한 준비서면을 제출하여야 한다.
   ① 원고(항소인)의 손해액 주장에 대한 답변
   ② 원고(항소인)가 주장하는 매출액 등 사실에 대한 구체적인 답변
   ③ 원고(항소인)의 석명사항에 대한 답변
   ④ 원고(항소인)가 제출을 요구하는 서류(자료)의 소지 여부, 임의 제출 가능 여부, 임의 제출이 불가능한 경우 그 구체적인 사유

5. 화상회의의 내용
   화상회의에서는 아래의 내용 및 일정에 대해 협의할 예정입니다. 효율적인 회의 진행을 위해 상대방 대리인과 아래 사항에 대해 미리 협의하시기 바랍니다.
   ① 피고(피항소인)의 임의 제출 서류(자료)의 종류 및 범위
   ② 서류(자료)제출명령의 신청 여부 및 범위
   ③ 주장 및 증거의 제출기한
   ④ 전문가증인, 감정 등 시일을 요하는 증거의 신청 여부 및 기한
   ⑤ 조정절차 회부 여부
   ⑥ 쟁점 확인 및 정리

6. 유의사항
   가. 주장 및 증거의 제출 기한 이후 주장을 추가·변경하거나 추가·변경된 주장에 대한 증거를 제출하기 위해서는 정당한 사유로 위 기간 이내에 제출하지 못하였음을 소명하여야 합니다. 정당한 사유가 소명되지 아니하는 경우 재판부는 민사소송법 제149조를 엄격히 적용할 예정입니다.
   나. 손해액에 관한 주장
      ① 손해액에 관한 원고의 주장은, 적용법조를 명시하고, 각 요건사실에 대한 주장에 관련되는 증거번호를 표시합니다.

② 손해액에 관한 피고의 답변은 원고 주장 사실에 대한 구체적인 반박을 기재합니다(구체적으로 부인하지 않은 사실에 대해서는 다툼이 없는 것으로 볼 수 있습니다). 특히 원고가 특허법 제128조 제1항에 기해 손해액을 주장하는 경우 원고 주장의 양도수량을 부인하는 답변에는 실제 양도수량을 기재하고, 원고가 동조 제3항에 기해 손해액을 주장하는 경우 원고 주장의 이익액을 부인하는 답변에는 실제 이익액과 그 산정의 근거가 되는 매출액, 경비, 이익률 등을 기재합니다.

다. 손해액을 증명하기 위한 증거가 일방 당사자에게 편재되어 있고, 이를 제출하지 아니하거나 폐기하는 등 증거조사에 협조하지 아니하여 특허법 제128조 제1항부터 제5항에 기해 손해액을 산정하는 것이 극히 곤란한 경우 법원은 같은 조 제6항에 기해 상당한 손해액을 인정함에 있어서 위와 같은 사정을 고려할 수 있습니다.

라. 특허법원에서는 ‘특허 등 침해소송 항소심 심리 매뉴얼’을 정하고 있습니다. 구체적인 내용은 홈페이지(http://patent.scourt.go.kr)를 참조하여 주십시오. 신속하고 효율적이며 충실한 재판 진행을 위해 위 매뉴얼의 내용을 숙지하고 이에 따라 주시기 바랍니다. 특히, 준비서면은 위 매뉴얼의 ‘제출서류의 작성방법’에 따라 작성하고, 증거는 ‘증거의 신청’ 방법에 따라 신청해 주시기 바랍니다.

[첨부 8]

전문가증인 기본 진술서

인적 사항	이름		생년월일	
	주소			

중립성

1	원·피고(회사인 경우 대표이사 및 임직원, 이하 같음)와 친인척관계에 있습니까?	Y	N
2	원·피고와 채권·채무관계에 있습니까?	Y	N
3	원·피고와 업무를 같이 하거나, 계약관계, 고용관계 기타 이에 준하는 관계에 있거나, 과거에 있었습니까?	Y	N
4	원·피고가 관여한 소송 또는 이 사건 특허/제품 등에 관한 소송에서 증인으로 증언한 바 있습니까?	Y	N
5	본건 소송과 관련하여 원·피고에게 자문을 한 바 있습니까?	Y	N

전문성

1	증인의 전문 분야를 구체적으로 기재해주십시오.
2	전문 분야에 관하여, ⑴ 현재 및 과거의 직업(재직기간, 직위/직책, 담당업무 포함)을 밝히고, ⑵ 학위/자격증, 논문/보고서, 기타 전문성을 확인할 수 있는 자료가 있다면, 그 내용을 구체적으로 기재해주십시오. *※ 아래 칸이 부족한 경우 별지로 첨부 가능*

전문가증인의 의무

전문가증인은 당사자 일방에 편향되지 않게 사실과 전문지식에 근거하여 진술하여야 합니다. 전문가증인은 해당 분야의 전문가로서 객관적으로 검증되고 해당 분야에서 널리 인정되는 사실/이론에 기초하여 진술하여야 하며, 자신의 주관적인 이론/해석에 기초하여 진술하여서는 안 됩니다.

위 기재사항은 모두 사실임을 진술합니다.

일 자 20 . . .

서 명

[첨부 9]

특 허 법 원

제 21 부

변론준비명령(전문가증인)

사　　　건　　2016나100001
원고(항소인)　　○○○ 귀하
피고(피항소인)　○○○ 귀하

2016. ○. ○. 변론기일에서의 증인신문과 관련하여 충실한 심리를 위해 아래 사항에 대해 준비를 명합니다.

다　　음

1. 원고(항소인)의 전문가증인 진술서 등 제출
   가. 원고(항소인)는 **2016. ○. ○.까지** 전문가증인 진술서 및 증인신문 사항을 제출하여야 한다. 주신문은 전문가증인 진술서의 범위 내에서 하여야 한다.
   나. 증인에게 주신문에서 제시하거나 인용하는 모든 자료(Family 특허, 번역문, 실물사진, 참고자료 포함)는 **2016. ○. ○.까지** 증거로 제출되어야 한다.

2. 증인에 대한 주신문과 반대신문은 각 20분 이내로 한다.

3. 당사자는 각 주신문과 반대신문을 위한 통역을 대동할 수 있다. 통역을 대동하지 못하는 경우 **2016. ○. ○.까지** 재판부에 이를 알리고 통역인 지정신청을 하여야 한다.

4. 전문가증인의 증언의 신빙성을 탄핵하는 주장 및 증거는 **2016. ○. ○.까지** 제출하여야 한다.

Guideline of Civil Appellate Practice and Procedure of the Patent Court of Korea

March 16, 2016, Patent Court

I. Purpose of the Guideline

The Guideline of Civil Practice and Procedure of the Patent Court of Korea(hereinafter to as "the Guideline") is prepared to facilitate expeditious and efficient civil appeal proceedings involving complex issues by prescribing matters such as procedural discussions, designation of deadlines for submitting arguments and rebuttal arguments, and focusing examination on disputed issues. In addition, by prescribing and publicly disclosing the hearing procedures and methods for requesting and examining evidence adapted to the nature of patent actions, the Guideline provides predictability to the interested parties and facilitates diligent preparation in appeal proceedings.

II. Petition of Appeal and Preparatory Order

1. Preparatory Order to Appellant

A. If a petition of appeal does not contain the statement of sufficient grounds of appeal, the Court issues a preparatory order requesting appellant to submit of a statement of grounds of appeal, immediately upon receiving the petition for appeal(See. Attachment 1).

B. No later than 3 weeks from receipt of the preparatory order, the appellant shall submit a statement of grounds of appeal including the following:

① Errors of fact and errors of law in the judgment of the lower courts;

② A summary of the factual and legal arguments made by the appellant and the appellee in the lower court, and undisputed facts among the appellee's arguments;

③ A summary of the evidence submitted in the lower court and the purport of the evidence;

④ New arguments raised in appeal, new evidence presented in appeal and the purport thereof, and the reason(s) for the failure to present the arguments and evidence in the lower court;

⑤ Notice of related cases [all cases pending in the Intellectual Property Trial and Appeal Board of the Korean Intellectual Property Office((hereinafter to as "the IPTAB") or in the court and involving the same patent, utility model, trademark or design shall be deemed to be related cases (including a case initiated by a petition for correction trial and a petition for correction). If the appellant fails to notice such cases without a justifiable cause, the cases may be not considered during the appeal proceedings]; and

⑥ Whether the appellant desires mediation or settlement.

2. Preparatory Order to Appellee

A. No later than 3 weeks from service of the appellant's brief containing the grounds for appeal, the appellee shall submit a statement of response including the following:

① Answer to the appellant's arguments and undisputed portions among the appellant's arguments;

② A summary of the evidence submitted in the lower court and the purport of the evidence;

③ New arguments raised in appeal, new evidence presented in appeal and the purport thereof, and the reason(s) for the failure to present the arguments and evidence in the lower court;

④ Notice of related cases [all cases pending in the IPTAB or in the court and involving the same patent, utility model, trademark or design shall be deemed to be related cases (including a case initiated by a petition for correction trial and a petition for correction). If the appellee fails to notice such cases without a justifiable cause, the cases may be not considered during the appeal proceedings]; and

⑤ Whether the appellee desires mediation or settlement.

B. If the appellee fails to submit a statement of response or answer to the ground of appeal is not sufficient in the statement of response, the Court may issue a preparatory order requesting appellee to submit a statement of response describing the purport of the response in detail(See. Attachment 2).

3. Instructions Relating to New Arguments and Evidence

In the case where the lower court held a preparatory hearing or designated a deadline for submission of arguments, if a party seeks to add new or modified arguments that had not been submitted by the conclusion of the preparatory hearing or the designated deadline in the lower court or to submit any evidence for the new or modified arguments, the party shall provide a detailed explanation for the failure to submit the argument or evidence within such period based on a justifiable cause, provided that submission of such argument or evidence does not cause a substantial delay in the appeal proceeding.

III. Classification of a Case and Pre-Hearing Procedure

1. Classification of a Case

Upon submission of a statement of the grounds for appeal, the presiding judge reviews the case based on the briefs and appeal record and classifies the case as a case requiring immediate designation of a hearing, a case requiring a case management conference or a preparatory hearing, or a case to be referred to an early mediation proceeding.

2. Preparatory Order for Hearing

For a case requiring immediate designation of a hearing, in order to conduct the proceedings in a diligent manner, the Court may issue a preparatory order to the appellant and the appellee designating deadlines for submission of arguments and evidence and for requests for evidence that require a substantial amount of time such as an expert witness(See. Attachment 3).

3. Video Conference for Case Management

A. After hearing opinions of the parties, the presiding judge may discuss procedural matters of the case with the parties simultaneously through video and audio communication means (hereinafter, "video conference for case management"). The presiding judge may designate the judge to be in charge of the above process.

B. The Court may notify the appellant and the appellee of the video conference and issue a preparatory order with regard to the conference(See. Attachment 4).

C. In a video conference for case management, the following matters may be discussed:

① Dates and the number of hearings, and disputed issues to be addressed in each of the hearings;

② Deadlines for submission of arguments and evidence (including deadlines for submission of comprehensive briefs and expert's statement, and the number or volume of briefs to be submitted);

③ Whether to request for evidence requiring a substantial amount of time, such as an expert witness, and the deadline for such a request;

④ Whether to hold a technical explanatory session by the parties;

⑤ Whether to refer the case to a mediation proceeding; and

⑥ Confirmation and summary of issues.

D. The Court may issue a preparatory order (scheduling order) based on the results of the video conference for case management(See. Attachment 5).

E. If the Court orders submission of comprehensive briefs in a preparatory order, the appellant shall submit a comprehensive brief no later than 3 weeks from the date of the video conference for case management (or a deadline designated in the preparatory order) and the appellee shall submit a comprehensive brief no later than 3 weeks from the date of the appellant's submission of its comprehensive brief (or a deadline designated in the preparatory order).

F. Each party shall describe all arguments in its comprehensive brief (including the arguments that were made in the lower court and not withdrawn) and submit main evidence for the arguments. If the Court has ordered submission of comprehensive briefs for specific issues, the comprehensive briefs shall include all arguments relating to the specific issues.

G. If a party seeks to add any new or modified argument or submit evidence for such argument after the deadline for submission of arguments and evidence designated in the preparatory order, the party shall provide an explanation for the failure to submit the argument or evidence within the designated period based on a justifiable cause [e.g., addition or modification of arguments such as an argument relating to the statement of claim or defense, an argument that changes the closest prior art ("main prior art") relating to novelty, inventive step or a free-to-practice technology defense or that adds or changes prior art and the combination relationship thereof, an argument for lack of sufficient description in the specification based on a different legal provision, an argument contrary to the judgment of the lower court, etc.].

4. Preparatory Hearing

A. The Court may hold a preparatory hearing and have the parties present in order to summarize the parties' arguments and evidence or to hold a technical explanatory session.

B. If a party seeks to add or modify an argument or submit evidence for such added or modified argument after the conclusion of the preparatory hearing, the party shall provide an explanation for the failure to submit the argument or evidence before the conclusion of the preparatory hearing based on a justifiable cause.

IV. Oral Hearings

1. Conduct of Oral Hearings

A. Each party shall present an oral argument for 15 minutes, in the order of the appellant and the appellee. Even when a party has retained more than one attorney-of-record, the party shall present its oral arguments within the above time period. If deemed necessary, the presiding judge may extend or shorten the time.

B. Any materials for oral arguments shall be submitted no later than 1 week before the designated date for each hearing.

C. If necessary, the parties shall bring the products directly related to the case (e.g., products implementing a patent in dispute, accused infringing products, etc.). The presiding judge may request the parties to explain or demonstrate the products.

2. Separate Oral Hearings according to Issues

A. If deemed necessary in any of the following cases, the Court may consult with the parties and hold the separate oral hearings according to issues:

① Where it is necessary to hold oral hearings according to specific claims or issues because several claims are consolidated or several issues are in dispute;[1)]

② Where a hearing for claim construction should be conducted first

---

1) < Operational Example > When the issues of infringement and the amount of damages are in dispute:
① Based on the discussion in a video conference for case management, the Court sets a schedule for the separate oral hearing according to issues and designates a deadline for submission of arguments and evidence on the infringement issue. ? The Court holds a first hearing directed to the infringement issue ? The Court may disclose its opinion on the infringement issue, either orally or in writing.
② If a prima facie case of infringement is established, a discussion is held during a preparatory proceeding for setting the deadlines for submission of arguments and evidence relating to the amount of damages, procedures and methods of examination of evidence, etc.
If infringement is not clear, a discussion is held during a preparatory proceeding for conducting additional examination on unclear portions in a second hearing.
③ The Court holds the second hearing directed to the disputed issue discussed in the preparatory hearing proceeding. ? The Court issues a judgment.

because the parties dispute the proper construction of the claims and the parties' arguments on other disputed issues may change according to the claim construction;[2] or

③ Where it is otherwise necessary to hold hearings directed to specific issues.

B. At each of the hearings, the scope of the hearing is limited to the disputed issue designated for that hearing.

C. After a hearing, the Court may disclose its opinion, either orally or in writing, regarding disputed issues on which examination has been completed. The above opinion can be changed later. The judge panel may order the parties to prepare for hearings on other remaining disputed issues based on the Court's opinion above(See. Attachment 6).

3. Hearings of an Infringement Action and a Cancellation of IPTAB Decision Action

A. If deemed necessary, such as when both an infringement action and a cancellation of IPTAB decision action involving same patent, utility model, trademark or design are filed together before the Court and are litigated by same parties and the attorneys-of-record, the Court may examine both actions in parallel.[3]

---

2) < Operational Example > When claim construction is in dispute:
① Based on the discussion in a video conference for case management, the Court sets a schedule for the construction of the asserted claims first and designates a deadline for submission of arguments and evidence for claim construction and other disputed issues. ? The Court holds a first hearing directed to construction of the claims in dispute.
② The Court discloses its opinion on the proper construction of claims, either orally or in writing, and orders the parties to prepare for a hearing directed to the other remaining disputed issues.
③ The Court holds a second hearing directed to the other remaining disputed issues. ? The Court issues a judgment.

B. If it is necessary to organize related arguments in an infringement action and a cancellation of IPT decision action, the Court may conduct preparatory proceedings for these actions in parallel.

V. Application and Examination of Evidence

1. Application to Adduce Evidence and its Admissibility

A. If a party makes an application to adduce new evidence in the appeal proceeding, the party shall provide a detailed explanation for the failure to submit the evidence in the lower court. The Court determines whether to admit the evidence in consideration of the circumstances, including whether a significant harm to the other party is expected from a delay in court proceedings or whether an expedited proceeding is necessary.

B. If a party makes an application to adduce evidence that is identical or similar, in the evidentiary purport, to the evidence that had been admitted and examined by the lower court (e.g., where the lower court appraised an amount of damages and a party files a request for a separate appraisal to impeach the appraised amount), the party shall provide a detailed explanation on the need for such evidence.

---

3) < Operational Example > When the infringement action and the cancellation of IPTAB Decision action are heard before the Court in parallel:
① The Court examines the issues of nullification (and infringement) in a first hearing. ? Regarding the cancellation action, the Court concludes a hearing or sets a hearing TBD.
② If the nullification is not recognized, the Court discloses its opinion on this (and may issue a judgment regarding the cancellation of decision action first) and discusses other remaining issues of the infringement action in a preparatory hearing. ? A second hearing ? The Court issues a judgment.
If the nullification is recognized, the Court discloses its opinion on this (and may issue a judgment regarding the cancellation of decision action). ? A second hearing ? The Court issues a judgment.

C. If a party makes an application to adduce evidence that had been filed but rejected by the lower court or voluntarily withdrawn by the party in the lower court, the party shall provide a detailed explanation on the need for such evidence.

D. If deemed necessary, the Court may conduct a preparatory proceeding for discussing evidence examination procedure. After hearing the parties' opinions, the presiding judge may discuss procedural matters via a video conference method set forth in Section III.3.A and, if deemed necessary, issue a preparatory order in relation thereto(See. Attachment 7).

2. Expert Witnesses

A. If a party files a request for an expert witness, the party shall attach a declaration that can confirm the expertise and objectivity of the witness(See. Attachment 8).

B. The Court may issue a preparatory order for examination of an expert witness (e.g. deadlines for submission of a statement of the expert witness and a questionnaire for the direct examination, limitation of the time for examination, and deadlines for submission of arguments and evidence for impeaching the credibility of the expert witness testimony) (See. Attachment 9).

C. The direct examination by the party who requests for the witness shall be made within the scope of the statement of the expert witness. All materials presented or cited in the direct examination shall be submitted as evidence before the date designated for examining the witness.

D. If an expert witness is a foreigner, the parties may be respectively accompanied by an interpreter for the direct and cross examinations. If a party cannot be accompanied by an interpreter, the party shall notify the Court of the same 4 weeks before the witness examination date and file a request for designation of an interpreter.

3. Order to Adduce Materials

A. According to a party's request, the Court may order the other party to submit documents or materials(including electronic documents) necessary for proving infringement or calculating the amount of damages occurred by the infringing act (e.g., accounting books, books relating to revenues or expenditures, contracts, tax invoices, tax returns, and statements of bank transactions). The Court may determine the types and scope of materials to be submitted by comparing the adverse impact that the requesting party would suffer due to the lack of access to materials and the adverse impact that disclosure of materials would have on the disclosing party. If the disclosing party presents justifiable grounds such as the documents contain sensitive personal information or information that is not relevant to proving infringement or calculating the amount of damages, the Court may permit submission of the documents by redacting corresponding portions according to the disclosing party's request.

B. If deemed necessary, the Court may, upon a request by a party, generally describe the purport of materials requested and the facts to be proved by the materials and order the other party to submit descriptions and purport of the materials in its possession that relate to the request.

C. If deemed necessary such as when it is disputed whether the other party is in possession of the materials, the Court may examine the parties or witnesses before issuing an order for production of materials.

D. If the other party refuses to produce the materials, the Court may request the party to provide the materials for the purpose of determining whether a justifiable cause exists for the refusal to produce the documents.

E. If the materials requested to be produced contain trade secret, the Court may, upon a request by the party in possession of the materials, order the requesting party or its counsel to keep the contents of the materials confidential by its ruling.

4. Appraisal

A. The Court may conduct an appraisal if an appraisal for calculating the amount of damages was not conducted in the lower court, the appraisal is necessary to determine a reasonable royalty or a contribution ratio of a patented invention, or the appraisal is otherwise acknowledged to be necessary.

B. The parties shall explain to the appraiser matters necessary for the appraisal of the damages amount.

5. Technical Advisors

A. If deemed necessary, the Court may hear opinions of the parties and designate one or more technical advisors.

B. A preparatory hearing may be held if it is deemed necessary for the technical advisors to understand the case. In the preparatory hearing, the technical advisors may directly question the parties with approval of the presiding judge. If it is necessary for a party to supplement its answer to a question from the technical advisors, the party shall submit its supplemental answer in writing to the Court by a deadline designated by the presiding judge.

6. Submission of Arguments and Evidence regarding an Amount of Damages

A. The respondent from whom compensation for damages is sought shall provide specific answers to the arguments of the petitioner, and if the petitioner's arguments are different from the facts, the respondent shall disclose the actual sales period of products, quantities sold, unit cost of sales, sales amount, manufacturing cost, and profit rate.

B. If account books or books relating to accounting or finance recording sales or expenditures are submitted, the disclosing party shall attach a written confirmation of the person who prepared the books (for a company, the chief executive officer and the chief accounting officer) verifying that the submitted documents are the original documents or copies of the original documents without any modification, deletion, or omission. If the other party raises a reasonable doubt on the authenticity of the account books, the disclosing party shall submit additional documents (bank or financial documents, etc.), which are the basis for preparing the books.

VI. Mediation

1. Early Mediation

A. Immediately upon receiving an appeal case or at an appropriate time, the presiding judge may determine whether the case is suitable for mediation and refer the case to an early mediation proceeding.

B. In principle, the mediation judge shall be in charge of cases referred to an early mediation proceeding. Upon discussions with the parties, the mediation judge may conduct mediation proceedings at suitable locations other than the Court.

2. Mediation after Hearing

Even after the first hearing, if deemed necessary, the presiding judge may refer the case to the mediation proceeding to enable the Patent Court Mediation Committee or the like to mediate the case.

VII. Preparing Documents for Submission

1. Briefs

A. Contents of Briefs

① If a brief of 20 or more pages is to be submitted, a table of contents shall be included at the beginning of the brief.

② If evidence supporting an argument is submitted, a number for the evidence shall be indicated in a corresponding portion of the brief.

③ Technical terms shall be defined in footnotes and the sources thereof shall be identified.

④ A comprehensive brief shall include, at the beginning thereof, a summary of all offensive and defensive arguments by a party in this action and main evidence (including prior arts) therefor.

⑤ In briefs other than the comprehensive briefs, arguments that have been previously made shall not be repeated.

B. Arguments regarding Inventive Step

① A specific combination relationship of prior arts and the reason for the ease in combining the prior arts shall be specified. It should be noted that if such an argument is not specified, it may be deemed that the argument had not been made.

Example) The inventive step of the Claim is denied by Prior Arts 1 to 3 (×). If the ○○ constitution of Prior Art 2 is added to Prior Art 1 which is the main prior art (or if the constitution 2 of Prior Art 1 is replaced with the ○○ constitution of Prior Art 2), the patented invention is derived. And since Prior Art 1 discloses a suggestion for such combination, a person of ordinary skill in the art could have easily conceived such combination and thus the inventive step of the patented invention is denied (○).

② A feature comparison chart comparing the corresponding features of the patented invention and each of the prior arts shall be submitted.

③ The features of prior arts shall be specified in detail. If a single document contains multiple inventions, it shall be clearly specified as to which of the multiple inventions is asserted to be a prior art.

④ The person of ordinary skill in the art and the level of ordinary skill in the art shall be specified in detail.

⑤ The foregoing requirements shall also apply to a free-to-practice technology defense.

C. An argument regarding a lack of written description in the specification shall specify an applicable legal provision on which the argument is based.

D. Arguments regarding Infringement

① Infringing products and methods shall be described specifically, individually, and factually to allow the enforcement agency to identify the same without a separate judgment in relation thereto (e.g., describing the names and model numbers of products with drawings or photos attached).

② Arguments regarding infringing products and methods shall be made in sufficient detail to allow comparison with the patented invention and the descriptions shall correspond to the products and methods practiced by the other party in factual aspects.

③ A feature comparison chart comparing the corresponding features of the patented invention and the infringing products and methods shall be submitted.

E. Arguments regarding an Amount of Damages

① Plaintiff's argument regarding the amount of damages shall indicate an applicable legal provision on which the argument is based and shall indicate an evidence number relating to an argument for each of the essential elements.

② Defendant's response relating to the amount of damages shall include a detailed rebuttal argument to the plaintiff's factual arguments (it should be noted that any fact not specifically denied may be deemed as being undisputed). In particular, if the plaintiff claims a damages amount based on Article 128(1) of the Patent Act, the defendant's response denying the transferred volume argued by the plaintiff shall state the actual transferred volume. If the plaintiff claims a damages amount based on Article 128(3) of the Patent Act, the defendant's response denying the profit amount argued by the plaintiff shall state the actual profit amount and the grounds for calculating the amount such as sales revenues, expenses, profit margins, etc.

2. Explanatory Documents for Evidence

A. Each item of evidence and the purport to be proved therefrom shall be briefly described.

B. If an item of evidence is submitted in relation to an argument regarding novelty, inventive step, or free-to-practice technology, it shall be clearly specified whether the evidentiary item is submitted as a prior art invention or as evidence of well-known prior art.

3. Documentary Evidence

A. Written documents in a foreign language shall be submitted with a translation attached thereto and the main evidence (e.g., prior arts, etc.) shall be submitted with a professional translation attached thereto. Machine(automatic) translations shall not be submitted.

B. A documentary evidence shall indicate a title if the title of the document exists, or a summary of the document, if the document has no title [e.g., "Product Catalogue of the Company ○○ (published on January 2, 2006)"]. A written evidence submitted as a prior art shall indicate the same [e.g., "(Prior Art 1) Registered Patent Publication No. 0012345"].

C. Each evidence shall contain only a single evidentiary item [e.g., in trademark cases, several blog postings shall be submitted as separate evidentiary documents; however, if they are related, they can be indicated as multi-level numbers (Plaintiff's Exhibit No. 2-1, 2-2, etc.)].

[Attachment 1]

PATENT COURT

The 21st Panel

Preparatory Order (Grounds for Appeal)

Case No. 2016 Na 100001
Plaintiff (Appellant) ○○○

According to the filing of your appeal, the litigation records of the case identified above have been submitted to this Court. Thus, the appellant is requested to submit a brief describing the specific grounds for appeal and the necessary evidence.

<u>Deadline for Submission: [*], 2016</u>

Preparatory Matters

1. The appellant is requested to submit a brief containing the following matters:

   ① Portions of the lower court's decision where the court is alleged to have erred in acknowledging facts or applying the law;

   ② A summary of the factual and legal arguments made by the appellant and the appellee in the lower court, and undisputed portions among the appellee's arguments;

   ③ A summary of the evidence submitted in the lower court and the purport of the evidence;

   ④ New arguments to be raised on appeal, new evidence to be presented on appeal and the purport thereof, and the reason(s) for the failure to present the arguments and evidence in the lower court;

⑤ A description of related cases [all cases pending in the Intellectual Property Trial and Appeal Board or any court that relate to the same patent, utility model, trademark or design shall be deemed as related cases (including a case initiated by a petition for correction trial or any claim for correction). If the appellant fails to describe such cases without a justifiable cause, the cases may be disregarded and not considered during the proceedings]; and

⑥ Whether the appellant desires mediation or settlement.

2. In the case where the lower court held a preparatory hearing or designated a deadline for submission of arguments, if the appellant seeks to add new or modified arguments or submit any evidence for the new or modified arguments that had not been submitted by the conclusion of the preparatory hearing date or the designated deadline in the lower court, the appellant shall provide a detailed explanation for the failure to submit the argument or evidence within such period based on a justifiable cause.

3. The Patent Court has established the "Guideline of Civil Appellate Practice and Procedure of the Patent Court of Korea." Please refer to the Patent Court website (http://patent.scourt.go.kr) for more details. For prompt, efficient, and diligent trial proceedings, please read the Manual carefully and comply with the provisions therein. In particular, briefs should be prepared in accordance with the section "Method of Preparing Documents for Submission" of the Manual and evidence should be requested in accordance with the section "Request for Investigation of Evidence" of the Manual.

4. The judicial panel will strictly apply Article 149 of the Civil Procedure Act against arguments or requests for evidence that are not in compliance with the foregoing matters.

[Attachment 2]

PATENT COURT

The 21st Panel

Preparatory Order (Response)

Case No. 2016 Na 100001

Defendant (Appellee) ○○○

The appellee is requested to submit a brief describing the detailed grounds of its response and the necessary evidence.

Deadline for Submission: [*], 2016

Preparatory Matters

1. The appellee is requested to submit a response containing the following matters:

   ① Answers to the appellant's arguments and undisputed portions among the appellant's arguments;

   ② A summary of the evidence submitted in the lower court and the purport of the evidence;

   ③ New arguments to be raised in appeal, new evidence to be presented in appeal and the purport thereof, and the reason(s) for the failure to present the arguments and evidence in the lower court;

   ④ Acceptance/denial of the evidentiary documents submitted by the other party;

   ⑤ A description of related cases [all cases pending in the Intellectual Property Trial and Appeal Board or any court that relate to the same patent, utility model, trademark or design shall be deemed as related cases (including a case initiated by a petition for correction trial or any claim for correction). If the appellant fails to describe such cases without a justifiable cause, the cases may be disregarded and not considered during the proceedings]; and

⑥ Whether the appellee desires mediation or settlement.

2. In the case where the lower court held a preparatory hearing or designated a deadline for submission of arguments, if the appellant seeks to add new or modified arguments or submit any evidence for the new or modified arguments that had not been submitted by the conclusion of the preparatory hearing date or the designated deadline in the lower court, the appellee shall provide a detailed explanation for the failure to submit the argument or evidence within such period based on a justifiable cause.

3. The Patent Court has established the "Guideline of Civil Appellate Practice and Procedure of the Patent Court of Korea." Please refer to the Patent Court website (http://patent.scourt.go.kr) for more details. For prompt, efficient, and diligent trial proceedings, please read the Manual carefully and comply with the provisions therein. In particular, briefs should be prepared in accordance with the section "Method of Preparing Documents for Submission" of the Manual and evidence should be requested in accordance with the section "Request for Investigation of Evidence" of the Manual.

4. The judicial panel will strictly apply Article 149 of the Civil Procedure Act against arguments or requests for evidence that are not in compliance with the foregoing matters.

[Attachment 3]

PATENT COURT

The 21st Panel

Designation of Hearing Date and Preparatory Order for Hearing

Case No. 2016 Na 100001
Plaintiff (Appellant) ○○○
Defendant (Appellee) ○○○

The Court hereby orders the parties to prepare for the following matters for the purpose of clarifying the parties' arguments and conducting diligent proceedings:

THE FOLLOWING

1. The first hearing date is designated to be held on [*], 2016, [*]AM/PM, at the courtroom [*] of the Patent Court.

2. The plaintiff (appellant) shall submit all of its arguments and main evidence therefor by [*], 2016.

3. The defendant (appellee) shall submit all of its arguments and main evidence therefor by [*], 2016.

4. A request for evidence that requires a substantial amount of time, such as a request for an expert witness or a request for an appraisal, shall be filed in writing by [*], 2016.

5. Instructions

A. A request for a change in the hearing date or for an extension of the deadline for submitting arguments and requesting evidence shall be filed in writing at least 1 week before the designated date with an explanation of a justifiable cause for the request.

B. If a party seeks to add any new or modified argument or submit any evidence for such argument after the deadline for submission of arguments and evidence designated in the preparatory order, the party shall provide an explanation for the failure to submit the argument or evidence within the designated period based on a justifiable cause (e.g., addition or modification of arguments such as an argument relating to the cause of action or defense, an argument that changes the primary prior art relating to novelty, inventive step or the defense of free-to-practice technology, or that adds or changes prior arts or the combination relationship thereof, an argument for deficient description in the specification based on a different legal provision, an argument contrary to the acknowledged facts or legal judgment of the lower court, an argument regarding the amount of damages based on a different legal provision, etc.). If an explanation of a justifiable cause is not provided, the judicial panel will strictly apply Article 149 of the Civil Procedure Act.

C. At the hearing, the appellant and the appellee will present oral arguments for 15 minutes each, in the respective order. Any materials for oral arguments shall be submitted no later than 1 week before the designated hearing date.

D. If necessary at the hearing, the parties shall bring the products (e.g., products implementing the patent in dispute, accused infringing products, etc.) directly related to the case.

E. The Patent Court has established the "Guideline of Civil Appellate Practice and Procedure of the Patent Court of Korea." Please refer to the Patent Court website (http://patent.scourt.go.kr) for more details. For prompt, efficient, and diligent trial proceedings, please read the Manual carefully and comply with the provisions therein. In particular, briefs should be prepared in accordance with the section "Method of Preparing Documents for Submission" of the Manual and evidence should be requested in accordance with the section "Request for Investigation of Evidence" of the Manual.

[Attachment 4]

PATENT COURT

The 21st Panel

Preparatory Order for Video Conference for Case Management

Case No. 2016 Na 100001
Plaintiff (Appellant) ○○○
Defendant (Appellee) ○○○

The Court hereby orders the parties to prepare for the preparatory matters below for the purpose of clarifying the parties' arguments and conducting diligent proceedings.

Preparatory Matters

1. Schedule of Video Conference for Case Management

   A video conference for case management will be held on [*], 2016, [*] AM/PM, via a video conference(Vidyo).4) The parties are requested to access Vidyo at least 5 minutes before the conference begins and complete verification of the setup for the video, speaker, and microphone.

2. Contents of Video Conference for Case Management
   In a video conference for case management, the below matters and schedules will be discussed. Since the subsequent trial will proceed in accordance with the matters and schedule discussed therein, the parties are requested to prepare for the arguments and evidence in advance (*see*

4) For the video conference, it is necessary to install the Vidyo program (downloadable from http://vc.scourt.go.kr) with equipment such as a web camera (webcam), a headset (speaker and microphone), etc.

Article 147 of the Civil Procedure Act). To facilitate efficient conference proceedings, the counsel for the parties are requested to have prior discussions with each other regarding the matters below.

① Dates and the number of hearings, and disputed issues to be addressed in each of the hearings;

② Deadlines for submission of arguments and evidence (including deadlines for submission of comprehensive briefs and any expert witness statement, and the number or volume of briefs to be submitted);

③ Whether to request for evidence requiring a substantial amount of time, such as an expert witness, and the deadline for such a request;

④ Whether to hold a technical presentation session by the parties;

⑤ Whether to transfer the case to a mediation proceeding; and

⑥ Confirmation and summary of the disputed issues.

3. Instructions

A. In order to facilitate the proceeding, the factual and legal issues disputed in this case shall be submitted at least 7 days before the conference date. In particular, if the parties are in dispute over the interpretation of claims, the parties shall submit the claims and terms (including phrases and paragraphs) at issue, as well as the proposed interpretation thereof.

B. If a party seeks to submit arguments or evidence after the deadline for submission designated in the preparatory order, the party shall provide an explanation for the failure to submit the argument or evidence within the designated period based on a justifiable cause. Any argument and evidence, for which a justifiable cause is not sufficiently explained, may be rejected under Article 147(2) and Article 149 of the Civil Procedure Act.

C. Arguments relating to grounds of invalidation of the patented invention shall contain the following matters and the party seeking to add or modify an argument concerning any of the following matters after the final deadline shall explain the existence of a justifiable cause for such addition or modification:

① The level of technical skill required of a person having ordinary skills in the art (including the level of education, qualification, and duration of work); and

② Prior arts: If the primary prior art is added or modified or the specific combination relationship of several prior arts is modified (Example of an argument denying inventive step: If the Element 2 of Prior Art 1, which is the primary prior art, is replaced with Element ○○ of Cited Reference 2, the patented invention is derived. In addition, since Prior Art 1 suggests such a combination, a person having ordinary skills in the art could have easily conceived such a combination and thus the inventive step of the patented invention is denied).

D. The Patent Court has established the "Guideline of Civil Appellate Practice and Procedure of the Patent Court of Korea." Please refer to the Patent Court website (http://patent.scourt.go.kr) for more details. For prompt, efficient, and diligent trial proceedings, please read the Manual carefully and comply with the provisions therein. In particular, briefs should be prepared in accordance with the section "Method of Preparing Documents for Submission" of the Manual and evidence should be requested in accordance with the section "Request for Investigation of Evidence" of the Manual.

[Attachment 5]

PATENT COURT

The 21st Panel

Designation of Hearing Date and Preparatory Order for Procedures

Case No. 2016 Na 100001
Plaintiff (Appellant) ○○○
Defendant (Appellee) ○○○

With respect to the case above, the Court hereby designates deadlines for submission of arguments and evidence and the hearing date based on the discussions from the video conference for case management held on 2016. ○. ○., as follows:

THE FOLLOWING

1. The deadline for submission of a comprehensive brief by the plaintiff (appellant) shall be [*], 2016.

In the comprehensive brief, the plaintiff (appellant) shall describe all arguments relating to the disputed issues referred to in paragraph 3.A and submit main evidence for the arguments. If the plaintiff (appellant) seeks to add any new or modified argument or submit any evidence for such argument after the submission of the brief, the plaintiff shall provide an explanation for the failure to submit the argument or evidence within the period based on a justifiable cause (e.g. addition or modification of arguments such as an argument relating to the cause of action or defense, an argument that changes the primary prior art relating to novelty, inventive step or the defense of free-to-practice technology, or that adds or changes prior arts or the combination relationship thereof, an argument for deficient description in the specification based on a different legal provision, an argument contrary to the acknowledged facts or legal judgment of the lower court, etc.).

2. The deadline for submission of a comprehensive brief by the defendant (appellee) shall be [*], 2016.

In the comprehensive brief, the defendant (appellee) shall describe all arguments relating to the disputed issues referred to in paragraph 3.A and submit main evidence for the arguments. If the defendant (appellee) seeks to add any new or modified argument or submit any evidence for such argument after the submission of the brief, the defendant shall provide an explanation for the failure to submit the argument or evidence within the period based on a justifiable cause.

3. The first hearing date is hereby designated to be held on [*], 2016, [*] AM/PM, at the courtroom ○○ of the Patent Court.

   A. The disputed issues to be discussed in the first hearing is whether Claim 1 of Patent No. 1234567 is invalid and whether the defendant's products fall within the scope of rights of the above patented invention.

   B. At the hearing, the plaintiff (appellant) and the defendant (appellee) will present oral arguments for 15 minutes each, in the respective order.

   C. Any materials for oral arguments shall be submitted no later than 1 week before the designated hearing date.

4. A request for an expert witness relating to the disputed issues referred to

in paragraph 3.A shall be filed by [*], 2016. The request for an expert witness shall be attached with a basic statement that can confirm the expertise and objectivity of the expert witness [*see* the Patent Court Website (http://patent.scourt.go.kr)].

※ If the requested expert witness is adopted and it is necessary to examine the witness in the first hearing, the first hearing date may be changed through discussion with the parties.

[Attachment 6]

PATENT COURT

The 21st Panel

Interpretation of Claims and Preparatory Order for Hearing

Case No. 2016 Na 100001
Plaintiff (Appellant) ○○○
Defendant (Appellee) ○○○

Considering all of the arguments and evidence submitted to date by the parties, the Court hereby interprets the major terms among the claims of the patented invention, of which interpretation is disputed, as follows. Accordingly, the parties are requested to prepare for the hearing based on the following interpretation.

THE FOLLOWING

1. Claim of the Patented Invention

【Claim 1】 ··· (omitted) ··· (hereinafter, the "Invention in Claim 1")

2. Interpretation of Major Terms in Invention in Claim 1

A. ○○○

Upon consideration, it is reasonable to deem that it means ··· (omitted)···.

(omitted)

[Attachment 7]

PATENT COURT

The 21st Panel

Preparatory Order for Video Conference

Case No. 2016 Na 100001
Plaintiff (Appellant) ○○○
Defendant (Appellee) ○○○

The Court hereby orders the parties to prepare for the following matters for the purpose of clarifying the parties' arguments and conducting diligent proceedings:

Preparatory Matters

1. Schedule of Video Conference

   A video conference for discussing the schedule of evidence investigation, etc. will be held on [*], 2016, [*] AM/PM, via a video conference (Vidyo).[5] The parties are requested to access Vidyo at least 5 minutes before the conference begins and complete verification of the setup for the video, speaker, and microphone.

2. The plaintiff (appellant) shall submit all arguments for the amount of damages and a plan of proof thereof by [*], 2016.

3. If the plaintiff (appellant) intends to request for clarification by the

5) For the video conference, it is necessary to install the Vidyo program (downloadable from http://vc.scourt.go.kr) with equipment such as a web camera (webcam) and headset (speaker and microphone), etc.

defendant (appellee) regarding factual requirements for calculation of damages and intends to seek documents (materials) from the defendant (appellee) for the calculation of damages, the plaintiff (appellant) shall submit a detailed request therefor in writing by [*], 2016.

4. The defendant (appellee) shall submit a brief containing the following matters by [*], 2016:

① A response to the amount of damages argued by the plaintiff (appellant);
② A detailed response to the facts argued by the plaintiff (appellant) such as sales revenues, etc.;
③ A response to the request for clarification by the plaintiff (appellant); and
④ Whether the defendant (appellee) is in possession of the documents (materials) requested by the plaintiff (appellant) and whether the documents (materials) can be submitted voluntarily, and if not, the specific reasons therefor.

5. Contents of Video Conference
In the video conference, the matters and schedule below will be discussed. To facilitate efficient conference proceedings, the counsels for the parties are requested to have prior discussions with each other regarding the matters below.

① The types and scope of documents (materials) to be voluntarily submitted by the defendant (appellee);
② Whether to file a request for an order to produce documents (materials) and the scope of such request;
③ Deadlines for submission of arguments and evidence;
④ Whether to file a request for evidence requiring a substantial amount of time, such as an expert witness, and the deadline for such request;

⑤ Whether to transfer the case to a mediation proceeding; and
⑥ Confirmation and summary of the disputed issues.

6. Instructions

A. If a party seeks to add a new or modified argument or submit any evidence for such argument after the deadline for submission of arguments and evidence, the party shall provide an explanation for the failure to submit the argument or evidence within the period based on a justifiable cause. If a justifiable cause is not sufficiently explained, the judicial panel will strictly apply Article 149 of the Civil Procedure Act.

B. Arguments Regarding Amount of Damages

① The plaintiff's argument regarding the amount of damages shall state an applicable legal provision on which the argument is based and shall indicate an evidence number relating to the argument for each of the required facts.
② The defendant's response relating to the amount of damages shall describe the defendant's specific rebuttal to the plaintiff's factual arguments (it should be noted that any fact not specifically denied may be deemed as being undisputed). In particular, if the plaintiff claims an amount of damages based on Article 128(1) of the Patent Act, the defendant's response denying the transferred volume argued by the plaintiff shall state the actual transferred volume. If the plaintiff claims an amount of damages based on Article 128(3) of the Patent Act, the defendant's response denying the profit amount argued by the plaintiff shall state the actual profit amount and the grounds for calculating the amount such as sales revenues, expenses, and profit margins, etc.

C. If any evidence for proving the amount of damages is in possession of one party and the party fails to cooperate with the evidence investigation by refusing to submit the evidence, destroying the evidence, etc., and therefore it is extremely difficult to calculate the damages amount under Paragraphs 1 to 5 of Article 128 of the Patent Act, the Court may consider such circumstances in acknowledging a considerable amount of damages under paragraph 6 of the same Article.

D. The Patent Court has established the "Guideline of Civil Appellate Practice and Procedure of the Patent Court of Korea." Please refer to the Patent Court website (http://patent.scourt.go.kr) for more details. For prompt, efficient, and diligent trial proceedings, please read the Manual carefully and comply with the provisions therein. In particular, briefs should be prepared in accordance with the section "Method of Preparing Documents for Submission" of the Manual and evidence should be requested in accordance with the section "Request for Investigation of Evidence" of the Manual.

[Attachment 8]

Basic Statement of Expert Witness

Personal Information	Name		Date of Birth	
	Address			

Neutrality			
1	Are you a relative of either the plaintiff or the defendant (if a party is a corporation, a chief executive, officer, or an employee; the same applies hereinafter)?	Y	N
2	Are you in a creditor-debtor relationship with either the plaintiff or the defendant?	Y	N
3	Have you ever worked or do you currently work with either the plaintiff or the defendant, or have you ever been or are you currently in a contractual, employment, or other similar relationships with either the plaintiff or the defendant?	Y	N
4	Have you ever provided testimony as a witness in a lawsuit involving either the plaintiff or the defendant or the patent/ products at issue?	Y	N
5	Have you ever provided consultation to either the plaintiff or the defendant with respect to this lawsuit?	Y	N

Expertise	
1	Describe your area of expertise specifically.
2	With regards to your area of expertise, specifically describe (1) your current and past occupations (including the duration of employment, position/title, and assigned duties) and (2) materials that can confirm your expertise, such as a diploma/license, papers/reports, among others. ※ *You may add a separate attachment may be added in case more space is needed.*

Obligation of Expert Witness
The expert witness shall make statements based on facts and special knowledge in a manner unbiased to any party. In addition, as an expert in the relevant area, the expert witness shall make statements based on the facts/theories objectively verified and widely acknowledged in the area and shall not make any statements based on his or her subjective theory/interpretation.

I hereby state that the foregoing statements are all true.

Date: ____________________

By: ____________________

[Attachment 9]

PATENT COURT

The 21st Panel

Preparatory Order for Hearing (Expert Witness)

Case No. 2016 Na 100001
Plaintiff (Appellant) ○○○
Defendant (Appellee) ○○○

The Court hereby orders the parties to prepare for the below matters for conducting a diligent examination of the witness in the hearing to be held on [*], 2016.

THE FOLLOWING

1. Submission of Expert Witness Statement by Plaintiff (Appellant)

   A. The plaintiff (appellant) shall submit a statement of its expert witness and questions for the expert witness by [*], 2016. A direct examination shall be conducted within the scope of the expert witness statement.

   B. Any and all materials to be presented or cited in the direct examination of the expert witness (including family patents, translations, photos of actual products and reference materials) shall be submitted as evidence by [*], 2016.

2. The direct examination and a cross examination of the witness shall be conducted within 20 minutes for each.

3. The parties may be accompanied by interpreters each for the direct and cross examinations. If a party cannot be accompanied by an interpreter, the party shall notify the Court of the fact by [*], 2016 and file a request for the designation of an interpreter.

4. Any arguments and evidence for impeaching the credibility of the testimony by the expert witness shall be submitted by [*], 2016.

2.

특허법원 심결취소소송 심리 매뉴얼

특허법원 심결취소소송 심리 매뉴얼

2016. 9. 1. 제정

I. 제정 취지

특허·실용신안·상표·디자인에 관한 심결취소소송 중 쟁점이 복잡한 사건에서 절차 협의, 주장·항변의 제출기한 지정, 쟁점별 집중 심리 등을 규정하여 신속하고 효율적인 소송절차의 진행을 가능하게 함과 아울러, 적절한 변론절차의 진행방법과 증거의 신청·조사방법 등을 규정하고 공개함으로써 사건관계인에게 예측가능성을 부여하며, 충실한 소송 준비를 할 수 있게 한다.

II. 소장의 제출과 서면 공방

1. 원고의 소장 제출

가. 원고는 소장에 다음의 사항을 구체적으로 기재하여야 한다.

① 특허청의 심사 및 특허심판원의 심판 절차의 경위

② 심결의 요지(심판 단계에서 당사자의 주장과 그에 관한 특허심판원의 판단)

③ 심결의 이유 중 인정하는 부분과 인정하지 않는 부분

④ 심결의 위법사유에 관한 모든 주장

⑤ 관련 사건의 표시(정정심판 및 정정청구를 포함한 관련 심판 및 심결취소소송, 관련 민사 본안 및 신청사건, 형사 사건의 진행 경과 및 그 결과 포함, 이를 기재하지 아니한 경우 소송절차의 진행에서 고려되지 않을 수 있음)

⑥ 증거신청 계획 등을 비롯한 소송 진행 전반에 관한 의견

나. 원고는 위 ① 내지 ⑥항에 대응하는 증거와 그 입증취지를 기재한 증거설명서를 제출하여야 한다. 특히 다음과 같은 기본적 서증과 소송위임장, 법인등기부등본 또는 법인국적증명서(당사자가 외국법인인 경우), 심결문송달증명원 등의 필수 첨부서류가 누락되지 않도록 주의하여야 한다.

① 거절결정 사건 : 심결문, 출원서, 의견제출통지서, 보정서, 의견서, 거절결정서

② 등록무효 사건 : 심결문, 등록원부, 등록공보, 선행발명(선행고안, 선등록상표, 선사용상표, 선행디자인)에 관한 증거

③ 권리범위확인 사건 : 심결문, 등록원부, 등록공보, 확인대상발명(확인대상고안, 확인대상상표, 확인대상디자인 등)의 설명서 및 도면

다. 소장에 가.항의 소장 기재 사항이 기재되지 않은 경우 또는 나.항의 기본적 서증이나 필수 첨부서류가 누락된 경우, 재판장 또는 재판장의 명을 받은 법원 사무관 등은 원고에게 이를 보완하는 준비서면 또는 기본적 서증이나 필수 첨부서류의 제출을 명하는 [첨부 1]의 보정명령을 한다. 원고는 보정명령 수령 후 3주 이내에 보정명령의 내용에 따라 준비서면, 증거 또는 서류 등을 제출하여야 한다.

2. 피고의 답변서 제출 등

가. 피고는 원고로부터 구체적 청구원인이 기재된 소장 또는 준비서면을 송달받은 때로부터 3주 이내에 [첨부 2]의 준비명령에 따라 다음의 사항이 포함된 답변서와 함께, 답변서에서 인용하고 있는 증거 및 증거설명서를 제출하여야 한다.

① 원고의 청구취지에 대한 답변

② 원고의 주장 중 인정하는 부분과 인정하지 않는 부분

③ 원고의 주장 중 인정하지 않는 부분에 대한 구체적인 반박

④ 그 밖에 심결의 적법 사유에 관한 모든 주장

⑤ 관련 사건의 표시(정정심판 및 정정청구를 포함한 관련 심판 및

심결취소소송, 관련 민사 본안 및 신청사건, 형사 사건의 진행 경과 및 그 결과 포함, 이를 기재하지 아니한 경우 소송절차의 진행에서 고려되지 않을 수 있음)

⑥ 원고가 제출한 서증에 대한 인부

⑦ 증거신청 계획 등을 비롯한 소송 진행 전반에 관한 의견

나. 재판장은 피고의 답변서 제출 후, 소장 및 답변서와 당사자들로부터 제출된 증거 등을 종합적으로 검토한 결과, 추가 서면 공방이 필요하다고 인정되는 경우, 원고에게 구체적인 반박, 증거의 추가 제출 등을 명하는 [첨부 3]의 준비명령을 한다. 원고는 준비명령 수령 후 3주 이내에 준비서면, 증거 또는 서류 등을 제출하여야 한다.

III. 사건의 분류와 변론의 준비

1. 사건 분류

재판장은 당사자 사이의 서면 공방이 완료되면, 당사자가 제출한 주장 서면과 증거를 토대로 절차 진행에 관한 사항의 협의나 구체적인 심리계획의 수립 등이 필요한 사건인지를 검토하여, ① 바로 변론기일을 지정할 사건과 ② 변론준비절차에 회부할 사건으로 분류한다.

2. 변론기일을 지정할 사건의 변론준비

바로 변론기일을 지정하는 사건에 대하여, 재판장은 충실한 심리를 위하여 원고 및 피고에게 [첨부 4]의 요약쟁점정리서면의 제출을 명하는 변론준비명령을 할 수 있다. 또한 재판장은 당사자의 서면 공방 결과를 참작하여 주장 및 증거의 제출기한, 전문가 증인 등 시일을 요하는 증거의 신청 기한 등을 정한 [첨부 5]의 변론준비명령을 할 수 있다.

3. 사건 관리를 위한 화상회의

가. 재판장은 영상·음성의 송수신에 의하여 동시에 통화를 할 수 있는 방법(이하 '사건관리 화상회의')으로 절차 진행에 관한 사항을 협의할 수 있다. 재판장은 수명법관을 지정하여 위 절차를 담당하게 할 수 있다.

나. 사건관리 화상회의를 개최하기로 한 사건에 대하여는 원고와 피고에게 화상회의의 개최사실을 통지하고, 그에 관한 [첨부 6]의 준비명령을 할 수 있다.

다. 사건관리 화상회의에서는 아래 사항을 협의할 수 있고, 협의된 내용에 대하여는 [첨부 7]의 준비명령을 할 수 있다.

① 변론기일 횟수 및 일자, 각 기일별 진행사항
② 주장 및 증거의 제출기한(종합준비서면의 제출기한, 전문가 진술서 제출기한, 준비서면의 제출횟수 및 분량 포함)
③ 검증·감정이나 전문가 증인 등 시일을 요하는 증거방법의 신청 여부 및 기한
④ 전문심리위원 지정 여부
⑤ 당사자에 의한 기술설명회의 실시 여부
⑥ 청구항 해석에 관한 심리를 선행하여 진행할 것인지 여부
⑦ 쟁점의 확인 및 정리

라. 전항의 준비명령에서 사건 전반 또는 특정 쟁점에 대하여 종합준비서면의 제출을 명한 경우, 원고는 사건관리 화상회의 후 3주(또는 준비명령에서 정한 기한) 이내에, 피고는 원고의 종합준비서면이 제출된 날로부터 3주(또는 준비명령에서 정한 기한) 이내에 각각 종합준비서면을 제출하여야 한다.

마. 준비명령에서 정한 주장 및 증거의 제출·신청 기한 이후 주장을 추가·변경하거나 추가·변경된 주장에 대한 증거를 제출·신청하기 위해서는 정당한 사유로 위 기간 이내에 제출·신청하지 못하였음을 소명하여야 한다(예를 들어, 청구원인이나 항변에 해당하는 주장, 신규성·진보성에 관한 주장 및 자유실시기술 항변에 있어서 가장 근접한 주된 선행발명을 변경하거나 선행발명들과 그 결합관계를 추가·변경하는

주장, 적용법조를 달리하는 명세서 기재불비 주장 등).

4. 변론준비기일

가. 위 제3의 다.항에 정한 사항을 협의하거나 증거조사 또는 기술설명회를 개최하기 위하여 필요한 경우 변론준비기일을 진행할 수 있다. 재판장은 수명법관을 지정하여 위 절차를 담당하게 할 수 있다.

나. 변론준비기일이 종결된 이후 주장을 추가·변경하거나 추가·변경된 주장에 대한 증거를 제출하기 위해서는 전항과 같이 정당한 사유로 변론준비기일 종결 전에 제출하지 못하였음을 소명하여야 한다.

IV. 변론기일의 운영

1. 변론의 진행

가. 원고, 피고의 순서로 각 20분 이내의 범위에서 구술로 변론한다. 수인의 소송대리인이 선임된 경우에도 위 시간 내에 변론하여야 한다. 다만, 구체적인 변론시간은 재판장이 필요하다고 판단하는 경우 변경할 수 있다.

나. 구술변론을 위한 변론자료와 요약쟁점정리서면 등은 변론기일 1주일 전까지 제출하여야 한다.

다. 당사자는 변론기일에 사건과 관련된 제품(등록특허·등록디자인, 선행특허, 확인대상발명·확인대상디자인의 실시품 등)을 지참하여 이를 시연하거나, 법정 컴퓨터, 실물화상기 등을 이용하여 관련 기술을 이해하는 데 도움을 줄 수 있는 동영상 자료를 재생하거나, 사진 등을 제시하는 방법으로 변론할 수 있다.

2. 쟁점별 집중 심리

가. 재판부는 여러 개의 쟁점이 존재하는 사건에서 쟁점별 집중심리의 필요성이 인정되는 경우 당사자와 협의하여 변론기일을 쟁점별로 운영할 수 있다.

(쟁점별 집중심리의 대상이 될 수 있는 사건의 예시) 청구항 해석이나 선행발명의 공지 여부 등이 선결문제가 되는 사건, 다수의 무효 사유가 주장되는 사건, 확인대상발명의 특정 및 실시 여부가 문제되는 사건

나. 각 변론기일에서는 각 변론기일에 심리하기로 한 쟁점에 한하여 심리한다.

다. 재판부는 변론기일에 심리를 마친 쟁점에 대하여 구술 또는 서면으로 견해를 밝힐 수 있고, 당사자에게 위 견해를 토대로 나머지 쟁점 등에 대한 변론을 준비할 것을 명할 수 있다.

3. 청구항 해석에 관한 심리

가. 당사자 사이에 청구항 등의 해석에 관하여 다툼이 있고, 그에 따라 나머지 쟁점에 대한 주장이나 증거관계가 달라질 수 있어, 청구항 해석에 관한 심리가 선행되어야 하는 사건의 경우, 재판장은 당사자와 협의하여 청구항 해석에 관한 공방을 다른 쟁점에 앞서 진행할 수 있다.

나. 당사자는 다툼의 대상이 되는 청구항 등에 관하여 정정심판, 정정청구 등이 진행되고 있는 경우 그 진행상황을 재판부에 알려야 하고, 향후 정정심판, 정정청구 등을 예정하고 있는 경우 정정심판, 정정청구 등에 관한 계획 및 의견을 구체적으로 밝혀야 한다.

다. 재판부는 청구항 등의 해석에 관하여 구술 또는 서면으로 견해를 밝힐 수 있고, 재판장은 당사자에게 위 견해를 토대로 나머지 쟁점 등에 대한 변론을 준비할 것을 명하는 [첨부 8]의 준비명령을 할 수 있다.

4. 심결취소소송과 관련 침해소송의 심리

가. 특허법원에 동일한 특허·실용신안·상표·디자인에 관한 심결취소소송과 침해소송이 함께 계속되어 있고, 양 사건의 당사자 및 소송대리인이 동일한 경우 등 필요하다고 인정되는 경우, 양 사건을 병행하여 심리할 수 있다.

나. 심결취소소송과 침해소송에서의 관련 주장을 정리할 필요가 있는 등의 경우에는 변론준비절차를 병행하여 진행할 수 있다.

V. 증거의 조사와 전문가의 참여

1. 증거의 신청 일반

가. 서증을 제출하거나, 증인, 사실조회, 문서인증등본 송부촉탁, 문서제출명령, 검증 및 감정 등을 신청하는 경우에는 그 증거방법에 의하여 입증하고자 하는 내용을 구체적으로 밝혀야 한다.

나. 재판장은 증거조사 절차의 협의를 위하여 필요한 경우 사건을 변론준비절차에 회부할 수 있다. 재판장은 당사자의 의견을 들어 화상회의의 방법으로 절차 협의를 할 수 있다.

2. 검증 및 감정

가. 재판부는 필요하다고 인정되는 경우 당사자의 신청에 따라 또는 직권으로 검증 및 감정절차를 진행할 수 있다.

나. 검증 및 감정의 채부, 검증 및 감정 사항과 방식의 결정, 전제사실의 확정 및 필요한 자료의 제공, 감정인의 선정 등을 위하여 필요한 경우 변론준비절차를 진행할 수 있다. 재판장은 당사자의 의견을 들어 화상회의의 방법으로 절차 협의를 할 수 있고, 필요한 경우 [첨부 9]의 준비명령을 할 수 있다.

다. 재판부는 정당한 이유가 있다고 인정되는 경우 결정으로 검증 및 감정 목적물의 제출을 명할 수 있다.

3. 전문가 증인

가. 전문가 증인을 신청할 때에는 증인의 전문성과 객관성을 확인할 수 있는 [첨부 10]의 전문가 증인 기본 사항 확인서를 첨부하여야 하고, 전문가 증인이 채택되면 전문가 증인의 증언이 담긴 증인 진술서와 증인신문사항을 제출하여야 한다.

나. 주신문은 전문가 증인의 증인 진술서의 범위 내에서 하여야 한다. 주신문에서 제시하거나 인용하는 모든 자료는 증인신문기일 전에 증거로 제출되어야 한다.

다. 전문가 증인이 외국인인 경우 당사자는 각 주신문과 반대신문을 위한 통역을 대동할 수 있다. 다만, 그 경우에도 통역인 지정과 비용예납 등을 위해 대동할 통역인의 인적 사항과 통역비용을 재판부에 알려야 한다. 당사자가 통역인을 대동할 수 없는 경우에는 증인신문기일 4주 전까지 재판부에 이러한 사정을 알리고 통역인 지정신청을 하여야 한다.

라. 재판장은 증인 진술서 및 증인신문사항의 제출기한, 증인신문시간의 제한, 전문가 증인의 증언의 신빙성을 탄핵하는 주장 및 증거의 제출기한 등 전문가 증인의 신문을 위하여 필요한 사항에 관하여 [첨부 11]의 변론준비명령을 할 수 있다.

4. 전문심리위원

가. 재판부는 필요하다고 인정되는 경우 당사자의 의견을 들어 1인 또는 수인의 전문심리위원을 지정할 수 있다.

나. 전문심리위원의 사건 파악 등을 위하여 필요한 경우에는 변론준비절차를 진행할 수 있다.

다. 전문심리위원은 변론기일 또는 변론준비기일에 재판장의 허가를 받아 당사자 등에게 직접 질문할 수 있다. 당사자는 전문심리위원의 질문에 대하여 추가로 답변할 필요가 있는 경우 재판장이 정한 기한 내에 서면으로 의견을 제출하여야 한다.

Ⅵ. 서류의 작성 및 서증의 제출

1. 소장, 답변서, 준비서면

가. 기재 방식 및 내용

① 서면의 크기는 A4 용지(가로 210㎜, 세로 297㎜)로 하고, 위쪽 45㎜, 왼쪽 및 오른쪽 각 20㎜, 아래쪽 30㎜(장수 표시 제외)의 여백을 둔다.

② 글자 크기는 12pt, 줄 간격은 200%, 또는 1.5줄 이상으로 한다.

③ 준비서면의 분량은 30쪽 이내로 한다. 재판장은 준비서면의 분량이 30쪽을 넘는 경우 당사자에게 해당 준비서면을 반환하고, 30쪽 이내로 줄여 제출하도록 명할 수 있다. 재판장은 당사자와 준비서면의 제출 분량 등에 대해 협의할 수 있고, 이에 관한 합의가 이루어진 경우 당사자는 그 합의에 따라 준비서면을 제출하여야 한다.

④ 주장을 뒷받침하는 증거가 제출된 경우 해당 부분에 증거번호를 표시한다.

⑤ 기술용어에 대하여는 각주로 그 용어의 정의를 기재하고, 출처를 명시한다.

⑥ 요약쟁점정리서면에는 [첨부 4]의 별지와 같이 원고의 심결취소 사유의 요지, 다툼 없는 사항, 쟁점정리표, 증거설명, 추가 제출 증거, 서증에 대한 인부, 석명사항, 소송진행에 대한 의견 등을 간명하게 기재한다.

⑦ 종합준비서면에는 종합준비서면의 제출을 명한 사항에 관한 모든 주장의 요지를 기재하고, 그에 대한 주된 증거를 제출하여야 한다.

⑧ 준비서면에는 소장, 답변서 또는 앞서 제출한 준비서면과 중복·유사한 내용을 불필요하게 반복 기재하거나 그 내용의 전부 또는 일부를 인용하여서는 아니 된다.

나. 유의할 사항

① 특허·실용신안의 청구항 및 명세서의 기재 내용이 보정 또는 정정청구 등에 의하여 변경된 경우, 그 변경 내역을 구체적으로 기재하고, 그중 소송의 대상이 되는 시점의 청구항 및 명세서의 기재 내용을 명시한다.

② 대상 특허·실용신안·상표·디자인의 권리관계가 변동된 경우 변동 내역과 최종 권리자를 기재한다.

③ 심판 단계에서 제출한 선행발명들 중 심결취소소송에서도 그대로 제출하는 것과 제출하지 않는 것을 구분하여 기재한다. 심결취소소송에서 제출하는 자료가 선행발명으로서 제출하는 것인지, 주지관용기술이나 기술상식, 기술수준 등을 입증하기 위하여 제출하는 것인지를 밝힌다. 하나의 문서에 수 개의 발명이 포함되어 있는 경우 그 중 어떤 것을 선행발명으로 주장하는 것인지 명확히 한다.

④ 선행발명의 구성을 구체적으로 특정하여 특허발명과 각 선행발명의 대응되는 구성을 대비한 구성대비표를 제출한다. 주지관용기술도 그 대비 대상이 되는 부분을 특정한다.

⑤ 진보성에 대한 주장, 자유실시기술 주장을 하는 경우 통상의 기술자가 누구인지와 그 기술수준을 구체적으로 기재한다.

⑥ 선행발명들의 결합에 의하여 진보성이 부정된다는 주장을 하는 경우 주된 선행발명을 선정하고 선행발명들 사이의 구체적인 결합관계 및 결합이 쉬운 이유를 명시한다.

(예시) 선행발명 1 내지 3에 의하여 진보성이 부정된다.(×)

주된 선행발명인 선행발명 1에 선행발명 2의 OOOO 구성을 부가(또는 선행발명 1의 구성 2를 선행발명 2의 OOOO 구성으로 대체)하면 특허발명이 도출되고, 선행발명 1에 그와 같은 결합에 대한 시사가 있어 통상의 기술자가 그러한 결

합을 쉽게 생각해낼 수 있으므로 특허발명의 진보성이 부정된다.(○)

⑦ 명세서 기재불비 주장은, 당해 특허·실용신안의 설명에 의하여 쉽게 실시가 가능한지 여부(특허법 제42조 제3항 제1호), 청구항이 당해 특허·실용신안의 설명에 의하여 뒷받침되는지 여부(특허법 제42조 제4항 제1호), 당해 특허·실용신안의 청구범위가 명확하게 기재되어 있는지 여부(특허법 제42조 제4항 제2호) 등을 적용법조를 명시하여 구체적으로 설시한다.

⑧ 청구항의 해석에 관한 심리가 선행될 필요가 있는 경우 그 이유를 밝히고, 청구항 해석이 필요한 문구, 해당 문구에 관련된 명세서 기재 내용, 당사자가 주장하는 청구항 해석 내용 및 구체적인 근거를 제시한다.

⑨ 거절결정에 대한 심결취소소송의 경우, 피고는 특허청 심사관의 의견제출통지, 거절결정, 심판원의 의견제출통지, 심결에서 나타난 거절 이유를 정리하여 기재하고, 소송 단계에서 주장하는 거절 이유가 그 중 무엇인지를 명확히 밝힌다.

2. 증거설명서

가. 증거설명서에는 당사자가 제출한 모든 증거를 명시하고, 이를 통하여 입증하고자 하는 바를 간략히 기재한다.

나. 신규성, 진보성, 자유실시기술 주장에 관한 증거를 제출하는 경우, 선행발명으로 제출하는 것인지, 주지관용기술의 증거로 제출하는 것인지 명확히 한다.

3. 서증 등

가. 당사자가 심사 및 심판 단계에서 제시한 자료라고 하더라도 소송절차에서 증거로 제출되지 않는 한 판단의 자료로 삼을 수 없으므로, 심사 및 심판 절차에서 제출된 자료들 중 필요한 자료들은 모두 증거로

제출하도록 하되, 상대방이 제출한 것과 중복되지 않도록 한다. 특히 아래 각 서류들은 소송절차에서도 중요한 판단 자료가 될 수 있으므로 누락되지 않도록 주의한다.

(예시) 심결문, 출원서 및 최초 명세서, 의견제출통지서, 보정서 및 의견서, 재심사청구서, 거절결정서, 정정청구서, 확인대상발명의 설명서 및 도면, 확인대상발명의 보정서, 선행기술문헌 등

나. 외국어로 된 서증은 번역문을 첨부하되, 기계 번역을 하여 제출하여서는 아니 된다. 특히 선행발명 등 주된 증거에 대하여는 발췌 번역문이 아닌 전문 번역문을 첨부하고, 그 중 입증취지와 관련된 부분은 밑줄 처리 등의 방법으로 강조하여 표시한다.

다. 서증명은 문서의 제목이 있는 경우에는 그 제목을 표시하고, 제목이 없는 경우에는 문서의 내용을 요약하여 기재한다. 선행발명으로 제출하는 증거는 서증명에 이를 명시한다.

(예시) OO회사의 상품 카탈로그(2006. 1. 2. 발행). 선행발명 1(등록특허공보 제OOOOO호)

라. 하나의 서증에는 하나의 증거만이 포함되어야 하고, 관련된 내용인 경우 가지번호로 표시한다(갑 제2호증의 1, 갑 제2호증의 2 등).

마. 심결취소소송에서 새롭게 제출하는 선행발명들은 혼란을 피하기 위하여 심판 단계에서 제출하였던 선행발명들의 번호 다음에 이어서 선행발명의 번호를 붙인다. 예를 들어 심판단계에서 선행발명 1, 2, 3이 제출되었는데, 심결취소소송에서 선행발명 1은 그대로 제출하되 선행발명 2, 3은 제출하지 않고 새로 선행발명을 제출하는 경우 이를 선행발명 4로 한다.

바. 특허·실용신안 등의 기술적인 내용이나 디자인의 구체적인 형상을 이해하는 데 도움이 되는 실시 제품이나 모형, 사진, 동영상 자료 등이 있는 경우 이를 증거로 제출한다. 상표·디자인 사건의 경우 원본이 컬러인 서증은 컬러 상태로 제출한다. (끝)

[첨부 1]

특 허 법 원

제 O 부

보 정 명 령

사 건 2016허OOOO 등록무효(특)
[원고 주식회사 OOO / 피고 OOO]
원고 소송대리인 변호사 OOO, 변리사 OOO (귀하)

원고 소송대리인은 이 명령을 받은 날로부터 21일 안에 소장에 포함되어야 하는 구체적인 기재사항이 기재된 준비서면을 제출하고, 심결문송달증명원, 원고의 법인국적증명서, 피고의 법인등기부등본을 참고자료로 제출하여 주시기 바랍니다.

2016. O. O.
법원사무관 OOO

◇ 유 의 사 항 ◇

※ 이 명령에 응하지 않을 경우에는 민사소송법 제254조 제2항에 의하여 소장이 각하될 수 있습니다.

※ 이 사건에 관하여 제출하는 서면에는 사건번호(2016허OOOO)를 기재하시기 바랍니다.

※ 특허법원에서는 '심결취소소송 심리 매뉴얼'을 정하고 있습니다. 구체적인 내용은 홈페이지(http://patent.scourt.go.kr)를 참조하여 주십시오. 신속하고 효율적이며 충실한 재판 진행을 위해 위 매뉴얼의 내용을 숙지하고 이에 따라 주시기 바랍니다.

※ **특히 구체적인 청구원인이 기재된 준비서면에는 위 심리 매뉴얼의 'II. 1. 가.항의 소장에 기재하여야 하는 사항이 포함되어야 하고, 나.항의**

기본적 서증과 필수 첨부서류가 제출되어야 합니다. 준비서면의 작성 및 증거의 신청은 민사소송규칙 및 위 매뉴얼에서 정한 제출서류의 작성 방법 및 증거의 신청 방법에 따라 주시기 바랍니다.

[첨부 2]

특 허 법 원

제 O 부

준 비 명 령

사 건 2016허OOOO 등록무효(특)
[원고 주식회사 OOO / 피고 OOO]

피고는 **2016. O. OO.**까지 다음 사항들이 포함된 답변서와 증거 등을 제출하여 주시기 바랍니다.

다 음

• 답변서의 제출
① 원고의 청구취지에 대한 답변
② 원고의 주장 중 인정하는 부분과 인정하지 않는 부분
③ 원고의 주장 중 인정하지 않는 부분에 대한 구체적인 반박
④ 그 밖에 심결의 적법 사유에 관한 모든 주장
⑤ 관련 사건의 표시(정정심판 및 정정청구를 포함한 관련 심판 및 심결취소소송, 관련 민사 본안 및 신청사건, 형사사건이 있는 경우에는 사건번호 및 사건명, 진행상황을 준비서면의 끝부분에 관련사건 항목을 마련해서 기재한다. 이를 기재하지 않는 경우 소송절차의 진행에서 고려되지 않을 수 있음)

• 위 • 항의 내용에 대응하는 증거방법 및 증거신청 계획(서증, 증인, 사실조회, 문서인증등본 송부촉탁 신청, 검증 및 감정 등. 다만, 서증은 상대방이 제출한 것과 중복되지 않도록 하고, 증인, 사실조회, 문서인증등본 송부촉탁을 신청하는 경우에는 그 증거방법에 의하여 입증하고자 하는 내용을 구체적으로 밝힐 것)

• 원고가 제출한 서증에 대한 인부서의 제출(진정성립을 인정할 수 없는

서증만 표시할 것)

• 외국어로 된 증거서류에 대한 번역문 제출(기계 번역문을 제출하여서는 아니 된다. 특히 선행발명 등 주된 증거에 대하여는 발췌 번역문이 아닌 전문 번역문을 첨부하고, 그 입증취지와 관련된 부분은 밑줄 처리 등의 방법으로 강조하여 표시할 것)

2016. O. O.

재판장 판사

◇ 유 의 사 항 ◇

이 사건에 관하여

① 우리 재판부는 당사자의 기일출석 횟수를 줄이면서도 충실한 변론이 이루어지도록 하기 위하여 집중심리를 실시합니다. 이 경우 특별한 사정이 없는 한 변론기일은 1회로 한정할 계획입니다.

② 그러므로 당사자 쌍방은 주장과 증거를 재판부가 지정한 기일까지 일괄하여 제출하여야 합니다. 만약 이 기일을 지키지 아니하여 소송을 지연시키는 것으로 인정되는 때에는 더 이상 주장과 증거를 제출할 수 없는 등 불이익을 받을 수 있으니 유의하시기 바랍니다.

④ 변론기일이나 변론준비기일의 변경신청은 사안이 복잡·난해하여 변론준비나 증거수집에 많은 기일이 소요되는 등 특별한 사정이 있는 경우 이외에는 가급적 삼가하여 주시기 바랍니다. 부득이 기일변경신청을 할 경우 사유를 명확히 기재하고 가능한 한 상대방과 협의한 희망기일을 표시하여 주시기 바랍니다.

※ 구체적인 내용은 홈페이지(http://patent.scourt.go.kr)에 게재된 '심결취소소송 심리 매뉴얼'을 참조하시기 바랍니다, 특히 답변서의 작성 및 증거의 신청은 민사소송규칙 및 위 매뉴얼에서 정한 제출서류의 작성 방법 및 증거의 신청 방법에 따라 주시기 바랍니다.

[첨부 3]

특 허 법 원

제 O 부

준 비 명 령

사 건 2016허OOOO 등록무효(특)
[원고 주식회사 OOO / 피고 OOO]

원고 소송대리인 변호사 OOO, 변리사 OOO (귀하)

원고 소송대리인은 **2016. O. OO.까지** 다음의 체크한 사항들이 포함된 준비서면과 증거를 제출하여 주시기 바랍니다.

다 음

☑ 피고의 답변서에 대한 구체적인 반박내용

☑ 피고가 제출한 서증에 대한 인부서의 제출(다만, 진정성립을 인정할 수 없는 서증만 표시할 것)

☑ 원고가 추가로 제출하거나 신청하는 증거와 그 입증취지(서증, 증인, 사실조회, 문서인증등본 송부촉탁 신청 등. 다만, 서증은 상대방이 제출한 것과 중복되지 않도록 하고, 증인, 사실조회, 문서인증등본 송부촉탁, 검증 및 감정 등을 신청하는 경우에는 그 증거방법에 의하여 입증하고자 하는 내용을 구체적으로 밝힐 것)

☑ 외국어로 된 증거서류에 대한 번역문 제출(기계 번역문을 제출하여서는 아니 된다. 특히 선행발명 등 주된 증거에 대하여는 발췌 번역문이 아닌 전문 번역문을 첨부하고, 그 입증취지와 관련된 부분은 밑줄 처리 등의 방법으로 강조하여 표시할 것)

2016. O. O.

재판장 판사

◇ 유 의 사 항 ◇

이 사건에 관하여

① 우리 재판부는 당사자의 기일출석 횟수를 줄이면서도 충실한 변론이 이루어지도록 하기 위하여 집중심리를 실시합니다. 이 경우 특별한 사정이 없는 한 변론기일은 1회로 한정할 계획입니다.

② 그러므로 당사자 쌍방은 주장과 증거를 재판부가 지정한 기일까지 일괄하여 제출하여야 합니다. 만약 이 기일을 지키지 아니하여 소송을 지연시키는 것으로 인정되는 때에는 더 이상 주장과 증거를 제출할 수 없는 등 불이익을 받을 수 있으니 유의하시기 바랍니다.

④ 변론기일이나 변론준비기일의 변경신청은 사안이 복잡·난해하여 변론준비나 증거수집에 많은 기일이 소요되는 등 특별한 사정이 있는 경우 이외에는 가급적 삼가하여 주시기 바랍니다. 부득이 기일변경신청을 할 경우 사유를 명확히 기재하고 가능한 한 상대방과 협의한 희망기일을 표시하여 주시기 바랍니다.

※ 구체적인 내용은 홈페이지(http://patent.scourt.go.kr)에 게재된 '심결취소소송 심리 매뉴얼'을 참조하시기 바랍니다. **특히 준비서면의분량은 30쪽을 넘을 수 없고,** 준비서면의 작성 및 증거의 신청은 민사소송규칙 및 위 매뉴얼에서 정한 제출서류의 작성 방법 및 증거의 신청 방법에 따라 주시기 바랍니다.

[첨부 4]

특　　허　　법　　원

제　O　부

변론준비명령

사　　　건	2016허OOOO　등록무효(특) [원고 OOO / 피고 OOO]
원고 소송대리인	변호사 OOO (귀하)
피고 소송대리인	변리사 OOO (귀하)

이 사건의 제1차 변론기일을 **2016. O. O. OO:OO** 특허법원 OOO호 법정으로 지정하였습니다. 소송관계를 명료하게 하기 위하여 원고와 피고 소송대리인은 **2016. O. OO.**까지 별지 요약쟁점정리서면의 작성요령에 따라 요약쟁점정리서면을 제출하여 주시기 바랍니다.

2016.　O.　O.

재판장　　　판사

〈별지〉

요약쟁점정리서면

- 사건번호 :
- 제출자 :

Ⅰ. 원고의 심결취소 사유의 요지

Ⅱ. 다툼 없는 사항

Ⅲ. 쟁점정리표

쟁점	쟁점에 대한 당사자의 주장 및 증거

Ⅳ. 제출 서증(전자문서) 중 주요변론 내용과 관련된 부분에 대한 증거설명

번호	서증의 이름	작성일	작성자	요지 및 입증취지

Ⅴ. 쟁점에 대한 당사자의 추가 제출 증거

증거방법	입증취지

Ⅵ. 상대방 제출 서증에 대한 인부 의견

Ⅶ. 상대방에 대한 석명사항

Ⅷ. 소송 진행에 대한 의견

※ 요약쟁점정리서면의 작성요령

요약쟁점정리서면은 재판의 원활한 진행과 충실한 심리를 도모하는 데에 활용될 예정이오니, 원고 및 피고는 아래 작성요령을 참고하여 1~2페이지 범위 내에서 작성·제출해 주시기 바랍니다. 그 밖에 서면의 작성·제출 방법에 관하여는 민사소송규칙 및 홈페이지(http://patent.scourt.go.kr)에 게재된 '심결취소소송 심리 매뉴얼'을 참조하시기 바랍니다.

1. "원고의 심결취소 사유의 요지"란에는 원고가 주장하는 심결의 구체적 위법사항을 간략하게 기재하되, 그 사항이 여러 개인 경우에는 항목을 나누어 기재함.

   예컨대, 심결이 진보성 유무에 관하여 판단을 한 경우에는 '심결이 진보성 유무에 관하여 잘못 판단하였다'라고 추상적으로 기재하지 말고 심결이 진보성 유무 판단을 하면서 구체적으로 어떠한 잘못을 하였는지를 기재하고, 심결이 상표의 유사 여부에 관하여 판단을 한 경우에는 '심결이 상표의 유사 여부에 관하여 잘못 판단하였다'라고 추상적으로 기재하지 말고, 심결이 상표의 유사 여부를 판단하면서 구체적으로 어떠한 잘못을 하였는지를 기재함

   [예시 1] 심결이 이 사건 특허발명의 청구항 1(이하 '청구항 1')의 진보성 유무를 판단하면서, 예컨대, ① 선행기술의 구성 1을 "A1"이라고 이해하여야 함에도 "A2"라고 잘못 이해하여 심결의 결론에 영향을 미친 위법이 있음, ② 청구항 1의 구성 1을 "B1"이라고 이해하여야 함에도 "B2"라고 잘못 이해하여 심결의 결론에 영향을 미친 위법이 있음, ③ 청구항 1의 구성 2와 선행기술의 구성 2가 상이함에도 불구하고 일치한다고 잘못 인정하여 심결의 결론에 영향을 미친 위법이 있음, ④ 청구항 1의 구성 3과 선행기술의 구성 3이 동일함에도 차이가 난다고 잘못 인정하여 심결의 결론에 영향을 미친 위법이 있음, ④ 청구항 1의 구성 3과 선행기술의 구성 3의 차이점을 P라고 파악하여야 함에도 K라고 잘못 파악하여 심결의 결론에 영향을 미친 위법이 있음, ⑤ 청구항 1과 선행기술의 차이점은 통

상의 기술자가 용이하게 극복할 수 있음에도 이와 달리 잘못 판단하여 심결의 결론에 영향을 미친 위법이 있음

[예시 2] 심결이 상표의 유사 여부를 판단하면서, 예컨대, ① 상표의 구성 중 "A"부분이 식별력이 없음에도 식별력이 있다고 잘못 판단하여 심결의 결론에 영향을 미친 위법이 있음, ② 이 사건 등록상표는 그 구성 "A"부분으로 분리관찰될 수 없음에도 분리관찰한 잘못으로 심결의 결론에 영향을 미친 위법이 있음, ③ 이 사건 등록상표의 호칭(또는 외관, 관념)과 선등록상표의 호칭(또는 외관, 관념)이 유사하지 아니함에도 유사하다고 잘못 판단하여 심결의 결론에 영향을 미친 위법이 있음, ④ 선등록상표의 지정상품 A와 이 사건 등록상표의 지정상품 K는 유사하지 아니함에도 유사하다고 잘못 판단하여 심결의 결론에 영향을 미친 위법이 있음

2. '쟁점'이란 당사자 사이에 다툼이 있는 사항 즉, 사실상 또는 법률상 쟁점을 의미하는바, 원고 및 피고는 소장, 답변서, 준비서면과 거기에 첨부되어 있는 증거자료 등을 검토한 다음, 당사자 사이에 다툼이 없는 사항과 당사자 사이에 다툼이 있는 사항을 추출하여 "당사자 사이에 다툼이 없는 사항" 및 "쟁점"란에 기재함(쟁점이 많은 경우에는 표를 더 추가할 수 있음)

[다툼 없는 사항의 예시] ① 심결에서 정정이 적법하다고 판단한 부분은 다투지 아니함, ② 심결에서 청구항 1의 구성 중 구성 1이 선행기술에 나타나 있거나 그로부터 용이하게 도출될 수 있다고 판단한 부분은 다투지 아니함, ③ 심결에서 청구항 2~5의 한정된 구성이 선행기술에 나타나 있거나 그로부터 용이하게 도출될 있다고 판단한 부분은 다투지 아니함

[쟁점의 예시 1] ① 선행기술의 구성 1을 "A1"이라고 이해하여야 할 것인지 아니면 "A2"라고 이해하여야 하는지 여부, ② 청구항 1의 구성 1을 "B1"이라고 이해하여야 하는지 아니면 "B2"라고 이해하여야 하는지 여부, ③ 청구항 1의 구성 2와 선행기술의 구성 2가 상이한지 여부, ④ 청구항 1의 구

성 3과 선행기술의 구성 3이 동일한지 여부, ④ 청구항 1의 구성 3과 선행기술의 구성 3의 차이점을 P라고 파악하여야 하는지 아니면 K라고 파악하여야 하는지 여부, ⑤ 청구항 1과 선행기술의 차이점은 통상의 기술자가 용이하게 극복할 수 있는 정도에 해당하는지 여부

[쟁점의 예시 2] ① 상표의 구성 중 "A"부분에 식별력이 있는지 여부, ② 이 사건 등록상표가 구성 "A"부분으로 분리관찰될 수 있는지 여부, ③ 이 사건 등록상표의 호칭과 선등록상표의 호칭이 유사한지 여부, ④ 선등록상표의 지정상품 A와 이 사건 등록상표의 지정상품 K가 유사한지 여부

3. "쟁점에 대한 당사자의 주장 및 증거"란에는 쟁점에 대한 당사자의 주장을 간략히 기재하고, 이를 뒷받침하는 증거를 기재함. 이 항목에서는 상세한 논거를 기재할 필요는 없고 당사자가 주장하는 사항의 개요만을 간략하게 기재하면 충분함

4. "제출 서증(전자문서) 중 주요변론 내용과 관련된 부분에 대한 증거설명"란에는 서증번호, 서증의 이름, 작성일, 작성자, 요지 및 입증취지 등을 기재하되, 다만 편의상 별도의 서면(증거설명서)으로 제출할 수 있음

5. "쟁점에 대한 당사자의 추가 제출 증거"란에는 이미 제출된 증거 이외에 추가로 제출할 증거의 유무를 밝히고 만일 추가로 제출할 증거가 있는 경우에는 그 증거방법 및 입증취지를 기재함. 추가제출 증거방법에 관하여는 반드시 증거신청서를 별도의 서면으로 제출하여야 적법한 증거신청이 된다는 점에 유의하고, 아울러 첫 기일에 모든 증거조사를 실시하므로, 요약쟁점정리서면을 제출할 때 추가제출 증거의 제출도 완료하여야 함

6. "상대방 제출 서증에 대한 인부 의견"란에는 문서의 성립을 인정하는 경우에는 성립인정, 성립을 다투는 문서에 대하여는 부인, 잘 모르는 문서에 대하여는 부지 등으로 기재함.

7. “상대방에 대한 석명사항”란에는 상대방에 대하여 석명을 구하는 사항을 기재함

8. “소송 진행에 대한 의견”란에는 기일 진행에 관한 당사자의 의견을 기재함

※ 기타사항

1. 변론의 진행순서 및 시간: 서면 및 증거의 확인, 원고의 심결취소사유 및 쟁점의 정리, 쟁점에 관한 당사자의 변론(각 20분 이내), 질의·답변, 보충변론 등의 순서로 진행되나, 사안에 따라서 진행순서 및 시간이 조금씩 달리될 수 있음

2. 변론 방법: 요약쟁점정리서면에 기재된 내용에 기초하여 쟁점에 관한 당사자의 주장과 증거를 중심으로 변론하여야 하고, 필요한 경우에는 PT자료를 활용한 변론을 하되, PT자료는 재판부에서 지정한 기한까지 제출하여야 함. 도면, 도표, 대비표, 증거 등을 법정스크린에 현출하여 놓고 변론하거나 증거설명 또는 증거탄핵 등을 하는 방식으로 변론하는 것을 권장함

3. 당사자의 주장 및 증거가 복잡하여 많은 변론시간이 소요되거나 진행순서를 달리할 필요가 있는 경우에는 사전에 재판부에 그 사정 및 필요한 예상 변론시간 등을 밝히면, 재판부에서 참고함 (끝)

[첨부 5]

특　　허　　법　　원

제 O 부

변론준비명령

사　　　건　　2016허OOOO　등록무효(특)
[원고 주식회사 OOO / 피고 OOO]
원고 소송대리인　변리사 OOO (귀하)
피고 소송대리인　변호사 OOO (귀하)

이 사건의 제1차 변론기일을 **2016. O. O. OO:OO** 특허법원 OOO호 법정으로 지정하였습니다. 당사자의 주장을 명확하게 하고, 충실한 심리를 위하여 원고와 피고 소송대리인에게 다음 사항에 대한 준비를 명합니다.

다　　음

1. 원고와 피고는 **2016. O. O.까지** 모든 주장 및 그에 대한 주된 증거를 제출·신청하여야 합니다.

2. 증인신청, 감정신청 등 시일을 요하는 증거의 신청은 **2016. O. O.까지** 서면으로 신청하여야 합니다.

3. 유의사항

가. 변론기일 변경 신청, 주장 및 증거의 제출·신청기한 연장신청은 기한이 도래하기 1주 전까지 정당한 사유를 소명하여 서면으로 신청하여야 합니다.

나. 주장 및 증거의 제출·신청 기한 이후 주장을 추가·변경하거나 추가·변경된 주장에 대한 증거를 제출·신청하기 위하여는 정당한 사유로 위 기간 내에 제출하지 못하였음을 소명하여야 합니다(예를

들어, 청구원인이나 항변에 해당하는 주장, 신규성·진보성에 관한 주장이나 자유실시기술 항변에서 주된 선행발명을 변경하거나 선행발명 및 그 결합관계를 추가·변경하는 주장, 적용법조를 달리하는 명세서 기재불비 주장, 심판단계에서 인정한 사실관계와 법적 판단에 반하는 주장 등). 정당한 사유가 소명되지 않는 경우 우리 재판부는 민사소송법 제149조를 엄격히 적용할 예정입니다.

다. 변론기일에는 특별한 사정이 없는 한 원고, 피고 순서로 각 20분 이내의 범위에서 구두 변론 시간이 허용될 예정입니다. 구술변론을 위한 변론자료 등은 변론기일 1주일 전까지 제출하여야 합니다.

라. 변론기일에는 필요한 경우 사건과 직접적으로 관련된 제품이나 모형, 관련 기술을 이해하는 데 도움을 줄 수 있는 사진이나 동영상 자료 등을 제시하여 주시기 바랍니다.

마. 특허법원에서는 '심결취소소송 심리 매뉴얼'을 정하고 있으므로, 구체적인 내용은 홈페이지(http://patent.scourt.go.kr)를 참조하여 주시고, 특히 **준비서면의 분량은 30쪽을 넘을 수 없고**, 준비서면의 작성 및 증거의 신청은 민사소송규칙 및 위 매뉴얼에서 정한 제출서류의 작성 방법 및 증거의 신청 방법에 따라 주시기 바랍니다.

2016. O. O.

재판장 판사

[첨부 6]

특　　허　　법　　원

제 O 부

사건관리 화상회의 준비명령

사　　건	2016허OOOO　등록무효(특) [원고 주식회사 OOO / 피고 OOO]
원고 소송대리인	변호사 OOO (귀하)
피고 소송대리인	변리사 OOO (귀하)

당사자의 주장을 명확하게 하고, 충실한 심리를 위하여 원고와 피고 소송대리인에게 다음 사항에 대한 준비를 명합니다.

다　　음

1. 사건관리 화상회의 일정

이 사건에 대한 사건관리 화상회의를 **2016. O. O. OO:OO**에 영상통화(원격영상증언시스템, vidyo) 방식으로 진행하고자 합니다.[1] 당사자 및 관계인은 회의 시작 5분 전까지 원격영상증언시스템(vidyo)에 접속하고, 영상 및 스피커, 마이크의 상태 점검을 마쳐주시기 바랍니다.

2. 사건관리 화상회의의 내용

사건관리 화상회의에서는 아래 내용 및 일정에 관하여 협의할 예정입니다. 이후의 소송절차는 협의된 내용 및 일정에 따라 진행되므로, 미리 주장과 신청할 증거를 준비하여 주시기 바랍니다(민사소송법 제147조 참조). 효율적인 회의의 진행을 위하여 상대방 대리인과 아래 사항에 관하

1) 화상회의를 위하여 "원격영상증언시스템(vidyo)" 프로그램의 설치(위 프로그램은 http://vc.scourt.go.kr URL 접속하여 다운받을 수 있습니다)와 웹 카메라(화상 카메라), 헤드셋(스피커, 마이크) 등의 장치가 필요합니다.

여 미리 협의하여 주시기 바랍니다.

가. 변론기일 일자 및 횟수, 각 기일별 변론 쟁점사항

나. 주장 및 증거의 제출기한(종합준비서면, 선행기술 관련 증거 등의 제출기한 포함)

다. 검증·감정이나 전문가 증인 등 시일을 요하는 증거방법의 신청 여부 및 기한

라. 전문심리위원 지정 여부

마. 당사자에 의한 기술설명회의 실시 여부

바. 청구항 해석에 관한 심리를 선행하여 진행할 것인지 여부

사. 쟁점의 확인 및 정리

3. 유의사항

가. 원활한 소송절차의 진행을 위하여 이 사건에서 다투는 사실관계 및 법적 쟁점을 화상회의일 7일 전까지 제출하여 주시기 바랍니다. 특히 청구항의 해석에 관하여 다툼이 있는 경우 해당 청구항, 용어(구, 절 포함) 등을 특정하여 주시고, 그에 대하여 주장하는 해석을 제출합니다.

나. 사건관리 화상회의 결과, 별도로 발령되는 준비명령에서 주장 및 증거의 제출기한을 정한 경우, 그 기한을 위반하여 주장 및 증거를 제출하고자 하는 당사자는 정당한 이유로 위 기간 내에 제출하지 못하였음을 소명하여야 하고, 정당한 이유가 소명되지 아니한 주장 및 증거는 민사소송법 제147조 제2항, 제149조에 의하여 각하될 수 있습니다.

다. 특허발명의 무효사유에 관한 주장은 아래 사항을 포함하여야 하며, 최종 기한 이후에 아래 사항에 대한 주장을 추가·변경하려면 정당한 사유가 있음을 소명하여야 합니다.

① 통상의 기술자의 기술수준(학력, 자격, 종사기간 등)

② 주된 선행발명의 특정

③ 선행발명을 결합함에 있어 구체적인 결합관계

라. 특허법원에서는 '심결취소소송 심리 매뉴얼'을 정하고 있으므로, 구

체적인 내용은 홈페이지(http://patent.scourt.go.kr)를 참조하여 주시고, 특히 준비서면의 작성 및 증거의 신청은 민사소송규칙 및 위 매뉴얼에서 정한 제출서류의 작성 방법 및 증거의 신청 방법에 따라 주시기 바랍니다.

2016. O. O.

재판장 판사

[첨부 7]

특　　허　　법　　원

제　O　부

절차에 관한 준비명령

사　　　건	2016허OOOO　등록무효(특) [원고 OOO / 피고 OOO]
원고 소송대리인	변호사 OOO (귀하)
피고 소송대리인	변리사 OOO (귀하)

위 사건에 관하여 2016. O. O. 사건관리 화상회의에서 당사자가 협의한 내용에 기초하여 주장 및 증거방법의 제출기한과 변론기일 등을 다음과 같이 정합니다.

다　　음

1. 원고의 종합준비서면 제출기한은 **<u>2016. O. O.까지</u>**로 합니다.
   종합준비서면에는 쟁점에 관한 모든 주장을 기재하고, 그에 대한 주된 증거를 제출하여야 합니다. 종합준비서면 제출 이후 주장을 추가·변경하거나 추가·변경된 주장을 뒷받침하기 위한 새로운 증거를 제출하려면, 정당한 이유로 위 기간 내에 제출하지 못하였음을 소명하여야 합니다(예를 들어, 청구원인이나 항변에 해당하는 주장, 신규성·진보성에 관한 주장이나 자유실시기술 항변에서 주된 선행발명을 추가·변경하거나 선행발명들 및 그 결합관계를 추가·변경하는 주장, 적용법조를 달리하는 명세서 기재불비 주장, 심판단계에서 인정한 사실관계와 법적 판단에 반하는 주장의 추가·변경 등).

2. 피고의 종합준비서면 제출기한은 **<u>2016. O. O.까지</u>**로 합니다.
   종합준비서면에는 쟁점에 관한 모든 주장을 기재하고, 그에 대한 주된 증거를 제출하여야 합니다. 종합준비서면 제출 이후 주장을 추가·변경하거나 추가·변경된 주장을 뒷받침하기 위한 새로운 증거를 제출하려면 정당한 이유로 위 기간 내에 제출하지 못하였음을 소명하여야 합니다.

3. 1차 변론기일은 **2016. O. O. OO:OO** 특허법원 OOO호 법정에서 진행합니다.
   가. 1차 변론기일에 논의할 쟁점은 특허번호 제OOOOO호 특허 중 청구항 1의 진보성 인정 여부입니다.
   나. 변론기일에는 원고, 피고 순서로 각 OO분간의 구두 변론이 예정되어 있습니다.
   다. 구두 변론을 위한 변론자료 등은 변론기일 1주일 전까지 제출하여야 합니다.

4. 쟁점에 관한 전문가 증인의 신청 기한은 **2016. O. O.**까지로 합니다. 전문가 증인 신청서에는 전문가 증인의 전문성과 객관성을 확인할 수 있는 전문가 증인 기본사항 확인서{특허법원 홈페이지(http://patent.scourt.go.kr) 참조}를 첨부하여야 합니다.

※ 전문가 증인이 채택되고, 1차 변론기일에 증인신문을 함께 할 필요가 있는 경우 원·피고 협의 하에 1회 변론기일을 변경할 수 있습니다.

※ 종합준비서면의 분량은 30쪽을 넘을 수 없고, 종합준비서면의 작성·제출, 전문가증인신청 절차는 민사소송규칙 및 위 홈페이지에 게재된 '심결취소소송 심리 매뉴얼'에서 정한 방법에 따라 주시기 바랍니다.

2016. O. O.

재판장 판사

[첨부 8]

특 허 법 원

제 O 부

청구항 해석 및 변론준비명령

사 건	2016허OOOO 등록무효(특) [원고 OOO / 피고 OOO]
원고 소송대리인	변호사 OOO (귀하)
피고 소송대리인	변리사 OOO (귀하)

당사자의 현재까지의 주장과 증거를 종합하여, 이 사건 특허발명의 청구항 O 중 그 해석에 다툼이 있는 주요 용어에 관하여 다음과 같이 해석합니다. 따라서 당사자들은 아래 해석에 기초하여 변론을 준비하여 주시기 바랍니다.

다 음

1. 이 사건 특허발명 중 청구항 1의 내용

【청구항 1】 패널의 테두리부에 각각 형성된 테두리 리브는 바닥면으로 갈수록 그 두께가 두꺼워지도록 일측면이 테이퍼면으로 구성되고, 상기 테두리부의 내부공간에는 격벽인 주 보강리브에 의해 분리되는 다수의 정방형 격자부가 형성되어지되, 그 격자 부의 내부공간에는 격자부의 내부를 4등분하는 보조 보강리브가 형성되어져 있으면서, 상기 각 보조 보강리브에 의해 4등분 된 격자부의 바닥층에는 다수개의 원형홈이 형성되어 상부로부터 가해지는 수직 하중과 편심 하중에 대한 지지력을 강화하도록 한 것을 특징으로 하는 고강도 패널

2. 청구항 1의 “격자부”에 관한 당사자의 주장 요지

가. 원 고

청구항 1의 “격자부”는 무늬형 패턴을 가지도록 패널에 형성되는 원형홈을 밀집시켜 그룹(group)화한 부분이다.

이와 같은 원고 주장의 근거는, …… 이다.

나. 피 고

청구항 1의 “격자부”는 격자 형태로 배치되는 리브에 의하여 구획되는 영역이다.

이와 같은 피고 주장의 근거는, …… 이다.

3. 청구항 1의 ‘격자부’에 대한 해석

가. (구체적인 판단 근거의 적시)

나. 따라서 청구항 1의 ‘격자부’는 ‘격자 형태로 배치되는 리브에 의하여 분리되는 영역’이라고 보는 것이 옳다.

2016. O. O.

재판장 판 사

[첨부 9]

특　허　법　원

제　O　부

화상회의 준비명령

사　　건	2016허OOOO　등록무효(특) [원고 OOO / 피고 OOO]
원고 소송대리인	변호사 OOO (귀하)
피고 소송대리인	변리사 OOO (귀하)

당사자의 주장을 명확하게 하고, 충실한 심리를 위하여 원고와 피고 소송대리인에게 다음 사항에 대한 준비를 명합니다.

다　음

1. 화상회의 일정

증거조사 일정 등의 협의를 위한 화상회의를 **2016. O. O. OO:OO**에 영상통화(원격영상증언시스템, vidyo) 방식으로 진행합니다.[2)] 당사자 및 관계인은 회의 시작 5분 전까지 원격영상증언시스템(vidyo)에 접속하고, 영상 및 스피커, 마이크의 상태 점검을 마쳐주시기 바랍니다.

2. 화상회의의 내용

가. 화상회의에서는 아래 사항에 대하여 협의할 예정입니다. 효율적인 회의 진행을 위하여 상대방 또는 상대방의 대리인과 아래 사항에 대하여 미리 협의하여 주시기 바랍니다.

① 감정 채부

---

2) 화상회의를 위하여는 "원격영상증언시스템(vidyo)" 프로그램의 설치(위 프로그램은 http://vc.scourt.go.kr URL 접속하여 다운받을 수 있습니다)와 웹 카메라(화상 카메라), 헤드셋(스피커, 마이크) 등의 장치가 필요합니다.

② 감정 사항과 방식

③ 전제사실의 확정 및 필요한 자료의 제공

④ 감정인 선정

3. 유의사항

가. 주장 및 증거의 제출 기한 이후 주장을 추가·변경하거나 추가·변경된 주장에 대한 증거를 제출하기 위하여는 정당한 사유로 위 기간 내에 제출하지 못하였음을 소명하여야 합니다. 정당한 사유가 소명되지 아니하는 경우 우리 재판부는 민사소송법 제149조를 엄격하게 적용할 예정입니다.

나. 특허법원에서는 '심결취소소송 심리 매뉴얼'을 정하고 있으므로, 구체적인 내용은 홈페이지(http://patent.scourt.go.kr)를 참조하여 주시고, 특히 준비서면의 작성 및 증거의 신청은 민사소송규칙 및 위 매뉴얼에서 정한 제출서류의 작성 방법 및 증거의 신청 방법에 따라 주시기 바랍니다.

2016. O. O.

재판장 판사

[첨부 10]

전문가 증인 기본 사항 확인서

인적사항	이름		생년월일	
	주소			

중립성

1	원·피고(회사인 경우 대표이사 및 임직원, 이하 같음)와 친인척관계에 있습니까?	Y	N
2	원·피고와 채권·채무관계에 있습니까?	Y	N
3	원·피고와 업무를 같이 하거나, 계약관계, 고용관계 기타 이에 준하는 관계에 있거나, 과거에 있었습니까?	Y	N
4	원·피고가 관여한 소송 또는 이 사건 특허/제품 등에 관한 소송에서 증인으로 증언한 바 있습니까?	Y	N
5	본건 소송과 관련하여 원·피고에게 자문을 한 바 있습니까?	Y	N

전문성

1	증인의 전문 분야를 구체적으로 기재해주십시오.
2	전문 분야에 관하여, (1) 현재 및 과거의 직업(재직기간, 직위/직책, 담당업무 포함)을 밝히고, (2) 학위/자격증, 논문/보고서, 기타 전문성을 확인할 수 있는 자료가 있다면, 그 내용을 구체적으로 기재해주십시오. *※ 아래 칸이 부족한 경우 별지로 첨부 가능*

전문가 증인의 의무

전문가 증인은 당사자 일방에 편향되지 않게 사실과 전문지식에 근거하여 진술하여야 합니다. 전문가 증인은 해당 분야의 전문가로서 객관적으로 검증되고 해당 분야에서 널리 인정되는 사실/이론에 기초하여 진술하여야 하며, 자신의 주관적인 이론/해석에 기초하여 진술하여서는 아니 됩니다.

위 기재사항은 모두 사실임을 확인합니다.

일 자 20. . .

서 명

[첨부 11]

특 허 법원

제O 부

변론준비명령(전문가 증인)

사 건	2016허OOOO 등록무효(특)
	[원고 OOO / 피고 OOO]
원고 소송대리인	변호사 OOO (귀하)
피고 소송대리인	변리사 OOO (귀하)

2016. O. O. OO:OO 변론기일에서의 전문가 증인에 대한 증인신문과 관련하여 충실한 심리를 위하여 원고와 피고 소송대리인에게 다음 사항에 대한 준비를 명합니다.

다음

1. 전문가 증인의 증인 진술서 등의 제출

   가. 원고는 **2016. O. O.까지** 전문가 증인의 증인 진술서와 증인신문사항을 제출하여야 합니다. 원고의 주신문은 증인 진술서의 범위 내에서 할 수 있습니다.

   나. 증인에게 주신문에서 제시하거나 인용하는 모든 자료(관련 선행기술, 번역문, 실물사진, 참고자료 포함)는 **2016. O. O.까지** 증거로 제출되어야 합니다.

2. 전문가 증인에 대한 주신문과 반대신문은 각 OO분 이내로 제한합니다.

3. 당사자는 전문가 증인이 외국인인 경우 주신문과 반대신문을 위하여 통역인을 대동할 수 있습니다. 다만, 그러한 경우에도 통역인 지정과 비용예납을 위해 **2016. O. O.까지** 대동할 통역인의 인적 사항과 통역

비용을 재판부에 알려야 합니다.

4. 당사자가 따로 통역인을 대동할 수 없는 경우, **<u>2016. O. O.까지</u>** 재판부에 그 내용을 알리고 통역인 지정신청을 하여야 합니다.

2016. O. O.

재판장 판사

Guideline of Practice and Procedure of Revocation Action in the Patent Court of Korea

September 1, 2016, Patent Court

Ⅰ. Purpose of the Guideline

The Guideline of Practice and Procedure of Revocation Action in the Patent Court of Korea (hereinafter, "Guideline") is prepared to facilitate expeditious and efficient cancellation proceedings involving complex issues regarding patents, utility models, trademarks or designs by prescribing matters such as procedural discussions, designation of deadlines for submitting arguments and rebuttal arguments, and focusing examination on disputed issues. In addition, by prescribing and publicly disclosing proper hearing procedures and methods for requesting and examining evidence, the Guideline provides predictability to the interested parties and facilitates diligent preparation in litigation proceedings.

Ⅱ. Submission of Petition and Brief

1. Submission of Petition by Plaintiff

A. The plaintiff shall set forth in detail the following matters in its petition:

① Procedural background on the examination of the Korean Intellectual Property Office (hereinafter, "KIPO") and the trial of the Intellectual Property Trial and Appeal Board of KIPO(hereinafter, "IPTAB");

② A summary of the decision (the arguments of the parties and the judgment thereon by the IPTAB at the trial stage);

③ Acknowledged parts and unacknowledged parts among the grounds for the decision;

④ All arguments relating to erroneous grounds of the decision;

⑤ Notice of related cases (inclusive of the progress and outcome of related trials and cancellation of decision actions including correction trials and petitions for correction, related civil cases on merits and petition cases, and criminal cases; if the plaintiff fails to notice such cases, the cases may be not considered during the litigation proceedings); and

⑥ Opinion on the overall litigation proceedings, including any plan for request for evidence.

B. The plaintiff shall submit evidence corresponding to items ① to ⑥ above and explanatory documents for evidence describing the purport of the evidence. In particular, the plaintiff shall be careful to ensure that the following basic evidentiary documents and requisite attachments thereto, such as a power of attorney for litigation, a corporate registry or a certificate of corporate nationality (if the party is a foreign corporation), and a certificate of service of a decision, are not omitted.

① Revocation of refusal decision case: Decision, application, preliminary rejection, amendment, opinion, and rejection decision;

② Revocation of invalidation decision case: Decision, original register, registration publication, evidence relating to prior art (including prior conception, prior-registered trademarks, prior-used trademarks, prior designs); and

③ Revocation of decision on scope of right case: Decision, original register, registration publication, explanatory documents and drawings of invention (including conception, trademark, design, etc.)

C. If the petition fails to set forth the requisite matters described in Paragraph A above or omits the basic evidentiary documents or requisite attachments thereto as described in Paragraph B above, the presiding judge or a court clerk authorized by the presiding judge issues an order to submit a supplemental brief or the omitted basic evidentiary documents or attachments. [See. Attachment 1] No later than 3 weeks after receipt of the order, the plaintiff shall submit a preparatory brief, evidence, or documents according to the order.

2. Submission of Response Brief by Defendant

A. No later than 3 weeks from service of the plaintiff's petition or brief containing specific grounds for petition, the defendant shall submit a response brief, including the following matters, together with cited evidence cited and explanatory documents for evidence, in accordance with a preparatory order. [See. Attachment 2]

① Response to the purport of petition ;

② Acknowledged parts and unacknowledged parts among the plaintiff's arguments;

③ Detailed rebuttal arguments on the unacknowledged parts of the plaintiff's arguments;

④ All additional arguments relating to proper grounds of the decision;

⑤ Notice of related cases (inclusive of the progress and outcome of relevant trials and revocation actions including correction trials and petitions for correction, related civil cases on merits and preliminary injunction cases, and criminal cases; if the plaintiff fails to provide a notice of such cases, the cases may be not considered.);

⑥ Statement on the evidentiary documents submitted by the plaintiff; and

⑦ Opinion on the overall litigation proceedings, including any plan for request for evidence.

B. The presiding judge may issue an order requesting the plaintiff to submit detailed rebuttal arguments; additional evidence, etc. [See. Attachment 3] No later than 3 weeks after receipt of the order, the plaintiff shall submit a preparatory brief, evidence or documents, etc.

Ⅲ. Classification of a Case and Pre-Hearing Procedure

1. Classification of a Case

Upon completion of written arguments, the presiding judge reviews the case based on the briefs and evidence, and classifies the case as (i) a case requiring immediate designation of a hearing or (ii) a case requiring a case management conference and preparatory hearing.

2. Preparatory Order for Hearing

For a case requiring immediate designation of a hearing, in order to conduct the proceedings in a diligent manner, the presiding judge may issue a preparatory order requesting the plaintiff and the defendant to submit a summary brief on disputed issues. [See. Attachment 4] In addition, the presiding judge may issue a preparatory order designating deadlines for submission of arguments and evidence and for request for evidence that require a substantial amount of time such as expert witnesses, etc. [See. Attachment 5]

3. Video Conference for Case Management

A. The presiding judge may discuss the procedural matters of the case with the parties simultaneously through video and audio communication means (hereinafter, “video conference for case management”). The presiding judge may designate a judge to be in charge of the above process.

B. The Court may notify the plaintiff and the defendant of the video conference and issue a preparatory order with regard to the conference. [See. Attachment 6]

C. In a video conference for case management, the following matters may be discussed and a preparatory order(scheduling order) may be issued based on the results of the discussion. [See. Attachment 7]

① The number and dates of hearings, and matters to be addressed for each hearing;

② Deadlines for submission of arguments and evidence (including deadlines for submission of comprehensive briefs and expert statements, and the number or volume of briefs to be submitted);

③ Whether to request for evidence requiring a substantial amount of time such as verification, appraisal, and expert witness, and the deadline for such request;

④ Whether to designate a technical advisor;

⑤ Whether to hold a technical explanatory session by the parties;

⑥ Whether to hold a claim construction hearing first; and

⑦ Confirmation and summary of issues.

D. If the Court orders submission of comprehensive briefs on the overall or particular issues of the case in a preparatory order, the plaintiff shall submit a comprehensive brief no later than 3 weeks from the date of the video conference for case management (or a deadline designated in the preparatory order), and the defendant shall submit a comprehensive brief no later than 3 weeks from the date of the plaintiff’s submission of its comprehensive brief (or a deadline designated in the preparatory order).

E. If a party seeks to add any new or modified argument or submit evidence for such argument after the deadline for submission of arguments and evidence designated in the preparatory order, the party shall provide an explanation for the failure to submit the argument or evidence within the designated period based on a justifiable cause [e.g., addition or modification of arguments such as an argument relating to the statement of claim or defense, an argument that changes the closest prior art relating to novelty, inventive step, and a free-to-practice technology defense or that adds or changes prior art and the combination relationship thereof, an argument for lack of sufficient description in the specification based on a different legal provision, etc.].

4. Preparatory Hearing

A. The Court may hold a preparatory hearing if deemed necessary for discussing the matters set forth in Section 3, Paragraph C above, examining evidence, or holding a technical explanatory session. The presiding judge may designate a judge to be in charge of the above process.

B. If a party seeks to add or modify an argument or submit evidence for such added or modified argument after the closing of the preparatory hearing, the party shall provide an explanation for the failure to submit the argument or evidence before the closing of the preparatory hearing based on a justifiable cause similar to the previous Section.

Ⅳ. Oral Hearings

1. Conduct of Oral Hearings

A. Each party shall present an oral argument for no longer than 20 minutes, in the order of the plaintiff and the defendant. Even when a party has retained more than one attorney-of-record, the party shall present its oral arguments within the above time period. If deemed necessary, the presiding judge may adjust the time.

B. Any materials, summary briefs on disputed issues, for oral arguments shall be submitted by no later than 1 week before the designated date for each hearing.

C. At hearings, the parties may present oral arguments by bringing and demonstrating the products related to the case (e.g., products implementing a registered patent/design, a prior art, an invention/design subject to confirmation, etc.), or by playing video materials or presenting photos, via a computer, a visual presenter, etc. at the court, which might be helpful in understanding related technologies.

2. Separate Oral Hearings according to Issues

A. Where it is deemed necessary to hold oral hearings according to specific issues because several issues are in dispute in the case, the Court may consult with the parties and hold separate oral hearings according to issues.

(Example cases eligible for separate oral hearings on an issue-by-issue basis) A case where claim construction or whether prior art was published is an issue to be resolved first; a case where multiple grounds for invalidation are asserted; and a case in which whether an invention subject to confirmation is specified and implemented is at issue.

B. At each of the hearings, the scope of the hearing is limited to the disputed issue designated for that hearing.

C. After a hearing, the Court may disclose its opinion, either orally or in writing, regarding disputed issues on which examination has been completed, and may order the parties to prepare for hearings on other remaining disputed issues based on the Court's opinion above.

3. Hearings for Claim Construction

A. In a case where the parties are in dispute over the claim construction, according to which the arguments or evidence concerning the remaining issues may be different, and thus a hearing for claim construction need to be conducted first, the presiding judge may conduct a hearing for claim construction upon consultation with the parties.

B. If there are any pending correction trial or petition for correction. relating to claims that are in dispute, the parties shall notify the Court of the progress of such trial or petition. The parties shall inform the Court of their plan on the correction trial or petition for trial in detail.

C. The Court may disclose its opinion on the claim construction, either orally or in writing, and order the parties to prepare for hearings directed to the other remaining disputed issues based on the Court's opinion above. [See. Attachment 8]

4. Hearings of an Infringement Action relating to Revocation of IPTAB Decision Action

A. If deemed necessary, such as when both a revocation of IPTAB decision action and an infringement action involving same patent, utility model, trademark or design are pending concurrently before the Court and are litigated by same parties and attorneys-of-record, the Court may examine both actions in parallel.

B. If it is necessary to organize related arguments in an infringement action and a revocation of IPTAB decision action, the Court may conduct preparatory proceedings for these actions in parallel.

V. Examination of Evidence and Participation of Experts

1. Application to Adduce Evidence in General

A. If a party submits any evidentiary documents or files a request for witness, inquiry of facts, certified copy of document, document submission order, verification, appraisal, etc., the party shall specify in detail what the party intends to prove by such evidentiary means.

B. If deemed necessary, the presiding judge may conduct a preparatory proceeding for discussing evidence examination procedure. The presiding judge may discuss procedural matters via a video conference upon consultation with the parties.

2. Verification and Appraisal

A. If deemed necessary, the Court may conduct verification or appraisal procedures either upon a party's request or on an ex officio basis.

B. If deemed necessary, the Court may conduct a preparatory proceeding. for the decision on the request, confirming objects and method of verification or appraisal, confirming a factual premise, providing necessary materials, selecting an appraiser, etc. The presiding judge may discuss procedural matters via a video conference upon consultation with the parties and issue a preparatory order. [See. Attachment 9]

C. If a reason is deemed to exist, the Court may order submission of the objects of verification or appraisal.

3. Expert Witnesses

A. If a party files a request for an expert witness, the party shall attach a basic declaration of the expert witness that can confirm the expertise and objectivity of the witness. [See. Attachment 10] If the request is accepted, the party shall submit a witness statement containing the testimony of the expert witness and a questionnaire for witness examination.

B. A direct examination of the expert witness shall be conducted within the scope of the statement of the expert witness. All materials presented or cited in the direct examination shall be submitted as evidence before the date designated for examining the witness.

C. If an expert witness is a foreigner, the parties may be respectively accompanied by an interpreter for direct and cross examinations. In such case, the parties shall notify the Court of the personal information and interpretation fees in advance, etc. If a party cannot be accompanied by an interpreter, the party shall notify the Court of the same 4 weeks before the witness examination date and file a request for designation of an interpreter.

D. The presiding judge may issue a preparatory order for examination of an expert witness including deadlines for submission of a statement of the expert witness and a questionnaire for the direct examination, limitation of the time for examination, and deadlines for submission of arguments and evidence for impeaching the credibility of the expert witness testimony. [See. Attachment 11]

4. Technical Advisors

A. If deemed necessary, the Court may hear opinions of the parties and designate one or more technical advisors.

B. A preparatory hearing may be held if it is deemed necessary for technical advisors to understand the case.

C. In a hearing or preparatory hearing, technical advisors may directly question the parties with approval of the presiding judge. If it is necessary for a party to supplement its answer to a question from the technical advisors, the party shall submit its opinion in writing by a deadline designated by the presiding judge.

Ⅵ. Preparation of Documents and Submission of Evidentiary Documents

1. Petitions, Responses, and Briefs

A. Forms and Contents

① The paper size of documents shall be A4 (210 mm * 297 mm) with a top margin of 45 mm, left and right margins of 20 mm, and a bottom margin of 30 mm (excluding a page numbering).

② The font size shall be 12pt, and there shall be a line space of no less than 200% or 1.5 lines.

③ The length of briefs shall not exceed 30 pages. If a brief of more than 30 pages is submitted, the presiding judge may return the brief and order the party to resubmit the brief by reducing to 30 pages or less. The presiding judge may discuss the length, etc. of briefs with the parties. If an agreement is reached during the discussion, the parties shall submit briefs in accordance with such agreement.

④ If any evidence supporting an argument is submitted, a number for the evidence shall be indicated on a corresponding portion thereof.

⑤ Technical terms shall be defined in footnotes and the sources thereof shall be identified.

⑥ Summary briefs on disputed issues shall briefly state a summary of the grounds for the plaintiff's petition for cancellation of decision, undisputed facts, a summary table of disputed issues, explanation of evidence, additional evidence to be submitted, acceptance/denial of evidentiary documents, clarification, opinion on litigation proceedings, etc. [See. Attachment 4]

⑦ Comprehensive briefs shall include a summary of all arguments regarding the issues on which the Court ordered, and main evidence for such arguments.

⑧ In briefs, contents identical or similar to those included in petitions, responses or previous briefs shall not be needlessly repeated, nor shall be cited in part or as a whole.

B. Instructive Note

① If any claims or descriptions in the specification of a patent or utility model are changed due to a petition for amendment or correction, such changes shall be stated in detail, and claims or descriptions in the specification subject to litigation shall be specified.

② If any rights relating to a patent, utility model, trademark or design at issue is changed, the details of such change and the ultimate holder of such rights shall be stated.

③ Among the prior arts submitted at the trial phase, those included in and excluded from the revocation action shall be stated separately. In addition, it shall be clearly specified whether an evidentiary material is submitted either as a prior art or evidence for proving well-known technologies, ordinary skill in the art, level of ordinary skill. If a single document contains multiple inventions, it shall be clearly specified as to which of the multiple inventions is asserted to be prior art.

④ The features of prior arts shall be specified in detail, and a feature comparison chart comparing the corresponding features of the patented invention and each of the prior arts shall be submitted. The comparable features of well-known technologies shall also be specified.

⑤ If an argument is made regarding inventive step or free-to-practice technology, the person of ordinary skill in the art and the level of ordinary skill in the art shall be specified in detail.

⑥ If an argument is made regarding denial of inventive step by a combination of prior arts, a main prior art shall be selected, and a specific combination relationship of the prior arts and the grounds for the ease in combining the prior arts shall be specified.

(Example) The inventive step of the Claim is denied by Prior Arts 1 to 3 (X).

If the feature ○○○○ of Prior Art 2 is added to Prior Art 1 which is the main prior art invention (or if the feature 2 of Prior Art 1 is replaced with the feature ○○○○ of Prior Art 2), the patented invention is derived. Since Prior Art 1 discloses a suggestion for such combination, a person of ordinary skill in the art could have easily conceived such combination, and thus the inventive step of the patented invention is denied (O).

⑦ An argument regarding a lack of written description in the specification shall specify an applicable legal provision on which the argument is based, such as whether the patent or utility model at issue can be readily practiced by the explanation therein (Article 42(3)1 of the Patent Act), whether a claim is supported by the explanation of the patent or utility model at issue (Article 42(4)1 of the Patent Act), whether the scope of a claim of the patent or utility model at issue is clearly specified (Article 42(4)2 of the Patent Act), etc.

⑧ If it is necessary to conduct a hearing for claim construction first, the grounds thereof shall be specified, and the terms for which claim construction is necessary, descriptions relating to such terms in the specification, the parties' proposed claim constructions, and specific grounds for such constructions shall be stated.

⑨ In case of a revocation action against a trial decision regarding examiner's rejection, the defendant shall state the grounds for rejection set forth in a preliminary rejection notice and a rejection decision issued by an examiner of KIPO, and a preliminary rejection notice and a rejection decision issued by IPTAB, and clearly specify which of the rejection grounds are asserted in the litigation proceedings.

2. Explanatory Documents for Evidence

A. All evidence submitted by a party shall be stated, and the purport to be proved therefrom shall be briefly described.

B. If evidence is submitted in relation to an argument regarding novelty, inventive step, or free-to-practice technology, it shall be clearly specified whether the evidence is submitted as a prior art or as evidence of a well-known technology.

3. Evidentiary Documents, Etc.

A. Even if a material was submitted by a party during the examination or trial stage, it may not serve as a basis for judgment unless such material is submitted as evidence during the litigation proceedings. Therefore, a party shall submit all necessary materials, however, that such materials shall not overlap with those submitted by the other party. In particular, each of the following documents shall not be omitted since they may serve as important basis for judgment during the litigation proceedings.

(Example) Decision, application and initial specification, preliminary rejection notice, amendment and response, petition for re-examination, examiner's rejection decision, petition for correction, explanatory document/drawing/amendment of invention subject to confirmation, prior art references, etc.

B. Written documents in a foreign language shall be submitted with a translation attached thereto; however, machine translations shall not be submitted. Particularly for main evidence such as prior arts the translations of the full text, not excerpted translations, shall be submitted. In the translations, the portions concerning evidentiary purport shall be highlighted by underlines, etc.

C. An evidentiary document shall indicate a title if the title of the document exists, or a summary of the document, if the document has no title. An evidentiary document submitted as a prior art shall indicate the same.
(Example) "Product Catalogue of Company ○○ (published on January 2, 2006)" and "Prior Art 1 (Registered Patent Publication No. 00000)."

D. Each evidentiary document shall contain only a single evidentiary item. If evidentiary items are mutually related, an evidentiary document shall indicate the evidentiary items as multi-level numbers (e.g., Plaintiff's Exhibit No. 2-1, 2-2, etc.).

E. For the avoidance of confusion, the numbers following those previously assigned to prior arts submitted at the trial stage shall be assigned to prior arts newly submitted in the revocation action. For example, if Prior Arts 1, 2, and 3 were submitted at the trial stage, and in the case where Prior Art 1 is to be submitted as it is and Prior Arts 2 and 3 are not to be submitted in the revocation action, a new prior art to be submitted should be designated as Prior Art 4.

F. If there is any product, model, photograph, video material, etc., which may facilitate understanding of the technical details of or the specific shape of the patent, utility model, etc., the parties shall submit the same as evidence. In a case concerning a trademark or design, if the original document is in color, the evidentiary document shall be submitted in color. (End)

[Attachment 1]

PATENT COURT

The [*] Panel

Amendment Order

Case No.:	2016*Heo***** Invalidation of Registration (Patent) [Plaintiff: Company ***; Defendant: ***]
Attorney for the plaintiff:	Attorney ***, Patent Attorney ***

The Court hereby orders the attorney for the plaintiff to submit a brief containing specific details required to be included in the petition within 21 days from the receipt of this order and submit, as reference materials, a certificate of service of administrative decision, a certificate of corporate nationality of the plaintiff, and the corporate registry of the defendant.

[*] [*], 2016

Court Clerk [***]

◇ Instructions ◇

※ If you fail to comply with this order, the petition may be rejected pursuant to Article 254(2) of the Civil Procedure Act.

※ Please include the case number (2016*Heo*****) in all briefs submitted in relation to this case.

※ The Patent Court has established the "GuidelineofPractice and Procedure of Revocation Action of the Patent Court of Korea." Please refer to the website of the Patent Court (http://patent.scourt.go.kr) for further details. For facilitating prompt, efficient, and diligent trial proceedings, please carefully read the Guideline and comply with the provisions therein.

※ **Particularly in case of a brief containing specific cause of action, the matters to be stated in the petition as set forth in Section Ⅱ. 1. A. of the Guideline shall be included, and the basic evidentiary documents and requisite attachments thereto, as set forth in Section Ⅱ. 1. B. of the Guideline, shall be submitted**. Please prepare briefs and request evidence in accordance with the method of preparing documents for submission and the method of requesting evidence, respectively, as set forth in the Civil Procedure Rules and the above Guideline.

[Attachment 2]

PATENT COURT

The [*] Panel

Preparatory Order

Case No.: 2016*Heo***** Invalidation of Registration (Patent)
[Plaintiff: Company ***; Defendant: ***]

The Court hereby orders the defendant to submit a response, evidence, etc. containing the following matters by **[*][*], 2016**.

THE FOLLOWING

1. Submission of Response
   ① Response to Plaintiff's Demand;
   ② Parts admitted and not admitted among the plaintiff's arguments;
   ③ Detailed rebuttal arguments on the unacknowledged parts of the plaintiff's arguments;
   ④ All additional arguments relating to whether the administrative decision complies with the law; and
   ⑤ Notice of related cases (If there are any relevant trials and cancellation of decision actions including correction trials and petitions for correction, related civil cases on merits and petition cases, and criminal cases, the case number, case name, and progress thereof shall be stated in a separate section provided at the end of a brief. If the defendant fails to provide a notice of such cases, the cases may be not considered during the litigation proceedings).

2. An evidentiary method and a plan to request for evidence for the matters

set forth in Paragraph 1 above (e.g., evidentiary documents, witnesses, inquiry of facts, a request for certified copy of document, verification, appraisal, etc. However, evidentiary documents shall not overlap with those submitted by the other party, and if the defendant requests a witness, inquiry of facts, or a certified copy of document, the content that the defendant intends to prove by such evidentiary method shall be specified in detail).

3. Acceptance/denial of evidentiary documents submitted by the plaintiff (Only the evidentiary documents of which authenticity cannot be accepted shall be indicated).

4. Translation of an evidentiary document prepared in a foreign language. (Machine translations shall not be submitted. Particularly for main evidence such as prior arts, etc., the translations of the full text, not excerpted translations, shall be submitted. In the translations, the portions concerning the purport of evidence shall be highlighted by an underline, etc.)

[*] [*], 2016

Presiding Judge [***]

◇ Instructions ◇

With respect to the above-referenced case, please note the following:

① The Court intends to conduct a focused examination so as to reduce the number of the parties' attendance at hearings and also ensure a diligent hearing procedure. In this case, the Court plans to limit the hearings to a single hearing in the absence of special circumstances.

② Therefore, both parties shall submit all arguments and evidence by a due date designated by the Court. Please note that if a party is deemed as delaying the litigation proceedings by failing to comply with such due dates, the party may be subject to disadvantages, such as a restriction on submission of any further argument, evidence among others.

③ Please refrain from applying for a change of the date of a hearing or a preparatory hearing in the absence of special circumstances such as where a substantial amount of time is required to prepare for the hearing or collect evidence due to the complexity and difficulty of the disputed issues, etc. If it is unavoidable to request such change of the hearing date, please clearly specify the reason and if possible, indicate a desired date upon consulting with the other party.

※ For further details, please refer to the "Guideline of Practice and Procedure of Revocation Action of the Patent Court of Korea" published on the website of the Patent Court (http://patent.scourt.go.kr). In particular, please prepare responses and request evidence in accordance with the method of preparing documents for submission and the method of requesting evidence, respectively, as set forth in the Civil Procedure Rules and the above Guideline.

[Attachment 3]

PATENT COURT

The [*] Panel

Preparatory Order

Case No.:	2016*Heo***** Invalidation of Registration (Patent) [Plaintiff: Company ***; Defendant: ***]
Attorney for the	Plaintiff: Attorney ***, Patent Attorney ***

The Court hereby orders the Attorney for the Plaintiff to submit a brief, evidence, etc. containing the matters checked below **by [*][*], 2016**.

THE FOLLOWING

□√ Detailed rebuttal to the defendant's response

□√ Submission of acceptance/denial regarding evidentiary documents submitted by the defendant (Only the evidentiary documents of which authenticity cannot be accepted shall be indicated).

□√ Additional evidence submitted or requested by the plaintiff and the evidentiary purport thereof (e.g., evidentiary documents, witnesses, inquiry of facts, request for certified copy of document, etc.; however, evidentiary documents shall not overlap with those submitted by the other party, and if the plaintiff requests a witness, inquiry of facts, a certified copy of document, verification, appraisal, etc., the content that the plaintiff intends to prove by such evidentiary method shall be specified in detail.)

□√ Submission of translation regarding an evidentiary document prepared in a foreign language (Machine translations shall not be submitted. Particularly for the main evidence such as prior arts, etc., the translations of the full text, not excerpted translations, shall be submitted. In the translations, the portions concerning evidentiary purport shall be highlighted such as by an underline).

[*] [*], 2016

Presiding Judge [***]

◇ Instructions ◇

With respect to the above-referenced case, please note the following:

① The Court intends to conduct a focused examination so as to reduce the number of the parties' attendance at hearings and also ensure a diligent hearing procedure. In this case, the Court plans to limit the hearings to a single hearing in the absence of special circumstances.

② Therefore, both parties shall submit all arguments and evidence by a due date designated by the Court. Please note that if a party is deemed as delaying the litigation proceedings by failing to comply with such due dates, the party may be subject to disadvantages, such as a restriction on submission of any further argument, evidence among others.

③ Please refrain from applying for a change of the date of a hearing or a preparatory hearing in the absence of special circumstances such as where a substantial amount of time is required to prepare for the hearing or collect evidence due to the complexity and difficulty of the disputed issues, etc. If it is unavoidable to request such change of the hearing date, please clearly specify the reason and if possible, indicate a desired date upon consulting the other party.

※ For further details, please refer to the "Guideline of Practice and Procedure of Revocation Action of the Patent Court of Korea" published on the website of the Patent Court (http://patent.scourt.go.kr). In particular, please prepare responses and request evidence in accordance with the method of preparing documents for submission and the method of requesting evidence, respectively, as set forth in the Civil Procedure Rules and the above Guideline.

[Attachment 4]

PATENT COURT

The [*] Panel

Preparatory Order for Hearing

Case No.:	2016*Heo***** Invalidation of Registration (Patent) [Plaintiff: ***; Defendant: ***]
Attorney for the plaintiff:	Attorney ***
Attorney for the defendant:	Patent Attorney ***

The Court has designated the first hearing to be held on **[*], 2016, [*] AM/PM** at the courtroom [*] of the Patent Court. In order to clarify the legal relationship in the litigation, the Court hereby requests the attorneys for the plaintiff and the defendant to submit a summary brief on the disputed issues by **[*], 2016** in accordance with the Drafting Guidelines for Summary Briefs on Disputed Issues as attached hereto as an annex.

[*] [*], 2016

Presiding Judge [***]

〈Annex〉

Summary Brief on Disputed Issues

○ Case No.:

○ Submitted by:

Ⅰ. Summary of the Plaintiff's Grounds for Revocation of Administrative Decision

Ⅱ. Undisputed Matters

Ⅲ. Summary Table of the Issues in Dispute.

Disputed Issues	The Party's Arguments and Evidence on the Disputed Issues

Ⅳ. Explanation on the Evidence for Main Arguments in Submitted Evidentiary Documents (Electronic Documents)

No.	Name of Evidentiary Document	Date of Preparation	Author	Summaryand Evidentiary Purport

Ⅴ. Additional Evidence for Submission on the Disputed Issues

Evidentiary Method	Evidentiary Purport

Ⅵ. Opinion on the Acceptance/Denial of Evidentiary Documents Submitted by the Other Party

Ⅶ. Request for Clarification to the Other Party

Ⅷ. Opinion on Litigation Proceedings

※ Drafting Guidelines for Summary Briefs on Disputed Issues

Summary briefs on disputed issues are intended to be utilized for the purpose of facilitating expeditious trial proceedings and conducting an examination in a diligent manner. Therefore, the plaintiff and the defendant should prepare and submit a summary brief on the disputed issues inone or two pages in accordance with the guidelines below. As for the guidelines on the preparation and submission of other documents, please refer to the Civil Procedure Rules and the "Guideline of Practice and Procedure of Revocation Action of the Patent Court of Korea" on the website of the Patent Court (http://patent.scourt.go.kr).

1. In the section "Summary of the Plaintiff's Grounds for Revocation of Administrative Decision," the plaintiff's argument on the specific error in the decision shall be briefly stated, but if multiple errors are alleged, such errors shall be stated in sub-sections.

For example, if a decision was made on whether an inventive step exists, a party shall not state that "the decision was erroneous in determining whether there was an inventive step" in an abstract manner, but shall specify the error in the decision in concrete details. Similarly, if a decision was made on the similarity of a trademark in dispute, a party shall not state that "the decision was erroneous in determining similarity of the trademark" in an abstract manner, but shall specify the error in the decision in concrete details.

[Example 1] In determining whether Claim 1 of the patented invention (hereinafter, "Claim 1") involves an inventive step in the decision, for example, ① although Element 1 of the prior art should be understood as "A1," it was erroneously understood as "A2" and thus unlawfully affected the outcome of the decision, ② although Element 1 of Claim 1 should be understood as "B1," it was erroneously understood as "B2" and thus unlawfully affected the outcome of the decision, ③ although Element 2 of Claim 1 and Element 2 of the prior art are different from each other, they were erroneously found to be identical and thus unlawfully affected the outcome of the decision, ④ although Element 3 of Claim 1 and Element 3 of the prior art are identical, they were erroneously found to be different and thus unlawfully affected the outcome of the decision, ⑤ although the difference between Element 3 of Claim 1 and Element 3 of the prior art should be understood as "P," it was erroneously understood as "K" and thus unlawfully affected the outcome of the decision, and ⑥ although a person having ordinary skills in the art could have easily overcome the difference between Claim 1 and the prior art, it was erroneously decided to the contrary and thus unlawfully affected the outcome of the decision.

[Example 2] In determining whether the subject registered trademark is similar to the prior registered trademark in the decision, for example, ① although the portion "A" of the registered trademark lacks distinctiveness, it was erroneously determined to have distinctiveness and thus unlawfully affected the outcome of the decision, ② although Element "A" of the subject registered trademark cannot be observed separately, it was erroneously observed separately and thus unlawfully affected the outcome of the decision, ③ although the pronunciation (appearance or concept) of the subject registered trademark is not similar to the pronunciation of the prior registered trademark, they were erroneously determined to be similar and thus unlawfully affected the outcome of the decision, and ④ although the designated product A of the prior registered trademark is not similar to the designated product K of the subject registered trademark, they were erroneously determined to be similar and thus unlawfully affected the outcome of the decision.

2. "Disputed issues" refer to issues as to which there is a factual or legal dispute between the parties. After reviewing the petition, response, briefs, evidentiary materials attached thereto, etc., the plaintiff and the defendant shall state matters as to which there is no dispute between the parties and

matters as to which there is a dispute between the parties separately in the sections "undisputed matters" and "disputed issues," respectively (If there are multiple disputed issues, additional rows may be inserted in the table).

[Example of Undisputed Matters] ① There is no dispute over the part in the decision that found the correction to be legally proper, ② there is no dispute over the part in the decision finding that Element 1 of Claim 1 is disclosed in or can be easily derived from the prior art, and ③ there is no dispute over the part in the decision finding that the limitations of Claims 2 to 5 are disclosed in or can be easily derived from the prior art.

[Example 1 of Disputed Issues] ① Whether Element 1 of the prior art should be understood as "A1" or "A2," ② whether Element 1 of Claim 1 should be understood as "B1" or "B2," ③ whether Element 2 of Claim 1 and Element 2 of the prior art differ from one another, ④ whether Element 3 of Claim 1 and Element 3 of the prior art are identical to one another, ⑤ whether the difference between Element 3 of Claim 1 and Element 3 of the prior art should be understood as "P" or "K," and ⑥ whether a person having ordinary skills in the art can easily overcome the difference between Claim 1 and the prior art.

[Example 2 of Disputed Issues] ① Whether the portion "A" of the trademark has distinctiveness, ② whether Element "A" of the subject registered trademark can be observed separately, ③ whether the pronunciation of the subject registered trademark is similar to the pronunciation of the prior registered trademark, and ④ whether the designated product A of the prior registered trademark is similar to the designated product K of the subject registered trademark.

3. In the column "The Party's Arguments and Evidence on the Disputed Issues," a party shall set forth arguments on the disputed issues briefly and state

evidence supporting the arguments. In this section, the party does not need to set out detailed grounds for the arguments and it is sufficient to briefly state the gist of the arguments.

4. In the section "Explanation on the Evidence for Main Arguments in Submitted Documentary Evidence," a party shall set forth a number, name, preparation date, author, gist, evidentiary purport, etc. of the evidentiary documents. For sake of convenience, however, the party may submit a separate document (i.e., an explanatory document for evidence) in lieu of the foregoing.

5. In the section "Additional Evidence Submitted on the Disputed Issues," a party shall clarify whether there is any additional evidence for submission aside from those submitted previously, and if so, the party shall set forth the evidentiary method and evidentiary purport of such additional evidence. Please note that a request for submission of additional evidence must be submitted as a separate written application in order to be a legally proper request for evidence. Please note also that since examination of all evidence is conducted at the first hearing, submission of all additional evidence must be completed when submitting a summary brief on disputed issues.

6. In the section "Opinion on the Acceptance/Denial of Evidentiary Documents Submitted by the Other Party," a party shall indicate "acceptance" if authenticity of an evidentiary document is accepted, "denial" if authenticity of an evidentiary document is denied, and "uncertain" if authenticity of an evidentiary document is not sufficiently known.

7. In the section "Request for Clarification to the Other Party," a party shall set forth the matters on to which the party seeks clarification from the other party.

8. In the section "Opinion on Litigation Proceedings," a party shall set forth its opinion on the hearing procedures.

※ Other Guidelines

1. Procedural Sequence and Duration of Hearing: A hearing is conducted in the following order: (i) confirmation of documents and evidence, (ii) review of the grounds for the plaintiff's petition for revocation of decision and disputed issues, (iii) the parties' oral arguments on disputed issues (within 20 minutes each), (iv) exchange of questions and answers, (v) supplemental arguments, etc. However, the sequence and duration of the hearing may be slightly adjusted on a case-by-case basis.

2. Method of Presenting Arguments: The parties shall present their arguments and evidence on disputed issues based on their summary briefs on disputed issues. If necessary, the parties may use presentation materials, but such presentation materials shall be submitted by a deadline designated by the Court. The Court recommends presenting arguments and explaining or impeaching evidence by displaying drawings, charts, comparison tables, evidence, etc. on a screen in the Court.

3. If the parties need more time for arguments or adjustment in the procedural sequence due to the complexity of their arguments and evidence, the parties may inform the Court in advance of such circumstances and the anticipated time necessary for presenting the arguments and evidence, which the Court will take into consideration. (End)

[Attachment 5]

PATENT COURT

The [*] Panel

Preparatory Order for Hearing

Case No.:	2016*Heo***** Invalidation of Registration(Patent) [Plaintiff: Company ***; Defendant: ***]
Attorney for the plaintiff:	Attorney ***
Attorney for the defendant:	Patent Attorney ***

The Court has designated the first hearing to be held on **[*], 2016, [*] AM/PM** at the courtroom [*] of the Patent Court In order to clarify the parties' arguments and facilitate diligent proceedings, the Court hereby orders the attorneys for the plaintiff and the defendant to prepare for the matters set forth below.

THE FOLLOWING

1. The plaintiff and the defendant shall submit all arguments and main evidence therefor **by[*], 2016**.

2. A request for evidence that requires a substantial amount of time, such as a request for a witness, a request for an appraisal, etc., shall be filed in writing **by[*],2016**.

3. Instructions
   A. A request for a change of the hearing date and a request for an extension of the deadline for submitting or requesting arguments and evidence shall be filed in writing at least one (1) week before the

designated date with an explanation of a justifiable cause for the request.

B. If a party seeks to add any new or modified argument or submit evidence for such argument after the expiration of the deadline for submission of arguments and evidence designated in the preparatory order, the party shall provide an explanation for the failure to submit the argument or evidence within the designated period based on a justifiable cause [e.g., addition or modification of arguments such as an argument relating to the cause of action or defense, an argument that changes the primary prior art relating to novelty, inventive step, and a freely exploited invention defense or that adds or modifies prior arts or the combination relationship thereof, an argument for deficient description in the specification based on a different legal provision, an argument contrary to the acknowledged facts or legal judgment in the trial stage, etc.]. If an explanation of a justifiable cause is not provided, the Court will strictly apply Article 149 of the Civil Procedure Act.

C. At the hearing, the plaintiff and the defendant will be allowed to present oral arguments for 20 minutes each in the respective order, in the absence of special circumstances. Any materials for oral arguments shall be submitted by no later than 1 week before the designated hearing date.

D. If necessary at the hearing, the parties may bring products or models that are directly related to the case at hand, or photos, video materials, etc. that may be helpful for understanding related technologies.

E. For further details, please refer to the “Guideline of Practice and Procedure of Revocation Action of the Patent Court of Korea” on the website of the Patent Court (http://patent.scourt.go.kr). In particular, the length of a brief shall not exceed 30 pages, and please prepare briefs and request evidence in accordance with the method of preparing documents for submission and the method of requesting evidence, as set forth in the Civil Procedure Rules and the Guideline.

[*] [*], 2016

Presiding Judge [***]

[Attachment 6]

PATENT COURT

The [*] Panel

Preparatory Order for Video Conference for Case Management

Case No.:	2016*Heo***** Invalidation of Registration (Patent) [Plaintiff: Company ***; Defendant: ***]
Attorney for the plaintiff:	Attorney ***
Attorney for the defendant:	Patent Attorney ***

In order to clarify the parties' arguments and facilitate diligent proceedings, the Court hereby orders the attorneys for the plaintiff and the defendant to prepare for the matters set forth below.

Preparatory Matters

1. Schedule for Case Management Video Conference

A video conference for case management will be held on **[*], 2016, [*] AM/PM**, via a video conference (Vidyo)[1]. The parties and interested persons are requested to access Vidyo at least 5 minutes before the conference begins and complete inspection of the setup for the video, speaker, and microphone.

2. Contents of Case Management Video Conference

In the case management video conference, the below matters and schedules will be discussed. Since the subsequent litigation proceedings will proceed in accordance with the matters and schedule discussed, the parties are requested to

1) For the video conference, it is necessary to install the Vidyo program (downloadable from http://vc.scourt.go.kr) with equipment such as a web camera (a webcam), a headset (a speaker and a microphone), etc.

prepare for the arguments and evidence in advance (see Article 147 of the Civil Procedure Act). To facilitate efficient conference proceedings, the counsels for the parties are requested to have prior discussions with each other regarding the matters set forth below.

A. The dates and number of hearings, and disputed issues to be addressed in each of the hearings;
B. Deadlines for submission of arguments and evidence (including deadlines for submission of comprehensive briefs and evidence relating to prior art technologies);
C. Whether to request an evidentiary method requiring a substantial amount of time, such as verification, appraisal, and an expert witness, and the deadline for such request;
D. Whether to designate a technical advisor;
E. Whether to hold a technical explanatory session by the parties;
F. Whether to conduct a hearing for claim construction first; and
G. Confirmation and summary of the disputed issues.

3. Instructions
   A. In order to facilitate the proceeding, the factual and legal issues disputed in this case shall be submitted at least 7 days before the conference date. In particular, if the parties are in dispute over the interpretation of claims, the parties shall submit the claims and terms (including phrases and paragraphs) at issue, as well as the proposed interpretation thereof.
   B. If a party seeks to submit arguments or evidence after the expiration of the deadline for submission designated in the preparatory order which issued separately as a result of a video conference for case management, the party shall provide an explanation for the failure to submit the argument or evidence within the designated period based on a justifiable cause. Any argument and evidence, for which a

justifiable cause is not sufficiently explained, may be rejected under Article 147(2) and Article 149 of the Civil Procedure Act.

C. Arguments relating to grounds of invalidation of the patented invention shall contain the matters set forth below, and the party seeking to add or modify an argument concerning any of the below matters after the final deadline shall provide an explanation for a justifiable cause thereof.

① The level of technical skill required of a person having ordinary skills in the art (including the level of education, qualification, and duration of work); and

② Identification of main prior art invention; and

③ Specific combination relationship in combination of reference.

D. The Patent Court has established the "Guideline of Practice and Procedure of Revocation Action." Please refer to the website of the Patent Court (http://patent.scourt.go.kr) for more details. In particular, please prepare briefs and request evidence in accordance with the method of preparing documents for submission and the method of requesting evidence as set forth in the Civil Procedure Rules and the Guideline.

[*] [*], 2016

Presiding Judge [***]

[Attachment 7]

PATENT COURT

The [*] Panel

Preparatory Order for Procedural Matters

Case No.:	2016*Heo***** Invalidation of Registration (Patent) [Plaintiff: ***; Defendant: ***]
Attorney for the plaintiff:	Attorney ***
Attorney for the defendant:	Patent Attorney ***

With respect to the case above, the Court hereby designates deadlines for submission of arguments and evidence and a hearing date based on the discussions held between the parties via the case management video conference on [*], 2016, as set forth below.

THE FOLLOWING

1. The deadline for submission of a comprehensive brief by the plaintiff shall be **[*], 2016**.

In the comprehensive brief, the plaintiff shall describe all arguments relating to the disputed issues and submit main evidence for the arguments. If the plaintiff seeks to add any new or modified argument or submit any new evidence to support such argument after the submission of the comprehensive brief, the plaintiff shall provide an explanation for the failure to submit the argument or evidence by the above deadline based on a justifiable cause (e.g. addition or modification of arguments such as an argument relating to the cause of action or defense, an argument that changes the primary prior art relating to novelty, inventive step or the defense of free-to-practice technology, or that adds or changes prior arts or the combination relationship thereof, an argument for deficient description in the specification based on a different legal provision, an argument contrary to the acknowledged facts or legal judgment in the administrative trial proceeding, etc.).

2. The deadline for submission of a comprehensive brief by the defendant shall be **[*], 2016**.

In the comprehensive brief, the defendant shall describe all arguments relating to the disputed issues and submit main evidence for the arguments. If the defendant seeks to add any new or modified argument or submit any new evidence to support such argument after the submission of the comprehensive brief, the defendant shall provide an explanation for the failure to submit the argument or evidence by the above deadline based on a justifiable cause.

3. The first hearing will be held on **[*], 2016, [*] AM/PM**, at the courtroom ○○ of the Patent Court.

A. The disputed issues to be discussed in the first hearing is whether Claim 1 of Patent No. [*****] has an inventive step.

B. At the hearing, the plaintiff and the defendant will present oral arguments for [*] minutes each, in the respective order.

C. Any materials for oral arguments shall be submitted no later than 1 week before the designated hearing date.

4. A request for an expert witness relating to the disputed issues referred to in paragraph 3.A shall be filed by [*],2016. The request for an expert witness shall be attached with a basic statement that can confirm the expertise and objectivity of the expert witness [*see* the Patent Court

website (http://patent.scourt.go.kr)].

※ If the requested expert witness is adopted and it is necessary to examine the witness in the first hearing, the date of the first hearing may be changed through discussions between the plaintiff and the defendant.

※ The length of a comprehensive brief shall not exceed 30 pages. The preparation and submission of comprehensive briefs and the procedure for requesting expert witnesses shall be in compliance with the "Guideline of Practice and Procedure of Revocation Action" published on the website of the Patent Court.

[*] [*], 2016

Presiding Judge [***]

[Attachment 8]

PATENT COURT

The [*] Panel

Claim Construction and Preparatory Order for Hearing

Case No.:	2016*Heo***** Invalidation of Registration (Patent) [Plaintiff: ***; Defendant: ***]
Attorney for the plaintiff:	Attorney ***
Attorney for the defendant:	Patent Attorney ***

Considering all of the arguments and evidence submitted to date by the parties, the Court hereby interprets the major terms among the claims of the patented invention, of which interpretation is disputed, as follows. Accordingly, the parties are requested to prepare for the hearing based on the following interpretation.

THE FOLLOWING

1. Claim 1 of the Patented Invention

【Claim 1】 A high-strength panel, characterized in that: a rim rib respectively formed on rim portion of the panel is configured so that one side of the rim rib is configured as a tapered surface to have increasing thickness as it gets nearer to the bottom layer; a plurality of square lattice sections that is divided by a main reinforcing rib serving as a partition is formed in the interior space of said rim portion; an auxiliary reinforcing rib which quadrisects the interior space of the lattice section are arranged in said interior space of the lattice section; and a plurality of circular recesses are formed on the bottom layer of the rim portion quadrisected by said respective auxiliary reinforcing rib to enhance supporting force resistant to vertical load and eccentric load applied from an upper portion.

2. Summary of the Parties' Arguments on the Term "lattice section" of Claim 1

A. Plaintiff

The "lattice section" of Claim 1 is a portion comprising a group of concentrated circular grooves formed on the panel to have a certain pattern.

The above construction of the plaintiff is based on the following grounds. (*omitted*)

B. Defendant

The "lattice section" of Claim 1 is a portion defined by a rib which is arranged in a lattice form.

The above construction of the defendant is based on the following grounds. (*omitted*)

3. Construction of the Term "lattice section" of Claim 1

A. (Concrete grounds for judgment)

B. Therefore, it is reasonable to construe the term "lattice section" of Claim 1 as "a portion which is divided by a rib arranged in a lattice form."

[*] [*], 2016

Presiding Judge [***]

[Attachment 9]

PATENT COURT

The [*] Panel

Preparatory Order for Video Conference

Case No.:	2016*Heo***** Invalidation of Registration (Patent) [Plaintiff: ***; Defendant: ***]
Attorney for the plaintiff:	Attorney ***
Attorney for the defendant:	Patent Attorney ***

In order to clarify the parties' arguments and facilitate diligent proceedings, the Court hereby orders the attorneys for the plaintiff and the defendant to prepare for the matters as set forth below.

Preparatory Matters

1. Schedule of Video Conference

A video conference for discussing the schedule of evidence investigation, etc. will be held on **[*], 2016, [*] AM/PM**, via a video communication means (Vidyo)[2]. The parties and interested persons are requested to access Vidyo at least 5 minutes before the conference begins and complete inspection of the setup for the video, speaker, and microphone.

2. Contents of Video Conference

In the video conference, the matters set forth below will be discussed. To

2) For the video conference, it is necessary to install the Vidyo program (downloadable from http://vc.scourt.go.kr) with equipment such as a web camera (a webcam), a headset (a speaker and a microphone), etc.

facilitate efficient conference proceedings, the parties or the counsels for the parties are requested to have prior discussions with each other regarding the matters below.

① Admissibility of appraisal;
② Matters and method of appraisal;
③ Confirmation of a factual premise and provision of necessary materials; and
④ Selection of an appraiser.

3. Instructions

A. If a party seeks to add a new or modified argument or submit any evidence for such argument after the deadline for submission of arguments and evidence, the party shall provide an explanation for the failure to submit the argument or evidence within the period based on a justifiable cause. If a justifiable cause is not sufficiently explained, the judicial panel will strictly apply Article 149 of the Civil Procedure Act.

B. The Patent Court has established "Guideline of Practice and Procedure of Revocation Action." Please refer to the website of the Patent Court (http://patent.scourt.go.kr) for further details. In particular, please prepare briefs and request evidence in accordance with the method of preparing documents for submission and the method of requesting evidence as set forth in the Civil Procedure Rules and the Guideline.

[*] [*], 2016

Presiding Judge [***]

[Attachment 10]

Basic Statement of Expert Witness

Personal Information	Name		Date of Birth	
	Address			

Neutrality			
1	Are you a relative of either the plaintiff or the defendant (if a party is a corporation, a chief executive, officer, or an employee; the same applies hereinafter)?	Y	N
2	Are you in a creditor-debtor relationship with either the plaintiff or the defendant?	Y	N
3	Have you ever worked or do you currently work with either the plaintiff or the defendant, or have you ever been or are you currently in a contractual, employment, or other similar relationships with either the plaintiff or the defendant?	Y	N
4	Have you ever provided testimony as a witness in a lawsuit involving either the plaintiff or the defendant, or the patent/products at issue?	Y	N
5	Have you ever provided consultation to either the plaintiff or the defendant with respect to this lawsuit?	Y	N

Expertise	
1	Describe your area of expertise specifically.
2	With regards to your area of expertise, specifically describe (1) your current and past occupations (including the duration of employment, position/title, and assigned duties) and (2) materials that can confirm your expertise, such as a diploma/license, papers/reports, among others. ※ *You may add a separate attachment in case more space is needed.*

Obligation of Expert Witness
The expert witness shall make statements based on facts and special knowledge in a manner unbiased to any party. In addition, as an expert in the relevant area, the expert witness shall make statements based on the facts/theories objectively verified and widely acknowledged in the area and shall not make any statements based on his or her subjective theory/interpretation.

I hereby state that the foregoing statements are all true.

Date: ____________________

By: ____________________

[Attachment 11]

PATENT COURT

The [*] Panel

Preparatory Order for Hearing (Expert Witness)

Case No.:	2016*Heo***** Invalidation of Registration (Patent) [Plaintiff: ***; Defendant: ***]
Attorney for the plaintiff:	Attorney ***
Attorney for the defendant:	Patent Attorney ***

The Court hereby orders the attorneys for the plaintiff and the defendant to prepare for the matters set forth below to facilitate a diligent examination of the expert witness in the hearing to be held **at [*] AM/PM on [*], 2016**.

THE FOLLOWING

1. Submission of Witness Statement of Expert Witness

A. The plaintiff shall submit a witness statement of its expert witness and an examination questionnaire for the expert witness **by [*], 2016**. A direct examination by the plaintiff shall be conducted within the scope of the witness statement.

B. All materials to be presented or cited in the direct examination of the expert witness (including related prior art technologies, translations, photos of actual products, and reference materials) shall be submitted as evidence **by [*], 2016**.

2. The direct examination and cross examination of the expert witness shall

be limited to [*] minutes each.

3. If the expert witness is a foreigner, the parties may be accompanied by interpreters each for direct and cross examinations. In such case, however, the parties shall notify the Court of the personal information and interpretation fees of the interpreter **by [*], 2016** for designating the interpreter and paying fees in advance.

4. If a party cannot be accompanied by an interpreter, the party shall notify the Court thereof **by [*], 2016** and file a request for designation of an interpreter.

[*] [*], 2016

Presiding Judge [***]

(한영, 영한) 지식재산 법률용어 사전

2017년 10월 27일 초판 인쇄
2017년 11월 10일 초판 발행

지은이 특허법원 국제 지식재산권법 연구센터
발행인 양진수
발행처 진원사
출판등록번호 제321-2512007002호
주 소 서울시 서초구 법원로2길 17-6(서초3동, 형덕빌딩 1층)
전 화 02.916.1850 팩 스 02.916.3442
홈페이지 http://www.jinwonsa.co.kr
http://www.lawbookstore.co.kr
이메일 hhansin@hanmail.net

ISBN 978-89-6346-512-8 91360
정 가 25,000원